# Hip Hop's Amnesia

# Hip Hop's Amnesia

## *From Blues and the Black Women's Club Movement to Rap and the Hip Hop Movement*

### Reiland Rabaka

LEXINGTON BOOKS
Lanham • Boulder • New York • Toronto • Plymouth, UK

Published by Lexington Books
A wholly owned subsidary of The Rowman & Littlefield Publishing Group, Inc.
4501 Forbes Boulevard, Suite 200, Lanham, Maryland 20706
www.rowman.com

10 Thornbury Road, Plymouth PL6 7PP, United Kingdom

Copyright © 2012 by Lexington Books

British Library Cataloguing in Publication Information Available

**Library of Congress Cataloging-in-Publication Data**

Rabaka, Reiland, 1972–
Hip hop's amnesia : from blues and the black women's club movement to rap and the hip hop movement / Reiland Rabaka.
p. cm.
Includes bibliographical references and index.
ISBN 978-0-7391-7491-3 (cloth : alk. paper) — ISBN 978-0-7391-7492-0 (pbk. : alk. paper) — ISBN 978-0-7391-7493-7 (electronic)
1. Rap (Music)—History and criticism. 2. Hip-hop—United States. I. Title.
ML3531.R225 2012
782.4216490973—dc23
2012000571

♾™ The paper used in this publication meets the minimum requirements of American National Standard for Information Sciences Permanence of Paper for Printed Library Materials, ANSI/NISO Z39.48-1992.

Printed in the United States of America

*For my father, Robert Dean Smith, in memoriam. You are my hero—you always have been, and you always will be. I love you. I love you endlessly and eternally. I love you with every word I write and every song I sing.*

*And, as with all of my work, for my mother, grandmothers, and great aunt: Marilyn Jean Giles, Lizzie Mae Davis, Elva Rita Warren, and Arcressia Charlene Connor*

*Lift Every Voice and Sing . . .*
*Nkosi Sikelel' iAfrika . . .*
*A luta continua . . .*

# Contents

# Introlude

## *Acknowledgments*

*Hip Hop's Amnesia* is meant to be a monument: a monument to the musicians and politicians, the musics and movements, the writers and revolutionaries, the preachers and teachers, the hipsters and hustlers, and, most of all, the ghetto youth and suburban youth who paved the way for rap music, hip hop culture, and, ultimately, *the Hip Hop Movement.* However, even more than a monument to hip hop's artistic ancestors and political antecedents, *Hip Hop's Amnesia* also stands as a testament to all the folk who contributed to my personal, professional, and radical political development. Every word, sentence, paragraph, and "remix" to follow bears the imprint of the diverse— although often disconnected—intellectual and political arenas and agendas I draw from and endeavor to establish critical dialogue with. As a consequence, the list of academics, organic intellectuals (including rappers, spoken-word artists, DJs, b-girls, b-boys, graffiti-writers, students, etc.), activists, archivists, institutions, and organizations to which I am indebted is, indeed, enormous. Such being the case, I hope I may be forgiven for deciding that the most appropriate way in which to acknowledge my sincere appreciation is simply to list them below without the protracted praise each has so solemnly earned.

My deepest gratitude and most heartfelt *asante sana* (a thousand thanks) is offered, first and foremost, to my family: my mother, Marilyn Giles; my father, Robert Smith I (deceased); my grandmothers, Lizzie Mae Davis (deceased) and Elva Rita Warren; my great aunt, Arcressia Charlene Connor; my older brother and his wife, Robert Smith II and Karen Smith; my younger brother, Dwight Randle Wellington Clewis; my nieces and nephews, Journée Clewis, Dominique Clewis, Kalyn Smith, Robert Smith III, Ryan Smith, and

Remington Smith; my grandfathers, Joseph Warren (deceased) and Jafari Jakuta Rabaka (deceased); my innumerable aunts, uncles, and cousins throughout the Americas, the Caribbean, and Africa; and, most especially, Dr. Stephanie Krusemark, whose incomparable intellect, extraordinary eloquence, grand sense of grace, soulful sophistication, and limitless love helped me research and write this book, as well as tend to my mind, body, heart, and soul (*nakupenda sana* Nzuri).

An undertaking as ambitious as *Hip Hop's Amnesia* would have been impossible without the assistance of colleagues and comrades, both far and wide. I express my earnest appreciation to the following fine folk, who each in their own special way contributed to the composition and completion of this book: W. E. B. Du Bois; Langston Hughes; Zora Neale Hurston; Claude McKay; James Baldwin; Sonia Sanchez; Amiri Baraka; Audre Lorde; Haki Madhubuti; June Jordan; Camille Paglia; Kariamu Welsh; Lucius Outlaw; Lewis Gordon; Tukufu Zuberi; Rhonda Tankerson; Nedra James; Vickie Washington; the faculty, staff, students, and alumni of the Booker T. Washington High School for the Performing and Visual Arts (Dallas, Texas); the faculty, staff, students, and alumni of the University for the Arts (Philadelphia, Pennsylvania); the faculty, staff, students, and alumni of the Department of African American Studies at Temple University (Philadelphia, Pennsylvania); Rev. L. R. Davis and the congregation of Galilee Missionary Baptist Church; Lamya Al-Kharusi; Denise Lovett; Adam Clark; Elzie Billops; Sigmund Washington; Patrick DeWalt; Awon Atuire; Stacey Smith; Toroitich Chereno; De Reef Jamison; Anthony Lemelle; Troy Barnes; Zachary Epps; Ursula Lindqvist; Tiya Trent; La'Neice Littleton; Radia Amari; Howard Wallen; Vincent Harding; Marvin Lynn; David Stovall; Gloria Ladson-Billings; Daniel Solórzano; George Junne; Eva Torres Henry; Stephany Hope Wilson; Vicki Carter; Richard Hodges; Stacy and Sekou Robertson; Gail Dennis; Bernard Robertson; Oliver Wang; Mark Anthony Neal; Bakari Kitwana; Jared Ball; Adam Bradley; M.K. Asante, Jr.; David Ferris; Chelsey Jennings; Mpozi Mshale Tolbert (deceased); Taharka Leophus King (deceased); the editorial board of the *Critical Africana Studies* book series (Stephanie Evans, Lewis Gordon, Martell Teasley, Christel Temple, and Deborah Whaley); the National Association for Ethnic Studies (NAES); and the Association for the Study of African American Life and History (ASALH).

I cannot adequately convey the depth of my gratitude to the National Council for Black Studies (NCBS) for providing me with the critical feedback and fora to deepen and develop my relationship with the wider world of American studies, critical race studies, cultural studies, popular music studies, women's studies, sexuality studies, postcolonial studies, black radical politics, and critical social theory. I have been presenting my research at NCBS's annual conferences for more than a decade. Along with saying *nashukuru sana* (very special thanks) to NCBS in general, I would be remiss not to single out several members whose key contributions and intellectual encouragement have made the present volume possible. I, therefore, express my earnest appreciation to the following NCBS colleagues and comrades: Molefi Asante; Maulana Karenga; James Turner; Delores Aldridge; James Stewart; Martell Teasley; Mark Christian; James Conyers; Charles Jones; Sundiata Cha-Jua; Perry Hall; Shirley Weber; Barbara Wheeler; Alfred Young; Bill Little (deceased); Munasha Furusa; Akinyele Umoja; Fred Hord; Terry Kershaw; Jeffrey Ogbar; Scot Brown; Alan Colon; Abdul Nanji; Christel Temple; Patricia Reid-Merritt; Kevin Cokley; Salim Faraji; Cecil Gray; and Ricky Jones.

The faculty, staff, students, and alumni of the Department of Ethnic Studies and the Center for Studies of Ethnicity and Race in America (CSERA) at the University of Colorado at Boulder deserve special thanks for their patience and critical support. *Nashukuru sana* to our steadfast staff, especially Sandra Lane, Jason Van Horn, and Tiya Trent, for always being there and lending a helping hand. I am also deeply indebted to my colleagues and comrades who selflessly serve on the faculty in the Department of Ethnic Studies, each of whom has patiently listened to me rant and rave about both the positives and negatives of rap music and hip hop culture over the last couple of years. I say *nashukuru sana*, especially, to professors William King, Ward Churchill, and Daryl Maeda, who have consistently supported both my teaching and research endeavors over the years.

Several libraries, research centers, special collections, and archives hosted and helped me transform this book from an inchoate idea into its fully realized form. I am indelibly indebted to the directors, research fellows, and staffs of: the Hip Hop Archive and the W. E. B. Du Bois Institute for African and African American Research, Harvard University; Arthur A. Houghton, Jr., Library, Harvard University; Arturo A. Schomburg Center for Research in Black Culture, New York Public Library; Nicholas Murray Butler Library, Columbia University; Institute for African American Affairs, New York University; Elmer Holmes Bobst Library, New York University; John Henrik Clarke Africana Library, Africana Studies and Research Center, Cornell University; Charles L. Blockson African American Collection, Temple University; Center for African American History and Culture, Temple University; Center for Africana Studies, University of Pennsylvania; August Wilson Center for African American Culture, Pittsburgh, Pennsylvania; Center for American Music, University of Pittsburgh; Center for Popular Culture Studies, Bowling Green State University; Center for Black Music Research, Columbia College Chicago; Karla Scherer Center for the Study of American Culture, University of Chicago; Center for Popular Music, Middle Tennessee State University; Center for the History of Music Theory and Literature, Jacobs School of Music, Indiana University; African American Cultural Cen-

ter, University of Illinois at Chicago; Bruce Nesbitt African American Cultu-
ral Center, University of Illinois at Urbana–Champaign; African American
Cultural Center, North Carolina State University; H. Fred Simons African
American Cultural Center, University of Connecticut at Storrs; Moorland-
Spingarn Research Center, Howard University; John Hope Franklin Collec-
tion for African and African American Documentation, Rare Book, Manu-
script, and Special Collections Library, Duke University; Carter G. Woodson
Center for African American and African Studies, University of Virginia;
Robert W. Woodruff Library, Atlanta University Center Archives; Manu-
script Sources for African American History, Special Collections, Emory
University; John L. Warfield Center for African and African American Stud-
ies, University of Texas at Austin; Center for African American Studies,
University of Houston; African and African American Collection, University
Library, University of California, Berkeley; Institute for Advanced Feminist
Research, University of California, Santa Cruz; Ralph J. Bunche Center for
African American Studies, University of California, Los Angeles; Blair-
Caldwell African American Research Library, Denver Public Library; Center
for Media, Arts, and Performance, Alliance for Technology, Learning, and
Society (ATLAS) Institute, University of Colorado at Boulder; American
Music Research Center, College of Music, University of Colorado at Boul-
der; Howard B. Waltz Music Library, College of Music, University of Colo-
rado at Boulder; Department of Musicology, College of Music, University of
Colorado at Boulder; African American Materials, Special Collections,
George Norlin Library, University of Colorado at Boulder.

*Hip Hop's Amnesia* could not have been researched and written without
the music and inspiration of the following singer-songwriters, rapper-rhyme
writers, and musician-magicians, several of whom were gracious enough to
grant interviews: Rhonda Nicole; Roy Hargrove; Keith Loftis; Sweet Honey
in the Rock; Vinx; Sharon Jones; Sade; Cassandra Wilson; Tracy Chapman;
Terence Trent D'Arby; Seal; Corey Harris; Lenny Kravitz; Ben Harper;
Cody Chesnutt; Angie Stone; Dionne Farris; Nadirah Shakoor; Erykah Badu;
N'dambi; Raphael Saadiq; Alicia Keys; Maxwell; Bilal; Ledisi; Donnie;
Macy Gray; Rahsaan Patterson; Van Hunt; Jill Scott; Anthony Hamilton;
John Legend; India.Arie; Musiq Soulchild; Chocolate Genius (a.k.a. Marc
Anthony Thompson); Goapele Mohlabane; Dwele; Raheem DeVaughn;
Me'Shell Ndegéocello; Michael Franti; Spearhead; Amel Larrieux; The
Roots (especially Tariq "Black Thought" Trotter and Ahmir "Questlove"
Thompson); Bahamadia; KRS-One; Public Enemy; Chuck D.; X-Clan; Ra-
kim Allah; Tupac Shakur (deceased); Common; Talib Kweli; Mos Def; Q-
Tip; A Tribe Called Quest; De La Soul; The Jungle Brothers; Brand Nubian;
Digable Planets; Arrested Development; Intelligent Hoodlum; Poor Right-
eous Teachers; Dream Warriors; Main Source; The Solsonics; NaS; OutKast;
Goodie Mob; Cee-Lo Green; Little Brother; Phonte Coleman; Jean Grae;

Dead Prez; M-1 (a.k.a. Mutulu Olugbala); K'naan; Medusa; The Coup; Paris; The Conscious Daughters; Wyclef Jean; Buju Banton; Gang Starr; and Guru (a.k.a. Keith Edward Elam [deceased]).

My publisher and I would like to thank and openly acknowledge Chelsey Jennings, who graciously granted permission to use her collage for the book cover. Majoring in both art and ethnic studies at the University of Colorado at Boulder, I have been able to witness Chelsey's extraordinary growth and development over the years. She is a gracious and gifted artist, poet, and writer, who skillfully brings an aesthetic approach to social science, and a social science approach to the arts. In my mind, her work is the epitome of the best of what hip hop culture has to offer, not simply the present, but the future.

My editor, Jana Hodges-Kluck, and the Lexington Books editorial board deserve very special thanks (*nashukuru sana*) for seeing the potential in this book project and gently prodding me along during the many months it took me to revise the manuscript and prepare it for production. Jana's keen eye and constructive criticisms of the manuscript have certainly helped me to compose what I believe to be my best book to date. I would like to formally thank Jana and, my publisher, Julie Kirsch for the promptness and professionalism with which they have handled my book projects, and for their patience with my extremely erratic (if not a bit eccentric) research and writing regimen, which in this instance took me to dozens of university and public libraries, archives, and research centers. I am not by any means the easiest person to correspond with when I am working, but throughout the entire research and writing process they calmly fielded my inquiries and coolly encouraged me to complete my book.

This book is offered as an emblem of my deep and abiding love and respect for my father, Robert Dean Smith, who, after a long and bitter bout with prostate and lung cancer, recently succumbed to the disease. I am at a loss for words to express the depth of my sorrow, my mourning, my grief. Suffice to say, he was my hero, even though he could be more or less characterized as a working-class or ghetto "anti-hero." Nonetheless, he was my hero—he always has been, and he always will be. In his own way, fatherly, musically, and otherwise, he helped to shape and remake the world that I live in today. Even in his absence I can feel his presence. *Death is dual: it is both an ending and a new beginning.* It is with this heartfelt belief that I have moved beyond sorrow toward celebration.

In short, *Hip Hop's Amnesia* can also be seen as a conversation between a once estranged father and son who learned to love (and actually like) each other by deciphering and sharing the coded messages in black popular music. Although he is not physically here with me anymore, spiritually and musically he is as alive and vibrant as ever. Every time I hear Bobby "Blue" Bland, Johnny Taylor, Z. Z. Hill, Al Green, or, his all-time favorite, Lou Rawls, I can still hear his gravel-voiced singing—sometimes sounding pretty good, and at other times, especially after he'd had a couple of drinks, sounding really bad. Somewhere between the saint and the sinner lies my father's life, or, rather, the life he lived. By continuing to decipher and share the music he shared with me, by sending him messages through the music, and by bringing the wider world into our conversation, I humbly invoke my father's spirit. I say to him softly and solemnly, like only a son can say to his father, I love you. I love you endlessly and eternally. I love you with every word I write and every song I sing.

If, then, my most respected readers, any inspiration or insights are gathered from my journey through the classic musics and movements that influenced rap music and hip hop culture, I pray you will attribute them to each of the aforementioned. However, if (and when) you find foibles and intellectual idiosyncrasies, I humbly hope you will neither associate them with any of the forenamed nor, most especially, the members of the Hip Hop Movement. I, and I alone, am responsible for the flows and flaws to follow. As is my custom, then, I begin by softly saying, almost silently singing my earnest and eternal prayers: *Lift Every Voice and Sing. Nkosi Sikelel' iAfrika. A luta continua.*

# Introduction

## *African American Movement Music: On Hip Hop's "Partial or Total Loss of Memory" Surrounding Classical Black Popular Music and Classical Black Popular Movements*

> And it seems to me that if the Negro represents, or is symbolic of, something in and about the nature of American culture, this certainly should be revealed by his characteristic music. In other words, I am saying that if the music of the Negro in America, in all its permutations, is subjected to a socio-anthropological as well as musical scrutiny, something about the essential nature of the Negro's existence in this country ought to be revealed, as well as something about the essential nature of this country, *i.e.*, society as a whole. —Amiri Baraka, *Blues People: Negro Music in White America*, ix–x

### FURTHER EXPLORATIONS OF HIP HOP'S INHERITANCE: ON "WHAT HAS BEEN FORGOTTEN BUT SHOULD BE REMEMBERED" ABOUT THE ROOTS OF RAP MUSIC AND HIP HOP CULTURE

Over the last decade or so, there has been a great deal of discussion concerning rap music's connections to earlier or, rather, "classical" forms of African American music. There have been scholarly studies of rap music's poetics, as well as several books centered around the "politics of rap music" or, rather, "rap music's politics."[1] Additionally, there have been studies that have examined the ways in which rap helped to revitalize the music industry at the end of the twentieth century, and other studies that have explored how certain forms of rap express regional culture, politics, and musical trends.[2] In spite of these very often innovative studies, most work within the world of Hip Hop Studies seems to only superficially treat the wider historical, cultural, social, political, economic, and aesthetic contexts from which rap music initially and more directly emerged.

Rap music did not fall out of the sky, like the erstwhile acorn in the Chicken Little tale. Even in light of all of its sonic, semantic, and social innovations, it is important to point to its musical and other aesthetic antecedents. Too often African American music is treated as though it exists outside of African American musical and other aesthetic traditions. This is not only unfortunate, it is extremely disingenuous, as it makes it seem as though each new form of black popular music is some sort of free-floating, "postmodern" sonic signifier, and not, as it most often is, deeply connected to and undeniably indicative of the origins and evolution of African American musical history and culture. Therefore, in order to really and truly understand rap music much must be understood about the history, culture, and ongoing struggles of its primary producers: black ghetto youth in specific, and black folk in general.

In often unrecognized ways, the origins and evolution of rap music have actually come to be treated or, rather, ill-treated much like African Americans—especially, black ghetto youth—in mainstream American history, culture, and society. Which is to say, there seems to be a serious *amnesia* surrounding the origins and evolution of rap music and the wider world of hip hop culture that rap music reflects. Conceptually *amnesia*, which according to *Merriam-Webster's Dictionary* means "a partial or total loss of memory," offers us an interesting angle to revisit, re-evaluate, and ultimately "remix" the origins and evolution of rap music and hip hop culture.

At this point it can be said with little or no fanfare that most work in Hip Hop Studies only anecdotally explores the origins and evolution of rap music and hip hop culture. Consequently, Hip Hop Studies stands in need of a serious scholarly work that transcends the anecdotal and critically engages not only hip hop's musical history, but also its intellectual, cultural, social, and political history. If, as most Hip Hop Studies scholars concede, rap music reflects more than merely the angst and ill-will of post–Civil Rights Movement black ghetto youth and white suburban youth, then a study that treats rap music as a reflection of the Hip Hop Generation's—however "politically incorrect"—politics is sorely needed. *Hip Hop's Amnesia* was researched, written, *and* remixed specifically with this dire need in mind.[3]

However, it should be sternly stated at the outset, *Hip Hop's Amnesia* is not merely about the ways that rap music reflects the Hip Hop Generation's politics. It is also a book about the *amnesia* surrounding the ways in which rap and other forms of hip hop music (e.g., neo-soul, reggaeton, rock rap, metal rap, punk rap, rapcore, glitch hop, trip hop, krunk, snap music, and wonky music) build on previous generations' black popular music and black popular culture. For example, in *Rap Music and the Poetics of Identity* (2000), music scholar Adam Krims asserted that a full-length study of hip hop culture that "theorize[s] its embeddedness or expressive value within African American traditions" would be "eminently worth while" and a much-needed contribution to the literature on hip hop culture and rap music (2). But, he writes, *Rap Music and the Poetics of Identity* "does not attempt to fill that gap" in Hip Hop Studies. Hence, *Hip Hop's Amnesia* is not just another book about rap music and hip hop culture in some isolated and ahistorical/apolitical amnestic sense, but arguably one of the first book-length studies to critically explore the musical, historical, cultural, social, and political roots of rap music and hip hop culture, which—as will be illustrated in the "remixes" (as opposed to chapters) to follow—reach all the way back to African American enslavement and post-enslavement or, rather, Reconstruction black popular music and black popular culture.

Moreover, recently I was extremely excited to read *Keep On Pushing: Black Power Music from Blues to Hip Hop* (2011) by renowned music journalist Denise Sullivan. But, in spite of its title, her study actually does not treat classic blues music in any substantial manner. In fact, even its discussion of jazz seems to completely overlook early jazz's extremely interesting origins and evolution, as *Keep On Pushing* takes late 1950s and early 1960s jazz as its point of departure. Sullivan's book, indeed, is an undeniable *tour de force*, but one that could have benefitted from a more accurate title and a more in-depth discussion of the ways in which rap music and hip hop culture built on the musics of the various 1950s, 1960s, and 1970s Freedom Movements (e.g., the Civil Rights Movement; the Black Power Movement; the Women's Liberation Movement; the Lesbian, Gay, Bisexual & Transgender Liberation Movement; the New Left Movement; and the Anti-War Movement).

As it stands, *Keep On Pushing* seems to meander from one musical moment to the next, covering a great deal of historical ground, but not really providing its readers with a much-needed window into the extra-musical, cultural, social, and political world of black America that coalesced to create modern (i.e., 1950 through 1980) and more contemporary (i.e., 1980 through the present) black popular music in specific, and black popular culture more generally. All of this is to say, no matter how brilliant Sullivan's book may very well be (and I honestly believe that it is a beautifully written book), yet and still, there is not a single serious scholarly work that sincerely grapples with and seeks to critically grasp *hip hop's inheritance* from previous African American musics *and* movements (see Rabaka 2011, forthcoming). Here we have yet another reason *Hip Hop's Amnesia* registers as more than merely another book on rap music and hip hop culture. When and where the fifth fundamental element of hip hop (i.e., knowledge) is brought into the mix, a qualitatively different history of hip hop emerges. In short, this is a book—and, even more, this is an organic intellectual "old school" mega-mix and mash-up—about what hip hop has lost and *why* it needs to be found and *how* it can be found—or, rather, rescued, reclaimed, and remixed.

The musics of the major African American social and political movements of the 1950s, 1960s, and 1970s were based and ultimately built on earlier forms of *African American movement music*. Therefore, in order to really and truly understand rap music and hip hop culture—let alone whether there really is such a thing as *the Hip Hop Movement* currently underway—we must critically examine both *classical African American musics* and the *classical African American movements* that these musics served as soundtracks for. This study will be primarily preoccupied with the ways in which post-enslavement black popular music and black popular culture frequently served as a soundtrack for and reflected the populist politics of post-enslavement African American social and political movements. Where many Hip Hop Studies scholars have made clever allusions to the ways in which rap music and hip hop culture are connected to and seem to innovatively evolve earlier forms of black popular music and black popular culture, *Hip Hop's Amnesia* moves beyond anecdotes and witty allusions and earnestly endeavors a full-fledged critical examination and re-evaluation of *hip hop's inheritance* from the major African American musics *and* movements roughly between 1900 and 1955.

It is generally accepted that black popular music and black popular culture frequently reflect the conservatism *and* radicalism, the moderatism *and* militantism of the major African American movement (or movements, plural) of the milieu in which they initially emerged. Bearing this in mind, *Hip Hop's Amnesia* critically explores how "old school" black popular musics—such as classic blues, ragtime, and jazz, essentially between the turn of the twentieth century through to the beginning of the Civil Rights Movement—were more or less *movement musics*—that is to say, *music that literally mirrored and served as mouthpieces for African American social and political movements*, again, roughly between 1900 and 1955. The sequel to *Hip Hop's Amnesia*, which is tentatively titled *The Hip Hop Movement: From R&B and the Civil Rights Movement to Rap and Obama's America*, will explore *hip hop's inheritance* from the major African American musics and movements between 1955 and 1980 (see Rabaka, forthcoming). The forthcoming study will ultimately provide an alternative history and critical theory of contemporary society that will highlight how rap music and hip hop culture, in their own often-warped and often-wicked ways, continues the African American movement music tradition, even though the Hip Hop Movement does not always and in every instance resemble the various cultural, social, and political major movements of the 1950s, 1960s, and 1970s.

Where *Hip Hop's Amnesia* examines classic blues, ragtime, and jazz, as well as the correlate African American socio-political movements that correspond with each of these classical black popular musics, *The Hip Hop Movement* will explore rhythm & blues, soul, funk, go-go, and disco, as well as the correlate African American socio-political movements that correspond with each of these more modern black popular musics.

There is, indeed, a serious need for more historically rooted, culturally relevant, and politically radical research within the world of Hip Hop Studies. Too often fans and critics listen to, speak of, and write about rap music and hip hop culture as though contemporary black popular music and contemporary black popular culture are not in any way connected to a historical and cultural continuum that can be easily traced back to African American enslavement and—most importantly with respect to the discussion at hand—*post-enslavement, turn of the twentieth century, and early twentieth century classical black popular music and classical black popular culture.*[4] As a matter of fact, I would go so far to wager that most of my readers have probably heard and, I would surmise, have some sort of relationship with blues, ragtime, and jazz music, but possibly know little or nothing about the historic movements these now much-touted musics sonically symbolized and aurally represented during their heydays.

For instance, I am almost certain that most folk would be hard-pressed to merely list without detailed explanation pre–Civil Rights Movement African American social and political movements. Of course, many would immediately invoke the Harlem Renaissance without realizing that it was actually the aesthetic arm of the New Negro Movement (see the fourth "remix" to follow). Citing the Harlem Renaissance as a social and political movement, without in any way referencing that the radicals of the Renaissance were actually most often directly reflecting and reacting to the ethos of the broader New Negro Movement, is tantamount to invoking the Black Arts Movement as though it was not an offshoot of the Black Power Movement, or invoking the Feminist Art Movement without acknowledging that it was a correlate of the Women's Liberation Movement.[5] In short, *Hip Hop's Amnesia* is a study about aesthetics *and* politics, music *and* social movements, as well as the ways in which African Americans' unique history and culture has consistently led them to create musics that have served as the soundtracks or, more or less, the *mouthpieces* for their socio-political aspirations and frustrations, their socio-political organizations and nationally-networked movements.

Obviously here the question becomes: "But, really now, which movement does rap music reflect?" This is the question that is at the heart of this book. It should be stated openly and outright: This is a very valid question. Indeed, it is a critical question that I am sincerely seeking to ask my generation, the so-called "Hip Hop Generation," throughout the following pages of this book. In a nutshell, what I have come to call the "Hip Hop Movement" actually does not rotely resemble any previous African American social and political movement. But, by the time my readers get to the fifth and final "remix" of this book they will see that, yet and still, there is a Hip Hop Movement afoot. As will be revealed in the five "remixes" to follow, truth be told, historic African American social and political movements have been neither identical nor have they had the exact same goals. Rapid and radical changes in "mainstream" American history, culture, politics, and society have made it such that there are great and often grave differences between successive generations of African Americans, including their aspirations and frustrations.[6]

*Hip Hop's Amnesia* argues that many of these "great and often grave differences" are easily observed in the history of black popular music and black popular culture, and that, even more, black popular music and black popular culture are often incomprehensible without some sort of working-knowledge of historic African American social and political movements. Taking this line of logic even further, *Hip Hop's Amnesia* contends that neither *hip hop's aesthetics* nor *hip hop's politics* can be adequately comprehended without some sort of working-knowledge of historic African American social and political movements. Ultimately, then, this is a book about "partial or total loss of memory" or, rather, *what has been forgotten but should be remembered* concerning the "old school" origins and evolution of rap music and hip hop culture.

In other words, *Hip Hop's Amnesia*, to put it plainly, is not only about *hip hop's amnesia* in some sort of literal sense, but also about the *amnesia surrounding hip hop*. It is a study about the Hip Hop Generation's "partial or total loss of memory" in terms of previous African American musics and movements, but also, and equally important here, it is a study about what hip hoppers' grandparents and parents have forgotten but should remember about previous African American musics and movements in relationship to the origins and evolution of rap music and hip hop culture. In so many words it could and, perhaps, *should* be said that rap music and hip hop culture's real "old school" roots have been routinely overlooked largely in favor of 1980-onward examinations of black popular music and black popular culture.

## MY "OLD SCHOOL" MIXTAPE MANIFESTO: ON THE FIVE REMIXES OF THE PRE–RHYTHM & BLUES AND PRE–CIVIL RIGHTS MOVEMENT ROOTS OF RAP MUSIC AND HIP HOP CULTURE TO FOLLOW

In lieu of "chapters" I have chosen to offer, quite literally, "remixes" of hip hop history and culture in the series of studies to follow. Opting for "remixes" instead of "chapters" speaks to the special efforts and intellectual labor-filled lengths I have gone through to really and truly make a contribution to the interdisciplinary and intersectional field of Hip Hop Studies. From my point of view, Hip Hop Studies is a wide-ranging and wide-reaching field of critical inquiry where contemporary black popular music and contemporary black popular culture are conceived of as "text" and (re)situated and (re)interpreted within the wider "context" of, first and foremost, African American and African diasporan history, culture, aesthetics, politics, and economics, and then ultimately broader national and international history, culture, aesthetics, politics, and economics. Within the world of Hip Hop Studies, then, black popular music and black popular culture can be said to represent an arena of "subjugated knowledge," which Michel Foucault (1977a, 1977b, 1988) essentially defined as ways of thinking and doing that have been eclipsed, devalued, or rendered invisible within the dominant institutions of power/knowledge.

When black popular music and black popular culture are conceived of as "subjugated knowledge," then it is possible to perceive the ways that they historically have and currently continue to indelibly influence and inform race relations, gender identity, sexual politics, class struggles, cultural conventions, social views, and broader political values. Revealingly, black popular music and black popular culture are often relegated to the realm of "low culture" (as opposed to "high culture"), which means they are frequently overlooked and, accordingly, under-scrutinized as "serious" sites of scholarly historical, cultural, social, and political study. This lame line of logic also overlooks the fact the black popular music and black popular culture, in their own sometimes warped and sometimes wicked ways, represent distinct sites of ideological and counter-ideological production, articulation, and contestation. Hence, the five "remixes" of hip hop history and culture to follow aim to critically engage the ideological and counter-ideological currents and undercurrents deeply embedded in pre–rhythm & blues black popular music and pre–Civil Rights Movement black popular movements that have been, however unheralded, handed down to rap music, hip hop culture, and the broader Hip Hop Movement.

To conceptually focus on *interdisciplinary and intersectional "remixes" of hip hop history and culture*, as opposed to taking a more musicological, monodisciplinary, and single-subject academic book-based approach to Hip Hop Studies, also enables me to illustrate the incredible intellectual depth and wide-reach of rap music and hip hop culture's contributions to contemporary history, culture, aesthetics, politics, and society. At this point Hip Hop Studies' interdisciplinary and intersectional emphasis is undeniably and rather easily detected in its utilization of myriad "remixed" epistemologies and methodologies from disciplines as far afield and far flung as: American Studies; African American Studies; Women's Studies; Sexuality Studies; Critical Race Studies; Cultural Studies; Postmodern Studies; Postcolonial Studies; and, of course, Popular Music Studies—as well as more conventional disciplines such as: sociology; anthropology; history; philosophy; religion; political science; economics; linguistics; English; comparative literature; communications; education; and, of course, musicology, among many others.

By the sheer fact of its ever-increasing cultural and socio-political impact over the last three decades, rap music and hip hop culture have proven to be much more than a passing postmodern cultural copy-cat or an erstwhile intellectual fad. As the "remixes" to follow will illustrate, the best hip hop intellectuals, artists, and activists are as adept at critiquing its flows and flaws as many of the most astute aficionados and entrants in any other genre of critical, cultural, musical, or aesthetic endeavor. Moreover, as Hip Hop Studies enters a new phase and heightens its critical acumen—which is to say, as it matures and moves to expand in new directions, as it discursively deepens and develops even more extensive areas of investigation and interrogation—hip hop scholars and students must grapple with and seek to seriously grasp the multidimensionality and mayhem, serious contributions and controversies of not merely rap music and hip hop culture, but the larger socio-political project and, perhaps even, the long-lasting legacy of *the Hip Hop Movement*.

In other words, hip hop scholarship—as opposed to either uncritical "hip hop cheerleading" or hardcore "hip hop hateration"—must do a much better job of conceptually capturing, critically reflecting, and frequently refracting the music, aesthetics, politics, and culture it aims to interrogate—critique and/or appreciate. Hip hop scholarship should always and everywhere have the very same characteristics as the most exemplary rap music and hip hop culture: poetic license; loaded-language and value-laden lyrics; marvelous sense of melody; irresistible trunk-rattling rhythms; head-bobbing beats; sophisticated yet soulful samples; and a kind of *aural alchemy* or, rather, *musical magic* that inspires its listeners to want more and more and to often place themselves within the world of the text. In a sense, more than anything else *Hip Hop's Amnesia* is emblematic of my ongoing efforts to bring some of the word-wizardry, rhetorical acrobatics, aural innovations, and sonic sophistication of rap music and hip hop culture into the American academy, if not ultimately into highbrow and highfalutin parliaments, parlors, and palaces around the world.

*Hip Hop's Amnesia* is also emblematic of my humble ongoing efforts to wrestle with the creative cultural and political expressions of very often degraded, if not outright dehumanized and *de-Africanized*, past and present black ghetto youth. As a matter of fact, it could be said that this is a book about denigrated and much-misunderstood black ghetto youth—again, past and present—who have "knuckled and brawled" (to borrow a favorite phrase from the rhetorical genius Black Thought of the Roots) to have their long-muted and long-disregarded voices heard, views acknowledged, and values taken seriously, both intra-racially and inter-racially, as well as nationally and internationally.[7] Bearing this in mind, in the five "remixes" to follow my readers will detect that I am up to much more than merely making connections between rap and classic blues, ragtime, and jazz.

There is admittedly, then, a deep socio-political dimension to this book, as each of the aforementioned musics will be "remixed" and (re)placed within the wider historical, cultural, social, and political contexts within which they initially emerged. Consequently, ultimately this means that I will re-situate and reinterpret these musics within the wider contexts of the socio-political movements they originally served as soundtracks or "mouthpieces" for. In this sense, I have several other objectives in mind here: to expose and explore the "old school," pre–rhythm & blues and pre–Civil Rights Movement roots of rap music and hip hop culture; to examine African American femininity, masculinity, gender relations, sexual politics, and class struggles within the world of pre–rhythm & blues black popular music and pre–Civil Rights Movement black popular culture in relationship to rap music and hip hop culture; to accent and amplify the unprecedented interracial alliances between African American and European American intellectual-artist-activists in pre–Civil Rights Movement America; and, to emphasize rap music and hip hop culture as "mouthpieces" and creative cultural expressions for the major post–Civil Rights Movement African American *and* multi-racial/multi-cultural/multi-issue youth movement of our era: *the Hip Hop Movement.*

In the five "remixes" that constitute the core of this text I seek to offer an intellectual-activist's version of a hip hop "mixtape"—à la Michael Eric Dyson (2007), Kevin Driscoll (2009), and my esteemed colleague Jared Ball (2009, 2011). However, what decidedly distinguishes my "mixtape manifesto"—to build on Ball's brilliant work—is that *Hip Hop's Amnesia* unerringly focuses on pre–rhythm & blues black popular music and pre–Civil Rights Movement black popular movements and critically engages their contributions to rap music, hip hop culture, and the Hip Hop Movement. Where the aforementioned works took a more or less theoretical and thematic angle in offering their intellectual-activist versions of a hip hop mixtape, *Hip Hop's Amnesia* endeavors a historical and critical theoretical approach that, literally, highlights what rap music, hip hop culture, and the Hip Hop Movement— either directly or indirectly—"inherited" from pre–rhythm & blues black popular music and pre–Civil Rights Movement black popular movements.

As is well-known, an authentic hip hop mixtape always and everywhere reflects the musical tastes and, to a certain extent, the political or even apolitical attitude of its compiler or, rather, its "mix-master," as we say in hip hop lingo. A hip hop mixtape can be a randomly selected compilation of the latest hot rap songs, or it can be a deeply-contemplated conceptual mix of a wide-range of songs—rap, classic soul, neo-soul, funk, jazz, blues, gospel, reggae, and rock, among other, songs—that are lyrically linked by a specific motif or mood. Recently, major rap artists, especially many of the more commercially successful rappers, have controversially used the mixtape format to release either more decadent or more politically charged music that their more "mainstream" and pop chart-obsessed record labels have either passed on or do not want to be linked to—for instance: G-Unit's *50 Cent Is The Future* (2002); T.I. and P.S.C.'s *In Da Streetz* (2003); Chamillionaire's *Mixtape Messiah* (2004); Beanie Sigel's *Public Enemy #1* (2004); Talib Kweli's *Right About Now!* (2005); Young Jeezy's *Trap Or Die* (2005); Juelz Santana's *Back Like Cooked Crack, Vol. 2* (2005); The Re-Up Gang's *We Got It For Cheap, Vol. 2* (2005); Lil' Wayne's *Dedication* (2006); Little Brother's *Separate But Equal* (2006); Talib Kweli's *Liberation!* (2006); Lil' Wayne's *Dedication 2* (2007), *Lyrical Homocide* (2007), *The Carter Files* (2007), and *New Orleans Millionaire* (2007); Little Brother's *And Justice For All* (2008); Lil' Wayne's *Dedication 3* (2008), *The Carter Show* (2008), *It's Weezy Baby!* (2008), and *The Greatest Rapper Alive* (2008); Gucci Mane's *Writing On the Wall* (2009); and Drake's *So Far Gone* (2009).

In keeping with most aspects of rap music and hip hop culture, mixtapes are usually intensely personal and nothing if not revelatory manifestos specifically tailored to the tape's intended individual recipient or target audience. Hence, in "The Digital Mix Tape Comes of Age," music critic Michael Resnick (2006) quoted the Library of America's editor-in-chief, Geoffrey O'Brien, as saying that the mixtape is "the most widely practiced American art form." With *Hip Hop's Amnesia* I seek to humbly share my mixtape manifesto about the real "old school" roots of rap music and hip hop culture; about the connections between rap and classic blues, ragtime, and jazz; and, about the connections between the Hip Hop Movement and the Black Women's Club Movement, the New Negro Movement, the Harlem Renaissance, the Lost Generation, the Bebop Movement, and the Beat Generation. The five extended "remixes" that constitute *Hip Hop's Amnesia*, therefore, seek to translate the energy and excitement, the contradictions and outright courting of controversy in rap music and hip hop culture's "commercial," "conscious," "alternative," and "underground" communities into book form, placing rap-styled remixes and homespun hip hop-inspired alternative histories, critical theories, and counter-narratives between the covers of a book and in the hands of the Hip Hop Generation.

As Russell Potter revealed in *Spectacular Vernaculars: Hip Hop and the Politics of Postmodernism* (1995), "[h]ip hop audiences do not, at any rate, merely *listen*—passive reception is no longer possible" (108, emphasis in original). The "remixes" of hip hop history and culture offered in *Hip Hop's Amnesia* are aimed at disrupting the longstanding amnestic relationship most hip hop fans and critics have with the real "old school" roots of rap music and hip hop culture, especially *pre–rhythm & blues and pre–Civil Rights Movement* African American history and culture. If, indeed, "passive reception [of rap and other hip hop music] is no longer possible," then I would like to bring some of the same (pro)active ethos and intellectually assertive energy into the field of Hip Hop Studies, where it is still very possible to passively claim to love rap music but actively hate black ghetto youth; where it remains possible to passively claim to love your mother and grandmother but actively hate your "baby-mama," girlfriend, or seemingly all hip hop women because they are perceived to be "chickenheads," "hood rats," and "gold diggers"; and, finally, where it is still possible to passively claim to love *all* people but openly and assertively hate homosexuals.

Potter contended that "[h]ip hop itself is not merely *music* (though it is certainly that)," but even more, in a certain sense, hip hop is a novel kind of "cultural recycling center" (108, emphasis in original). Well, in a nutshell, *Hip Hop's Amnesia* is about the specific aspects of *pre–rhythm & blues and pre–Civil Rights Movement* African American culture, music, and movements that historically have been and currently continue to be radically "recycled" and "remixed" by rap music, hip hop culture, and the Hip Hop Movement. In keeping with the hip hop mixtape motif, the five "remixes" to follow offer alternative histories and critical theories of the "old school" roots of rap music and hip hop culture, classic blues queens and the Black Women's Club Movement, classic jazz and the New Negro Movement, and bebop and the Bebop Movement in relationship to rap, other hip hop music, hip hop culture, and ultimately the Hip Hop Movement. Indeed, the real power of these "remixes" will hit home and be heartfelt only if my readers have a clear sense of what is at stake in each of the subsequent aural and intellectual excursions. Hence, here I will briefly outline the five "remixes" to follow.

The first "remix," "'Back to the Old School!': On the 'Old School' Origins and Evolution of Rap Music, Hip Hop Culture, and the Hip Hop Movement," will explore the "old school" roots of rap music and hip hop culture more generally. It emphasizes that rap music and hip hop culture are regularly judged or, rather, misjudged—both hailed and hated on—using criteria that actually have little or nothing to do with it or the historical, cultural, musical, social, and political world that it was formed in and directly grew out of. Returning to the notion that Hip Hop Studies is a wide-ranging and wide-reaching field of critical inquiry where contemporary black popular music and contemporary black popular culture are conceived of as "text" and (re)situated and (re)interpreted within the wider "context" of, first and foremost, African American and African diasporan history, culture, aesthetics, politics, and economics, and then ultimately broader national and international history, culture, aesthetics, politics, and economics, here *the text/context concept* is discursively deepened and developed. Similar to the cadre of youth it primarily represents—that is, black ghetto youth—the first "remix" ultimately argues that rap music and hip hop culture are much-misunderstood, both nationally and internationally, in large part as a consequence of the ongoing amnesia or outright ignorance surrounding African American history, culture, and contemporary struggles. If rap music and hip hop culture appear to be contradictory, the first "remix" strongly stresses, we should refrain from condemning the whole of hip hop culture prior to thoroughly probing its pre–Civil Rights Movement, Civil Rights Movement, and post–Civil Rights Movement antecedents. How might many of hip hop culture's contradictions have been handed down by earlier black ghetto youth, generation after generation, who, for whatever reason, found black popular music and black popular culture to be the most viable mediums through which to express their aspirations and frustrations, their love and hate, their spirituality and sexuality, their embrace of democracy and outright rejection of hypocrisy, and on and on *ad infinitum*?

Growing out of the first "remix," the second "remix," "'Lifting As We Climb!': Classic Blues Queens and the Black Women's Club Movement, Neo-Soul Sistas and the Hip Hop Women's Movement," will examine the connections between classic blues women, classic black clubwomen, and contemporary hip hop women. It seeks to circumvent *hip hop's amnesia* with regard to blues music, the blues aesthetic, and blues culture by critically engaging classic blues women's controversial and contradictory black feminism in contrast to the historically celebrated and more socially acceptable forms of black feminism that emerged from the Black Women's Club Movement. It demonstrates that, where most members of the Black Women's Club Movement shunned classic blues women, and classic black popular culture more generally, most members of the Hip Hop Women's Movement by contrast embrace—even as they remain highly critical of—many elements of contemporary black popular music and contemporary black popular culture, going so far as to dub themselves "hip hop feminists" who are leading a "Hip Hop Feminist Movement." The second "remix" ultimately centers on continuity and discontinuity within African American women's popular movement politics and solemnly calls into question the connections between the first major African American women's movement (i.e., the Black Women's Club Movement) and the most recent major African American women's movement (i.e., the Hip Hop Women's Movement). What did the Hip Hop Women's Movement "inherit" from the Black Women's Club Movement? Which parts of its "inheritance" has it outright rejected or ingeniously "remixed" in its ongoing efforts to speak to the special needs of young African American and other (especially non-white) women at the turn of the twenty-first century?

In the ongoing effort to either locate or create an antidote for *hip hop's amnesia* the third "remix," "Jazzmatazz: From Classic Jazz and Bebop to Jazz Rap and Hip Hop," focuses on classic jazz's contributions to rap music and hip hop culture in general, and the 1990s "jazz rap" phenomenon in particular. Here the main point is to critically examine how jazz *as music, aesthetics, poetics, politics, and culture* has indelibly influenced the origins and evolution of rap music and hip hop culture. Certainly it will not be as difficult to demonstrate the connections between jazz and rap as compared to the almost unheard of connections between classic blues—especially classic blues queens—and rap discussed in the second "remix." However, and this should be sternly stated at the outset, this jazz rap "remix" is not simply about the connections between jazz and rap, but also about the ways in which jazz music, jazz dance, jazz films, jazz novels, jazz poetry, and jazz politics uneasily served as an inspiration and soundtrack for multiple major countercultural movements, including: the New Negro Movement, the Harlem Renaissance, the Lost Generation, the Hipster Movement, the Zoot Suit Riots, the Bebop Movement, and the Beat Generation. Each of these jazz-influenced countercultural movements has, however unheralded, contributed to the Hip Hop Movement in one way or another, which means, it will be argued, jazz's influence on rap music and hip hop culture has been both direct and indirect, and perhaps a lot deeper and a lot more prevalent than previously believed.

The fourth "remix," "'If We Must Die!': The New Negro Movement, the Harlem Renaissance, and the Homosexual Hip Hop Movement," offers alternative histories and critical theories of the New Negro Movement and the Harlem Renaissance with a keen eye on what has been passed on to the Hip Hop Movement. The first section of the "remix" provides a succinct survey of the New Negro Movement that sheds light on the ways that its sometimes moderate, and sometimes militant civil rights activism laid a foundation for the Hip Hop Movement's, truth be told, "sometimes moderate, and sometimes militant" civil rights and social justice activism. The second section develops a discourse on the aesthetics, poetics, and sexual politics of the Harlem Renaissance. It seeks to accent the often-overlooked links between Renaissance music, aesthetics, poetics, and politics in light of its unprecedented *interracial heterosexual-homosexual alliances*. Building on the previous sections, the fourth "remix's" final section turns readers' attention to the simple—but still controversial in many quarters—fact that the Homosexual Hip Hop Movement, as quiet as it has been kept, may actually embody much of what can be considered "real" hip hop culture—especially "real" hip hop poetics, politics, and social activism—in light of its incessant emphasis on openness to and acceptance of difference, whether that "difference" is sexual, cultural, racial, gender, economic, or religious.

The fifth and final "remix," "The Hip Hop Movement: From Merely Rap Music to a Major Multi-Issue Socio-Political Movement," takes up the issues surrounding the over-emphasis on previous black popular music and the de-emphasis on previous black socio-political movements—especially pre–rhythm & blues black popular music and pre–Civil Rights Movement black popular movements—in the conventional histories of rap music and hip hop culture in light of "remixes" 1 through 4. Even though many know a great deal about classic blues, ragtime, classic jazz, and bebop, there has been a marked tendency to downplay, if not outright disassociate, these classic musics from the classic movements—that is to say, the Black Women's Club Movement, the New Negro Movement, the Harlem Renaissance, and the Bebop Movement—that most often inspired them and that they were in daily dialogue with. Moreover, the final "remix" reveals that there is a similar, extremely tired tendency to downplay and disassociate rap music, hip hop culture, and the Hip Hop Movement from these classic black popular musics and classic black socio-political movements. Ultimately this callous custom makes it appear as though rap music, hip hop culture, and the Hip Hop Movement are complete anomalies instead of, at least in part, logical extensions and expansions of previous black popular music, black popular culture, and black popular movements.

As with previous black popular music and black popular movements, this "remix" reveals that now rap music is being distanced from the Hip Hop Movement, and that even invoking such a thing as a "Hip Hop Movement" may cause many to laugh in disbelief, as if rap—similar to classic blues, classic jazz, and bebop, among other black popular musics—does not have any social or political impulse, and does not serve as a soundtrack for the Hip Hop Movement. Indeed, this book concludes by emphasizing the often-overlooked fact that hip hop youth, African American or otherwise, could possibly learn a great deal from pre–rhythm & blues black popular music and pre–Civil Rights Movement black socio-political movements, especially their discursively deep and undeniably inextricable _musical mouthpiece-and-socio-political movement relationship_—which is to say, their _black popular music as the soundtrack and/or mouthpiece for black popular movements' relationship_. We begin, then, with an alternative remix and mash-up of the "old school" roots of rap music, neo-soul, hip hop culture, and the broader Hip Hop Movement.

# NOTES

1. For further discussion of rap music's poetics and politics, and for the most noteworthy works that informed my analysis here, see Bradley (2009), Hendershott (2004), Krims (2000), Murray (1998), Ogbar (2007), and Perry (2004).

2. For further discussion of the ways in which rap helped to revitalize the music industry at the end of the twentieth century, as well as the ways in which certain forms of rap express regional culture, politics, and musical trends, and for the most noteworthy works that informed my analysis here, see Basu and Lemelle (2006), Charnas (2010), Mitchell (2001), Negus (1999), Ogg (2001), and Watkins (2005).

3. It is important, here at the outset, to openly acknowledge that what we now call "hip hop" or "hip hop culture" initially had four fundamental elements, according to Afrika Bambaataa: MCing (i.e., "rapping"), DJing, break-dancing (i.e., "breaking"), and graffiti-writing (i.e., "writing"). According to Jeff Chang, in *Can't Stop Won't Stop: A History of the Hip Hop Generation* (2005), when hip hop "lost its way" Bambaataa ingeniously added a fifth fundamental element of hip hop culture: "knowledge" (90). It is extremely important, therefore, to acknowledge that instead of being "anti-intellectual," which is one of the common stereotypes about the Hip Hop Generation, one of the core elements of authentic hip hop culture is its emphasis on *the acquisition, production, and dissemination of knowledge*. Chang quoted Bambaataa as having stated that "real hip hop" is about having "right knowledge, right wisdom, right 'overstanding' and right sound reasoning—meaning that we want our people to deal with factuality versus beliefs, factology versus beliefs" (90). Although all five forms of the culture continue to survive today, in the early 1980s rap music, which synthesizes both MCing and DJing, entered into a love/hate relationship with corporate America and mainstream American popular culture, effectively eclipsing break-dancing, graffiti-writing, and, to a certain extent, the fifth fundamental element of "knowledge." In chapter 5 of my book *Hip Hop's Inheritance* I developed a critique of the "hyper-corporate colonization of hip hop culture" where I critically explored how late 1970s and early 1980s African American underclass and other working-class youth culture, which was initially thought to be nothing more than a mere passing ghetto fad and poor young folks' foolishness, evolved into an artistic and socio-political force of great significance, not only nationally but internationally (Rabaka 2011, 189–220). Hence, with its increasing cultural clout, by the mid-1980s corporate America began to take notice and perceive the "mad" money-making potential in hip hop culture, initially elevating rapping and break-dancing over the other five fundamental elements of hip hop culture. After a brief period of competing with rap music as the most identifiable public emblem or social symbol of hip hop culture, break-dancing fell to the wayside and the "hyper-corporate colonization of hip hop culture," mostly centering around all manner of schemes to market and commercialize rap music, began in earnest (Fricke and Ahearn 2002; Kugelberg 2007). It is important, yet and still, to emphasize the prominence of break-dancing and b-boys and b-girls (i.e., "break-dancing boys" and "break-dancing girls") in early hip hop culture. In fact, many of my readers may be too young to recall how break-dancing films—such as *Wild Style* (1983), *Breakin'* (1984), *Breakin' 2: Electric Boogaloo* (1984), *Beat Street* (1984), *Body Shock* (1984), *Krush Groove* (1985), and *Rappin'* (1985)—took the nation, and later the world, by storm. Along with several of the major scholarly studies of break-dancing (e.g., Alford 1984; Bramwell and Green 2003; Franklin and Watkins 1984; Hazzard-Gordon 1990; Huntington 2007; Schloss 2009), I have relied on the following critically acclaimed documentaries for my interpretation of "breakin'" here: Celia Ipiotis's *Popular Culture in Dance: The World of Hip Hop* (1984), Israel's *The Freshest Kids: A History of the B-Boy* (2002), and Benson Lee's *Planet B-Boy: Breakdance Has Evolved* (2008). Moreover, graffiti-writing has made many inroads from the dark and dirty inner-city streets of its origins to several of the most prestigious contemporary art galleries around the world. But, truth be told, a greater appreciation of graffiti *as art* outside of the bourgeois "high art" versus "low art" distinctions germane to mainstream middle-class aesthetics remains desperately needed. For further discussion of the origins and evolution of hip hop-styled graffiti-writing, and for the major works which have influenced my interpretation here, see Austin (2001), Castleman (1982), Cooper and Chalfant (1984), Felisbret and Felisbret

(2009), Gastman and Neelon (2010), Hager (1984), S. A. Phillips (1999), Rahn (2002), and Wimsatt (2003). Finally, in terms of the fifth fundamental element of hip hop culture, "knowledge," a tug-of-war of sorts has been taking place between those who, on the one hand, see rap music as a pop cultural and commercial gold mine and those who, on the other hand, strongly believe that rap music should radically reflect the "knowledge," as well as the politics, culture, and impecunious communities, of its primary producers and practitioners: black ghetto youth. Needless to say, Hip Hop Studies is part and parcel of the discourse and debates surrounding the fifth fundamental element of hip hop culture (i.e., "knowledge"), and this book is specifically aimed at addressing the "knowledge" that has been handed down to the Hip Hop Generation from previous generations of black ghetto youth via their popular music, popular culture, and participation in popular movements during the first half of the twentieth century, roughly from 1900 to 1955.

    4. For further discussion of post-enslavement, turn of the twentieth century, and early twentieth century classical black popular music and classical black popular culture, and for the most noteworthy works that informed my analysis here, see Abbott and Seroff (2002), Banfield (2010), Burnim and Maultsby (2006), N. T. Davis (1996), Peretti (2009), and Small (1998a).

    5. In *Hip Hop's Inheritance* (2011) I critically explored the relationships between rap music and hip hop culture and several major—even though mostly marginalized—African American, black feminist/womanist, and homosexual cultural aesthetic movements. For instance, the Harlem Renaissance, Black Arts Movement, and Feminist Art Movement were engaged as the artistic arms of the New Negro Movement, Black Power Movement, and Women's Liberation Movement, respectively. Bearing the historic—and equally *herstoric*—connections between socio-political and cultural aesthetic movements in mind, *Hip Hop's Amnesia*, in a sense, deepens and develops the analysis presented in *Hip Hop's Inheritance* by methodically returning to the "old school," pre–rhythm & blues black popular music and pre–Civil Rights Movement black popular movement "roots" of rap music, hip hop culture, and, ultimately, the Hip Hop Movement.

    6. For further discussion of the pre–Hip Hop Movement historic African American social and political movements, and for the most noteworthy works that informed my analysis here, see D. W. Aldridge (2011), Franklin (1984), Giddings (1984), Harding (1981), Hine and Thompson (1998), Kelley and Lewis (2000), Marable and Mullings (2000), Payne and Green (2003), Singh (2004), and Walters (1993).

    7. With regard to Black Thought's phrase "knuckle and brawl," see the track "Long Time" on the Roots's *Game Theory* (2006) compact disc. He also used the phrase "knuckle and brawl" in his rhyme on the track "Duck Down!" on the Roots's *Tipping Point* (2004) compact disc. Obviously I have a particular predilection for a certain conscious rapper whose stage name is Black Thought (government name: Tariq Trotter) and who fronts the most famous acoustic hip hop band in the land. Those readers unaware of the Roots, their music *and* politics, and curious about conscious rap *and* acoustic hip hop music, should also spin their discs *Things Fall Apart* (1999), *The Roots Come Alive* (1999), *Phrenology* (2002), *Rising Down* (2008), *How I Got Over* (2010), and *Undun* (2011).

*Remix 1*

# "Back to the Old School!" [1]

## *On the "Old School" Origins and Evolution of Rap Music, Hip Hop Culture, and the Hip Hop Movement*

By appropriating and signifying upon beats, melodies, and any number of other recorded sounds, DJs and producers can assume the role of historians, using those sonic files as primary sources to create a historical narrative and to introduce audiences to political figures of the past and present; or, they can assume the role of cultural critic, using music as a method to construct and deconstruct historical narratives. —Charise Cheney, *Brothers Gonna Work It Out: Sexual Politics in the Golden Age of Rap Nationalism*, 10

### RAP MUSIC: MORE THAN MERELY "MEAN-MUGGING," "BITCH-BEATING," "PIMP-SLAPPING," "HO-SMACKING," AND "HOMOSEXUAL-HATING" MUSIC

Rap music and hip hop culture amazingly embody many aspects of the African American art, dance, literature, music, politics, and social move-ments that preceded it. But, because so little is known about the African American art, dance, literature, music, politics, and social movements that preceded it, sad to say, rap music and hip hop culture, for the most part, seem to remain a mystery to most of its fans and critics. That is to say, when we move beyond the booming beats, seemingly schizophrenic rhetoric, "mean-mugging," "bitch-beating," "pimp-slapping," "ho-smacking," and "homo-sexual-hating" in much of rap music and hip hop culture there are myriad ways in which contemporary black popular music and contemporary black popular culture, however unheralded, conceptually connect with and boldly

1

builds on classical black popular music and classical black popular culture. Moreover, it is important here to reiterate that it would be difficult to identify previous major forms of black popular music and black popular culture that were not in one way or another reflective of previous major African American social and political movements.

Hence, when all of the smoke clears and all of the dust settles, there very well may be a sense in which rap music and hip hop culture symbolize a *Hip Hop Movement*—a new form of African American political thought and a novel social movement that is profoundly indebted to earlier forms of both black popular music and black popular culture, *as well as* earlier forms of black political culture and black social movements. Furthermore, to be completely candid here, many of my readers may be amazed to discover that classic blues, ragtime, and jazz all in their own unique ways harbored a lot of booming beats, seemingly schizophrenic rhetoric, "mean-mugging," "bitch-beating," "pimp-slapping," "ho-smacking," and "homosexual-hating." Moreover, my readers might also find it interesting that each of the aforementioned forms of music were initially understood to be—by both the black and white well-to-do—nothing more than "lowdown," "sinful sounds," and "nigger noise" emerging from the black ghettos, slums, and juke joints.

Therefore, tensions between black popular music and black popular culture, on the one hand, and African American socio-political leaders and movements, on the other hand, did not begin and, truth be told, probably will not end with either rap music and hip hop culture or, even more, the wider Hip Hop Movement. *Hip Hop's Amnesia*, consequently, is not only about what hip hop "inherited" from previous African American musics and movements, but also about the historical relationship between black popular music and black socio-political movements. Over and above that, *Hip Hop's Amnesia* is almost unerringly about how rap music and the Hip Hop Movement are continuing the African American movement and African American "movement music" tradition.

Over the years within the world of Hip Hop Studies there has developed a marked tendency to go back only as far as there is easily identifiable evidence to support claims concerning rap and other hip hop music's indebtedness to earlier forms of African American music. This has, however unwittingly, created a situation where most Hip Hop Studies scholars go back only as far as rhythm & blues in their efforts to make connections between rap and other hip hop music and earlier—that is to say, pre–Civil Rights Movement—forms of African American music. Furthermore, even when and where Civil Rights Movement and post–Civil Rights Movement African American music is explored, because Hip Hop Studies scholars and critics most often have no working understanding or intricate knowledge of pre–Civil Rights Movement African American musics *and* movements they routinely offer what can only be called *amnestic analyses* of contemporary black popular music and contemporary black popular culture, which is arguably best embodied in rap music and hip hop culture.

In so many words I am saying that, indeed, the Hip Hop Generation seems to have a "partial or total loss of memory" surrounding the past— African American or otherwise, and musical or otherwise. However, here I also wish to imply that *there has been much that has been forgotten but should be remembered about classical black popular music and classical black popular culture in relationship to classical black political culture and classical black social movements.* Rap music and hip hop culture are regularly judged or, rather, misjudged—both hailed and hated on—using criteria that actually have little or nothing to do with it or the historical, cultural, musical, social, and political world that it was formed in and directly grew out of.

Similar to the cadre of youth it primarily represents—that is, black ghetto youth—rap music and hip hop culture is much misunderstood, both nationally and internationally, in large part as a consequence of the ongoing amnesia or outright ignorance surrounding African American history, culture, and contemporary struggles. If, as will be discussed in the four "remixes" to follow, rap music and hip hop culture appear to be contradictory, we should refrain from condemning the whole of hip hop culture prior to thoroughly probing its pre–Civil Rights Movement, Civil Rights Movement, and post–Civil Rights Movement antecedents. How might many of hip hop culture's contradictions have been handed down by earlier black ghetto youth, generation after generation, who, for whatever reason, found black popular music and black popular culture to be the most viable mediums through which to express their aspirations and frustrations, their love and hate, their spirituality and sexuality, their embrace of democracy and outright rejection of hypocrisy, and on and on *ad infinitum*?

Instead of symbolizing a mindless mass of ghetto youth, what if rap music and hip hop culture actually represent a kind of unprecedented uprising on the part of an oppressed group who have been traditionally relegated to the margins of post–Civil Rights Movement social and political discourse? What if rap represents more than merely the mad-wonderings and warped worldview of ghetto youth? What if the controversies surrounding rap—and, more specifically, "pop," "commercial," or "gangsta" rap—have consistently overshadowed the political character and social vision of hip hop culture and the wider world of the Hip Hop Movement? What if, when it is all said and done, rap music and hip hop culture actually accurately reflect the complexities, controversies, and contradictions of turn of the twenty-first century America, roughly between 1980 and the present? Is it feasible that we might actually have a deeper understanding of rap music and hip hop culture by critically exploring the musics *and* movements that surreptitiously serve as the foundation for contemporary black popular music and black popular culture?

*Hip Hop's Amnesia* sheds light on the "old school" origins and evolution of rap music and hip hop culture by critically examining the origins and evolution of classical black popular music and classical black popular culture in relationship to classical black political culture and classical black social movements. This book's emphasis on black popular music and black popular culture in connection with black political culture and black social movements is not new and can be traced back to, among others, Amiri Baraka's dictum in his classic work on black music, *Blues People* (1963), where he asserted, "it seems to me that if the Negro represents, or is symbolic of, something in and about the nature of American culture, this certainly should be revealed by his characteristic music" (ix). In other words, he continued, "I am saying that if the music of the Negro in America, in all its permutations, is subjected to a socio-anthropological as well as musical scrutiny, something about the essential nature of the Negro's existence in this country ought to be revealed, as well as something about the essential nature of this country, *i.e.*, society as a whole" (ix-x, emphasis in original).

At this point it is almost undeniable that rap and other forms of hip hop music, however roguishly, reveal "something about the essential nature of [African American] existence in this country," as well as "something about the essential nature of this country, *i.e.*, [mainstream] society as a whole." Frequently what rap and other forms of hip hop music reveal about both African American *and* mainstream American history, culture, politics, and society is overlooked in favor of uncritical blanket condemnations of each and every aspect of contemporary black ghetto youth music and culture. Most often it seems as though *there simply is no socially acceptable way to be a black ghetto youth in America.*[2]

Everything meaningful in black ghetto youth's lives—from their music to their behavior at shopping malls, from their language to their sex lives, from their sense of fashion to their "soul food" (à la Goodie Mob)—is deemed degenerate. Accordingly, then, faced with the "damned if you do, and damned if you don't" lame logic of middle-class black America and mainstream white America, most black ghetto youth turn to each other for sustenance. Their world is one that is almost completely devoid of the privileges and luxuries most middle-class Americans take for granted on a daily basis. Consequently, it is not a coincidence that black ghetto youth's popular music and popular culture seem to be preoccupied with the trauma and drama of ghetto life; with "movin' up out da hood and livin' good" (to quote Biggie Smalls); with "makin' it big," "mad money," and material possessions; and with drugs, alcohol, and sex.

The irony at the heart of *Hip Hop's Amnesia* is that, when classical black popular music and classical black popular culture are critically engaged, one discovers that it would be extremely difficult, if not impossible, to find a major form of black popular music and black popular culture that has not been preoccupied with each and every one of the issues and ills mentioned above. One of the reasons for this thematic continuity, even in the midst of well-documented and undeniably unprecedented black musical diversity, roughly between 1900 and 2000, might have something to do with the simple fact that very little has actually changed for the majority of African Americans since the issuing of the Emancipation Proclamation and the end of the Civil War. We would do well to take the post–Civil War, post-Reconstruction, and, yes, post–Civil Rights Movement cries of desperation and aural outrage emerging from black popular music and black popular culture seriously. Indeed, we would do well to earnestly ask: "What has really and truly changed for the majority of African Americans—especially the black masses—since the end of the Civil War, Reconstruction or, even, the Civil Rights Movement?"

Not in any way wanting to sound depressing, but solemnly guided by my conscience to "keep it real" on behalf of the black ghetto youth who continue to be the primary producers and practitioners of rap music and hip hop culture, several pertinent points should be made here concerning the realities of contemporary African American life and culture: *African Americans continue to have some of the highest school drop-out rates, infant mortality rates, unemployment rates, incarceration rates, gun-related death rates, sexually transmitted disease rates, and HIV/AIDS rates in the nation.*[3] *They are collectively more likely to die from one of the Center for Disease Control and Prevention's regularly listed "10 leading causes of death" than any other demographic in the United States.*[4] *By and large African Americans continue to go to substandard public schools, live in substandard public housing, receive substandard public medical care, and eat substandard public (or "welfare") food.* Consequently, just as classic blues, ragtime, and jazz at each of their emergences reflected the aspirations and frustrations of the majority of African Americans—who were then, as they are now, callously quarantined to the ghettos, slums, and barrios—rap and other forms of hip hop music primarily reflect the triumphs and tragedies, the ecstasies and agonies of contemporary black ghetto life and culture.

It is important here to observe that *Hip Hop's Amnesia* is not a book about rap, or any other form of hip hop music, as an unmitigated and unambiguous form of "pure" and "perfect" black radicalism (*or* "critical multiculturalism," *or* "radical humanism," as many would have it). Truth be told, rap music does not sonically symbolize or aurally articulate "pure" and "perfect" anything, and neither does what I am wont to call the Hip Hop Movement. Rap music and hip hop culture mirror contemporary American history, culture, politics, and society far too closely, and its core ethos, consequently, is far too contradictory for it to fall into the lazy dichotomous logic of being *either* all good, *or* all bad.

To be completely open and honest here, rap music and hip hop culture are quite often *both* good *and* bad, which is one of the reasons that by the time my readers get to the fifth and final "remix" of this book they will detect a strong stress on rap music and the Hip Hop Movement's "schizophrenic progressive/regressive tendencies." By emphasizing rap music and the Hip Hop Movement's "schizophrenic progressive/regressive tendencies" I do not wish to imply that rap music and hip hop culture are somehow "crazy," as many may misinterpret the term "schizophrenic" here, but to simply point out that rap music and hip hop culture are *essentially shared human projects that yield shared human products.* Hence, similar to each and every truly self-actualizing human being, rap music and hip hop culture are a lot more complex and complicated than many of their erstwhile fans and critics may be aware of.

As a critical social theorist, I can certainly understand why so many hip hop fans and critics would like to read rap music and hip hop culture as a form of neo-black radicalism, or critical multiculturalism, or, even, radical humanism. But the truth of the matter is that rap music and hip hop culture are quite complex and complicated, and made all the more complex and complicated by the longstanding and very tired tendency to over-emphasize its expressions of homophobia, misogyny, and materialism while de-emphasizing its expressions of anti-racism, anti-sexism, anti-capitalism, anti-imperialism, moral outrage, principled militantism, democratic radicalism, and political progressivism. In short, it can be said with a calm and clear conscience that *rap is more than merely "mean-mugging," "bitch-beating," "pimp-slapping," "ho-smacking," and "homosexual-hating" music.*

## POLITICS, POETICS, AND POPULAR CULTURE: ON RAP MUSIC'S RADICALISM AND HIP HOP CULTURE'S CONSERVATISM

*Hip Hop's Amnesia* strives to maintain a balance between those interpretations of rap music and hip hop culture that, on the one hand, see it as nothing more than babble over bangin' beats, and those interpretations, on the other hand, that perceive it to be some sort of "hardcore" or "pristine" expression of black ghetto youth radicalism and white suburban youth militant multiculturalism. In complete agreement with Adam Krims in *Rap Music and the Poetics of Identity* (2000), I utterly understand that "there can be little doubt that rap is extremely appropriate music for modeling what it is that cultural theorists like about 'resistant' culture" (8). But, by the same token, it can be said with some certainty that "a strong case could be made that the history of hip hop culture demonstrates precisely how marginalized cultural practices can be deployed to reinforce, at least as much as to challenge, dominant discourses (so-called 'gangsta rap' being only the most famous example)" (8). After we explore the ways that classic blues, ragtime, and jazz each in their own unique way lyrically and musically captured the aspirations and frustrations of African America—again, especially black ghetto youth—between 1900 and 1955, the lyrics, music, and sadomasochistic *and* schizophrenic progressive/regressive politics of gangsta rap may sound decidedly different—even if it, by and large, remains morally repugnant and ethically reprehensible to our ears and inner wisdom. The fifth and final "remix," accordingly, at least in part, will undertake an analysis of gangsta rap and what is generally called "hardcore" hip hop culture in light of what was once understood to be the vulgar and vice-laden lyrics and music of classic blues, ragtime, and jazz at their respective moments of emergence and periods of greatest popularity.

Indeed, we should not lose sight of the often-overlooked fact that "the history of hip hop culture demonstrates precisely how marginalized cultural practices can be deployed to reinforce, at least as much as to challenge, dominant discourses." Something very similar could and, I honestly believe, *should* be said about each and every major form of black popular music and black popular culture. As mentioned above, we should be wary of those interpretations of rap music and hip hop culture that over-emphasize its expressions of homophobia, misogyny, and materialism while de-emphasizing its expressions of anti-racism, anti-sexism, anti-capitalism, anti-imperialism, moral outrage, principled militantism, democratic radicalism, and political progressivism. But, conversely, we should be equally wary of those fans and critics who over-emphasize or outright romanticize rap music and hip hop culture's supposed multi-racial radicalism, political progressivism, and social activism while de-emphasizing its morally repugnant and ethically reprehensible misogyny, materialism, and heterosexism. Continuing this line of logic, in her watershed work *Brothers Gonna Work It Out: Sexual Politics in the Golden Age of Rap Nationalism* (2005), Charise Cheney offered further insight:

> It is important, therefore, not to overstate the case for the existence of seditious thinking within hip hop culture. While the power of rap music lies in its ability to articulate the hidden transcript of black cultural expression, not all rap music is counter-discourse. There is much within hip hop culture in general, and rap music specifically, that supports mainstream American social, political, economic, and cultural values. The widespread endorsement of conventional gender roles, the rampant heterosexism and homophobia, and the romanticization of capitalist pursuit and conspicuous consumption are all, in fact, conservative elements of hip hop culture. The most sensational aspects of

rap music that reflect cultural hegemony, however, are sexism and misogyny; and the rap music genre most known for these social offenses is "gangsta rap." (5)[5]

Above I asserted that it is generally accepted that black popular music and black popular culture frequently reflect the conservatism *and* radicalism, the moderatism *and* militantism of the major African American political thought and social movement of the milieu in which it initially emerged. In the "remixes" to follow, to reiterate, I seek a balanced approach to rap music and hip hop culture in light of classical black popular music and classical black popular culture in relationship to classical black political culture and classical black social movements. Rap music and hip hop culture may or may not be more conservative or more radical than any previous form of black popular music and black popular culture. But there is one thing that is certain at this point: we will never really know if we do not critically engage and cautiously interpret previous forms of black popular music and black popular culture.

Even as we critically engage and cautiously interpret previous forms of black popular music and black popular culture, we must solemnly bear one of Cheney's (2005) heartfelt questions in mind: "What are the (dis)advantages to having politics mediated through popular culture" (2)? Unlike several critically acclaimed scholars who have undertaken studies of rap music as a form of political critique and social commentary (e.g., Banjoko 2004; Dyson 1997; Kitwana 2002; Railton and Watson 2011; Reeves 2008; Rose 1994; Spencer 1991), here it is not my contention that *all* rap music and hip hop culture should be read as some postmodern or postcolonial, new-fangled form of political critique and social commentary. Furthermore, in the four "remixes" to follow I do not put into play the foolhardy and hype-filled impulse to search for political critique and social commentary in rap music and hip hop culture where they quite simply do not exist. Throughout *Hip Hop's Amnesia*, I call a spade a spade: *Misogyny is as morally repugnant in rap music as it is in most religious cultures and institutions in America. Homophobia is as ethically reprehensible in hip hop culture as it is in mainstream American culture. Bourgeois materialism or, rather, as Cheney put it above, the "romanticization of capitalist pursuit and conspicuous consumption" are as ostentatious, obscene, and absurd in rap music and hip hop culture as they are in virtually each and every lily-white suburban home and hamlet in America.*

All of this is to say that I utterly understand the impulse to defend and validate a music and culture that has been under attack seemingly since the very first second of its inception, especially when the attacks, for the most part, frequently—even if unwittingly—express their own postmodern, postcolonial, and/or "post-racial," new-fangled forms of anti-black racism, racialized sexism, racialized eroticism, racialized exoticism, and anti-poor people attitudes. However, the kind of extreme inclusiveness momentarily exhibited in, for instance, Tricia Rose's *Black Noise: Rap Music and Black Culture in Contemporary America* (1994), where she claimed that "rap lyrics, style, music, and social weight are predominantly counter-hegemonic," seeks to deconstruct and reconstruct or, rather, stridently *stretch* the "political" in order to include forms of rap music and hip hop culture that are in fact quite conservative and staunchly—even if often unwittingly—in favor of the established order and current status quo.

In arguing that the definition of the "political" should be, at liberty, enlarged to include all aspects of hip hop culture—which absolutely is *not* what Rose argued overall in her groundbreaking book—both dilutes rap music's salience as the major soundtrack for the Hip Hop Movement and outright misrepresents hip hop's origins and evolution by reducing it to a reactionary "subculture" that emerged exclusively as a response to the dominant issues and ills of turn of the twenty-first century America—for example: racism; Reaganism; Bushism; Clintonism; Bushism II; the right-wing rolling back of the women's rights gains of the Women's Liberation Movement; the escalation of homophobia and hate crimes against homosexuals; magnified militarism and amplified American imperialism; heightened jingoism, xenophobia, and religious intolerance (especially with respect to Islam—i.e., Islamophobia); the 1980's and 1990's "War on Poverty" (which was actually a *war against the poor*); the government's almost complete abandonment of its commitment to public housing and the growing tidal wave of gentrification allowed to overrun low-income urban areas traditionally occupied by working-class and poverty-stricken people; the under-funding of public education in urban environments and the over-funding of public and private education in suburban enclaves; increased drug abuse (especially crack cocaine and other "new" designer drugs); gang violence (especially gunplay and gun-related deaths); unabated unemployment; and rising incarceration rates. [6]

Although they mean well, most hip hop scholars and fans do not seem to fully comprehend the pitfalls of positivist pandering concerning *all* rap music's allegedly "counter-hegemonic" or "radical politics," as this spurious species of homespun positivism inevitably over-estimates and grossly exaggerates hip hop's "real"—as in authentic, genuine, or true—"radical politics." Moreover, the contention that each and every form of rap or hip hop music is somehow "political," or "radical," or even "subversive" actually undermines the social, political, cultural, and aesthetic authority of the rap and other hip hop artists whose music, poetics, and politics unambiguously and unapologetically, mindfully and critically engage the ongoing issues surrounding human liberation and radical democratic social transformation—especially in the interest of black ghetto youth in particular, and African Americans in general. A critical read of Rose's early work actually shows that even prior to the hyper-commercialization of rap music and hip hop culture—in fact, as far back as the mid-1990s—she astutely understood all too well that "[n]ot all forms of rap transcripts directly critique all forms of domination," and that many genres of rap actually "support and affirm aspects of current social power inequalities" (100, 103).

In so many words, Krims, Cheney, Rose, and I are all asserting that hip hop scholars and fans must be wary of "the populist optimism of cultural studies," as Jody Berland (1998) boldly put it, and side-step the longstanding tendency to read rap music and hip hop culture as *either* politically progressive *or* politically regressive in a hard and fast fashion (138). Very often, as the "remixes" to follow will reveal, rap music and hip hop culture harbor both progressive *and* regressive, radical *and* conservative elements—many of which are not unlike, and may very well be deeply connected to, those conspicuously found in classical forms of black popular music and black popular culture that actually pre-date the national emergence of rhythm & blues and the Civil Rights Movement in the mid-1950s.

## WHERE POSTMODERNISM MEETS THE POST-SOUL AND POST–CIVIL RIGHTS MOVEMENT: ON RAP MUSIC AND HIP HOP CULTURE AS A "CULTURAL RECYCLING CENTER"

Instead of over-determining the "political" or the "radical" or even more the "radical political" in rap music and hip hop culture, *Hip Hop's Amnesia* seeks to offer a radically "remixed" alternative history and critical theory of how rap music and hip hop culture have been ineradicably informed and influenced by classical black popular music and classical black popular culture—their perceived positives and negatives, as well as their historic controversies and contradictions. *Hip Hop's Amnesia* also seeks to illustrate how the Hip Hop Movement's often-overlooked relationships with previous African American social and political movements currently informs and influences the race, gender, class, and sexuality consciousness and politics of not only black ghetto youth, but also suburban white, poor white, Native American, Asian American, Caribbean American, and Latino youth—and that is whether Hip Hop Studies, African American Studies, American Studies, Ethnic Studies, Cultural Studies, Women's Studies, and Sexuality Studies scholars comprehend rap music and hip hop culture to be politically progressive or politically regressive, socially constructive or socially destructive or not.[7] Although I understand rap music and hip hop culture to be emblematic of much more than the sonic equivalent to, or patchwork soundtrack for, "postmodern" society, à la Russell Potter in *Spectacular Vernacu-*

*lars: Hip Hop and the Politics of Postmodernism* (1995), I will quickly concede that it can be characterized as a kind of "cultural recycling center," as he perceptively put it:

> Yet in a crucial sense, I would argue, the history of African American cultures provides the most astonishing and empowering account of resistance, and of a resistance which from its earliest days has consisted of strategies for forming and sustaining a culture *against* the dominant, using materials at hand. Deprived by the Middle Passage and slavery of a unified cultural identity, African American cultures have mobilized, via a network of localized sites and nomadic incursions, cultures of the *found*, the *revalued*, the *used*—and cultures, moreover, which have continually transfigured and transformed objects of *consumption* into sites of *production*.

> This remaking, this *revaluation*, is especially evident in hip hop; through its appropriation of the detritus of "pop" culture and use of the African American tradition of Signifyin(g), it hollows out a fallout shelter where the ostensible, "official" significance of words and pictures is made shiftable, mutable, unreliable. A television jingle for a breakfast cereal, a drum-break from Booker T. and the MG's, the William Tell overture, a speech by Huey Newton or Louis Farrakhan—all these are intermingled and layered together in a musical fusion that transforms and transposes, in the process constructing its own internal modes of Signifyin(g). These modes are not only constructed, but endlessly form and repeat an "open," *reconstructable* structure—since the rhythm track, the words, or the mix of Funkadelic may be sampled by Digital Underground, which in turn will be sampled by Craig G., which in turn will be sampled by. . . . Hip hop audiences do not, at any rate, merely *listen*—passive reception is no longer possible. Layer upon layer—one to dance to, one to think on, one to add to the din. Hip Hop itself is not merely *music* (though it is certainly that); it is a cultural recycling center, a social heterolect, a field of contest, even a form of psychological warfare. When a jeep loaded with speakers powered by a bank of car batteries blasts "Gangsta Gangsta" over the lawns of the "vanilla suburbs" of the "chocolate cities" (the phrases are George Clinton's) it is not to sell ice cream. (108, all emphasis in original)[8]

From my vantage point, to listen to, speak of, or write about rap music and hip hop culture as a postmodern "social heterolect," which is to say a wide-open "field of contest" or "even a form of psychological warfare," without first critically comprehending it within the distinct African American musical *and* movement traditions it was created in and, consequently, initially grew out of is yet another example of what I am wont to call *hip hop's amnesia* and *the amnesia surrounding hip hop* throughout the series of studies or, rather, the "remixes" to follow. How are our eager readers to grasp and seriously grapple with the pastiche, parody, play, and "panoply of symbols and signs" (à la Jacques Derrida in *De la grammatologie* [1967]) characteristic of postmodernism to be found in rap music and hip hop culture if they are not also exposed to the appropriations, extensions, and outright deconstructions and reconstructions of earlier forms of black popular music and black popular culture, most importantly, in relationship to the earlier forms of black political culture and black social movements these classic musics and cultures served as soundtracks and aesthetic outlets for, respectively? That is to say, even within the world of postmodernism there is a need to understand individual works of art within their original historical and cultural contexts in order to adequately appreciate their significance in the new or "remixed" postmodern, pastiche art.

Indeed, here we might recall Derrida's famous—if not now *infamous*—statement in *Of Grammatology* (1976) where he iconoclastically asserted "*il n'ya pas de hors-texte*" (translation: "there is nothing outside of the text"). By which he meant "there is no such a thing as out-of-the-text" and, consequently, "there is nothing"—implying, no intelligible or accurate interpretation—"outside context" (158–59, 163).[9] In other words, to "deconstruct" (à la Derrida) and break this down even further, the milieu or context of a text is an integral aspect of, and essential for critically comprehending, the text—whether one is examining a literary text, historical text, cultural text, social text, political text, musical text, or any other form of aesthetic text.

Hence, it is extremely important for us to openly observe at the outset that rap music and hip hop culture draw from more than merely earlier forms of European and European American popular music and popular culture, as well as Eurocentric conceptions of "high culture" and "low culture." Although it probably need not be said, I will say it anyway: rap music and hip hop culture also draw from more than merely those aspects of earlier forms of black popular music and black popular culture that have, for whatever reason, registered in and seem to continue to resonate with white America, especially white youth. In truth, then, text *and* context are inextricable and of prime importance here, and those who would have more than merely a superficial relationship with rap music and hip hop culture, or, even more, the Hip Hop Movement, would do well to place rap and other hip hop musical and cultural texts within the broader—both African American *and* mainstream American—historical, cultural, social, and political contexts they have been indelibly informed and undeniably influenced by.

To be clear here, I am not in any way taking issue with postmodern reads of rap music and hip hop culture, but simply and solemnly questioning whether it makes historical, cultural, epistemological, and methodological sense that postmodern reads of rap music and hip hop culture have been routinely privileged over and seem more prevalent than more historically rooted, culturally relevant, and politically radical reads of rap music and hip hop culture as, for instance, unambiguous forms of *post-soul black popular music* and *post–Civil Rights Movement black popular culture*. Anyone who carefully reads the rap music and hip hop culture "remixes" to follow will be able to easily detect my sympathy for postmodern (and postcolonial, post-feminist, post-Marxist, etc.) reads within the world of Hip Hop Studies. Here, I am simply emphasizing that most postmodern reads of rap music and hip hop culture frequently free-float or precariously hover above the actual— and, let it be said, distinctly *African American*—history, culture, politics, and social movements that have indelibly informed and deeply influenced the origins and evolution of rap music and hip hop culture. In other words, even when and where hip hop scholars and critics have acknowledged the need to contextualize rap music and hip hop culture there has been, and there remains, a marked tendency for most of these scholars and critics to privilege more "mainstream" (read: predominantly white or European) American historical, cultural, social, political, musical, and other artistic events, contexts, and movements over the distinctly African American historical, cultural, social, political, musical, and other artistic events, contexts, and movements that have historically served and currently continue to serve as the central paradigms and primary points of departure for rap music and hip hop culture, as well as the overarching Hip Hop Movement.

Even more directly, I must admit that I thoroughly enjoy and learn a great deal from engaging postmodern reads of rap music and hip hop culture—and I especially have in mind here Russell Potter's *Spectacular Vernaculars* (1995). However, in all honesty, I believe that I was able to more profoundly appreciate Potter's postmodern read of rap music and hip hop culture because I came to the text with a, however humble, pre-existing working knowledge of the distinctly *African American* history, culture, politics, and social movements that have indelibly informed and deeply influenced the origins and evolution of rap music and hip hop culture. For instance, Potter's contention that rap music and hip hop culture essentially "turn the tables" on "previous black traditions, making a future out of fragments from the archive of the past," as he poetically put it (18), really resonated with me. But, after critically reading *Spectacular Vernaculars* from cover to cover, I was left wondering and sincerely wanting to know more about rap music and hip hop culture in relationship to those often-mentioned "previous black traditions"—"traditions" which have been frequently forgotten, erased, rendered invisible, or appropriated as someone else's, and especially those "traditions" that decidedly and in the most defiant manner imaginable pre-date the national emergence of rhythm & blues and the Civil Rights Movement in the mid-1950s. It has long seemed to me that hip hop scholars, students, fans, and critics' *amnesia*, their "partial or total loss of memory," is even more acute—I would even go so far to say *chronic*—when and where we come to *pre–rhythm & blues black popular music* and *pre–Civil Rights Movement black popular culture.*

As a matter of fact, as I read, re-read, and pondered *Spectacular Vernaculars* I kept asking the text, myself, and erstwhile others unfortunate enough to be nearby at the time key questions, such as: What is rap's relationship with earlier, more "classical" forms of black popular music and black popular culture, such as classic blues, ragtime, and jazz? What did rap music, hip hop culture, and the broader Hip Hop Movement "inherit" from earlier, more or less, "classical" forms of black political culture and black social movements, such as the Black Women's Club Movement, the New Negro Movement, the Hipster Movement, and the Bebop Movement, among other early twentieth century, pre–Civil Rights Movement African American movements? And, to come back to Cheney's crucial question above: "What are the (dis)advantages to having politics mediated through popular culture?" In addition, we should also earnestly ask the inverse: "What are the (dis)advantages to having popular culture mediated through politics?"

At this point few will deny that hip hop DJs and producers are artists, even though many still will not concede that rap is really music (but, truth be told, to properly address this asininity and outright ignorance would require more space than I have here and ultimately take us far beyond the scope of this book; suffice to say, there are several more or less sophisticated Hip Hop Studies that take up this issue or, rather, this *ignorance*).[10] Indeed, hip hop DJs and producers are artists, but—along with the neo-soul singers, rappers, spoken-word artists, jazz musicians, and rock musicians, among many others, who blaze and bellow over their beats—they also often serve as historians, cultural critics, psychologists, sociologists, and political activists. For example, and speaking directly to the *DJ, producer, and rapper as intellectual-artist-activist* point, Cheney (2005) went so far to say: "By appropriating and signifying upon beats, melodies, and any number of other recorded sounds, DJs and producers can assume the role of historians, using those sonic files as primary sources to create a historical narrative and to introduce audiences to political figures of the past and present; or, they can assume the role of cultural critic, using music as a method to construct and deconstruct historical narratives" (10).[11]

Who can deny the myriad ways that Jay-Z and Kanye West used "sonic files as primary sources to create a historical narrative and to introduce audiences to [musical *and*] political figures of the past" on their critically acclaimed collaborative album *Watch the Throne* (2011)? Essentially songs such as "Otis," "Gotta Have It," and "The Joy," where they "chopped and screwed"—or, rather, "slowed and throwed"—Otis Redding's "Try A Little Tenderness," "Jigga-ed" and jacked-up James Brown's "People Get Up and Drive Your Funky Soul," and "Kanyeezyed," krumped, and krunked Curtis Mayfield's "The Makings of You," respectively, all bear the poetic and sonic signs of two enormously talented hip hop historians and cultural critics who used "music as a method to construct and deconstruct historical narratives" about what it means to be "African American" at the turn of the twenty-first century in contrast to what it meant to be "black and proud" in the middle of the twentieth century. Even though Redding, Brown, and Mayfield, for the most part, have much more musical and lyrical depth than Jay-Z and Kanye West's rhymes on *Watch the Throne*—rhymes that were dubbed "relentless capitalism" by Rob Harvilla of *Spin* and "luxury rap" by Ross Green of *Tiny Mix Tapes*—Jigga and Yeezy's reverence for these iconic musical *and* "political figures of the past" has not gone unacknowledged by even their most vociferous critics and hardcore haters. I was particularly struck by their open and unapologetic references to "Black Power" throughout the album, but most especially on the monster track "Murder to Excellence," where they sampled Quincy Jones's "Katutoka Corrine" (from Alice Walker and Steven Spielberg's 1985 film *The Color Purple*) alongside a Romanian folk song entitled "La, La, La."

Indeed, when we take the *DJ, producer, and rapper as intellectual-artist-activist* idea seriously there are innumerable instances where hip hoppers with neither high school diplomas nor college degrees—as Kanye West's *The College Dropout* (2004), *Late Registration* (2005), and *Graduation* (2007) trilogy playfully and painfully points out—can be said to serve as homespun historians, cultural critics, organic intellectuals, psychologists, sociologists, and political activists who, again, utilizing "sonic files as primary sources to create a historical narrative and to introduce audiences to [musical *and*] political figures of the past and present," in their own unique way, "assume the role of cultural critic, using music as a method to construct and deconstruct historical narratives." Who can deny that this is precisely what DJ Hi-Tek and rapper Talib Kweli did on their Reflection Eternal debut *Train of Thought* (2000), where they ingeniously remade Nina Simone's 1965 classic "Four Women"? When most people—obviously including Jigga and Yeezy on *Watch the Throne*—think of black popular music in the 1960s, which is to say during the Civil Rights Movement and later the Black Power Movement, they probably think first and foremost about Motown, Stax, Atlantic, Brunswick, Chess, Dial, Minit-Instant, James Brown, Aretha Franklin, or Curtis Mayfield. Few would invoke an iconoclastic, genre-jumping, and soul-searching singer and social activist like Nina Simone.[12]

Hi-Tek and Kweli introduce their audience to a musical *and* political figure from the past and also "construct and deconstruct historical narratives" about black popular music by highlighting an under-appreciated icon like Nina Simone. Equally—if not even more—important, Hi-Tek and Kweli introduce their audience to a black feminist musical *and* political figure from the past and also "construct and deconstruct historical narratives" about African American women's *herstory* from enslavement through to the Hip Hop Movement by rewriting and updating Simone's "Four Women" narrative, which originally painted a poetic portrait of African American women's lives and struggles from enslavement through to the Black Power Movement and Women's Liberation Movement. [13]

Many of hip hop's "hardcore" critics have consistently been able to make blanket condemnations about rap music and hip hop culture by turning a blind eye to the more politically progressive aspects of the music and culture. This not only makes their knee-jerk criticisms of rap music and hip hop culture suspect, but it also illustrates that more than a highfalutin form of "amnesia" is at play and plaguing hip hop's fans and critics. There is a sense in which it can be said that both hip hop's fans and critics are suffering from "a partial or total loss of memory" when and where we come to the "real" roots of rap music and hip hop culture, which extend back much further than the Sugarhill Gang's 1979 classic "Rapper's Delight," and actually can be found in the earliest forms of post-enslavement black popular music and black popular culture: classic blues, ragtime, and jazz.

Even more, if there is any impulse on the part of my readers to accept the fact that rap music and hip hop culture are actually emblematic of much more than merely contemporary black popular music and contemporary black popular culture, and actually serve as the major soundtrack and cultural aesthetic outlet for what should be more properly termed the "Hip Hop Movement," then we would do well to also critically engage the classical black political culture and classical black social movements that the Hip Hop Movement's "real" roots can be said to lie in: the Black Women's Club Movement, the New Negro Movement, and the Bebop Movement. Something should also be said about the ways in which European American avant-garde and counter-cultural movements, such as the Lost Generation and the Beat Generation, have been indelibly influenced by and, in turn, undeniably influential on black popular music and black popular culture—and all of this in spite of the long and shameful shadow cast by the distinctly *American* apartheid that derailed American democracy during the first half of the twentieth century. Bearing all of this in mind, now we turn our attention to arguably rap music and the Hip Hop Movement's most unheralded classical popular music and classical popular movement models: the blues and the Black Women's Club Movement.

## NOTES

1. The title, "Back to the Old School," is obviously a shameless reference to Just-Ice's groundbreaking album *Back to the Old School* (1986). Even though many believed that he resembled Mike Tyson with his mounds of muscles, mouth full of gold teeth, and distinctive tattoos, Just-Ice actually possessed remarkable skills as a rapper. Even with its often "down-and-dirty" sound, *Back to the Old School*'s sonic brilliance could hardly be denied at the time of its release. Perhaps best characterized by its fast and forceful rhymes, fresh human beat-

boxing (provided by the legendary beat-box—not the rapper—DMX), and the unique production of Mantronix's Kurtis Mantronik, ironically *Back to the Old School* lyrically and musically foreshadowed both "conscious" and "gangsta" rap. Widely credited with being the first MC to embrace the esoteric teachings of the Nation of Gods and Earths or, rather, the Five Percent Nation (or, even still more colloquially, the "Five Percenters"), Just-Ice's reggae dancehall-style DJing or toasting over hip hop beats would influence countless rappers who came after him—from Busta Rhymes and Kool G Rap to Canibus and Jadakiss. On the one hand, with the tracks "Cold Gettin' Dumb," "Back to the Old School," and "Little Bad Johnny," Ice proved to be a fairly perceptive ghetto social commentator, and in many senses prefigured and laid a foundation for "conscious" rap. On the other hand, with the tracks "Gangster of Hip Hop," "Latoya," and "That Girl is a Slut" he undeniably contributed to the genesis of what would quickly come to be called "gangsta" rap. For further discussion of Just-Ice and *Back to the Old School*, among his other classic albums (especially *Kool & Deadly* [1987]), see P. Shapiro (2005a, 201–2), Woodstra, Bush, and Erlewine (2008, 45), and Bogdanov, Woodstra, Erlewine, and Bush (2003, 249–50). Hence, it is in the sense that *Back to the Old School* captured both the contributions *and* contradictions of rap music and hip hop culture that I begin my most beloved little book: *Selah.*

2. In the four "remixes" to follow we will note how the idea that "there simply is no socially acceptable way to be a black ghetto youth in America" historically—or, rather, *her-storically*—reaches all the way back to the very first form of post-enslavement black popular music and black popular culture, the blues, and rears its ugly head and shows its fiendish face and fangs in each and every form of black popular music and black popular culture that followed in the aftermath of the blues's emergence and greatest period of popularity. I, especially, have in mind here ragtime, classic jazz, and bebop, but honestly believe that we would do well to observe this *anti-black ghetto youth impulse* in the discourse surrounding and constant condemnation of rhythm & blues, soul, funk, go-go, disco, reggae, and, ultimately, rap. For further discussion of the anti-black ghetto youth impulse in the discourse surrounding post-bebop black popular music (i.e., rhythm & blues, soul, funk, go-go, disco, and reggae), see my previously mentioned forthcoming book *The Hip Hop Movement.*

3. In terms of each of these major issues and ills plaguing African Americans at increasingly alarming rates, my interpretation here is based on the following: school drop-out rate (Rovai, Gallien, and Stiff-Williams 2007; Simpson 2004; Thernstrom and Thernstrom 1997); infant mortality rate (Ahmed 1992; Boone 1989; Braithwaite and Taylor 1992); unemployment rate (Freeman and Holzer 1986; Glasgow 1981; Schwartzman 1997); incarceration rate (Bhui 2009; Dyer 2000; Gabbidon 2010; Inciardi 1980; Sulton 1996); gun-related death rate (Hall, Cassidy, and Stevenson 2008; Nielsen, Martinez, and Rosenfeld 2005; Zimmerman, Steinman, and Rowe 1999); sexually transmitted disease rate (Buntin 1988; C. F. Collins 2006; Hampton, Gullotta, and Crowel 2010); and HIV/AIDS rate (C. J. Cohen 1999; McCree, Jones, and O'Leary 2010; Robertson 2006). It is interesting to observe how frequently each of these issues is referenced—even if often uncritically—in rap music and hip hop culture. That is to say, even though much of middle-class and mainstream America may be able to turn a blind eye to these issues, black ghetto youth cannot and have not because of their (and their loved ones') intense intimacy with these problems. Again, it is important here to invoke the fifth fundamental element of hip hop culture, "knowledge"—both "book knowledge" and "street knowledge" (or, rather, "ghetto knowledge")—bearing in mind the ways in which it plays itself out in rap music, hip hop culture, and throughout the wider Hip Hop Movement. Obviously rappers' and other hip hoppers' ongoing cognizance of these ruinous rates and their impact on African America— *and*, very often, multicultural and multiracial America—is an irrefutable example of the fifth fundamental element of hip hop culture at work. This is, in part, one of the reasons that "message," "political," or "conscious" rap has never fallen out of favor with the masses of black ghetto youth. For further discussion of black ghetto youth's production of and relationship with conscious rap, and for the most noteworthy works that informed my analysis here, see Eure and Spady (1991), Keyes (2002), McQuillar (2007), Spady, Dupres, and Lee (1995), Spady, Lee, and Alim (1999), and Spady, Alim, and Meghelli (2006).

4.   Among the Center for Disease Control and Prevention's regularly listed "10 leading causes of death" between 2000 and 2010 were: (1) heart disease; (2) cancer; (3) stroke; (4) chronic lower respiratory diseases; (5) accidents; (6) Alzheimer's disease; (7) diabetes; (8) influenza and pneumonia; (9) nephritis, nephritic syndrome, and nephrosis; and (10) septicemia. For further discussion, see www.cdc.gov/nchs/fastats/lcod.htm.

5.   For further discussion of sexism and misogyny in rap music, as well as hip hop culture more generally, and for the most noteworthy works that informed my analysis here, see Adams and Fuller (2006), Barongan and Hall (1995), Larsen (2006), Oware (2011), Sharpley-Whiting (2007), and Weitzer and Kubrin (2009).

6.   My interpretation of mainstream American history, culture, politics, and society between 1980 and 2000 obviously challenges those "good boy" histories of this time period that consistently overlook the major issues and ills impacting U.S. ghettos, barrios, and slums. For the most noteworthy works I consulted, see Alexander (2010), Bogazianos (2011), Ehrman (2005), Kelley and Lewis (2000), Marable (1983, 2007), Martin (2011), Minkler and Roe (1993), Oliver and Shapiro (1995), Omi and Winant (1994), Schulman (2001), T. M. Shapiro (2004), Sterk (1999), Vergara (1995), and Webb (1998).

7.   For further discussion of the ways in which rap music and hip hop culture have influenced European American, Native American, Asian American, Caribbean American, and Latino rich *and* poor, heterosexual *and* homosexual, Christian *and* non-Christian youth, and for the most noteworthy works that informed my analysis here, see Bynoe (2006), Chang (2006), Forman and Neal (2004, 2012), Hadley and Yancy (2011), Hess (2007a), Pride (2007), and Strode and Wood (2008).

8.   For further discussion of rap music and hip hop culture in relationship to postmodernism, and for the most noteworthy works that informed my analysis here, see Baker (1993), Bayles (1994), Gilroy (1993), Grandt (2009), Hess (2005), Lipsitz (1994), M. A. Neal (1998, 2002), Rodriquez (2006), and Walcott (1996).

9.   For further discussion of Jacques Derrida's life and philosophical legacy, and for the most noteworthy secondary sources and critical commentary that informed my analysis here, see Beardsworth (1996), T. Cohen (2001), Royle (2003), Silverman (1989), and D. Wood (1992).

10.   For examples of the studies that take up the issue as to whether or not rap is really music, and for the most noteworthy works that informed my analysis here, see Bradley (2009), Dyson (1997, 2007), Keyes (2002), Krims (2000), Mook (2007), Ramsey (2003), Rose (1994, 2008), Schloss (2004), and Schur (2009).

11.   . For further discussion of the hip hop *DJ, producer, and rapper as intellectual-artist-activists*, and for the most noteworthy works that informed my analysis here, see Bailey (2011), Boyd (1997), Chang (2005), Demers (2001, 2002, 2003), Dyson (2002), Dyson and Daulatzai (2010), George (1999), Light (1999), Ogbar (2007), Schloss (2004), Schumacher (1995), and Watkins (1998, 2005).

12.   . For further discussion of Nina Simone's life and legacy, and for the most noteworthy works that informed my analysis here, see Brun-Lambert (2009), Cohodas (2010), Hampton and Nathan (2004), Simone (2003b), and R. Williams (2002).

13.   . At this point my readers have, perhaps, detected that I am a serious Nina Simone fanatic. Indeed, I would be remiss if I did not refer my readers to her classic album *Wild is the Wind* (1966), which features "Four Women," and the jaw-dropping and genre-jumping four compact disc box set, *Four Women: The Nina Simone Philips Recordings* (2003a), released as a posthumous tribute. Although her 1960s Verve/Philips recordings, to my ears, simply cannot be recommended highly enough, yet and still, those wanting a sampling of her work post–Verve/Philips work should consult the Grammy Award–winning three compact disc box set, *To Be Free: The Nina Simone Story* (2008).

*Remix 2*

# "Lifting As We Climb!"

*Classic Blues Queens and the Black Women's Club Movement, Neo-Soul Sistas and the Hip Hop Women's Movement*

Today, as we reflect on the process of empowering Afro-American women, our most efficacious strategies remain those that are guided by the principle used by black women in the club movement. We must strive to "lift as we climb." In other words, we must climb in such a way as to guarantee that all of our sisters, regardless of class, and indeed all of our brothers, climb with us. This must be the essential dynamic of our quest for power—a principle that must not only determine our struggles as Afro-American women, but also govern all authentic struggles of disposed people. Indeed, the overall battle for equality can be profoundly enhanced by embracing this principle. —Angela Davis, *Women, Culture, and Politics*, 5

## INTRODUCTION: BLUES WOMEN, BLACK CLUBWOMEN, AND HIP HOP WOMEN

In many ways African American women have suffered similar fates when and where we come to their contributions to the origins and evolution of both black popular music and black popular movements. With regard to the latter, whether one speaks of the Abolitionist Movement or the New Negro Movement, the Civil Rights Movement or the Black Power Movement, there is a tired tendency to either *marginalize* or *masculinize* African American women's distinct donations to African American social and political history, culture, and struggle (Guy-Sheftall 1995; Hull, Scott, and Smith 1982; James,

Smith, and Guy-Sheftall 2009; Springer 1999). In terms of black popular music, sadly, something very similar could be said. Although African American women have been seminal participants in the creation, production, and dissemination of every major form of African American music—from work songs and spirituals to blues and jazz, from rhythm & blues and rock & roll to funk and rap—their contributions to the successive soundtracks to the ever-evolving African American experience have been repeatedly erased or attributed to African American male "musical geniuses" (Barnett 2007; Burnim and Maultsby 2006; Hayes 2010; Hayes and Williams 2007; Walker-Hill 2007).

Very few folk outside of African American Studies and Women's Studies have acknowledged the enormous impact and continued influence African American women musicians have had on the development of black popular music in specific, and black popular culture in general. Moreover, since black popular culture has long put the premium on what is distinctly "American" about American popular culture, it is extremely important to emphasize the ways in which African American women's marginalization within the world of African American music mirrors their marginalization within the wider world of U.S. history, culture, politics, and society.[1] Hence, it may not come as a shock to my readers to reveal that African American women were central to the first major post-enslavement African American social movement, commonly called *the Black Women's Club Movement*, and similarly central to the first major post-enslavement African American musical form, *the blues*.

Just as work songs and the spirituals could be said to have served as the soundtrack for African American enslavement and jazz the musical accompaniment for the New Negro Movement and the Harlem Renaissance, here I would like to suggest that the blues served not simply as the soundtrack for black life during the Reconstruction and post-Reconstruction years that ushered in the twentieth century but also, and more specifically, classic blues women's work served as a *counter-herstory* and counter-narrative to the frequently Eurocentric and bourgeois conceptions of womanhood articulated and touted by the Black Women's Club Movement. For instance, in *Too Heavy A Load: Black Women in Defense of Themselves, 1894–1994* (1999), historian Deborah Gray White wrote, "The club leaders' frequent calls for black female unity were more a political strategy than practical reality. Unity was neither existent nor anticipated, and this was recognized by club leaders again and again" (77).

Most black clubwomen, who were largely college-educated, upper-class and middle-class churchwomen, sought to distance themselves from working-class and poor black women. This distancing on the part of the clubwomen was undertaken because of what they perceived to be the immoral or "bad" behavior on the part of lower-class African American women. Much of what was interpreted as poor black women's "unladylike" and "bad" behavior stemmed from their embrace of late nineteenth century and early twentieth century black popular culture, especially as found in minstrel, medicine, tent, and vaudeville shows. [2]

"Lifting As We Climb" was the motto of the Black Women's Club Movement, and it essentially meant that clubwomen "pledged to help others as they helped themselves" (54). The irony here, however, is that the clubwomen paternalistically believed that they knew what was best for poor black women, and that poor black women should "climb" only as directed and sanctioned by nobly "lifting" clubwomen. Similar to the current trend among many black feminist academics to speak about and write on behalf of working-class and poor African American women, classic black clubwomen "did not hesitate to represent poor black women, few of whom belonged to their organization[s]. Proud of their work on behalf of their less fortunate sisters, they felt it a duty to speak for them" (55). One has to wonder how the clubwomen could possibly speak for poor black women when clubwomen almost outright rejected poor African American women's "lowdown" language, lifestyle, and, most especially, their "lewd" music—primarily, *the blues.*

The blues, with its emphasis on the issues and ills of working-class black culture, emerged as the soundtrack to seemingly every aspect of lower-class African American life at the turn of the twentieth century: from spirituality and sexuality to death and disease, from racism and sexism to classism and American militarism. In other words, classic blues consistently touched on topics that the black bourgeoisie's polite politics woefully left in the lurch. While the Black Women's Club Movement undoubtedly made major contributions to the Suffrage Movement, the Civil Rights Movement, and early movements to empower the poor, it did so from within the framework of a decidedly condescending, Eurocentric, and bourgeois ideology based on upper-class and middle-class white women's conceptions and articulations of the "cult of True Womanhood" (to be discussed in greater detail below).

"Certainly the [National] Association [of Colored Women]," the premier nationally organized black women's club institution, "did accomplish much," Deborah White openly asserts. However, she critically continues:

> We need to understand that the different classes of black women were allied, not united; that their alliance was based on race and sex sameness and the sentiments that flowed from this kinship—not on social or cultural unity. Most black women were poor. They lived lives weighed down by agricultural and domestic labor. Pervasive discrimination left them with few choices. They did not have time to read, much less to cultivate an appreciation for Beethoven. For most, the church served an emotional need. It provided social activities, and the moral code they lived by. The clubwoman's intolerance for difference blinded them to these realities. Like white female reformers who heaped criti-

cism on ["ethnic" European] immigrants for holding on to their old culture, black women reformers lacked compassion and a concept of cultural relativism. Given their program, the NACW motto "Lifting As We Climb" presumed race and sex sameness, but social and cultural distance. (78)

White's work points to the pitfalls of elite and college-educated African American women uncritically utilizing bourgeois European American standards in their efforts to "uplift" poor and working-class African American women. As quiet as it has been kept, this is a theme that runs throughout the history of African American social and political movements, whether moderate or militant, black feminist nationalist or black masculinist nationalist.[3] Black clubwomen's "intolerance for difference blinded them" to the realities of the masses of black women, who held a profound respect for the African American church, but who knew firsthand that the church was not free from its own controversies and contradictions.

Upper-class and middle-class black churchwomen and black clubwomen's lack of "compassion and a concept of cultural relativism" with respect to the life-worlds and life-struggles of working-class and poor black women ultimately relegated lower-class African American women to the realm of licentious, evil, ignorant, and immoral womanhood—which, rather ironically, mirrored college-educated upper-class and middle-class white men and women's views regarding black women at the turn of the twentieth century.[4] What is more, *blues women*, which is to say, *women steeped in turn of the twentieth century black popular music and black popular culture*, were singled out as especially egregious examples of wanton womanhood because their maddening music and "unrefined" manners, their lustful lyrics and "lowdown" lives seemed to celebrate many of the immoralities and indignities of lower-class African American life and culture—in short, immoralities and indignities that upper-class and middle-class black and white folk flippantly would rather not be bothered with.

Here it is important to stretch White's work, and to critically question whether something very similar to the turn of the twentieth century ostracization of blues women (i.e., primarily poor and working-class black women) is taking place at the turn of the twenty-first century with respect to the ostracization of *hip hop women*, which is to say, *primarily poor and working-class women steeped in turn of the twenty-first century black popular music and black popular culture*. Although there is no institutionally organized African American women's movement on the grand scale of the Black Women's Club Movement taking place in our time, there has long been an intra-racial tendency among older African Americans in general, and older African American women in specific, to lambaste hip hop women for their embrace of hip hop culture, and especially rap music and videos (e.g., C. DeLores Tucker, Calvin O. Butts, and John McWhorter). Admittedly, several pre–Hip

Hop Generation African American women have offered many very valid critiques to hip hop women in specific, and hip hop culture in general (e.g., scholars Patricia Hill Collins [2006], Angela Davis [1998b], and bell hooks [1994b], as well as poets Nikki Giovanni, June Jordan, and Sonia Sanchez). However, what distinguishes their *constructive criticisms* from the more common *destructive criticisms* of hip hop women and hip hop culture is the fact that they comprehend rap music and hip hop culture to be an important part of the African American cultural continuum. [5]

When the African American cultural continuum is seriously taken into consideration, rap music and hip hop culture are seen to be no more vulgar and vice-filled than blues, ragtime, jazz, rhythm & blues, rock & roll, soul, funk, go-go, and disco at each of their outsets. In fact, it could be said that what truly distinguishes rap music and hip hop culture is not so much its controversial musical topics and innovative musical techniques but, even more, its widespread digital dissemination; its schizophrenic sonic and social relationships with both postmodernism and postcolonialism; and, perhaps most importantly, the fact that it is the first major African American musical form to emerge in the aftermath of the 1950s, 1960s, and 1970s Civil Rights Movement, Black Power Movement, Free Speech Movement, Anti-War Movement, Women's Liberation Movement, and Lesbian, Gay, Bisexual & Transgender Liberation Movement. Rap music and hip hop culture also seem to controversially capture black and other youth life lived in the age of HIV/ AIDS, the "War on Drugs," and the increasing privatization of the U.S. prison system (i.e., the now fully established prison industrial complex). In sum, it could be said that rap music and hip hop culture sonically symbolize and ingeniously encapsulate the sights and sounds of a legally "desegregated" and thoroughly "integrated" U.S. in the process of deconstructing and reconstructing itself (i.e., "American democracy") at the turn of the twenty-first century. Needless to say, differing factions of U.S. citizens harbor a wide-range of conceptions concerning what it means to really and truly deconstruct and reconstruct American democracy, including the quickly coming of age "Hip Hop Generation" (Butler 2009; Kitwana 2002; Ogbar 2007; Perry 2004; Rose 2008; Watkins 2005).

Never before have so many working-class and underclass African Americans had such a wide-ranging and far-reaching platform to speak their special truths free from the censoring conservatism of both the white and black bourgeoisies. This is not to say that rap music represents "authentic" and "unmitigated" African American thought and culture—truth be told, most of what passes nowadays for rap music and hip hop culture is absolutely inauthentic and often anti-black racist or, rather, *postmillennial minstrelism* (see Rabaka 2011, 49–57). However, it has become something of a trend for even the most commercially successful rappers to release "mixtapes" and "underground joints" with harder-hitting beats and frequently either more politically or sexually charged material for their die-hard fan base. It is this aspect of rap music and hip hop culture that makes so much of contemporary black popular music and black popular culture seem schizophrenic and boldly blurs the lines between "commercial" and "conscious" rap music and hip hop culture. Hence, both white and black bourgeois conservatives' one-dimensional critiques of rap music and hip hop culture as patently patriarchal or homophobic or what have you mindlessly downplay the depth and double meanings at the heart of hip hop culture without in any significant way historically and culturally connecting rap music's misogyny or hip hop's heterosexism to mainstream America's longstanding misogyny, heteronormativity, and wholesale homophobia. This, it would seem to me, is an instance where the pot is calling the kettle black, to employ the old adage.

Unorganized though they may be, the black bourgeoisie is more powerful and seemingly more condescending toward working-class and poor blacks (i.e., the primary producers of rap music and hip hop culture) than ever before.[6] Returning the focus to African American women, and especially hip hop women, it is hard not to apply Deborah White's words to hip hop women's world. Again, she contends, "[m]ost black women were poor. They lived lives weighed down by agricultural and domestic labor. Pervasive discrimination left them with few choices. They did not have time to read, much less to cultivate an appreciation for Beethoven"—it would seem that only the most stubborn and stiff-necked among us would deny the ways in which most hip hop women's life-worlds and life-struggles eerily echo classic blues women's life-worlds and life-struggles. Certainly not every aspect of White's analysis is applicable to hip hop women (obviously most hip hop women are not "weighed down by agricultural . . . labor"), but the bulk of her commentary here does indeed help to provide a heretofore overlooked connection between African American women's lives at the turn of both the twentieth century and the twenty-first century.

This "remix," therefore, will explore the connections between classic blues women and contemporary hip hop women. It seeks to circumvent *hip hop's amnesia* with regard to blues music, the blues aesthetic, and blues culture by critically examining classic blues women's controversial and contradictory black feminism in contrast to the historically celebrated and more socially acceptable forms of black feminism that emerged from the Black Women's Club Movement. As discussed above, the Black Women's Club Movement was primarily a church-going and college-educated, upper-class and middle-class African American women's movement. Although its ideological framework was not identical to the parallel White Women's Club Movement, nevertheless, excluding its emphasis on race and class, its conceptions of womanhood, wifehood, and motherhood closely mirrored the views and values (i.e., the elitism, genteelism, and Victorianism) of upper-class and middle-class white women at the turn of the twentieth century.[7]

Here I would like to suggest that classic blues women at the turn of the twentieth century were looked down on in much the same way that contemporary hip hop women are misunderstood and looked down on at the turn of the twenty-first century. My primary preoccupation in this "remix" revolves around the ways in which elite and college-educated, upper-class and middle-class African American women perceive and, even more ironically, devalue working-class and poor African American women. By embracing Eurocentric and bourgeois views and values, and by encouraging lower-class African American women to adhere to white men and white women's standards of womanhood, wifehood, and motherhood, one wonders whether black clubwomen realized that they unwittingly became compradors for Eurocentrism, embourgeoisement, and, ultimately, the continuation of *the de-Africanization of African American women*, which stretched back to the stench and stain of the African holocaust and African American enslavement. Although often overlooked, there remains a tendency today for upper-class, middle-class, and/or college-educated African American women to, however unwittingly, become contemporary neocolonial compradors for Eurocentrism, embourgeoisement, and, ultimately, the continuation of *the de-Africanization of African American women*.

Why is the (often foible-filled) feminism of elite and college-educated African American women considered more valuable and valid than the admittedly controversial and contradictory, arguably "unacademic" and outright "organic" womanism emerging from the life-worlds and life-struggles of working-class and poor African American women? Why is the feminist theory and praxis of college-educated African American women consistently privileged over the womanist work, artistry, and activism of African American women who have not had the opportunity to receive "higher education," let alone master "fly" feminist epistemologies and methodologies in prestigious Women's Studies programs and departments? Is feminism only to be found in often esoteric academic books, or can it also be observed in cyber-space, social media, populist politics, music, film, fashion, fiction, art, theater, dance, and athletics, among other aspects of popular culture? If, indeed, "feminism is for everybody," as bell hooks (2000b) proclaimed in one of her watershed works, then can everybody contribute to feminism? These are the crucial questions this "remix" seeks to resolve or, at the very least, offer adequate answers to. [8]

Utilizing Patricia Hill Collins's *Black Feminist Thought: Knowledge, Consciousness, and the Politics of Empowerment* (2000) as one of its primary points of departure, this "remix" in many senses "remixes" Collins's contention that "[d]eveloping black feminist thought also involves searching for its expression in alternative institutional locations and among women who are not commonly perceived as intellectuals. . . . Black women intellectuals are neither all academics nor found primarily in the black middle-class"

(14). With these weighted words Collins challenges us to not only sift through and search for the philosophical foundations of black feminism amongst the members of the greatly esteemed Black Women's Club Movement, but her heartfelt words also open us to the idea that the classic blues women and their work invariably represent equally important expressions of classical black feminism and seminal contributions to contemporary black feminism, hip hop feminism, and the "organic" womanism of hip hop women. Faithfully following Collins, in this "remix" "all U.S. black women who somehow contribute to black feminist thought as critical social theory are deemed to be 'intellectuals.' They may be highly educated," as with the classic black clubwomen (and contemporary black feminist academics). Although, as with the classic blues women (and contemporary hip hop women), "[m]any are not" (14).

It is important to further emphasize the ways in which this "remix" is undergirded by Collins's groundbreaking conception of "black feminist thought as critical social theory" and her unequivocal inclusion of "unsophisticated," "uneducated," working-class, and poor African American women—including "[m]usicians, vocalists, poets, writers, and other artists"—in her articulation of what it means to be an intellectual. Moving away from the hyperbole and high-sounding notions that usually accompany contemporary ideas revolving around what it means to be an intellectual, Collins importantly continues:

> Developing black feminist thought as critical social theory involves including the ideas of black women not previously considered intellectuals—many of whom may be working-class women with jobs outside academia—as well as those ideas emanating from more formal, legitimated scholarship. The ideas we share with one another as mothers in extended families, as othermothers in black communities, as members of black churches, and as teachers to the black community's children have formed one pivotal area where African American women have hammered out a multifaceted black women's standpoint. Musicians, vocalists, poets, writers, and other artists constitute another group from which black women intellectuals have emerged. Building on African-influenced oral traditions, musicians in particular have enjoyed close association with the larger community of African American women constituting their audience. Through their words and actions, grassroots political activists also contribute to black women's intellectual traditions. Producing intellectual work is generally not attributed to black women artists and political activists. Especially in elite institutions of higher education, such women are typically viewed as objects of study, a classification that creates a false dichotomy between scholarship and activism, between thinking and doing. In contrast, examining the ideas and actions of these excluded groups in a way that views them as subjects reveals a world in which behavior is a statement of philosophy and in which a vibrant, both/and, scholar/activist tradition remains intact. (16–17)

What I am most interested in here is the "multifaceted black women's stand-point" that Collins contends emerges from middle-class *and* working-class, college-educated *and* so-called "uneducated" African American women's lives and struggles. I am also interested in challenging the "false dichotomy between scholarship and activism, between thinking and doing" by bringing African American women who are typically not thought of as contributors to black feminist theory and praxis (i.e., classic blues women and contemporary hip hop women) into critical dialogue with the unusual suspects (i.e., classic black clubwomen and contemporary black feminist academics) in conventional explorations of the intellectual origins and philosophical foundations of black feminism. In examining both the *academic intellectual* and the *organic intellectual* origins and evolution of black feminism we are provided with a paradigm that will enable us to critically comprehend and, perhaps even, appreciate the many faces and multiple forms of contemporary black feminism/womanism, hip hop feminism/womanism, and the Hip Hop Women's Movement.

By bringing the feminism of the black clubwomen and the womanism of the classic blues women into critical dialogue, in this "remix" I intend to demonstrate that different classes of African American women have long-held divergent conceptions of "feminism," "womanism," "women's liberation," and "gender justice"—even though, admittedly and quite ironically, most African American women outside of the academy do not use any of these terms with any regularity.[9] Also, I intend to illustrate the ways in which class and class-based ideology continue to be a barrier in contemporary black feminist theory and praxis by ultimately focusing my discussion on the frequently ragged relationship between black feminist academics and hip hop women. The main points here are to: (1) extend and expand the range and meaning of black feminism to include working-class and poor African American women's contributions, which frequently grow out of their creation of and participation in black popular music and black popular culture; (2) utilize African American women's contributions to classical black popular music and black popular culture to combat *hip hop's amnesia* with respect to African American women's contributions to both classical and contemporary black popular music and black popular culture; and (3) identify and analyze a body of knowledge, set of cultural practices, and recurring themes that demonstrate the continuity and distinctiveness of black feminist theory and praxis—both classical *and* contemporary, academic *and* organic, and elite *and* underclass.

Bearing the foregoing in mind, the next section provides a brief history of classic blues women. It primarily focuses on the ways in which these women's lyrics, music, and aesthetics offer alternative and often-overlooked forms of black feminism and social criticism at the turn of the twentieth century. The subsequent section offers an abridged exploration of the Black

Women's Club Movement. It essentially concentrates on how the clubwomen's politics and social programs often overlapped with the blues women's lyrics, music, and aesthetics. The final section examines classic blues women's work—their unacademic and organic black feminism—as the unrecognized soundtrack for the Black Women's Club Movement, and the ways in which contemporary hip hop women's work—again, their unacademic and organic black feminism—bears the influence of and eerily echoes the classic blues queens' contributions to black popular music and black popular movements.

Ultimately, the last section emphasizes what both the classic blues women and black clubwomen contributed to contemporary hip hop women, and how hip hop women's music and culture is providing an often unacknowledged soundtrack for turn of the twenty-first century black feminism in specific, and contemporary U.S. feminism in general. The premise for the remainder of this "remix" is predicated on the notion that privileging elite and academic black feminism over the "organic" black feminism to be found in black popular music and black popular culture, or vice versa, in the end only offers us a lame and lopsided, "false dichotomy" form of black feminism. By moving away from the longstanding tendency to take the black bourgeoisie as the ideal agents of African American thought and practices; by freeing myself from the frame of reference that seems to incessantly downplay and diminish the politics of African American aesthetics (especially black popular music and black popular culture); and, lastly, by intensely probing the blues from a black feminist perspective and the Black Women's Club Movement from working-class and poor black women's perspective—I honestly believe that *hip hop's amnesia* with respect to the blues, classic blues women, the Black Women's Club Movement, and African American women's contributions to the soundtracks for African American socio-political movements will be undeniably apparent.

## BLUES FOR THE OFTEN-UNACKNOWLEDGED BLACK FEMINIST FOREMOTHERS: BLUES QUEENS, RAGTIME KINGS, AND THE BEGINNINGS OF BLACK POPULAR MUSIC AND BLACK POPULAR CULTURE

One of the hallmarks of classical African griots, priests, praise singers, and dirge singers was their ability to express profoundly personal emotions and offer them up in a way that deeply resonated with their communities. They possessed an *aesthetic alchemy* that enabled them to translate individual experience—their own and others'—into collective music and communal expressions. Similar to contemporary African singers—for example, Fela

Kuti, Youssou N'Dour, Angélique Kidjo, Thomas Mapfumo, Ladysmith Black Mambazo, Salif Keita, Miriam Makeba, Cheikh Lô, Baaba Maal, and Césaria Évora—classical African singers took seemingly simple lyrics and loaded them with intense and animated emotion, multiple metaphors, indigenous figures of speech, folk philosophy, political ideology, and religious references.[10]

The spirituals and the blues built on and went beyond the classical African lyrical tradition by incorporating proverbs, double entendres, and allegories that grew out of the African American experience during enslavement, Reconstruction, and post-Reconstruction. During enslavement the spirituals represented African American sacred music, while work songs and field hollers symbolized African American secular music (W. F. Allen 1995; M. M. Fisher 1998; Work 1998). It is important to observe that each of the aforementioned musics contained improvisational elements that enabled them to be formulated and reformulated or, rather, mixed and *remixed* according to the spiritual, psychological, and physical needs of the enslaved—much like every major form of African American music that followed in their wake, including rap and other forms of hip hop music.

The deep double entendres of early African American spirituals, field hollers, work songs, and party songs frequently masked the complexity and hidden meanings of the music. Early African American music was usually draped in seemingly "primitive" lyrics and "simple" melodies—that is, of course, purportedly "primitive" lyrics and "simple" melodies when compared with European and European American lyrics and melodies, and not traditional African lyrics and melodies. However, when the lyrics, melodies, and rhythms of the enslaved are scrutinized they reveal music of profound spiritual substance and exceptional insight that often escaped the understanding of outsiders—especially anti-African, enslaving, and colonizing "outsiders."

Like all other major African American musical forms, work songs and spirituals mean more to those who have some working knowledge of the lives and struggles of the people who produced them. Hence, the body of lyrical literature and beautiful "sorrow songs" that have been handed down to us speak volumes about the ingenuity and intelligence of an alleged "illiterate," "unintelligent," and "primitive" people. That these songs continue to be movingly sung (and, at times, seemingly employed in African American Christian-styled séances) to this day, indeed, says something about the humble humanity and innovative artistry of the people who produced them.[11]

The multiple meanings and multiple purposes of African American music were sonically intensified and socially amplified with the emergence of the blues at the end of the nineteenth century. The blues was the first major African American musical form produced in the post-enslavement period. Which is to say, the blues was conceptually conceived and birthed during the

Reconstruction and post-Reconstruction years, roughly between 1865 and 1900. Where work songs, field hollers, and the spirituals could be considered primarily communal music that expressed life lived in the face of the hard labor, harsh realities, and the other innumerable horrors African American enslavement entailed, the blues encapsulated the experiences and emotions of individual African Americans who were "freed from the bonds of slavery" but still bound by the Black Codes, the Ku Klux Klan, Jim Crow laws, lynching, the peonage system, the sharecropping system, and the convict-lease system—in other words, what is currently more commonly called "American apartheid."[12]

The blues developed into a dynamic musical and cultural aesthetic form that harbored an ingenious improvisational element that mutated and translated contingent on the artist, audience, environment, occasion, and venue. Hence, blues music and blues musicians have an extremely fluid or, rather, jazz-like rapport that is incessantly altered by any number of the aforementioned elements (i.e., the artist, audience, environment, occasion, or venue). It is ironic that the very post-enslavement racism, poverty, and anti-black racist violence that blocked African Americans from untold educational, economic, and political opportunities ended up providing them with the wherewithal to create a majestic musical form and cultural aesthetic that continue to reverberate around the world.

Although women have been recurringly erased from the history of the blues, as with most other major African American musical forms, they undoubtedly played a pivotal role in its origins and evolution. Most blues scholars concede that there is no empirical evidence that provides us with clear-cut proof of *when*, *where*, *why*, and *by whom* the blues was invented, but musical and historical artifacts reveal that women were deeply involved as both singers and instrumentalists from its inception. What we do know with some certainty is that African American women were the first to record and popularize the blues.

As has been recounted in almost every major book about the blues, Mamie Smith's version of Perry Bradford's "Crazy Blues" in 1920 was the first identifiable—at least by modern and postmodern sonic sensibilities—blues recording. The song was so popular that it sold more than 75,000 copies within the first month of its release—no small feat in 1920. The success of "Crazy Blues" sent shock waves through both black and white America. It represented something new. It announced the emergence of a "New Negro" identity to America and, even more, a new expression of black womanhood that was free from the conservatism of the "cult of True Womanhood" that plagued both white and black middle-class women in the first quarter of the twentieth century (F. Davis 1995; Harrison 1988; B. Jackson 2005).

We should take care here to note that the blues was given its first popular expression by African American women. Even though it eventually (and incorrectly) came to be seen as a marker—if not for some folk a *maker*—of black masculinity, similar to the origins and evolution of rap music and hip hop culture, at its heart the blues is a transgender and transgenerational art form that initially served as a soundtrack for turn of the twentieth century African American socio-political movements and a new epoch in U.S. history and culture. In other words, according to Francis Davis in *The History of the Blues* (1995), the blues "provides a kind of soundtrack to the gradual urbanization of a once largely rural people" (46).

The blues is the music of a people on the move. It is the sound African Americans created to capture their tribulation-filled transition from the nineteenth century to the twentieth century, from the South to the North, from agricultural labor to industrial labor. The blues, therefore, was what it sounded like to live at the crossroads, somewhere between heaven and hell, spirituality and sexuality, life and death, slavery and freedom, Africa and America, and the oldness and the newness of the African American experience.[13]

I am often amazed by the myriad ways the blues resembles rap music and hip hop culture or, rather, I should more accurately say, vice versa. Rap music and hip hop culture sonically and socially represent to African Americans at the turn of the twenty-first century what blues music and blues culture represented to black folk at the turn of the twentieth century. The major difference between blues music, the blues aesthetic, and blues culture and hip hop music, the hip hop aesthetic, and hip hop culture revolves around the incredible breakthroughs in civil rights, women's rights, homosexual rights, technology, and telecommunications that took place in the twentieth century. However, even in light of the aforementioned "breakthroughs," many of the same themes found in turn of the twentieth century blues continue to dominate hip hop discourse, so much so that any serious student or scholar of black popular music and black popular culture should solemnly question exactly how life is qualitatively different for working-class and poor black people at the turn of the twenty-first century.

It would seem that working-class and poor black people, the exiles and outcasts of both "mainstream" *and* middle-class white *and* black America, have consistently created the major African American musical forms—again, including rap and other hip hop music. Therefore, the class-based character of African American music should not be overlooked. Art, especially popular music, has long been one of the few avenues open to working-class and underclass African Americans. It has often appeared to be the only medium through which poor black folk could get upper-class and middle-class white and black America to recognize the humble humanity, the tragedy, and the comedy of the life-worlds and life-struggles of the black masses (M. Ellison 1989; Ferris 2009; Sanger 1995; J. M. Spencer 1990).

Because the blues was the music that initially painted a sonic portrait of turn of the twentieth century minstrel, medicine, tent, and vaudeville shows, as well as both urban and rural black nightlife (including Jim Crowed juke joints, brothels, dancehalls, clubs, and bars), it was shunned by the emerging and extremely uppity African American middle class. At the turn of the twentieth century the black bourgeoisie preferred the solemn singing of the spirituals or the refined sounds of ragtime over the blues. Even though ragtime began as a form of red-light district dance music, whose origins have been traced back to African Americans in St. Louis and New Orleans circa 1897, it ultimately achieved widespread respectability and popularity among whites when it became available as sheet music for the piano (Berlin 1980; Hasse 1985; Schafer and Riedel 1973).

In its "purest" form ragtime is not improvised, which not only made it appear to many to be America's equivalent to European classical music, but its general lack of any form of improvisation clearly distinguished it from early jazz. Undoubtedly an influence on the early development of jazz, ragtime was primarily a vehicle for solo pianists, although several banjoists, such as Vess Ossman and Fred Van Eps, made numerous recordings. Among the three most renowned ragtime composers, Scott Joplin, James Scott, and Joseph Lamb, two were African American, Joplin and Scott respectively. The African American middle class, as to be expected, reveled in the fact that Scott Joplin was universally crowned the "King of Ragtime" and, even more, they delighted in the fact that his "piano rags" were repeatedly offered up as the American equivalent of minuets by Mozart, mazurkas by Chopin, or waltzes by Brahms. Great pride was also taken when European classical composers, such as Claude Debussy, Igor Stravinsky and Ferruccio Busoni, acknowledged the influence of ragtime music (Argyle 2009; Berlin 1994; Curtis 1994; Gammond 1975).

Where the spirituals and ragtime initially sonically represented African American "hyper-religiosity" and African American "hyper-sexuality," respectively, because European Americans became enamored with these black musical forms the black middle class apishly followed suit. The blues, on the other hand, was supposedly everything that the spirituals and ragtime were not: The spirituals and ragtime were sophisticated. The blues was unsophisticated. The spirituals and ragtime represented African American "high culture." The blues represented African American "low culture." The spirituals and ragtime were performed in prestigious churches and majestic concert halls. The blues was performed in juke joints and brothels—but the breakaway success of Mamie Smith's "Crazy Blues" in 1920 challenged and eventually changed the national perception and cultural reception of the blues.

After a prolonged period of gestation, the blues had finally arrived on the national scene, sensuously feminine and fully formed, flamboyant and colorful, with flowing robes, satins, and sequins—not in dirty denim overalls, brogan boots, and a snaggle-toothed smile. The early American recording industry clearly comprehended that there was money to be made from this dark and mysterious music that seemed simultaneously ancient *and* futuristic. In many ways the blues harked back and heaved forward all at once: *back* to the "slavery days" and the "failures of Reconstruction and post-Reconstruction," and *forward* to the jazz of the New Negro Movement, the rhythm & blues of the Civil Rights Movement, the soul music of the Black Power Movement, the myriad musics (e.g., soul, funk, and disco) of the Black Women's Liberation Movement and, of course, the rap and neo-soul music of the Hip Hop Movement.

Smith's "Crazy Blues" was a boon to both the blues and the then fledgling recording industry. The success of "Crazy Blues" demonstrated the *trans-cultural* and *trans-class* characteristics of the blues, if not early black popular music and early black popular culture. In other words, although the blues was created by a particular *race*, black folk, and a specific *class* within the African American community, working-class and underclass black folk, the lyrics, music, and overall aesthetic nonetheless hit a national nerve that transcended race and class as the 1920s progressed. In many ways the blues provided the first major model for what has come to be called "black popular music" and "black popular culture."

To this day, African American expressive culture is, however unwittingly, rooted in blues music, the blues aesthetic, and blues culture. What Mamie Smith and the classic blues women of the 1920s actually popularized were the sights, sounds, and sorrows of an emerging African American post-enslavement and post-Reconstruction worldview (Bourgeois 2004; J. Brown 2008; S. Vogel 2009; Willis and Williams 2002). A worldview that was both divinely and demonically dancing with a distinct African American dialectic that W. E. B. Du Bois conceived of as "double-consciousness" in his 1903 classic *The Souls of Black Folk.* "After the Egyptian and Indian, the Greek and Roman, the Teuton and Mongolian," Du Bois (1903b) famously declared:

> The Negro is a sort of seventh son, born with a veil, and gifted with second-sight in this American world,—a world which yields him no true self-consciousness, but only lets him see himself through the revelation of the other world. It is a peculiar sensation, this double-consciousness, this sense of always looking at one's self through the eyes of others, of measuring one's soul by the tape of a world that looks on in amused contempt and pity. One ever feels his two-ness,—an American, a Negro; two souls, two thoughts, two unreconciled strivings; two warring ideals in one dark body, whose dogged strength alone keeps it from being torn asunder.

The history of the American Negro is the history of this strife,—this longing to attain self-conscious manhood, to merge his double self into a better and truer self. In this merging he wishes neither of the older selves to be lost. He would not Africanize America, for America has too much to teach the world and Africa. He would not bleach his Negro soul in a flood of white Americanism, for he knows that Negro blood has a message for the world. He simply wishes to make it possible for a man to be both a Negro and an American, without being cursed and spit upon by his fellows, without having the doors of Opportunity closed roughly in his face. (3–4; see also Rabaka 2007, 2008, 2010a, 2010c)

The blues sonically and succinctly captures "double-consciousness." It represents the cultural, musical, and aesthetic aftermath of centuries of enslavement, racial colonization, racial segregation, and American apartheid. It is what being emancipated and recurringly re-enslaved sounds like. It is African Americans expressing that "peculiar sensation," that "sense of always looking at one's self through the eyes of others, of measuring one's soul by the tape of a world that looks on in amused contempt and pity."

The blues excruciatingly encompasses African Americans' feelings of perpetual "two-ness" and dividedness, their quests to see themselves as they actually are, not as others would like for them to be. The blues, then, is fundamentally about truth, about black folk speaking their special truths to each other and to the world at large. Part of African Americans' distinct truth undeniably involves the struggle to come to terms with their "American[ness]" and their "Negro[ness]," their "two souls, two thoughts," their "two unreconciled strivings," their "two warring ideals in one dark body, whose dogged strength alone keeps it from being torn asunder."

The blues is a musical and cultural manifestation of African Americans' "dogged strength." It represents a secularization of the deep double entendres of the spirituals and, as with all other forms of African American music, it makes the music mean one thing to those who have not *lived* the music and wholly another to those who have. *Living the music* and having an authentic relationship—or, rather, "keeping it real"—with the culture and community, or the experiences, individuals, and institutions that one is singing or rapping about represents both the *leitmotif* and *sine qua non* of black popular music and black popular culture. In other words, both the artist and the audience have got to *feel* the realness of the lyrics and music. If the lyrics and music do not conjure up and sonically capture the African American experience in a highly original and thoroughly individual way they do not register as "real," or "authentic," or—yes, I am about to boldly say it—"soulful."

It is the mystical and almost magical category of "soul" that has determined the fate more than a few would-be iconic African American artists. In African America, as in Africa, an artist must do more than represent themselves. They must also "rep" (i.e., represent) their community and culture.

They must speak the special truth of their community and culture to the wider world. No matter how technically proficient one may be on their chosen instrument. No matter how much facility one has to sing high or low, or rap fast or slow, without "soul," that *je ne sais quoi* of both continental and diasporan African art, there would be nothing truly distinct or, more to the point, "African" about African American music. [14]

Arguably one of the most "African" of all of African American music, as it was with classical African music, in the early blues aesthetic *sonic individuality* and *sonic originality* were not only greatly valued but, even more, they were greatly expected in anything that would pass itself off as "the blues." As with both classical and contemporary African music, even in a group setting each singer or instrumentalist is expected to make their special contribution to the collective sound. The emphasis on honing and harnessing a highly personal sound, an extremely individualized instrumental voice, no matter what the cost, was carried over from the traditional African music aesthetic and can be found in every major African American musical form: from work songs and field hollers to spirituals and gospel, from blues and jazz to rhythm & blues and rock & roll, from soul and funk to rap and neo-soul.

This emphasis on developing a distinct musical voice and soulful sound had an unfathomable impact on the early blues aesthetic. Even if we were to limit our discussion to classic blues women, which is what I have done here in this "remix," it could be sarcastically said that only a deaf person would fail to hear the distinct differences between the musical genius of Ma Rainey, Bessie Smith, Sarah Martin, Maggie Jones, Lucille Bogan, Martha Copeland, Eva Taylor, Bessie Tucker, Mildred Bailey, and Alberta Hunter. The African and African American traditions of composing and performing extremely personal music, music that moves the heart and the soul, was fundamental to classic blues women's work. The blues provided these women with a medium through which to express thoughts, feelings, and viewpoints usually silenced or ignored in almost all other areas of African American and mainstream U.S. culture during the first decades of the twentieth century.

To put it plainly, as a musical and cultural forum for individual expression, the blues quite simply has no equal. In fact, even when compared with the musical genres that directly built on the blues aesthetic (e.g., jazz, rhythm & blues, rock & roll, and soul), no other form of black popular music has provided so many poverty-stricken, socially segregated, and racistly ridiculed black folk with a medium through which to express their thoughts, feelings, and viewpoints—well, I am wont to say, that is until the emergence of rap music. Here we have hit on the peculiar political economy of black popular music.

As stated above, all major forms of African American music essentially have been created by poor black people, which leads us to critically question: What is it about working-class and poor African Americans' lives that compels them to create soundtrack after soundtrack to accompany their life struggles? What does it say about the universality of their lived experiences that so many people, both nationally and internationally, strongly identify with the music working-class and poor black people have created and contributed? And, lastly, what does it say about the persistence of anti-black racism and the racist nature of capitalism that seemingly most African American recording artists have been and continue to be exploited at the hands of European American musicians and record labels?

The exploitative musicians or "musical cultural bandits" are too numerous to name, but it might interest my readers to know that between 1988 and 1998 there were six major record labels in the United States: Warner Music Group, EMI, Sony Music, BMG Music, Universal Music Group, and Polygram. The years 1998 through 2004 saw Universal Music Group "absorb" Polygram, and between 2004 and 2008 Sony and BMG merged to become Sony/BMG. As of 2009 the four major labels are Sony Music Entertainment, EMI Group, Warner Music Group, and Universal Music Group, and they collectively control 70 percent of the world's music market and 80 percent of the music market in the United States.

One would be hard-pressed to find one of these record labels or the record companies they "absorbed" that has not super-exploited almost every major form of African American music, even as they have distanced themselves from anything and everything about black popular music (and African American culture in general) that mainstream and thoroughly middle-class America finds distasteful: from the classic blues women's lyrics about sex and their reportedly raunchy concerts to gangsta rappers' rhymes about pimps, "hoes" (i.e., whores), drugs, drunkenness, guns, and the ghetto (Shuker 2001; Suisman 2009; Toynbee 2000). As will be discussed in greater detail below, in many ways the blues lyrically and musically provided rap music with its "in yo' face!" ethos and "keep it real" criteria. Like gangsta rap and other forms of commercial rap in comparison with 1960s and 1970s soul music, the blues shifted black popular music from spirituality to sexuality, from the sacred to the secular, from the religious to the irreligious.

Comparable to its rap music offspring, the blues is an open expression of those heartfelt feelings that most folk, especially upper-class and middle-class folk, bury deep within and, in this sense, the blues can be said to be a collective exorcism of "double-consciousness" and other repressed emotions intimately experienced by and shared between the artist and their audience. Tragedy and comedy, domination and liberation, racism and sexism, spirituality and sexuality, poverty and unemployment, imprudence and violence, alcoholism and drug addiction, enslavement and imprisonment—the blues, as with every major form of African American music initiated in its aftermath, is the sonic and socio-cultural symbol of many things that polite middle-class people would much rather forget, and that is why the blues and most other forms of black popular music and black popular culture have been consistently shunned by the bourgeoisie at their (i.e., both the various black popular musics' and black popular cultures') inceptions.

At the turn of the twentieth century most upper-class and middle-class women in the United States were embracing and articulating the "cult of True Womanhood" ideology (Blair 1980; Donnelly 1986; Welter 1976). Both white and black bourgeois women looked down on women who did not meet "their" Eurocentric and middle-class standards. I have placed the word "their" in quotes in the preceding sentence because from a radical black feminist and revolutionary womanist perspective one wonders whether well-to-do white women realized how many of "their" standards of womanhood were actually the standards of white middle-class patriarchal men. And, equally important, one wonders how many of the black bourgeois women realized that most of "their" standards were actually patriarchal and Eurocentric "codes of honor" and "codes of behavior" borrowed from mainstream and middle-class European America.

Classic blues women, then, were the bane of both white and black bourgeois women. However, as is often the case when an aspect of a culture is hyper-commodified, capitalist political economy took precedence over social conventions. As in our own epoch, women of wealth or, at the least, women with access to wealth were considered "high-class," "respectable," and cultured "ladies" with low libidos, where working-class and poor women were considered unusually erotic and sometimes extremely exotic, as well as licentious and disreputable (Caplan 1987; P. H. Collins 2005; Kline 2001; Vance 1984; Weitz 1998).

After Mamie Smith's success every major and minor record company in America sent scouts down South to "discover" the next Mamie Smith (Brooks 2008; Miller 2010; Radano 2000, 2003). Although socially unacceptable in some "high-class" circles and socially celebrated in most "low-class" circles, the classic blues women were in vogue in the 1920s, and their "discovery" began a two-way flow of music and culture between the South and the North that has been replicated in almost each and every major form of African American music that rose in the aftermath of the classic blues queens' heyday. Henceforth, the blues would have both Southern *and* Northern expressions, rural *and* urban articulations or, rather, what has come to be called "country blues" *and* "urban blues" traditions.[15]

The shared family backgrounds and commonality of experiences of the first wave of blues women indicate that the combination of raw talent and deep desire to express themselves and perform took precedence over the pressures to conform to the social mores and communal taboos surrounding African American women prevalent during the first decades of the twentieth century. In their efforts to escape and overcome the innumerable issues and ills plaguing poor black women's lives at the outset of the twentieth century, the first wave of blues women was drawn to what they perceived to be the glamorous life, at first, on the vaudeville stage and, then later, on the blues revue circuit. The already powerful images produced with early photographic technology and proudly promoted by the recording industry presented simultaneously gorgeous and sensuous representations of blues women that attracted throngs of poverty-stricken young African American women to blues music, the blues aesthetic, and blues culture. For most of these young women the blues was not merely a career but, even more, a sacred calling that would enable them to, night after night, offer up their truths about what it meant to be *poor*, *black*, and *women* in early twentieth century America.

For example, when asked for a definition of the blues, iconic blues woman Alberta Hunter, whose awe-inspiring seventy-five year career stretched all the way from 1909 to her death in 1984, responded, "Why the blues are a part of me. . . . When we sing the blues, we're singin' out our hearts, we're singin' out our feelings. Maybe we're hurt and we just can't answer back, then we sing or maybe even hum the blues. Yes, to us the blues are sacred." She eloquently continued, "When I sing, 'I walk the floor, wring my hands and cry,' what I'm doing is letting my soul out" (quoted in Shapiro and Hentoff 1966, 246–47; see also Taylor and Cook 1987). Observe Hunter's emphasis on expressing her innermost "feelings" and what is in her "heart," and "letting [her] soul out."

Many of the singers and players of the spirituals and gospel music describe their relationship to their hallowed music in much the same way. Hunter could not have hit the nail on the head any harder than when she exclaimed, "Yes, to us the blues are sacred." The sanctity of the blues should not be overlooked, as James Cone contended in his classic *The Spirituals and The Blues* (1972):

> The blues are "secular spirituals." They are *secular* in the sense that they confine their attention solely to the immediate and affirm the bodily expression of black soul, including its sexual manifestations. They are *spirituals* because they are impelled by the same search for the truth of black experience. Yet despite the fact that the blues and the spirituals partake of the same Black Essence, there are important differences between them. The spirituals are *slave songs*, and they deal with historical realities that are pre–Civil War. They were created and sung by the group. The blues, while having some pre–Civil War roots, are essentially post–Civil War in consciousness. They reflect experience that issued from Emancipation, the Reconstruction Period, and segregation laws. . . . Also, in contrast to the group singing of the spirituals, the blues are intensely personal and individualistic. (112, all emphasis in original)

The sacred character of African American secular music should be borne in mind here and throughout the "remixes" to follow. Black secular music is inextricable from black sacred music, and it is only by critically engaging both that we will have some sense of the profundity of the African American experience and why this experience continues to astonish and intrigue people all over the world. Here we also have a sense of the connection between the Black Women's Club Movement and the first wave of blues women.

As discussed above, the Black Women's Club Movement primarily consisted of upper-class and middle-class churchwomen. Studies that focus exclusively and hard and fast on classic black clubwomen *or* classic blues women without bringing their womanist work into critical dialogue are usually lopsided, as they either negate the major articulations of working-class and poor black women (i.e., the blues women) or upper-class and middle-class black churchwomen (i.e., the clubwomen). Hence, a lot of hip hoppers' *amnesia* or fragmented knowledge regarding African American women's classical contributions to rap music and hip hop culture stems from one-dimensional interpretations or, rather, misinterpretations of African American women's history, culture, and struggle.

There has been a longstanding tendency, within both African American Studies and Women's Studies, to privilege the discourse of black clubwomen over classic blues women, or classic blues women over black clubwomen. Here I seek to comprehend the discourses of *both* the blues women *and* the clubwomen as discursively distinct parts of a—although at times terribly tension-filled—unified whole. Obviously this approach is not free from its own pitfalls. But, here I honestly believe that we will walk away with a fuller picture of what turn of the twentieth century black women involved in both political culture and popular culture contributed to turn of the twenty-first century women involved in both political culture and popular culture. Speaking directly to our need to move beyond the dichotomous discourse surrounding the black church and the blues and, in a sense, the fractious relationship between black churchwomen and classic blues women, Cone candidly wrote:

> Unfortunately, it is true that many black church people at first condemned the blues as vulgar and indecent. But that was because they did not understand them rightly. If the blues are viewed in the proper perspective, it is clear that their mood is very similar to the ethos of the spirituals. Indeed, I contend that the blues and the spirituals flow from the same bedrock of experience, and neither is an adequate interpretation of black life without the commentary of the other. (111; see also J. M. Spencer 1993)

Part of my overall argument throughout this book is that the major African American musical forms "flow from the same bedrock of experience, and [none] is an adequate interpretation of black life without the commentary of the other[s]." At the heart of my argument is also the contention that African American music reflects much more than the changing *sonic landscape* in black America, but also the changing *social landscape* in black America and the wider world of U.S. history, culture, politics, and society. Consequently, to reiterate, each major African American musical form can be said to mirror a major African American socio-political movement, sometimes serving as the official and, at other times, the unofficial soundtrack to the trauma and drama of black life during a particular period in African American history, culture, politics, and social struggle.

Above Cone alluded to the fact that African American music to a certain extent can be understood to be "commentary" on black life. It may be relatively easy for my readers to see how different genres of rap music serve as "commentary" on contemporary African American life. For example, *conscious rap* mirrors the 1980s and 1990s critique of Reaganism, the first Bush administration, the Clinton administration's "three strikes law," and increasing American militarism; *gangsta rap* coincides with the rise of the "War on Drugs," gang violence, and the predatory nature of the prison industrial complex at the end of the twentieth century; and *underground and alternative rap* speaks to many hip hoppers' disillusionment with the hyper-commercialization and corporate colonization of rap music and hip hop culture at the turn of the twenty-first century. However, it may be more difficult for many of my readers to perceive the ingenious ways classic blues women's music served as the soundtrack for most African American women's lives during the first decades of the twentieth century and, even more, how their work represents an unofficial soundtrack to the underside of the Black Women's Club Movement. Just as it can be said that there is a class-based character to all major African American musical forms, there seems to be a class-based character to what constitutes "black feminism" and who counts as a "black feminist."

In *Blues Legacies and Black Feminism: Gertrude "Ma" Rainey, Bessie Smith, and Billie Holiday* (1998b), Angela Davis asserted, "To a large extent . . . what are constituted as black feminist traditions tend to exclude ideas produced by and within poor and working-class communities, where women historically have not had the means or access to publish written texts" (xi–xii). However, similar to many hip hop women, many early twentieth century working-class and poor African American women (i.e., blues women) "did have access to publishers of *oral* texts." In fact, in the 1920s, "many black women were sought after—and often exploited by—burgeoning recording companies" (xii, emphasis in original). When African American women's written *and* oral texts are brought into critical dialogue a whole new archive is opened up and a more comprehensive portrait of African American women emerges.

However, even within the world of the classic blues women, deeper distinctions should be made. They should not all be lumped together, as is so often the case when and where we come to African American women, if not African Americans in general. In many ways mirroring the diversity of thought and practices within the world of the Black Women's Club Movement and the wider Women's Suffrage Movement, the classic blues women and their audiences made clear distinctions between "country" and "city" blues women, gospel and jazz blues women, and Mississippi Delta and Chicago blues women, et cetera (Bourgeois 2004; Carby 1991, 1998; B. Jackson 2005).

The style of blues sung and played by women most often reflected their seminal musical experiences during their formative years, the types of venues where they performed, and the composition of their audiences. For many of the classic blues women the road to stardom ran through minstrel, medicine, tent, and vaudeville shows. For instance, classic blues queens such as Mamie Smith, Ma Rainey, Bessie Smith, Ida Cox, Lizzie Miles, Clara Smith, Beulah "Sippie" Wallace, Bertha "Chippie" Hill, Victoria Spivey, and Trixie Smith all began their illustrious careers in such shows.

The early traveling revues—such as the Rabbit Foot Minstrels, Tolliver's Circus and Musical Extravaganza, the C. W. Parker Show, the Al Gaines Show, and the Silas Green Show—usually featured a guitar or "jug" (i.e., home-made instruments) band with a female singer.[16] Early blues women also sang and played in juke joints, bootleg whiskey watering-holes, whore houses, gambling dens, and at house parties. Accordingly, observe that even though these women's artistry was created in environments where there was all manner of illicit and illegal activities, their work has withstood the test of time and continues to influence contemporary popular music and popular culture—including rap music and hip hop culture.

Moreover, like many of the jazz, rhythm & blues, soul, and hip hop women who would come after them, most of the classic blues women got their start performing in the church. In fact, Sarah Martin, one of the most prolific classic blues women (recording more than sixty sides for the Okeh record label between 1922 and 1927), returned to singing gospel music full-time in the late 1930s (Bogdanov, Woodstra, and Erlewine 2003a; Russell and Smith 2006). Likewise, after her undisputed acknowledgment as the "Mother of the Blues" and a long and colorful career that reached back to 1900 by most estimates, Ma Rainey retired from the blues and "got religion" in 1935. By the time of her death from a massive heart attack in 1939 she was devoutly religious (P. J. Harris 1994; Lieb 1981; Stewart-Baxter 1970).

Even Bessie Smith, the "Empress of the Blues," as she continues to be hailed to this day, did not escape the influence of the African American church. Commenting on her *secularized spirituality* and innovative use of the African American call-and-response technique, in *The Devil's Music: A History of the Blues* (1997), British blues scholar Giles Oakley asserted:

> Women had always played a big part in the black church and many singers came from religious households. No one could have been more "secular" in private life than Bessie Smith, but even at the height of her career she would

always try to get to church on Sunday when on tour, and she often sang hymns around the house. Everyone who saw her perform agrees that her movements and vocal style evoked the fervor of a Southern Baptist Church. . . . Several of Bessie's generation did in fact turn to religion, and Ethel Waters, after a long career as a jazz singer and film star, came to sing religious songs for the Billy Graham Crusade. (104–5)[17]

Therefore, the connection that I am making between churchwomen, club-women, and blues women is quite real. Whichever way one looks at it, either from the point of view of the "sorrowful nature of the spirituals" (à la W.E.B. Du Bois's interpretation of the "sorrow songs" in *The Souls of Black Folk*) or the "sacred character of the blues" (à la James Cone's contentions above in *The Spirituals and The Blues*), there are overlapping and recurring themes that run throughout African American women's political discourse and popular culture during the first decades of the twentieth century. Black clubwomen's and classic blues women's work was not so much separate entities as much as it was different strategies and tactics to quite often address identical, if not at the least extremely similar, issues confronting African American women and the African American community as a whole in the early twentieth century.

## THE BLACK WOMEN'S CLUB MOVEMENT: AUTHENTIC WOMANIST ALTRUISM AND ELITE BLACK FEMINISM IN FULL EFFECT

Because black clubwomen were also black churchwomen, they had an extremely contentious relationship with classic blues women in particular, and classic blues culture in general. Blues women represented the black masses, who were—as they remain—primarily poor and working-class. Black clubwomen and black churchwomen, virtually being one and the same, shunned black popular music and black popular culture, which they perceived to be extremely vulgar and vice-laden. Instead they, for the most part, embraced European and European American music and culture in keeping with the "politics of respectability" (A. P. Long 2004; Parker and Cole 2000; E. F. White 2001).

The black churchwomen and clubwomen's preoccupation with respectability reflected a Eurocentric and bourgeois vision that incessantly vacillated between a constructive critique of the United States for not living up to its democratic ideals of freedom, justice and equality, and a concerted critique of the values, vernacular, and overall "lowdown" lifestyle of the black masses for not living up to white middle-class values, morals, and culture. Hence, black churchwomen and clubwomen's proclamations appeared to, almost schizophrenically, swing from "radical" to "conservative." It is the sheer range of the black churchwomen and clubwomen's politics, their radicalism *and* conservatism, that seems to mirror many of the views and values of contemporary black feminist academics in relationship to hip hop women, if not hip hop culture more generally.

The argument here is not that contemporary black feminist academics hold each and every view and value that has been handed down by classic black churchwomen and clubwomen. However, the argument here *is* that there seems to be enough of a similarity between many contemporary black feminist academics' rejection of hip hop women—if not rap music and hip hop culture in general—to warrant comparisons with the ragged relationship between classic black clubwomen and classic blues women. In more ways than one, classic black clubwomen and contemporary black feminist academics can be said to represent elite and college-educated African American women, where classic blues women and contemporary hip hop women disproportionately represent working-class and poor African American women.

Where classic black clubwomen and contemporary black feminists largely operate from within the hallowed walls of the African American church and the American academy, respectively, classic blues women and contemporary hip hop women work within the world of black vernacular culture, black popular music, and black popular culture. The preoccupation in this section, then, is with the ways in which the class-based character of certain forms of late nineteenth century and early twentieth century black feminism frequently produced *enmity instead of solidarity* and *conflict instead of cooperation* among African American women. One cannot help but to sincerely wonder whether a similar situation is brewing or, even more, already playing itself out between most contemporary black feminist academics and hip hop women.

Similar to classic black clubwomen, contemporary black feminist academics seem to harbor elements of what could be considered both "radical" and "conservative" thought in their rapport with hip hop women. In order for us to adequately understand the roots of the rift between contemporary black feminist academics and hip hop women it may not be going too far to say that we need to understand the relationship between the first acknowledged black feminist movement, the Black Women's Club Movement, and the black women involved in the first acknowledged black popular music and black popular culture, classic blues women. At this point, we have a working understanding of the centrality of African American women with respect to the creation and popularization of the blues. Now what we need to develop is a working understanding of both the radicalism *and* conservatism of the Black Women's Club Movement. This will provide us with an understanding of the major point of departure for contemporary academic black feminism in much the same way that the previous section provided us with a discussion of the world of classic blues women in order to *herstorically* comprehend the world of hip hop women.

To dive deeper into our discussion, first, it is important for us to be clear on black clubwomen's schizophrenic radicalism *and* conservatism. Most Black Women's Club Movement scholars agree that the clubwomen had relatively progressive politics when it came to issues revolving around anti-black racism, civil rights, and social justice. For instance, in *To Better Our World: Black Women in Organized Reform, 1890–1920* (1990), Dorothy Salem stated, "The formation of the National Association of Colored Women represented the black female elite's attempt to combat the growing racism of the late nineteenth century, to build a national female reform network, and to meet the changing needs of the black community" (7). It is laudable, to say the least, that less than thirty years after the issuing of the Emancipation Proclamation African American women organized a nationally networked movement against ongoing anti-black racism, human rights transgressions, and civil rights violations. Far from taking a backseat to late nineteenth century black male leadership, even though they were "[s]eparated along denominational, community, and ideological lines," Salem continued, "black women together faced the necessity of cooperating for their own self-interest and for the betterment of the race. They were both pushed and pulled into an organized reform role during the thirty-year period from 1890 to 1920" (7).

The rising tide of late nineteenth century and early twentieth century racism shockingly shook the African American elite's faith in the American Dream. Booker T. Washington's extremely popular advocation of the Protestant ethic of hard work, thriftiness, and individual initiative for African Americans had encouraged a historic drive for exemplary education, middle-class material comforts, and the other accoutrements of American upward mobility among black folk in both the North and the South. For most African Americans during the decades that closed the nineteenth century and opened the twentieth century it appeared as though every social breakthrough was met with a social setback. As the conditions grew grimmer and grimmer for African Americans in employment, education, public accommodations, politics, popular image, and the legal system, each favorable gain seemed to be foiled by the pigheaded persistence of anti-black racism (Fredrickson 1987; Jordan 1968; Litwack 1979, 1998; Meier 1963).

Truth be told, the Black Women's Club Movement was initiated as a result of problems both external and internal to African American communities. Which is to say, it is important for my readers to bear in mind that the black women's clubs, as Salem said, "were neither imitations of white women's groups nor formed solely as reactions to discrimination." It should be stated outright: The White Women's Club Movement "found race a controversial issue to be ignored or handled tactfully in order to gain members and support" (11–12). Therefore, the uninformed and disingenuous thought that black clubwomen were merely mindlessly imitating white clubwomen should be wiped out of our minds altogether.

As with the Black Women's Liberation Movement of the 1960s and 1970s, it was the black clubwomen's anti-racism, as well as their struggles against other socio-political problems, that decidedly distinguished their club movement from that of white clubwomen. We witness here, then, that the external political problems and social pressures that lead to the formation of the Black Women's Club Movement did not simply issue from suffrage, Christian benevolence, and temperance or, what is more, anti-black racism in a general sense, but also from anti-black racism on the part of white women in general, and white clubwomen in specific. Salem eloquently elaborated:

> Black women were in a paradoxical position. On the one hand, women, especially middle-class, educated women, were increasingly drawn into participation in organized reform. On the other hand, blacks were increasingly rejected as equal participants in these movements. For middle-class, educated black women the situation was filled with conflict or potential conflict. Depending on local conditions and leadership, most black women organized to meet immediate local needs, as did their white counterparts. Expanding beyond the denominational or social restrictions of the female church or literary organizations, black women formed clubs to improve themselves and their communities. As clubwork spread among white women, a similar movement, though different in content, emerged among the black women of the major black communities. (11)[18]

It is important to keep in mind that the Black Women's Club Movement was "a similar movement, though different in content" when compared with the White Women's Club Movement. Just as white clubwomen by and large excluded African American women from their clubs, many African American men sought to exclude African American women from the realm of social leadership and political activism. During the decades that closed the nineteenth century and opened the twentieth century many black men perceived black women the way most white folk perceived them—that is, as de-feminized, dirty, and promiscuous half-woman and half-animal creatures profoundly in touch with the sordid side of human nature. Here, then, is an example of one of the main problems internal to African American communities that led to the establishment of the Black Women's Club Movement. In other words, it was a movement not only against *external* white supremacy, but also against *internal* sexism or, rather, *black male supremacy*.

Perhaps, the best (and most egregious) example of black men's internalization of Eurocentric and misogynistic conceptions of African American women at the turn of the twentieth century is William Hannibal Thomas's infamous *The American Negro, What He Was, What He Is, and What He*

*May Become* (1901). Thomas was born in Ohio in 1843 to formerly enslaved folk of African descent, although he made it a point to imperiously note that most of his ancestors were white. In 1871 he relocated to the South to teach the formerly enslaved, and in 1873 he earned a license to practice law in South Carolina, where he later became a trial justice and a member of the state legislature. His views on African Americans, and African American women in specific, were strongly criticized by prominent New Negro males, such as Charles Chesnutt, Booker T. Washington, W. E. B. Du Bois, and Kelly Miller (J. D. Smith 2000).

Thomas's work, as to be imagined, was extremely popular among white racists and frequently cited to support their abhorrent arguments for white superiority and black inferiority. Part of what made his commentary so salient is that he argued that he observed firsthand the "sinful" nature of African Americans—and, again, African American women in particular. In many white folks' minds this, therefore, was not mere hearsay, but empirical evidence of and the undiluted truth about African American women. Ultimately, his early twentieth century exposé argued that the destiny of a people is inextricably connected to the character and condition of its women and, consequently, African Americans were doomed because of their extremely "immoral" and "licentious" women. In his own wicked words:

> We shall, however, in view of all the known facts at our command, be justified in assuming that not only are fully ninety per cent of the Negro women of America lascivious by instinct and in bondage to physical pleasure, but that the social degradation of our freed-women is without a parallel in modern civilization. . . . The moral status of a race is fixed by the character of its women; but, as moral rectitude is not a predominant trait in Negro nature, female chastity is not one of its endowments. (Thomas 1901, 195, 197)

Notice how in Thomas's twisted logic the "Negro race" either rises or falls based on the sexual purity of African American women, a group of women who U.S. history reveals to have been repeatedly (and anti-black racistly) raped and sexually exploited for more than 350 years at the hands of the very Christian white folk that Thomas, among other misguided "Negroes" at the time, believed to be intellectually, culturally, and morally superior to African Americans in general, and African American women in particular. Thomas took his lame logic further, focusing on the alleged licentious nature of "American Negro women":

> It is, therefore, almost impossible to find a person of either sex, over fifteen years of age, who has not had actual carnal knowledge. . . . Innate modesty is not a characteristic of American Negro women. On the contrary, there is observable among them a willing susceptibility to the blandishments of licentious men, together with widespread distribution of physical favors among

their male friends. . . . Marriage is no barrier to illicit sexual indulgence, and both men and women maintain such relations in utter disregard of their plighted troth. In fact, so deeply rooted in immorality are our Negro people that they turn in aversion from any sexual relation which does not invite sensuous embraces, and seize with feverish avidity upon every opportunity that promises personal gratification. Women unresistingly betray their wifely honor to satisfy a bestial instinct, and though there may be times when a morbid sentimental remorse reminds them for a brief period of their folly, yet every notion of marital duty and fidelity is cast to the winds when the next moment of passion arrives. (182–84)

According to Thomas and those of his ilk, it was not simply working-class and poor African American women who embraced immorality, but also upper-class and middle-class African American women. "Marital immoralities," he exclaimed, "are not confined to the poor, the ignorant, and the degraded among the freed people, but are equally common among those who presume to be educated and refined" (184). In so many words, Thomas said that all African American women, regardless of their education and class, are promiscuous and unprincipled. It is here that we have a bird's-eye view of why black clubwomen took exception to Thomas's commentary and the black men, white men, and white women who embraced and espoused his views as the gospel truth about African American women. White men at the time may have thought of white women as "the weaker sex" and, consequently, unable to perform work requiring muscular and intellectual development, but scathing attacks against all white women, especially upper-class and middle-class white women, and their much vaunted chastity and morality were virtually unheard of in the United States.[19]

Anti-black racism and the sordid details of African American women's sexual history (again, at the hands of the very Christian white folk who set the standards for "American womanhood") distinguished African American women's lives from European American women's lives, even working-class and poor white women. Here we have come back to the tired tendency to lump all African American women together, regardless of their education, income, employment, or social environment. Sad to say, this is a prickly practice that continues to this day and, also, one that continues to be constructively critiqued and combated by both black feminist academics and hip hop feminists.

As in our epoch, *African American women's womanhood, wifehood, and motherhood* were given special attention by early twentieth century Eurocentric patriarchs and their mindless minions. Long before the heated debates concerning "welfare queens" and the "baby-mama drama" of hip hop culture that closed the twentieth century and opened the twenty-first century, it is absolutely amazing to read tirades against African American womanhood, wifehood, and motherhood from the turn of the twentieth century. Almost perfectly encapsulating the major arguments against African American womanhood, wifehood, and motherhood during his day, Thomas was convinced that black women were miserable failures as women, wives, and mothers:

> Negro women, however, have but dim notions of the nature and obligations of wifehood. . . . So visibly universal is the strife for personal adornment that Negro mothers cannot be held blameless for the immoralities of their daughters, and there is at least ground for believing that sexual impurity is deliberately inculcated in them, since in many instances, their maternal guardians appear so pleased as when the physical charms of their daughters have procured for them dress and jewels beyond the ability of their parents to provide. Nor do the girls themselves appear to be abashed by any publicity of their immoralities. On the contrary, they are conspicuous in the social gatherings of their people, and parade with shameless audacity their wanton finery before their envious and less successful female friends. These facts would be incredible did we not realize that Negro women are admittedly weak in purpose, timid in execution, superstitious in thought, lascivious in conduct, and signally lacking in those enduring qualities which make for morality, thrift, and industry. (184, 197–98)

Not only does Thomas, in so many words, call African American women whores who have illicit sex for "dress and jewels," but he also blames their mothers for "pimping them out" and turning them into "gold-diggers" (à la Kanye West and Jamie Foxx's famous song), so to speak. No matter how difficult this may be for us to read, it is important for us to seriously consider Thomas's ideas because, as quiet as it has been kept, they not only represent the culmination of Eurocentric and patriarchal thought concerning African American women for an entire epoch, but also his ideas have been, however hidden, handed down to rap music and hip hop culture. Think for a moment. Think about the ways in which Thomas's words continue to be echoed in half-hearted critiques of hip hop women, if not working-class and poor African American women in general. Think about how many contemporary black men, white men, and white women continue to blame black mothers for the disfunctionality of the African American family—as if 350 years of enslavement, laws against African Americans marrying, whites selling off black mothers' children to the highest bidder, anti-black racist rape, consensual concubinage, and domestic violence would not affect any other human groups' marital traditions, familial structure, and parenting practices?

It is not a coincidence that the Black Women's Club Movement sought to rescue and reclaim African American womanhood, wifehood, and motherhood. Thomas and those who subscribed to his thought charged that black women had not sufficiently embraced and internalized the "True Woman ideal," which was put forward by upper-class and middle-class, formerly black folk–enslaving whites. As it remains in the twenty-first century, in the late nineteenth century and early twentieth century order of things, upper-class and middle-class white women were held up as the paragons of moral-ity and universal models for womanhood, wifehood, and motherhood that black (among other non-white) women should emulate. In an effort to coun-ter the concerted assaults on African American women, black clubwomen wrote articles defending *their* character—"their character," meaning upper-class and middle-class, well-educated, well-read, well-traveled, well-be-haved, and well-dressed black churchwomen. In fact, Dorothy Salem (1990) shared, "[i]t was a slanderous letter [written by a white man named James W. Jacks] about the character of black women that served as the catalyst to the calling of a national conference," and that *herstoric* conference eventually lead to the founding of the National Association of Colored Women (NACW) in 1896 (20).

While most of their responses to anti-black racism could be considered "radical" by the standards of their time, yet and still, there was much about black clubwomen's critiques of anti-black racist representations of black women that harbored the stench and stain of their conservatism and class bias against working-class and poor African American women. Salem important-ly observed:

> The national club movement among black women was the culmination of three factors. First, by 1890 the women had developed local leadership at-tempting to respond to specific community needs. Second, common interests and/or issues brought women together as a group above denominational or regional rivalries. Finally, several incidents demonstrated the need for a na-tional organization to promote a positive image of black women, to preserve their relatively privileged status, and to provide moral and educational guid-ance to the less privileged in their communities. (12)

It is the final factor that I would like to focus on here. In their efforts to counter negative images of African American women, black clubwomen frequently and openly embraced upper-class and middle-class white wom-en's standards for womanhood, wifehood, and motherhood. This means, then, at the very least some of their conservatism is attributable to their, however unwitting, internalization of Eurocentric and patriarchal concep-tions of womanhood, wifehood, and motherhood. Their obviously "radical" (again within the context of their time) critique of *anti-black racist sexism* and their obviously "conservative" and bourgeois embrace of Eurocentric and patriarchal conceptions of womanhood, wifehood, and motherhood created a tacit tension in their club work and between themselves and lower-class African American women.

As we have hopefully learned from hip hop feminism, not all working-class and poor African American women share the exact same views and values on everything. Ironically, while most black clubwomen rejected thought and commentary that aggregated all African American women into a single (most often negative) category, they themselves consistently embraced the inclination to view all working-class and poor African American women as a homogeneous and undifferentiated mass. Undoubtedly, according to Salem, the "Victorian model of the lady influenced the behavior of the black elite women. Columns in the black press frequently quoted white women's magazines about appropriate dress, language, demeanor, and values" (30). Ironically, and in no uncertain terms, black clubwomen sought to emulate white clubwomen in almost everything except their (i.e., white clubwomen's) anti-black racism and complicity in the violation of African Americans' human rights, civil rights, and voting rights.

For black clubwomen, it was plain and simple: "Good manners, social purity, cleanliness, and home-care would eventually demonstrate the inaccuracy of the white conception of the black woman as immoral." In a way, black clubwomen sought to offer up their lives as exemplary examples of African American womanhood, wifehood, and motherhood. The problem with them employing their own lives as ideal examples of black womanhood is that they perniciously and perfunctorily excluded examples of African American womanhood, wifehood, and motherhood emerging from the lives of working-class and poor black women.

Salem did not pull any punches when she asserted that the "members of the NACW believed in the women's sphere, which emphasized women's moral superiority, nurturance of children and social inferiors, and imposition of middle-class standards on lower classes" (30). It is when and where we come to the black clubwomen's "nurturance of . . . social inferiors" and their "imposition of middle-class standards on lower classes" that we are provided with irrefutable evidence of their Eurocentrism, elitism, bourgeoisism, paternalism, and conservatism. Obviously their embrace of "the Victorian model of the lady" was simultaneously Eurocentric, bourgeois, and patriarchal since it outright reflected "American Victorianism" with its mindless mimicry of British dress, mannerisms, and morality. [20]

Black women's club work was inextricable from their church work. As stated above, black churchwomen and black clubwomen were virtually one and the same, which is one of the reasons black churchwomen and black clubwomen have resembling relationships with classic blues women and classic blues culture. For instance, in *Righteous Discontent: The Women's Movement in the Black Baptist Church, 1880–1920* (1993), Evelyn Brooks Higginbotham revealingly wrote, "Although women's historians tend to focus overwhelmingly on the secular club movement, especially the National Association of Colored Women, as exemplary of black women's activism, clubwomen themselves readily admitted to the precedent of church work in fostering both 'women's consciousness' and a racial understanding of the 'common good'" (16–17). Going even further to emphasize the religious roots of the Black Women's Club Movement, Higginbotham continued:

The club movement among black women owed its very existence to the groundwork of organizational skills and leadership training gained through women's church societies. Missionary societies had early on brought together women with little knowledge of each other and created bonds of sisterly cooperation at the city and state levels. Not only Baptists but black Methodists, Presbyterians, and women in other denominations came together in associations that transformed unknown and unconfident women into leaders and agents of social service and racial self-help in their communities. For black Baptist women during the 1880s, the formation of state societies nurtured skills of networking and fund-raising. For more than a decade before the founding of the National Association of Colored Women, church-related societies had introduced mothers' training schools and social service programs, many of which were later adopted into the programs of secular women's clubs. (17; see also Collier-Thomas 2010)

It could be said that it is the religious roots of both the classic black clubwomen and classic blues women that simultaneously connected and disconnected their respective discourses. In much the same way that I argued above, Higginbotham cautions us against hard and fast or, rather, dichotomous thinking with respect to African American women's social and political activism at the turn of the twentieth century. Speaking directly to the tendency to divorce the activities of black churchwomen from black clubwomen, she offered remarkable insight:

> More than mere precursors to secular reform and women's rights activism, black women's religious organizations undergirded and formed an identifiable part of what is erroneously assumed to be "secular." The black Baptist women's convention thrust itself into the mainstream of Progressive reform, and conversely such clubs as those constituting the secular-oriented National Association of Colored Women included church work as integral and salient to their purpose. This complexity precludes attempts to bifurcate black women's activities neatly into dichotomous categories such as religious versus secular, private versus public, or accommodation versus resistance. (Higginbotham 1993, 17)

In complete agreement with Higginbotham, what I am emphasizing here is that along with the inclination on the part of most Black Women's Club Movement scholars to "bifurcate black women's activities neatly into dichotomous categories such as religious versus secular, private versus public, or accommodation versus resistance," there is also a longstanding tendency to discursively delink black clubwomen's social criticism and political activism from classic blues women's social criticism and aesthetic activism. The ongoing penchant to privilege the theories and praxes of elite, church-going, and college-educated African American women over the theories and praxes of working-class and poor African American women, in its own special way, speaks volumes about the ways in which most Black Women's Club Move-

ment scholars appear to have internalized the Eurocentrism, elitism, bourgeoisism, paternalism, and conservatism of classic black clubwomen. How else
could we explain most Black Women's Club Movement scholars' longstanding and ongoing erasure of working-class and poor African American wom-
en's—that is to say, classic blues women's—social commentary, political
criticism, and aesthetic activism?

To her credit, Higginbotham critically acknowledged classic black
churchwomen and black clubwomen's Eurocentrism, elitism, bourgeoisism,
conservatism, and paternalism. For example, she sternly stated, the "zealous
efforts of black women's religious organizations to transform certain behavior patterns of their people disavowed and opposed the culture of the 'folk'—
the expressive culture of many poor, uneducated, and 'unassimilated' black
men and women dispersed throughout the rural South or newly huddled in
urban centers" (15). Obviously Higginbotham is hinting at the issue that is at
the heart of this "remix," and it is the black churchwomen and black clubwomen's disavowal and staunch opposition to "the culture of the 'folk'"—
which is to say, classic blues culture in this instance—that appears to have
been passed on to most of the elite and college-educated African American
women who were born after the heyday of the Black Women's Club Movement.

By disavowing and distancing themselves from the "expressive culture of
many poor, uneducated, and 'unassimilated' black men and women," late
nineteenth century and early twentieth century black churchwomen and black
clubwomen disavowed and distanced themselves from black vernacular culture, which Houston Baker, in *Blues, Ideology, and Afro-American Literature: A Vernacular Theory* (1984), characterized as the "quotidian sound of
every day life" (11). "During their heyday," Baker went on, "the blues unequivocally signified a ludic predominance of the vernacular with that sassy,
growling, moaning, whooping confidence that marks their finest performances" (12). Likewise, in *Drylongso: A Self-Portrait of Black America*
(1980), John Langston Gwaltney contended that the "folk" culture of contemporary urban environments is essentially "core black culture," which is
"more than ad hoc synchronic adaptive survival" (xxv–xxvii). All of this is to
say that it is actually the culture of working-class and poor black folk that
really constitutes the "core" of African American culture. Because the black
bourgeoisie has consistently disowned the culture of the black masses, their
mimicry of white middle-class culture is not authentic African American
culture but, rather, *white middle-class culture in blackface.*[21]

Ironically, the black bourgeoisie at the turn of the twenty-first century
continues to take issue with black vernacular culture, black popular culture,
and black popular music in much the same way that the black bourgeoisie did
at the turn of the twentieth century. An identifiable difference, however,
stems from the inroads African Americans have made into the American

academy in the twentieth century. Along with the critiques of black popular culture and black popular music spewing out of most African American churches, now—mostly middle class or petit bourgeois—African American academics offer half-hearted critiques of black popular culture and black popular music—that is, if they acknowledge contemporary black popular music and black popular culture at all. Working-class and poor black folk— their language, customs of dress, mannerisms, popular music, and popular culture—have long served as a source of embarrassment for upper-class and middle-class African Americans. For the most part, elite and college-educated African Americans would much rather working-class and poor black folk assimilate into white middle-class culture and "mainstream" America as quickly and surreptitiously as possible.[22]

Black churchwomen and black clubwomen at the turn of the twentieth century whole-heartedly embraced the idea that working-class and poor black folk needed to assimilate in order for African Americans to be respected by white folk. Higginbotham (1993) helps to drive this point home:

> This educated female elite, frequently consisting of teachers or wives of ministers associated with educational institutions, promoted middle-class ideals among the masses of blacks in the belief that such ideals ensured the dual goals of racial self-help and respect from white America. Especially in the roles of missionary and teacher, black churchwomen were conveyers of culture and vital contributors to the fostering of middle-class ideals and aspirations in the black community. Duty-bound to teach the value of religion, education, and hard work, the women of the black Baptist church adhered to a politics of respectability that equated public behavior with individual self-respect and with the advancement of African Americans as a group. They felt certain that "respectable" behavior in public would earn their people a measure of esteem from white America, and hence they strove to win the black lower class's psychological allegiance to temperance, industriousness, thrift, refined manners, and Victorian sexual morals. (14)

Many African Americans continue to embrace a "politics of respectability," and many well-to-do black folk are still embarrassed by black popular culture and black popular music. It is amazing that almost a century after the Black Women's Club Movement's peak period so many African Americans have an acute form of *amnesia* when and where we come to the ways in which turn of the twentieth century black churchwomen and black clubwomen's Eurocentrism, elitism, bourgeoisism, paternalism, and conservatism continues to inform our understandings of, and relationships with, working-class and poor black women, black popular culture, and black popular music. To reiterate, the Black Women's Club Movement contained elements of what could be considered both "radicalism" and "conservatism": "radicalism" with regard to issues revolving around anti-black racism, civil rights, and social justice, and "conservatism" in terms of their embrace of upper-class and middle-class white women's conceptions of womanhood, wifehood, and motherhood, as well as their (i.e., black clubwomen's) contemptuous relationship with working-class and poor black folk and their unique culture.

In particular, I would like to suggest that black churchwomen and black clubwomen's relationship with classic blues women at the turn of the twentieth century has been, to a certain extent, replicated in most contemporary black churchwomen and black feminist academics' relationship with hip hop women at the turn of the twenty-first century. Again, the argument here is not that each and every facet of classic black churchwomen and black clubwomen's relationship with classic blues women has been handed down to contemporary black churchwomen and black feminist academics in their relationship with hip hop women, but that there are enough similarities to suggest that a critical examination may prove beneficial to contemporary black churchwomen, black feminist academics, and hip hop women in particular, and hip hop culture in general.

In light of the foregoing sections, the concluding section of this "remix" explores *hip hop's amnesia* with respect to the relationship between classic blues women, classic black clubwomen, and contemporary hip hop women. The key questions are as follows: Is there a new twenty-first century form of the "politics of respectability" and the "cult of True Womanhood" playing itself out in African America, especially when and where we come to older black churchwomen and black feminist academics, on the one hand, and young African American women, rap music, and hip hop culture, on the other hand? If so, in what ways is this new twenty-first century form of the "politics of respectability" and the "cult of True Womanhood" rooted in the "conservative" views and values of the Black Women's Club Movement in specific, and the late nineteenth century and early twentieth century black bourgeoisie in general? How could contemporary black feminism, as it is most often articulated by elite and college-educated African American women, benefit from a "remix" that brings it into critical dialogue with hip hop women, hip hop feminism, and the Hip Hop Women's Movement?

## MOTHERS OF THE BLUES AND MIDWIVES OF RAP MUSIC: CLASSIC BLUES QUEENS AND THE BLACK WOMEN'S CLUB MOVEMENT, WOMEN-CENTERED RAP AND THE HIP HOP WOMEN'S MOVEMENT

In his influential work, *What the Music Said: Black Popular Music and Black Popular Culture* (1998), Mark Anthony Neal identified two early African American institutions that ultimately lead to the establishment of the "Black

Public Sphere" of the twentieth century and, truth be told, the twenty-first century as well: the African American church and the juke joint.[23] The classic black church was primarily dominated by the black bourgeoisie, where the juke joint was presided over by working-class and poor black folk. The black church supposedly represented African American sacred culture, where the juke joint reputedly symbolized African American secular culture. In a nutshell, the black church was rich and spiritual, and the juke joint was poor and sexual. Neal noted:

> To a large extent the black church, despite the economic diversity contained within it, privileged the sensibilities of the liberal bourgeois, in that the liberal bourgeois establishment provided the most likely conduit for African American integration into American public life. It is not my intention to characterize the totality of the black church tradition in this way, but rather to highlight the general privileging among African Americans of bourgeois models within the black community. The liberal bourgeois model functioned within the Black Public Sphere as a formalized and public expression of African American political and social sensibilities, that by definition would create alternative and informal spheres of expression and critique. (6)[24]

Above we have witnessed firsthand the "general privileging among African Americans of bourgeois models within the black community." It is important to observe that Neal and I are in agreement that because the black bourgeoisie dominates the black church, and African American religious discourse in general, for the most part the black church has developed a middle-class character that is patently paternalistic toward the humble humanity of working-class and poor black folk. It is ironic that, even in an institution where they are undoubtedly the majority, working-class and poor black folk are found wanting and made to feel unworthy. Many grow frustrated fast, while others (who sincerely "wanna be like Jesus," as it were) are long-suffering and willing to accept the insults of the black bourgeoisie. Eventually the frustrated and alienated, both within the white world and the black church, find comfort and camaraderie in the "first secular cultural institution to emerge after emancipation—the jook." In *Jookin': The Rise of Social Dance Formations in African American Culture* (1990), Katrina Hazzard-Gordon explained the social significance of the juke joint:

> Precisely because gatherings of slaves or free people of African descent were illegal, slavery fostered black social institutions that defied white control, and thus helped create a recurrent pattern of covert social activity. During the post-Reconstruction era, African Americans saw a need—and an opportunity—to relocate the clandestine social activities and dances of the plantation days. Their freedom, the reorganized labor system, and their cultural past deter-

mined the shape of the first secular cultural institution to emerge after emancipation—the jook. Like the blues, the jook gave rise to and rejuvenated a
variety of cultural forms. (76–77)[25]

The blues was the incipient soundtrack to the "first secular cultural institution to emerge after emancipation—the jook." As an institution within
African America, initially the juke joint symbolized a series of transgressive
traditions that defied white and black bourgeois culture and morality. For
instance, in the decades immediately following African American enslavement leisure time and amusements were still virtually unheard of within
working-class communities in the United States, and the overt and aggressive
search for leisure activities—that is, of course, except during holidays and
community-sanctioned special occasions—was almost always acknowledged
as transgressive or, actually, straight-up "bad" behavior among African
Americans. As a result, the juke joint operated as an illusive institution that
was understood to be intrinsically taboo and, even more, the opposite of the
black church with its primarily black (and white) bourgeois sensibilities.

Undeniably, during the enslavement and post-enslavement years the
African American church was the central "sacred" institution in African
America, and it served multiple purposes—spiritual, social, political, cultural, economic, educational, recreational, aesthetic, etc. Bearing in mind what
Hazzard-Gordon wrote above concerning it being "the first secular cultural
institution to emerge after emancipation," the juke joint was the major "secular" early incubator for black popular music and black popular culture. In this
sense, similar to the African American church, the juke joint prefigured and
provided a foundation for every major form of black popular music and black
popular culture, including contemporary rap music and hip hop culture.

When viewed from this angle, the juke joint registers as a source of solace
and a site of resistance to issues and ills often overlooked or downplayed by
the African American church as a consequence of its insidious inclination
toward the "liberal bourgeois model" Neal discussed above. In short, the juke
joint, including its innumerable twentieth century and twenty-first century
manifestations, is unequivocally in contest with the black church as the "official" site and source of African American authenticity and African American
culture. Here, my readers should bear in mind that the juke joint, above and
beyond its role as a covert social and political space, was also a unique
cultural aesthetic arena that revitalized an inchoate post-enslavement African
American aesthetic tradition, specifically in the realms of black popular music, theater, and dance. These black aesthetic forms were obviously and
rather roguishly restricted during enslavement, except when their performance entertained or in some way bolstered the black folk–enslaving Southern white elite and their Northern business associates. This is all to say, from
the spirituals and field hollers to neo-soul and hip hop, from blackface min-

strel and vaudeville shows to Spike Lee's and Tyler Perry's movies, and from tap-dancing and the cakewalk to the moonwalk and the crip walk, the incubative influence of the juke joint reaches across several centuries and resolutely remains with us in the twenty-first century.

During the Reconstruction and post-Reconstruction years the emergence of the juke joint, however intra-racially furtive and extra-racially secretive, bluntly registers the appearance of class schisms within post-enslavement African America. As quiet as it has been kept, these early class schisms continue to haunt African America and, even more, twenty-first century man-ifestations of the African American church and the juke joint. However, even as I write all of this I do not intend to conceptually construct the African American church and the juke joint as hard and fast binary opposites that can be nicely and neatly reduced to the high-handed sensibilities of the black bourgeoisie, on the one hand, and the "profane" predilections of the black working-class and the black poor, on the other hand.

Hence, to get right to the meat of the matter, my main point here is to intensely emphasize the transgenerational and extremely imaginative social and political construction of these pillar African American institutions vis-à-vis the perceptions of the black bourgeoisie, the black working-class, and the black poor *and*, equally important, the white bourgeoisie, the white working-class, and the white poor. Obviously there is a tendency to privilege both white and black bourgeois thought and culture when and where we come to African American social movements, political thought, popular music, and popular culture. I seek to discursively disrupt this prickly practice by high-lighting poor and working-class black folk's contributions to African American social movements, political thought, popular music, and popular culture via arguably one of the only institutions in U.S. history that has unceasingly accepted them on their own terms (as opposed to on white or black bourgeois terms) and that they have consistently had control over—*the juke joint*, which is also to say, the main discursive domain of black popular music and black popular culture.

It will not be going too far to say that the African American church, with its predominantly black (and white) bourgeois views and values, put the premium on the range and reach of African American social and political culture. In no uncertain terms, the juke joint has consistently and very crea-tively challenged the black (and white) bourgeois values and vision of the African American church. Consequently, this historic contestation between the church and the juke joint inadvertently created a core set of democratic and distinctly *African American* values within the juke joint, much like those found in African American churches free from black bourgeois leadership, that ironically celebrated the distinctiveness of working-class and poor black folk's—that is, the black masses'—humble humanity in the midst of American apartheid and black bourgeois Eurocentrism, elitism, bourgeois-ism, conservatism, and paternalism.

Late nineteenth century and early twentieth century African American women played a pivotal role in both the external struggle for civil rights, women's rights, and voting rights and the internal struggle against colorism, sexism, and classism. In this sense, then, classic black clubwomen and clas-sic blues women represent much more than merely "old school" black bour-geois and black proletarian feminist foremothers but, even more, precursors to the 1920s and 1930s New Negro women and jazz women, the 1950s and 1960s civil rights sisters and rhythm & blues women, the 1960s and 1970s Black Power pantherettes and soul sisters, the 1960s and 1970s women's liberationists, black feminist funksters, and black disco divas, and—yes, of course—the Obama America female rappers, neo-soul sisters, and hip hop feminist-activists of the twenty-first century.

As discussed above, turn of the twentieth century black clubwomen sought to deconstruct and reconstruct the white public's perception of black womanhood, wifehood, and motherhood. Indeed, within the context of turn of the twentieth century America the Black Women's Club Movement's overarching political goals and social programs were quite "radical," even though they were very often marred by the conservatism of the bulk of their bourgeois views and values. For instance, in *Toward a Tenderer Humanity and a Nobler Womanhood: African American Women's Clubs in Turn of the Twentieth Century Chicago* (1996), Anne Meis Knupfer provides us with a sense of the wide range and reach of black clubwomen's "radical" politics and social programs:

> Clubwomen made tremendous contributions to their communities, contribu-
> tions that have yet to be fully documented, chronicled, and analyzed. Such
> contributions included the founding and sustenance of non-formal community
> facilities, such as kindergartens, day nurseries, reading rooms, employment
> agencies, homes for the elderly and infirm[ed], homes for working girls, youth
> clubs, settlements, and summer outings and camps for children. Working in
> conjunction with local churches, businesses, and urban chapters of national
> organizations, African American women participated in numerous educational
> and social uplift activities. Presentations through forums, debates, discussions,
> oratories, addresses, and lyceums not only gave voice to the clubwomen's
> perspectives on community concerns, but also socialized young girls into po-
> litical and social consciousness. Through fund-raising activities as various as
> bazaars, raffles, picnics, dances, theater productions, and musical concerts,
> clubwomen financially supported the institutions they created and provided in-
> kind gifts and moneys to poorer African Americans. . . . Furthermore, such
> occasions provided rich contexts for celebrating African American traditions
> and culture. (2; see also Knupfer 2006)

The first thing that it is important to observe here is that no matter what anyone might say about the conservative nature of some of the Black Women's Club Movement's politics and programs, they indeed did make "tremendous contributions to their communities." Secondly, they understood themselves to working in the best interest of African Americans, particularly poor black folk. This is extremely important to emphasize, or else some of my readers might misinterpret my critical comments concerning the Black Women's Club Movement in the previous section as a complete rejection of their contributions to ongoing African American history, culture, and struggle—including hip hop women, hip hop feminism, and the Hip Hop Women's Movement more generally. Far from rejecting the Black Women's Club Movement and writing them off as "old school" and "conservative" black bourgeois feminist foremothers, my analysis instead highlights their simultaneous radicalism *and* conservatism.

Indeed, when the majority of the well-to-do folk (i.e., upper-class and middle-class white folk) of their era turned a blind eye to post-enslavement and post-Reconstruction black suffering and social misery, the Black Women's Club Movement established "non-formal community facilities, such as kindergartens, day nurseries, reading rooms, employment agencies, homes for the elderly and infirm[ed], homes for working girls, youth clubs, settlements, and summer outings and camps for children." Obviously the Black Women's Club Movement was not so Eurocentric and bourgeois that it was willing to callously turn its back on the black working-class and the black poor. This should be strongly stressed, or many may misunderstand why I honestly believe that, along with classic blues women and the early blues aesthetic in general, the Black Women's Club Movement is a major sociopolitical and cultural movement that most hip hoppers *have forgotten but desperately need to remember* in order for us to re-radicalize and re-politicize rap music, hip hop culture, and the wider Hip Hop Movement.

Above and beyond emphasizing that the Black Women's Club Movement "socialized young girls into political and social consciousness," it is significant to highlight *how* they "socialized young girls into political and social consciousness." Notice that Knupfer was keen to comment on the clubwomen's utilization of "bazaars, raffles, picnics, dances, theater productions, and musical concerts" to "socialize . . . young girls into political and social consciousness." Just as both classic black clubwomen and classic blues women had a common connection in the African American church, they also shared a commitment to "celebrating African American traditions and culture."

At the very least, according to Knupfer's research, some of the African American "traditions and culture" that the clubwomen sought to celebrate emerged from African American musical, theatrical, and dance traditions. This means, then, on top of being connected through their respective relationships with the African American church, classic clubwomen and classic blues women were also connected through their celebrations of African American musical, theatrical, and dance traditions. This is something that has been directly handed down to hip hop women and the Hip Hop Women's Movement, especially when we observe how contemporary African American women, both in black communities and on college campuses, employ rap music and hip hop culture to not only raise awareness about issues impacting African American women's lives and struggles in the twenty-first century, but also to raise much needed support and funds to aid poor African Americans and underfunded community institutions that assist young, old, and infirmed poor black folk.

In this sense, the connections that I am making between classic black clubwomen, classic blues women, and contemporary hip hop women are quite real. However, these connections will remain unacknowledged so long as we overlook working-class and poor African American women's contributions to classical and contemporary African American feminist/womanist thought, politics, and social movements, as well as classical and contemporary black popular music and black popular culture. The full range and reach of African American women's thought and practices, whether we would like to call them "black feminist" or "womanist," will not be critically comprehended without, first, thoroughly engaging working-class and poor African American women's contributions and, second, bringing their unique contributions into critical dialogue with the contributions of upper-class and middle-class, college-educated African American women. My line of logic here has been profoundly influenced by Daphne Duval Harrison's watershed work, *Black Pearls: Blues Queens of the 1920s* (1988), where she critically examined 1920s classic blues women as "pivotal figures in the assertion of black women's ideas and ideals from the standpoint of the working-class and the poor":

> It reveals their dynamic role as spokespersons and interpreters of the dreams, harsh realities, and tragicomedies of the black experience in the first three decades of [the twentieth] century; their role in the continuation and development of black music in America; [and] their contributions to blues poetry and performance. Further, it expands the base of knowledge about the role of black women in the creation and development of American popular culture; illustrates their modes and means for coping successfully with gender-related discrimination and exploitation; and demonstrates an emerging model for the working woman—one who is sexually independent, self-sufficient, creative, assertive, and trend-setting. (10)

It would be virtually impossible to deny that the most representative "feminist" or "womanist" rappers, neo-soul sisters, and hip hop women are positioned in a "dynamic role as spokespersons and interpreters of the dreams, harsh realities, and tragicomedies of the black experience" in twenty-first century America. It would be equally difficult to deny the fact that classic black clubwomen understood themselves to be "spokespersons and interpreters of the dreams, harsh realities, and tragicomedies of the black experience" in late nineteenth century and early twentieth century America. Moreover, mirroring the classic blues women, contemporary hip hop women—whether rappers, neo-soul singers, musicians, producers, DJs, or music critics—are making their own unique contributions to the "continuation and development of black music in America." At this point it is undeniable that their work "expands the base of knowledge about the role of black women in the creation and development of American popular culture; illustrates their modes and means for coping successfully with gender-related discrimination and exploitation; and demonstrates an emerging model for the working woman— one who is sexually independent, self-sufficient, creative, assertive, and trend-setting."

Where the classic black clubwomen may have put the premium on what it meant to be African American *and* a "respectable" middle-class lady, the classic blues women's lyrics, music, and lifestyles testified to the "dreams, harsh realities, and tragicomedies" of what it meant to be an African American "working woman." The connections between the classic blues women's articulation of the turn of the twentieth century "working woman" as a woman who is "sexually independent, self-sufficient, creative, assertive, and trend-setting," and hip hop women's articulation of the "around the way girl" (à la LL Cool J's classic rap song) as a woman who is confident, independent, intelligent (i.e., book-smart), and street-smart should not be lost on my readers. Hip hop women have more in common with classic blues women than previously acknowledged, and where most classic blues women felt constrained by the bourgeois beliefs and politics of the turn of the twentieth century African American church, many hip hop women feel restricted by the religious conservatism and bourgeoisism of most African American churches at the turn of the twenty-first century. Just as classic blues women broached subjects that impacted turn of the twentieth century African American women that classic black clubwomen believed to be impolite and viciously vulgar, hip hop women have consistently taken up topics that the contemporary black bourgeoisie and many black feminist academics have ignobly ignored. It would seem to me that much of the work of the classic blues women and contemporary hip hop women is simultaneously culturally and aesthetically audacious, boldly blurring the lines between politics and aesthetics and, ultimately, providing us with *the art of African American women's decolonization and liberation.*

In the African American church at large the discourse on the most pressing problems confronting African America is often dampened by religious restrictions and bourgeois conservatism. This is not in any way to suggest

that there is not a strong tradition of religious radicalism that has significantly impacted African American history, culture, and struggle, including black
popular music and black popular culture.[26] Nevertheless, African American
religious radicalism has always appeared to take a backseat to the piousness
and religious conservatism of the black bourgeoisie, who, once again, have
long presided over and been the primary leaders of the African American
church. It is not as though African Americans did not want or need to publicly discuss what were perceived to be "impolite" issues, but the fact that the
black church forbade discussion of taboo topics.

Taboo topics, consequently, were taken up in African American secular
institutions and discourse, specifically those emerging from the juke joint.
Emphasizing the African American women-centered character of classic
blues women's work, Harrison (1988) helps to highlight how their lyrics,
music, and lifestyles provide us with a working understanding of the range
and reach of African American secular discourse:

> They dealt openly with the issues that were of particular concern to black
> women in the urban setting—freedom from social and religious constraints,
> sexual and economic independence, alcoholism and drugs. Issues of sexuality
> and sex were addressed directly and indirectly in their lifestyles and their
> blues. The desire to find and express affection, love, and sensuality in various
> ways and under less scrutiny was a central issue for them. Lesbianism was
> practiced and sung about by such diverse singers as Bessie Smith, Ma Rainey,
> and Gladys Bentley—the last was known as a tough-talking, singing piano
> player who some believed to be a male transvestite and others, a lesbian.
> (13–14)

Although the classic black clubwomen sought to help poverty-stricken
African American women, in many ways their efforts were limited by their
bourgeois beliefs and conservative conceptions of "respectable" womanhood. Obviously they were aware of many of the dire issues confronting
working-class and poor black women, but often their pretensions to respectability proved abstract and impractical to African American "working wom-
en." Instead of constructively and instructively utilizing turn of the twentieth
century black "working women's" popular music and popular culture, classic
black clubwomen for the most part kept up a condescending relationship
with the language, culture, and music of working-class and poor black folk.

Had classic black clubwomen suspended their Eurocentric elitism and
actually took the time to develop their own mutually respectful relationships
with classic blues women's work they would have discovered that there was
a significant number of *black feminist blues songs* or, rather, *black women-
centered blues songs* concerned with racial segregation, poverty, employment, imprisonment, domestic violence, prostitution, alcoholism, drug addiction, natural disasters, and other issues that, when taken together, creatively

constitute a *mélange* social, political, and cultural history of African Americans, especially African American "working women," during the decades that closed the nineteenth century and opened the twentieth century. Similar to the political protest and social critique found in hip hop women's work, most often the political protest and social critique elements in classic blues women's work were entwined with themes of love, romance, sexuality, and the like. This is something that has caused quite a few fairly competent blues scholars to misinterpret blues in general, and classic blues women's work in particular.

As with many hip hop scholars and critics, there has been a longstanding inclination on the part of blues scholars and critics to argue that the blues aesthetic, which essentially demands an intense emotional intimacy and vocal vulnerability on the part of the individual composer or performer, is virtually free from political protest and social critique. For example, "[t]here is little social protest in the blues," imperiously declared Samuel Charters in *The Poetry of the Blues* (1963, 152). How Charters can be considered a renowned blues scholar and either overlook or surreptitiously seek to downplay one of the core characteristics of the blues is beyond me. He seems to be completely oblivious to the deep double entendres inherent in most African American musical expressions.

As it was with work songs and the spirituals, and as it remains with rap and neo-soul, the blues may very well mean one thing to folk unfamiliar with the intricacies and intimacies of the African American experience, and wholly another thing to those of us who share the sights, sounds, sensualities, sorrows, and celebrations of the blues composers and performers. Continuing his efforts to discursively de-politicize the blues, Charters further stated:

> There is often a note of anger and frustration; sometimes the poverty and the rootlessness in which the singer has lived his life is evident in a word or a phrase, but there is little open protest at the social conditions under which a Negro in the United States is forced to live. There is complaint, but protest has been stifled. . . . It is almost impossible for the white American to realize how tightly he has united against his black fellow citizens. The oppressive weight of prejudice is so constricting that it is not surprising to find little protest in the blues. It is surprising to find even an indirect protest. (152)

One earnestly wonders what kind of "blues" Charters was listening to when he came up with his commentary here. "It is surprising to find even an indirect protest" in the blues. This, quite simply, is madness, and a gross misinterpretation of the music. As with contemporary rap and neo-soul, especially when and where we come to women's work, I am not in any way arguing that each and every blues song should be seen as some sort of sonic protest. However, I would like to strongly stress the multiple meanings and innate innuendo in black popular music in particular, and black popular culture in general. The fact of the matter is that African American music is often much more than it seems and, equally important, it represents much more than the "distinct voice" or "unique sound" of this or that individual musician.

The blues is not commonly characterized as a "happy music," even though it is the music of both African American sorrow *and* African American celebration. Because the blues is not commonly characterized as a "happy music," and considering the fact that it is the first major musical form to emerge after African American enslavement, it is puzzling to me that Charters cannot hear the subtleties of political protest and social critique in a musical form that came into being during one of the darkest and most doom-filled periods in African American history. Does Charters not realize that the blues appeared during the same epoch that witnessed the end of Reconstruction, the terrorism of the Ku Klux Klan and the Black Codes, the rise of lynching and other forms of anti-black racist violence, and the horrors of the peonage system, the sharecropping system, the convict-lease system, and the chain gang? If, indeed, Charters does not realize this, or if, for whatever reason, he did not take all of this into consideration when he came up with his analysis above, then he should respectfully refrain from writing about the blues, or any form of black popular music for that matter.

It is extremely offensive that so many European and European American "black music" scholars and critics seem to go out of their way to disassociate "black music" from the lives and struggles of black people. They would not dare dream of putting this prickly practice into play when and where we come to the music of Bach, Beethoven, Handel, Mozart, Vivaldi, or Verdi. In fact, it is almost universally accepted at this point—especially within the world of Eurocentric musicology—that in order to really and truly appreciate European classical music, one must, at the very least, have a novice's knowledge of the history, culture, and politics of the period in which the composer created their most beloved music. Why, then, does it seem strange that the same holds true for African American composers and music? Needless to say, Charters's analysis above fails to consider the *interpretive audience* that the blues initially was and primarily remains directed at—working-class and poor black folk. Consequently, Charters engaged blues protest from the very whitewashed, Eurocentric ahistorical and apolitical point of view of the very white folk who, first, enslaved and, later, racially segregated, lynched, and otherwise terrorized African Americans during the early developmental phase of the blues.

As with most white scholars of black music who define themselves and their work as "anti-racist," especially those of the 1960s and 1970s, Charters's work here puts forward conceptions of black subjectivity that are flawed because they are, however unwittingly, predicated on Eurocentrism and paternalism. I will make no mention of the fact that they are also rooted in deep-seated notions of "black exoticism" and "black eroticism." Similar to Charters, in *The Meaning of the Blues* (1960) the British blues scholar Paul Oliver went so far as to develop an argument to explain exactly why there was a lack of protest in the blues. In so many words, he brusquely announced that African Americans are essentially nothing more than the by-product of their physical environments and their material circumstances.

In essence Oliver's argument is that history changes African Americans. They do not and cannot change history. Whites, in other words, have defined the world once and for all. Blacks (among other non-whites), therefore, must suffer through the racist reality that whites have socially, politically, economically, and culturally constructed. Oliver observed:

> That the number of protest blues is small is in part the result of the Negro's acceptance of the stereotypes that have been cut for him. In rural areas where education is meager and the colored people have known no better environment, there is little with which to compare the mode of life. They are primarily concerned with the business of living from day to day, of "getting along" with the whites, of conforming and making the best of their circumstances. As surely as the Southern white intends them to "keep their place" the majority of Negroes are prepared to accept it. They know that they cannot change the world but they have to live in it. An apathy develops which the racial leaders find exasperatingly hard to break, and even when aggravation reaches the point where the spirit of revolt against the system arises, this is often soon dissolved in minor personal disruption and eventual disregard. (322–23)

Oliver painted a picture of African Americans that, in more ways than one, robbed them of both their subjectivity and agency. It is shocking that a book written on the blues and published in 1960 argued that the "masses" of Southern black folk were essentially apathetic, inert, and "primarily concerned with the business of living from day to day, of 'getting along' with the whites." By disassociating the blues from African American history, culture, and struggle Oliver created a blackface minstrelesque caricature of the blues and, unwittingly I honestly believe, dehumanized African Americans. Why did he, and blues critics of his ilk, feel the need to represent African Americans as apathetic, inert, and politically immature?

As with Charters's (mis)conception of the blues, Oliver's articulation of the blues ignores all of the blues protest songs that critiqued: 1920s and 1930s Wall Street and the "Great Depression" (e.g., "Down and Out Blues" by Scrapper Blackwell, "Starvation Blues" by Big Bill Broonzy, "Tough Times Blues" by Charley Jordan, "Hard Time Blues" by Carrie Edwards, "The Panic Is On" by Jimmy McCracklin, and "Depression Blues" by Clarence Gatemouth Brown); the policies of Presidents Herbert Hoover, Harry Truman, and Dwight Eisenhower (e.g., "Hobo Jungle Blues" by Sleepy John Estes, "Hard Times Ain't Gone Nowhere" by Lonnie Johnson, "Unemployment Stomp" by Big Bill Broonzy, "Welfare Blues" by Calvin Frazier, and "Eisenhower Blues" by J.B. Lenoir); and the Red Cross, the New Deal, the Public Works Administration, and the Works Progress Administration (e.g., "W.P.A. Blues" by Casey Bill Weldon, "Don't Take Away My W.P.A." by Jimmie Gordon, "Working for the W.P.A." by Black Ivory King, and "High Cost, Low Pay Blues" by Ivory Joe Hunter).

Between 1924 and 1954 African Americans composed, recorded, and performed hundreds of blues protest songs. How Charters and Oliver could have missed all of this provocative protest music and still be regarded as renowned blues scholars continues to escape me. The only way any of this makes sense is by following the sneaky suspicion that Charters and Oliver are writing what those who have the power to deem someone a "renowned" blues scholar would like to read concerning black folk and the blues.

Hence, this could be a simple case of someone finding exactly what they are looking for. It will be recalled that President Abraham Lincoln allegedly said: "If you look for the bad in people expecting to find it, you surely will." Here, we might paraphrase President Lincoln and say, "If you look for a lack of protest in the blues, and in black music in general, you will surely find it." Instead of suspending preconceived notions concerning African Americans and the blues, it seems that all most folk want to hear in the blues is indifference, abject poverty, ongoing agony, illicit sex, and tale after tale of unrequited love. But, as with rap (including gangsta rap [see the fifth "remix" to follow]), the blues, both sonically and socially, represents much more than any of the aforementioned.

Considering the fact that both Charters's and Oliver's books on the blues were published in the early 1960s it is even more astounding that they sought to characterize African Americans as "primarily concerned with the business of living from day to day, of 'getting along' with the whites." The 1950s and 1960s Civil Rights Movement demonstrated loud and clear that African Americans were interested in much more than "living from day to day" and merely "'getting along' with the whites." There was a concerted effort and extremely *radical* political demand on the part of African Americans to deconstruct and reconstruct American democracy and extend it to all U.S. citizens, without regard to race, gender, class, sexual orientation, or religious affiliation. In no uncertain terms, the Civil Rights Movement radically altered U.S. history, culture, politics, and society, and it is extremely offensive that European and European American "black music" scholars can write "respected" books on African American music that, however surreptitiously, simultaneously *de-politicize black music* and *dehumanize black people*. The blues, as it actually is and not as seemingly most European and European American "black music" scholars imagine it to be, in truth reveals a great deal about turn of the twentieth century African American music, politics, and social movements.

What Charters and Oliver fail to understand is that "protest" for oppressed people most often looks, sounds, and feels different than the "protest" of an oppressing people—or, at the least, people who are not oppressed or privileged as a result of their ancestors, great-grandparents, grandparents, or parents' participation in the enslavement, colonization, exploitation, violation, and oppression of others. As a matter of fact, the alleged absence of what Charters, Oliver, and several other white blues critics call "direct social protest" in blues songs can be easily explained without denying or denigrating the songs' powerful, even if implicit, political elements and social commentary. Here it is important to go back to Oliver's assertion that "when aggravation reaches the point where the spirit of revolt against the system arises, this is often soon dissolved in minor personal disruption and eventual disregard." It should be said, as sincerely and solemnly as possible, the Civil Rights Movement was not "minor personal disruption," but a wide-ranging and wide-reaching collective and communal social revolution that undeniably transfigured American democracy.

According to *Webster's Dictionary*, "protest" implies "an organized public demonstration expressing strong objection to a policy or course of action adopted by those in authority." Whether we turn to the 1910s, 1920s, 1930s, 1940s, or 1950s, and all the way up to the decade in which Charters and Oliver published their books, the 1960s, African Americans consistently protested U.S. anti-black racism in law, politics, social relations, the military, religion, education, entertainment, and athletics, etc. For instance, the Black Women's Club Movement and New Negro Movement opened the twentieth century; the NAACP, Garvey Movement, and Pan-African Movement helped to usher in the Jazz Age and Harlem Renaissance years; and the Congress of Racial Equality, Montgomery Bus Boycott, Sit-In Movement, Freedom Riders Movement, Southern Christian Leadership Conference, and Nation of Islam laid the foundation for the Civil Rights Movement of the 1950s and 1960s.[27]

Unlike most forms of political protest, *aesthetic protest* is very rarely a direct call to action. Even so, critical aesthetic representation of socio-political problems, political aesthetics, and social realism in the context of African American artistic traditions must be comprehended as constituting extremely powerful social and political ideas and acts. Samuel Charters, Paul Oliver, and other blues scholars might interpret instances of protest in blues songs as "complaint," but by the very fact that the alleged "complaint" is publicly articulated to such an eloquent extent that even blues music's most ahistorical and apolitical interpreters understand it to be "complaint" illustrates that blues protest, indeed, is a form of contestation of oppressive and exploitive conditions even when it does not directly translate into "organized public demonstration." This is part of the distinct power of black popular music, if not black popular culture in general. Indirectly responding to Charters and

Oliver's de-politicization of the blues and helping to drive my point home about blues protest, in *Black Culture and Black Consciousness: Afro-American Folk Thought from Slavery to Freedom* (1977), Lawrence Levine offered remarkable insight:

> To state that black song constituted a form of black protest and resistance does not mean that it necessarily led to or even called for any tangible and specific actions, but rather that it served as a mechanism by which Negroes could be relatively candid in a society that rarely accorded them that privilege, could communicate this candor to others whom they would in no other way be able to reach, and, in the face of the sanctions of the white majority, could assert their own individuality, aspirations, and sense of being. Certainly, if nothing else, black song makes it difficult to believe that Negroes internalized their situation so completely, accepted the values of the larger society so totally, or manifested so pervasive an apathy as we have been led to believe. . . . The African tradition of being able to verbalize publicly in song what could not be said to a person's face, not only lived on among Afro-Americans throughout slavery but continued to be a central feature of black expressive culture in freedom. (239–40, 247)

It is Levine's last sentence that directly connects with classic blues women and contemporary hip hop women's work. When he reminds us that the "African tradition of being able to verbalize publicly in song what could not be said to a person's face, not only lived on among Afro-Americans throughout slavery but continued to be a central feature of black expressive culture in freedom," he hints at how generation after generation of black pop music divas have, literally, utilized music as a medium to constructively critique their enslavers, oppressors, and abusers, both within and without African American communities. It is also important for us to keep in mind that the contention that "black song constituted a form of black protest and resistance does not mean that it necessarily led to or even called for any tangible and specific actions." As with hip hoppers and contemporary African American socio-political movements, classic blues folk's "protest and resistance" may not have nicely and neatly paralleled the "protest and resistance" emerging from the dominant African American socio-political movements of their epoch (e.g., the Black Women's Club Movement and the New Negro Movement). But, make no mistake about it, classic blues folk, as Levine noted, indeed did protest and resist by way of black popular music and black popular culture, among other political and aesthetic avenues.

Most of classic blues women and contemporary hip hop women's political protest and social critique did not and has not translated into "organized public demonstration," especially not on the grand level of the Black Women's Club Movement or the Black Women's Liberation Movement. However, that does not mean that classic blues women and contemporary hip hop women have not protested and critiqued. Because most contemporary black feminist academics usually utilize the Black Women's Club Movement and the Black Women's Liberation Movement as core models to measure whether authentic black feminist/womanist struggle has transpired, classic blues women and contemporary hip hop women's contributions to *African American women's decolonization and liberation* are often overlooked. Classic blues women's sonic protests and social critiques and, even more, the ways in which their work prefigures and provides an aesthetic palette for female rappers, neo-soul sisters, hip hop feminists, and hip hop women in general are often ignored in favor of those forms of "black feminism" that most closely resemble elite and college-educated white women's feminism.[28]

When and where we break away from most black feminist academics' whitewashed models of "black feminism" we are able to see how classic blues women, whether directly or indirectly, provided political paradigms and aesthetic archetypes for contemporary female rappers and neo-soul sisters. As discussed above, the typical classic blues woman embraced and primarily sang about what it meant to be an early twentieth century African American "working woman—one who is sexually independent, self-sufficient, creative, assertive, and trend-setting." In "Empowering Self, Making Choices, Creating Spaces: Black Female Identity via Rap Music Performance" (2000), acclaimed ethnomusicologist Cheryl Keyes identified four distinct categories of women rappers: the "Queen Mother," the "Fly Girl," the "Sista With an Attitude," and the "Lesbian" (256). Each of these conceptions of contemporary women rappers coincides, admittedly often incongruently, with an archetype offered up by classic blues women. As with the multidimensionality of almost every other aspect of African American women's lives, Keyes cautioned us to keep in mind that African American women rappers can and frequently do "shift between these categories or belong to more than one simultaneously. More importantly, each category mirrors certain images, voices, and lifestyles of African American women in contemporary urban society" (256).

As Daphne Harrison's research in *Black Pearls* revealed, classic blues women were frequently given titles, such as "Queen," "Mother," "Ma," "Sister" or, in Bessie Smith's case, "Empress." The female rappers who broke onto the scene in the late 1980s and 1990s with rap aliases with either "Queen" or some other "royal" or "queenly" name were, however unwittingly, carrying on a tradition that began back at the turn of the twentieth century—interestingly, the royal or queenly sounding name phenomenon is also quite prevalent in contemporary womanist reggae; see the work of artists such as Ivy Queen, Lady Saw, Kingston Ladies, Patra (short for "Cleopatra"), Sister Breeze, Sister Carol, Sister Nancy, and Sister Nyanda.[29] Keyes goes even further to assert that "it is certainly possible that female rap artists may know of the historical significance of African queens; women in this category adorn their bodies with royal or Kente cloth strips, African head-dresses, goddess braid styles, and ankh-stylized jewelry. Their rhymes embrace Black female empowerment and spirituality, making clear their self-identification as African, woman, warrior, priestess, and queen" (257). Echoing Keyes, although focusing primarily on Queen Latifah, in "'Ladies First': Queen Latifah's Afrocentric Feminist Music Video" (1994), Robin Roberts wrote:

> Through her name and emphases Queen Latifah draws upon a tradition of African music and culture to make her criticism of sexism and racism. Latifah—whose name means "delicate and sensitive" in Arabic—was born Dana Owens in East Orange, NJ. (She added to *Latifah*, a name conferred upon her by a friend, the word *Queen* when she became a professional rapper.) Her name suggests the Afrocentric nature of her performances, for, as Angela Davis explains, "according to African tradition, one's name is supposed to capture the essence of one's being." (246, all emphasis in original; see also A. Y. Davis, 1989, 100)[30]

It is generally understood that what is called "womanism," as opposed to "feminism," is primarily predicated on women, especially women of African descent, practicing *self-determination, self-definition, and self-naming*. Notice that "self-naming" is important enough to womanists that it is included in their core beliefs and that this element of their thought directly challenges notions that African American women's liberation thought and practices are derivative of European and European American women's feminism (i.e., "white feminism") (Hewitt 2010; Newman 1999). Admittedly, womanism indeed does share many of the core concerns of feminism, whether white or black feminism, but often what unambiguously distinguishes womanism is its emphasis on and utilization of African and African diasporan history, culture, and struggle as its point of departure. Truth be told, black feminism with its characteristic focus on African American women's life-worlds and life-struggles is often indistinguishable from womanism, but yet and still the womanists' emphasis on "self-naming" seems to have hit a nerve with many women of African descent.[31]

However, even though there is significant overlap between the womanist tradition of "self-naming" and the more recent practice of "self-naming" within the Hip Hop Women's Movement, it is important to acknowledge that most Hip Hop Women's Studies scholars continue to utilize Eurocentric and bourgeois feminist theories and methodologies to evaluate and critically engage hip hop women and the Hip Hop Women's Movement. Which is also to say, when and where women's decolonization and women's liberation thought and practices are detected within the world of hip hop women they are generally characterized as "hip hop feminism" and "feminist rap." According to Roberts (1994), "feminist rap" is "rap that focuses on promoting women's importance," rap "that demands equal treatment for women," and rap "that demonstrates the need for women to support each other" (245).

Well aware of the problems involved in embracing and articulating feminism via rap music and other forms of black popular music, Roberts asserted that rap, "like all other forms of popular music, is not inherently feminist, but in this genre, as in other popular genres, female performers use specific generic qualities to promote a feminist message. Rap is noted for its emphasis on lyrics, and through the lyrics, female rappers make explicit assertions of female strength and autonomy" (246). Challenging what Donna Troka referred to as "the male-centered master narrative of rap music" in "'You Heard My Gun Cock': Female Agency and Aggression in Contemporary Rap Music" (2002), Roberts's work helps to highlight how women rappers have re-appropriated rap for their specific womanist/feminist purposes (82). Roberts (1994) revealed that "by using the very forms that are used (by many male rappers) to denigrate women," Queen Latifah, among other female rappers, is "reclaiming those forms for women":

> At the same time, by using rap and Afrocentricity, she asserts the centrality of women to an Afrocentric outlook. Being feminist does not mean abandoning her African heritage; instead, it becomes an additional source of strength and power. Her attire, in particular, reveals the way in which an African-based clothing style can assert an eroticism that resists the nakedness and exposure of Western styles for women (such as the dresses and high heels worn by Tina Turner). (247)

Rappers within the "Queen Mother" category, then, often inadvertently acknowledge their "inheritance" from the classic blues queens via their "queenly" names, women-centered lyrics, and "African-based clothing style." On this last point (i.e., their "African-based clothing style") it is important to bear in mind how "erotic," "exotic," "flamboyant," and "bohemian" classic blues queens' (among other black pop divas', such as Josephine Baker's, Ethel Waters', and Adelaide Hall's) costumes were within the context of 1920s and 1930s America. In many ways their "erotic" and "exotic" wardrobes challenged Victorian conceptions of what wealthy women in the public eye ought to look like, what they ought to wear, and how they ought to behave.[32]

Although they might take exception to being labeled both "feminist" and "Afrocentric" (à la Roberts's mid-1990s research), along with Queen Latifah, rappers such as Nefertiti, Queen Kenya, Isis, Sister Souljah, Queen Mother Rage, Queen Pen, Medusa, and Bahamadia have all put their special womanist spin on culturally rooted and socially relevant hip hop music and style. Additionally, several neo-soul singers—such as Dionne Farris, Nadirah Shakoor, Erykah Badu, India.Arie, Jill Scott, Macy Gray, Amel Larrieux, Hil St.

Soul, and Kwanza Jones—have radically "remixed" and produced critically acclaimed turn of the twenty-first century *African American women-centered soul music*, replete with head-nodding hip hop beats and copious references to everything from HIV/AIDS and domestic violence to monogamy and sexual agency, from prostitution and the prison industrial complex to underdevelopment in Africa and overdevelopment in America.

Although "fly" is a term that usually describes someone sporting the latest cosmetics, clothes, hairstyle, jewelry, and digital gadgets, rap's "fly girl" image is much more than a dated whim because it "highlights aspects of black women's bodies considered undesirable by American mainstream standards of beauty" (Keyes 2000, 260). Womanist rappers such as Sha Rock, Sequence, Lady B., L'Trimm, Salt-N-Pepa, Queen Latifah, MC Lyte, Monie Love, J.J. Fad, TLC, Oaktown's 357, Lauryn Hill, and Missy Elliott fall within this category. More significantly, it is interesting to note that as hip hop culture developed in the 1990s and there was, rather ironically, the rise of both "conscious" and "gangsta" rap, both harboring their own brands of male supremacy and musical misogyny, more hip hop women turned away from the "old school" definition of "fly girl" that revolved around trendy fashions and increasingly turned to women-centered rap, spoken-word, and neo-soul to articulate a new form of "fly girl[hood]" that emphasized "aspects of black women's bodies considered undesirable by American mainstream standards of beauty."

Far from silently accepting or timidly taking a back seat to the "boys club" clannishness that has developed within the rap music and hip hop culture industries, hip hop women have produced women-centered rap, spoken-word, and neo-soul that has radically deconstructed and reconstructed male-centered misconceptions and misrepresentations of African American women's bodies and sexuality. For example, in "Can't Touch This!: Representations of the African American Female Body in Urban Rap Videos" (1997), Marla Shelton observed:

> African American women in rap music find themselves in a unique position in terms of the production of music and image; they must struggle for control and expression in a predominantly white and patriarchal culture industry on the one hand and a system of management controlled predominantly by African American males on the other (e.g., Russell Simmons, Dr. Dre, and Ice Cube). While the past 15 years have witnessed the expansion of entertainment media into large networks with a great deal more diversity than was true in the past, the decision-making power still remains largely the privilege of a small number of men. Hence, rap has become synonymous with masculine "core" culture in spite of the popularity of artists such as TLC, Salt-N-Pepa, Queen Latifah, and MC Lyte. Nevertheless, female music producers such as Sylvia Rhone, Pat Charbonnet, and Jean Riggins, among others, are infiltrating the music business and actively promoting women artists in rap. These pioneering cultural

producers ongoingly confront ideologies and visual paradigms in the industry
that hinder production of enlightened images of African American women.
(107)[33]

Shelton's emphasis on hip hop women as "pioneering cultural producers"
who consistently "confront ideologies and visual paradigms" that "hinder
[the] production of enlightened images of African American women" in the
rap music and hip hop culture industries speaks volumes about the ways in
which hip hop women have challenged "the male-centered master narrative
of rap music" (à la Donna Troka), if not hip hop culture in general. Deftly
demonstrating that rap music and hip hop culture are much more than merely
"masculine 'core' culture," women-centered rap, spoken-word, and neo-soul
gives voice to hip hop women's views and values. Moreover, hip hop wom-
en's music videos in specific often directly deconstruct and reconstruct racial
and patriarchal "ideologies and visual paradigms" that present African
American women in *highly sexual* or *highly asexual, highly maternal* or
*highly malevolent*, wicked and almost anti-woman—if not unhuman *and*
inhuman—ways. As Shelton perceptively shared:

> Considered vital to a rapper's public recognition, a music video represents a
> synthesis of soundtrack and visual narrative that mediates a female-gendered
> voice and body in and out of American urban landscapes. As a location for
> ideological struggle, music video is a key site for the workings of sexism,
> racism, and classism as well as a site for resistance. While record labels con-
> tinue to urge artists to make live appearances for promotional considerations,
> female performers confront several stultifying stigmas when exposing their
> body to the consuming eye. In popular culture, African American women's
> bodies are often subject to sexual imagery with connotations of "the celibate
> mammie" or "the hyper-sexual tragic mulatto," "the weak hysteric," or "the
> welfare mother." Because representation is bound by racial and gender stereo-
> types, female rappers must invert stigmas, redefine feminine subjectivity, and
> repossess the gaze in order to gain respect. (108)

Hip hop women's practice of "invert[ing] stigmas, redefin[ing] feminine
subjectivity, and repossess[ing] the gaze in order to gain respect" unambiguously links them to classic black clubwomen, and, ultimately, the overarching African American feminist/womanist tradition. As discussed above, the
late nineteenth century genesis of the Black Women's Club Movement can
be traced back to a slanderous letter written by James W. Jacks, a white male
newspaper editor in Missouri, who called into question black women's
"character," callously claiming that all African American women were liars,
prostitutes, and thieves (see also F. Morgan 2005, 128–30, 219). Also discussed above was William Hannibal Thomas's infamous *The American Negro, What He Was, What He Is, and What He May Become* (1901), where he
made particularly damaging observations concerning African American

women's sexuality—indeed, their supposed *hyper-sexuality*—from an allegedly "insider's point of view" because he was partially black and, therefore, had access to the inner workings of African America. Needless to say, as the above discussion illustrated, black clubwomen were particularly keen on confronting the racial and patriarchal "ideologies and visual paradigms" surrounding African American women in their era, for the most part speaking, dressing, and generally behaving in the most conservative and socially acceptable white middle-class manners as possible. Nevertheless, their efforts to—however Eurocentrically and conservatively—challenge anti-black racist and anti-black sexist turn of the twentieth century misconceptions and misrepresentations of African American womanhood, wifehood, and motherhood should not be downplayed, diminished, or discarded.

Again, seeking to counter the tired tendency to focus exclusively on elite and college-educated African American women's contributions to women's decolonization and women's liberation, here it will be important to explore and emphasize the rarely discussed ways in which classic blues women countered anti-black racist and anti-black sexist misconceptions and misrepresentations of African American women at the turn of the twentieth century. In many senses it could be said that classic blues queens created and contributed several of the central political paradigms and aesthetic criteria on which contemporary hip hop women have built and innovatively gone beyond in their efforts to "invert stigmas, redefine feminine subjectivity, and repossess the gaze in order to gain respect" at the turn of the twenty-first century. Bearing in mind Shelton's assertion that hip hop women "confront several stultifying stigmas when exposing their body to the consuming eye" and "African American women's bodies are often subject to sexual imagery with connotations of 'the celibate mammie' or 'the hyper-sexual tragic mulatto,' 'the weak hysteric,' or 'the welfare mother,'" it is likewise important to observe how classic blues queens' bodies were viewed both intra-racially (i.e., inside their race) and inter-racially (i.e., outside of their race).

For instance, in *A Bad Woman Feeling Good: Blues and the Women Who Sing Them* (2005), Buzzy Jackson revealingly wrote about Bessie Smith taking special pleasure in challenging Eurocentric beauty standards, so much so that "a special appreciation of her beauty was a common one among Bessie Smith fans, who recognized that her physical attributes clashed with prevailing standards of beauty for the era," yet and still, her fans "loved her all the more for it" (70–71). Jackson importantly continued, "Among the anorectic flappers and slinky vamps of the age, Smith's ebony skin and generous size set her apart, proudly. . . . The self-satisfaction that Smith exuded was a huge part of her appeal to her listeners, male and female" (71).[34]

Indeed, there were countless classic blues women whose "ebony skin and generous size set [them] apart, proudly." Moreover, contemporary female rappers, spoken-word womanists, and neo-soul sisters, such as Ms. Melodie, Sister Souljah, Nikki D., Rah Digga, Missy Elliot, Sarah Jones, Jessica Care Moore, Caron Wheeler, Jill Scott, Angie Stone, and India.Arie, all continue to challenge the "prevailing standards of beauty." Therefore, they indispensably provide women who are not wealthy, white, and thin with alternative avenues to embrace and eloquently express their distinct womanhood and sisterhood. India.Arie in particular has waged an unmistakable one-woman war against contemporary "prevailing standards of beauty" with her albums *Acoustic Soul* (2001), *Voyage to India* (2002), *Testimony, Vol.1: Life & Relationships* (2006), and *Testimony, Vol.2: Love & Politics* (2009), and more specifically hit neo-soul songs such as "Video," "Brown Skin," "Beautiful," "Private Party" and, of course, "I Am Not My Hair."

Shifting the focus from African America's body image and sexuality, the third major hip hop women's archetype that can be said to have been handed down from and concretely coincide with classic blues women's myriad expressions of *black and blues womanhood* is the rap or neo-soul "sista with an attitude." In the most general sense a "sista with an attitude" is a female rapper or neo-soul singer "who value[s] attitude as a means of empowerment and present[s] themselves accordingly" (Keyes 2000, 262). Obviously what many hip hop women refer to as "attitude" has something to do with their critical posture or oppositional stance toward the established order. Frequently their critiques touch on racism, at other times on sexism, and still others on classism. Their music is, literally, the soundtrack to what the black feminist sociologist Deborah King has dubbed the "multiple jeopardy" of African American women's lives. In her groundbreaking article, "Multiple Jeopardy, Multiple Consciousness: The Context of a Black Feminist Ideology" (1988), King innovatively contended:

> The triple jeopardy of racism, sexism, and classism is now widely accepted and used as the conceptualization of black women's status. However, while advancing our understanding beyond the erasure of black women within the confines of the race-sex analogy, it does not yet fully convey the dynamics of multiple forms of discrimination. Unfortunately, most applications of the concepts of double and triple jeopardy have been overly simplistic in assuming that the relationships among the various discriminations are merely additive. These relationships are interpreted as equivalent to the mathematical equation, racism plus sexism plus classism equals triple jeopardy. In this instance, each discrimination has a single, direct, and independent effect on status, wherein the relative contribution of each is readily apparent. This simple incremental process does not represent the nature of black women's oppression but, rather, I would contend, leads to non-productive assertions that one factor can and should supplant the other. . . . The modifier "multiple" refers not only to

several, simultaneous oppressions but to the multiplicative relationships among them as well. In other words, the equivalent formulation is racism multiplied by sexism multiplied by classism. (46–47)

Part of the distinctiveness of black feminist thought revolves around its un-apologetic engagement of the most pressing problems confronting African American women, and African Americans in general. In the *Holy Bible* it says "[o]ppression makes a wise man mad" (Ecclesiastes 7:7); the "sistas with an attitude," therefore, are understandably angry—or, rather, *morally outraged*—about and critical of the multiple oppressions that African American women and girls face on a daily basis and, truth be told, both within and without African American communities. Through women-centered rap, spoken-word, and neo-soul—as well as other aspects of hip hop culture (e.g., break-dancing, graffiti-writing, playwriting, screenwriting, fiction-writing, social media, cyber-politics, and more conventional political activism)—hip hop women are utilizing arguably the only available means they have to express themselves and articulate their unique life-worlds and life-struggles—their undeniably distinct lived-experiences and lived-endurances that, according to Tricia Rose (1994, 148) and Donna Troka (2002, 83), place them "in 'dialogue' with several different ideologies and communities: black male rappers, dominant notions of femininity, feminism, and black female sexuality."

It is no secret that African American women's lives have been recurringly robbed of specificity and subjectivity by both white feminist and black masculinist academics and pundits. In fact, it may not be going too far to say that the only place African American women's lives have been rendered in their complete and complicated, ugly and beautiful, sophisticated and unsophisticated soulfulness is within the context of black feminist/womanist thought and practice. "The experience of black women is apparently assumed, though never explicitly stated, to be synonymous with that of either black males or white females," King (1988) asserted, and "since the experiences of both are equivalent, a discussion of black women in particular is superfluous. It is mistakenly granted that either there is no difference in being black and female from being generically black (i.e., male) or generically female (i.e., white)" (45). Hence, here we have come back to the notion of "the male-centered master narrative of rap music" (à la Donna Troka) and the erroneous thought that rap music and hip hop culture are ultimately "synonymous with masculine 'core' culture" (à la Marla Shelton) when and where rap music and hip hop culture are acknowledged and openly celebrated as "black"— meaning essentially, *black male*—popular music and popular culture.

It should be stated outright: African American women's political protest and social critique frequently differs from both African American men and European American women's political protest and social critique. Elite and college-educated African American women's political protest and social critique decidedly differs from that of working-class and poor African American women. Furthermore, classical African American women's protest and critique in many senses diverges from contemporary African American women's protest and critique.

Just as there is no monolithic form of black feminism or womanism that each and every black woman adheres to, there is no single form of political protest and social critique that each and every black woman embraces. What provides the diverse forms of black feminism with discursive coherence is that "black feminist ideology fundamentally challenges the interstructure of the oppressions of racism, sexism, and classism both in the dominant society and within movements for liberation." As a matter of fact, "[i]t is in confrontation with multiple jeopardy that black women define and sustain a multiple consciousness essential for our liberation, of which feminist consciousness is an integral part" (72).

African American women's political protest and social critique is as diverse as African American women's lives and struggles, as well as their complexions, body types, heights, and hair textures. Class, cultural geography, social ecology, and sexuality impact black women's views and values just as much as their race and gender. Hence, King's conception of "multiple jeopardy" directly speaks to my emphasis on the alternative forms of black feminism found in classic blues women's and contemporary hip hop women's lyrics, music, politics, and lifestyles. "In the interactive model, the relative significance of race, sex, or class in determining the conditions of black women's lives is neither fixed nor absolute but, rather," King continued, "is dependent on the socio-historical context and the social phenomenon under consideration. These interactions also produce what to some appears a seemingly confounding set of social roles and political attitudes among black women" (49).

The contemporary hip hop "sistas with an attitude" are extending and expanding a tradition that began with classic blues "sistas with an attitude." These "sistas'" "multiple consciousness" of the ways in which they are oppressed and exploited on the basis of their race, gender, class, and sexuality has lead them to develop *a distinct African American women-centered style of insurgent intersectional critique.* After listening to classic blues women's and contemporary hip hop women's work, who can deny that this is precisely what the classic blues women did during their day and what many contemporary hip hop women are doing during our day—protesting and critiquing, with a healthy dose of African American women-centered "sistaly" attitude?

For instance, few will deny that Bessie Smith's 1928 classics "Poor Man's Blues" and "Washwoman's Blues" are early ancestors to the social protest genre in black popular music. "Poor Man's Blues" openly indicts the upper class and middle class for the increasing exploitation and poverty of the poor, where "Washwoman's Blues" critiques the exploitive conditions under which most African American women were forced to work during the first decades of the twentieth century.[35] Smith's iconic sonic protests also included critiques of the chain gang, the convict-lease system, and capital punishment in classic songs such as "Jail House Blues," "Work House Blues," "Sing Sing Prison Blues," and "Send Me to the 'Lectric Chair." Ma Rainey, Bessie Smith's mentor, also offered sonic protest and social critique, with "Chain Gang Blues," "Hustlin' Blues," "Tough Luck Blues," "Slave to the Blues," and "Yonder Come the Blues," unequivocally critiquing the chain gang, the convict-lease system, prostitution, poverty, sexism and racism, respectively.

Obviously there are countless hip hop women, both women-centered rappers and neo-soul singers, who have carried on the sonic protest and social critique tradition that classic blues women such as Ma Rainey and Bessie Smith initiated. Hip hop women, such as Harmony, Yo-Yo, Jill Scott, Amel Larrieux, Alicia Keys, Eve, Ledisi, Erykah Badu, Angie Stone, and Me'Shell Ndegéocello, however unwittingly, have effectively built on and went beyond many of the issues and ills that the classic blues women addressed in their work. For instance, Eve engaged the issue of domestic violence with her 1999 hit song and video "Love is Blind," and over a decade later Rihanna continued the critique of domestic violence with her controversial song and video "Man Down." Alicia Keys delivered a subtle critique of the ways the prison system (i.e., now the prison industrial complex) continues to impact African Americans and African American relationships with her runaway hits "Fallin'" and "A Woman's Worth."

Several neo-soul sistas, deftly demonstrating the transgender and transcendent range and reach of hip hop womanism, have critiqued the hardships African American men face as a consequence of their race, gender, class, and sexuality. For example, Erykah Badu's "Other Side of the Game," Jill Scott's "Brotha," Angie Stone's "Soul Brotha," and Marsha Ambrosius's "Far Away" each acknowledge many of the major issues confronting hip hop men and lovingly celebrate their "brothas'" triumph over tragedy. Moreover, genre-jumping rapper, singer, and multi-instrumentalist Me'Shell Ndegéocello has taken up everything from prison and prostitution to poverty and homosexuality on innovative albums such as *Plantation Lullabies* (1993), *Peace Beyond Passion* (1996), *Bitter* (1999), *Cookie: The Anthropological Mixtape* (2002), *Comfort Woman* (2003), *The World Has Made Me the Man of My Dreams* (2007), *Devil's Halo* (2009), and *Weather* (2011).

Indeed, as Daphne Brooks observed in "'All That You Can't Leave Behind': Black Female Soul Singing and the Politics of Surrogation in the Age of Catastrophe" (2008), these hip hop soul sistas' work "creates a particular kind of black feminist surrogation." That is to say, "an embodied cultural act that articulates black women's distinct forms of palpable socio-political loss and grief, as well as spirited dissent and dissonance. Their combined efforts mark a new era of protest singing that sonically resists, revises, and reinvents the politics of black female hyper-visibility in the American cultural imaginary" (183).

Similar to the classic blues "sistas with an attitude," contemporary hip hop "sistas with an attitude" frequently blur the lines between the spiritual and the sexual, the personal and the political, the public and the private by embedding their sonic protests and social critiques in songs that seem to fall squarely within the world of rhythm & blues—both flamboyant and flaccid—balladry. The public and socio-political voices of African American female discontent is often difficult to detect in black popular music in particular, and black popular culture more generally, because of a unique form of what could be characterized as "double-consciousness" (à la W.E.B. Du Bois in *The Souls of Black Folk*) in which African American women self-consciously struggle to avoid being labeled "the angry black woman" both intra-racially and inter-racially—that is to say, by both African American men and the ever-onlooking white world at large. Brooks broached this extremely taboo topic, audaciously asserting that "crafting a voice of black female discontent in black female popular culture is, however, a slippery slope if one aims to avoid the caricature of 'the angry black woman'—immortalized by everyone from Hattie McDaniel's simmering and contemptuous cinematic characters to the sour squint of genius comic LaWanda Page or, of late, the wickedly 'sick and tired' stand-up of Wanda Sykes" (184). Moving from African American women's discontent in black popular culture to African American women's discontent in black popular music, and directly hitting at the heart of our discussion here, Brooks continued:

> In contemporary pop music, black female (socio-political) discontent is even trickier to trace. Certainly eclectic performer Nina Simone's songbook ranged from the sly, oblique, and ironic critique in classics such as "I Hold No Grudge" ("I hold no grudge/There's no resentment und'neath/I'll extend the laurel wreath and we'll be friends/But right there is where it ends") to the searing political satire of the civil rights "showtune" "Mississippi Goddam." But while Simone and Odetta remain forebears of a certain kind of critical voice that emerged as the cultural arm of the Civil Rights and Anti-War Movements, twenty-first-century black female pop stars—save for folkies like Tracy Chapman, bohemian rebels like Me'Shell Ndegéocello, or sharp and powerful emcees like early MC Lyte, Lauryn Hill, and Jean Grae—are more likely to couch their dissatisfaction in domestic, romantic, and/or gospel-religious R&B zones. (185; Harris-Perry 2011; Jones and Shorter-Gooden 2003)

We see here, then, that "attitude"—especially an anti-racist, anti-sexist, and sometimes even an obscured anti-capitalist attitude—is an important ingredient in African American women's popular music and popular culture. Hence, classic blues queens handed down more than merely music to contemporary hip hop women. "Attitude," although often overlooked, is a unique part of hip hop women's "inheritance" from blues women. Again, because black popular music is more than merely music, *hip hop's inheritance* from previous forms of black popular music is simultaneously musical *and* extra-musical.

Here it is important to emphasize the ways in which black popular music has consistently revealed the social, political, and cultural desires of African Americans and the astonishing irony that these sonically registered desires remain largely overlooked and under-theorized in a wide range of academic disciplines, including African American Studies, American Studies, Cultural Studies, and Popular Music Studies. An equally indicting observation could be made about the ways in which "sistas with an attitude" and, more specifically, African American women's discontent in popular music and popular culture has been largely overlooked and under-theorized in Women's Studies. All of this is to say, very few critics have critically engaged the ways in which blues women, jazz women, rhythm & blues women, soul women, funk women, disco women, and hip hop women, as well as their legions of fans, have historically contributed and currently continue to contribute to black feminism/womanism and produce public records of African American women's deep-seated social, political, cultural, spiritual, and sexual desires. In other words, African American women's musical subcultures—from classic blues to contemporary neo-soul—insist that we take them much more seriously in light of the fact that they, however "unconventionally" from Eurocentric, bourgeois, and patriarchal points of view, actually articulate overt and covert common desires and shared dreams that run like a fast-flowing river through the peaks and valleys, the high points and low points of African American history, culture, and struggle.

The fourth and final category of hip hop womanhood that Cheryl Keyes identified above was the hip hop lesbian or, rather, hip hop lesbianism. Corroborating Keyes, in "Like an Old Soul Record: Black Feminism, Queer Sexuality, and the Hip Hop Generation" (2007b), Andreana Clay emphasized "queerness in hip hop culture" by offering an innovative analysis of arguably the most popular and most outspoken homosexual of the Hip Hop Generation: Me'Shell Ndegéocello (58). Clay boldly claimed:

> Academic examinations of queerness in hip hop culture are fairly recent. However, Me'shell Ndegéocello's impact on women in hip hop culture and on a generation of black feminists continues to be overlooked. While important works have been written in recent years on the relationship between hip hop and feminism, there is little to no mention of Ndegéocello, particularly of her work at bridging these two cultural and political movements. While mainstream media contains images of white lesbians (e.g., Ellen [DeGeneres] and

her girlfriend, Portia de Rossi; Melissa Etheridge; and Rosie O'Donnell), black
lesbians in popular culture are virtually nonexistent, or remain closeted. This
absence persists in academia as well. (58–59)[36]

For the most part African American lesbians have been either rendered invisible or erased altogether from the discursive domains of African American Studies, Women's Studies, and, ironically, sometimes even Lesbian, Gay, Bisexual, and Transgender Studies as well. Unfortunately Hip Hop Studies, in large part, has followed suit. Where mainstream rap music and hip hop culture seem to be much more explicit in their condemnation of homosexuality (especially lesbianism), taken as a whole, Hip Hop Studies—except in extremely rare instances—seems to have fallen silent on the issue of homosexuality (again, especially lesbianism). As Tracy Sharpley-Whiting contended in *Pimps Up, Ho's Down: Hip Hop's Hold on Young Black Women* (2007),"[v]iewed through the prism of the hyper-masculine culture of hip hop, lesbians and lesbianism are in some respects the final frontier of conquest. The prevailing mentality is that all lesbians need is a 'good stiff one' to set them on a 'straight' (or at the very least, bisexual) course" (15). Although its connections with hip hop music and hip hop culture have not been explored in-depth previously, expressions of African American lesbianism have been prevalent in black popular music and black popular culture since the very first post-enslavement black popular music and black popular culture: the blues and blues culture.

Consequently, even when and where Me'Shell Ndegéocello broaches the still taboo topic of homosexuality, in songs such as "Leviticus: Faggot," "Barry Farms," and "Trust" (and there are many, many others), she still stands within the tradition that was handed down by the classic blues women. As Harrison noted above, the "desire to find and express affection, love, and sensuality in various ways and under less scrutiny was a central issue" for classic blues women. As a matter of fact, "[l]esbianism was practiced and sung about by such diverse [classic blues] singers as Bessie Smith, Ma Rainey, and Gladys Bentley." Moreover, in "It Jus' Be's Dat Way Sometime: The Sexual Politics of Women's Blues" (1998), Hazel Carby went so far to assert:

> Ma Rainey's strongest assertion of female sexual autonomy is a song she composed herself, "Prove It On Me Blues". . . . "Prove It On Me Blues" was an assertion and an affirmation of lesbianism. Though condemned by society for her sexual preference, the singer wants the whole world to know that she chooses women rather than men. The language of "Prove It On Me Blues" engages directly in defining issues of sexual preference as a contradictory struggle of social relations. Both Ma Rainey and Bessie Smith had lesbian relationships and "Prove It On Me Blues" vacillates between the subversive hidden activity of women loving women with a public declaration of lesbian-

ism. The words express a contempt for a society that rejected lesbians. "They say I do it/Ain't nobody caught me/They sure got to prove it on me." But at the same time the song is a reclamation of lesbianism as long as the woman publicly names her sexual preference for herself in the repetition of lines about the friends who "must've been women, cause I don't like no men." (479; see also Chapman 2011; B. Wilson 2009)

As discussed in my previous work, *Hip Hop's Inheritance*, hip hop has always had many homoerotic tendencies, and a vibrant Homosexual Hip Hop Movement has been underway since 1999 (Rabaka 2011, 49–82). Therefore, it is important to juxtapose contemporary expressions of homosexuality with classical expressions of homosexuality in black popular music and black popular culture. The homosexual hip hoppers are not the first generation of young black folk to embrace and practice homosexuality, and it is extremely important for us to bear this in mind as we sincerely seek to remedy *hip hop's amnesia*. Accordingly, the "amnesia" that I write of here—and, again, throughout this book—does not simply invoke and involve past black popular music and black popular culture but, even more, the forgotten history and traditions of past African American social, political, educational, sexual, and religious movements.

African Americans are not now, and never have been, all heterosexuals. Hence, it is important as we acknowledge classical contributors to rap music and hip hop culture that we not ignore or erase the contributions of our homosexual ancestors. It would, indeed, be a travesty to argue that we need to seriously take into consideration working-class and poor black folk's contributions to past and present black popular music and black popular culture and then turn around and neglect the contributions, innovations, and expressions of African American, among other, homosexuals.

It is only when we take into consideration the most marginalized among us, their humble life-worlds and heartfelt life-struggles, that we have some sense of who we are and what we are struggling for. The same could (and should) be said concerning the past: *It is only when we take into consideration the most marginalized aspects of the African American experience of the past that we have a real sense of the African American experience in the present.* Going back to Rainey's "Prove It On Me Blues," Angela Davis (1998b) argued that it is a "cultural precursor to the lesbian cultural movement of the 1970s, which began to crystallize around the performance and recording of lesbian-affirming songs" (40). Obviously contemporary folk/blues/rock women, such as Joan Armatrading, Tracy Chapman, and Billie Myers, and neo-soul/rap/hip hop women, such as Me'Shell Ndegéocello, Feloni, and Queen Pen, demonstrate that just as it was important for many classic blues women to express their lesbianism or bisexuality in their music, it continues to have sonic significance at the turn of the twenty-first century.

Clay (2007b) went so far as to say that "female hip hop artists take on a role similar to that of blues women in their discussion of politics and sexuality" (63). And, more specifically, "Me'Shell Ndegéocello's work is similar to that of the women in blues in that her message is both (homo)sexually explicit and marked by social protest" (64). Again, the connections between classic blues women and contemporary hip hop women are concrete, as opposed to abstract, and blues women, however unbeknownst to most hip hoppers, actually bequeathed much more than blues music to hip hop culture.

Echoing Clay, in "Me'Shell Ndegéocello: Musical Articulations of Black Feminism" (2007), Martha Mockus asserted that "[c]entral to her [Ndegéocello's] musical ethnography are political convictions about the search for freedom and the struggles against capitalism, racism, sexism, and homophobia in African American cultural history" (82). When we bring Me'Shell Ndegéocello into dialogue with Ma Rainey the connections between blues women and hip hop women are even clearer. Both women critiqued anti-black racism. Both women critiqued sexism. Both women critiqued capitalism, especially its extra-economic exploitation of working-class and poor African American women. Both women critiqued police brutality and the prison system. And both women critiqued homophobia and heterosexism. In short, even when and where we come to the controversial issue of homosexuality (and lesbianism in particular) within the world of hip hop culture, the women-centered musical and extra-musical concepts and criteria classic blues women contributed continue to reverberate and ring true.

Continuing in this vein, Angela Davis (1998b) innovatively demonstrated the ways in which classic blues women, especially Ma Rainey with her song "Prove It On Me Blues," contributed to the jazz women, rhythm & blues women, rock & roll women, soul women, funk women, disco women, and hip hop women who came after them:

> "Prove It On Me Blues" suggests how the iconoclastic blues women of the twenties were pioneers for later historical developments. The response to this song also suggests that homophobia within the black community did not prevent blues women from challenging stereotypical conceptions of women's lives. They did not allow themselves to be enshrined by the silence imposed by mainstream society. (40)[37]

One honestly wonders how Ma Rainey and Bessie Smith might feel to know that one of their hip hop progeny, Me'Shell Ndegéocello, has not only been hailed as one of the pioneers of the Neo-Soul Movement, but continues to make innovative music on her own women-centered and openly bisexual terms. As a matter of fact, in "The Last Maverick: Me'Shell Ndegéocello and the Burden of Vision" (2004), Amy Linden lauded, "From the moment she stepped in the arena, with her potent debut *Plantation Lullabies*, and continuing through her latest release *Cookie: The Anthropological Mixtape*,

Me'Shell Ndegéocello has defied categorization and sent any number of
critics and industry executives scrambling to dig deeper into their respective
trick bags to find a neat, simplistic description that would suit her. Or maybe
just suit them" (185). Linden colorfully continued:

> She's been lumped in with progressive artists, both black and white, female
> musicians, gay musicians, gay single mother musicians, pop, jazz, funk, rock,
> R&B, hip hop, and any possible netherland that manages to bridge all of those
> and anything else that might slip between the cracks. She carries the double-
> edged sword of not only being a female musician but a black one who is not
> traditionally R&B or hip hop—the two entry-level positions most accessible to
> women of color. Defiantly, Me'Shell answers to no one except for what she
> instinctively senses sounds good and feels right. She's recorded with a dispar-
> ate array of musicians from Scritti Politti, to Roy Hargrove, Citizen Cope, and
> John Mellencamp and seems as at ease being the focus of the record as she
> does keeping it rock steady in the background. She is that most odd of birds: a
> star who behaves like a session player and a session player with the undeniable
> charisma and chops to become a star. Me'Shell's ability—hell, one might even
> declare it a mission—to make music that does what it needs to do regardless of
> what it happens to sound like has been instrumental (no pun intended) in
> sealing her position as one of the most consistently inconsistent artists of the
> past ten years. That is a good thing, unless, of course, you have the unenviable
> task of creeping over to the studio to let someone know that, "Wow, you know,
> I'm not really sure I hear a single." (185–86)

Drawing from everything from blues and jazz to rock & roll and soul, from
reggae and rap to gospel and rhythm & blues, Ndegéocello—constantly
"def[ying] categorization" and undoubtedly "one of the most consistently
inconsistent artists of the past ten years"—has a whopping ten career Grammy Award nominations. She is arguably one of the most noted contemporary
exponents of the special truths that classic blues women spoke to the world.
It has been, and remains, her willingness to take up taboo topics and insur-
gently embrace sonic experimentation that places her squarely in the tradition
established by the classic blues queens and the long line of black pop music
divas who rose in their wake.

   "The blues idiom requires absolute honesty in the portrayal of black life,"
Angela Davis (1998b) observed. "It is an idiom that does not recognize
taboos: whatever figures into the larger picture of working-class African
American realities—however morally repugnant it may be to the dominant
culture or to the black bourgeoisie—is an appropriate subject of blues discourse" (107). The exact same thing could be said about hip hop discourse, if
not black popular music in general.

   Narrative, storytelling, signifying, testifying, and witnessing are all at the
heart of the African American call-and-response tradition, including the religious, rhetorical, intellectual, and musical strands of this tradition. It is a

tradition that is predicated on a certain kind of social, political, and cultural realism. Whether one engages the iconic artistry of Ma Rainey or Bessie Smith, Billie Holiday or Nina Simone, Aretha Franklin or Etta James, Cassandra Wilson or Erykah Badu, Me'Shell Ndegéocello or Amel Larrieux, what one is really being exposed to are the long-erased or long-ignored stories—the *womanist signifying, testifying,* and *witnessing*—that emerged from African American women's unique life-worlds and life-struggles.

Classic blues women firmly believed that their lives, the lives of their working-class and poor sisters, and the stories that grew out of their lived-experiences and lived-endurances were just as worthy of publication as those of early twentieth century white and black bourgeois clubwomen. In this sense, Lawrence Levine was absolutely on point in *Black Culture and Black Consciousness* (1977) when he eloquently observed:

> The blues insisted that the fate of the individual black man or woman, what happened in their everyday "trivial affairs," what took place within them—their yearnings, their problems, their frustrations, their dreams—were important, were worth taking note of and sharing in song. Stressing individual expression and group coherence at one and the same time, the blues was an inward-looking music which insisted upon the meaningfulness of black lives. In these respects it was not only the more obviously angry work songs but the blues as well, that were subversive of the American racial order and proved to be an important portent of what was to come in a very few decades. (269–70)

After the sonic revolutions of the classic blues women, there were jazz women, rhythm & blues women, rock & roll women, soul women, funk women, disco women, and hip hop women, and each of these women put into play their very own brand of womanist storytelling, womanist signifying, womanist testifying, and womanist witnessing—audaciously "insist[ing] that the fate of the individual black . . . woman, what happened in their everyday 'trivial affairs,' what took place within them—their yearnings, their problems, their frustrations, their dreams—were important, were worth taking note of and sharing in song." Because the bulk of these women usually hail from working-class and poor African American communities, and also because their primary audience was and remains working-class and poor black folk, they used the *lingua franca* (i.e., the common language) or, rather, the vernacular of working-class and poor black folk. Their public personas and stage presences also reflected the mores—which is to say, the common customs and conventions—of working-class and poor black folk. This is an aspect of classic blues women's culture that has trickled down to hip hop women.

Many of the hip hop "sistas" have attempted (unsuccessfully I honestly believe) to "flip da script" or deconstruct and reconstruct the word "bitch," Cheryl Keyes (2000) claimed, "viewing it as positive rather than negative and using the term to entertain or provide cathartic release. Other sistas in the interpretive community are troubled by that view" (262). Still others, both within and without the hip hop community, are equally troubled by what they perceive to be many hip hop women's vulgar lyrics, language, and lifestyle. Whether we agree or disagree with the way many hip hop women present or "represent" (in the hip hop sense) themselves it is important for us to acknowledge how their "vulgar" lyrics, language, and lifestyles are deeply rooted in classic blues women's work—and, also, the wider world of African American and "mainstream" American popular culture.

"Some audiences expected raunchy lyrics and singers gave them what they wanted, from [Ma] Rainey to Bessie Smith to Edith Wilson and Gladys Bentley," Daphne Harrison (1988) reported (100). Connected to Keyes's contention that many hip hop women use the word "bitch" and other colorful language in their poetry, lyrics, and everyday language to "entertain or provide cathartic release," Harrison similarly argued that for classic blues women "[s]inging lewd or raunchy blues provided a form of release for pent-up feelings which were repressed by social norms that prohibited open discussion of sex" (109). As with contemporary hip hop women, classic blues women could be as "dirty" and derogatory as classic blues men, often employing elements from black male vernacular, "flippin' da script" on maculinist metaphors, and innovatively opening up new avenues *and* arenas for African American women to express their unique power as women, their deep sexual desires, and their sexual subjectivity in general. Harrison importantly observed:

> Women also employed the bragging, signifying language of males to boast of fine physical attributes and high-powered sexual ability. In these blues are found metaphors that liken automobiles, foods, weapons, trains, and animals to the sex act or genitals. The prurient nature of many of these blues led to a spate of community activities seeking to ban them. Black newspapers waged the battle against performers who included them in their repertoire and accused them of using lewd lyrics as a substitute for talent. This was clearly not the case because the best of the blues women sang sexual blues sometimes. Admittedly, some were openly lascivious and left little to the imagination. (106)

Classic blues women's sexually explicit braggadocio can be said to have opened the way and provided hip hop women with a *herstoric* foundation for their sexually explicit boasting and bragging. Many of the "gangsta" and hyper-sexual hip hop women have been accused of "employ[ing] the bragging, signifying language of males to boast of fine physical attributes and high-powered sexual ability." A quick listen to the work of hyper-sexual hip hop women, such as Lil' Kim's *Hard Core* (1996), Foxy Brown's *Ill Na Na* (1996), Trina's *Da Baddest Bitch* (2000), Khia's *Thug Misses* (2001), Jacki-O's *Poe Little Rich Girl* (2004), or Nicki Minaj's *Pink Friday* (2010), will immediately quell any lingering confusion. With regard to "gangsta" women's work, one should consult L.A. Star's *Poetess* (1990), Da Brat's *Funkdafied* (1994), The Lady of Rage's *Necessary Roughness* (1997), Mia X's *Unlady Like* (1997), Gangsta Boo's *Enquiring Minds* (1998), and La Chat's *Murder She Spoke* (2001). In the collective rhymes of the "gangsta" and hyper-sexual hip hop women one will surely find what many believe to be *faux* hip hop feminist flipped-out and tricked-out "metaphors that liken automobiles, foods, weapons, trains, and animals to the sex act or genitals."[38]

No matter what we may think of all of this, the reality of the matter is that contemporary hip hop women have actually inherited a great deal from classic blues women in specific, and classic blues culture in general. It could be said that hip hop women seem to have inherited more from classic blues women than classic black clubwomen. But, I honestly believe, this is all beside the point. Here my main objective has been to combat *hip hop's amnesia* with respect to the contributions of both the classic blues women and classic black clubwomen. When all the smoke clears and all the dust settles, I continue to solemnly believe that both classic blues women and classic black clubwomen have contributed to hip hop women in specific, and hip hop culture in general. Consequently, disingenuous efforts to privilege the contributions of one coterie of classic African American women over the contributions of another coterie of classic African American women misses the main point and central purpose of this "remix," if not this book.

When it is all said and done, the Hip Hop Generation, my most beloved and most troubled generation, is long overdue in acknowledging the full range and reach of classic African American women's contributions to rap music, hip hop culture, and the wider Hip Hop Movement. We should not privilege the contributions of the classic black clubwomen over those of the classic blues women, because the classic blues women, as we have hopefully witnessed above, have much to teach us about the first generation of black women to put the premium on what it meant to be an African American "working woman—one who is sexually independent, self-sufficient, creative, assertive, and trend-setting." Equally important, we should not privilege the contributions of the classic blues women over those of the classic black clubwomen, because the classic black clubwomen, as Anne Knupfer noted above, "made tremendous contributions to their communities"; they established "non-formal community facilities, such as kindergartens, day nurseries, reading rooms, employment agencies, homes for the elderly and infirm[ed], homes for working girls, youth clubs, settlements, and summer outings and camps for children"; and they made "[p]resentations through forums, debates, discussions, oratories, addresses, and lyceums [that] not only gave voice to the clubwomen's perspectives on community concerns, but also socialized young girls into political and social consciousness."

Turning our attention to working-class and poor African American women's plight, in their own unique way contemporary hip hop women continue what classic blues women and classic black clubwomen started. Even though most of their lyrics, music, and lifestyle would be more than likely shunned by classic black clubwomen, as was the case with classic blues women, it is important to recognize that the Black Women's Club Movement was a movement primarily directed at uplifting working-class and poor African American women. Indeed, it is ironic that a women's movement that took as its motto "Lifting As We Climb" would practice any form of elitism or paternalism. But, just as history is not written with "clean hands and pure hearts" (Psalm 24:4), it is equally true that history is not made or "performed" by perfect people.

What we must do is critically engage the contributions of the classic blues women and the classic black clubwomen always bearing in mind that at their best they, literally, "lifted as they climbed." We must do more than read their words and listen to their music. We must utilize their lives and legacies as models—exploring the lyricism and musicality of the classic black clubwomen, and the intellectual and political ethos of the classic blues women. Indeed, there was music in the Black Women's Club Movement, just as there were new forms of black feminism and womanism to be found in the lyrics, music, and lifestyles of the classic blues queens.

How might hip hop culture be enhanced if hip hoppers, both female and male, took the collective work of the classic blues women and classic black clubwomen to heart? How might we be able to more quickly re-radicalize and re-politicize rap music and hip hop culture if we were to take stock of the ways in which classic blues women and classic black clubwomen's relationship with one another in many senses mirrors the relationship between contemporary black feminist academics and hip hop women? And, finally, how might we remedy *hip hop's amnesia* with respect to the contributions of both the classic blues women and the classic black clubwomen by openly acknowledging that both coteries of early twentieth century African American women created thoughts and practices that remain relevant, especially with respect to the Hip Hop Movement?

It is important here to observe that, whether hip hop women are aware of it or not, African American women at the turn of the twentieth century faced a similar situation with respect to anti-black sexist misrepresentations and gross mischaracterizations of African American womanhood in what was then an emerging mass media and culture industry. As discussed above, Harriet Tubman, Margaret Murray Washington, Frances E.W. Harper, Ida B. Wells, Josephine Ruffin, and Mary Church Terrell established the National Association of Colored Women (NACW) in 1896, which was not only committed to the uplift of African American women, but also preoccupied with repudiating anti-black sexist caricatures of African American women in the then materializing mass media. Similar to their womanist/black feminist foremothers in the Black Women's Club Movement, then, the women of the Hip Hop Women's Movement find themselves fighting the simultaneously anti-black racist *and* anti-black sexist stereotypes incessantly being hurled at them. Most of the women of the Hip Hop Generation who have been able to engage and ultimately embrace feminism or womanism strongly stress the necessity of sensibly utilizing hip hop culture, especially rap music and videos, as a critical consciousness-raising conduit, an anti-racist womanist/ feminist forum that exposes the young women (and men) of the Hip Hop Generation to what non-white and non-elite feminism/womanism has to of-fer—that is to say, as we have seen above, the very kind of womanism/black feminism put forward and practiced not only by classic black clubwomen but also by classic blues women.

Most contemporary cultural critics and cultural studies scholars agree that hip hop is the late twentieth century/early twenty-first century generation's signature socio-cultural contribution (or "damned" deprivation, depending on who you ask), so it should not shock anyone, least of all those of us working in the fields of African American Studies and Women's Studies, that a new form of feminism—that is, *hip hop feminism*—has arisen from the underbelly or entrails of hip hop culture. In addition, none of this should shock and awe any of us when we bear in mind something that Frantz Fanon demonstrated in *The Wretched of the Earth* (1968) in his discussion of the ways in which violence, colonization, exploitation, and oppression often unwittingly gives rise to radical, if not revolutionary, forms of resistance (see also Rabaka 2010b). Men, and least of all the men of the Hip Hop Generation, do not have a monopoly on radicalism or revolutionary thought and praxis, which is also to say that the hyper-masculinism, misogyny, and male supremacy seemingly at the center of commercial rap music and hip hop culture has only inten-sified many young women's decolonial desire(s) to critique and combat pa-triarchy or, rather, *patriarchal colonialism*.

The non-white women of the Hip Hop Generation whose gender con-sciousness has been heightened as a result of their exposure to feminist ideas within Women's Studies classrooms often use their newfound knowledge in ways comparably different than most of their contemporary white counter-parts, because their daily lives and struggles, their lived-experiences and lived-endurances, demand not only that they be fluent in womanist/feminist theory and praxis, but also in critical race theory, Marxist (and other anti-capitalist) theory, and queer (and other anti-heterosexist) theory (R. A. Ber-nard 2009; Johnson and Henderson 2005; Pough 2002, 2003, 2004; Rojas 2009; Sharpley-Whiting 2007). Many of these women are able to detect early on the deficiencies of feminism as a stand-alone theory and usually they quickly tire of all of the "academic talk" of feminism. Hence, when they put feminist theory into praxis, they usually turn to the issues and terrain that they feel strongest about and are most familiar with. As a result of their coming of age during a period of intense technological revolution—for instance, from the Sony Walkman to Apple's iPod, from car phones to cellular phones, and from the Commodore 64 computer to Apple's iPad—the women of the Hip Hop Generation, as with the Hip Hop Generation in general, have been inundated with the explosion of social media and popular culture that took place during the 1980s, 1990s, and early 2000s. Consequently, social media and popular culture have become important sites and sources for hip hop feminism, and often these new-fangled feminists (albeit, many would argue, "feminists" nonetheless) make important connections between "old school" grassroots politics and Hip Hop Generation cyber-politics, between 1960s and 1970s–styled politicization and late twentieth century/early twenty-first century new multi-issue social movement mobilization (Hindman 2009; Jenkins 2006, 2009; Runell 2008; Shirky 2008; Spence 2011; Watkins 2009).

Even if we were to focus our discussion primarily on the hip hop feminists featured in Gwendolyn Pough, Elaine Richardson, Aisha Durham, and Rachel Raimist's groundbreaking edited volume, *Home Girls Make Some Noise!: A Hip Hop Feminism Anthology* (2007), we can deduce that hip hop feminism critically engages music, film, fashion, fiction, poetry, spoken-word, dance, theater, and visual art, as well as other aspects of popular culture, as essential arenas for feminist politicization and mobilization. Which is also to say, when compared with the feminist mobilization of the classic black clubwomen and classic blues women, the majority of hip hop feminist mobilization at the present moment seems to emerge from cyber-social networks, mass media, and popular culture, rather than nationally networked women's organizations based in religious, government, academic, or male-dominated leftist bureaucracies.

Undeniably, hip hop culture touches the lives of many more young non-white women, and even the lives of many young white women, than the feminism coming out of Women's Studies classes and the American academy in general. This means, then, that those of us who would truly like to reach and radicalize the women of the Hip Hop Generation will have to come to the realization that whether we like it or not hip hop feminists, and even more the "around the way girls" (i.e., streetwise hip hop women), have developed what I am wont to call *the Hip Hop Women's Movement*. We might even go so far to say that for many of the women of the Hip Hop Generation their women-centered politics reflect the fact that the majority of non-white women regularly receive substandard education in the public school system and, therefore, school has ceased to serve as the place where they learn literacy, sociality, and politics. Instead, for many, if not for most, cyber-social networks, mass media, and popular culture have, literally, become their classroom and, not seeking to sound supercilious, little or no distinction is made between uncritical information and authentic critical education.[39]

In observing the fact that hip hop culture currently reaches more young non-white women, especially black and brown women, than the feminism found in the academy of the twenty-first century, I am not in any way arguing that hip hop, and specifically rap music and videos, is not full of controversy and contradictions when and where we come to the ways in which women (again, especially black and brown women) are represented or, rather, misrepresented within the world of hip hop. Instead, I am emphasizing the fact that rap music and hip hop culture are malleable and mobile enough to be adapted to a wide-range of ideas and actions, a wealth of theories and praxes—some progressive, while others regressive; some truly remarkable, while others merely mediocre; and some liberating, while others incarcerating.

Taking into consideration the contradictory ability of hip hop culture to simultaneously imprison and emancipate women, most hip hop womanists' theories and praxes revolve around their relationships with and critiques of the racial-patriarchal-capitalist political economy of cyber-social networks, mass media, and popular culture, as well as more conventional cultural and socio-political institutions. All of this makes perfect sense when one contemplates the often-overlooked fact that the hyper-masculinism, misogyny, and bourgeoisism seemingly inherent in the most popular expressions of hip hop culture—for example, commercial rap music and videos—mirrors the hyper-masculinism, misogyny, and bourgeoisism seemingly inherent in U.S. history, culture, politics, and society. Were we to focus specifically on African American women's ragged relationship with rap music and videos, then and there we would be able to easily see the often conflicted connections many women of the Hip Hop Generation make between rap music and hip hop culture, on the one hand, and womanism/feminism, anti-racism, and anti-capitalism, on the other hand.[40]

When hip hop feminism and the wider Hip Hop Women's Movement is viewed against the backdrop of the Black Women's Club Movement and the contributions of the classic blues queens we come to comprehend the Hip Hop Women's Movement as the culmination of more than a century of African American women-centered—whether understood to be "black feminist" or "womanist"—work. Hence, instead of an either/or approach to African American women's lives and struggles that privileges politics over music, or music over politics, the Hip Hop Women's Movement synthesizes black women's popular music with black women's popular movements in ways that are unprecedented and awe inspiring.

At the heart of the Hip Hop Women's Movement seems to be a critical understanding of the fact that "the experiences of hip hop or contemporary feminists are often overlooked or misunderstood because they do not fall within traditional feminist analysis" and praxis (Clay 2007b, 69). As witnessed above, something very similar could be said about the experiences and contributions of classic black clubwomen and, most especially, classic blues women. Whether conscious of it or not, hip hop women have been influenced by, and have indeed "inherited" much from, classic black clubwomen *and* classic blues women. In the final analysis it would seem that all of these women collectively embrace the classic black clubwomen's principle of "Lifting As We Climb." Perhaps, Angela Davis in *Women, Culture, and Politics* (1989) put it best when she ardently asserted:

> Today, as we reflect on the process of empowering Afro-American women, our most efficacious strategies remain those that are guided by the principle used by black women in the club movement. We must strive to "lift as we climb." In other words, we must climb in such a way as to guarantee that all of our sisters, regardless of class, and indeed all of our brothers, climb with us. This must be the essential dynamic of our quest for power—a principle that must not only determine our struggles as Afro-American women, but also govern all authentic struggles of disposed people. Indeed, the overall battle for equality can be profoundly enhanced by embracing this principle. (5)

The influence of the classic blues queens and classic black clubwomen should not be limited to African American women's popular music and popular movements. Just as we conceded their influence on hip hop women and the Hip Hop Women's Movement it is equally important to acknowledge the ways in which classic blues women and classic black clubwomen's aesthetics and politics were central to and provided a philosophical foundation for arguably each and every form of black popular music and black popular movement that followed. As mentioned in the previous "remix," there is a longstanding tendency to delink and dissociate black popular music from black popular movements. Likewise, there is a longstanding tendency to delink and dissociate black popular movements, as if they are not in fact deeply connected and, ultimately, part of a historical and cultural continuum that can be traced back to the Abolitionist Movement during the period of African American enslavement.

In the next "remix" we will explore the ways in which classic blues and the blues aesthetic gave way to classic jazz and the jazz aesthetic. Building on and going on beyond the blues, classic jazz in many senses eclipsed the blues in the mainstream American mindset of the 1920s and 1930s and ushered in a wholly new pop culture complex that intertwined race, gender, class, and sexuality. Arguably even more than the blues, jazz has handed down much to the Hip Hop Generation. As easily observed in the "jazz rap" genre, hip hoppers have openly acknowledged the influence of jazz on rap music. However, most hip hoppers continue to have an acute *amnesia* with regard to how jazz's musical evolution, jazz aesthetics, jazz politics, and the broader jazz culture continues to factor into and indelibly influence not merely rap music, but almost each and every aspect of what we have come to call hip hop culture. The next "remix," therefore, demonstrates *what the Hip Hop Generation has forgotten but should remember* about black popular music and black popular culture during the Jazz Age and, more generally, during the first half of the twentieth century.

## NOTES

1.  For further discussion of the enormous influence and impact of black popular music and black popular culture on the wider world of U.S. popular music and popular culture, and for the most noteworthy works that informed my analysis here, see Boyd (1997), Dent (1992), Elam and Jackson (2005), Iton (2008), M. A. Neal (1998), Phinney (2005), and Pollard (1999).
2.  For further discussion of minstrel, medicine, tent, and vaudeville shows during the Reconstruction and post-Reconstruction years, and for the most noteworthy works that informed my analysis here, see Bean, Hatch, and McNamara (1996), DiMeglio (1973), R. M. Lewis (2003), E. Lott (1993), Nowatzki (2010), and Toll (1974, 1976). And, for an engagement of "hip hop's inheritance" from blackface minstrelism in particular, see my book *Hip Hop's Inheritance* (Rabaka 2011, 49–57).
3.  It would seem that African American Studies scholars have been more prone to acknowledge the ways in which African American social and political movements have been divided along gender lines, but not necessarily class lines. The question here has to do with the difference that class makes in African American life, culture, and leadership. Without in any way wanting to give the impression that the contention here is that *all* upper-class and middle-class African Americans are somehow brainwashed (or, rather, "whitewashed," as we commonly say within the African American community), yet and still I believe that it is extremely important to acknowledge the high levels of Eurocentrism and intense internalization of bourgeoisism on the part of the black bourgeoisie. Because the black bourgeoisie, like all other bourgeoisies around the world, has sought to lead in the most white middle-class manner imaginable, because they have never bothered to study or develop an authentic appreciation of any aspect of working-class and underclass African American thought and culture (i.e., from an African American point of view), most often the black bourgeoisie has used its considerable influence, talent, and resources to encourage working-class and poor black folk to Eurocentrically assimilate as quickly as possible. For further discussion of the trials and tribulations surrounding black bourgeois leadership and their historic domination of African American institutions and socio-political movements, see S. M. Collins (1997), Coner-Edwards and Spurlock (1988), Dyson (2005), Frazier (1962), Fulwood (1996), Lacy (2007), Landry (1987), Pattillo (2000), Summers (2004), and Tye (2004).
4.  For further discussion of the *anti-black sexist* disdain most upper-class and middle-class whites held black women in, and for the most noteworthy works that informed my analysis here, see A. Y. Davis (1981), Giddings (1984), Guy-Sheftall (1990), Hine (1990a, 1990b), Hine and Gaspar (1996, 2004), Hine, King, and Reed (1995), Hine and Thompson (1998), hooks (1981), St. Jean and Feagin (1998), and Vaz (1995).
5.  For further discussion of the African American cultural aesthetic continuum, from enslavement through to rap music and hip hop culture, see Sam Pollard's award-winning six-part documentary *I'll Make Me a World: African-American Artists in the Twentieth Century* (1999).
6.  Once again it is important to acknowledge class struggle within African America. The black bourgeoisie of the present unapologetically continues the Eurocentric and schizophrenic legacy of the black bourgeoisie of the past. Their major preoccupation is not simply *de-Africanization* and assimilation into European America as quickly as possible, but also distancing themselves from working-class and poor black folk, the very same folk the black bourgeoi-

sie often claims to be leading out of the "burdens of blackness." Obviously W. E. B. Du Bois' concept of "double-consciousness"—discussed below—continues to plague African America, especially the African American middle class.

7.  For further discussion of the White Women's Club Movement, and specifically its conservative conceptions of womanhood, wifehood, and motherhood, and for the most noteworthy works that informed my analysis here, see Bleser (1991), Gere (1997), Houde (1989), Martin (1987), Smith-Rosenberg (1985), Steinschneider (1994), and Wells (1953).

8.  These questions, and the answers offered to them below, have been indelibly influenced by Joan Morgan's watershed work, *When Chickenheads Come Home to Roost: A Hip Hop Feminist Breaks It Down* (1999), where she revealingly wrote: "feminism's ivory tower elitism excludes the masses . . . black women simply 'didn't have time for all that shit'" (53). She continued, "[l]ack of college education explains why 'round-the-way girls aren't reading bell hooks." However, it does not adequately explain why "even the gainfully degreed (self included) would rather trick away our last twenty-five dollars on that new nineties black girl fiction (trife as some of it may be) than some of those good, but let's face it, laboriously academic black feminist texts" (53). Morgan has hit at the heart of the issue here, and it involves not only white women's (including self-proclaimed white feminists') anti-black racism (however inadvertent and unconscious), but also, and rather ironically, seemingly most middle-class and college-educated black women's (including self-proclaimed black feminists') elitism, bourgeoisism, and paternalism toward working-class and poor African American women. Below we will witness what can be considered the origins and early evolution of the rift between upper-class and middle-class African American women and working-class and underclass African American women and their distinct forms of black feminism/womanism: the Black Women's Club Movement.

9.  In *When Chickenheads Come Home to Roost* (1999), Joan Morgan contended that white women's (including self-proclaimed white feminists') racism, as well as racism within the wider Women's Liberation Movement, "may explain the justifiable bad taste the f-word leaves in the mouths of women who are over thirty-five," but for the women of the Hip Hop Generation these are merely "abstractions drawn from someone else's history" (53). As a hip hop woman, Morgan wants to embrace a form of feminism that doesn't feel like "white women's shit," a form of feminism "that would allow me to explore who we are as women—not as victims. One that claimed the powerful richness and delicious complexities inherent in being black girls now—sistas of the post-Civil Rights, post-feminist, post-soul, Hip Hop Generation" (36, 57). However, where Morgan—along with other young black feminist academics and college-educated hip hop women—is willing to embrace the term feminist, especially the term "hip hop feminist," most hip hop women seem to outright reject "the f-word." For instance, in *Black Noise: Rap Music and Black Culture in Contemporary America* (1994), Tricia Rose wrote, "during my conversations with Salt, MC Lyte, and Queen Latifah it became clear that these women were uncomfortable with being labeled feminist and perceived feminism as a signifier for a movement related specifically to white women" (176). Rose candidly continued:

> For these women rappers, and many other black women, feminism is the label for members of a white women's social movement that has no concrete link to black women or the black community. Feminism signifies allegiance to historically specific movements whose histories have long been the source of frustration for women of color. Similar criticisms of women's social movements have been made vociferously by many black feminists. As they have argued, race and gender are inextricably linked for black women. This is the case for both black and white women. However, in the case of black women, the realities of racism link black women to black men in a way that challenges cross-racial sisterhood. Sisterhood among and between black and white women will not be achieved at the expense of black women's racial identity. (177; see also Newman 1999)

All of this is to say, more or less academic terms such as "feminism" and "womanism" are "*academic* intellectual" terms frequently utilized in efforts to conceptually capture the thought and practices of "*organic* intellectuals," such as the African American women artists, political activists, and workers Patricia Hill Collins seeks to include in her definition of what it means to be an "intellectual" and contributor to the black feminist tradition in *Black Feminist Thought* (2000).

10.  For further discussion of classical and contemporary African music, and for the most noteworthy works that informed my analysis here, see Bebey (1999), Bender (1991), Chernoff (1979), Ewens (1992), Nketia (1974), Stone (2008), and Tenaille (2002). Several (ethno)musicological studies have explored the "African roots" of the blues and made more general connections between continental and diasporan African music, see Charters (1981), Floyd (1995), Kubik (1999), and Palmer (1981).

11.  For further discussion of early African American music, during and after enslavement, and for the most noteworthy works that informed my analysis here, see Abbott and Seroff (2002), Burnim and Maultsby (2006), Du Bois (1903b), Epstein (2003), Floyd (1995), Johnson and Johnson (2002), Parrish (1992), Peretti (2009), Ramey (2008), Southern (1997), and Spencer (1990, 1993, 1995).

12.  For further discussion of Reconstruction and post-Reconstruction anti-black racism and its impact on post-enslavement African American music and culture, and for the most noteworthy works that informed my analysis here, see Abbott and Seroff (2007), Brundage (2011), Du Bois (1995a), Lawson (2010), Lhamon (1998, 2003), E. Lott (1993), Miller (2010), Sotiropoulos (2006), Wondrich (2003), and Wormser (2002).

13.  For further discussion of the Great Migration and African American labor at the turn of and during the first decades of the twentieth century, and for the most noteworthy works that informed my analysis here, see Hahn (2003), A. Harrison (1991), Lemann (1991), Marks (1989), Trotter (1991), and Wilkerson (2010).

14.  For further discussion of authenticity, "realness," and "soulfulness" within the world of black popular music and black popular culture, and for the most noteworthy works that informed my analysis here, see Banfield (2010), Bracey (2003), Moten (2003), Nielsen (1997), and R. F. Thompson (1974, 1983).

15.  For further discussion of the various blues traditions and expressions (i.e., lyrical, musical, political, and philosophical), and for the most noteworthy works that informed my analysis here, see Charters (1975, 2005), Keil (1991), Oliver (1970, 2006, 2009), and Oster (1969).

16.  Minstrel, medicine, tent, and vaudeville shows were touched on above; therefore there is no need to rehearse the whole of our discussion here. However, for further discussion of the relationship between blues and jug music, and for the most noteworthy works that informed my analysis here, see Bogdanov, Woodstra and Erlewine (2003a), Olsson (1970), Stambler and Stambler (2001), and Wright (1993).

17.  For further discussion of Bessie Smith's life and legacy, to get a clearer sense of how and why she arguably eclipsed her mentor Ma Rainey ("the undisputed Mother of the Blues"), and for those sincerely seeking to explore the mystery and mayhem surrounding the "first major blues and jazz singer on record and one of the most powerful of all time," see Albertson (2003), Feinstein (1985), Grimes (2000), and Scott (2008). The influence of these works on my interpretation of Bessie Smith cannot be overstated.

18.  For further discussion of the Black Women's Club Movement, its origins and evolution, and for the most noteworthy works that informed my analysis here, see Cash (1986, 2001), E. L. Davis (1996), Dickson (1982), Dublin, Arias, and Carreras (2003), Guy-Sheftall (1990), Hendricks (1998), Jenkins (1984), J. M. Johnson (2004), Shaw (1991), S. L. Smith (1986), and Wesley (1984).

19.  For further discussion of African American women's civil rights, voting rights, and women's rights struggles at the turn of the twentieth century, as well as the "women-are-the-weaker-sex" argument popular in Europe and European America at the time, and for the most noteworthy works that informed my analysis here, see Dudden (2011), Gilmore (1996), Gordon and Collier-Thomas (1997), Koehler (1980), Materson (2009), and Terborg-Penn (1998).

20.  For further discussion of Victorian America and "American Victorianism," and for the most noteworthy works that informed my analysis here, see Blodgett and Howe (1976), Green and Perry (1983), Schlereth (1992), Smith-Rosenberg (1985), and K. White (2000).

21.  For further discussion of black vernacular culture, which is alternatively called "black expressive culture," and for the most noteworthy works that informed my analysis here, see Caponi-Tabery (1999), Gilroy (1993), Gundaker (1998), T. L. Lott (1999), Oboe and Scacchi (2008), and White and White (1998).

22.  For further discussion of the distinct disdain and special kind of contempt that upper-class and middle-class African Americans most often hold working-class and underclass African Americans—again, their language, customs of dress, mannerisms, popular music, and popular culture—in, and for the most noteworthy works that informed my analysis here, see, first and foremost, E. Franklin Frazier's classic *The Black Bourgeoisie: The Rise of a New Middle-Class in the United States* (1962), especially "Part II: The World of Make-Believe" (153–238), as well as more recent research, such as Cose (1993), Feagin and Sikes (1994), Gatewood (1990), Graham (1999, 2006), and L. B. Thompson (2009).

23.  For further discussion of the black public sphere, and for the most noteworthy works that informed my analysis here, see E. Anderson (1999), Black Public Sphere Collective (1995), Corbould (2009), Dawson (2001, 2011), Doreski (1998), H.S. Gray (1995, 2005), Harris-Perry (2004), and Iton (2008).

24.  For further discussion of the "liberal bourgeois" tendencies of the African American church (including the more recent African American "mega-church" phenomenon), and for the most noteworthy works that informed my analysis here, see Barnes (2010), Billingsley (1999), Irvin (1992), Lincoln and Mamiya (1990), Nelsen, Yokley, and Nelsen (1971), Pinn (2010), Pinn and Pinn (2002), and Tucker-Worgs (2011).

25.  For further discussion of the origins and evolution of the juke joint, as well as other manifestations of African American dancehalls and nightclubs, and for the most noteworthy works that informed my analysis here, see Grazian (2003), R. B. Hayes (2008), M.A. Hunter (2010), Imes (2003), and Peretti (1992).

26.  For further discussion of African American religious radicalism, and for the most noteworthy works that informed my analysis here, see J. K. Carter (2008), Cone (1969, 1970, 1975), Cone and Wilmore (1993), Fulop and Raboteau (1996), Pinn (1998, 2006), Raboteau (1978, 1995, 1999), and Wilmore (1983, 1989). And, for more detailed discussion of the connections between African American religious culture and hip hop culture, see Knight (2007), Miyakawa (2005), Pinn (2003, 2009), Pinn and Valentin (2009), and Smith and Jackson (2005).

27.  There is, obviously, an abundance of research on the Civil Rights Movement. However, most of this work has had a tendency to downplay the connections between the Civil Rights Movement and previous African American social and political movements, most especially the Black Women's Club Movement, the New Negro Movement, and the Harlem Renaissance. For works that cogently connect previous (i.e., pre–Civil Rights Movement) African American social and political movements with the Civil Rights Movement, and for the most noteworthy works that informed my analysis here, see Aldridge (2011), Collier-Thomas and Franklin (2001), Crawford, Rouse, and Woods (1990), J. E. Davis (2001), Franklin (1984), Harding (1981), Joseph (2006a, 2006b), Kelley and Lewis (2000), Morris (1984), Ogbar (2004), Singh (2004), and Tuck (2010). As mentioned in this book's introduction, my next book project, *The Hip Hop Movement: From R&B and the Civil Rights Movement to Rap and Obama's America*, will explore *hip hop's inheritance* from the major African American musics and movements between 1955 and 1980 (see Rabaka, forthcoming).

28.  In *Hip Hop's Inheritance*, in the chapter "'The Personal Is Political!': From the Black Women's Liberation and Feminist Art Movements to the Hip Hop Feminist Movement," I examined "hip hop's inheritance" from the Black Women's Liberation Movement and the Feminist Art Movement (Rabaka 2011, 129–88). However, for those seeking scholarly overviews of the Black Women's Liberation Movement of the 1960s and 1970s independent of the Hip Hop Movement, and for the most noteworthy works that informed my analysis here, see Breines (2006), P. H. Collins (1998, 2000), A. Y. Davis (1981, 1989), hooks (1981, 1984, 1989, 1990, 1991), Lorde (1984, 1996, 2009), Roth (1999a, 1999b, 2004), and Springer (2001, 2002, 2005).

29. For further discussion of reggae women, as well as "Rasta women" (i.e., women within the Rastafari Movement), and for the most noteworthy works that informed my analysis here, see Chevannes (1998), Christensen (2003), C. J. Cooper (1995, 2004), Lake (1998), Ray (1998), Waagbø (2007), and Walker (2005).

30. It is interesting to observe that most of what is now called "conscious rap," "alternative rap," "jazz rap," "feminist rap," and "women-centered rap" produced in the late 1980s and throughout the 1990s was labeled "Afrocentric." In the simplest terms, "Afrocentricity" involves viewing phenomena—especially African phenomenon, such as continental and disporan African history, culture, and struggles—from an African perspective, as opposed to the conventional Eurocentric perspective that predominates in Europe, America, and the rest of the racially colonized world (i.e., Africa, Asia, Australia, the Caribbean, and Latin America). For further discussion of Afrocentricity, and for the most noteworthy works that informed my analysis here, see Asante (1988, 1990, 1998, 1999, 2007), G. J. Giddings (2003), C. C. Gray (2001), Hamlet (1998), Mazama (2002), Schiele (2000), and Walters (1993). And, for the most noteworthy works that examine Afrocentricity within or, rather, the Afrocentric elements and expressions of rap music and hip hop culture, see Amatokwu (2009), Boone (2008), Ginwright (2004), Stephens (1996), and T. R. Walker (1998).

31. For further discussion of womanism and how it is, according to self-described womanists, different from feminism, especially what they term "white feminism," and for the most noteworthy works that informed my analysis here, see Charles (1990), Eaton (2008), Heilmann (2003), Hudson-Weems (1995, 2004), Kolawole (1997), Mathew (2007), L. Phillips (2006), and Phillips, Reddick-Morgan, and Stephens (2005).

32. For further discussion of blues women's performance, fashion, and visual culture, as well as African American women's performance, fashion, and visual culture in general, and for the most noteworthy works that informed my analysis here, see Brooks (2006), J. Brown (2008), Brundage (2011), Fleetwood (2011), Nyongó (2009), and S. Vogel (2009).

33. For further discussion of hip hop women's body image, colorism, sexuality, and hypersexualization within rap music videos, as well as hip hop culture more generally, and for the most noteworthy works that informed my analysis here, see Bost (2001), Conrad, Dixon and Zhang (2009), Emerson (2002), Hobson (2003), Miller-Young (2008), M. Morgan (2005), Muñoz-Laboy, Weinstein, and Parker (2007), Parasecoli (2007), Railton and Watson (2011), Stephens and Few (2007a, 2007b), and Zhang, Dixon, and Conrad (2009, 2010).

34. For further discussion of the ways in which Bessie Smith challenged Eurocentric beauty standards, and how her challenge was greatly appreciated by her fans (female and male), it is important to turn to arguably the best work to date on "Ms. Bessie" (as we say within the African American community), Chris Albertson's *Bessie* (2003), where he wrote of how Bessie's beauty was rebuffed early in her career but eventually accepted because of the power of and piercing pathos in her voice. For instance, in 1912 Smith was a member of Irvin C. Miller's touring show in the South. Albertson quoted Miller as saying that "[s]he was a natural singer, but we stressed beauty in the chorus line and Bessie did not meet my standards as far as looks were concerned. I told the manager to get rid of her, which he did" (14). Albertson further stated that "Miller's failure to see Bessie's physical beauty is explained by his well-known slogan, the theme of all his shows: 'Glorifying the Brownskin Girl.' To put it plainly, Bessie was too black" (14). By 1924, when Smith headlined Cincinnati's Roosevelt Theater, "she brought a show that was worthy of the theater's splendid interior, including a variety of imaginative, dazzling costumes and headgear." Albertson offered more insight:

> Her personal favorite . . . was a white and blue satin dress with a moderate hoop skirt, adorned with strands of pearls and imitation rubies. To complement that, she wore headgear that resembled a cross between a football helmet and a tasseled lampshade. The flashy outfits offered fans a momentary escape from everyday reality, but the lyrics to Bessie's songs soon brought them back down to earth, and they seem to have loved the contrast. (66–67)

Even though Bessie Smith was considered "too big" and "too black" by most people (including many siddity African Americans) within the entertainment industry of the 1920s and 1930s, observe that her legions of working-class and poor African American fans "seem to have loved the contrast" she presented to mainstream white standards of beauty. Indeed, Smith set into motion a challenge to Eurocentric and bourgeois standards of beauty that continues to reverberate throughout women-centered rap, neo-soul, and hip hop culture more generally.

35.    For further discussion of working-class and poor African American women's lives as laborers, especially in domestic service, during the first decades of the twentieth century, and for the most noteworthy works that informed my analysis here, see Branch (2011), Dill (1994), T. W. Hunter (1997), J. Jones (1985), Rollins (1985), and S. Tucker (1988).

36.    For more detailed discussion of African American lesbian's lives and struggles, and for the most noteworthy works that informed my analysis here, see Battle and Barnes (2010), Bowleg (2008), Carbado, McBride and Weise (2002), Cornwell (1983), James (2007), McKinley and DeLaney (1995), Moore (1997), B. Smith (1983), and B. Wilson (2009).

37.    For further discussion of homophobia and heterosexism in African American history, culture, politics, and communities, and for the most noteworthy works that informed my analysis here, see Boykin (1996), Brandt (1999), Chapman (2011), Constantine-Simms (2001), Ferguson (2004), A. C. Harris (2009), E. P. Johnson (2008), Johnson and Henderson (2005), and Loiacano (1989).

38.    Unfortunately, there is not to my knowledge a single book-length study devoted to female and women-centered rappers in general, and hyper-sexual and gangsta female rappers in particular. However, there have been several eye-opening journal articles and book chapters. Consequently, here my analysis has greatly benefitted from and builds on groundbreaking contributions provided by Goodall (1994), Haugen (2003), Oware (2009), Phillips, Pough (2004), Reddick-Morgan and Stephens (2005), Roberts (1994), Rose (1994), Skeggs (1993), and Troka (2002).

39.    For further discussion of the ways in which contemporary black popular culture, and hip hop culture in particular, has been and continues to be utilized as a teaching tool and in educational environments, and for the most noteworthy works that informed my analysis here, see Alim (2005), R. N. Brown (2008), Comissiong (2007), Dimitriadis (2009), Ginwright (2004), Hill (2009), Parmar (2009), Powell (1991), Runell (2008), Runell and Diaz (2007), and Seidel (2011).

40.    For further discussion of what I am referring to as "African American women's ragged relationship with rap music and videos," specifically the ways in which they are (mis)represented (i.e., objectified and hyper-sexualized) in seemingly most rap music videos, how women-centered rappers' videos frequently "flip da script" on hyper-masculine misrepresentations of African American women, and for the most noteworthy works that informed my analysis here, see Balaji (2010), Emerson (2002), Gan, Zillmann, and Mitrook (1997), Reid-Brinkley (2008), Roberts (1991, 1994), and Shelton (1997).

*Remix 3*

# Jazzmatazz

*From Classic Jazz and Bebop to Jazz Rap and Hip Hop*

The so-called jazz hip hop movement is about bringing jazz back to the streets. It got taken away, made into some elite, sophisticated music. It's bringing jazz back where it belongs. —Guru

### INTRODUCTION: ON HOW JAZZ AS MUSIC, AESTHETICS, POLITICS, AND CULTURE HAS INFLUENCED RAP MUSIC AND HIP HOP CULTURE

Rap music and hip hop culture have, however unheralded, inherited much from jazz and the parallel African American arts and civil rights movements of the so-called "Jazz Age" (i.e., the Harlem Renaissance and the New Negro Movement, respectively). On the one hand, this is not in any way a revelatory assertion, as anyone who has heard the early jazz narratives and jazz poetry of Duke Ellington's *Black, Brown and Beige* (1943) and *A Drum is a Woman* (1956), Langston Hughes and Charles Mingus's *Weary Blues* (1958), Max Roach's *We Insist!: The Freedom Now Suite* (1960) and *Percussion Bitter Sweet* (1961), or Sterling Brown's *The Poetry of Sterling Brown* (1995) will attest. Moreover, jazz scholars have long made much of Louis Armstrong's "scat singing," Cab Calloway's "vocalese," Lester Young's "jive talk," and Dizzy Gillespie's "bop talk"—as is well-known, what came to be called "bop talk" was initially referred to as "hepcat talk" and, later, "hipster talk" and concretely coincided with late 1940s and early 1950s African American hipster music, hipster culture, and the wider Hipster Movement. [1]

Traces of Hughes, Armstrong, Brown, Young, Calloway, and Gillespie's utilization of the polyvocality and cadences of African American vernacular—including their collective use of the glissandos, arpeggios, and rhetorical rhythms of African American urban "folk" speech—can be easily detected in classic jazz rap albums, such as A Tribe Called Quest's *People's Instinctive Travels and the Paths of Rhythm* (1990), Main Source's *Breaking Atoms* (1991), Gang Starr's *Daily Operation* (1992), Digable Planets' *Reachin': A New Refutation of Time and Space* (1993), Guru's *Jazzmatazz, Vol. 1* (1993), Us3's *Hands on the Torch* (1994), and the critically-acclaimed various artists HIV/AIDS awareness project *Stolen Moments: Red Hot + Cool* (1994). On the other hand, what might really strike and puzzle most of my readers is the exact extent to which rap, especially jazz rap and other jazz hip hop hybrids, has been indelibly informed by jazz and, even more, the jazz poetry tradition extending all the way back to the Jazz Age, the Harlem Renaissance, and the New Negro Movement.

The jazz and poetry, as well as the political aesthetic and artistic activism in general, of the Harlem Renaissance ran parallel to and were unmistakably impacted by the social and political aspirations of the New Negro Movement. Indeed, after 350 years of enslavement it would seem that late nineteenth century and early twentieth century African Americans established several simultaneous socio-political and artistic movements. As discussed in the previous "remix," classic blues women's music and the Black Women's Club Movement, as well as their relationship with each other, provides us with one of the earliest models for *the re-gendering, re-politicization, and re-radicalization of rap music and hip hop culture.* It could be said that jazz music, the Harlem Renaissance, and the New Negro Movement grew out of or, at the least, were inspired by classic blues women's music and the Black Women's Club Movement. The overlap between these musics and movements, therefore, should be strongly stressed because it illustrates the multiple issues and the multiple ways that African Americans confronted collective problems at the turn of the twentieth century. This overlap also points to and prefigures the artistic archetypes, political paradigms, and philosophical foundations of rap music and hip hop culture at the turn of the twenty-first century.

In the ongoing and earnest effort to either locate or create an antidote for *hip hop's amnesia* this "remix" focuses on jazz's contributions to rap music and hip hop culture. Hip hop's "poetic inheritance" from the Harlem Renaissance and "political inheritance" from the New Negro Movement will be the main subject of the subsequent "remix." Hence, here the main point is to critically examine how jazz *as music, aesthetics, politics, and culture* has—again, however unheralded—indelibly influenced the origins and evolution of rap music and hip hop culture. Certainly it will not be as difficult to demonstrate the connections between jazz and rap as compared to the almost unheard of connections between blues and rap discussed in the foregoing "remix." However, and this should be sternly stated at the outset, this "remix" is not simply about the connections between jazz and rap, but also about the ways in which jazz music, jazz poetry, and jazz politics uneasily served as an inspiration and soundtrack for multiple major countercultural movements, including: the Lost Generation, the Harlem Renaissance, the New Negro Movement, the Bebop Movement, the Hipster Movement, the Zoot Suit Riots, and the Beat Generation.

Hip hop culture and the controversial and contradictory character of rap music did not develop in a historical, cultural, social, and political vacuum. As with jazz music, jazz poetry, and jazz politics during the Jazz Age and the Bebop Movement, rap music and hip hop culture reflect—more than anything else—the angst-filled feelings of the first generation of African Americans to come of age after the Civil Rights Movement, Black Power Movement, Black Arts Movement, Women's Liberation Movement, and Feminist Art Movement, among other 1960s and 1970s radical political and countercultural movements. Poetically and sonically surveying both the breakthroughs and the setbacks of the 1960s and 1970s, rap music and hip hop culture simultaneously register and represent the bright optimism *and* gloomy pessimism, the transcendent triumphs *and* transgressive tragedies of the post–Civil Rights, post–Black Power, post–Women's Liberation, "post-feminist," "post-Marxists," post-etc., turn-of-the-twenty-first-century generation—which is to say, the much-heralded and, let it be duly noted, the much-hated Hip Hop Generation.

However, in order to really and truly understand the origins and evolution of rap music and hip hop culture it is of paramount importance for us to "keep conscious," "do the knowledge," and go above and beyond the musics and movements of the 1960s and 1970s. The whole history and scope of black popular music and black popular culture, as well as more "mainstream" popular music and popular culture, must be critically engaged if we are to comprehend the novel *poetic perceptiveness* and *sonic inventiveness* of rap music and hip hop culture. In other words, more than anything else, this means we must explore the blues and the blues aesthetic, as we did in the previous "remix," and jazz and the jazz aesthetic, as will be the primary preoccupation of the present "remix." We must also examine the major African American social and political movements these musics and cultural aesthetics directly correspond with—that is to say, the Black Women's Club Movement, the New Negro Movement, the Harlem Renaissance, the Bebop Movement, and the Hipster Movement, respectively. As the Black Women's Club Movement's contributions to rap music and hip hop culture were taken up in the preceding "remix," the succeeding "remix" will identify and analyze hip hop's "poetic inheritance" from the Harlem Renaissance and "political inheritance" from the New Negro Movement, among other pre–Civil Rights Movement poetic and political movements.

Emerging at the end of the nineteenth century, and in many ways mirroring the development of classic urban blues and ragtime, jazz music, the jazz aesthetic, and jazz culture was perceived to be more "upbeat" than classic blues and to offer a wider improvisational range than ragtime. In this sense, classic jazz symbolizes a shift in African America, one that sonically marks the transition from rural to urban music, and a greater acknowledgment of the power of black popular music by both the white and black bourgeoisies. These early twentieth century modulations in black popular music in particular, and black popular culture in general, continue to revealingly reverberate throughout early twenty-first century black popular music and black popular culture in general, and rap music and hip hop culture in particular.

Hence, to get right into the thick of things, the key queries guiding our discussion in this "remix" are as follows: What did classic jazz music and classic jazz poetry contribute to rap music and hip hop culture? How might the relationship between classic jazz and the New Negro Movement mirror the relationship between rap music and the Hip Hop Movement? How did classic jazz inspire the Lost Generation, and how might the Lost Generation's relationship with classic jazz eerily parallel contemporary white youths' relationship with rap music? What did bebop music and the Bebop Movement bequeath to rap music and the Hip Hop Movement? In what ways does 1940s and 1950s bebop *as music, aesthetics, politics, and culture* mirror the emergence of "alternative" rap and "conscious" rap in relation to the rise of "hardcore" rap and "gangsta" rap in the late 1980s and early 1990s? How did bebop inspire the Beat Generation, and how might the Beat Generation's relationship with bebop and the Bebop Movement eerily parallel contemporary white youths' relationship with rap music and the Hip Hop Movement? Exactly what aspects of jazz does jazz rap draw from, or is jazz rap really nothing more than another corporate American crossover dream and get-rich-quick-scheme? What are rap artists, hip hop producers, and hip hop heads' perceptions of jazz? How do jazz musicians, both jazz legends and "Young Lions," perceive the jazz rap phenomenon? Finally, which artistic archetypes, political paradigms, and philosophical foundations from classic jazz, the Jazz Age, and the Bebop Movement might contemporary "conscious" hip hoppers build on in our efforts to counteract *hip hop's amnesia* and re-politicize and re-radicalize the Hip Hop Movement? All that being said (or, rather, *asked*), the following sections seek to provide earnest answers to these crucial questions.

The subsequent section, "'It Don't Mean A Thing (If It Ain't Got That Swing!)': Revealing Rap & Hip Hop's Roots in Classic Jazz," offers a brief overview of classic jazz, its origins, and evolution. The next section, "Tales of the Jazz Age: On Jazz's Influence on the Jazz Age & the Lost Generation," provides a succinct survey of the Lost Generation and their relationship with classic jazz. Because the emphasis in this section will be on the ways in which jazz provided inspiration and a soundtrack for the more "mainstream" Jazz Age and Lost Generation, the main focus will be on those European American intellectuals and artists who utilized—even if unwittingly or only indirectly—the jazz aesthetic (or, rather, "jazz codes") in their literary and other artistic endeavors. The following section, "To Be, Or Not . . . To Bop: The Bebop Movement, Black Popular Music & Black Popular Culture in the 1940s & 1950s," examines the evolution of mid–twentieth century jazz *as music, aesthetics, politics, and culture* by focusing on the Bebop Movement and its popularization of the late 1940s and early 1950s Hipster Movement and its corollary aesthetics, politics, colloquialisms, and culture. Then, the closely associated—albeit abbreviated—ensuing section "On 'White Negroes' & 'Wiggers': From the Beat Generation & the Bebop Movement to the Millennial Generation & the Hip Hop Movement" discusses the Bebop Movement's influence on the Beat Generation in general, and beat poetry and beat literature in particular. The final section, "'Relaying a Message, Revealing the Essence of a Jazz Thing!': On Jazz Rap's Lyrical Leaps, Sonic Radicalism, and Other Aural Innovations," explores jazz's often-overlooked contributions to rap music, hip hop culture, and the Hip Hop Movement in general, and the jazz rap phenomenon and the offshoot "alternative" rap and "conscious" rap styles in specific.

## "IT DON'T MEAN A THING (IF IT AIN'T GOT THAT SWING!)": REVEALING RAP & HIP HOP'S ROOTS IN CLASSIC JAZZ

The origins and evolution of jazz amazingly mirrors the ebb and flow of African American life and culture at the turn of the twentieth century through to the turn of the twenty-first century. Although jazz achieved an unprecedented level of renown and respectability by the end of the twentieth century (e.g., jazz programs and concert series at prestigious venues such as Carnegie Hall, the Lincoln Center, the Kennedy Center, the Los Angeles Philharmonic, and the San Francisco Jazz Center), at the beginning of the century it was regarded as a "primitive" and "sinful sound" (not music!)—or, rather, even more crudely, "nigger noise"—compared to the more sedate dance music, marches, ragtime, and European classical music of its initial epoch. A number of social and political forces have influenced the dynamic evolution of jazz over the years, including racism, classism, urbanization, the rise of recording and broadcasting technology, the New Negro Movement, the Harlem Renaissance, World War I and II, the Great Depression, the Hipster Movement, the Civil Rights Movement, the Black Power Movement, and the Black Arts Movement, among many others. Jazz, much like African Americans themselves, is a music composed of many disparate parts (i.e.,

African, European, Caribbean, and Latin, etc.), but sonically synthesized so as to create a wholly new mosaic-esque music. Early jazz drew from work songs, field hollers, spirituals, blues, ragtime, European classical music, marches, and the other popular music of its incubative period.[2]

Classic jazz has been characterized as the instrumental alter ego of classic blues, but that kind of over-simplified description reduces and robs both classic jazz and classic blues of their distinctiveness. Indeed, one of the trademarks of the jazz tradition is its blues feeling and blue notes, which it undoubtedly borrows from the blues tradition. However, jazz's other hallmarks, such as improvisation, syncopation, an infectious rhythmic thrust known as "swing," and its harmonic complexity clearly distinguish it from the blues and other forms of African American music. Jazz is further distinguished by its longstanding emphasis on instrumental rather than vocal performances. Obviously there have been countless pioneering and iconic jazz vocalists, including Louis Armstrong, Ella Fitzgerald, Billie Holiday, Jimmy Rushing, Sarah Vaughan, Billy Eckstine, Dinah Washington, Joe Williams, Nancy Wilson, Jon Hendricks, Betty Carter, and Abbey Lincoln. However, unlike most other African American musical genres, vocal jazz has never been privileged over instrumental jazz and, as a matter of fact, many have argued that much of jazz's distinctiveness is best observed in instrumental jazz performances where jazz instrumentalists capture the tone and timbre of the human voice, especially the melody and melancholia of African American voices and vernacular.[3]

There is something profound to be said about jazz's instrumental emphasis. Call it "instrumental abstraction." Call it "sonic cerebrality." Call it "jive talk." Nevertheless, during its developmental phase jazz sought to express aspects of African American life, culture, and struggle that its creators felt simply could not be conveyed—*je ne sais quoi*—via words (à la Frantz Fanon's famous discussion of "The Black Man and Language" in his 1952 classic *Black Skin, White Masks* [1967]). This is unambiguously jazz's crowning achievement, because where other African American music genres harbor emphases on improvisation, it could be said that the heart and soul of jazz is the expectation that each individual jazz musician develop a distinct improvisational approach to harmony, melody, and rhythm, most often through intentional variations and distortions of time, tone, and timbre.

Emerging around the turn of the twentieth century in New Orleans, early jazz harbored the high levels of hybridity that distinguished turn of the twentieth century New Orleans from almost every other city in the United States, especially other cities in the South. Native American, African, Caribbean, French, Spanish, Irish, and German elements combined to create a new— albeit thoroughly "American" with its adherence to Jim Crow segregation and the Black Codes—creolized culture. Within the social world of African Americans in New Orleans at the turn of the twentieth century a crude kind of colorism and classism divided poorer and "darker" blacks from richer and "lighter" mixed race creoles. The blacks lived uptown, beyond Canal Street, and the creoles lived downtown, in the French Quarter. Much has been made of the fact that early black jazz musicians generally could not read music and, likewise, early creole jazz musicians frequently received "formal" music training.[4]

Classic black jazz musicians, such as trumpeters Buddy Bolden, Joseph "King" Oliver, and Louis Armstrong, were allegedly not as well schooled in reading music and, consequently, they privileged playing by ear and "feeling" the music over reading music. Classic creole jazz musicians, such as trumpeter Oscar "Papa" Celestin, clarinetist and soprano saxophonist Sidney Bechet, and clarinetist and tenor saxophonist Barney Bigard, were able to read music and participated in well-established creole musical traditions and events, including creole cotillions, balls, and galas. A core catalyst for jazz was undoubtedly the growing social and cultural contact between black and creole musicians around the turn of the twentieth century as a consequence of Jim Crow segregation and the Black Codes, which essentially removed the previous social distinctions between blacks and creoles.

In 1894 New Orleans gave into the longstanding tidal wave sweeping across the South that embraced new forms of post-enslavement American Apartheid (e.g., Jim Crow segregation, the Black Codes, the peonage system, the sharecropping system, and the convict-lease system, among others) by passing rigid segregation legislation that reclassified creoles (the so-called *gens de couleur*—a French phrase meaning "people of color") as "plain-old" black folk. Downtown creoles, previously welcomed (and revered) in white brass, string, and marching bands, suddenly had no other recourse but to make common cause with arguably New Orleans' ultimate underclass, the poorer and darker uptown blacks. Rather reductively, the emergence of jazz has often been characterized as the meeting and merging of the uptown black brass, string, and marching band tradition of church frenzy-filled, blues-laden, and vernacular-inflected music, with the downtown creole band tradition of instrumental virtuosity, musical literacy, and thorough training in European classical music. However, as with all abridged histories, especially when and where we come to black popular music and black popular culture, this abbreviated history of the origins and early evolution of jazz simplifies a much more complex and complicated reality that includes musically literate black musicians and, correspondingly, creole musicians who played by ear and were unable to read music.

Much like other forms of black popular music—especially, classic blues, rhythm & blues, soul, funk, and rap—early jazz was perceived as the soundtrack for lower-class African American life. Additionally, because it was the music that most commonly accompanied the festivities in juke joints, honkytonks, and whorehouses in Storyville, New Orleans's legendary red-light district, many creoles and most whites viewed jazz as "outlaw," "sinful," or "ghetto" music—again, much like rap music, as will be discussed in detail below. Hence, when creole musicians, such as Jelly Roll Morton, Kid Ory, Barney Bigard, and the immortal Sidney Bechet, embraced jazz they simultaneously breached social, cultural, and musical boundaries (Gushee 2005).

However, it is generally accepted that a black musician named Buddy Bolden led the first jazz band (Marquis 2005). Bolden's legend rests on his pioneering playing, which reportedly contained a deep blues feeling, an intense improvisational elaboration of melodies, and an ability to play loud enough to be heard from extremely far distances. For the most part, by the early years of the twentieth century most jazz scholars agree that New Orleans jazz featured the blues-drenched and vernacular-inflected feeling of uptown African Americans and the instrumental virtuosity and musical literacy of downtown creoles, woven together with a distinct improvisational style and a new rhythmic interpretation that innovatively transformed the basic march beat into either a "slow drag" or an up-tempo strut, the two most noted rhythmic trends of the original New Orleans jazz style. [5]

During the first quarter of the twentieth century, jazz traveled out of New Orleans and spread throughout the United States and Europe. Many prominent jazz musicians left New Orleans during the first two decades of the twentieth century, and where they went jazz faithfully followed, although not without major modifications. For instance, in 1904 Jelly Roll Morton, widely considered the first great jazz composer, became a peripatetic piano player, providing music mostly for minstrel, medicine, vaudeville, and tent shows in St. Louis and New York City, as well as throughout the South. He settled in Chicago between 1911 and 1915, where he performed with a small ensemble. He played in Los Angeles from 1917 to 1922 and then returned to Chicago where, for the next six years, he was at his music history-making peak. Throughout his pinnacle years in Chicago Morton's band, the Red Hot Peppers, boasted a number of early jazz luminaries, including: trumpeters Sidney DeParis, Red Rossiter, and George Mitchell; trombonists Kid Ory, Geechie Fields, and Gerald Reeves; clarinetists Johnny Dodds, Barney Bigard, Omer Simeon, Stomp Evans, and Darnell Howard; saxophonists Russell Procope, Happy Caldwell, and Paul Barnes; banjoists Johnny St. Cyr, Buddy Scott, and Lawrence Lucie; bassists John Lindsey and Wellman Braud; and drummers Baby Dodds, Zutty Singleton, and Andrew Hilaire. [6]

Ironically, the majority of the recordings documenting the classic New Orleans jazz sound, including the groundbreaking work of luminaries such as King Oliver and Louis Armstrong, took place in or near Chicago. Oliver arrived in Chicago in 1918, and Armstrong joined Oliver's band in 1922. Their classic recordings together, including "Dippermouth Blues," "Snake Rag," "High Society," "Sobbin' Blues" and "Sugar Foot Stomp," helped to popularize jazz and move it from the local and regional level to a national and international phenomenon (S. B. Charters 2008; M. T. Williams 1960; Yanow 2001b).

Louis Armstrong is widely regarded as the first great jazz soloist on record and, along with Duke Ellington, the most influential musician in jazz history. A true trumpet virtuoso, his colorful playing and overall musical charisma, dating back to his watershed studio work with his 1920s Hot Five and Hot Seven ensembles, literally, laid the foundation for the future development of jazz. Almost all subsequent styles of jazz—from big band to swing, bebop to hard bop, Dixieland to Latin, modal to modern creative jazz—are indebted to Armstrong's highly imaginative and emotionally charged soloing and gruff-voiced singing. [7]

Although Armstrong's breakthroughs as an improvising soloist undoubtedly represent one of the great distinctions of jazz, it is equally important to observe that the evolution of the jazz ensemble, both large and small, contributes to the uniqueness of jazz. As a matter of fact, the particular and often times peculiar sound produced by the blending of the striking rhythmic, melodic, harmonic, and timbral vocabularies of the ensemble are as crucial to defining the jazz sound as improvisation. Among the jazz composers and arrangers who marked and molded the early jazz sound were Jelly Roll Morton, Fletcher Henderson, Don Redman, and the incomparable Duke Ellington. In his classic recordings with his Red Hot Peppers band, Morton prefigured the ubiquitous "shout-chorus" of big band and swing arrangements. His music also offers one of the earliest examples of how, arguably, one of the top-tier rhythm sections sounded during jazz's early recording years, with Morton on piano; Johnny St. Cyr on banjo; John Lindsey on bass; and Andrew Hilaire on drums.

Georgia-born Fletcher Henderson, generally regarded as the first great big band leader, and West Virginia–born Don Redman, widely considered the first great arranger in jazz history, symbolize both tradition and innovation in jazz history. Over the years Henderson's big band incorporated a number of improvisational geniuses, including trumpeters Louis Armstrong, Joe Smith, Tommy Ladnier, Rex Stewart, Bobby Stark, Cootie Williams, Red Allen, and Roy Eldridge; trombonists Charlie Green, Benny Morton, Jimmy Harrison, Sandy Williams, J. C. Higginbottham, and Dickie Wells; clarinetists Buster Bailey and Don Pasquall; alto saxophonists Benny Carter, Russell Procope, and Hilton Jefferson; tenor saxophonists Coleman Hawkins, Ben Webster, Lester Young, and Chu Berry; bassists John Kirby and Israel Crosby; and drummers Sid Catlett, Walter Johnson, and Kaiser Marshall. A much larger ensemble than the typical New Orleans jazz band, Henderson's big band usually featured three trumpets, a trombone, three reeds, and a rhythm section (Hennessey 1994; Magee 2005).

Foreshadowing Duke Ellington and Billy Strayhorn's history-making musical experiments, Henderson and Redman worked as a team, developing an innovative arranging style that featured call-and-response between the brass and reed sections and the use of one instrumental choir as a background accompaniment (often employing a riff) for the other. One of Redman's sonic signatures was his ability to write intricate ensemble sections in the style of improvised jazz solos. Needless to say, all of these distinctly "jazz" techniques and devices became trademarks of the 1930s big band arranging style.

Long regarded as the most important composer in jazz history, Edward Kennedy "Duke" Ellington led his jazz orchestra for over fifty years—from 1923 until his death in 1974. He innovatively used his band as a musical laboratory for his new compositions and shaped his writing specifically to showcase the talents of his legendary band members, many of whom remained with him through thick and thin. Ellington's music drew from several different genres, and not all of them distinctly "African American" and, equally important, not all of them musical. Running the musical gamut from spirituals to blues, ragtime to rhythm & blues, European classical to Latin American music, Ellington's experimentalism, eloquence, and extraordinary charisma—both on and off the stage—seemed to single-handedly elevate jazz to an art form on par with other more renowned and respected genres of music. However, Ellington's music also bears the influence of great politicians, painters, playwrights, poets, novelists, dancers, and, most importantly, everyday people (see his recordings *Black, Brown and Beige* [1943], *The Deep South Suite* [1947], *The Liberian Suite* [1947], *Jump for Joy* [1950], *The Shakespearean Suite/Such Sweet Thunder* [1957], *The Queen's Suite* [1959], *Three Suites* [1960], *Afro-Bossa* [1963], *My People: A Century of Negro Progress* [1963], *The Far East Suite* [1967], *The Degas Suite* [1968], *The Latin American Suite* [1970], *The New Orleans Suite* [1970], *The River Suite* [1970], *Togo Brava Suite* [1971], and *Afro-Eurasian Eclipse* [1971]).[8]

Remarking on the occasion of Ellington's centennial in 1999 in the *Boston Globe* acclaimed jazz scholar Bob Blumenthal wrote: "In the century since his birth, there has been no greater composer, American or otherwise, than Edward Kennedy Ellington." Also, in celebrating his centennial in 1999 the prestigious Pulitzer Prize Board honored Ellington with a special posthumous award. His singular sound combined the New Orleans classic jazz style, the gut-bucket blues style, and the "sweet" dance band style with his own ragtime-derived, stride-strewn, and boogie-woogie–based piano style. His was a wholly "urban" and "modern" jazz sound—a history-making sound and corollary style that ultimately placed intensely studying *and* listening to music on the same level.

At the age of seven Ellington began taking piano lessons. Although in his autobiography, *Music is My Mistress* (1973), he revealed that he missed more lessons than he attended, feeling at the time that playing piano was not his shtick. Around age fourteen he started sneaking into Frank Holiday's Poolroom, where he heard poolroom pianists play with both intelligence and emotional exuberance. It was the poolroom pianists, above and beyond all others, who ignited Ellington's intense interest in and, ultimately, life-long love for the piano and its unfathomable improvisational and compositional possibilities. From the summer of 1914 onward Ellington took his piano studies very seriously, and part of his unique course of pianistic studies involved long hours of listening to poolroom pianists, among other popular pianists. The innumerable poolroom and popular pianists he intently listened to included icons such as Doc Perry, Lester Dishman, Louis Brown, Turner Layton, Gertie Wells, Clarence Bowser, Sticky Mack, Blind Johnny, Cliff Jackson, Claude Hopkins, Luckey Roberts, Eubie Blake, Joe Rochester, and Harvey Brooks (see Ellington 1973, 1993).

Around this time Ellington also became aware of ragtime pianists. In his autobiography he reported that he began to obsessively listen to, watch, and try his darnedest to imitate (and even emulate) ragtime pianists. After studying harmony with Henry Lee Grant and music reading with Doc Perry, Ellington encountered stride pianists James P. Johnson and Luckey Roberts. At this point old enough to travel on his own to New York, which was then quickly becoming the jazz capital of the country, Ellington solicited advice from jazz legends Will Marion Cook, Fats Waller, and Sidney Bechet. Even though he was a gifted enough visual artist to receive an art scholarship to the prestigious Pratt Institute in Brooklyn in 1916, the multi-talented Ellington turned once and for all to music and ultimately brought a painterly approach and unique sonic color palette to jazz pianism, jazz composition, and jazz orchestration.

Ellington's experimentalism led him to develop one of the most distinctive orchestras and orchestral sounds in jazz history. He carefully composed with the specific style, skill set, and temperament of his individual band members in mind. Here we see, then, that jazz also reflects an ongoing tension between individual improvised expression and composed collective structure. This is, perhaps, best observed in the constantly shifting emphasis between the spontaneously improvising soloist, on the one hand, and the composed and arranged ensemble music, on the other hand. Hence, classic examples of Ellington compositions which were composed with specific orchestra members in mind include: "Jeep's Blues" for Johnny Hodges, "Concerto for Cootie" for Cootie Williams, and "The Mooche" for Joe "Tricky Sam" Nanton and James "Bubber" Miley.

Extremely "unorthodox" in his compositional methods, Ellington composed the famous jazz standard "It Don't Mean a Thing (If It Ain't Got That
Swing!)" between intermissions while he was performing at Chicago's Lincoln Tavern in 1931. Not only did he compose the song with both Johnny
Hodges and Tricky Sam Nanton in mind, but also as a tribute to his then
terminally ill twenty-seven year old trumpeter Bubber Miley, who was
stricken with tuberculosis and who frequently stated the phrase as a kind of
credo. Regularly lauded in jazz lore, "It Don't Mean a Thing (If It Ain't Got
That Swing!)" has been recognized as the first song to use the word "swing"
in its title, consequently introducing, popularizing, and translating the term—
and the "new" jazz music, aesthetic, and culture it implied—into "mainstream" American colloquial and popular culture, and prophetically presaging the Swing Era by about five years.

Therefore, it was Ellington who opened the Swing Era and paved the way
for both swing pioneers and swing posers, such as: Count Basie, Billie Holiday, Ella Fitzgerald, Benny Carter, Benny Goodman, Charlie Christian,
Frank Sinatra, Mary Lou Williams, Glen Miller, Jay McShann, Jimmy Dorsey, Tommy Dorsey, Roy Eldridge, Harry "Sweets" Edison, Buck Clayton,
Lionel Hampton, Artie Shaw, Coleman Hawkins, Lester Young, Ben Webster, Chu Berry, Illinois Jacquet, Chick Webb, Woody Herman, Harry James,
and Andy Kirk, among others. Here, it is also important to point out that
Ellington recorded and popularized several songs written by his bandsmen
and the man he called his "writing and arranging companion," openly homosexual composer-arranger-pianist Billy Strayhorn. For example, Ellington
recorded and regularly performed "Caravan" and "Perdido," both written by
Juan Tizol, and the Strayhorn compositions—although there still exists the
longstanding tendency to think of them as Ellington compositions—"Take
the 'A' Train," "Lush Life," "Day Dream," "A Flower is a Lovesome
Thing," "Lotus Blossom," "Rain Check," "Johnny Come Lately," "Something to Live For," and "Blood Count," among countless others.[9]

## TALES OF THE JAZZ AGE: ON JAZZ'S INFLUENCE ON THE JAZZ AGE & THE LOST GENERATION

By the 1920s jazz had become such a dominant force in U.S. popular culture
that the prodigious F. Scott Fitzgerald cashed in on the country's fascination
with the newness of the twentieth century by referring to the "roaring twenties" as the "Jazz Age" and publishing a classic work of short stories under
the title *Tales of the Jazz Age* in 1922. Although, it should be quickly observed, the 1920s European American generation—also referred to as the
"Lost Generation" by Gertrude Stein and Ernest Hemingway—was nostalgi-

cally thought of as a highly hedonistic generation by the immediately ensuing generations who had to live through the horrors and unspeakable aftermaths of the Great Depression and World War II. The term the "Lost Generation" generally refers to those who were members of the age groups called to duty in what was then called the "Great War" or, rather, World War I, which lasted from the summer of 1914 until the signing of the Treaty of Versailles in June of 1919. A short list of the distinguished intellectuals and artists of this generation usually includes Ernest Hemingway, F. Scott Fitzgerald, T. S. Eliot, Malcolm Cowley, John Dos Passos, Waldo Peirce, Alan Seeger, and Erich Maria Remarque. It must be noted that not a single African American is included in the "Lost Generation" cohort, even though renowned and well-respected writers, artists and intellectuals, such as W. E. B. Du Bois, Langston Hughes, Zora Neale Hurston, Alain Locke, Aaron Douglass, Charles Johnson, Countee Cullen, Jacob Lawrence, Jessie Fauset, Claude McKay, Nella Larsen, A. Philip Randolph, Jean Toomer, Sterling Brown, Augusta Savage, Richard Bruce Nugent, and Wallace Thurman, were effulgently plying their crafts during the same era.[10]

Even in the early years of the twentieth century it would seem that black popular music, especially jazz, resonated with whites in a way that African American literature, visual art, dance, theater, and scholarship simply did not. The "Lost Generation" was especially interested in jazz—albeit, *merely as music*—because they believed that it coincided with their articulation of an alternative value system they youthfully hoped would challenge "mainstream" America's—that is, their parents and grandparents'—confidence in commercialism and other remnants of bourgeois materialism. They were self-described "non-conformists" who, many believed rather naïvely, registered their resistance to the increasing opulence of American society through artistic expression and the sybaritic and seemingly incessant pursuit of sexual liberation, drinking, smoking, dancing, and the embrace of the other *accoutré mon* of the 1920s version of the "fast life"—all of which continue to be hallowed hallmarks of contemporary European American youths' increasing consumption of rap music and hip hop culture. For the "Lost Generation" jazz became a sonic symbol of rebellion and a clear marker of how much America and the world had changed during and in the wobbling wake of World War I.[11]

Hence, many of the stodgy stereotypes about the "Lost Generation" may be based on blurred truths, but history and reality-based truths nonetheless. Also, and there should be no mistakes made about it, there was much more to the 1920s and 1930s than contemporary audiences have been habitually exposed to in lily-white or, rather, whitewashed Hollywood movies depicting the era (e.g., just peep at *The Jazz Age* [1929], *Some Like It Hot* [1959], *The Great Gatsby* [1974], *The Moderns* [1988], *Mobsters* [1991], and *Chicago* [2002]). Furthermore, there was much more to jazz, the Harlem Renaissance, and the New Negro Movement than the "Lost Generation" and successive generations of black and white intellectuals, artists, and activists have been led to believe or doggedly disbelieve, ignore, or outright erase. As a matter of fact, it was classic blues and classic jazz that audaciously announced that there was such a thing as a "New Negro Movement" afoot in America. Here, then, the term "classic jazz" essentially refers to jazz music from the 1920s and 1930s era, as well as later 1940s and 1950s revivals and recreations, that overlap with New Orleans, Dixieland, and "hot" jazz, and ultimately encompasses jazz music, jazz literature (especially jazz poetry), the jazz aesthetic, and jazz culture between 1900 and 1950.

The 1920s were arguably the most important decade in the history of jazz. For instance, in 1920 jazz was largely unknown to the general public, and those that knew of it often disapproved of and outright despised it. Many considered it "barbaric" "nigger noise" and particularly depraved compared to the "sweet" and "soft" sounds of European and European American classical, dance, brass and march music. By the early 1930s, even though it was still not taken seriously as an art form, jazz had become a permanent and undeniable influence on "mainstream" popular culture and popular music, and it was danced to by a countless number of people who had never heard of Buddy Bolden, King Oliver, Jelly Roll Morton, or Sidney Bechet.

The number of significant developments that occurred during the first decade of jazz recording is nothing short of remarkable. It was during the 1920s that important soloists first emerged in jazz, causing the music to develop beyond its New Orleans brass band roots (where all of the musicians generally played at the same time—i.e., collective composition and collective improvisation) into an ingenious vehicle for creative composing and soloing virtuosos. Musicians began to phrase differently, changing from a staccato to a legato approach and play either slightly ahead of or behind the beat—in other words, not predictably playing each and every note right on the beat.

Arrangers began to infuse dance band arrangements with the "swing" rhythm and phrasing of jazz, leaving room for soloists. In fact, even most of the more commercial orchestras at the time featured a brief trumpet or saxophone solo after the vocalist. Also during this period, the recording industry grew drastically, propelled by the change in the mid-1920s (mostly between 1925 and 1927) from an acoustic to an electric process, which greatly improved the technical and sound quality of recordings. And, perhaps, most importantly, it was in the 1920s that the top African American jazz musicians began to record and tour (Cooke and Horn 2002; Driggs and Lewine 1982; Kirchner 2000).

As with the emergence of the blues as the first major genre of (secular) black popular music, jazz seemed to continue the tradition of controversial beginnings that have marked the origins of every major form of black popular music since the birth of the blues. It was when the "blues craze" was at its height in the early 1920s that jazz began to emerge more forcefully on record and in the public eye. Even though several white jazz musicians and bands (e.g., Paul Whiteman, Phil Napoleon, the Original Dixieland Jazz Band, the New Orleans Rhythm Kings, and the Original Memphis Five) recorded what might be considered "jazz" first, it is extremely important for us to bear in mind something Kathy Ogren emphasized in *The Jazz Revolution: Twenties America & the Meaning of Jazz* (1989):

> However successful such groups [i.e., early white jazz bands] may have been, jazz was obviously a music in which blacks were the primary creators and whites often the imitators. Black and white musicians generally did not play in the same ensembles during jazz's formative years, although performers often heard each other's performances. Equally obvious, jazz was a music of raw emotions—of hard luck and good times, of lust and loneliness. At first, neither jazz nor the places where it was played fell under the control of respectable whites. The morally and culturally subversive aspects of jazz stirred anxieties that fueled a long-running public controversy in the 1920s. (12)[12]

The first thing we might observe is how rap music's origins seem to closely mirror jazz's origins. Who can deny that early rap was a music in which "blacks were the primary creators and whites often the imitators" (e.g., the Beastie Boys, Vanilla Ice, Snow, 3rd Bass, House of Pain, Marky Mark & the Funky Bunch, Kid Rock, Haystak, Bubba Sparxxx, and, of course, Eminem)? Can the *musical segregation* of rap's formative years be denied, where even as late as the late-1970s the "ghetto music" moniker continued to plague new forms of black popular music? Can rap music's "raw emotions" be denied? Or the fact that more than thirty years after its inception it continues to be looked down on by "respectable whites" and, consequent to its "morally and culturally subversive aspects," viewed as the culprit behind a "long-running public controversy" that closed the twentieth century and opened the twenty-first century?

Truth be told, rap music inherited much more than music from jazz. It also inherited aspects of jazz literature (again, especially jazz poetry) and the jazz aesthetic. And, just as early on jazz was seen as a threat to "Lost Generation" white youth's morals and values, in our day rap music serves as the contemporary black popular music culprit which "mature" white America has deemed to be corroding the lily-white lives, views, and values of turn of the twenty-first century white youth. By critically engaging what was called the "jazz controversy" in the 1920s we will be able to see that the war of words surrounding rap music and hip hop culture is not new, but a more or less roguishly recycled version of turn of the twentieth century "mainstream" America's misinterpretation and minstrelesque fantasies about black people, black popular music, and black popular culture.

The pride of place given to jazz in U.S. historical and cultural memory is neither an accident nor a facile custom derived from the previously mentioned "roaring twenties" and "Lost Generation" stereotypes. Jazz and the young radicals of the Harlem Renaissance were central to and deeply influenced by the unprecedented changes occurring in the first quarter of the twentieth century. As with the recurring contemporary references to "Generation X," "Generation Y," and the "Millennial Generation" (or, rather more simply, the "Millennials"), even though African Americans were central to and patently participated in the epoch-making changes that marked the first quarter of the twentieth century, their contributions have been mainly marginalized and rotely reduced to their music, dance, and other artistic contributions.

Hence, references to the "Jazz Age" often disingenuously acknowledge African Americans' increasing influence on American popular music and popular culture while subtly either ignoring or outright erasing their contributions to politics, law, labor, education, science, the military, industrialization, and a host of other areas *beyond* race relations, civil rights, and social justice. That is to say, explorations of African Americans' social and political culture, their intellectual and employment innovations, their history-making militarism, and contributions in the court of law are rarely, if ever, engaged to the depth, with the critical detail, and with the infectious enthusiasm with which black popular music and black popular culture is. In other words, *hip hop's amnesia*, to put it plainly, is not the Hip Hop Generation's alone, but symptomatic of successive generations of U.S. citizens' acute amnesia surrounding all-encompassing and authentic African American history, culture, and struggle.[13]

What is frequently overlooked when and where we come to the "jazz controversy" of the "roaring twenties" is the fact that most members of the "Lost Generation," and, truth be told, most 1920s and 1930s white Americans in general, failed to understand that jazz music in and of itself—its origination and evolution, as well as the sordid circumstances under which it continued to develop and to be performed—served as a sonic symbol of and intensely embodied African Americans' thoughts and feelings about the new and novel social, political, and cultural changes of the 1920s and 1930s. Along with "mainstream" jazz (both jazz music and jazz dance), there are countless polemics, paintings, poems, plays, essays, novels, political treatises, and scholarly volumes that eloquently illustrate how the members of the New Negro Movement and the radicals of the Harlem Renaissance perceived the "Jazz Age." Moreover, most of the intellectual and artistic work produced by African Americans during the "Jazz Age" is grounded in and directly mirrors the evolution of jazz *as music, aesthetics, politics, and culture* during the 1920s and 1930s, which is one of the reasons it is imperative for the Hip Hop Generation to consciously counteract its amnesia not only with regard to jazz but also with respect to the New Negro Movement and its aesthetic arm, the Harlem Renaissance.[14]

Similar to rap music, especially early rap, early jazz was believed to impart negative or "Negro" (read: "backwards," "bad," and "primitive") qualities to its white listeners, especially "extremely impressionable" white youth. Which is also to say, even though there has been and remains a longstanding tendency to view African Americans as an inert and impotent social and political group, when and where we come to African American art, especially black popular music, there is allegedly a kind of *aesthetic alchemy* or *musical magic*, a spooky spellbinding that takes place that induces whites—again, especially "extremely impressionable" white youth—to renounce the "civilized" and "highly cultured" social conventions of white America in favor of the "barbarism" and "backwardness" of black America. As with many "mature" European Americans at the turn of the twenty-first century, during the Jazz Age most "mature" white Americans, according to Ogren, "shared a common perception that jazz had transforming qualities that could last beyond the time of a song and the space of a cabaret act. For many [white] Americans, to argue about jazz was to argue about the nature of change itself" (6–7).

This is all very interesting because many of the asinine anti-jazz arguments from the turn of the twentieth century have been rudely recycled into anti-rap arguments at the turn of the twenty-first century. The same folk who are willing to eagerly acknowledge the power of black popular music often deny the social, political, and intellectual power *and* agency of black people. Again, Ogren offered insights:

> Jazz was indeed a powerful new music, characterized by syncopation, poly- rhythm, improvisation, blue tonalities, and a strong beat. It rose to popularity amidst strident criticism and extravagant praise. Detractors criticized jazz's musical characteristics—unless they dismissed it as noise—and its origins in lower-class black culture. Jazz lovers hailed the same sounds as everything from exciting entertainment to an antidote for repressive industrial society. Americans on all sides of the jazz debate found the music symbolic of funda- mental—and provocative—changes they were experiencing in the maturing post–World War I urban and industrial society. The music represented the end of an earlier era and the transition to a modern one. . . .What is striking about the jazz controversy is that jazz communicated change across vast racial and cultural dividing lines, despite its development from a participatory and dis- tinct black musical culture. (7)[15]

What is it about black popular music that enables it to communicate "across vast racial and cultural dividing lines, despite its development from a partici- patory and distinct black musical culture?" Why is African American music understood to be more or less "universal" but African Americans' calls for civil rights, social justice, and an end to their longstanding economic exploitation perceived as "particular," if not patently parochial? How can African American music be raised up and revered as the epitome of "American" modernism but yet African Americans themselves continue to be thought of in the most primitivist and provincial terms? Finally, how is it possible for so many people to "respect" black popular music but "disrespect" black people by not adequately acknowledging or critically engaging the culture and the frequently hostile conditions under which their most beloved music was and continues to be produced? As Ralph Ellison wrote in his classic 1970 *Time* magazine essay, "What Would America Be Like Without Blacks?," these crucial questions point to what can only be tersely termed white America's "tricky magic" when and where we come to the way black popular music is generally privileged over the human suffering and social misery of flesh and blood black people (see also R. W. Ellison 1995, 2001).

The Lost Generation, and indeed the whites of the Jazz Age in general, marked the beginning of the Jazz Age with the emergence of mainstream radio and the end of World War I. On their interpretation, the era understandably ended with the onset of the Great Depression consequent to the stock market crash on what is generally—and rather ironically I believe—referred to as "Black Tuesday" (i.e., 29 October 1929). Jazz music and dance ushered in an entirely new cultural movement, not only in America but also on the other side of the Atlantic, especially in England, France, and even Nazi Germany, as depicted in films such as *La Revue des Revues* (1927), *La Sirène des Tropiques* (1927), *Picadilly* (1929), *Swing Kids* (1993), and *Bright Young Things* (2003), as well as a wide range of scholarly research.[16] Ironically, even though African Americans undeniably invented jazz it was the above-mentioned white writers and performers who popularized jazz among whites.

Although jazz music and dance was enthusiastically embraced by well-to-do and middle-class whites, in its own unique way "white jazz" (or, rather, "soft" and "sweet" jazz) helped to facilitate the synthesis of African American culture and conventions with European American middle-class culture and conventions. Similar to contemporary white hip hop youth, the Lost Generation, literally, used jazz to rebel against the culture and conventions of previous (white middle-class and upward mobility-obsessed) generations. The white youth rebellion of the Jazz Age went hand-in-hand with fads like bold fashion statements (e.g, the flappers, the "modern girl," the "New Woman," "Oxford Bags," knickerbockers, sailor suits, Homburg hats, and fedoras) and new radio concerts.[17] As jazz's popularity increased, European American elites who preferred European classical music and "soft" dance band sounds sought to expand the listenership of their favored genre, ungraciously hoping that jazz would not become "mainstream."

Despite steep competition with European classical music, as the 1920s wore on jazz increasingly rose in popularity and helped to generate a genuine cultural shift. Hence, the time-honored epithet, the "Jazz Age." Jazz dances, such as the cakewalk, the black bottom, the Charleston, the boogie-woogie, swing dance, and the related lindy hop, exploded in popularity among the Lost Generation. In 1922 large-scale radio broadcasts brought the urbanity and infectious energy of "live" jazz music into suburban homes without white youth ever having stepped a foot into a jazz club—much like early twenty-first century suburban white youth's consumption of "underground" and "live" rap music and concerts via DVDs, streaming videos, and satellite and cable television. These were heady times indeed, and the new radio culture provided both white and black Americans with an *au courant* avenue for exploring each other and communicating with the wider world through broadcasts and concerts from the comfort of their living rooms.[18]

Even though legendary blues and jazz artists, such as Bessie Smith and Louis Armstrong, initially received very little airtime because most stations embraced the "race records" and "musical segregation" mentality of the era and preferred to play the music of white jazz singers and musicians, ultimately black jazz singers and musicians eclipsed the frequently watered-down and "soft" sounds of early white jazz singers and musicians. When jazz took the new radio airwaves by storm and outdistanced everything from European classical music to classic blues, it sonically symbolized African Americans further integration into mainstream American popular music and popular culture, as well as African American popular music's awe-inspiring ability to breakdown racial and sonic barriers *and* breakthrough cultural and social scenes predominately and "traditionally" dominated by whites.[19]

Needless to say, African Americans' sonic civil rights breakthroughs during the Jazz Age foreshadowed their social and political civil rights breakthroughs during the 1950s, 1960s, and 1970s. However, even before the civil rights breakthroughs of the 1950s, 1960s, and 1970s an extremely important genre of jazz developed that symbolized African Americans' continued challenge to the musical segregation mentality and what many African American jazz musicians perceived to be *the ongoing European Americanization or "whitewashing" of jazz*. I am, of course, referring to the first major genre of jazz to emerge in the aftermath of the Great Depression: "bebop" or, rather more simply, "bop."

Bebop is distinguished from big band, swing, and other forms of pre–World War II jazz by its instrumental virtuosity, extended improvisations based on a combination of melody and harmony, and its extremely fast tempos. Already developing in the late 1930s, bebop was in full swing by the early 1940s and so popular by the end of World War II that it seemed to eclipse all previous forms of jazz music. In fact, bebop increasingly became synonymous with what it means to play or listen to "modern" jazz, and every major development in jazz music from 1945 forward is, in one way or another, deeply indebted to bebop and the musical/cultural revolution—that is to say, the Bebop Movement—it inaugurated.

## TO BE, OR NOT . . . TO BOP: THE BEBOP MOVEMENT, BLACK POPULAR MUSIC & BLACK POPULAR CULTURE IN THE 1940S & 1950S

The origins of bebop have been traced back to Coleman Hawkins's immortal 1938 recording of "Body and Soul." Straying, however briefly, from the then commonplace "swing" resolution of the musical themes and playfully jumping to double-time, Hawkins's rendition of the song boldly signaled a new direction in jazz. His version of "Body and Soul" was extremely popular, especially among the younger generation of jazz musicians at the time who felt fenced in by the limitations of the big band and swing dance–oriented jazz popular in the 1930s. These younger and decidedly more austere jazz musicians felt that swing and "hot" jazz had been diluted to a meaningless form of popular and "sweet" dance music—more akin to the "society orchestras" of the 1910s and 1920s—and, consequently, swing and "hot" jazz had come to an artistic cul-de-sac. [20]

The beboppers loathed the "light" jazz of so-called "sweet" dance bands, including the extremely popular bands led by: Guy Lombardo, Les Brown, Harry James, Glen Gray, Paul Whiteman, Tex Beneke, Kay Kyser, Fred Waring, Jan Garber, Les Elgart, and Horace Heidt, among others. Primarily influenced by the preceding generation's most innovative and adventurous "hot" jazz and hard-swinging composers and improvisers—including tenor saxophonists Coleman Hawkins, Lester Young, Ben Webster, Chu Berry, and Don Byas, trumpeters Roy Eldridge, Harry "Sweets" Edison, Buck Clayton, and Oran "Hot Lips" Page, and pianists Art Tatum, Thomas "Fats" Waller, Earl Hines, and Duke Ellington—the bebop generation of jazz musicians culled a new style out of the increasingly predictable swing and "sweet" music of the 1930s. As a matter of fact, two of the leading lights of bebop, Charlie Parker and Dizzy Gillespie, initially began collaborating in the Earl Hines band in the early 1940s. [21]

During the late 1930s and early 1940s, working with pre-bop masters such as Jay McShann, Noble Sissle, Frank Fairfax, Edgar Hayes, Teddy Hill, Cab Calloway, Ella Fitzgerald, and Billy Eckstine, Parker and Gillespie both developed key chordal and harmonic innovations while working with a number of bassists in their respective employers' bands, most notably Gillespie with Milton Hinton during his stay with Calloway, and Parker with Gene Ramey while he was with McShann. Other eminent beboppers include: trumpeters Kenny Dorham, Fats Navarro, Miles Davis, Howard McGhee, and Red Rodney; trombonists J.J. Johnson, Slide Hampton, and Frank Rosolino; alto saxophonists Sonny Stitt, Lou Donaldson, Jackie McLean, Frank Morgan, and Phil Woods; tenor saxophonists Gene Ammons, Dexter Gordon, Wardell Gray, Lucky Thompson, and Teddy Edwards; pianists Thelonious Monk, Bud Powell, Elmo Hope, Herbie Nichols, Tadd Dameron, Duke Jordan, John Lewis, George Wallington, and Lee Tristano; guitarists Charlie Christian, Herb Ellis, Barney Kessel, Kenny Burrell, and Chuck Wayne; bassists Oscar Pettiford, Ray Brown, Percy Heath, and Charles Mingus; drummers Kenny Clarke, Max Roach, Art Blakey, Buddy Rich, and Louie Bellson; and vocalists Billy Eckstine, Ella Fitzgerald, Billie Holiday, and Sarah Vaughn. These artists understood themselves to be advocates of a more advanced (compositionally speaking) and more adventurous (improvisationally speaking) music, and between 1939 and 1945 they knuckled and brawled to aurally eke out and audaciously bring their new sonic conception (i.e., *bebop music*) and socio-political values and vision (i.e., *the Bebop Movement*) into being.[22]

Flying in the face of the apolitical nature of mainstream jazz by the end of the 1930s, beboppers were decidedly political and extremely outspoken with respect to their philosophical, political, and cultural views and values, particularly those that pertained to racism, economic exploitation, and the artistic merits of African American music and African American musicians. For instance, the beboppers regarded themselves as artists and their most beloved music as an art form—in the *par excellence* sense of the term. Although they were not opposed to jazz musicians profiting from their musical endeavors, they mocked jazz musicians who "sold out" or commercially exploited jazz with little or no concern for the artistic merit and ongoing evolution of the music. Furthermore, they had no patience for musicians who criticized bebop and, it should be strongly stressed, attacks from "old school" musicians grounded in classic jazz, big band, and swing were quite common during bebop's golden years, from 1945 to 1955.

Beboppers were especially intolerant of African American musicians who they perceived to be presenting themselves in ways that reinforced Eurocentric stereotypical images of African Americans in order to make themselves more marketable and artistically acceptable to white America. The aforementioned images were obviously anchored in nineteenth century blackface minstrelsy—along with its corollary vaudeville, medicine, and tent shows—and early twentieth century movies, radio, white musicals, and white-produced so-called "black musicals" and "black theater," which continued to misrepresent African Americans in racially demeaning and culturally denigrating ways. The beboppers passionately believed that the perpetuation of anti-black racist images of African Americans by jazz musicians, as well as by

African American musicians in general, impeded their earnest efforts to render bebop, and jazz in general, with long-overdue and much-deserved respect.

In *To Be, or Not . . . to Bop* (1979), Dizzy Gillespie went so far as to criticize jazz's arch-patriarch Louis Armstrong for "grinning in the face of white racism":

> I criticized Louis [Armstrong] for . . . his "plantation image." We didn't appreciate that about Louis Armstrong, and if anybody asked me about a certain public image of him, handkerchief over his head, grinning in the face of white racism, I never hesitated to say I didn't like it. I didn't want the white man to expect me to allow the same things Louis Armstrong did. Hell, I had my own way of "Tomming." Every generation of blacks since slavery has had to develop its own way of Tomming, of accommodating itself to a basically unjust situation. (295–96)[23]

We must keep in mind here that Louis Armstrong was one of the greatest innovators in jazz history, and that Gillespie's "throw-the-baby-out-with-the-bathwater" attitude, although highly commendable from a 1960s and 1970s cultural nationalist point of view, seems to negate the fact that in the 1920s Armstrong was undeniably seen as a great source of racial and cultural pride for African Americans. Admittedly, by the 1940s many of Armstrong's stage mannerisms were quite antiquated, yet and still he soldiered on, conquering new aural and interracial terrain and laying the classic jazz foundation upon which the Bebop Movement was built. Ever perceptive and a serious student of jazz history, eventually Gillespie came to recognize Armstrong's enormous musical *and* political innovations and contributions, openly observing: "Later on, I began to recognize what I had considered Pop's grinning in the face of racism as his absolute refusal to let anything, even anger about racism, steal the joy from his life and erase his fantastic smile. Coming from a younger generation, I misjudged him" (296).

Although it may be purely conjectural, in the 1950s Armstrong offered several scathing critiques of anti-black racism that may be related to the beboppers' criticisms of his "Tomming" and perceived kowtowing to white America at the expense of civil rights for black America. For example, in 1957 Armstrong openly and audaciously called President Eisenhower "two-faced" and "gutless" because of his stammering inaction during the history-making conflict surrounding school desegregation in Little Rock, Arkansas. As a protest Armstrong (1957) unprecedentedly canceled a U.S. State Department–sponsored tour of the Soviet Union, sternly stating: "The way they're treating my people in the South, the government can go to hell!" He went on to say that he could not represent his government abroad when it was in conflict with its own people at home (see also Margolick 2007).

As Frank Kofsky has revealed with respect to 1960s jazz in *Black Nationalism and the Revolution in Music* (1970) and even more fastidiously in *John Coltrane and the Jazz Revolution of the 1960s* (1998), in the 1940s and 1950s Islam made many inroads into the African American community. As a matter of fact, it could be said that the Bebop Movement's origins and evolution mirror a parallel Muslim Movement in African America occurring during the same time span. Islam influenced the beboppers, and "modern" jazz music in general, in a number of ways. To begin, it is important to understand that early on bebop was associated, at least in the minds of many in white America, with Islam.[24]

As Francis Davis (1992) recalled in one of his classic essays from *Atlantic Monthly*, the Bebop Movement had several stereotypes surrounding it, one of them being Islam. According to Davis, bebop "was identified in the public imagination with such stereotypes as berets, goatees, dark glasses, Meerschaum pipes, Islam, and flatted fifths—that day's equivalents of baseball caps turned backward, 'fade' haircuts, sneakers, hood ornaments worn as medallions, Afrocentricism, and DJ mixes" (116). All of which is to say, there is a definite and undeniable link between the Bebop Movement and the Hip Hop Movement, and both movements' connections to Islam, although Davis does not hint at Islam's influence on hip hop, especially the jazz rap phenomenon.[25]

Continuing to explain Islam's influence on the Bebop Movement, in his autobiography Dizzy Gillespie (1979) shrewdly shared: "For social and religious reasons, a large number of modern jazz musicians did begin to turn toward Islam during the forties, a movement completely in line with the idea of freedom of religion" (291). It was clarinetist and saxophonist Rudy Powell who was the first jazz musician Gillespie knew to accept Islam, and countless other musicians soon followed. However, beboppers converted to Islam, Gillespie emphasized again, "for social rather than religious reasons, if you can separate the two." He anecdotally further explained:

> "Man, if you join the Muslim faith, you ain't colored no more, you'll be white," they'd say. "You get a new name and you don't have to be a nigger no more." So everybody started joining, because they considered it a big advantage not to be black during the time of segregation. I thought of joining, but it occurred to me that a lot of them spooks were simply trying to be anything other than a spook at that time. They had no idea of black consciousness; all they were trying to do was escape the stigma of being "colored." (291)

Many 1940s and 1950s jazz musicians, as with many mid–twentieth century African Americans in general, converted to Islam because they believed that it did not discriminate amongst its adherents and that, ultimately, it was less contradictory and less hypocritical in its precepts and practices than "American" Christianity, which they understood to be an utterly racialized and horribly Eurocentric version of Christianity, if an authentic form of Christianity at all (e.g., Malcolm X, Betty Shabazz, Muhammad Ali, H. Rap Brown [a.k.a. Jamil Abdullah Al-Amin], Kareem Abdul-Jabbar, and Mumia Abu-Jamal). In arguably one of the best scholarly sources on jazz and Islam, "Prophetics in the Key of Allah: Towards an Understanding of Islam in Jazz" (2010), Christopher Chase asserted: "Just as African American Protestant Christians have built enormous institutions of influence and power by critiquing the notion of America as a promised land of freedom and opportunity, so have jazz musicians appropriated Islam in different ways to generate their own nascent discourses" (157). Prefiguring the discussion below concerning bebop as the foundation for every major genre of jazz produced from the middle of the twentieth century to the present, here it is important for us to engage the religious or spiritual influence of the Bebop Movement on subsequent generations of jazz musicians.

Drawing from Christopher Small's provocative musicological concept of "musicking," in *Musicking: The Meanings of Performing and Listening* (1998b), where he reexamined old assumptions about the nature and role of music within specific socio-cultural and politico-economic contexts, we may conclude that music is much more than music but also aural representations of socio-cultural and politico-economic realities. That is to say, if we interpret music not as an absolute *sui generis* aural activity, but instead perceive of "musicking" as another type of historical, cultural, social, and political production, it becomes possible to move beyond mere musical formalism and the study of scores toward an interdisciplinary and intersectional examination of wider systems of historical, cultural, social, and political relationships in which music is always already embedded. Looking at the influence of the Muslim Movement in African America in the 1940s and 1950s and its influence on the Bebop Movement, it is important to reemphasize the ways in which black popular music frequently aurally reflects wider systems of historical, cultural, social, and political relationships. Continuing to accent Islam's often-unacknowledged influence on jazz, Chase (2010) observed:

> There is no question that some of the greatest performers in American jazz either converted to—or have been indelibly shaped by—Islam, even if the specific musical impacts of this association are not immediately apparent. For instance, William Huddleston, a noted bebop saxophonist and cohort of Cannonball Adderley, converted in 1950 and took the name Yusef A. Lateef. Drummer Kenny Clarke, known for his work with Miles Davis and the early Modern Jazz Quartet, converted between 1943 and 1946, taking the name Liaquat Ali Salaam. Hard bop drummer Art Blakey, who later formed one of jazz's great "incubators," the Jazz Messengers, converted to Islam after traveling to Africa in the late 1940s to study religion and philosophy. He changed his name to Abdullah Ibn Buhaina. Other prominent Muslim musicians, such

as Ahmad Jamal, McCoy Tyner, and Idris Muhammad, have been important as
well. And even those jazz greats who did not convert—such as John Coltrane—nonetheless bear the stamp of Islam's influence. (158–59)

The influence of Islam on bebop is easily ascertained by the titles of several
bebop classics, such as "A Night in Tunisia" by Dizzy Gillespie, "Dance of
the Infidels" by Bud Powell, "Introspection" by Thelonious Monk, "The
Moors" and "Ballad to the East" by Sahib Shihab, and "Deciphering the
Message" by Hank Mobley. A number of bebop and post-bebop (i.e., post-
bop) jazz musicians, often privately, embraced Islam, among them: Kenny
Clarke (a.k.a. Liaquat Ali Salaam); Art Blakey (a.k.a. Abdullah Ibn Buhai-
na); William Emanuel Huddleston (a.k.a. Yusef Lateef); Frederick Russell
Jones (a.k.a. Ahmad Jamal); McCoy Tyner (a.k.a. Sulaimon Saud); Adolph
Johannes Brand (a.k.a. Abdullah Ibrahim); Jaki Byard (a.k.a. Jamil Bashir);
Walter Bishop (a.k.a. Ibrahim Ibn Ismail); Jackie McLean (a.k.a. Omar Ah-
med Abdul Kariem); Larry Young (a.k.a. Khilad Yasin); Leo Morris (a.k.a.
Idris Muhammad); Robert Patterson (a.k.a. Rashied Ali); Ben Dixon (a.k.a.
Qaadir Almubeen Muhammad); Gigi Gryce (a.k.a. Basheer Qusim); Leonard
Graham (a.k.a. Idrees Sulieman); Rudy McDaniel (a.k.a. Jamaaladeen Tacu-
ma); James Blood Ulmer (a.k.a. Damu Mustafa Abdul Musawir); and Leo
Smith (a.k.a. Ishmael Wadada Leo Smith).

From all of this we may gather that bebop was much more than music to
the musicians who invented and evolved it. In many senses, it served as both
an internal and external critique. On the one hand, it was a critique of those
inside the jazz world who were understood to be exploiting and making a
mockery of jazz music. On the other hand, it was a critique of those social
and political forces outside of the jazz world that denied African Americans
their human, civil, and voting rights. Hence, the Bebop Movement was just
as much a socio-political movement as it was a musical movement.

With respect to bebop as a musical movement, the beboppers were interested in developing jazz, not merely making money by playing "sweet,"
"swinging," or "background" dance music for audiences who did not really
listen to or seem to authentically appreciate the music. In order to develop
jazz they intensely studied advanced harmonies, complex syncopation, altered chords, and chord substitutions. Anyone who would be a bebopper
embraced and unapologetically advanced these techniques in a fluid, free-
wheeling, intricate, and often esoteric manner, controversially bringing the
music back to the musicians and, perhaps even more importantly, bringing
the music back to its roots as a mouthpiece for black America—all of this,
even though the Bebop Movement featured many prominent (and most could
be characterized as "progressive") white beboppers, such as Phil Woods, Red
Rodney, George Wallington, Lee Tristano, Herb Ellis, Barney Kessel, Buddy
Rich, and Louie Bellson (Gerard 1998; Porter 2002; Sudhalter 1999).

Here we have come back to Ogren's wisdom-filled words above when she commented on the origins and early evolution of jazz. We might paraphrase her words to make them more specific to the origins and evolution of bebop by conceding that bebop "was obviously a music in which blacks were the primary creators and whites often the imitators." This assertion does not in anyway deny the European American innovators of the bebop idiom, but is emphasized only to remind my readers that it was African Americans who invented and initially evolved the idiom in which white beboppers based their styles on and to which they offered their invaluable innovations.

A similar situation is currently afoot within the world of hip hop, where more and more white rappers are scoring hit songs and making serious contributions to rap music. The general thought here is that it is extremely important to acknowledge the origins and early evolution of whatever form of black popular music we are listening to or scrutinizing in a scholarly fashion. This is extremely important because so often in American history and contemporary society African Americans' innovations and contributions are either erased or appropriated *and* "whitewashed," and ultimately made to appear to be European American innovations and contributions.

With regard to the origins and early evolution of bebop, it is not in any way a coincidence that bebop was birthed in Harlem, and at the famed Minton's Playhouse, Monroe's Uptown House, and Small's Paradise, to be more historically and aesthetically accurate.[26] Minton's, Monroe's, and Small's were each, in essence, ultimately efforts to recreate and translate the juke joints of the agricultural and rural South into the increasingly industrial and urban North. In other words, bebop sonically symbolizes not only 1940s and 1950s African American quests to reclaim and resuscitate "real" jazz, but also—and especially considering its requisite *accoutré mon* of jive talk, goatee beards, berets, zoot suits, and heroin—an attempt to sonically subvert and, thereby, transgress and transcend the *extra-communal* (e.g., racism, capitalism, and commercialism) and *intra-communal* (e.g., conservatism, classism, and colorism) impositions of race, space, place, and time. Helping to drive this point home, in arguably one of the finest cultural critiques of bebop ever published, "Double V, Double-Time: Bebop's Politics of Style" (1995), Eric Lott asserted:

All of this does merit the spin of subculture theory: zoot, lip, smack, and double-time became the stylistic answer to social contradictions (having mainly to do with generational difference and migration) experienced by the makers and followers of bop. Further, we need to restore the political edge to a music that has been so absorbed into the contemporary jazz language that it seems as safe as much of the current scene—the spate of jazz reissues, the deluge of "standards" records, Bud Powell on CD—certainly an unfortunate historical irony. For in the mid-forties, [Charlie] Parker, Dizzy Gillespie, Thelonious Monk and the rest were tearing it up with such speed and irreverence—sometimes so acrobatic as to feel unfinished, often world-historical—that pre-war life seemed like a long, long time ago. In hindsight there may appear to be other more radical breaks with jazz's past, but to an America fed on Bing [Crosby] and "Marezy Doats" bebop was the war come home. Listen to the fury as Parker roars into "Bird Gets the Worm," or to the way he and Fats Navarro suddenly transpose the head of "Move" to minor on *One Night in Birdland* [1950], or even to Monk's derangement of "April in Paris," and it's clear why white music writers trying to preserve a sense of professional balance resorted to the plum tones of "this is the sort of bad taste and ill-advised fanaticism that has thrown innumerable impressionable young musicians out of stride." Brilliantly outside, bebop was intimately if indirectly related to the militancy of its moment. Militancy and music were undergirded by the same social facts; the music attempted to resolve at the level of style what the militancy combated in the streets. If bebop didn't offer a call to arms, as one writer has said in another context, it at least acknowledged that the call had been made. (245–47; see also DeVeaux 1997; E. Lott 1988; Owens 1995; Porter 2002)

I could not agree more with Lott and, in addition, his contention that post–World War II African American "[m]ilitancy and music were undergirded by the same social facts" is one of the recurring themes of this "remix" and, truth be told, each and every word of this book. Even after jazz's whitewashing and commercialization in the 1930s, progressive African American jazz musicians sought to re-politicize and re-radicalize the music, turning it away from the "sweet," "sedate," and "soft" sounds that big band and swing had been boiled down to in the 1930s. Beboppers, as with contemporary conscious rappers and other progressive hip hoppers, summoned black and other forward-thinking folk through searing songs—"hot" and hard swinging jazz as opposed to "cool" and "soft" swinging jazz—so innovative in their aural avant-gardism, social critique, and political commentary that seven decades later they continue to be shrouded in cultural and musical mystery and, for many of us, *majesty.*

All of this means, then, that jazz in general, and bebop in particular, provides the Hip Hop Generation with not simply viable musical models, but also other aesthetic archetypes, cultural codes, and political paradigms to re-politicize and re-radicalize rap music and the whole of hip hop culture. The Hip Hop Generation is not the first generation to suffer from the hyper-commercialization and corporate colonization of their popular music and popular culture. To counteract *hip hop's amnesia* hip hoppers need to know about bebop *as music, aesthetics, politics, and culture,* and how the jazz youth of the 1940s and 1950s decisively rescued and reclaimed jazz and, consequently, saved it from the sudden death that seems to be an integral part of commercialization in America.

It has been said that Minton's, Monroe's, and Small's served as sonic laboratories of sorts, where the pioneers of bebop, luminaries such as Charlie Parker, Dizzy Gillespie, Thelonious Monk, Don Byas, and Charlie Christian, came together and conceived a new and, at the time, avant-garde form of jazz that challenged what they understood to be the dilution and hyper-commercialization of jazz. Ironically, it could be said that bebop is, partially, the offspring of the musical segregation that privileged frequently mediocre white jazz musicians over bona fide black jazz geniuses. Experiencing an intense alienation (and anti-black racism, even if a form of "soft," "cultural," or merely "musical" racism) within the 1930s jazz world—once again, a world created by African Americans but sonically colonized by European Americans—bebop *as music, aesthetics, politics, and culture* contributed to the *élan* and modernization of post–World War II juke joint culture not only in the urban North, but in the rural South as well.

While it is certainly debatable as to whether bebop was directly inspired by African Americans' wartime and post–World War II experiences or simply appropriated as the soundtrack of a restive, creative, and self-assertive group of black youth, what we can say with certainty is that bebop was intentionally developed to go above and beyond the realm of what was understood to be a stale "jazz" marketplace by the early 1940s. Correspondingly, despite the anti-black racist implications of the American Federation of Musicians' recording ban in 1942 (which lasted until 1944), which made it even more difficult for black musicians in the already extremely sonically segregated 1940s music industry, the ban unintentionally provided the fertile ground for bebop to be birthed (DeVeaux 1988; Kofsky 2008; Miller 2010). Tellingly, in the 1940s when the white jazz world of highbrow jazz magazines such as *Metronome, Down Beat, Esquire's Jazz Book, Jazz Journal, Jazz Forum*, and *Jazz Quarterly* were fervently debating the merits of New Orleans jazz and swing, many of the young black jazz musicians unceremoniously and unpretentiously returned to jazz's roots in the African American community, specifically in black clubs predominantly frequented by working-class and poor black folk.

Similar to contemporary rap music and hip hop culture, early on bebop music and culture was associated with violence, specifically the Harlem riot of 1943. Although—as with the relationship between Tupac Shakur's "anti-police" raps on *2Pacalypse Now* (1991) and Ronald Ray Howard's fatal shooting of Texas State Trooper Bill Davidson, or gangsta rap and the Los Angeles riots as a result of the Rodney King verdict, both of which took place in April of 1992—the real relationship between bebop and the Harlem riot of 1943 is circumstantial at best, as both arguably represent re-articulations of African American economic and political interests within the world of America's ever-homogenizing mass market and criminal justice system culture. In probably the definitive scholarly source on the subject, *The Har-*

*lem Riot of 1943* (1977), Domenic Capeci argues that the 1943 riot in Harlem was the first clear-cut example of what he termed a "commodity riot"—which is to say, a riot where the main focus of the violence is on the destruction of property—in U.S. history.

The Harlem riot of 1943, unlike the Harlem riot of 1935 or the Detroit riot of 1943, was sparked by a white policeman intentionally striking an African American woman in the face as she was being arrested for "disturbing the peace" at the Braddock Hotel in Harlem. At that point an African American soldier in the U.S. Army, Robert Bandy, attempted to stop the police officer from repeatedly hitting the woman. The situation quickly escalated, and the policeman ultimately shot Bandy in the shoulder. Bandy was taken to the hospital, but word of the shooting spread fast. Soon Bandy's shot in the shoulder, growing with each retelling as the news made its way through the Harlem grapevine, became a fatal shot in the heart. The crowd that gathered, as can be imagined based on the "grapevine" (mis)information they had heard, was absolutely outraged.[27]

The rioters targeted policemen and mainly white-owned businesses over a three-day period (1–3 August 1943), which left six people dead, five hundred injured, and more than five hundred behind bars with riot-related charges. Capeci's research suggests that the act of looting—which has been integral to acts of urban unrest from the 1965 Watts rebellion and the 1967 Newark rebellion to the 1968 riots in the aftermath of Martin Luther King's assassination and the 1977 New York City "blackout" riots—is, in fact, part and parcel of working-class and poor people's efforts to redefine property rights. Consequently, when considering any of the "riots" that have taken place since the emergence of rap music and hip hop culture (e.g., the Miami riot of 1980, the Crown Heights riot of 1991, the Los Angeles riots of 1992, or even the widespread "looting" that took place in the wake of Hurricane Katrina in 2005) it is extremely important to bear Capeci's caveat in mind.[28]

Whether serving as an "official" or "unofficial" soundtrack for the Harlem riot of 1943, in many ways bebop could be characterized as a kind of "musical mayhem" or "musical looting" that not only provided the foundation for what was called "free" jazz or "avant-garde" jazz in the 1960s, but bebop also provided a forum where increasingly marginalized young black jazz musicians could participate in a collective effort to deconstruct and reconstruct the property rights of jazz *as music, aesthetics, politics, and culture.*[29] Initially bebop exploded on the American music scene as a conscious effort on the part of black youth to *re-politicize* and *re-radicalize* jazz, indeed black popular music in general, and rescue and reclaim it from the grips of an increasingly lily-white, commercial, indifferent, and exploiting music marketplace. The complex melodic, harmonic, and rhythmic structures of bebop, with its intricate chord inversions and adventurous improvisations, offered up an aural terrain that privileged African American autonomy, originality, individuality, and community over the growing predictability and placidness of the immediate post–World War II American music marketplace (e.g., "old school" big bands, "sweet" jazz bands, and "soft" swing bands). In the face of the polite predictability that big band and swing had been reduced to by the 1940s, bebop gave jazz a sense of surprise again, and the new music seemed to be as unusual and unpredictable as the black jazz youth who were its primary pioneers and popularizers.

One of the main differences between bebop and swing is that the soloists engage in chordal (rather than melodic) improvisation, often discarding the melody altogether after the first chorus and using the chords as the basis for the solo. Bebop bands were essentially combos (usually five to seven musicians), in marked contrast to the popular big bands, swing bands, and "sweet" bands of the 1930s. Moving away from melodic improvisation, bebop soloists were free to improvise as long and as adventurously as possible, of course, as long as the overall improvisation fit within the chord structure.

As to be imagined, as bebop virtuosos moved further and further away from the melody in their often searing solos many listeners began to question the music, often irksomely asking, "Where's the melody?" Along with its innovations in jazz improvisation, bebop was frequently played very fast. As a consequence, it divorced itself not only from big bands, "sweet" bands, and swing, but also from 1940s popular music and the then in vogue dance scene. Ironically, it helped to raise jazz to the realm of modern "art music," but also cut deeply and almost decisively into what might have been its "commercial" and more "mainstream" success.

It would seem that one of the quintessential quirks of jazz history is that from about 1950 forward the once extremely radical compositional and improvisational bebop style, in many ways, became the foundation for all of the "modern" jazz innovations that followed in its wake and, even more incongruously, now bebop is generally thought of as "old school" or "mainstream" jazz music. Although often overlooked, as with many of the more historically rooted, culturally grounded, and politically charged aspects of black popular music, it can now be said without hyperbole and high-sounding words that bebop is the bedrock upon which all jazz created in the second half of the twentieth century and up to the present moment has been, whether consciously or unconsciously, based. Which is also to say, innovative jazz genres— from "mainstream" jazz and "cool" jazz to "hard bop" jazz and "bossa nova" jazz, from "modal" jazz and "free" jazz to "soul" jazz and "groove" jazz, from "fusion" jazz and "Afro-Brazilian" jazz to "Afro-Cuban" jazz and "post-bop" jazz—all, in one way or another, reach back to their roots in bebop—*as music, aesthetics, politics, and culture.*[30]

Bebop *as music, aesthetics, politics, and culture* served as the soundtrack for African American youths' popular culture *and* political culture in the 1940s and 1950s. It was part aesthetics and part politics, even though its critique of American society and the racial status quo did not always and in every way resemble the 1920s and 1930s "New Negro" and classic jazz crowd's anti-racist activism and aesthetics. Similar to rap music and hip hop culture in the aftermath of the Crown Heights riot of 1991 and the Los Angeles riots of 1992, many meanings were conjectured about bebop and black youth culture in light of the Harlem and Detroit riots of 1943 and, to a certain extent, the Zoot Suit riots in Los Angeles, also in 1943.[31] In many ways the Bebop Movement represented a complex historical, cultural, social, and political moment in which the militancy that was widespread throughout 1940s and 1950s African American life ingeniously manifested itself in youthful and flamboyant ways, artistic innovations and cultural advances, frequently unconventional behavior and outright criminal resistance, and myriad other new and novel challenges to both musical *and* social segregation in mid–twentieth century America. However, within the world of the African American community the Bebop Movement also accentuated a seemingly ever-widening and wildly yawning chasm between the sensibilities and social mores of the "old guard" and more politically conservative black bourgeoisie and the more black masses–identified black youth, their popular music, and their popular culture.

The 1940s and 1950s chasm between the conservatism of the black bourgeoisie–identified elder leadership and the radicalism of the black masses–identified youth obviously set into motion a political pattern in African American life and culture that has been handed down to the Hip Hop Generation. As is well-known, during the Civil Rights Movement the moderatism of the elder leadership ultimately clashed with the militancy of the youth, which lead the younger activists to defiantly initiate both the Sit-In Movement in 1960 and the Freedom Rider Movement in 1961.[32] The militancy of the Sit-In Movement and Freedom Rider Movement, as well as the increasing conservatism of the elder leadership and the increasing radicalism of the youth activists during the Civil Rights Movement, in time led to the more militant Black Power Movement.[33] As I discussed in *Hip Hop's Inheritance*, the concrete connections between the Black Power Movement and the Hip Hop Movement are both political and aesthetic. Moreover, I would go so far to say that rap music, hip hop culture, and the Hip Hop Movement are actually incomprehensible without some sense of the music, paintings, poetry, plays, novels, and other aesthetic innovations of the Black Arts Movement (i.e., the artistic arm of the Black Power Movement).[34]

All of this is to say, in order to really and truly understand rap and neo-soul as the soundtrack of the Hip Hop Movement—as well as rhythm & blues as the soundtrack of the Civil Rights Movement or, even more, soul music as the soundtrack of the Black Power Movement—we need to understand bebop *as music, aesthetics, politics, and culture*—especially notice here that there is an even stronger stress on "bebop as politics" or, rather, the "politics of bebop." My thinking here has been indelibly influenced by Ralph Ellison's classic and often-quoted riddle concerning the politics of black popular culture. Although Ellison was referring to the then recent spate of riots in his 1943 editorial comments in the *Negro Digest* (which was resurrected and renamed *The Black World* in 1970), his weighted words continue to ring true within the contemporary world of rap music and hip hop culture: "Much in Negro life remains a mystery; perhaps the zoot suit conceals profound political meaning; perhaps the symmetrical frenzy of the lindy-hop conceals clues to great potential power—if only Negro leaders would solve this riddle" (R. W. Ellison 1943, 300–1; see also R. W. Ellison 2001).

In other words, instead of incessantly denouncing and distancing themselves from each and every aspect of rap music and hip hop culture, current African American leaders—many of whom were the militant youths who participated in the Civil Rights Movement, Black Power Movement, and Black Arts Movement—ought to critically engage contemporary black popular music and black popular culture from an African American (as opposed to a Eurocentric or European American middle-class) perspective that is sensitive to the social and political implications of black popular music and black popular culture. Part of what makes Ellison's riddle so salient in the context of rap music and hip hop culture is that he eloquently articulates an issue that continues to plague us concerning black youth culture and elite black leadership. In so many words, he suggested that 1940s "mainstream," moderate, and middle-class black leadership was either inept or outright unwilling to understand or adequately address the increasing stratification within the African American community and the grim reality that this distance would eventually obstruct comprehensive communal empowerment as African American youth would increasingly be socially and politically marginalized within both European American society *and* the African American community.

After the recording ban between 1942 and 1944 came to an end, bebop was recorded and introduced to audiences outside of the African American community and, equally important, outside of New York City. It seemed to burst onto the scene in a no-holds-barred way, taking no prisoners, and shunning anything and everything about classic jazz, big band, sweet bands, dance bands, and swing not deemed in the best interest of African Americans and the development of jazz as an art form, not merely background music and erstwhile entertainment for wealthy whites. No longer existing only in smoky jazz clubs and recreated juke joints uptown in Harlem, consequent to its recording and wide distribution bebop began to be commodified and, ultimately, codified.

As to be imagined, the commodification and codification of bebop meant that in the minds of the emerging post–World War II middle-class white youth, most notably the so-called "Beat Generation," bebop was viewed as a new and novel medium through which they could tap into their deeper sensu-al, sexual, and spiritual pretensions and passions. As with the Lost Genera-tion of the Jazz Age, the Beat Generation of *the Bebop Age* faithfully fol-lowed early twentieth century suburban white youths' tendency to regard black popular music and black popular culture as a conduit for them to connect, *not* with authentic African American history, culture, and struggle, but with their own brand of new bohemian hedonism. As is well-known, Norman Mailer famously captured and critiqued this phenomenon, specifi-cally in reference to jazz culture, in his classic book *The White Negro: Superficial Reflections on the Hipster* (1957).

Bebop's popularity and subsequent move from Harlem's club scene to Manhattan's 52nd Street club scene eventually problematized and seriously troubled the already ragged—because of the whitewashing of big band and swing—relationship between "modern" jazz and the working-class and poor black communities where it originated and initially evolved. In *Gigs: Jazz and the Cabaret Laws in New York City* (2005), Paul Chevigny commented on the distinctly *African American* communal and collective nature of "ur-ban" juke joint jazz, its origins, and intriguing evolution:

> Harlem was showing the perennial elements of a strong jazz environment. The clubs not only supported the musicians, but gave them places to hone their skills and learn from one another. The complexity of learning to improvise, to make use of new rhythmic patterns and at the same time play with others, made for a difficult art that, to a large extent, had to be shaped in a group. Hours of playing together made good musicians able to react to nuances of style from others. They communicated excitement to one another, and to an audience, who then communicated a little of it back to them. The relation between the audience and the orchestras at the huge Savoy Ballroom in Har-lem was legendary. Performance could create a tremendous sense of common emotional understanding and release. (24–25)

The "common emotional understanding and release" that bebop radically registered began to seriously suffer by the early 1950s as its predominant patronage shifted from Harlem hipsters and hustlers to Greenwich Village bohemians and proto-hippies. In many ways building on the interracial alli-ances of the Harlem Renaissance, to be discussed in the subsequent "remix," and prefiguring the interracial alliances of the Civil Rights Movement and the Black Power Movement (e.g., the Congress of Racial Equality, the Stu-dent Non-Violent Coordinating Committee, Students for a Democratic Soci-ety, the Weather Underground Organization, and the Symbionese Liberation Army), in the 1940s and 1950s bebop *as music, aesthetics, politics, and culture* came to boldly blur the "color-line"—as Du Bois declared in *The Souls of Black Folk*—between black radical youth and white radical youth. However, truth be told, bebop paid a heavy price for crossing the "color-line," ultimately losing touch with the cultural nuances and perspicacity of the Harlem juke joint jazz scene that selflessly served as its incubator, early goad, and vigilant guide. Undoubtedly, the most notable manifestation of the Bebop Movement crossing the "color-line" and inspiring white radical youth in the 1940s and 1950s is what is often referred to as the "Beat Generation."

## ON "WHITE NEGROES" & "WIGGERS": FROM THE BEAT GENERATION & THE BEBOP MOVEMENT TO THE MILLENIAL GENERATION & THE HIP HOP MOVEMENT

Bebop's impact and influence went well beyond the world of music. For instance, even though what came to be called the "bebop style" in the fashion world was reduced to Dizzy Gillespie's trademark beret and goatee beard during the 1940s, its influence on American culture was actually much more profound. Like rap music and hip hop culture, in the "mainstream" American mindset bebop was associated with non-conformity (to both white *and* black bourgeois views and values), alcoholism, drug addiction, and promiscuity, among other ills. As with the Lost Generation of the 1920s, in the mid-1940s a group of mostly middle-class, young, white dissidents inaugurated a move-ment that heavily drew from jazz and black popular culture in their efforts to rebel against the established order. Greatly based on bebop *as music, aesthet-ics, politics, and culture*, the Beat Generation was more or less the Lost Generation of the post–World War II period. Elements central to the Beat Movement included a rejection of materialism, experimentation with drugs and alternative forms of sexuality, an interest in Eastern and "non-tradition-al" religions, and the idealization of exuberant and uncensored means of expression and modes of being.[35]

The most famous works of the Beat Movement are undoubtedly Allen Ginsberg's *Howl* (1956), Jack Kerouac's *On the Road* (1957), and William S. Burroughs's *Naked Lunch* (1959) (see also Gewirtz 2007; Raskin 2004; Skerl and Lydenberg 1991). Because of the homosexual, bisexual, and other anti-establishment elements in *Howl* and *Naked Lunch* both were the focus of extensive obscenity trials that, in the long run, significantly aided in liberaliz-ing the publishing industry in the United States. As a consequence of the obscenity trials and other "eccentric" behavior, members of the Beat Genera-tion gained reputations as new bohemian hedonists who championed non-conformity (actually *anti-conformity*) and, faithfully following the Bebop Movement, greatly valued spontaneous creativity. According to Ann Char-ters in *The Portable Beat Reader* (2003), the word "beat" was primarily in use after World War II by bebop and other jazz musicians, as well as African American hipsters and hustlers, who utilized it as a slang term to mean "down and out" or "poor and exhausted" (xvii; see also A. Charters 1986). Moreover, in his jazz literature classic, *Really the Blues* (1990), jazz clarinetist, saxophonist, and raconteur Mezz Mezzrow creatively combined "beat" with other words, to coin now common phrases such as "deadbeat" (169).

It was Jack Kerouac who gave the Beat Generation its moniker, introducing the phrase in 1948 to characterize what he understood to be an emerging underground, avant-garde, and anti-conformist white youth movement in New York City. Initially he explained that colloquially "beat" could mean "tired" or "beat down," but eventually Kerouac extended and expanded the meaning to include the more positive connotations "upbeat," "beatific," and, again closely following the Bebop Movement, the musical association of being "on the beat." The influence of the Bebop Movement, especially Charlie Parker, on the Beat Generation can sadly be seen in the beats' excessive use of a number of different drugs, including alcohol, marijuana, Benzedrine, morphine, and, later, psychedelic drugs, such as peyote, yagé (i.e., "ayahuasca" or "ayawaska"), and LSD. Reportedly, the beats' usage was "experimental," in the sense that initially they did not have the foggiest idea of the effects (or side effects) of most of these drugs. It has been said, rather apologetically, that they were initially inspired by "intellectual" interests, as well as bohemian hedonistic interests.

As with the thousands of young jazz musicians who heard that it was Charlie Parker's heroin use that made him play with such fire and fury and, consequently, followed his example by abusing drugs (e.g., Miles Davis, Sonny Rollins, John Coltrane, Jackie McLean, Dexter Gordon, Gene Ammons, Hampton Hawes, Chet Baker, Stan Getz, Art Pepper, and Joe Pass, among many others), members of the Beat Generation bought into similar claims that drugs could enhance their insight, creativity, and productivity.[36] Just as recreational drug use was an enormous influence on the social and cultural events of the time, "experimental" and "alternative" forms of sexuality also factored into the social and cultural fabric of the post–World War II period. As is well known, several of the core members of the Beat Generation were either homosexual or bisexual, and some of them quite openly so, including two of the most prominent writers of the movement, Ginsberg and Burroughs. As a matter of fact, many of the beats initially met in homosexual haunts and often engaged in what has repeatedly been described as "alternative sexual practices," which were later alluded to in Ginsberg's poem *Howl* and Burroughs's novel *Naked Lunch*. Although *Naked Lunch* obviously focuses on drug abuse, its homosexual content and frequently graphic descriptions of "alternative sexual practices" marked it for censor in the conservative, post-McCarthyism mindset of late 1950s and early 1960s America.[37]

It is extremely interesting that among the Beat Generation's major influences the Bebop Movement is often curiously omitted. Beat scholars regularly rattle off major Beat Generation influences, including: Romanticism (e.g.,

Percy Shelley, William Blake, and John Keats); classic European American writers (e.g., Henry David Thoreau, Ralph Waldo Emerson, Herman Melville, Edgar Allan Poe, Emily Dickinson, and Walt Whitman); French Surrealism (e.g., André Breton, Antonin Artaud, Marcel Duchamp, Guillaume Apollinaire, Arthur Rimbaud, and Charles Baudelaire); and American modernist poets (e.g., Ezra Pound, William Carlos Williams, Hilda Doolittle, and Gertrude Stein). As with early 1920s jazz *as music, aesthetics, politics, and culture* and its unfathomable impact on the Lost Generation, the Bebop Movement's influence on the Beat Generation is most often given short shrift, if it is acknowledged at all. This is extremely unfortunate because ignoring the Bebop Movement's influence on the Beat Generation, however unwittingly, contributes to America's ongoing cultural amnesia surrounding African America's influence on and concrete contributions to U.S. history, culture, society, politics, and aesthetics.

In terms of both the Lost Generation of the 1920s and 1930s and the Beat Generation of the 1940s and 1950s, because they are most often disassociated from the African American *youth militancy, youth movements, and youth musics* that initially inspired them, they are often erroneously believed to have jumpstarted the Harlem Renaissance and the Bebop Movement, respectively, when, truth be told, it was actually and much more accurately the other way around. Hence, faithfully following W. E. B. Du Bois in *The Gift of Black Folk* (1924), here I openly and audaciously challenge the longstanding tendency in mainstream America to view anything viable and deemed valuable offered up by African Americans as somehow derivative of European American (mostly middle-class) thought and culture. The Lost Generation, the Beat Generation, the authentic white anti-racists of the Civil Rights Movement, Students for a Democratic Society, the Weather Underground Organization, the progressive brothers and sisters of the Hippie Movement, and, of course, the white youth of the Hip Hop Generation speak volumes about the ways in which white youths have been regularly inspired by and derived their popular cultures and popular movements from *black youths' militancy, black youths' movements, and black youths' music*, as well as African American social and political movements in general. Here, once again, we are haunted by Norman Mailer's *The White Negro: Superficial Reflections on the Hipster* (1957), which seems to patently prefigure contemporary discourse on whites who emulate black speaking styles, black fashion styles, and other aspects of black popular culture. In other words, although often overlooked, there is a strange symmetry between Norman Mailer's *The White Negro* and Bakari Kitwana's "wiggers" in his *Why White Kids Love Hip Hop: Wangstas, Wiggers, Wannabes, and the New Reality of Race in America* (2005).

Borrowing from a concept that Cornel West ingeniously came up with in *Race Matters* (1993), although applying it in a completely different context, we might call this the *African Americanization* of white youth militancy, movements, and music (88). Indeed, there is something to be said about the initial emergence and popularity of classic jazz and the Harlem Renaissance in the aftermath of World War I and its direct influence on the emergence of the Lost Generation, the "Jazz Age," and the "roaring twenties." Obviously, jazz's initial explosion onto the American musical and cultural scene touched a national nerve, just as bebop and hard bop would in the 1940s and 1950s, rhythm & blues and soul would in the 1960s and 1970s, and rap and neo-soul would in the 1980s, 1990s, and early 2000s.

Closely mirroring the emergence of classic jazz and the "jazz controversy" in the aftermath of World War I in the 1920s, the emergence of bebop during and, especially, in the wake of World War II suggests that at the very moment that many Americans were valiantly fighting and dying for freedom abroad, there were parallel struggles taking place at home where many were valiantly fighting and dying for freedom—*domestic freedom, social freedom, political freedom, cultural freedom, sexual freedom,* and, indeed, *artistic freedom.* In an almost cyclical fashion, the Beat Generation seems to symbolize white youth's, once again and however surreptitiously, turning to *black youths' militancy, black youths' movements, and black youths' music,* in the wake of yet another World War. Where the Lost Generation turned to the classic jazz music and culture of the 1920s, the Beat Generation turned to the colorful bebop music, culture, and language of the 1940s, which they correctly understood to be a rebellion of sorts against the sterilities and stoicism pervading 1940s and 1950s American society, including the elite and "old school" world of 1940s and 1950s African American society.

When and where we acknowledge bebop's influence (again, *as music, aesthetics, politics, and culture*) on the emergence of the Beat Generation, then—and, perhaps, only then—a whole new conception and comprehension of the Beat Generation is offered up. If, after it is all said and done, we concede that the Beat Generation was to a certain extent inspired by the Bebop Movement or, at the least, there were high levels of mutual influence and acknowledgment flowing between these movements, then we must also acknowledge the Bebop Movement's influence on "mainstream" 1960s and 1970s counterculture: from the Dizzy Gillespie-inspired beret and goatee beard-sporting "beatniks" who emotionally recited quasi-political poetry and uncontrollably played bongos, to the much-misunderstood Hippie Movement that directly grew out of the Beat (and, later, the media-created "Beatnik") Movement. For instance, in Lisa Phillips's *Beat Culture and the New America, 1950–1965* (1995), the Beat Movement is given credit for inspiring several significant social, political, cultural, and even musical movements in the 1960s and 1970s: spiritual liberation; sexual liberation; homosexual liberation; liberation from censorship; the decriminalization of marijuana and other drugs; the Environmental Movement; the Anti-War Movement; and the evolution of rhythm & blues into rock & roll via the influence of Beat culture–inspired musicians, most notably the Beatles and Bob Dylan (19, 184–85; see also Sterritt 2004).

Any remaining doubts concerning the Bebop Movement's influence on the Beat Generation, or the fundamental meaning and mission of the Beat Generation, can be quickly and easily laid to rest by turning to Jack Kerouac's classic 1957 "About the Beat Generation" essay (which was retitled and republished in *Esquire* magazine as "Aftermath: The Philosophy of the Beat Generation" in 1958), where he beautifully and revealingly wrote:

> The Beat Generation, that was a vision that we had, John Clellon Holmes and I, and Allen Ginsberg in an even wilder way, in the late Forties, of a generation of crazy, illuminated hipsters suddenly rising and roaming America, serious, curious, bumming and hitchhiking everywhere, ragged, beatific, beautiful in an ugly graceful new way—a vision gleaned from the way we had heard the word "beat" spoken on street corners on Times Square and in the Village, in other cities in the downtown-city-night of postwar America—*beat*, meaning down and out but full of intense conviction—We'd even heard old 1910 Daddy Hipsters of the streets speak the word that way, with a melancholy sneer— It never meant juvenile delinquents, it meant characters of a special spirituality who didn't gang up but were solitary Bartlebies staring out the dead wall window of our civilization—the subterranean heroes who'd finally turned from the "freedom" machine of the West and were taking drugs, digging bop, having flashes of insight, experiencing the "derangement of the senses," talking strange, being poor and glad, prophesying a new style for American culture, a new style (we thought) completely free from European influences (unlike the Lost Generation), *a new incantation*—The same thing was almost going on in the postwar France of Sartre and Genet and what's more we knew about it—But as to the actual existence of a Beat Generation, chances are it was really just an idea in our minds—We'd stay up 24 hours drinking cup after cup of black coffee, playing record after record of Wardell Gray, Lester Young, Dexter Gordon, Willis Jackson, Lennie Tristano and all the rest, talking madly about that holy new feeling out there in the streets—We'd write stories about some strange beatific Negro hepcat saint with goatee hitchhiking across Iowa with taped up horn bringing the secret message of *blowing* to other coasts, other cities, like a veritable Walter the Penniless leading an invisible First Crusade—We had our mystic heroes and wrote, nay *sung* novels about them, erected long poems celebrating the new "angels" of the American underground—In actuality there was only a handful of real hip swinging cats and what there was vanished mighty swiftly during the Korean War when (and after) a sinister new kind of efficiency appeared in America, maybe it was the result of the universalization of Television and nothing else (the Polite Total Police Control of Dragnet's "peace" officers), but the beat characters after 1950 vanished into jails and madhouses, or were shamed into silent confor-

mity, the generation itself was short-lived and small in number. (Kerouac 2007, 559–60, all emphasis in original; see also A. Charters 1994; Charters and Charters 2010; Kerouac 1958)

Unambiguously acknowledging the African American influence on the Beat Generation, from the colloquialisms of the "Daddy Hipsters of the streets" and "digging bop" to celebrating "some strange beatific Negro hepcat saint with goatee," from the aural innovations of Lester Young and Wardell Gray to the musical mayhem of Dexter Gordon and Willis Jackson, none other than Jack Kerouac—the "hepcat" savant that gave the Beat Generation its name—placed the African American influences on the Beat Generation right alongside its European and European American influences (e.g., the Lost Generation, Jean-Paul Sartre, and Jean Genet). Further demonstrating his comprehension of and complete agreement with the philosophy of the Bebop Movement, Kerouac candidly wrote that his cohort was interested in "experiencing the 'derangement of the senses,' talking strange, being poor and glad, prophesying a new style for American culture, a new style (we thought) completely free from European influences (unlike the Lost Generation), a new incantation." Philosophically speaking, this is a bebop sentence if ever there was one. It speaks volumes about the ways in which the Bebop Movement provided much more than musical inspiration for the Beat Generation, but spiritual, intellectual, cultural, social and political inspiration as well.

It is extremely important for us to accent the African American influence on and contributions to both the Lost Generation and the Beat Generation, because without understanding the significance of this influence and these contributions African Americans will continue to be repeatedly robbed of their historical and cultural contributions, and *hip hop's amnesia*—which is actually nothing more than a code-word for *contemporary multiracial and multicultural American youths' amnesia* surrounding not only popular culture but also social and political culture—will go on unabated into the foreseeable future. In the final analysis, what I am asserting here is actually rather simple: when the music, militancy, *and* movements that "real" jazz sonically symbolizes is viewed within the context of African American history, culture and struggle, along with the specific aural environs where it originated and first evolved, a decidedly different portrait of the first fifty years of jazz emerges. In fact, we might go so far as to softly say, *any interpretation of jazz during the Jazz Age and the Bebop Movement that does not demonstrate a historically and culturally grounded understanding of the unprecedented changes taking place, first and foremost, in African America during the 1910s, 1920s, 1930s, 1940s, and 1950s is not really an interpretation of jazz at all, but rather a whitewashing and misinterpretation of jazz, its inventors, and its major innovators in light of individuals and events external to its origins and early evolution.* All of this is to say, jazz music, jazz dance, jazz literature, jazz aesthetics, jazz politics, and other diverse aspects of jazz culture are incomprehensible without a historically and culturally grounded understanding of the major African American socio-political and cultural aesthetics movements stirring from the Jazz Age through to the Bebop Movement: the New Negro Movement and the Harlem Renaissance, respectively.

Although, it should be emphasized, the Bebop Movement actually emerged in the aftermath of the New Negro Movement and the Harlem Renaissance, it is important to emphasize here because it provides us with a sense of continuity and cultural legacy. The Bebop Movement deftly demonstrates that many of the major breakthroughs and core concepts of the New Negro Movement and the Harlem Renaissance were actually only temporarily interrupted by the Great Depression and World War II. In fact, just as the Bebop Movement in many ways represented a resurgence of certain elements of the classic jazz aesthetic of the 1920s, the "jazz rap" subgenre of the Hip Hop Movement can be said to sonically symbolize a reemergence of many of the major motifs of classic jazz, bebop, and the subsequent subgenres of "modern" jazz that have come to prominence in their wake.

## "RELAYING A MESSAGE, REVEALING THE ESSENCE OF A JAZZ THING!": ON JAZZ RAP'S LYRICAL LEAPS, SONIC RADICALISM, AND OTHER AURAL INNOVATIONS

In a 1994 interview in *Vibe* magazine the innovative and openly jazz-influenced rapper Guru proclaimed: "The so-called jazz hip hop movement is about bringing jazz back to the streets. It got taken away, made into some elite, sophisticated music. It's bringing jazz back where it belongs" (quoted in D. Smith 1994, 88). Remarkably similar to the sentiments of the Bebop Movement, the members of the jazz rap subgenre understood jazz to have been whitewashed and taken away from the people who invented and initially developed it: primarily working-class and poor black folk. Jazz rap does not have the pride of place in contemporary hip hop discourse that it once enjoyed, especially in the 1990s, but its comprehension is crucial for any critical understanding of what is currently called "alternative" rap, "underground" rap, and, more frequently, "conscious" rap.[38]

Although often explained as a merging of jazz with hip hop's sonic sensibilities (especially "hip hop beats"), jazz rap is perhaps more deeply grounded in the African American poetic tradition, especially the tradition of African American folk (or "street") poetry as opposed to the African American academic poetic tradition. In its heyday there was a tendency for some fans and critics of jazz rap to privilege the lyrical message over the music, or vice versa. Taken as a whole, jazz rap actually celebrates and reinvigorates jazz by bringing the jazz aesthetic into dialogue with the hip hop aesthetic.

Additionally, jazz rap innovatively expands rap music by providing rappers with a wider and more historically grounded palette anchored in the rich colors and flamboyant creativity of the jazz poetry tradition, which was pioneered by Langston Hughes (see his classic volume of verse *The Weary Blues* [1926] and his proto-jazz rap album, with Charles Mingus, among others, *The Weary Blues* [1958]). The jazz poetry tradition was subsequently expanded by Sterling Brown (see *Southern Road* [1932]) in the 1930s before being taken up by arguably the greatest exponent of the jazz poetry tradition in the second half of the twentieth century, Amiri Baraka (see *Preface to a Twenty-Volume Suicide Note* [1961], *Black Magic: Collected Poetry, 1961–1967* [1969], *It's Nation Time!* [1970a], *In Our Terribleness* [1970b], *Spirit Reach* [1972], *Hard Facts* [1975], *The Selected Poetry of Amiri Baraka/LeRoi Jones* [1978], and *Transbluesency: The Selected Poems of Amiri Baraka/LeRoi Jones* [1995]). Baraka boldly pushed the jazz poetry envelope, adding hard bop, post-bop, and avant-garde jazz influences along with Civil Rights Movement sensibilities and Black Power Movement politics to the jazz poetry tradition. Other major contributors to the jazz poetry tradition in the 1960s and early 1970s include African American literary icons, such as A. B. Spellman (see *The Beautiful Days* [1965]), Sonia Sanchez (see *Homecoming* [1969]), Larry Neal (see *Black Boogaloo: Notes on Black Liberation* [1969]), Jayne Cortez (see *Pisstained Stairs and the Monkey Man's Wares* [1969]), Askia Touré (see *Juju: Magic Songs for the Black Nation* [1970]), Michael S. Harper (see *Dear John, Dear Coltrane* [1970]), and Gil Scott-Heron (see *Pieces of a Man* [1971]).

Jazz poetry also made many inroads into white America in the 1950s and 1960s when it was popularized by several bebop, "cool," and "west coast" jazz-influenced Beat Generation poets, such as Bob Kaufman, Lawrence Ferlinghetti, Philip Lamantia, Michael McClure, Kenneth Patchen, Kenneth Rexroth, Gary Snyder, Lew Welch, and Philip Whalen (A. Charters 2003, 227–30). Harlem Renaissance music and poetry proved to be so provocative, so unprecedented that Langston Hughes's innovative technique of anchoring poetic form and influencing performance structure in response to the sonorities of blues and jazz was handed down to subsequent generations of poets and spoken-word artists—both black and white, and especially including the Hip Hop Generation's *Def Poetry Jam* and *Brave New Voices* television shows.[39] As a matter of fact, Hughes's breakthrough extended well beyond the African American poetic tradition early on and, according to Stephen Henderson in *Understanding the New Black Poetry: Black Speech and Black Music as Poetic References* (1973), the beat poets in specific were "enamored of jazz in particular and the black life-style in general, and at times sought to communicate . . . a 'black feeling' in their work. Often their formal model was alleged to be jazz" (30–31). By the time jazz rap began to emerge on the scene in the mid to late 1980s, as Guru's quote above reveals, jazz had been "taken away" from working-class and poor black folk and "made into some elite, sophisticated music."[40]

Unlike the "new" and "cutting-edge" jazz of the Bebop Movement, the jazz of the "Jazz Renaissance" of the 1980s was preoccupied with resurrecting older—essentially pre-1970s "electric" jazz or "fusion" jazz—jazz styles. Proponents of what Gary Giddins, in *Rhythm-a-ning: Jazz Tradition and Innovation in the '80s* (1985), termed the "neo-classical" and "conservative" (as opposed to "progressive") jazz style—often called the "Young Lions" (e.g., Wynton Marsalis, Joshua Redman, Wallace Roney, Terence Blanchard, Donald Harrison, Christian McBride, Roy Hargrove, Antonio Hart, Brad Mehldau, Jacky Terrasson, Marlon Jordan, Tim Warfield, Terell Stafford, Cyrus Chestnut, Nicholas Payton, Marcus Roberts, the Harper Brothers, Wes Anderson, Jesse Davis, Javon Jackson, Stephen Scott, and Eric Reed)— directly contributed to a public discourse that emphasized jazz as serious "art music" (xi–xv). The impulse to emphasize jazz as a serious art form can be easily traced back to the Bebop Movement, as can much of the neo-classical jazz schools' repertoire. However, even before the Bebop Movement several jazz aficionados and critics supported the idea of jazz as an elite art form, specifically in Europe, and most often focusing on Duke Ellington's enormous and extremely influential oeuvre.[41]

By the 1980s jazz had once again moved, both musically and physically. As will be recalled, in the late 1940s jazz made the move from the uptown juke joints of Harlem to the downtown dives on 52nd Street. In the 1980s after the jazz rock and jazz fusion experiments of the 1970s, acoustic jazz returned with a vengeance, migrating from dark, dank clubs to the bright lights of prestigious concert halls, academic institutions, and to within often uncomfortably close proximity of the European classical section of most music stores. As was the case during both the Jazz Age and the Bebop Movement, jazz became a sonic symbol for many things, some involving aesthetics but many others encompassing politics: American democracy, African American culture, civil rights, anti-Reaganism, artistic license, and highbrow art music. In terms of style, the jazz revival of the 1980s might be more properly termed "neo-hard bop" or even "neo-post-bop" because it frequently either overlooked or outright dismissed innovative jazz history-making post-bop jazz subgenres such as free jazz and avant-garde jazz, and particularly the work of free-wheeling and forward-thinking jazz musicians such as Sun Ra, Ornette Coleman, Don Cherry, Cecil Taylor, Jimmy Lyons, Muhal Richard Abrams, Bill Dixon, Anthony Braxton, Albert Ayler, the Art Ensemble of Chicago, Prince Lasha, Sonny Simmons, Jimmy Woods, Dewey Redman, Alice Coltrane, Pharoah Sanders, Archie Shepp, Sam Rivers, Amina Claudine Myers, Marion Brown, John Tchicai, Makanda Ken McIntyre, Frank Lowe, Charles Gayle, Sonny Sharrock, James "Blood" Ulmer, and the Association for the Advancement of Creative Musicians (AACM).[42]

The Jazz Renaissance of the 1980s was sparked not simply by the youthful exuberance of adolescent jazz musicians, but by the hardcore economic interests of corporate America via the music industry. It seemed that every youngster who could hold a horn in their hands without either drooling on it or dropping it was put before the public and hailed as the next "great" jazz prodigy. Many of these youngsters, mostly men, were quite talented, but they should not be mistaken for jazz innovators of any sort.

In fact, coming on the scene in the aftermath of the explosive aural adventures of the free jazz and avant-garde jazz of the 1960s and 1970s, the young neo-classicists of the 1980s sound quite conservative and out of touch with jazz history, especially the evolution of jazz after 1965. Instead of moving jazz *forward*, it seemed that these youngsters and their elder handlers and producers were dead-set on taking jazz *backward*: nostalgistically backward to the jazz history-making sonic breakthroughs of Louis Armstrong, Jelly Roll Morton, Duke Ellington, Count Basie, Fats Waller, Art Tatum, Coleman Hawkins, Lester Young, Ben Webster, Earl Hines, Thelonious Monk, Bud Powell, Oscar Peterson, Charlie Christian, Charlie Parker, Dizzy Gillespie, J.J. Johnson, Sonny Rollins, Miles Davis, John Coltrane, Horace Silver, Art Blakey, Hank Mobley, Wynton Kelly, Clifford Brown, Max Roach, Bill Evans, Jackie McLean, Curtis Fuller, Lee Morgan, Freddie Hubbard, Donald Byrd, Herbie Hancock, Wayne Shorter, Ron Carter, Tony Williams, Cannonball Adderley, Wes Montgomery, Grant Green, McCoy Tyner, Keith Jarrett, Chick Corea, and on and on *ad infinitum*.

Along with aggressive marketing campaigns to keep the "Young Lions" in the public eye, including high-profile tours and photo-spreads in jazz magazines and more mainstream media, recording companies began unprecedented reissue campaigns that saw the compact disc release of many of the most coveted jazz classics. In the 1980s jazz was, in a way, "upgraded" and it seemed that America had caught the jazz bug again. Several feature films cashed in on the nation's nostalgia surrounding jazz: *The Jazz Singer* (1980), *The Cotton Club* (1984), *The Gig* (1985), *'Round Midnight* (1986), *Bird* (1987), *Mo' Better Blues* (1990), and *Tune in Tomorrow* (1990).

On one level, these films more or less romanticized the lives of jazz musicians and the jazz world. But, on another level, these films helped to introduce the Hip Hop Generation to jazz *as music, aesthetics, politics, and culture*. Although extremely superficial, these films seemed to suggest that jazz was highbrow culture, and the images they projected were often in stark contrast to the "hood" film genre that boomed in the late 1980s and throughout the 1990s, which included genre classics such as: *Colors* (1988); *Do the Right Thing* (1989); *Boyz n the Hood* (1991); *New Jack City* (1991); *Juice*

(1992); *South Central* (1992); *Menace II Society* (1993); *Poetic Justice* (1993); *Strapped* (1993); *Sugar Hill* (1994); *Above the Rim* (1994); *Fresh* (1994); *Jason's Lyric* (1994); *Clockers* (1995); *Dead Presidents* (1995); *New Jersey Drive* (1995); *Set It Off* (1996); *One Eight Seven* (1997); *He Got Game* (1998); *Belly* (1998); and *Caught Up* (1998).[43]

As Grover Sales's *Jazz: America's Classical Music* (1984) audaciously announced, jazz was now being touted as "America's classical music." Undoubtedly, nothing better symbolizes jazz's newfound respectability (and unapologetic conservatism, according to his critics) than Wynton Marsalis's work in the 1980s and 1990s. Born in New Orleans in 1961, Marsalis began trumpet studies early, performing with the New Orleans Philharmonic at fourteen, and the New Orleans Symphony Brass Quintet, New Orleans Community Concert Band, New Orleans Youth Orchestra, and New Orleans Symphony, among others, during his high school years. In 1979 he moved to New York City to continue his studies at Juilliard, and by 1980 he was touring with the famed Art Blakey and the Jazz Messengers (Gourse 1999).

At first sounding like a combination of Clifford Brown, Booker Little, Freddie Hubbard, and Woody Shaw and, years later, pre–*Bitches Brew* "acoustic" Miles Davis, Marsalis's virtuosic technique was almost immediately apparent. In 1983 he became the only artist ever to win Grammy Awards for both jazz and classical albums in the same year (a feat he amazingly repeated in 1984), and he is the only artist to win Grammy Awards for five consecutive years (from 1983 to 1988). Steadily growing in popularity, by 1987 Marsalis was tapped to co-found a jazz program at the Lincoln Center for the Performing Arts, and by 1996 "Jazz at the Lincoln Center" was installed under his leadership as a new constituent of the Lincoln Center. In 1997 he received the high honor of being the first jazz musician to win the Pulitzer Prize for Music (for his epic oratorio on African American enslavement, *Blood on the Fields* [1997]). To close and celebrate jazz's first century, in 1999 Marsalis released a phenomenal ten albums, totaling fifteen compact discs: *The Marciac Suite*; *Standard Time, Vol. 4: Marsalis Plays Monk*; *At the Octoroon Balls*; *Fiddler's Tale*; *Big Train*; *Sweet Release & Ghost Story*; *Standard Time, Vol. 6: Mr. Jelly Lord!*; *Reeltime*; and the seven compact disc box set *Live at the Village Vanguard*.

Bearing in mind the simple fact that no time and place is ever really and truly homogenous, in the 1980s and 1990s jazz, to a certain extent, became synonymous with sophistication, affluence, and a highbrow aesthetic. For all intents and purposes, jazz during Marsalis's heyday disrupted its previous perception as "popular music." Disassociated from the 1980s and 1990s discourse surrounding black popular music and black popular culture (i.e., rap music and hip hop culture), jazz was once again perceived of as part of the white cultural mainstream, as was the case with big band and swing in the

1930s and early 1940s, and the political and cultural legitimacy of jazz—its "upgraded" and upstanding status—was attributed to those who borrowed from or "sampled" (to use hip hop lingo) the music and aesthetics of jazz.

Just as Wynton Marsalis and his cohort of "Young Lions" sought to distance themselves from pop music in general, and black popular music in particular, jazz rappers sought to distance themselves from mainstream pop music. For instance, Q-Tip famously took a swipe at both Michael Jackson and Bobby Brown on "Excursions" (the first track on A Tribe Called Quest's *The Low End Theory* [1991]). Rhythmically rhyming over a solo acoustic or "jazz" bass accompaniment, he skillfully recreated a conversation he and his father had about black popular music from bebop to hip hop. In essence, the "realness" of bebop and hip hop are contrasted with the pop pretensions of Michael Jackson and Bobby Brown, among others. *The Low End Theory* begins by acknowledging the African American aesthetic lineage from bebop to hip hop. However, even at the outset, A Tribe Called Quest wants its listeners to recognize that they are not a "boy band" or a black pop group (à la contemporaries New Edition, New Kids on the Block, Menudo, Guy, Boyz II Men, Color Me Badd, All-4-One, the Backstreet Boys, and, of course, *NSYNC).

On "Check the Rhyme," also on *The Low End Theory*, Q-Tip further distinguishes between his "conscious" or "jazz" rap and MC Hammer's "pop" or "commercial" rap—and we may include the entire genre of "commercial" rap—when he critiques the commercialization of rap, rhyming: "Industry rule number four thousand and eighty/Record company people are shady./So kids watch your back 'cause I think they smoke crack/I don't doubt it. Look at how they act./Off to better things like a hip hop forum./Pass me the rock and I'll storm with the crew and . . ./Proper. What you say Hammer? Proper./Rap is not pop, if you call it that then stop."

As we witnessed above, the distancing of "authentic" African American music from pop music had been a *recurring aural ritual* long before jazz rap. For instance, after the Jazz Age Louis Armstrong was routinely criticized for surviving the Great Depression—"in style" I might add—when he had to resort to singing Broadway and Tin Pan Alley tunes in the 1930s and 1940s. Recall, bebop musicians distanced their distinct jazz from the "popular" or "commercial" big band, "sweet" band, and swing jazz of the 1930s and 1940s, and classic rhythm & blues and soul singers and musicians went out of their way to distinguish their music from that of 1960s and 1970s pop singers and musicians in their lyrics, performances, and interviews.[44]

In a sense it could be said that the young rappers, especially the pioneers of jazz rap, inherited far more from the aesthetics and politics of the Bebop Movement than did Wynton Marsalis's Young Lions Movement of the 1980s and 1990s. For one thing, similar to bebop, jazz rap sought to "bring . . . jazz back to the streets," and "bring . . . jazz back where it belongs" in the African

American community. However, as Gang Starr and Guru himself came to painfully realize, because of jazz's newfound "upgraded" and upstanding status in the 1980s and 1990s those hip hoppers who borrowed from jazz ultimately had the highbrow aesthetic projected onto them and their music and not the cultural nationalist or, rather, "Afrocentric" aesthetic they embraced and passionately espoused. It was a cold catch-22. Even though jazz was created and initially developed by African Americans, because of its high-profile in the 1980s and 1990s—not to mention during the 1920s and 1930s big band, "sweet" band, and swing eras—it had multiple musical and cultural meanings irrespective of those jazz rappers in particular, and African Americans in general imbued it with.

It is interesting to note that, while the rhythms of jazz rap came almost entirely from hip hop's aural terrain, the samples and sonic textures were drawn primarily from several different jazz genres, including bebop, hard bop, post-bop, cool jazz, soul jazz, free jazz, funk jazz, and fusion jazz. Jazz rap is often described as being "cooler" and more cerebral than other styles of rap. Consequently, jazz rap came to be stereotypically thought of as "college kids' rap" or, more tellingly, the "thinking man's rap music." Coupled with the fact that the large majority of the artists in the jazz rap genre embraced what can be loosely termed an "Afrocentric" or "quasi-black nationalist" cultural, social, and political consciousness and consistently put forward generally positive messages in their music, eventually it emerged as an uplifting alternative to the "hardcore" rap and "gangsta" rap aurally ascending in the early to mid 1990s. Where hardcore rap and gangsta rap seemed to be preoccupied with drug-dealing, gang-banging, and gunplay, jazz rap appeared to be preoccupied with offering its listeners alternatives, both lyrically and musically, to the increasing verbal violence, mean-mugging, ghetto gangsterism, sonic softcore/hardcore porn, and simple sounding music popular in early gangsta rap.

The main audience for the "learned" lyrics of jazz rap was the college crowd, rap-rock fans, alternative rock fans, and young postmodern-bohemians in general. Initially evolving out of Afrika Bambaataa's New York City–based revolving-door collective of rap groups dubbed the "Native Tongues Posse," this hip hop history-making collaborative was without a doubt the seminal and most significant cooperative in terms of the origins and early evolution of what is currently called "alternative" rap, "conscious" rap, and, most importantly with regard to the discussion at hand, "jazz" rap. A group of inspired, ambitious, and like-minded rap artists, the Native Tongues Posse brought abstract, eloquent, and open-minded lyricism to rap music by addressing a wide range of topics: from spirituality to sexuality, racism to capitalism, and partying to politicking. Along with their utilization of eclectic samples and jazz-influenced beats that increasingly embraced a "jazzy" hip hop sound, the Native Tongues collective established an alternative lyrical and musical path for rap artists in the 1990s and, in the process, pioneered "alternative" rap, "conscious" rap, and "jazz" rap. The Native Tongues collective included the Jungle Brothers, De La Soul, A Tribe Called Quest, Queen Latifah, Monie Love, Mos Def, Talib Kweli, Common, Black Sheep, Da Bush Bees, Fu-Schickens, Truth Enola, and Chi-Ali (Bynoe 2006; Hess 2007; Light 1999; P. Shapiro 2001, 2005a).

The Native Tongues' alternative jazz hip hop vibe was introduced with the Jungle Brothers' groundbreaking recording *Straight Out the Jungle* (1988) and its follow-up *Done by the Forces of Nature* (1989); De La Soul's *3 Feet High and Rising* (1989), *De La Soul is Dead* (1991), and *Buhloone Mindstate* (1993); Queen Latifah's *All Hail The Queen* (1989) and *Nature of a Sista* (1991); Monie Love's *Down to Earth* (1990) and *In a Word or 2* (1993); and, of course, A Tribe Called Quest's *People's Instinctive Travels and the Paths of Rhythm* (1990), *The Low End Theory* (1991), and *Midnight Marauders* (1993). The work of A Tribe Called Quest and De La Soul in particular stands out and offers us stunning examples of jazz rap. A Tribe Called Quest's *The Low End Theory* is widely regarded as one of the first records to synthesize hip hop with a so-called "laid-back" jazz sound, with jazz and jazz poetry samples that include: "Time" by the Last Poets; "Tribute to Obabi" by the Last Poets; "A Chant for Bu" by Art Blakey and the Jazz Messengers; "Minya's the Mooch" by Jack DeJohnette; "Spinning Wheel" by Lonnie Liston Smith; "Gentle Smiles" by Gary Bartz; "Upon This Rock" by Joe Farrell; "Down Here on the Ground" by Grant Green; "The Steam Drill" by Cannonball Adderley; "North Carolina" by Les McCann; "Hydra" by Grover Washington, Jr.; "Red Clay" by Freddie Hubbard; "On Green Dolphin Street" by Lucky Thompson; "17 West" by Eric Dolphy; "So What" by Miles Davis; and "Oblighetto" by Jack McDuff. A Tribe Called Quest was even able to persuade Miles Davis's former bassist Ron Carter to play acoustic bass on "Verses from the Abstract," provided there would be no profanity on the track and they addressed what he termed "serious issues" (Sansevere and Farber 1993; S. Taylor 2007).

On De La Soul's second album, *De La Soul Is Dead*, they sampled such jazz classics as "Stretchin'" by Art Blakey and the Jazz Messengers, "In All My Wildest Dreams" by Joe Sample, and "It's Your Thing!" by Lou Donaldson. However, it was their third album, the rap classic *Buhloone Mindstate*, that really showed their jazz roots, with samples from "People Make the World Go Round" by Milt Jackson, "Ground Hog" by Duke Pearson, "Hot Dog" by Lou Donaldson, and "The Next Band" by the immortal Eddie Harris. Picking up on the trend began by A Tribe Called Quest where they featured Ron Carter's "live"—as opposed to "sampled"—bass on *The Low End Theory*, De La Soul cajoled James Brown's legendary horn-men Maceo Parker, Fred Wesley, and Pee Wee Ellis to perform on their album (see the tracks "Pattie Dooke," "I Be Blowin'," and "I Am I Be"). The results are nothing short of remarkable, and the group's lyrical and aural innovations have garnered the album an uncontested place in hip hop history.

Although overshadowed by De La Soul's *3 Feet High and Rising*, in 1989 the rap group Gang Starr (with MC Guru and DJ Premier) helped to inaugurate and made significant contributions to the jazz rap subgenre. Their debut, *No More Mr. Nice Guy* (1989), and classic hit single "Jazz Thing," which was featured on the soundtrack for Spike Lee's jazz movie *Mo' Better Blues*, was as explosive as anything on the rap scene at the end of the 1980s. For example, on "Jazz Thing," along with saxophonist Branford Marsalis's "live" improvisations, Gang Starr sampled "Cool Blues" by Charlie Parker, "Light Blue" by Thelonious Monk, "Shadows" by Lonnie Liston Smith, and "Great Gorge" by Joe Farrell. Now widely considered one of the most influential MC-and-DJ tandems of the 1990s, Gang Starr's *Step in the Arena* (1991), *Daily Operation* (1992), *Hard to Earn* (1994), and *Moment of Truth* (1998), along with Guru's groundbreaking solo albums *Jazzmatazz, Vol. 1* (1993), *Jazzmatazz, Vol. 2: The New Reality* (1995), *Jazzmatazz, Vol. 3: Streetsoul* (2000), *Baldhead Slick & da Click* (2001), and *Jazzmatazz, Vol. 4: The Hip Hop Jazz Messenger* (2007), not only helped to popularize jazz rap but kept the genre alive when most of the other major figures in the field had either fallen by the wayside or musically moved in the direction of hardcore or gangsta rap.

Guru (a.k.a. Keith Edward Elam), whose stage name is a backronym that stands for "Gifted Unlimited Rhymes Universal" or, initially, "God is Universal; he is the Ruler Universal" (both of which are references to the teachings of the Nation of Gods and Earths or, rather, the more commonly called "Five-Percent Nation"), is rightly regarded as the quintessential jazz rapper. More than any other figure in the field of jazz rap, with his history-making *Jazzmatazz* series Guru consistently brought jazz artists, rap artists, DJs, and hip hop producers into dialogue, into the recording studio together, and onto the stages of jazz and hip hop clubs worldwide. *Jazzmatazz, Vol. 1* was the first full-length jazz rap album (as opposed to a song or two) to combine a "live" and intensely improvising jazz band with hip hop production techniques (predating the various artists effort *Stolen Moments: Red Hot + Cool* [1994] by more than a year). Featuring legendary jazz artists such as trumpeter Donald Byrd, pianist Lonnie Liston Smith, vibraphonist Roy Ayers, guitarist Ronny Jordan, saxophonist Courtney Pine, and saxophonist Branford Marsalis, the album also sampled several jazz classics, including "Povo" by Freddie Hubbard, "Mosadi (Woman)" by the Crusaders, "The Book of Slim" by Gene Harris and the Three Sounds, and "It Feels So Good" by Grover Washington, Jr.

It was not merely the music on *Jazzmatazz, Vol. 1* that brought the jazz vibe to the album, but Guru's contemplative lyrics also seemed to nod to earlier forms of jazz poetry, specifically the work of Langston Hughes, Amiri Baraka, Sonia Sanchez, Ishmael Reed, Jayne Cortez, Gil Scott-Heron, Gylan Kain, the Last Poets, and the Watts Prophets. Lyrically illustrating that rap's roots extend further back than 1960s and 1970s rhythm & blues, soul, and funk, Guru rhymed about inner-city life, drug addiction, poverty, crime, violence, and sex, among other topics—all issues addressed previously in the jazz poetry tradition: from Langston Hughes through to Gil Scott-Heron. Indeed, jazz rap might actually be nothing more than the Hip Hop Generation's jazz poetry, as it would seem that since jazz's emergence each generation of black youth has faithfully put its own special spin on the jazz poetry tradition.[45]

On *Jazzmatazz, Vol. 2: The New Reality* Guru added a slightly more "acid" or "funk" jazz edge to the album's sound—hence the album's subtitle, "The New Reality." Along with Donald Byrd, Branford Marsalis, Courtney Pine, and Ronny Jordan reprising their roles from *Jazzmatazz, Vol. 1*, jazz legends trumpeter Freddie Hubbard, pianist Ramsey Lewis, saxophonist Kenny Garrett, guitarist Marc Antoine, organist Reuben Wilson, bassist Me'Shell Ndegéocello, and drummer Bernard "Pretty" Purdie were added to the aurally amazing mix. *Jazzmatazz, Vol. 2*'s jazz samples were drawn from "Django" by Cal Tjader, "What You Won't Do For Love" by Bobby Caldwell, "You Are My Starship" by Norman Connors, and "The Midnight Sun Will Never Set" by Quincy Jones.

Fans and critics consider *Jazzmatazz, Vol. 2* a bold move forward for Guru, both lyrically and musically, because, while Brand New Heavies diva N'Dea Davenport and acid jazz queen Carleen Anderson were featured on *Jazzmatazz, Vol. 1*, the sequel took what might be loosely termed the "hip hop feminist" vibe further by featuring Chaka Khan, Bahamadia, Patra, Me'Shell Ndegéocello, Mica Paris, and Shara Nelson, each contributing much more than a hip hop feminist ambience on their respective tracks but, even more, openly addressing a range of black feminist and hip hop feminist issues. Overall, it was once again Guru's ingenious synthesis of "live" jazz (or, rather, "acid" jazz), conscious rap, and new hip hop production techniques that made *Jazzmatazz, Vol. 2* special. There is something breathtakingly brilliant about Guru's sonic sagacity and the way his wisdom-filled words rhythmically ride and musically mesh with the in-studio or "live" legendary jazz musicians' obbligatos and improvisations on *Jazzmatazz, Vol. 2*.

Moving even further away from the jazz vibe heard on *Jazzmatazz, Vols. 1* and *2*, on *Jazzmatazz, Vol. 3: Streetsoul*, as the album's subtitle implies, a kind of soul jazz and neo-soul sound dominated the proceedings. To be sure, jazz is still very much a part of the mix, but this time around Guru drew more heavily from the soul jazz and fusion jazz traditions, featuring the "live" obbligatos and improvisations of jazz legends Herbie Hancock and Bobbi Humphrey, among others, and little or no jazz sampling. With respect to sampling, it is important to emphasize the history and political economy of sampling here, because by 2000 it was extremely difficult to gain permission and much more expensive to sample classic songs. Therefore, Guru's sonic shift of focus on *Jazzmatazz, Vol. 3* can be easily explained. Along with the issues surrounding sampling, by 2000—the year *Jazzmatazz, Vol. 3* appeared—jazz rap was almost as antiquated as the 1960s and 1970s soul jazz, funk jazz, and fusion jazz sound it helped to resurrect—under the guise of "acid jazz"—in the late 1980s and early 1990s.[46]

By the turn of the millennium, the Jungle Brothers and Monie Love had had neither a major record deal nor a hit single since 1993. A Tribe Called Quest had broken up in 1998. De La Soul was on the verge of losing its major recording contract. Queen Latifah had turned to acting, hosting her own television show, *The Queen Latifah Show*, and, later, singing classic soul and jazz standards. Acid jazz was all but long gone, and neo-soul and gangsta rap were all the rage. Hence, leaving gangsta rap to the gangsta rappers, Guru opted to sonically move in the direction of the Neo-Soul Movement. Consequently, *Jazzmatazz, Vol. 3* featured undisputed neo-soul divas Erykah Badu, Macy Gray, Amel Larrieux, Les Nubians, Kelis, and Angie Stone, neo-soul romeos Bilal, Donell Jones, and David Craig, and classic soul icon Isaac Hayes. Helping to give credence to Guru's hip hop credentials—keep in mind that he had been making albums for more than a decade by 2000—was none other than hip hop's most famous "acoustic" and undeniably jazz-influenced Grammy Award-winning band, the Roots, as well as top producers J Dilla, Pharrell Williams, the Neptunes, James Poyser, and Chad Hugo, among others.

Ultimately more of a "soul" rap rather than a jazz rap record, *Jazzmatazz, Vol. 3* nonetheless demonstrated that the jazz rap genre could, both lyrically and musically, change with the times and expand its topical base. By 2000, Guru, in many ways, was a man dancing to the (albeit decidedly *hip hop*) beat of a different drum. Reflecting on his history-making *Jazzmatazz* series in *Blues & Soul* magazine in 2009, Guru gushed:

> Back around '93—when I first came up with the *Jazzmatazz* concept—I was noticing how a lot of cats were digging in the crates and sampling jazz breaks to make hip hop records. But, while I thought that was cool, I wanted to take it to the next level and actually create a new genre by getting the actual dudes we were sampling into the studio to jam over hip hop beats with some of the top vocalists of the time. You know, the whole thing was experimental, but I knew it was an idea that would spawn some historic music. (quoted in P. Lewis 2009, 1)

Here is Guru's *Jazzmatazz* "genius move," stripped down and laid bare for all the world to witness. At a time when others were simply "sampling" or occasionally bringing jazz artists and rap artists into the studio together, Guru conceived of an entire album—or, rather, a series of albums—where jazz artists and rap artists would innovatively "take it to the next level and actually create a new genre by getting the actual dudes we were sampling into the studio to jam over hip hop beats." Ahead of the "live" hip hop band trend as a consequence of the series of law suits surrounding rap music and sampling in the 1990s, Guru was a musical visionary who, literally, helped to "create a new genre" by bringing improvisation back to black popular music during a period where most other rap artists and producers where content to digitally dodge the issue of musical originality and shamelessly sample someone else's music (most often without permission). Obviously sampling has a historic place in hip hop history and culture, and can be considered the Hip Hop Generation's way of *sonically signifyin'* on any number of issues the sampled songs might suggest or often cryptically capture. However, there is something to be said about the low level of musicianship among the Hip Hop Generation if the bulk of their music is based off of the soundtracks of past artistic, social, and political movements, specifically the Bebop Movement, the Hard Bop Movement, the Post-Bop Movement, the Civil Rights Movement, the Black Power Movement, and the Black Arts Movement.

Even as early as the late 1980s, do we detect a high level of nostalgia on the part of the youngsters of the Hip Hop Generation? From the point of view of sociology of music, we might also ask: Why would so many folk who were either not born or toddlers feel so connected to the popular music and popular culture of their grandparents and parents' youth years? What was going on socially and politically in African America in the late 1980s and early 1990s? What was going on culturally and artistically in African America in the late 1980s and early 1990s? Quick answers to these questions would more than likely have something to do with: the Reagan administration; the Bush administration; the cutting back of social services, recreation centers, and arts initiatives for inner-city youth; the new political ethos revolving around what was then considered the "radical" politics of Jesse Jackson and Louis Farrakhan; the rise of the Jazz Renaissance of the 1980s and 1990s; the digitization and over-production of rhythm & blues; and the postmoderniza-tion of African American visual art.

Although he placed another volume in the *Jazzmatazz* series—*Jazzmatazz, Vol. 4: The Hip Hop Jazz Messenger*, which featured the "live" improvisations of jazz luminaries such as David Sanborn, Ronnie Laws, and Bob James—it is generally agreed that the first three volumes of the series have achieved rap classics status. Because it was grounded in what many fans and critics (myself included) believe to be the bedrock of contemporary black popular music, soul music, *Jazzmatazz, Vol. 3* seems to simultaneously, and ingeniously I might add, look backward (to soul jazz and jazz poetry) and forward (to neo-soul and the evolution of conscious rap). Seeming to tap into some of the more rhythm & blues and soul music-influenced poetry of the 1960s and 1970s, at times *Jazzmatazz, Vol. 3* bears, however faint, echoes of the radical poetic inclinations of icons such as Sun Ra, Gil Scott-Heron, Millie Jackson, Haki Madhubuti, Etheridge Knight, Sonia Sanchez, Amiri Baraka, Nikki Giovanni, the Last Poets, and the Watts Prophets. Sonic echoes from the classic soul music tradition were eclectically drawn from Nina Simone, Etta James, Curtis Mayfield, Roberta Flack, James Brown, Donny Hathaway, Marvin Gaye, Aretha Franklin, Johnny Adams, Irma Thomas, Stevie Wonder, Gladys Knight, Al Green, Ann Peebles, Luther Ingram, Bobby Womack, Betty Wright, Tyrone Davis, James Carr, O.V. Wright, and Billy Paul.

Outside of the Native Tongues Posse's jazz hip hop hybrids, Guru was not alone. In fact, the group that arguably did the most to popularize the jazz rap genre was Digable Planets (a trio, with group members Butterfly, Ladybug, and Doodlebug). Although they only released two albums in the early 1990s, *Reachin': A New Refutation of Time and Space* (1993) and *Blowout Comb* (1994), Digable Planets has the distinction of bringing an updated version of "bop talk" or "jive talk" to the Hip Hop Generation. Primarily produced by musical mastermind Butterfly, *Reachin'* featured post-bop, soul jazz, funk jazz, and fusion jazz samples from several classics, including: "Rain Dance" by Herbie Hancock, "Black Satin" by Miles Davis, "Samba de Orpheus" by Grant Green, "Devika (Goddess)" by Lonnie Liston Smith, "Mystique Blues" by the Crusaders, "Superfluous" by Eddie Harris, "Mambo Bounce" by Sonny Rollins, "Blow Your Head" by Fred Wesley and the J.B.'s, "Stretchin'" by Art Blakey and the Jazz Messengers, "Lilies of the Nile" by the Crusaders, "Watermelon Man" by Herbie Hancock, "Black-nuss" by Rahsaan Roland Kirk, "Push Push" by Herbie Mann, and "Listen and You'll See" by the Crusaders. *Reachin'* also sampled the soul jazz poetry of the Last Poets (i.e., "Jazzoetry" and "The Black Is Chant") and former Last Poet Gylan Kain (i.e., "Black Satin Amazon Fire Engine Cry Baby"), along with classic soul and funk songs by James Brown (i.e., "Funky Drummer"), Parliament (i.e., "The Mothership Connection"), Curtis Mayfield (i.e., "Give Me Your Love"), Earth, Wind & Fire (i.e., "Saxophone Interlude"), Archie Bell & the Drells (i.e., "Tighten Up"), the Ohio Players (i.e., "Funky Worm"), and the Honey Drippers (i.e., "Impeach the President").

An incredibly imaginative and extremely innovative album, both lyrically and musically, Butterfly's production techniques gave the sample-saturated album a sense of originality and cohesion that many, both within and without the jazz rap community, came to copy. Lyrically taking up a wide range of topics, including the hipness or, rather, the "coolness" of Digable Planets (i.e., "The Rebirth of Slick (Cool Like Dat)"), abortion (i.e., "La Femme

Fétal"), and the similarities between potent marijuana and funky music (i.e., "Nickel Bags"), Digable Planets was unambiguously "cool" and "laid-back" when early hardcore and gangsta rap was "hot" and aurally aggressive. It was a striking contrast, and one that was not lost on their legions of fans and copious critics. The album was certified Gold by the Recording Industry Association of America (RIAA) in 1993, and the hit single "The Rebirth of Slick (Cool Like Dat)" was so well-received and resonated so widely that it won the "Grammy Award for Best Rap Performance by a Duo or Group" in 1994.

*Reachin'*, perhaps, could not have been released at a better time than the early 1990s. Along with the headway made by the jazz hip hop hybrid sounds of the Jungle Brothers, De La Soul, A Tribe Called Quest, and Gang Starr, among others, the so-called "alternative scene" was gaining more and more traction. A large cross-section of indie rockers, alternative rockers, heavy metal freaks (and geeks), grunge (and grime) groupies, New Jack Swing burn-outs, and new "old school" hip hop heads identified with Digable Planets's "alternative" vision and version of rap music (and hip hop culture). In a way, the hit single "The Rebirth of Slick (Cool Like Dat)" paints the perfect picture and lays the philosophical foundation for the other tracks on the album.

Similar to "The Rebirth of Slick (Cool Like Dat)," songs like "What Cool Breezes Do," "Escapism (Gettin' Free)," "Appointment at the Fat Clinic" and "Examination of What," replete with ample classic jazz samples and contemplative catchy rhymes, most of these tracks effortlessly *reach* (pun intended) across the early hip hop spectrum: from braggadocio and illegal drug use to political awareness and body image issues. Again, undoubtedly part of the seemingly universal appeal of *Reachin'* revolves around Ladybug, Doodlebug, and Butterfly's "smooth" and "jazzy" rap delivery in juxtaposition to the "hot" and "hype" rhymes of the hardcore and gangsta rappers at the time. Amazingly seeming simultaneously indifferent and impassioned, sometimes thoughtless and thoughtful, Digable Planets' *Reachin'* was able to be aurally "heavy" (i.e., "La Femme Fétal," "Pacifics," and "Swoon Units") and "light" ("It's Good To Be Here," "Last of the Spiddyocks," and "Examination of What") in a way rarely achieved on a rap record up to that point—obviously, Tupac, Jay-Z, NaS, Lauryn Hill, Wyclef Jean, Missy Elliott, and, of course, Lil' Wayne, among others, have perfected the "simultaneously indifferent and impassioned, sometimes thoughtless and thoughtful" vibe in the years following Digable Planets' demise.

In fact, of all the jazz rappers and jazz rap groups of the 1990s, Digable Planets arguably flaunted and consistently flashed their connections to jazz *as music, aesthetics, politics, and culture*, mostly via overt references to legendary jazz musicians in their lyrics and by sampling a generous amount of jazz classics. Their *Afro-boho* (i.e., "African American bohemian" or "black bohemian") image, which unambiguously borrowed from the Bebop Movement and the African American hipster culture of the 1940s and 1950s, was easily apparent in their incessant utilization of bebop-based terminology, including words such as "cool," "cat," "hip," "dig," "boogie," and "fizz." Their record company (Pendulum, a subsidiary of Elektra Records at the time) also used jazz to aggressively market the group.

For instance, their first music video, which was for the hit single "The Rebirth of Slick (Cool Like Dat)," featured Digable Planets performing in a smoky jazz club in New York City, and bebop cultural references abound, as do visual references to 1940s and 1950s African American hipster culture. Also, the overall advertisement campaign for *Reachin'* was squarely situated within the world of jazz culture. For example, an ad for *Reachin'* in *The Source* magazine in April of 1993 included the headline "jazz, jive, poetry & style." Hence, it is fairly easy to see how jazz, rather than hardcore or gangsta rap, provided the primary criteria through which to critique, review, interview, and listen to Digable Planets.

Perhaps more than any other jazz rap group, Digable Planets helps to highlight the often-overlooked fact that even though jazz and rap are usually treated as completely separate musical and cultural entities (à la Stanley Crouch, Wynton Marsalis, and their legions of minions), the jazz rap sonic syntheses and aural innovations of the 1990s acted as a symbolic musical and cultural exchange, a *trans-generational trading* of sights and sounds, music and mayhem, politics and poetry that ultimately increased or, rather, "upgraded" the social, cultural, and communicative capital of both jazz and rap at the close of the twentieth century. Furthermore, when we move beyond the more immediate engagement of the music and classic jazz, soul, and funk samples on *Reachin'* a serious listen to and look at the lyrics reveal myriad references to black popular music, black popular culture, and, equally important, *black political culture*, especially *the black radical politics of the 1950s, 1960s, and 1970s*. The cultural references to and complex collage of "bop talk," "jive talk," and other African American colloquialisms frequently buried in their lyrics were borrowed from an amazingly wide range of countercultures, including: the Hipster Movement, Bebop Movement, Civil Rights Movement, Beat Generation, Black Power Movement, Hippie Movement, Women's Liberation Movement, Five Percent Nation, "old school" hip hop (e.g., Fab 5 Freddie, Crazy Legs of the Rock Steady Crew, Sugarhill Records, and Grandmaster Flash and the Furious Five), and the panorama of 1960s and 1970s African American poetry (e.g., Margaret Walker, Gwendolyn Brooks, Bob Kaufman, Amiri Baraka, Sonia Sanchez, Haki Madhubuti, Nikki Giovanni, Maya Angelou, Audre Lorde, Lucille Clifton, June Jordan, Gil Scott-Heron, the Last Poets, and the Watts Prophets).

Digable Planets' lyrics also referenced classic jazz (mostly bebop and hard bop) musicians (such as Charlie Parker, Dizzy Gillespie, Thelonious Monk, Charles Mingus, Max Roach, Billie Holiday, Sonny Rollins, Miles Davis, John Coltrane, and Hank Mobley), 1970s blaxploitation films (such as *Superfly, Shaft, Foxy Brown, Cleopatra Jones*, and *The Spook Who Sat by the Door*), and signified on other aspects of African American culture and identity (such as Afros and other African American hairstyles, as well as the hardships of working-class and poor black folk). In line with other countercultures, especially the African American countercultures of the 1940s, 1950s, 1960s, and 1970s (i.e., the Hipster Movement, Bebop Movement, Black Power Movement, and Black Arts Movement), copious references to drugs were sprinkled throughout their lyrics and interlaced with anti-conformist and anti-establishment ideology, at times directly commenting on and critiquing "Uncle Sam," the "pigs" (i.e., the police), and "fascist" right-wing conservatives, just as the hipsters and beboppers had in the 1940s and 1950s and the activists and artists of the Black Power Movement and Black Arts Movement had in the 1960s and 1970s. In Digable Planets' lyrics references to bebop and hard bop, the Civil Rights Movement and the Black Power Movement, the Nation of Islam and the Five Percent Nation boldly stood side by side with their unique articulation of Marxist and existential philosophy. Clever lyrical allusions to Karl Marx, Jean-Paul Sartre, and Albert Camus, as well as Ladybug's much-acclaimed contribution of "female energy" and emphasis on "female issues" (again, see "La Femme Fétal"), were hailed by fans and critics just as much as their "laid-back" and "cool" jazz hip hop hybrid style.

The sequel to *Reachin'*, the undisputed rap classic, *Blowout Comb*, amazingly improved on the aural innovations of Digable Planets' debut. The cryptic album title wasn't so cryptic after all, as it was a clever cultural reference to a "natural" or undeniably African American non-synthetic style. In order to properly "pick" an "Afro" or a "natural"—the African American hairstyle popular in the late 1960s and 1970s—one needed an "Afro pick" or "blowout comb." Side-stepping the "sophomore slump" syndrome that has plagued so many throughout the history of hip hop, the Grammy Award–winning Digable Planets set out to prove that they deserved the accolades and attention their debut had garnered. Although a criminally under-rated successor, *Blowout Comb* carried over the contemplative catchy lyrics and memorable melodies of *Reachin'* and offered unambiguous answers to their fans and critics who questioned whether they were "real" enough or "hard" enough to represent the rising hip hop nation—or, rather, the meteorically rising *Hip Hop Movement* of the 1990s.

Apart from an at times indecipherable track entitled "Dial 7 (Axioms of Creamy Spies)," *Blowout Comb* sonically succeeded in bumping great jazz-based grooves over atmospheric political and party rhymes, somehow simultaneously softening *and* hardening their political critique and social commentary on standout tracks such as "The May 4th Movement," "Black Ego," and "Blowing Down." With their upgraded status as "Grammy Award winners," the awesome threesome invited, literally, dozens of musicians into the studio to "nice up" a more "natural" (meaning, a more "acoustic," "organic," and "soulful") jazz hip hop hybrid sound, including: trumpeter Gerald Brazel; trombonist Tim "T-Bone" Williams; saxophonists Donald Harrison and David Lee Jones; guitarist Huey Cox; keyboardist Dave Darlington; vibraphonists Carla Leighton and Shi Reltub; cellist Beth Russo; bassists Dwayne Burno, Alan Goldsher, David Chalice, and Carl Carter; and a battalion of background vocalists (simply too numerous to name here). To give the album more of a "live" jazz jam session feel, the classic jazz samples were kept to a minimum, but importantly included: "Ebony Blaze," "Slow Motion," and "We Live in Brooklyn" by Roy Ayers; "Soul Pride," an infectious free-flowing instrumental, by James Brown (see his *Soul Pride: The Instrumentals, 1960 – 1969* [1993] box set); "Blow Your Head" by Fred Wesley and the J.B.'s; "Black & Blues" and "Jasper Country Man" by Bobbi Humphrey; "Get On Up and Dance" by Eddie Harris; "Blue Lick" by Bob James; "God Made Me Funky" by the Headhunters; and "Luanna's Theme" by Grant Green.

Although *Blowout Comb* was not as commercially successful as *Reachin'*, Digable Planets nonetheless upped their game by directly responding to fans and critics who questioned whether an "Afro-boho" jazz rap group could really and truly represent the rising Hip Hop Movement in the 1990s. In particular, they deftly demonstrated their growth—lyrically, musically, *and* politically—in the two main areas discerning fans and critics found *Reachin'* woefully weak: beats and rhymes. After all, aren't *beats* and *rhymes* two of the core elements of rap music? What else are we talking about when we speak of critiquing (i.e., "feelin'" or not "feelin'") a rap song or album if we are not ultimately discussing the quality of the beats and the caliber of the rhymes? It should be stated outright, the beats on *Blowout Comb* are by far some of the best to ever bump, rattle, and roll on a rap record, specifically the early jazz–inflected hip hop "hyped-up" version of the—even if off-kilter— classic New Orleans second-line funk beat on "Black Ego," where Digable Planets samples "Here Comes the Metermen" by the Meters, "Luanna's Theme" by Grant Green, and "Generator Pop" by the P-Funk All-Stars.

On *Blowout Comb* the production duties were handled collectively by Digable Planets (as opposed to solely by Butterfly, as on *Reachin'*), and most serious hip hoppers concur that almost every track on the album actually greatly benefits from not pandering to corporate American music industry "crossover" schemes and "mainstream" dreams. Music critics almost universally lauded the album, and rap fans and critics alike immediately recognized *Blowout Comb* as unequivocally heads and shoulders above most of the rap music (including other jazz rap records) during the early to mid 1990s. In terms of their rhymes, again rapping about a wide-range of issues affecting African Americans—from inner-city ills and the increase in black youth incarceration to black nationalism and the Five Percent Nation—although by no means "hardcore" or "gangsta," blazoning across *Blowout Comb* are lively, even though "learned," raps that flipped, flopped, and flowed better than almost every track on *Reachin'*. Where *Reachin'* ultimately registered as an undisputed jazz rap classic, *Blowout Comb* is now rightly regarded as a timeless *rap classic* (as opposed to merely a "jazz rap" classic) that sonically captures the core beliefs and politics of hip hop culture.

By moving beyond the critical discussion surrounding what musicologist Justin Williams in "The Construction of Jazz Rap as High Art in Hip Hop Music" (2010a) called "jazz codes" (i.e., "walking acoustic bass, saxophones, trumpet with Harmon mute, and jazz guitar," etc.) in jazz rap, here I have decidedly gone against the longstanding tendency to analyze African American music with little or no reference to African American politics (443; see also J. A. Williams 2010b). When jazz rap is situated within a more historically and culturally grounded, socially and politically sensitive narrative of black popular music and black popular culture, an entirely new interpretation and, perhaps, a long overdue respect for the genre emerges. The jazz rap phenomenon was actually much more widespread than many contemporary hip hoppers may remember (or, truth be told, even wanna remember). However—and here's where we get "deep" and "do the knowledge"—in *The Rough Guide to Hip Hop* (2005a), renowned music critic Peter Shapiro got it right when he openly admitted that albums like *The Low End Theory*, *Breaking Atoms*, *Buhloone Mindstate*, *Blowout Comb*, and *Jazzmatazz* ingeniously "demonstrated that hip hop was an aesthetic every bit as deep, serious and worth cherishing as any in a century plus of African American music . . . giving rap the same aesthetic weight as a Coltrane solo" (363, 365).

As a matter of fact, for all of the newfound respectability and air of affluence that jazz achieved by the end of the twentieth century, in the early 1990s jazz rap was so influential that none other than jazz legend Miles Davis devoted his last album, *Doo-Bop* (released posthumously in 1992), to the phenomenon. *Doo-Bop* won the "Grammy Award for the Best R&B Instrumental Performance" in 1993. Following Miles Davis's lead, a slew of jazz musicians—both legends and "Young Lions" alike—began to record jazz hip hop hybrid albums, including: pianist Herbie Hancock with his album *Dis Is Da Drum* (1994); saxophonist Branford Marsalis with his albums *Buckshot LeFonque*(1994) and *Music Evolution* (1997); saxophonist Courtney Pine with his albums *Modern Day Jazz Stories* (1995), *Underground* (1997), and *Back in the Day* (2000); trumpeter Russell Gunn with his albums *Ethnomusicology, Vol.1* (1999), *Ethnomusicology, Vol. 2* (2001),

*Ethnomusicology, Vol. 3* (2003), *Ethnomusicology, Vol. 4: Live in Atlanta* (2005), *Ethnomusicology, Vol. 5: Krunk Jazz* (2007), and *Ethnomusicology, Vol. 6: The Return of Gunn Fu* (2010); trumpeter Roy Hargrove with his albums *Hard Groove* (2003), *Strength* (2004), and *Distractions* (2006); pianist Robert Glasper with his albums *Canvas* (2005), *In My Element* (2007), and *Double-Booked* (2009); and, of course, trumpeter Christian Scott with his albums *Rewind That!* (2006), *Anthem* (2007), *Live at Newport* (2008), and *Yesterday You Said Tomorrow* (2010).

In discussing the two-way backlash against jazz musicians for making overtures to hip hop culture and hip hop producers for making overtures to jazz culture, Justin Williams (2010a) contended that "the less conservative jazz musician who used elements from hip hop or the hip hop producer who digitally sampled from jazz records might be accused of gravitating to whatever was commercially popular and profitable at the time" (456). Bear in mind that like bebop in the 1940s and 1950s, especially as represented in 1950s *film noir* and "crime jazz" flicks (e.g., *The Wild One*, *The Man with the Golden Arm*, *Peter Gunn*, and *Odds Against Tomorrow*), from the late 1980s onward rap music represented little more than black youths' soundtrack for illicit sex, illegal drugs, crime, and violence to sanctimonious suburban conservatives and their political pundits who frequently and unwittingly made little or no distinction between "pop" rappers (e.g., Kris Kross, MC Hammer, and Sir-Mix-A-Lot), "jazz" or "alternative" rappers (e.g., De La Soul, A Tribe Called Quest, Digable Planets, and Guru), and "hardcore" or "gangsta" rappers (e.g., Ice-T, Too Short, N.W.A., 2 Live Crew, and the Geto Boys).

However, there was also understood to be a subtle political economy to the jazz hip hop hybrid phenomenon in that "[r]ecord labels, by the same token, could be [and were] criticized for fostering hip hop and jazz collaborations in order to rebrand an old genre and thus sell back catalogues." Missing the main point, as self-righteous, close-minded, and close-eared conservatives have a tendency to do, jazz rap was so much more than a corporate-sponsored get-rich-quick-scheme or crossover dream. The same generation that has been constantly accused of *historical* and *cultural amnesia* was, in its own off-kilter albeit extremely innovative way, demonstrating that it had a sense of history, even if only African American *musical* history. Where was the support and encouragement that so many of the *Little House on the Prairie* and *Leave It to Beaver*–loving Baby Boomer conservatives incessantly proclaimed that they had for Generation X, the Millennial Generation, and, by default, the Hip Hop Generation?

The jazz rap phenomenon was a reality check for both the "old school" soul brothers and sisters of the 1960s and 1970s and the rap and neo-soul hip hoppers of the 1980s and 1990s. Truth be told, there was something very "real," very "authentic," and very "soulful" about much of the music this phenomenon produced, and even though it has fallen out of favor there remains a body of work—a body of bold beats and often "radical" rhymes— that continue to rival contemporary rap classics. However, and we should be clear here, it was not merely the rap artists who benefitted by incorporating jazz into their aural landscapes. The forward-thinking jazz musicians who were bold enough to blur the lines between jazz and hip hop also benefitted by incorporating hip hop's sonic sensibilities into their sounds. Once again, Williams's words find their way into the fray: "At best, jazz musicians who borrowed and collaborated with hip hop could be said to improve the genre, staying close to their musical lineage while trying something new in the spirit of jazz as a verb rather than a noun. Thus, whereas jazz codes added a degree of sophistication and cultural elevation to rap, hip hop codes, such as turntable scratches and hiss from sampled vinyl, could be heard on a number of jazz recordings as 'sub-cultural capital' said to signify hipness or coolness" (456).

What Williams terms "hip hop codes" (i.e., "turntable scratches and hiss from sampled vinyl") can now be heard in most major forms of popular music in America, and, by the same token, without a doubt "jazz codes" continue to creep into rap and other forms of hip hop music, especially neo-soul. Even though jazz rap is no longer fashionable its influence continues to shape and shade contemporary black popular music: from the legendary Roots crew's Lonnie Liston Smith–like singular "soul jazz" sound (especially on their innovative early albums *Organix* [1993], *Do You Want More?!!!* [1995], *Illadelph Halflife* [1996], *Things Fall Apart* [1999], and *The Roots Come Alive* [1999]) to Erykah Badu's Billie Holiday–influenced vocal acrobatics (especially on her groundbreaking albums *Baduizm* [1997], *Mama's Gun* [2000], *Worldwide Underground* [2003], *New Amerykah, Pt.1* [2008], and *New Amerykah, Pt. 2* [2010]). Indeed, there is an interesting, even if often-overlooked, connection between jazz and rap that is frequently forgone in favor of the more readily apparent and more immediate rhythm & blues, soul, funk, go-go, disco, and reggae contributions to and connections with rap music and hip hop culture.

However, those of us honestly interested in combating *hip hop's amnesia* (and the amnesia surrounding hip hop culture) have come to the, however unpopular and impolite, conclusion that part of the antidote for *hip hop's amnesia* lies beyond the borders and boundaries of the history of black popular music and more than likely rests in the herstory/history of African American—among other oppressed and marginalized groups'—social and political movements. It is only when and where we understand black popular music and black popular culture in relationship with African American political culture and African American socio-political movements that we can truly comprehend the myriad messages in African American music, and African American aesthetics more generally. In other words, the "sound bite" approach to black popular music only exacerbates *hip hop's amnesia.*

Even with regard to the musical elements of hip hop culture, there is a longstanding tendency to go back only as far as those poetic and sonic contributions that fans and critics can easily ascertain while sitting in the comfort of their upscale living-rooms or the coziness of their luxury cars. However, no matter how many rhythm & blues, soul, funk, go-go, disco, and reggae influences listeners are able to easily detect in rap and neo-soul, it is extremely important to have some sonic cognizance of black popular music prior to the emergence of rhythm & blues in the middle of the twentieth century (i.e., between 1945 and 1955). Awareness of the aural imprint of classic blues and jazz on rap and neo-soul will enable us to combat not only the *musical amnesia* that has beset so many in the Hip Hop Generation, but also it will more than likely aid in counteracting historical and cultural amnesia among the Hip Hop Generation by inspiring "conscious" hip hoppers to explore the history, culture, politics, and social movements that classic blues and jazz emerged from—as has been the case with regard to the present author.

It is as if an entirely new aural terrain is opened up when and where neo-soul and rap's roots in classic blues and jazz are revealed and intently explored. For instance, when the improvisational aspects of jazz are explored and really understood, then connections between instrumental and other jazz improvisational elements (especially "cutting contests," scat singing, vocalese, "bop talk," and "jive talk") and "battle" rap, "freestyle" rap, and "cypherin'" are more correctly comprehended as part of a long musical and colloquial continuum that reaches all the way back to ancient African *jeliyas* (now *djalis*) or so-called "griots." Moreover, it has been generally accepted that rap has roots in the colloquial contests commonly called the "dozens," "playin' the dozens" or "doin' the dozens," and sometimes even the "dirty dozens" that African Americans created during their ignoble enslavement. However, there is also a sense in which "battle" rap may be connected to other, non-African American poetic traditions (specifically "poetic jousts") that have been more or less *African Americanized,* such as the Japanese poetic genres haiku, renku (i.e., haikai no renga), haibun, haiga, and senryū, as well as the European poetic tradition of "flyting."[47]

We see here, then, that rap's roots, and hip hop culture in general, is not a series of uninterrupted, straight, and narrow lines grounded in and flowing from one form of black popular music to another, but also bears the unmistakable influence of political, poetic, and linguistic traditions that are as diverse as *the multicultural, multi-racial, multi-national, multi-lingual, and multi-religious masses* who currently constitute the Hip Hop Generation. Nonetheless, in keeping with the focus of this "remix," I would like to conclude by re-emphasizing the roots of jazz rap, and subsequent forms of "alternative" and "conscious" rap. Writing about the direct connections between jazz and rap in particular, Justin Williams (2010a) judiciously observed:

> Both hip hop and jazz had their origins as dance music; they were largely the product of African American urban creativity and innovation, and they shared rhythmic similarities: hip hop and hard bop jazz of the 1950s and 60s were stylistically defined by a dominance of the beat. Bebop jazz was a source of inspiration for many 1950s hipsters and beat poets, and poetry was often recited with jazz accompaniment (almost as a proto-rap form). Improvisation (more specifically, the ability to improvise in the generic idiom) was linked to authenticity in both jazz and hip hop. For mainstream jazz, in addition to the technical mastery of one's craft, it was what one did with the past that made one authentic, and battles (or "cutting contests") were not uncommon in the early days of jazz as a way to gain respect (and gigs) in the musical community; in certain subgenres of hip hop, one's ability to freestyle (improvise raps on the spot) and to "battle" rap are sure signs of authenticity in certain "underground" rap and DJ circles. (441; see also K. Fitzgerald 2004; Spirer 1997, 2005, 2006)

Moving away from the focus on rap's musical roots in jazz to rap's political and poetic roots in the Jazz Age, here it is important to bear in mind that even more than classic blues classic jazz, bebop, and hard bop synthesized the sonic with the poetic, the musical with the lyrical. After acknowledging both hard bop and hip hop's intense emphasis on the beat, notice how Williams highlights how bebop "was a source of inspiration for many 1950s hipsters and beat poets, and poetry was often recited with jazz accompaniment (almost as a proto-rap form)." Going back, but not going far enough, Williams's work—unwittingly I honestly believe—ignores and, therefore, erases the fact that it was actually Langston Hughes and other poets of the Harlem Renaissance who first translated black popular music, specifically classic blues and classic jazz, into poetry. For instance, Hughes's iconic volumes of verse *The Weary Blues* (1926), *Fine Clothes to the Jew* (1927), *Shakespeare in Harlem* (1942), *Montage of a Dream Deferred* (1951), and *Ask Your Mama!: 12 Moods for Jazz* (1961) each skillfully synthesized poetry and black folk philosophy with black popular music two decades prior to the heydays of the Hipster Movement and the Bebop Movement. In this sense, although Williams's work is certainly groundbreaking in that it links jazz and rap and offers provocative concepts such as "jazz codes" and "hip hop codes," it is woefully weak when and where we come to hip hop's *poetic inheritance* from the Harlem Renaissance and its *political inheritance* from the New Negro Movement.

Williams is a musicologist and, at least academically speaking, is not expected to be able to critically engage the deep double entendres and pure "folk" poetry at the heart of black popular (especially hip hop) music. Nevertheless, an interdisciplinary (arts, humanities, *and* social science) approach to hip hop's poetic *and* political inheritance from the major African American arts movement and civil rights movement of the Jazz Age (i.e., the Harlem Renaissance and the New Negro Movement, respectively) would be not simply a serious contribution to the Hip Hop Generation, but also a major move forward for those of us earnestly searching for an antidote for *hip hop's amnesia*.

Suffice to say, all of the foregoing point to several pertinent points with respect to the origins and evolution of rap, and jazz rap in particular. First, rap is nothing more than the latest sonic and poetic contribution from a long line of diverse African American poets, from the Harlem Renaissance poets onward, who have creatively combined black popular music and black folk philosophy with poetry. Second, and core to the current "remix," jazz *as music, aesthetics, politics, and culture* has indelibly influenced the literary and performatory aspects of post–Harlem Renaissance African American poetry in ways conducive to the synthesis and ongoing development of both—and it is extremely important to observe that both the origins and early evolution of jazz *and* post–Harlem Renaissance African American poetry were indelibly influenced by the little-known (i.e., outside of African American Studies) New Negro Movement. Third, syntheses of African American poetry with African American music were routinely undertaken long before and actually directly influenced the inauguration of rap music and, truth be told, each successive poetic and sonic synthesis either spawned or influenced the origins and evolution of the ensuing poetic and sonic syntheses.

To a certain extent it might be argued that rappers are actually more in line with the African American poetic tradition than the African American musical tradition. For the sake of argument, that being accepted as (at least partially) the case, rappers should be viewed as contemporary exponents of the African American poetic and sonic synthesis tradition—a tradition, as will be discussed in the following Harlem Renaissance "remix," that has undeniable roots in the work of Harlem Renaissance poets and in the more militant politics of the New Negro Movement. The main difference between previous syntheses of African American music and poetry and rap music essentially lies in the fact that its inventors and key exponents principally emanate from African American folk (or "street") poetic traditions rather than primarily the African American academic poetic tradition.

Even a cursory perusal of the intellectual pedigrees of the great poetic trinity of the Harlem Renaissance—Langston Hughes, Claude McKay, and Countee Cullen—will reveal that Hughes earned his bachelors degree from

Lincoln University, McKay studied at Tuskegee University and Kansas State University, and Cullen received his bachelor's degree from New York University and his master's degree from Harvard University. Prior to rap music there has not been such a high volume of "untrained," "untutored," or "unlettered" African American poets with access to the largess and luxuries of corporate America, which previously have been haughtily reserved only for the most renowned (mostly European American or either college-educated African American) poets. However, too much should not be made of the differences between so-called "tutored" African American academic poets and "untutored" African American "street" poets (or, quite simply, "rappers"), because both groups of poets proudly and heavily draw from African American "folk" speech and African American "folk" philosophy, as well as black popular music and black popular culture.

In the end, it can be said simply: Rap's roots are not merely musical, but also political and poetic. Hence, deeply connected to rap's *musical inheritance* from jazz is its *poetic inheritance* from the Harlem Renaissance and its *political inheritance* from the New Negro Movement. In fact, it can be said without innuendo or the slightest trace of ambiguity, many of the major breakthroughs and core concepts of the New Negro Movement and the Harlem Renaissance continue to inspire and influence contemporary rap music and hip hop culture—just as much as (and sometimes even more than) jazz has. Consequently, the next "remix" will provide a brief overview of the New Negro Movement and the Harlem Renaissance with an eye toward what these history-making movements contributed, however unheralded, to rap music, hip hop culture, and the Hip Hop Movement.

## NOTES

1. For further discussion of jazz "jive talk," "bop talk," "hepcat talk," and what was later termed "hipster talk," as well as 1940s and 1950s hipster music, hipster culture, and the wider Hipster Movement, and for the most noteworthy works that informed my analysis here, see D. H. Daniels (1985, 2002), Farrell and Johnson (1981), Gold (1957), A. Green (2009), Heise (2011), Leland (2004), Leonard (1986), McCann (2008), McRae (2001), Moten (2003), Porter (1999), and R. J. Smith (2006).

2. For further discussion of what is variously referred to as "early jazz" and "classic jazz," and for the most noteworthy works that informed my analysis here, see Bogdanov, Woodstra, and Erlewine (2002), Carney (2009), Cooke and Horn (2002), Gioia (2011), Kirchner (2000), Schuller (1986), Ward (2000), M. T. Williams (1970b, 1985), and Yanow (2001a).

3. For further discussion of the jazz vocal tradition and the major iconic jazz vocalists, and for the most noteworthy works that informed my analysis here, see Crowther and Pinfold (1986), F. Davis (1990), M. Evans (1999), Friedwald (1996, 2010), Gourse (1984), Grime (1983), Roland (2000), and Yanow (2008).

4. For further discussion of "creole New Orleans," "black New Orleans," and the birth of jazz around the turn of the twentieth century, and for the most noteworthy works that informed my analysis here, see Bell (1997), Blassingame (1973), Hersch (2007), Hirsch and Logsdon (1992), and S. E. Thompson (2009).

5. For further discussion of classic New Orleans jazz and its association with illicit life-styles, and for the most noteworthy works that informed my analysis here, see Brothers (2006), S. B. Charters (2008), Longstreet (1965), Schafer and Allen (1977), and M. T. Williams (1959, 1967).

6. For further discussion of Jelly Roll Morton's music and colorful life, and for the most noteworthy works that informed my analysis here, see Albertson (1979), Lomax (1973), Reich and Gaines (2003), Pastras (2001), Schafer (2008), and M. T. Williams (1962).

7. For further discussion of Louis Armstrong's music and legendary life, and for the most noteworthy works that informed my analysis here, see Armstrong (1999), Bergreen (1997), Collier (1983), Giddins (1988), Jones and Chilton (1971), Riccardi (2011), and Teachout (2009).

8. For further discussion of Duke Ellington's music and extraordinary life, and for the most noteworthy works that informed my analysis here, see Collier (1987), Dance (2000), Ellington (1973, 1993), Hasse (1993), Jewell (1977), and Rattenbury (1990).

9. For further discussion of Billy Strayhorn's music and "lush life," see Hajdu (1996) and Leur (2002). And, for the most noteworthy works on the Swing and Big Band Era that informed my analysis here, see Erenberg (1998), Schuller (1989a, 1989b), and Yanow (2000b).

10. For further discussion of the Lost Generation, and for the most noteworthy works that informed my analysis here, see Aldridge (1985), Cowley (1973), Dolan (1996), Monk (2008), and Wohl (1979).

11. For further discussion of the Lost Generation's relationship with jazz and its conception of the word "jazz" in the moniker the "Jazz Age," and for the most noteworthy works that informed my analysis here, see Barrett (1959), Boardman (1968), D.J. Goldberg (1999), Newton-Matza (2009), Riley (2004), A. Shaw (1987, 1998), and Studlar (1996).

12. For further discussion of early white jazz musicians and their music, as well as the ways in which race and racism factored into jazz's origins and early evolution (i.e., 1900 to 1950), and for the most noteworthy works that informed my analysis here, see Austerlitz (2005), N. M. Evans (2000), Gerard (1998), Kennedy (1994), Lees (1994), Leonard (1962), Peretti (1992), Sandke (2010), Sengstock (2004), Sudhalter (1999), and Yaffe (2006).

13. For further discussion of African American history, culture, and struggle during the first half of the twentieth century (i.e., before the Civil Rights Movement), and for the most noteworthy works that informed my analysis here, see Hornsby (2005), Hurt (2003), Kelley and Lewis (2000), Painter (2006), Payne and Green (2003), Taylor and Hill (2000), and Trotter (2001).

14. For further discussion of the New Negro Movement and Harlem Renaissance in relationship to jazz, rap, and hip hop culture, see the subsequent "remix."

15. For further discussion of jazz's impact on American culture, especially American popular music and popular culture, and for the most noteworthy works that informed my analysis here, see Gioia (1988, 2011), O'Meally (1998), Panish (1997), Salamone (2009), Townsend (2000), and M. T. Williams (1970b, 1985, 1989, 1992).

16. For further discussion of Europe's perception and cultural reception of jazz in the Jazz Age, especially in England, France, and even Nazi Germany, and for the most noteworthy works that informed my analysis here, see Berliner (2002), Budds (2002), M. F. Jordan (2010), Kater (1992), Parsonage (2005), C. A. Riley (2004), Ross (2003), Shack (2001), Sternfeld (2007), D. J. Taylor (2009), and Wipplinger (2006).

17. For further discussion of fashion during the Jazz Age, and for the most noteworthy works that informed my analysis here, see Chadwick and Latimer (2003), Hannel (2002, 2006), and Steele (1985).

18. For further discussion of the origins and early evolution of radio broadcasting in America, and for the most noteworthy works that informed my analysis here, see Barfield (1996), Douglas (1987), Hilmes and Loviglio (2002), LaFollette (2008), and Smulyan (1994).

19. For further discussion of the "musical segregation" and white domination of early radio broadcasting in America, and for the most noteworthy works that informed my analysis here, see George (1988), Miller (2010), Savage (1999), Suisman (2009), and Ward (2004).

20. For further discussion of Coleman Hawkins, swing, "sweet," "hot," and big band jazz in the 1930s and 1940s, and for the most noteworthy works that informed my analysis here, see Caponi-Tabery (2008), Chilton (1990), Gitler (1985), Griffiths (1998), McClellan (2004), Oliphant (2002), Schuller (1989b), A. Shaw (1998), Stowe (1994), and Tumpak (2008).

21. For further discussion of Charlie Parker and Dizzy Gillespie, and for the most noteworthy works that informed my analysis here, see Horricks (1984), Koch (1988), Maggin (2005), Reisner (1977), R. Russell (1996), Shipton (1999), Vail (2003), and Woideck (1996).

22. For further discussion of bebop as both music *and* movement, and for the most noteworthy works that informed my analysis here, see DeVeaux (1997), Gitler (2001), Korall (2002), MacAdams (2001), Mathieson (1999), Meadows (2003), Oliphant (1994), Owens (1995), and Yanow (2000a).

23. For further discussion of the "Uncle Tom" (or, rather, the "Tommin'") image, expressions, and white construction of African Americans, which was based on Harriet Beecher Stowe's *Uncle Tom's Cabin* (1852), and for the most noteworthy works that informed my analysis here, see Bogle (2000, 2001, 2005), Gabbard (2004), Gossett (1985), Meer (2005), and Rocchio (2000).

24. For further discussion of Islam's influence on bebop and jazz in general, and for the most noteworthy works that informed my analysis here, see Bowen (2011), Chase (2010), Fanusie (2007), Macias (2010), and D. W. Stowe (2004, 2010). And, for the most noteworthy works I have relied on to develop my interpretation of the 1940s and 1950s Muslim Movement in African America, as well as African American Islam more generally, see Dannin (2002), Gomez (2005), S. A. Jackson (2005), Marable and Aidi (2009), McCloud (1995), and Turner (2003).

25. For further discussion of Islam's influence on rap music and hip hop culture, and for the most noteworthy works that informed my analysis here, see Cooke and Lawrence (2005), Knight (2007), Malik (2009), Miyakawa (2005), and Nieuwkerk (2011).

26. For further discussion of the birth of bebop uptown in Harlem (especially in clubs such as Minton's, Monroe's, and Small's) in particular and New York City more generally, and for the most noteworthy works that informed my analysis here, see J. Anderson (1993), Burke (2008), Griffiths (1998), Longstreet (1986), O'Neal (2009), Ostransky (1978), and A. Shaw (1977).

27. For further discussion of the Harlem riot of 1943, as well as other significant "race riots" during the first half of the twentieth century, and for the most noteworthy works that informed my analysis here along with Capeci (1977), see Abu-Lughod (2007), M. S. Johnson (1998), Knopf (2006), Masotti and Bowen (1968), Mitchell (1970), and Rucker and Upton (2007).

28. For further discussion of the "race riots," urban rebellions, and natural disasters impacting African America in the second half of the twentieth century and reaching into the early years of the twenty-first century (i.e., between the 1960s and Hurricane Katrina in 2005), and for the most noteworthy works that informed my analysis here, see Dyson (2006), Goldschmidt (2006), Gooding-Williams (1993), Horne (1995), Marable and Clarke-Avery (2008), Mumford (2007), Porter and Dunn (1984), Rucker and Upton (2007), and E. S. Shapiro (2006).

29. For further discussion of the connections between 1940s and 1950s bebop and 1960s and 1970s "free" or "avant-garde" jazz, and for the most noteworthy works that informed my analysis here, see I. Anderson (2007), Giddins and DeVeaux (2009), Jost (1981), G. Lewis (2008), Litweiler (1984, 1992), MacAdams (2001), Mandel (2007), Mathieson (1999), Whitehead (2011), M. T. Williams (1970a, 1970b, 1989), and P. N. Wilson (1999).

30. For further discussion of the various genres of jazz (especially post-bebop jazz), and for the most noteworthy works that informed my analysis here, see Bogdanov, Woodstra, and Erlewine (2002), Cooke and Horn (2002), Giddins (1998), Gioia (2011), Hasse (2000), Kirchner (2000), Meeder (2008), Schuller (1989a, 1989b), Shipton (2007), and M. T. Williams (1970b, 1985, 1989, 1992).

31. For further discussion of the Detroit and Zoot Suit (i.e., Los Angeles) riots of 1943, and for the most noteworthy works that informed my analysis here, see Alvarez (2008), Capeci and Wilkerson (1991), Daniels (2002), Mazón (1984), and Pagán (2003).

32.  For further discussion of the early 1960s Sit-In Movement and Freedom Rider Movement, and for the most noteworthy works that informed my analysis here, see Arsenault (2006), Carson, Garrow, Gill, Harding, and Hine (1997), Morris (1981, 1984), Nelson (2011), and J. Williams (1987).

33.  For further discussion of the Black Power Movement, and for the most noteworthy works that informed my analysis here, see Glaude (2002), Joseph (2006a, 2006b), Ogbar (2004), Olsson (2011), and Van Deburg (1992).

34.  For further discussion of the Black Arts Movement and its enormous influence on rap music, hip hop culture, and the Hip Hop Movement, see "'Say It Loud!—I'm Black and I'm Proud!': From the Black Arts Movement and Blaxploitation Films to the Conscious and Commercial Rap of the Hip Hop Generation" in Rabaka (2011, 83–128).

35.  For further discussion of the Beat Generation, and for the most noteworthy works that informed my analysis here, see Campbell (2001), A. Charters (1983, 1986, 1993, 2001, 2003), Cook (1971), George-Warren (1999), Maynard (1991), McDarrah and McDarrah (2001), B. Morgan (2010), Myrsiades (2002), S. Watson (1995a), and Zott (2003).

36.  For further discussion of the interconnections between the Bebop Movement, the Beat Generation, and drug abuse, and for the most noteworthy works that informed my analysis here, see A. Charters (1994), Erbsen (1968), Izant (2008), Lawlor (2005), Long (2005), Singer and Mirhe (2006), F. J. Spencer (2002), Tolson and Cuyjet (2007), and Warner (2007).

37.  For further discussion of the Beat Generation's homosexual, bisexual, and so-called "alternative sexual practices," and for the most noteworthy works that informed my analysis here, see Davenport (1995), O. C. G. Harris (1999), Marler (2004), J. Russell (2001), Sondergard (2003), Stimpson (1983), and Stone and Ward (2011).

38.  For further discussion of the various styles of rap music, and for the most noteworthy works that informed my analysis here, see Bogdanov, Woodstra, Erlewine and Bush (2003), Bynoe (2006), Hess (2007b), P. Shapiro (2001, 2005a), and Wang (2003).

39.  For further discussion of Langston Hughes's blues and jazz poetry, as well as its influence on subsequent generations' poets, and for the most noteworthy works that informed my analysis here, see Bonner (1996), Jemie (1976), M. D. Jones (2011), Komunyakaa (2002), Patterson (2000), Tracy (2001), and Waldron (1971).

40.  For further discussion of jazz in the 1980s and 1990s, and for the most noteworthy works that informed my analysis here, see F. Davis (1988), Giddins (1985, 1998), Hasse (2000), Meeder (2008), Nicholson (1995), and Shipton (2007).

41.  For further discussion of what is commonly called "concert jazz," which is usually thought of as a hybrid between jazz and European classical music, and for the most noteworthy works that informed my analysis here, see Collier (1975), Hobsbawm (1993), Howland (2009), and Shreffler (1997).

42.  For further discussion of the free jazz and avant-garde jazz subgenres that most of the 1980s and 1990s "neo-hard boppers" and "neo-post-boppers" either ignored or altogether erased from their hallowed histories of jazz, and for the most noteworthy works that informed my analysis here, see T. S. Jenkins (2004), Mazzola and Cherlin (2009), Nicholson (2005), Peterson (2006), Sportis (1990), Such (1993), and Wilmer (1992).

43.  For further discussion of "hood" films, or what are alternatively called "hip hop" films, and for the most noteworthy works that informed my analysis here, see Boyd (1997, 2002, 2003), Covington (2010), Donalson (2007), George (1994), Guerrero (1993), K. M. Harris (2006), Massood (2003), Sieving (2011), Smith-Shomade (2003), and Watkins (1998, 2005).

44.  For further discussion of the longstanding distinctions many African American musicians made and continue to make between "authentic" African American music and "crossover" pop "muzak," and for the most noteworthy works that informed my analysis here, see Floyd (1995), Miller (2010), Neal (1998, 2002, 2003), Phinney (2005), Ramsey (2003), and A. Shaw (1970, 1978, 1986, 1987, 1998).

45.  For further discussion of the jazz poetry tradition, and for the most noteworthy works that informed my analysis here, see T. J. Anderson (2004), Feinstein (1997), Feinstein and Komunyakaa (1991, 1996), Frost (1999), Hartman (1991), M. D. Jones (2011), and Wallenstein (1980, 1991).

46. For further discussion of sampling in rap and other forms of hip hop music, and for the most noteworthy works that informed my analysis here, see Demers (2001, 2002, 2003), Haupt (2008), Kaplicer (2001), Marshall (2006), Schloss (2004), and Schumacher (1995).

47. For further discussion of rap music's roots in previous African American socio-linguistic, cultural linguistic, and other communicative traditions and practices, especially "cutting contests" and the "dozens," and for the most noteworthy works that informed my analysis here, see Alim (2004, 2006), Alim, Ibrahim, and Pennycook (2009), L. J. Green (2002), Rickford (1999), Rickford, Mufwene, Bailey, and Baugh (1998), Rickford and Rickford (2000), and Smitherman (1975, 1986, 2000, 2006).

*Remix 4*

# "If We Must Die!"

*The New Negro Movement, the Harlem Renaissance, and the Homosexual Hip Hop Movement*

Significantly, attitudes toward sexuality and sexual preference are changing. There is greater acknowledgement that people have different sexual preferences and diverse sexual practices. Given this reality, it is a waste of energy for anyone to assume that their condemnation will ensure that people do not express varied sexual preferences. Many gay people of all races, raised within this homophobic society, struggle to confront and accept themselves, to recover or gain the core of self-love and well-being that is constantly threatened and attacked both from within and without. This is particularly true for people of color who are gay. It is essential that non-gay black people recognize and respect the hardships, the difficulties gay black people experience, extending love and understanding that is essential for the making of authentic black community. One way we show our care is by vigilant protest of homophobia. By acknowledging the union between black liberation struggle and gay liberation struggle, we strengthen our solidarity, enhance the scope and power of our allegiances, and further our resistance. —bell hooks, *Talking Back: Thinking Feminist, Thinking Black*, 125–26

## EPITAPHS OF THE OLD NEGRO: NEW NEGROES, RENAISSANCE RADICALS, AND HIP HOPPERS

In his history-making volume *The New Negro* (1925), Alain Locke, the long-acknowledged impresario of the Harlem Renaissance, made it known that "the Old Negro had long become more of a myth than a man" (3). He continued, "[f]or the younger generation is vibrant with a new psychology;

167

the new spirit is awake in the masses, and under the very eyes of the professional observers is transforming what has been a perennial problem into the progressive phases of contemporary Negro life" (3). For most of nineteenth century America, whether we speak of white America or otherwise, the general impression and image of African Americans long lodged in their minds revolved around "Negroes" as "black slaves" or "blackface minstrels." No longer content with being thought of as a "perennial problem," Locke emphasized that the "New Negro" of 1925 was not only "younger," but also that she or he was either a part of or deeply identified with "the masses."[1]

Prophetically prefiguring the politics of the Hip Hop Movement, Locke articulated the general mood and sentiments of many of the more artistically and politically inclined members of the New Negro Movement. "In a real sense it is the rank and file who are leading," he wrote, "and the leaders who are following. A transformed and transforming psychology permeates the masses" (7). As with the Civil Rights Movement, Black Power Movement, and Hip Hop Movement, each of which emerged in the aftermath of the New Negro Movement, Locke was keen to emphasize the role that both the black masses in general, and black youth in particular, played in the civil rights and social justice struggles of the early twentieth century.

Although each of the previously mentioned movements was more or less aimed at achieving human recognition and civil rights for African Americans, among other oppressed groups, it is important for us to accent the often-overlooked fact that each of the previously mentioned movements decidedly differed in terms of their strategies and tactics. We might go so far to say that even though the overarching goal of almost all African American social and political movements have remained relatively unchanged since the Reconstruction years (i.e., 1865–1877), the policy and basic battle plan to obtain civil rights and a higher level of human life have noticeably changed, and changed drastically. Hence, in its own unique way the Hip Hop Movement registers as a continuation of black youth movement and leadership and, most especially, positive proof that a "transformed and transforming psychology permeates the masses" in the early twenty-first century. Truth be told, then, there is a great deal of what is currently considered "real" hip hop that, to put it plainly, has "real" roots in the *politics* of the New Negro Movement and the *poetics* of the Harlem Renaissance.

"Each generation," Locke declared, "will have its creed, and that of the present is the belief in the efficacy of collective effort, in race cooperation" (11). Unambiguously presaging Hip Hop Generation social and political thought, especially the neo-black nationalism and "Afrocentrism" of the 1980s and 1990s (i.e., the "Golden Age of Hip Hop"), Locke's words provide a link between the ethos and overall agenda of the New Negro Movement of the past and the Hip Hop Movement of the present. The long-overlooked similarities between these movements is both startling and stunning. For instance, like the Hip Hop Movement in relationship to the Civil Rights Movement, and to a certain extent the Black Power Movement, the young artists, intellectuals, and activists of the Harlem Renaissance in many senses represented a "second wave" of early twentieth century civil rights soldiers within the context of the New Negro Movement. Which is also to say, similar to the Black Arts Movement in relationship to the Black Power Movement, the Harlem Renaissance should be regarded as the cultural aesthetic arm of the New Negro Movement, which was more or less a social and political movement aimed at securing African Americans' human and civil rights.

What obviously distinguishes the Harlem Renaissance from the New Negro Movement is the former's emphasis on utilizing art (i.e., artistic activism) to obtain human recognition and civil rights, and the latter's emphasis on utilizing politics and social organization (i.e., socio-political activism) to achieve human recognition and civil rights. What needs to be observed at the outset, however, is that many of the discursive distinctions currently being made between the members of the New Negro Movement and the radicals of the Harlem Renaissance are frequently nothing more than academic and extremely abstract hair splitting. As many of the major works of the Harlem Renaissance reveal, the members of the New Negro Movement and the radicals of the Harlem Renaissance were almost invariably one and the same.

For example, several prominent members of arguably the preeminent civil rights organization of the New Negro Movement, the National Association for the Advancement of Colored People (NAACP), were either pivotal participants in or, at the least, constructively contributed to the Harlem Renaissance, including: W.E.B. Du Bois (see his novels and other creative writings, *The Quest of the Silver Fleece* [1911], *Dark Princess* [1928], *The Selected Poems of W.E.B. Du Bois* [1964] and *Creative Writings by W.E.B. Du Bois* [1985]; James Weldon Johnson (see his novel and poetry, *The Autobiography of an Ex-Colored Man* [1912], *Fifty Years and Other Poems* [1917], *God's Trombones* [1927], and *The Complete Poems* [2000]); Jessie Fauset (see her novels, *There Is Confusion* [1924], *Plum Bun* [1928], and *The Chinaberry Tree* [1931]); and Walter White (see his novels, *Fire in the Flint* [1924] and *Flight* [1926]). As a matter of fact, when and where authentic distinctions are made between the New Negro Movement and the Harlem Renaissance they almost always revolve around those "New Negroes" who were the first generation born after African American enslavement and who seemed to privilege more "conventional" politics and civil rights activism, in contrast to those who were slightly younger than the first wave of New Negroes and who seemed to privilege "Negro art" and artistic activism in the civil rights struggle. All that being said, yet and still, it should be strongly stressed that one of the most distinctive aspects of both the New Negro

Movement and the Harlem Renaissance was the simultaneous *aestheticiza-tion of the African American civil rights struggle* and *the radical politiciza-tion of African American art.*

As with contemporary black popular music and black popular culture, most of the older, elite, and college-educated leaders of the New Negro Movement were embarrassed by and sought to distance themselves from the black popular music and black popular culture of their era (i.e., classic blues, classic jazz, and the more politically and aesthetically radical aspects of the Harlem Renaissance). Similar to the Black Women's Club Movement, which preceded it and indelibly influenced it, the New Negro Movement had both "conservative" and "radical" elements. In many ways, the artists of the Har-lem Renaissance represented the younger and more radical "second wave" of the New Negro Movement, although ultimately the Harlem Renaissance came to embody both conservative and radical politics and aesthetics as well. A cadre of the Harlem Renaissance quickly became disgusted with the Euro-centric and bourgeois condescending attitude of the elite and older New Negro leaders toward black popular music and black popular culture, and they took it upon themselves to audaciously document, lament, and celebrate the African American experience in its full, deep depth and torrid totality.

It is the work of the young radicals of the Harlem Renaissance that pro-vides the primary link between the New Negro Movement and the Hip Hop Movement. Renaissance radicals such as Wallace Thurman, Zora Neale Hurston, Langston Hughes, Richard Bruce Nugent, Gwendolyn Bennett, and Aaron Douglas sought to raise issues impacting African Americans that the elite and older New Negro leaders left in the lurch. For example, the young radicals' work frequently explored taboo topics such as homosexuality, bi-sexuality, promiscuity, prostitution, drug abuse, domestic violence, interra-cial relationships, and both classism and colorism within the African American community. Their collective work, as with the best work in black radical politics and critical social theory, provided both an external and inter-nal critique of the issues and ills besetting African America. It unrepentantly engaged the controversies and contradictions surrounding African American life and culture during the early decades of the twentieth century.

Representing much more than a critique of early twentieth century anti-black racism, lynching, and economic exploitation, the work of the young radicals of the Harlem Renaissance also served as an innovative commentary on and critique of the increasing conservatism and bourgeoisism of the New Negro Movement and, truth be told, some erstwhile elements of the Harlem Renaissance itself. As the elite and older New Negro leaders decried the vulgarity and vice-filled nature of working-class and poor black folk's cul-ture, much of which revolved around black popular music and black popular culture, the radicals of the Renaissance sought to celebrate both the beautiful-ness and ugliness, the triumphs and the tragedies of what it meant to be black, especially poor and black, in early twentieth century America. The Renaissance radicals forcefully challenged the Victorianism, bourgeoisism, and general Eurocentrism of the elite and older New Negro leaders, reminding them that the majority of African Americans were, as they remain in the twenty-first century, members of the working class and the underclass. Consequently, authentic African American art and expressive culture, the Renaissance radicals ardently believed, need not always but should in some sufficient way seek to grasp and seriously grapple with the lives and struggles of the black masses, who, to reiterate, historically have been and remain working class and patently poverty stricken.

It could be easily argued that at its best rap music and hip hop culture documents, laments, and celebrates the wide range and full reach of the African American experience in several ways that demonstrate its indebtedness to the aesthetics of the Harlem Renaissance and the politics of the New Negro Movement. Without in any way diminishing the distinct differences between the New Negro Movement and the Harlem Renaissance, which mostly revolve around emphasis on either politics or aesthetics, respectively, this "remix" endeavors to explore what has been, however unheralded, handed down to rap music and hip hop culture from the New Negroes and Renaissance radicals. It is interesting to note, as in the broader context of contemporary hip hop culture, New Negroes and Renaissance radicals were almost uniformly engrossed in public dialogues, academic debates, and artistic activities revolving around the very same intersectional issues that continue to preoccupy most progressive hip hoppers: race, gender, class, sexuality, spirituality, religion, education, artistic license, etc. That being the case, it could be said that the connections between both the New Negro Movement and the Harlem Renaissance *and* rap music, hip hop culture, and the Hip Hop Movement are direct (as opposed to merely indirect), concrete (as opposed to simply abstract), and more than meaningful enough to warrant deeper critical examination.

The subsequent sections of this "remix" will offer alternative histories and critical theories of the New Negro Movement and the Harlem Renaissance with an astute eye on what has been—again, even though unsung—passed on to rap music, hip hop culture, and the Hip Hop Movement. The following section, "The New Negro Movement: Conservatism and Radicalism in Early Twentieth Century African America," provides a succinct survey of the New Negro Movement that sheds light on the ways in which its sometimes moderate, and sometimes militant civil rights activism laid a foundation for the Hip Hop Movement's, truth be told, "sometimes moderate, and sometimes militant" civil rights and social justice activism. The succeeding section, "The Harlem Renaissance: On the Niggerati, Rap Music's Feminist Roots, and the Homo-Hoppers of the Hip Hop Generation," develops a discourse on the aesthetics, poetics, and sexual politics of the

Harlem Renaissance. It seeks to accent the often-overlooked links between Renaissance music, aesthetics, poetics, and politics in light of its unprecedented *interracial heterosexual-homosexual alliances*. Building on the previous sections, the final section, "The Homosexual Hip Hop Movement: The Transgressive Sexual Radicalism of the Harlem Renaissance Revisited and Remixed," turns readers' attention to the simple—but still controversial in many quarters—fact that the Homosexual Hip Hop Movement, as quiet as it has been kept, may actually embody much of what can be considered "real" hip hop culture—especially "real" hip hop poetics, politics, and social activism—in light of its incessant emphasis on openness to and acceptance of difference, whether that "difference" is sexual, cultural, racial, gender, economic, or religious. Although the Homosexual Hip Hop Movement is not completely free from many of the same issues that plague the wider world of hip hop (i.e., sexism, subtle racism, and classism, etc.), yet and still, the final section suggests that there may be much the Hip Hop Movement as a whole can learn from the unique poetics and politics of the Homosexual Hip Hop Movement. We begin, then, with an abbreviated overview of the New Negro Movement, which, along with the Black Women's Club Movement, can be said to provide the Hip Hop Movement with one of the major pillars of its politics.

## THE NEW NEGRO MOVEMENT: CONSERVATISM AND RADICALISM IN EARLY TWENTIETH CENTURY AFRICAN AMERICA

As with the Lost Generation, World War I had a profound impact on the young radicals of the Harlem Renaissance. Following W. E. B. Du Bois's 1918 *Crisis* dictum "Close Ranks," African Americans faithfully joined the war effort, genuinely believing that fighting for freedom and democracy abroad would translate into freedom and democracy for black folk back home (see Du Bois 1995b, 697). Sadly, nothing could have been further from the truth. The Great War's ending was in many ways the beginning of what James Weldon Johnson termed the "Red Summer of 1919."[2]

Several factors contributed to the situation where more than three dozen U.S. cities erupted in anti-black racist violence in 1919. First, there was the Great Migration of African Americans out of the rural South to the urban North between 1910 and 1930. Reports from this period estimate that between two and three million African Americans moved North during the first three decades of the twentieth century; a second Great Migration took place between 1940 and 1970 in which five million or more African Americans moved to even more diverse destinations, including the Midwest, the Southwest, and the far West.[3]

As African Americans fanned out across the country in the early years of the twentieth century most thought very little of the Red Scare of 1919, but anti-communism quickly translated into xenophobia, and xenophobia almost immediately mutated into fickle forms of anti-black racist violence that in many ways rivaled the horrors African Americans endured during the 1880s and 1890s—a period that noted historian Rayford Logan, in *The Negro in American Life and Thought: The Nadir, 1877–1901* (1954), famously characterized as "the nadir of American race relations." African Americans had many reasons for migrating to the North, including to escape lynching, Jim Crow laws, anti-black racist restrictions on their voting and civil rights, and the collapsing economy of the rural South, where the boll weevil was devastating cotton crops. By most accounts the Red Summer of 1919 began in May in Charleston, North Carolina, where a white sailor shot an African American civilian to death. The "race riot" that ensued left seven African Americans dead and more than thirty-five wounded, as well as three white sailors and one policeman injured.

Ellisville, Mississippi, exploded in late June. There a fanatical gang of white men fatally wounded an alleged black rapist by the name of John Hartfield as he sought to escape from capture by way of a cane field. Reports indicate that a local white physician fiendishly kept Hartfield alive so that he could be "properly" lynched the next day. The local newspapers gleefully announced the time and place of Hartfield's lynching, while the then governor of Mississippi, Theodore Bilbo, callously remarked that "[n]obody can keep the inevitable from happening." On the day after Hartfield's lynching the local newspapers shamelessly reported that more than three thousand townspeople and "upstanding" citizens gathered at the appointed tree and, after fervently debating the "best" way to torture him before they killed him, Hartfield's executioners hanged, burned, and then, for good measure, repeatedly shot his lifeless and brutally charred and bludgeoned body.

By summer's end this sickening scene was repeated in more than three dozen U.S. cities, including the nation's capital. In response to the carnage one of the leading lights of the Harlem Renaissance, Claude McKay, drummed out his most defiant and most famous poem, the immortal "If We Must Die." It became both the battle oath and battle anthem of the New Negro Movement: "If we must die, let it not be like hogs/ Hunted and penned in an inglorious spot/ While round us bark the mad and hungry dogs/ Making their mock at our accursed lot." Indeed, this was not Paul Laurence Dunbar's much-heralded "dialect poetry." It represented something altogether different, something clearly distinguished from even those race-conscious writings offered up by notable nineteenth century black radicals, such as Frederick Douglass, Frances Ellen Watkins Harper, Martin Delany, Alexander Crummell, Pauline Hopkins, and Bishop Henry McNeal Turner.[4]

McKay's words deftly helped to mark the new militancy of the New Negro Movement. In the summer of 1918 Frank Harris, the noted editor of *Pearson's Magazine, Fortnightly Review*, and *Saturday Review*, as well as the publisher of such talents as Oscar Wilde, George Bernard Shaw, and H.G. Wells, urged McKay not to mute and mask his true feelings concerning the swelling mob violence against African Americans. According to Wayne Cooper in *Claude McKay: Rebel Sojourner in the Harlem Renaissance* (1987), Harris admonished McKay not to hold back, but to "rise and storm the heights, like Milton when he wrote 'On the Late Massacre in Piedmont'" (100). Cooper eruditiously continued:

> Harris had pointed specifically to McKay's sonnet "The Lynching" as an example of a poem whose expressed sentiments did not really plumb the horror of racial repression in the United States. In it McKay had compared the mutilated black victim of a lynching to a Christ figure and had commented upon the satanic, unearthly "glee" with which men, women, and children went through the rites of crucifixion. Harris had objected that "a sonnet like this, after reading the report of the St. Louis Massacre of 1917 . . . sounds like an anti-climax." He had then quoted Milton: "Avenge O Lord! They slaughtered Saints whose bones/ Lie scattered on the Alpine mountains cold." Those lines, Harris had stated, "have the sublime human cry of anguish and hate against man's inhumanity to man. Some day you will rip it out of your guts!" (100)

In "If We Must Die" McKay's outrage was palpable. Gone was the muted tone and timbre of many of his early poems (e.g., see *Songs of Jamaica* and *Constab Ballads*, both published in 1912; see also W. James 2000; McKay 1973, 2004). With this anguish-filled and decidedly defiant poem he etched his name into the annals of African American literature, even though he, like Marcus Garvey, had been born in Jamaica and frequently felt alienated as a result of African Americans' peculiar intra-racial colorism and classism. McKay's poem became the mouthpiece for millions of African Americans, and he responded to the dire circumstances of his newfound people with an uncompromising and unapologetic condemnation of those responsible for the violence against black folk.

He appealed directly to African Americans in "If We Must Die," exhorting them to resist anti-black racist violence with courage and coordinated determination. This poem, perhaps more than any other poem, novel, play, painting, or essay produced during the Harlem Renaissance, eloquently expressed African America's disposition toward desperation and undeniable defiance that long, hot, and holocaustic summer. As David Levering Lewis declared in *When Harlem Was in Vogue* (1989), for African Americans the

"'Red Summer' was a *Gehenna* [i.e., 'hell' in Judaism and the New Testament], compared to which the [Red Scare] ordeal of anarchists, communists, socialists, immigrants, and white workers was merely scarifying" (17–18).

No matter what McKay's critics may have said about the shortcomings in the construction and the deficiencies in the diction of "If We Must Die," no matter the traces of the heroic sentimentalism of Victorianism one may hear in it, when it is all said and done, he had composed a poem that immediately garnered a permanent place in the historical and cultural memory of a besieged and much-maligned people. In fact, it has been said that "If We Must Die" helped McKay forfeit whatever echoes of foreignness (i.e., "Jamaicanness" or, rather, "Caribbeanness") he once had from African Americans' point of view and henceforth he came to be claimed as one of their own, right along with renowned Harlem Renaissance poets Langston Hughes and Countee Cullen. In one of his autobiographies, *A Long Way From Home* (1937), McKay went so far as to say that "If We Must Die," that "one grand outburst," is African Americans' "sole standard of appraising my poetry" (31).

From 1919 forward, McKay's poems not only reviled racial oppression, but they also renounced the whole social, political, and economic order that enabled ongoing racial oppression and economic exploitation. In this way, his work was in line with other U.S. radicals, black and white, who after World War I perceived the Bolshevik Revolution in Russia as a fundamental example of how to attain the unfulfilled aspirations of the "old regimes" throughout Europe and America. Similar to other radicals, McKay deeply hoped for a reconstructed Western world where African Americans, along with all other cultural groups, could live unmolested lives in dignity and true democracy. McKay's critique of Europe and European America was therefore based on his heartfelt belief that in a future democratic socialist society, which would be unerringly dedicated to the workers and not the capitalists, black and white workers would no longer feel compelled to compete for the "almighty dollar" but could work in harmony striving for a classless society. In other words, at this point McKay believed that only through a democratic communist reconstruction of society could either blacks or whites achieve dignity and America's much-heralded democracy.

Emphasis should be placed on the fact that the most important and long-lasting ideological aspect of McKay's poetic rebellion was his fiercely felt and firm allegiance to the working-class and poor "common people" among African Americans. At times his allegiance to working-class and poor black folk translated into an inchoate black nationalism that seemed to contradict other aspects of his thought and completely confound his readers. Between 1919 and 1923 McKay would unmask his utter disdain for racial oppression and economic exploitation in America with poems such as "To the White Friends," "The Dominant White," "A Capitalist at Dinner," "The Little Peoples," "Song of the New Soldier and Worker," "The Beast," "Negro Spiritual," "The White House," and "To the Entrenched Classes" (see McKay 1953, 1973, 2004). In his poetry McKay took the United States to task with a vigorous and unmitigated moral outrage that was unprecedented for any American writer, black or white, at the time. By the same token, he did not refrain from mercilessly criticizing the colorism, classism, and outright elitism of the black bourgeoisie, which he felt had long been timid in the face of anti-black racism and had betrayed working-class and poor black folk by embracing capitalism.

In many ways McKay's work helps to highlight several of the core differences between the more moderate New Negroes and the more militant New Negroes. As with the Hip Hop Movement, it is possible that each member of the New Negro Movement adhered to both collective and individual interpretations of the fundamental message and mission of the movement. Logically, this leads us to a more in-depth discussion of the New Negro Movement, its politics, and the myriad ways its politics informed the poetics and overall aesthetics of the artists of the Harlem Renaissance. To begin, it might be helpful for us to bear in mind something Eric Walrond wrote in his classic *Vanity Fair* essay, "Enter the New Negro, A Distinctive Type Recently Created by the Colored Cabaret Belt in New York" (1924):

> The effortless New York Public, revolving always with the fairest wind, has recently discovered a new brand of Negro entertainer. Not the old type, of course. The lullaby-singer has gone. Also the plantation darky. And, out of the welter of sentimentality which the old types created, the Negro now emerges as an individual, an individual as brisk and as actual as your own next-door neighbor. He no longer has to be either a Pullman car porter, or over-fond of watermelon, in order to be a successful type on our stage. He is a personality, always, and frequently an artist. (61)

Walrond's emphasis on the "old types" of Negroes is extremely important, as it speaks to the ways in which the New Negro Movement and the Harlem Renaissance, both politically and aesthetically, registered as critical responses to antebellum, Reconstruction, and post-Reconstruction anti-black racism—*literal* and *literary*, *political* and *musical* anti-black racism. Perhaps there is no better example of the literal and literary, political and musical anti-black racism that served as a backdrop to the New Negro Movement and the Harlem Renaissance than the infamous—albeit still invisible to most white Americans, especially the white youth of the Hip Hop Generation—blackface minstrel show. In their efforts to provide more "authentic" and "realistic" portrayals of African American life and culture, the New Negroes and Renaissance radicals firmly felt they needed to *deconstruct* the "Old Negro," primarily associated with African American enslavement and blackface minstrelism, and *reconstruct* a "New Negro," who was "an individual as brisk and as actual as your own next-door neighbor." Like the politically-progressive hip hoppers of the early twenty-first century, the New Negroes of the early twentieth century understood that covert racism was just as harmful as overt racism, literary racism was just as damaging as literal racism, musical racism was just as detrimental as social or political racism—*ad infinitum.*

Although hip hop culture did not emerge in earnest until the last quarter of the twentieth century, it is extremely important to acknowledge its cultural and aesthetic antecedents. As I argued in *Hip Hop's Inheritance,* hip hop's aesthetic ancestors extend well beyond the artists and activists of the Black Arts Movement. As quiet as it has been kept, the Hip Hop Generation's social, political, cultural, and artistic consciousness is actually linked to much earlier forms of African American expressive culture, some reaching all the way back to the era of minstrelsy. Minstrelsy or the minstrel show, as discussed in "remix" 2, was one of the earliest authentically "American" forms of entertainment. It incorporated comedy routines, dancing, singing, and variety acts performed by whites in blackface or, especially during the Reconstruction and post-Reconstruction periods, blacks in blackface.[5]

The minstrel show arose as a counter to the efforts of the abolitionists, both black and white, who argued that enslaved Africans should be emancipated. In essence, minstrel shows caricatured enslaved Africans as ignorant, lazy, dirty, buffoonish, superstitious, ever-joyous, and ever-musical (Bean, Hatch, and McNamara 1996; Brundage 2011; Nowatzki 2010). In many senses, materializing as a response to the Haitian Revolution (1791–1804) and the consecutive revolts of Gabriel Prosser, Chatham Manor, George Boxley, Denmark Vessey, Nat Turner, and the *La Amistad* rebellion in the 1830s, the minstrel show grew out of brief burlesques and comic *entr'actes,* and evolved and eventually took shape as a fully formed musical review by the beginning of the 1840s.[6]

From the 1830s through to the 1930s minstrel shows were utilized for every propagandistic or, rather, every anti-black racist purpose imaginable. To be sure, several stock characters manifested themselves in minstrel shows, such as the "happy slave," the "dandy," the "coon," the "mammy," the "old darky," the "mulatto wench," and the buffoonish black soldier (Browder 2000). Minstrels, again, mostly whites until about the last quarter of the nineteenth century, insistently asserted that their characters, songs, and dances were based on "real" black folkways and "real" black folk culture, but the extent of the exact influence of authentic African American culture on blackface minstrelsy has long remained a point of contention. What has been historically documented, however, is that when the spirituals began to be sung in minstrel shows in the 1870s, it marked the first time that unmistakably African American music entered into the minstrel show's musical repertoire (Abbott and Seroff 2002; Lhamon 2003).

No matter what the Hip Hop Generation may make of all of this, one thing is for certain, and that is that blackface minstrelsy was undeniably the first distinctly "American" theatrical form (R. M. Lewis 2003; C. J. Robinson 2007; Sotiropoulos 2006). Moreover, blackface minstrelsy was the motor inside the machine that not only led to the emergence of, but also consistently powered the American music industry during its most formative phase of development (Crawford 2005; A. Shaw 1986; Werner 2006). Although often downplayed, it should be emphasized that American popular music and popular culture came into being by mercilessly mocking blacks and their blackness. When minstrel shows spread from the South to the North in the early 1840s, it marked a significant turning point in the marketing of minstrelsy and it opened up an entirely new age that saw the meteoric rise, widespread commercialization, and institutionalization of blackface minstrelsy.

With its caricatures of African American singing, dancing and speaking styles, blackface minstrelsy ensured that the most popular image of blacks in the white social imagination was one of them (i.e., blacks) as infantile and pathological brutes (Strausbaugh 2006). Hence, even in so-called "freedom" (i.e., even in the post-Emancipation period), African Americans were frequently referred to and reproached as the "Negro Problem."[7] They were seen as a social menace, in many senses, because their lives and struggles impugned the longstanding lie of lily-white democracy in America. And, even more, they were a constant reminder that race and its corollary racism has always been, and will remain for the foreseeable future, part and parcel of American citizenship and democracy. Beginning in the Jacksonian era, an age which extended voting rights to all white men by eliminating property laws and other qualifications, the omnipresent image of the blackface minstrel incessantly announced that black men—white and non-white women would not gain the right to vote until 1920—were utterly unqualified to contribute to, or participate in American democracy in any meaningful way (R. L. Jackson 2006; Tucker 2007). What, pray tell, many whites asked, did ignorant, infantile, and indolent "slaves" and "former slaves" have to do with the august tradition of American citizenship and democracy?

As with many of the most questionable aspects of rap music and hip hop culture, whites, to put it plainly, were mesmerized by blackface minstrelsy. It was as though they were on safari, journeying through a jungle world filled with black (among other non-white) half-human and half-animal creatures who were as "savage" as they were sad. And, it was this white supremacist and anti-black racist construction of blacks that was celebrated and sold to whites and, truth be told, to other non-whites, nationally and internationally, as "authentic blackness."

It is extremely interesting to observe that a wide range of whites, from Abraham Lincoln and Mark Twain to newly arrived "ethnic" European immigrants in Northern ghettoes and poor whites in the Southern states, were among the most ardent admirers of the minstrel show. In this sense, then, the impact of blackface minstrelsy was, and covertly continues to be, both profound and pervasive. For instance, in *The Rise and Fall of the White Republic: Class, Politics, and Mass Culture in Nineteenth Century America*, Alexander Saxton (1990) observed, "[p]aced by the extraordinary popularity of blackface minstrelsy, theater expanded into an industry of mass entertainment" (109).

Furthermore, whites' fascination with, combined with the widespread popularity of, blackface minstrelsy served as a recurring anti-black racist reference point for whites of seemingly all social classes. Ironically, blackface minstrelsy, both wittingly and unwittingly, aided and abetted the spread of the "whiteness as property" ethos and white racial egalitarianism, irrespective of social, political, regional, and religious differences (Du Bois 1920; C. I. Harris 1993; Roediger 2005). Whiteness, in and of itself, was henceforth and seemingly forevermore the only qualification to be met to make one an authentic "citizen" and beneficiary of all that American citizenship and democracy had to offer.[8]

Additional emphasis should be placed on the foregoing contention that the anti-black racist representations of blacks and blackness propagated in blackface minstrelsy aided and abetted the creation of previously nonexistent alliances between the national white bourgeoisie and both Northern and Southern white workers by affirming a nationwide "racial contract" and socio-political commitment to *the diabolical dialectic of white superiority and black inferiority*.[9] In essence, blackface minstrelsy was the public theater space where whites' private fears and misunderstandings, not only about blacks, but also, on an even deeper level, about each other, were played out. For example, by embracing blackface minstrelsy Northern whites proved to Southern whites that they too could be just as unsympathetic to black suffering and black social misery, while white Southerners demonstrated to white Northerners that they still had a sense of humor after the devastating defeat they suffered in the Civil War. After all, both sides seemed to be saying to each other with their participation in, and perpetuation of the fiendish dehumanizing and recolonizing free-for-all that was blackface minstrelsy, what still mattered most with respect to American citizenship and democracy was not one's wealth or status as a worker, but one's "God-given" whiteness; hence, here we return to Cheryl Harris's (1993) groundbreaking discourse on "whiteness as property."

As Saxton observed above, the meteoric rise of blackface minstrelsy facilitated the popularization of theater throughout the United States, while also widening theater patronage beyond the bourgeoisie. In other words, to reiterate, blackface minstrelsy was the first authentically "American" popular culture. It was a simultaneously trans-class, trans-occupation, trans-education, trans-ethnic, and trans-regional space, which—for the first time—allowed whites to commingle on *their* hard won "American" common ground—that is, the common ground of their whiteness and all of its prickly proprietary rights.

Although blacks did participate in blackface minstrelsy from the late 1870s through to the 1910s, it is important to emphasize that whites constituted the overwhelming majority of blackface minstrel performers and patrons. Considering the fact that more than 90 percent of African Americans were enslaved and the few emancipated African Americans in the United States were not allowed to attend white theaters consequent to Black Codes and Jim Crow laws, during its more than a century of existence the minstrel show was an almost exclusively white cultural aesthetic arena where whites' commodified and consumed anti-black racist representations of blacks, blackness, and black performance. In fact, one of the distinguishing factors of authentically "American" music, theater, dance, children's stories, and literature by the late nineteenth century was its recurring and increasing reliance on anti-black racist representations of blacks, blackness, and black performance (i.e., caricatures of African Americans and their culture).

Various genres of "American" performing arts provided whites with myriad mediums through which to commodify and consume black caricatures, ironically enabling whites to feel as though they really and truly had been exposed to, and knew firsthand authentic African American culture. In reality, of course, they were consuming figments of other white folks' imaginations and not authentic African American culture in any way whatsoever. White blackface minstrels' anti-black racist representations of blacks, blackness, and black performance was as close as most whites, generation after jostling generation, would ever come to African Americans and African American culture. Which is also to say, the minstrel show was nothing other than a century-spanning public discourse on *the diabolical dialectic of white superiority and black inferiority.* In *The Hip Hop Revolution: The Culture and Politics of Rap*, Jeffrey Ogbar (2007) observed:

> The purpose of the minstrel was twofold. Minstrels provided easy and immediate entertainment to whites who simultaneously enjoyed the construction and dissemination of an ostensibly white American character by being the antithesis of the minstrel. The minstrel, or coon, was, in effect, an inversion of the white man. While white America prided itself on its scientific and technological achievements at world fairs, in government, in scholarship, and in other arenas, the carefree, happy, and irresponsible Negro offered a sharp contrast to articulations of whiteness and national identity. Additionally, the minstrel justified the socio-political and economic structure in the United States. The most important function of the minstrel was its role in rationalizing white supremacy. The enduring image of the happy, docile, cowardly, and shiftless coon insisted that black people were fundamentally ill-equipped to compete with white people in any meaningful way. Blacks were barred from equal access to

jobs, education, housing, military service, and democracy. The coon, there-fore, assuaged the conscience of many whites who reasoned that things could not be too terrible if blacks were always happy. (14)

There is a sense in which Ogbar's comments help to unambiguously accent the ways in which *the diabolical dialectic of white superiority and black inferiority* played itself out in the ubiquitous figure of the minstrel—a figure, he highlights, that existed long before and long after the Civil War, the Emancipation Proclamation, and Reconstruction. The blackface minstrel has been either rendered allusive to, or outright hidden from, the Hip Hop Gener-ation, just as most of the pertinent details about the African holocaust, the Middle Passage, African American enslavement, and the emergence of American apartheid during the post-Reconstruction period. Exposing the Hip Hop Generation to the minstrel show will hopefully enable us to critically comprehend that it is possible for African Americans to suffer and experi-ence a great deal of social misery even though prominent hip hoppers and the moguls of the music, movie, and fashion industries are commodifying and advocating increasing commercialization of rap music and hip hop culture, both of which are unequivocally rooted in and rose out of African American popular culture. The main point here is that simply because black performers are socially visible or high profile does not mean that black economic exploi-tation, black suffering, and black social misery is actually being critically engaged or, even more, consciously eradicated.

It could be argued that African Americans were socially visible and gar-nered a great deal of public attention during the century of blackface min-strelism that took place between 1830 and 1930. However, as with the New Negroes and Renaissance radicals of the past, progressive hip hoppers in the present need to critically question the quality and overall character of the representations of African Americans, whether they are put forward by whites or blacks, because African Americans historically have and, however covertly, continue to internalize anti-black racist conceptions of themselves and their culture. Moreover, this means that the Hip Hop Generation could and, indeed, *should* utilize the social, political, and cultural criticism be-queathed by the New Negro Movement and the Harlem Renaissance in our efforts to bring into being a truly culturally pluralist and radically democratic America.

In other words, our "inheritance" (à la my book, *Hip Hop's Inheritance*) from the New Negro Movement and the Harlem Renaissance must be under-stood to be much more than music, dance, theater, literature, and art, but also radical politics and models for multi-issue social movements. Obviously the rebellious intellectuals and artists of the Harlem Renaissance proved that African American music, dance, theater, literature, and art can be used to combat anti-black racism. But, the progressive hip hoppers of the present should bear in mind that there simply is no adequate substitute for the kinds of social organization, political activism, cultural criticism, and intellectual leadership now needed to combat the even more insidious forms and forces of anti-black racism contemporary African American youth and their authentic anti-racist allies are inundated with in the midst of Obama's America and during the post–Obama's America era.

At the turn of the twentieth century, New Negroes first impulse was not to sing, dance, write a poem, or paint in the face of the rising tide of post-Reconstruction anti-black racism. In light of the Hayes-Tilden Compromise of 1877, which withdrew federal troops from the South; the emergence and unyielding implementation of Black Codes and Jim Crow laws, which sought to control the labor, migration, and other activities of newly-freed "slaves" and which brought into being what can only be termed "American apartheid"; the convict-lease system; the peonage system; the sharecropping system; poll taxes; literacy tests; widespread lynching; and, culminating with the infamous 1896 *Plessy v. Ferguson* Supreme Court decision, which virtually wiped out each and every gain African Americans had made with the passage of the Fourteenth and Fifteenth Amendments—turn of the twentieth century New Negroes decidedly turned to political agitation, social organization, and civil rights activism, whether under the guise of the Black Women's Club Movement, as we witnessed in "remix" 2, or under the aegis of Booker T. Washington's accommodationism and Tuskegee Machine, or following the lead of W. E. B. Du Bois's Talented Tenth and Niagara Movement. In the minds of the first wave of New Negroes there were definite distinctions that needed to be made between the anti-black racist fictions and fantasies surrounding their "Old Negro," formerly-enslaved grandparents and parents and their decidedly "New Negro," purportedly more sophisticated and certainly more *siddity* selves.

Indeed, it would be extremely difficult to understand the artistic radicalism of the Harlem Renaissance without critically comprehending turn of the twentieth century "New Negroes," both their politics and their aesthetics. The New Negro Movement, of which the Harlem Renaissance was its artistic apogee, is commonly understood to have taken place between the mid-1890s and the late 1930s, or 1940 at the latest. Ironically, considering the incessant celebrations of, and expatiations on, black masculinity and "race men" throughout both the New Negro Movement and the Harlem Renaissance, it was the unequivocal black feminism of the Black Women's Club Movement that helped to spark what ultimately came to be known as the New Negro Movement. Although the term "New Negro" had been used prior to the mid-1890s, it is interesting to note some of the major historical (and *herstorical*) events that signaled, quite literally, a *new* "Negro" cultural consciousness and political presence in the United States.[10]

First, and as discussed in "remix" 2, the evolution of the Black Women's Club Movement, specifically the National Association of Colored Women (NACW), from the Woman's Era Club of Boston and the various Dorcas societies of Philadelphia in the early 1890s to the National Federation of Afro-American Women (NFAAW) in the mid-1890s, proved pivotal. In their own unique way, by establishing the first nationally networked "racial uplift" organization among African Americans, classic black clubwomen—along with their correlate classic blues queens—can be said to have ushered in *the Age of the New Negro* or, rather, *the New Negro Age*. This is a point that should be emphasized because time and time again black women's contributions to both the New Negro Movement and, especially, the Harlem Renaissance have been either downplayed or erased altogether—that is, of course, with the exception of a few notable "race women" sprinkled here and there (e.g., Frances Harper, Anna Julia Cooper, Ida B. Wells, Mary Church Terrell, Amy Jacques Garvey, Zora Neale Hurston, Bessie Smith, and Josephine Baker).[11]

Below we will witness how the colonization or complete erasure of black women's contributions, lives, and struggles continues to haunt rap music and hip hop culture. At this point, however, it is important for us to have an informed understanding of how hip hop's colonization or outright erasure of African American women's contributions, lives, and struggles has roots in the New Negro Movement in general, and the Harlem Renaissance in particular. For instance, in her groundbreaking book, *Portraits of the New Negro Woman: Visual and Literary Culture in the Harlem Renaissance* (2007), Cherene Sherrard-Johnson revealingly wrote:

From the 1890s through 1940, a period roughly spanning the end of Reconstruction to the end of the Harlem Renaissance, many black writers and visual artists fought a war of images in their effort to rewrite and re-envision black representation in high art and popular culture. In their attempts to counter stereotypes of black women as subhuman, immoral, and hypersexual, early African American fiction writers continued the project of reconstructing black womanhood begun by nineteenth century authors of slave narratives and anti-slavery rhetoricians. Black artists and thinkers were deeply invested in presenting a new African American identity and culture at the dawn of the twentieth century. The spirit of self-invention and optimism for the future of blacks in the United States gave birth to the New Negro Movement and the subsequent artistic explosion known as the Harlem Renaissance. Unfortunately, these concentrated narrative and visual efforts to christen the New Negro as a race leader cast the New Negro woman (frequently portrayed as ambiguously raced) in a supporting role. This was actually a regression from the more prominent political visibility of activist-writers such as Ida B. Wells and Frances Harper, who worked side by side with male abolitionists and took on the perils and pitfalls of the Reconstruction era firsthand. (xviii–xix)

Along with being portrayed as "ambiguously raced," New Negro women were also depicted as little more than chocolate-covered middle-class white women, including the requisite Victorianism, elitism, genteelism, and bourgeoisism that accompanied the mannerism and social mores of such women. As discussed in depth in "remix" 2, New Negro women, who were primarily conceived of as classic black clubwomen and not classic blues women, importantly jumpstarted and continuously contributed to the New Negro cause, even though they often schizophrenically embraced and rejected working-class and poor black folk, especially working-class and poor black women (i.e., blues women). Obviously the burgeoning black bourgeoisie of the New Negro Movement has handed down much to the growing black bourgeoisie of the Hip Hop Movement, who often affectionately rap and write about the ghetto or the "brothers and sisters on the block," but who seem to want to incessantly distance themselves from anything and everything about ghetto life that does not translate into increased album, concert, book, magazine, and movie ticket sales. Again, we see that *hip hop's amnesia* does not simply revolve around the history of African American social and political movements, but also has to do with the history of African American intra-racial class struggle, or what could be called "black classism."

In critically examining the literary and visual representations of the New Negro woman, Sherrard-Johnson went further to assert that the New Negro woman was "beautiful, educated, middle-class, and usually engaged in a charitable, conscientious trade such as nursing, library science, or teaching" (10–11). The problem with this portrayal of the New Negro woman is that, ultimately, "the idealization of black women as mulattas, madonnas, teachers, or socialites in the Harlem Renaissance literature, visual art, periodicals, and aesthetic discourse established parameters that restricted artistic expression and agency for black women." Furthermore, she continued, "it implied that a woman could not engage in anti-racist work unless she fit the prevailing class and color standards of respectability—standards that would have eliminated the majority of black women," including classic blues queens and the emerging jazz divas (11). Here we have come back to the ways in which colorism and classism *herstorically* have and currently continue to impact African American women's liberation movements, from the Black Women's Club Movement through to the Hip Hop Women's Movement. As discussed in greater detail in "remix" 2, it is not difficult to discern that in many ways contemporary black feminist academics' relationship with hip hop women—whether self-described "hip hop feminists" or not—seems to parallel classic black clubwomen's relationship with classic blues queens and poor black women.

Frederick Douglass's death on 20 February 1895 marked the second significant event influencing the emergence of the New Negro. In the wake of Douglass's death two of the major male figures of the New Negro Movement began their ascent to national prominence: W. E. B. Du Bois and Booker T. Washington. An avowed admirer of Douglass, Du Bois had long aspired to liberate and lead his beloved black folk. In his autobiography, *The Autobiography of W.E.B. Du Bois* (1968), he made clear that his deepest desire was to use what he had gained from his studies at Fisk, Harvard, and the University of Berlin in the best interest of black liberation. As the first African American to earn a Ph.D. from Harvard University in May of 1895, he believed that he was the ideal candidate to fill the leadership void left as a result of Douglass's death. However, Washington's accommodationism and tentacle-like Tuskegee Machine quickly dashed Du Bois's ambitious dream (D. L. Lewis 1993, 2000; Rabaka 2007, 2008, 2010a, 2010c).

In September of 1895 Booker T. Washington delivered what has been infamously referred to as "The Atlanta Compromise Address," where, in so many words, he told wealthy white capitalists that black workers would accommodate their (i.e., wealthy whites') interests. In the same speech he told blacks that they should focus their energies on manual labor and leave mental labor to wealthy whites and their minions. His rhetoric of accommodation simultaneously won him many wealthy white friends and alienated him from many black leaders, especially turn of the twentieth century black liberals and black radicals (e.g., Du Bois, William Monroe Trotter, Gertrude Morgan, John Hope, Ida Bailey, Frederick McGhee, and Charlotte Hershaw). However, because Washington's associations with rich whites increased his national influence and political power, many of his critics, both black and white, were silenced in one way or another (Harlan 1972, 1982, 1983; Meier 1963; Rabaka 2008).

The New Negro Movement, then, meant many things to many different people, and from its inception there were, at the least, two distinct conceptions. On the one hand, there was *the Washingtonian conservative conception*, which advocated that African Americans turn their attention to the employment and economic aspects of what was then referred to as the "Negro Problem." And, on the other hand, there was *the Du Boisian liberal-radical conception*, which exhorted African Americans to not only attend to the employment and economic aspects, but also the myriad social, political, legal, intellectual, and cultural issues inherent in the "Negro Problem" and, even more, in authentic African American and Pan-African liberation.

Washington, Du Bois, and the leaders of the Black Women's Club Movement, most of whom held conceptions of the New Negro woman or "race woman" somewhere between Washington and Du Bois's articulations of the New Negro, represented the first generation of African Americans to collectively express the social, political, and educational aspirations of black folk—indeed, of the *New* Negroes (Dublin, Arias, and Carreras 2003). From the time of Washington's rise to national prominence in 1895 to his untimely death in 1915, the New Negro Movement's main focus was on securing

African Americans' civil rights, social wealth, and political power. But, Washington's accommodationism and railroading of seemingly all blacks into the realm of manual labor increasingly rubbed more and more New Negroes the wrong way. Leading Booker T. Washington scholar Louis Harlan (1982) sensitively wrote on this subject:

> Washington's outright critics and enemies were called "radicals" because they challenged Washington's conservatism and bossism, though their tactics of verbal protest would seem moderate indeed to a later generation of activists. They were the college-educated blacks, engaged in professional pursuits, and proud of their membership in an elite class—what one of them [i.e., W. E. B. Du Bois] called the Talented Tenth. The strong holds of the radicals were the northern cities and southern black colleges. They stood for full political and civil rights, liberal education, free expression, and aspiration. They dreamed of a better world and believed Booker T. Washington was a menace to its achievement. (6)

Perhaps, no other New Negro—William Monroe Trotter withstanding (see Du Bois 1934; Fox 1970; Worthy 1952)—disagreed with Washington more than Du Bois. In his classic essay, "The Evolution of Negro Leadership" (1901), which was a critical book review of Booker T. Washington's autobiography, *Up From Slavery* (1901), Du Bois developed a sociology of African American politics that identified three basic trends: revolt and revenge; accommodation to the established order of the ruling race/class; and dogged social development and cultural survival, "in spite of environing discouragements and prejudice" (Du Bois 1977, 4). From the perspective of Du Bois's sociology of African American politics, Washington's leadership paradigm was simply one of three possible choices. For instance, Toussaint L'Ouverture, Richard Allen, Nat Turner, Blanche Bruce, Frederick Douglass, and John Mercer Langston—and Du Bois mentions several more "race leaders"—provided African Americans, an "imprisoned group" or "a group within a group," with alternative leadership models (4). Du Bois further calmly declared:

> Mr. Washington came with a clear simple program, at the psychological moment; at a time when the nation was a little ashamed of having bestowed so much sentiment on Negroes and was concentrating its energies on Dollars. The industrial training of Negro youth was not an idea originating with Mr. Washington, nor was the policy of conciliating the white South wholly his. But he first put life, unlimited energy, and perfect faith into this program; he changed it from an article of belief into a whole creed; he broadened it from a by-path into a veritable Way of Life. And the method by which he accomplished this is an interesting study of human life. (4)

With his characteristic literary brevity and conceptual economy, Du Bois went on to lay out the crux of the opposition to Washington's accommodationism, which must have shocked and worried more than a few white readers unaware of the history and diversity of African American social and political thought. On behalf of the opposition, Du Bois stated, "[w]e may not agree with the man at all points, but we admire him and cooperate with him so far as we conscientiously can" (5). However, Washington's increasing silencing of "the voice of criticism" in the African American community was more than the allegedly "admiring" opposition could bear (Du Bois 1986, 398). Du Bois, who had long held his tongue and, since his youth, gravitated toward the unrestrained social criticism and radical political activism of Frederick Douglass, fired his opening salvo at Washington and his tyrannical Tuskegee Machine. With passionate, but weighted words, Du Bois (1977) daringly wrote:

> Among the Negroes, Mr. Washington is still far from a popular leader. Educated and thoughtful Negroes everywhere are glad to honor him and aid him, but all cannot agree with him. He represents in Negro thought the old attitude of adjustment to environment, emphasizing the economic phase; but the two other strong currents of feeling, descended from the past, still oppose him. One is the thought of a small but not unimportant group, unfortunate in their choice of spokesman, but nevertheless of much weight, who represent the old ideas of revolt and revenge, and see in migration alone an outlet for the Negro people. The second attitude is that of the large and important group represented by Dunbar, Tanner, Chestnutt, Miller, and the Grimkés, who, without any single definite program, and with complex aims, seek nevertheless that self-development and self-realization in all lines of human endeavor which they believe will eventually place the Negro beside the other races. While these men respect the Hampton-Tuskegee idea to a degree, they believe it falls far short of a complete program. They believe, therefore, also in the higher education of Fisk and Atlanta Universities; they believe in self-assertion and ambition; and they believe in the right of suffrage for blacks on the same terms with whites. (5)

With these words an infamous episode in the history of African American social and political thought was born; the war between Washington and Du Bois, between the Tuskegee Machine and the Talented Tenth, would be waged not simply by these two social and political leaders, but by most of black America and, if the truth be told, many parts of white America as well. Du Bois audaciously challenged Washington and, in doing so, developed one of his most significant (and most misinterpreted) contributions to the New Negro Movement in particular, and African American social and political thought in general—that is to say, his much-heralded theory of the Talented Tenth. In a nutshell, the Talented Tenth theory argued that at the very least 10 percent of African Americans ought to have access to higher education, receiving concentrated training in medicine, law, politics, economics, sociology, psychology, history, and philosophy, so that African Americans can lead themselves and solve their own problems. As Du Bois observed above, many whites interpreted Washington's accommodationist politics and rhetoric as African Americans' collective embrace of the industrial education or manual labor model. Du Bois and his more militant New Negro cohort, therefore, critiqued what they perceived to be Washington's "Uncle Tomming," as well as white folks' ongoing anti-black racism, especially as found in turn of the twentieth century Black Codes, Jim Crow laws, lynching, literature, theater, and minstrel song lyrics and dances (R. Carroll 2003, 2006).

Hence, in response to the growing disdain for Washington's accommodationist politics and rhetoric, Du Bois co-founded, first, the Niagara Movement and, then, the National Association for the Advancement of Colored People (NAACP), which unambiguously laid the foundation for arguably every major form of civil rights activism and movement that has emerged since its inception.[12] Paralleling the phenomenal rise of the Black Women's Club Movement, the New Negro Movement sought to dialectically rupture African Americans' relationship with the bondage of their enslaved past and provide a bridge to the promised freedom of their future. In this sense, Washington, Du Bois, and the members of the Black Women's Club Movement all understood themselves to be breaking free from the stereotypical image of the "Old Negro," the "black slave," and the blackface minstrel, which had long dominated mainstream American discourse on black folk and their much-blighted blackness.

It was almost as if even in Reconstruction and post-Reconstruction "freedom" African Americans remained chained and bound, freeze-framed as perpetual "slaves," "darkies," and minstrels. This kind of "freedom," truth be told, was a farce. *New* Negroes would have none of it. After centuries of the most excruciating and unforgiving enslavement and blackface minstrel mockery imaginable, they put forward their own homespun critical social theory and counter-ideology.

In other words, to offset the fictions and fantasies of white supremacy and the anti-black racist ideology of the "Old Negro" archetype, turn of the twentieth century African Americans discursively developed *New Negro critical social theory and counter-ideology*.[13] Writing on this very issue in their groundbreaking volume, *The New Negro: Readings on Race, Representation, and African American Culture, 1892–1938*, Henry Louis Gates and Gene Andrew Jarrett (2007) declared:

> In an accurate, if humorous, sense, blacks have felt the need to attempt to "reconstruct" their image probably since that dreadful day in 1619, when the first boatload of Africans disembarked in Virginia. Africans and their descen-

dants commenced their cultural lives in this hemisphere as veritable deconstructions of all that the West so ardently wished itself to be. Almost as soon as
blacks could write, it seems, they set out to redefine—against already received
racist stereotypes—who and what a black person was, and how unlike the
racist stereotype the black original actually could be. To counter these racist
stereotypes, white and black writers erred on the side of nobility, and posited
equally fictitious black archetypes, from Oroonoko in 1688 to Kunte Kinte in
more recent times. If various Western cultures constructed blackness as an
absence, then various generations of black authors have attempted to reconstruct blackness as a presence. (3)

After two decades dominated by Washington's seemingly schizophrenic embrace and rejection of the "Old Negro" archetype, and also in light of the
increase in lynching and other forms of anti-black racist violence, the years
leading up to World War I and immediately following Washington's death in
1915 proved to be an unprecedented turning point in African American history, culture, and struggle. Years and years of New Negro accommodation and
acquiescence (à la Washington) and New Negro agitation and activism (à la
Du Bois) gave way to an innovative and distinctly *African American* expressive culture: the artistic, political, and rhetorical radicalism of the Harlem
Renaissance. Washington's death ended the bitter ideological battle between
he and Du Bois over the best New Negro leadership strategy for black liberation.

However, even before Washington's death Du Bois had begun to dabble
in the arts, writing short stories and poems and publishing his first novel, *The
Quest of the Silver Fleece*, in 1911. Challenging white constructions of
"blackness as an absence," Du Bois was among the first generation of
African American authors to consciously attempt to "reconstruct blackness
as a presence." Unlike any of the other major African American post-Reconstruction writers, including Charles Chesnutt, Pauline Hopkins, Sutton E.
Griggs, Frances Ellen Watkins Harper, and Paul Laurence Dunbar, Du Bois's
work had a direct impact on the overall New Negro Movement *and* its radical
aesthetic explosion under the guise of the Harlem Renaissance.[14]

According to David Levering Lewis in *When Harlem Was in Vogue*
(1989), the social and political focus of the New Negro Movement gradually
shifted from an accommodationism-cum-civil rights initiative (à la Washington) and an activism-cum-civil rights initiative (à la Du Bois) to an "arts-
cum-civil rights" initiative (à la the intellectuals, artists, and activists of the
Harlem Renaissance) (xvi). In other words, the Harlem Renaissance represents the New Negro Movement modified or "remixed," if you will. The
social and political focus of the movement remained on securing African
Americans' civil rights, but newfound cultural and aesthetic avenues were
utilized in ongoing efforts to achieve, not simply civil rights, but also to
contribute to the deconstruction and reconstruction of "citizenship" and "de-

mocracy" in the United States. Lewis, perhaps, put it best when he argued that the Harlem Renaissance's main motto could be paraphrased as: "civil rights by copyright" (xvi). This apt phrase, it seems to me, best summarizes the ways in which the New Negro Movement and Harlem Renaissance critically converged and diverged.

All of this means that here the Harlem Renaissance is not seen as a completely separate movement when compared with the New Negro Movement. Following many of the major Harlem Renaissance Studies scholars, I understand the Harlem Renaissance to be indicative of the evolution or, even more, the cultural aesthetic maturation of the New Negro Movement, just as most Black Power Studies scholars understand the Black Arts Movement to be the cultural aesthetic outlet of the Black Power Movement. Part of the confusion surrounding interpreting the connections between the New Negro Movement and the Harlem Renaissance may have to do with the fact that Black Studies was not established within the American academy until a quarter of a century after both the New Negro Movement and Harlem Renaissance had ended. Therefore, the abundance of theory and research methods currently utilized to critique and/or appreciate African American intellectual and cultural history was not available to the early advocates of what has come to be called "African American Studies"—and, with greater and greater frequency in the twenty-first century, "Africana Studies" (i.e., continental and diasporan African Studies).

In a sense, the Black Power Movement and the Black Arts Movement, being the most recent socio-political and cultural aesthetic paradigms offered by the generation that immediately preceded the Hip Hop Generation, represent more "modern" and seemingly more "concrete" models of black radical politics and cultural aesthetics. However, hip hoppers should not lamely limit themselves to the most immediate moments in African American—and national or, even more, international—history, culture, politics, society, and aesthetics. The only way that *hip hop's amnesia* can really and truly be combated is by going above and beyond the everyday-average, mass media (mis)understanding of African American—and, again, national or, even more, international—history, culture, politics, society, and aesthetics.

It should also be observed that generation after generation of African Americans have, whether consciously or unconsciously, followed in the footsteps of the New Negroes, who in forming their movement understood themselves to be breaking with the "Old Negro," "black slave," and/or blackface minstrel archetype. The intellectuals, artists, and activists of the Harlem Renaissance conceived of themselves, initially, as breaking with the Washingtonian New Negro, and then eventually the Du Boisian New Negro. The young, insurgent intellectuals and artistic radicals of the Harlem Renaissance sought to deconstruct and reconstruct not simply American "citizenship" and "democracy," but the very notion of what it meant to be an "American Negro" (or, rather, a "Negro American"). The radicals of the Harlem Renaissance were yet and still "New Negroes," but they were decidedly "New Negroes" with a twist—in a word, they were *neo–New Negroes*. As Jeffrey Stewart (2007) stated in "The New Negro as Citizen," for neo–New Negroes being "New Negroes" was "never simply" about "racial identities, but new, more complex personalities, black individuals, sparkling in their multifarious talents, inclinations, and aspirations"—in a word, "modern black people" (18).

Stewart went on to offer a stunning description of the neo–New Negroes of the Harlem Renaissance that subtly sounds as though he could be describing twenty-first century Hip Hop Movement intellectuals, artists, and activists: "Here was an outstanding group of intellectuals as well as artists, men and women as comfortable in the white intellectual world as the black, yet grounded by a commitment to try and find in the black experience a new voice of America. A new kind of enlightened American citizen had emerged—the race cosmopolitan, who was able to discuss the national literary and intellectual heritage in black and white, exhibit a worldliness and breadth of influences less evident in the black nationalisms of the 1960s, yet remain committed to the race and the transformation of America through the culture of the black community" (19). Clearly, again, whether consciously or unconsciously, the intellectuals, artists, and activists of the Hip Hop Movement have been influenced by the neo–New Negroes of the Harlem Renaissance, if not the New Negro Movement in general. In fact, one of the major distinguishing factors between the Black Arts Movement of the 1960s and 1970s and the Hip Hop Movement may very well be the hip hoppers' emphasis on "race cosmopolitan[ism]."

As the first generation of African Americans to come of age after the Civil Rights Movement, Black Power Movement, and Women's Liberation Movement, the Hip Hop Generation appears to be deeply "committed to the race and the transformation of America through the culture of the black community." However, as with other social, political, cultural, and artistic movements that emerged in the midst of postmodernism, postcolonialism, postfeminism, and post-Marxism, the Hip Hop Movement's politics are often muted and masked, fragmented and freakish. Young black folk are not passionately singing "We Shall Overcome!" or shouting "Black Power!" in the streets the way they did during the turbulent years of the 1960s and 1970s. But, there should be no mistake made about it, the Hip Hop Generation and, even more, the Hip Hop Movement *is* political. In fact, considering the wide range of 1960s and 1970s multi-issue movements that advocated for authentic multiracial and multicultural democracy in America it is not at all surprising that the Hip Hop Movement's major cultural and aesthetic motifs have provided the multiracial and multicultural foundation on which most twenty-first century popular culture, national and international, has been based.[15]

## THE HARLEM RENAISSANCE: ON THE NIGGERATI, RAP
## MUSIC'S FEMINIST ROOTS, AND THE HOMO-HOPPERS OF THE
## HIP HOP GENERATION

What is particularly troubling about the bulk of the Hip Hop Generation's politics, although their multiculturalism and cultural pluralism is quite commendable, is their often-unapologetic embrace of several of the "isms" and insidious ideologies of the past. Where most hip hoppers seem willing, at least musically, to cross the "color-line"—to employ Du Bois's apt phrase from *The Souls of Black Folk* here—they do not appear to be eager to cross the *gender-line*. That is to say, most hip hoppers appear to be completely reluctant to engage the ways that racism is almost always inextricable from, and intensely intertwined with, sexism (e.g., patriarchy and misogyny). Furthermore, where many hip hoppers seem to have some semblance of sensitivity to poor and poverty-stricken people's lives and struggles, they appear to be almost utterly insensitive to the struggles of homosexuals in a world decidedly dominated by heterosexuals and heteronormativity (e.g, both covert and overt homophobia and heterosexism).

Further amplifying and intensifying the critique of the Hip Hop Generation's historical and cultural amnesia, there is a sense in which the revolt of the neo–New Negroes of the Harlem Renaissance, those whom Zora Neale Hurston and Wallace Thurman with deliberate irony dubbed the "Niggerati," might be able to provide progressive hip hoppers with models for the kinds of contemporary, not simply "race cosmopolitans" but, even more, *race, gender, class, and sexuality cosmopolitans* who are so desperately needed now—especially in hip hop communities in the United States. [16] Once again, Stewart offers insight, observing: "Despite the legitimate criticisms of the New Negro as largely a male and heterosexist cultural icon, it should be remembered that many talented women, gay, and lesbian intellectuals and artists found themselves in the New Negro Movement" (19). Accordingly, a couple of questions quickly beg: Aren't hip hoppers frequently criticized for being "largely . . . male and heterosexist cultural icon[s]?" And, more importantly, how many "talented women, gay, and lesbian intellectuals and artists [have] found themselves" silenced or rendered utterly invisible within the worlds of rap music and hip hop culture?

The revolt of the "Niggerati" of the Harlem Renaissance was not only a rebellion against the "Old Negro" and blackface minstrel archetype, but also, to reiterate, the Washingtonian New Negro and the Du Boisian New Negro. As Martha Jane Nadell noted in *Enter the New Negroes: Images of Race in American Culture* (2004):

Scholars Henry Louis Gates Jr. and Eric Sundquist point to the fluidity of the term "New Negro," a fluidity that in turn affects its partner, the term "Old Negro." In the decade before "New Negro" came to be associated with the cultural agenda of the Harlem Renaissance, the term suggested a radical political orientation. Consider, for example, a cartoon published in the *Messenger* in 1919, a mere six years before Locke published his anthology of literature and art, *The New Negro: An Interpretation.* The image depicts the Old/New Negro dichotomy in terms of black leadership. The New Negroes are radicals who brandish guns to defend themselves against mob violence. W.E.B. Du Bois and Booker T. Washington stand for the "old crowd Negro," whose sentiments—"Close ranks. Let us forget our grievances" and "Be modest and unassuming"—the radical magazine rejected. Yet Du Bois and Washington, Old Negroes in 1919, had been new a mere nineteen years before, when Washington had published *A New Negro for a New Century*, a collection of essays and photographs depicting the "Upward Struggles of the Negro Race." (11; see also Locke 1925; B. T. Washington 1900)

It is important here to re-emphasize that the Harlem Renaissance was the artistic outgrowth of the New Negro Movement, and, where the New Negro Movement more or less sought social, political, and legal solutions to African American problems, the Harlem Renaissance aimed to offer up cultural, musical, theatrical, literary, poetic, and aesthetic solutions to African American problems. The primary goal for both movements was in fact African American civil rights and social justice. However, they harbored enough distinct differences so as to constitute, in some senses, two *simultaneous yet separate* movements: one socio-political (i.e., the New Negro Movement) and the other cultural aesthetic (i.e., the Harlem Renaissance). Although, truth be told, both movements gravitated toward relatively radical politics *and* emancipatory aesthetics. As a matter of fact, in many ways the Harlem Renaissance was a logical extension—in the areas of music, dance, theater, literature, and art—of the New Negro leaders and foot soldiers' newfound racial, cultural, historical, religious, educational, social, and political consciousness and thought.

To get a grasp of the overlapping timeline shared between the New Negro Movement and the Harlem Renaissance it might be helpful to point to the fact that most New Negro scholars agree that the New Negro Movement was underway no later than 1895 and extended through the years of the Great Depression. Most Harlem Renaissance scholars locate its genesis somewhere between the beginning of World War I in 1914 and the publication of Claude McKay's classic poem "Harlem Dancer" in 1917. Where most Harlem Renaissance scholars concur that Zora Neale Hurston's 1937 classic novel *Their Eyes Were Watching God* was arguably the last major work of the Harlem Renaissance, there is almost unanimous consensus that, by the time Richard

Wright published his classic novel *Native Son* in 1940, the Harlem Renaissance was over and a new phase of mid-century "modern" social realism in African American writing and rhetoric had begun.

The politics and rhetoric of the New Negro Movement was put forward through several major mouthpieces, for example: the National Association for the Advancement of Colored People and its publication the *Crisis*, edited by W. E. B. Du Bois; the National Urban League and its publication *Opportunity: A Journal of Negro Life*, edited by Charles Spurgeon Johnson; Marcus Garvey's Universal Negro Improvement Association and its publication the *Negro World*; the African Blood Brotherhood and its decidedly democratic socialist publication the *Crusader*, edited by Cyril Briggs; and, finally, A. Philip Randolph and Chandler Owen's decidedly democratic socialist the *Messenger* magazine (Goeser 2007; Vincent 1990; T. Vogel 2001). Other more mainstream journals and magazines that either published New Negroes or were in someway associated with the New Negro Movement included the *Nation, Modern Quarterly, New Republic, Survey Graphic*, and *Saturday Review*.

Although they sought to distance themselves from much of the politics and rhetoric of the "old" New Negro leaders, especially Washington, Du Bois, and the conservatism of the Black Women's Club Movement, it is extremely important to understand that the young radicals of the Harlem Renaissance conceived of their artistic creations as activism. According to Cherene Sherrard-Johnson (2007), the Harlem Renaissance artists and intellectuals "perceived the literary, musical, and visual art explosion of the twenties and thirties as artistic activism. They hoped that their achievements would result in political and social change" (16).

In the previous "remixes" we have discussed the major musics of the Black Women's Club Movement, the New Negro Movement, and the Harlem Renaissance (i.e., classic blues and classic jazz); here we turn our attention to the poetics, rhetorics, politics, and social movements that informed those musics, and vice versa. It is one thing to flippantly say that classic blues and classic jazz served as the soundtracks to the Black Women's Club Movement, the New Negro Movement, and the Harlem Renaissance, and wholly another thing to critically connect the musics to the politics, poetics, and rhetorics of these movements. The Harlem Renaissance represents, or rather *should* represent, much more than music, dance, theater, literature, and art. In many ways it was a rebellion against both whites' anti-black racism *and* increasing black—i.e., "old" New Negro—conservatism.

For more than two decades before the Harlem Renaissance came into being—again, circa 1914 to 1917—"old" New Negroes, such as Washington, Du Bois, and most members of the Black Women's Club Movement, had critiqued and protested anti-black racism in U.S. medicine, law, employment, education, religion, real estate, and the military, etc. The "Niggerati" of the

Harlem Renaissance aimed to critique and protest whites' anti-black racism *and* blacks' increasing conservatism in and via music, dance, theater, literature, and art, etc. As Martha Jane Nadell (2004) importantly asserted, "[i]f a central part of the invention of the New Negro was the creation of an appropriate and useful racial aesthetic for the era, another equally important part was the articulation of an Old Negro, who was not quite invented but rather culled from a wide variety of nineteenth century literary and visual images of African Americans" (10–11).[17]

In terms of the "wide variety of nineteenth century literary and visual images of African Americans" which Nadell notes that the "Old Negro" archetype was gleaned from, it is important for us to openly acknowledge how these literary and visual images of African Americans were, literally, used *against* African Americans and their quest for freedom. When the New Negro Movement is unambiguously understood to be the major social and political movement out of which the Harlem Renaissance emerged, an almost entirely new historical and cultural archive is offered to Harlem Renaissance scholars and students in their earnest efforts to understand, not only the New Negro aesthetic, but also the radical New Negro politics of the Harlem Renaissance. Discursively dovetailing with Nadell's contention concerning the literary and visual images that the "Old Negro" archetype was culled from, in *Word, Image, and the New Negro: Representation and Identity in the Harlem Renaissance* (2005), Anne Elizabeth Carroll importantly asserted:

> The Harlem Renaissance is a crucial moment in African Americans' attempts to define themselves and to engage in broader discourses about racial identity, but that effort has roots in the years before the movement. In the eighteenth, nineteenth, and early twentieth centuries, American popular culture presented overwhelmingly negative ideas about African Americans. African Americans, as part of the rationale used to justify slavery, were defined as strikingly different from white Americans and as incapable of significant intellectual, economic, or moral advancement, and thus incapable of assimilation. Even worse, African Americans were believed by many to be threats to national social order, with racial violence—including lynching—defended as necessary to the maintenance of white Americans' security, and with the deportation of African Americans seen as possibly necessary for the assertion and development of American unity and culture. Even liberal white Americans, who believed that African Americans were capable of at least some progress and growth, generally assumed that African Americans were inferior to white Americans. (5–6)

It is a hard and bitter historical truth, but one that must be acknowledged in order to really comprehend the canvas that the insurgent artists and activists of the Harlem Renaissance were painting on. The post-Reconstruction social and political scene that the New Negroes entered into was one where even the most liberal European Americans seemed to lovingly long for those "good ole" slavery days, replete with plantations and, of course, "Old Negro" "uncles" and "aunties." For instance, in *Negro Art: Past and Present* (1936), Alain Locke audaciously expressed the New Negro position on the post-antebellum "Plantation School" of writers—which infamously included Harriet Beecher Stowe, Joel Chandler Harris, George Washington Cable, Thomas Nelson Page, and Thomas Dixon—when he daringly declared: "The 'old faithful uncle,'—latter Uncle Tom, Uncle Ned, and Uncle Remus, the broad expansive "mammy" from Aunt Chloe to Aunt Jemima, the jiggling plantation hand in tattered jeans and the sprawling pickaninnies all became the typical stereotypes," and, he critically continued, "scarcely any nineteenth century art show was without its genre portrait study of one or more of these types or its realistically painted or sketched portrayal of '*The Plantation Quarters*' or '*Ole Virginia Life*' or some such glorification" (9).

Whether we speak of stereotype, caricature, or other forms of figurative representation, both literary and visual texts rely on readability, recognizability, and perceived realism—which is to say, once again, that the Hip Hop Generation's fascination with "keeping it real," "street credibility," and authenticity may be nothing more than an outgrowth of and a holdover from New Negro aesthetics or, going back even further, as Gates and Jarrett asserted above, abolitionist and enslaved African Americans' impulse to "redefine—against already received racist stereotypes—who and what a black person was, and how unlike the racist stereotype the black original actually could be." Also, similar to the genre of portraiture, stereotype and caricature, in specific, portray their subjects so that their respective audiences can identify the representative images with the objectified subjects to which they allude. However, where caricature usually functions by exaggerating the gestures, physiognomy, physiology, and behavior of the human figure, frequently pushing these to seemingly impossible and unreal extremes, stereotype hinges on a pretense of verisimilitude and gross repetition. At the heart of the problem here is that even though it maintains some semblance of reality (i.e., verisimilitude) through manipulated aesthetic strategies that enable figures to appear familiar—behaviorally, emotionally, physiognomically, or physiologically—and, therefore, "real" or authentic, stereotype inherently renders invisible or outright erases individuality and the particulars of human personality.

After being inundated with literary and visual text after text, the "Niggerati" New Negroes of the Harlem Renaissance came to believe that "if negative images of African Americans could justify or even encourage racism and violence against African Americans," according to Anne Elizabeth Carroll (2005), "the reverse might also be true: alternative images of African Americans might have an ameliorating effect on racism and its manifestations" (7). In other words, prefiguring the Hip Hop Generation discourse on black-on-black violence, Harlem Renaissance radicals sought to use the literary and visual representations of the militant New Negro to combat and ultimately *conceptually kill* or, rather, *commit conceptual homicide* against the literary and visual representations of the "Old Negro." And, as quiet as it has been kept, it was these both literary and visual representations of "Old Negroes" and "New Negroes" that Nadell (2004) insists "formed an unstable yet productive dialectic that engendered ideas about race, realism, and stereotype—ideas that would inform the work of writers and artists for generations to come" (11).

Obviously the members of the Civil Rights Movement and the Black Power Movement constitute two generations who continued to make distinctions between moderate "Old Negroes" and militant "New Negroes"—that is, of course, with the Black Power radicals ultimately leaving the word "Negro" in the discursive dustbin once and for all. However, the ways in which the Hip Hop Generation has inherited and, in their own newfangled ways, continued the New Negro Movement/Harlem Renaissance tradition of making distinctions between moderate "Old Negroes" and militant "New Negroes" should not be downplayed or diminished—and all of this, even though the word "Negro" is not commonly used within the hip hop community and many hip hoppers controversially call each other "niggers" often à la the "Niggerati" of the Harlem Renaissance. In terms of the Hip Hop Generation's continued utilization of the New Negro Movement/Harlem Renaissance trans-generational tradition of making distinctions between moderate "Old Negroes" and militant "New Negroes, " for instance, who can deny that in many ways "pop" rap, or what we currently call "commercial" rap music, and hip hop culture seem to mirror the white folk–friendly, moderate "Old Negro" aesthetic, where the "political" or "conscious" rap school almost patently parallels the black radical and more militant "New Negro" or "Niggerati" aesthetic of the Harlem Renaissance—not to mention the "Black Aesthetic" of the Black Arts Movement?

What needs to be reiterated here is that the "newness" of the "Niggerati" New Negro second wave of the Harlem Renaissance meant something almost completely different from—if not, in many senses, outright the opposite of—the "newness" of the "old New Negro" first wave, who witnessed firsthand the phenomenal rise of the Black Women's Club Movement and the history-making war of words between, and the correlate movements lead by, Booker T. Washington and W. E. B. Du Bois. Ultimately, this means that the first wave of New Negroes who set into motion the New Negro Movement in 1895 held a distinctly different conception of what it meant to be a New Negro in comparison with the second wave of relatively younger, self-described "Niggerati" New Negroes who audaciously inaugurated and advanced the Harlem Renaissance. I cannot help but to wonder whether something similar is beginning to take place within the world of hip hop, where more and more frequently discussions concerning "old school" rap music and hip hop culture may come to refer to *commercial, materialistic, misogynistic, and homophobic rap music and hip hop culture*, and "new school" rap music and hip hop culture may ultimately mean *race, gender, class, and sexuality sensitive and progressive rap music and hip hop culture*. I can only solemnly hope and sincerely pray that with every word written and every argument developed herein rap music and hip hop culture move away from the former and unapologetically embrace the latter. *Insha'Allah. Selah.*

Even though it was, in essence, called into being by Du Bois (e.g., see "Possibilities of the Negro: The Advance Guard of the Race," "The Talented Tenth," and, of course, his immortal *The Souls of Black Folk*, all published in 1903), the Harlem Renaissance was also a revolt against first wave New Negroes' increasing embrace of white middle-class culture and morality, specifically its simultaneously Eurocentric and thoroughly bourgeois obsession with genteelism and Victorianism (see Du Bois 1903a, 1903b, 1903c). Returning to the idea that the second wave New Negroes of the Harlem Renaissance sought to be not only "race cosmopolitans" but, even more, *race, gender, class, and sexuality cosmopolitans*, it is important to re-emphasize that of all the things that distinguish the Harlem Renaissance from the New Negro Movement, when it is all said and done, it may very well be the Renaissance radicals' unrepentant embrace of certain aspects of artistic activism, democratic socialism, feminism/womanism, and homosexuality that prove pivotal. Building on the New Negro Movement's critiques of anti-black racism and, to a certain extent, African American economic exploitation at the hands of white capitalists, the Harlem Renaissance radicals markedly added gender and sexuality to the New Negro Movement's history-making race/class critiques.

Obviously, as with the Black Women's Club Movement, the New Negro Movement's gender and sexual politics were, to some degree, influenced by the views and values of upper-class and middle-class whites. Which is to say, both of the major African American social and political movements that immediately preceded and profoundly influenced the Harlem Renaissance were more or less *intellectually emancipated* in terms of their critiques of anti-black racism and widespread white supremacy but, truth be told, appallingly *conceptually incarcerated* in many respects with regard to gender, class, and sexuality. Hence, for the "Niggerati" New Negroes of the Harlem Renaissance what it meant to really and truly be both "New" *and* "Negro" entailed not simply a break with the "Old Negro" and blackface minstrel archetype, as well as the Washingtonian and Du Boisian conceptions of the New Negro, but also a radical rupture with past gender, class, and sexual relations—especially as articulated and put into play by the "old New Negroes" of the Black Women's Club Movement and the first wave of the New Negro Movement. In this regard, Jeffrey Stewart (2007) importantly asserted:

To be New Negro [for the "Niggerati" radicals of the Harlem Renaissance] meant to live in the present with echoes of past crimes and silenced communities echoing in one's head, regardless of what the rest of the nation thought of it. And it meant dreaming in the 1920s of a new kind of citizenship, of at-homeness, grounded in a capacious black urban community that was far more advanced in its foregrounding of feminist and homosexual identities than the rest of the nation. It meant the courage to resist not only 100 percent Americanism, but also gender bias and homophobia within a black community in transition. (19)

When we survey the current Hip Hop Studies scene it appears as though the Harlem Renaissance has had little or no impact on the Hip Hop Movement. However, as I discussed in chapter 3 of *Hip Hop's Inheritance*, if several Hip Hop Studies scholars are correct when they connect hip hop's aesthetics to the cultural aesthetics of the Black Arts Movement, then it should also be acknowledged that the members of the Black Arts Movement were influenced by—even as they sought to radically rupture their relationships with—the artist-activist legacies of the New Negroes of the Harlem Renaissance. Why is it that so many other aspects of the artist-activist legacies of the New Negroes of the Harlem Renaissance have been, however surreptitiously, handed down to the Hip Hop Movement, but not their distinct conceptions of American citizenship and democracy? Is it possibly because their distinct conceptions of American citizenship and democracy were unambiguously anti-sexist and anti-heterosexist or, as Stewart stated above, completely and compassionately open to "feminist and homosexual identities?" How many hip hoppers, especially African American hip hoppers, can relate to the "Niggerati" radicals' daring definition above of what it meant to be a "New Negro?" How many, truth be told, would much rather start and stop with the first sentence, "[t]o be [a hip hopper] mean[s] to live in the present with echoes of past crimes and silenced communities echoing in one's head, regardless of what the rest of the nation [thinks] of it," ultimately excising any and all references to "feminist and homosexual identities"?

In her watershed work, *Gay Voices of the Harlem Renaissance* (2003), A. B. Christa Schwarz emphasized the centrality of bisexuality, homosexuality, and transgressive sexuality within the world of the Harlem Renaissance. Her expert analysis accented the double meanings (i.e., the homo-double entendre and homoeroticism) of much of the artistry of several of the major "Niggerati" New Negroes of the Harlem Renaissance. Moreover, in her explorative essay, "Transgressive Sexuality and the Literature of the Harlem Renaissance," Schwarz (2007) contended that "[m]any Renaissance participants were indeed same-sex interested. Most of them were covertly gay (for example, Alain Locke and Countee Cullen) or bisexual (for example, Claude McKay and Wallace Thurman)" (142). This means, then, that most of the bisexuality, homosexuality, and transgressive sexuality of the Harlem Renaissance was masked, except in the case of Richard Bruce Nugent. Schwarz candidly continued, "[o]nly the bohemian Richard Bruce Nugent dared to openly display his same-sex desire" (142).[18]

The bisexual and homosexual women of the Harlem Renaissance could be said to have muted and masked their same-sex desire even more than the males of the Renaissance on account of both the sexism and heterosexism of the white and black bourgeoisies, who were the primary patrons of the Renaissance. Schwarz (2007) shared, "faced with gender discrimination and often burdened with family obligations, female Renaissance authors in general experienced more repressive living and writing conditions than their male counterparts" (142). Same-sex interested Renaissance women such as Angelina Weld Grimké and Alice Dunbar-Nelson's homoeroticism was also hampered by the longstanding myths surrounding African American women's lasciviousness and promiscuousness discussed in "remix" 2, which, it will be recalled, was propagated during and after African American enslavement.

From the skewed point of view of the black bourgeoisie, African American women who embraced transgressive sexuality, especially lesbianism, were, in essence, exacerbating and perpetuating the myth of black women's lasciviousness and promiscuousness. By publicly announcing or "parading" their same-sex desire African American bisexual and homosexual women artists were aiding and abetting anti-black racism and fueling fictions about black women, or so the conservatism of the New Negro black bourgeoisie led them to believe. "The black bourgeoisie strove to control black women's sexual image," Schwarz stated, and Grimké, Dunbar-Nelson, Zora Neale Hurston, Nella Larsen, Ma Rainey, Bessie Smith, and Josephine Baker, among many others, challenged the colonization of African American women's sexuality by either the white or black bourgeoisie (143).[19]

It is interesting to observe the ways in which homosexuality and homoeroticism were hidden during the Harlem Renaissance, similar to the ways they are frequently hidden in contemporary rap music and hip hop culture. For instance, in "It's All One!: A Conversation," Homosexual Hip Hop Movement (i.e., Homo-Hop Movement) founders Juba Kalamka and Tim'm West (2006) argued that the history of hip hop "is incomplete until the presence of Queerness within is acknowledged" (198). Contesting the notion that hip hop culture is somehow incompatible with queerness, Kalamka and West accented *hip hop's amnesia* when they asserted that the "hip hop-is-incompatible-with-being-Queer" contention "springs from a very typical romanticism and nostalgia and lack of memory that's a component of most pop-cultural pop discourse, especially around music" (199).

Consequently, many, if not most, so-called hip hop "purists" have long pandered to extremely *heteronormative*, *hyper-heterosexual*, and *hyper-masculine* conceptions of hip hop culture without in any way critically coming to terms with the ways in which hip hop has been and remains profoundly influenced by homosexual culture. Here, by "heteronormative" I wish to suggest the wild-eyed, unyielding—even though unfounded—belief that heterosexuality is the "normal" and most socially acceptable sexual orientation, and homosexuality is the "abnormal" and, therefore, most socially unacceptable sexual orientation. By "hyper-heterosexual" here, I mean to accent the homophobic over-embrace, and the above and beyond the heteronormative "norm" declarations and incessant celebrations of heterosexuality by, whether conscious or unconscious, heterosexist heterosexuals. In terms of my use of the word "hyper-masculine" here, I seek to accent and critically call into question the version of masculinity—in this case, hip hop masculinity—that exaggerates stereotypical male behavior, such as an over-emphasis on physical strength, aggression, body hair, body odor, and virility. In other words, by "hyper-masculinity" here I wish to reveal an extremely reductive form of masculinity that really is nothing more than degenerate *muscles/penis/testicles–obsessed masculinity*, to put it properly albeit crudely.

Homosexual hip hoppers—that is to say, "homo-hoppers"—were a part of rap music and hip hop culture long before the recent Homo-Hop Movement.[20] As a matter of fact, one of the problematics of the more recent discourse surrounding "the gay rapper" is that it negates the significance of "closeted" versus "out" hip hoppers, not to mention the importance of the entire "coming out" and unapologetic-embrace-of-queerness process. Kalamka and West argue that "[w]hile we too are men on the mic, it is taken for granted that this man with a mic is straight, urban, masculine, and any other number of adjectives that fall in the lazy categorical imperatives associated with the MC" (199). However, critical questions concerning sexuality, especially transgressive sexuality, in hip hop culture extend well beyond MCs ("the dudes holding phallic symbols at their mouths") and help to complicate and provide counter-histories of hip hop producers, DJs, graffiti artists, b-boys, b-girls, intellectuals, journalists, and activists.[21]

The truth is, hip hop has always had transgressive sexualities. The issue here is the simple fact that most heterosexuals have refused to acknowledge the diversity of *hip hop sexualities*—recall this was one of the major issues the second wave "Niggerati" New Negroes of the Harlem Renaissance had with the first wave "old New Negroes" of the New Negro Movement. In other words, a hard-line *heterosexualization and hyper-masculinization of hip hop* has taken place, and this heterosexualization and hyper-masculinization of hip hop hinges on a distinctly heteronormative, hyper-heterosexual, and hyper-masculine historical amnesia that completely downplays and diminishes how flamboyant, feminist, and queer musical forms—such as funk, punk, new wave, disco, techno, electronica, and house music—directly contributed to the development of rap music and hip hop culture. Kalamka and West, once again, offer weighted words:

If you want to get even deeper—what kind of conversation about authenticity and maleness/masculinity, and by extension the absence of women and Queers, would we have if we talked about the Sugarhill Gang being the brain-child of soul singer and label owner Sylvia Robinson? How do we talk about the place of said maleness when the same woman is responsible for bringing Grandmaster Flash and the Furious Five to international attention? Or what about Blondie and lead singer Deborah Harry's contribution to hip hop's mainstreaming with the single "Rapture"? Or Talking Heads bassist Tina Weymouth and her Tom Tom Club's "Genius of Love" being the basis for The Furious Five's "It's Nasty"? Who "belongs" in hip hop then? Who's "real"? Are straight black men who sample records by white women "real" b-boys? The line is clearly arbitrary and glaringly ahistorical. (200)

Hence, we witness here that what I am calling *hip hop's amnesia* is not isolated to African American social and political history, but also entails women's and homosexuals' contributions to the origins and evolution of rap music and hip hop culture. To complicate matters even more, the overt sexism and heterosexism exhibited by most mainstream (or, rather, *male*stream) hip hoppers, no matter how "progressive" they claim to be, actually resembles nothing more than an unrefined, "remixed" version of the conservative gender and sexual politics of both the white and black bourgeoisies of the turn of the twentieth century. In other words, there is a lot of the upper-class and middle-class American "old school" still haunting and secretly hidden within the world of hip hop's supposedly "new school." Consequently, we must ask: "How genuinely 'new' is hip hop culture if it so closely mirrors and mindlessly mimics turn of the twentieth century bourgeois mores and morality?"

Here we witness where *hip hop's amnesia* is not simply historical, cultural, social, political, and aesthetic, but also *hyper-masculine* (i.e., gendered) and *hyper-heterosexual* (i.e., sexual). How might being exposed to the fact that the first rap record and rap group was the "brainchild" of an African American woman, Sylvia Robinson, have altered our current relationships with rap music and hip hop culture? What about the fact that the same Sylvia Robinson not only produced the world's first rap record, "Rapper's Delight" by the Sugarhill Gang in 1979, but also prefigured what is commonly referred to as the "Golden Age of Rap" (i.e., "political," "conscious," or "message" rap music, from 1987 to 1999) by masterminding "The Message" by Grandmaster Flash and the Furious Five in 1982? What about being aware of white women's unique contributions to the early development and popularization of rap music as well? How many postmillennial hip hoppers "big up" or give long-overdue "props" (i.e., maximum respect) to Deborah Harry or Tina Weymouth? The history *and* "herstory" of hip hop is much more complicated than previously imagined when we look at it through the illuminat-

ing lenses of feminism, womanism, and the contemporary Women's Liberation Movement now known as the Hip Hop Women's Movement, which was
discussed in detail in "remix" 2.

Acknowledging these "herstorical" and musical facts will only help rap
music and hip hop culture return to its *real* roots, which it must do if it
intends to re-politicize and re-radicalize itself and contribute more than merely corporatized/colonized song after song singing sexism and heterosexism's
praises. To speak freely here, I have often wondered about how Sylvia Robinson, Deborah Harry, and Tina Weymouth, among other hip hop feminist
foremothers, might feel about the sexism they hear spewing from their children's or, perhaps, their grandchildren's iPod, iPhone, and iPad speakers
(i.e., assuming they have children or grandchildren). It is, to say the least, a
bit ironic, if not outright absurd, that although hip hop's real roots are undeniably feminist/womanist it has evolved into one of the most hyper-masculinist and misogynistic musics in national and international history/herstory
(Babb 2002; R. N. Brown 2008; J. Morgan 1995, 1999; Osayande 2008).
This is an issue that all hip hoppers, not just hip hop women or hip hop
feminists, must raise everywhere and every time hyper-masculinist histories
of rap music and hip hop culture are put forward. What I am humbly calling
for here could be called *counter-herstories of hip hop culture*—that is, *unapologetically woman-centered or womanist histories of hip hop culture
which highlight women's distinct contributions to the discourse and ongoing
development of rap music, hip hop culture, and the wider Hip Hop Movement.*

For Kalamka and West, the conversation around hip hop's sexual diversity "is not just about the reclamation of hip hop by Queers, as is seen in the
budding gay hip hop and Homo-Hop Movement in the U.S., but a reexamina-
tion of how we've imagined hip hop in ways that have de-emphasized and
discounted Queer presence." They candidly continued, "[s]imilar counter-
histories are being explored with the military and professional sports, but I
think that hip hop, like these others I've mentioned, is the last stubborn
bastion of self-congratulating homophobia" (200).[22] Here, we could also
speak of hip hop as one of "the last stubborn bastion[s] of self-congratulating
[sexism, and specifically patriarchy]."

The issue I am raising here centers around the following questions; questions I have raised with recurrence throughout this book, my previous book,
*Hip Hop's Inheritance*, as well as my forthcoming book, *The Hip Hop Movement*: Are the currently accepted histories of hip hop, however sometimes
surreptitiously, hyper-masculinist? Do they, in fact, render invisible and utterly erase the "Queer presence" in, and the "Queer elements" of, rap music
and hip hop culture? How do the women and homosexuals of the Hip Hop
Generation feel about hip hop's homespun sexism and heterosexism? And,
what can we all—that is to say, women *and* men, homosexuals *and* hetero-

sexuals—*do* to deconstruct and reconstruct rap music and hip hop culture to reflect the dreams and realities, as well as the ecstasy and agony of what it means to be the first generation to pass through adolescence and come into adulthood in the "postmodern," "postcolonial," "postfeminist," "post-Marxist," "post–Civil Rights," "post–Black Power," "post–Women's Liberation," "post-AIDS," etc., poverty-stricken and war-torn world of the twenty-first century?

One of the many reasons I believe that more connections need to be made between the Harlem Renaissance and the Hip Hop Movement is because, for all of its faults (e.g., its sometimes subtle embrace of blackface minstrelsy, internalized black primitivism, and often intense Eurocentrism), the Harlem Renaissance represents one of the first times in U.S. history where black *and* white, male *and* female, heterosexuals *and* homosexuals created an alliance. Of course, as discussed below, much of the homosexuality of the Harlem Renaissance was "covert" and couched in "coded language," but, yet and still, I honestly believe that the *heterosexual-homosexual alliance* of the Harlem Renaissance provides the truly progressive of the Hip Hop Movement with much to build on. Both the black radicals and the authentic white anti-racist allies of the Harlem Renaissance offer examples, however imperfect, of what an authentic male-female/heterosexual-homosexual alliance is capable of producing. Tellingly, I write all of this solemnly bearing in mind pioneering Harlem Renaissance scholar Nathan Huggins's heartfelt words in *Voices from the Harlem Renaissance* (1976):

> Symbolically, then, the Harlem Renaissance stands for something more than the actual works of art it produced. Like all symbols, its primary significance is the deep emotional force it embodies, both for those whose experience it was and for those of us who find in it an important moment in our past. It is for us a principal emotional source, verifying our manliness and womanliness. Through the impact of it, we re-experience the triumph of that time and emerge as sensitive, sophisticated, complicated, and resourceful human beings who are capable of tolerance, cooperation, and love, but who also have ample capacity for anger, hatred, resentment, and retaliation. The experience of the Harlem Renaissance tells us that we are to be taken seriously—by ourselves as well as by others. (4; see also Huggins 1971)

Huggins's weighted words help to highlight the fact that moral outrage and, even more, anger directed at sexism and/or heterosexism is nothing new in African American cultural aesthetic movements. As was mentioned above, feminist and homosexual contributions frequently have been either completely erased or completely co-opted as male contributions in the hyper-masculine, hyper-heterosexual, and heteronormative narratives of generation after generation of historians. Huggins's words also emphasize movement member's capacity for "tolerance, cooperation, and love." Indeed, as stated above, the Harlem Renaissance is much more than the music, theater, dance, litera-ture, and art that have become its calling card. It is also "an important mo-ment in our past" that, if earnestly engaged from radical humanist as opposed to hyper-masculinist and/or heteronormative perspectives, has the potential to fundamentally alter contemporary rap music, hip hop culture, and the broader Hip Hop Movement. This reclamation of the Harlem Renaissance is not advocated only to highlight its "Queer elements," but also to reclaim its history-making heterosexual-homosexual alliances, its openness to feminist/womanist artistry and culture, and its receptiveness to authentic white anti-racist civil rights radicalism.

Here, the Harlem Renaissance is offered up as a model movement that provides important paradigmatic perspectives for the progressives of the Hip Hop Movement. Admittedly, the alliances between the blacks and whites, men and women, as well as the heterosexuals and homosexuals of the Har-lem Renaissance were fraught with great difficulties and disappointments. However, as a hip hop intellectual-activist indelibly influenced by contempo-rary radical politics and critical social theory, I understand these "great diffi-culties and disappointments" to be indicative of the radicals of the Harlem Renaissance "keeping it real" with one another and "being true to the game" of their time. Authenticity has always been important in African American cultural aesthetic movements, which is one of the reasons so many hip hop-pers have no respect for folk who "fake the funk!"—that is, people who are hip hop posers, and who really only embrace certain elements of hip hop culture because they are in vogue (i.e., pop, commercial, or mainstream rap music and hip hop culture). "Keeping it real" when and where we come to the setbacks that the radicals of the Renaissance suffered means that we are bringing the dialectic to bear and consciously seeking to develop *both* an appreciative *and* critical relationship with the radicalism of the Harlem Ren-aissance, which is also something we must do with regard to our relation-ships with every aspect of hip hop culture (and, again, this includes unrepen-tant critiques of hip hop's sexism and heterosexism).

What I seek to do here is offer tangible, more concrete examples of the kinds of work we must solemnly endeavor if we are to truly deconstruct and reconstruct hip hop culture, and extend and expand it to include *all* hip hoppers, and not simply those who are male and heterosexual. At the heart of my conception of critical social theory (i.e., Africana critical theory) is an emphasis on the critique of the insidious ideologies of the established order (e.g., racism, sexism, heterosexism, capitalism, colonialism, and religious bias, etc.). Ironically, even though hip hop began as a critique of the ideolo-gies of the established order, over the years, especially since its so-called "Golden Age" (1987–1999), it has increasingly backslid and retreated to the lame logic of the U.S. status quo, which has long been, however sometimes subtly, simultaneously racist, sexist, heterosexist capitalist, and colonialist.

At its inception, hip hop was decidedly critical of each of these *interlocking ideologies*, which have long constituted *overlapping and incessantly intersecting systems of exploitation, oppression, and violence* (P. H. Collins 1998, 2000, 2003, 2005, 2006, 2007).

In this early postmillennial moment it would appear as though hip hop culture has been co-opted and corporatized/colonized. At least in the most popular and socially visible manifestation of hip hop culture, commercial or mainstream rap music, hip hop seems to have morphed and moved away from being the polyvocal voice of the voiceless, the mouthpiece of the oppressed "minorities," and the neo-sorrow songs of human suffering and postmodern social misery, and bemoaningly become the unrepentant representative of the cultural voyeurism of corporate America, the soundtrack to suburban America's ghetto safari, and the crude cultural and musical accompaniment to the seemingly never-ending postmillennial neo–minstrel show.

Returning to the emphasis on the seminal nature of the Harlem Renaissance with regard to the Hip Hop Movement, it is important to accent the ways in which the radicals of the Renaissance sought to consciously go against the status quo of their epoch. Of course, much has been written about the anti-racist, anti-capitalist, and anti-colonialist artistry and activism of the radicals of the Renaissance. However, those Renaissance radicals who embraced explicitly feminist/womanist and homosexual identities have very rarely been revered for their heroism and key contributions to the Renaissance and the wider struggle for civil rights and social justice. Moreover, several Renaissance radicals were simultaneously committed to the struggles for civil rights, women's rights, *and* homosexual rights.

What is even more amazing are the myriad issues that the homosexual rebels of the Harlem Renaissance raised that have recently come to haunt the Hip Hop Movement. For instance, Schwarz (2007) wrote of how many Renaissance radicals were "covertly gay," wrote in "coded language," and whose corpuses are strewn with "camouflaged gay reference[s]" (142, 150–51). After screening *Pick Up the Mic!: The (R)Evolution of the Homo-Hop Movement* by Alex Hinton (2006) I have no doubt that there are many bisexual and homosexual hip hoppers out there who feel forced to choose between their queer identity or their hip hop identity (see also, Phipps 1992, 1993; Welbon 1993). Here it is important for us to return to Audre Lorde's *Sister Outsider* (1984), where she revealingly wrote:

> As a black lesbian feminist comfortable with many different ingredients of my identity, and a woman committed to racial and sexual freedom from oppression, I find I am constantly being encouraged to pluck out some one aspect of myself and present this as the meaningful whole, eclipsing or denying the other parts of self. But this is a destructive and fragmenting way to live. My fullest concentration of energy is available to me only when I integrate all the parts of who I am, openly, allowing power from particular sources of my

living to flow back and forth freely through all my different selves, without the restrictions of externally imposed definition. Only then can I bring myself and my energies as a whole to the service of those struggles which I embrace as part of my living. (120–21)[23]

The "Niggerati" New Negroes of the Harlem Renaissance rejected the "restrictions of externally imposed definition[s]," as put forward by the New Negro black bourgeoisie, of who and what a "New Negro" was and how they should live, love, and express themselves. Additionally, Audre Lorde, among others, audaciously challenged the sexism and heterosexism of both the Black Power Movement and the Black Arts Movement. Therefore, the homosexuals of the Hip Hop Movement have models and need not feel like political and/or aesthetic orphans.

The "Niggerati" radicals of the Harlem Renaissance have bequeathed much to the Hip Hop Movement, and part of *hip hop's inheritance* hinges on an unfettered and principled expression of sexuality: bisexuality, homosexuality, heterosexuality, and transgressive sexuality. Lorde's heartfelt words help to capture a vision of the kind of *transfigured selves* (i.e., *homosexual rights–* and *sexual orientation sensitive–selves*) that all so-called "progressive" hip hoppers should be striving towards. Her weighted words also help to highlight the activist dimension that needs to be brought back to the heart of hip hop culture, and not just activism on behalf of the issues that effect us personally but, on the most hallowed radical humanist principles, activism on behalf of those who might have very different issues and struggles than our own, or, rather, the heteronormative, hyper-heterosexual, and hyper-masculine majority of hip hop.[24]

Although much has been made of it as of late, it is also interesting to note that the "Niggerati" of the Harlem Renaissance were the first to touch on black bisexuality, especially black male bisexuality (Dean 2009). In fact, the entire "on the down low" phenomenon seems to have been prefigured by several Renaissance writers, especially Claude McKay in his novels *Home to Harlem* (1928), *Banjo* (1929), *Banana Bottom* (1933), and *Romance in Marseilles* (written in 1934, but not published until 1995), where he recurringly depicted "manly" black men's "[c]asual sexual involvement with pansies" and "painted boys" (Schwarz 2007, 147; see also Holcomb 2007). As *Pick Up the Mic!* demonstrated with the controversy surrounding the bisexual white rapper and producer Dutchboy, bisexuality—not to mention "bi-curious," "homoflexible," and "heteroflexible"—continues to be a contentious topic in the homosexual hip hop community. Similar to the politics of the truly "progressive"—as opposed to the merely *rhetorically radical*—of the Hip Hop Movement, the radicalism of the Harlem Renaissance was not simply centered around anti-racism, class struggle, and cultural aesthetics, but also deeply entrenched in women's liberation and homosexual liberation.

As a matter of fact, in "The Black Man's Burden" (1993), no less a savant than Henry Louis Gates went so far as to say that, as quiet as it has been kept, the Harlem Renaissance "was surely as gay as it was black" (233). Moreover, in *When Harlem Was in Vogue* (1989), the ever-scrupulous and cool-penned David Levering Lewis observed the "aesthetic straight-jacketing" of the younger New Negroes who eventually formed the "Niggerati" and published *Fire!!!* and *Harlem*, which simultaneously lamented Harlem being turned into the "white man's house of assignations" and warmly welcomed authentic "Negrotarians" (i.e., whites who supported not simply the cultural aesthetics of the Harlem Renaissance, but also the New Negro Movement's overall quest for civil rights and social justice) (141, 165; see also S. Watson 1995b, 95–103).

*Fire!!!* and *Harlem* contained pieces that were more or less "pointillistic soft pornography," Lewis (1989) nervously noted, which unrepentantly celebrated the increasingly common "transvestite floor shows, sex circuses, and marijuana parlors along 140th Street" (197, 211). Undoubtedly, then, sexuality and, as Lorde said above, "sexual freedom" was at the heart of the aesthetic radicalism of the Harlem Renaissance, and homosexuals and their distinct expressions of their homosexuality played a pivotal role which should not be downplayed or diminished. As Lorde (1984) insightfully exclaimed:

> By ignoring the past, we are encouraged to repeat its mistakes. The "generation gap" is an important social tool for any repressive society. If younger members of a community view older members as contemptible or suspect or excess, they will never be able to join hands and examine the living memories of the community, nor ask the all important question, "Why?" This gives rise to a historical amnesia that keeps us working to invent the wheel every time we have to go to the store for bread. (117).

By bringing to light the Harlem Renaissance's contributions to rap music, hip hop culture, and the Hip Hop Movement I honestly believe that hip hoppers can cease the silly cycle that has long had us "working to invent the wheel every time we have to go to the store for bread." In the final analysis, the Harlem Renaissance handed down much more than music, theater, dance, literature, and art to the Hip Hop Movement. Building on the foregoing sections, the final section focuses specifically on the ways in which the hip hoppers of the Homosexual Hip Hop Movement, arguably more than any other hip hop community, have in their own novel ways honored the cultural, musical, social, and political legacy of the "Niggerati" radicals of the Harlem Renaissance by unapologetically embracing not only diverse racial, cultural, political, and musical identities, but also—and this is of paramount importance—"feminist and homosexual identities."

## THE HOMOSEXUAL HIP HOP MOVEMENT: THE TRANSGRESSIVE SEXUAL RADICALISM OF THE HARLEM RENAISSANCE REVISITED AND REMIXED

Feminist and homosexual radicals were at the heart of the revolt of the "Niggerati" of the Harlem Renaissance, just as many feminist and homosexual radicals have historically contributed and currently continue to contribute to rap music, hip hop culture, and the overarching Hip Hop Movement. To put it plainly, if indeed hip hop constitutes a culture, instead of a group of "largely . . . male and heterosexist cultural icon[s]" or, rather, a *sexist and heterosexist cult,* then, progressive male and heterosexual hip hoppers must honestly open themselves to the lives and struggles of female and homosexual hip hoppers. Once they open themselves, then it is important to solemnly open others, especially their friends and family members, to the lives and struggles of the women and homosexuals of the Hip Hop Movement. It is not, and never will be, enough for male and heterosexual purportedly "progressive" hip hoppers to rant and rave about the multiple ways that racism and capitalism are corroding American citizenship, democracy, politics, and society. Sexism and heterosexism are equally important issues that must be critically engaged and combated by *all* genuinely progressive and forward-thinking hip hoppers.

Similar to the radicals of the Harlem Renaissance, especially the "Niggerati" New Negroes, truly progressive hip hoppers must be willing to extend and expand what it means to be a hip hopper. Men do not have a monopoly on what it means to be a hip hopper anymore than heterosexuals have a monopoly on love, marriage, or religion. Where the "Niggerati" of the Harlem Renaissance deconstructed and reconstructed the moniker "New Negro" to include women and homosexuals, as well as "the low-down folks, the so-called common element," as Langston Hughes (1997) roared in his classic "The Negro Artist and the Racial Mountain," *it is time for hip hoppers to radically embrace humanism* (53). Moreover, it is time for *hip hop radical humanists* to either deconstruct and reconstruct hip hop culture to make it inclusive of hip hop feminists and hip hop homosexuals or—and I say this quite solemnly and quite sincerely—leave the world of hip hop altogether and create a new, authentically humanist *post–hip hop culture,* if not, indeed, a new authentically humanist *post–Hip Hip Movement.*[25]

There are many lessons that hip hop radical humanists can and, indeed, *should* learn from the revolt of the "Niggerati" of the Harlem Renaissance, especially Langston Hughes's 1926 classic "The Negro Artist and the Racial Mountain," where he audaciously asserted:

We younger Negro artists who create now intend to express our individual dark-skinned selves without fear or shame. If white people are pleased we are glad. If they are not, it doesn't matter. We know we are beautiful. And ugly too. The tom-tom cries and the tom-tom laughs. If colored people are pleased we are glad. If they are not, their displeasure doesn't matter either. We build our temples for tomorrow, strong as we know how, and we stand on top of the mountain, free within ourselves. (56; see also Rampersad 2002a, 2002b)

Faithfully following—and to paraphrase—Hughes, hip hop radical humanists should say, in so many words: "We [hip hop radical humanists] who create now intend to express our individual [feminist, homosexual, etc.] selves without fear or shame. If [male hip hoppers] are pleased we are glad. If they are not, it doesn't matter. We know we are beautiful. And ugly too. . . . If [heterosexual hip hoppers] are pleased we are glad. If they are not, their displeasure doesn't matter either. We build our temples for tomorrow, strong as we know how, and we stand on top of the mountain, free within ourselves." The best of hip hop is about being "free within ourselves" and standing in solidarity with oppressed and honorably struggling others, especially others whose lives and struggles might be or, in fact, are very different from our own. This is so because "real" hip hop and "real" humanism has always been about daringly breaking down barriers and consciously crossing borders—à la the "Niggerati" of the Harlem Renaissance.

Radical humanist hip hoppers, both heterosexual and homosexual, must end hip hop's longstanding "don't ask, don't tell" policy. It is time to acknowledge our full inheritance from our cultural aesthetic ancestors, especially the radicals of the Harlem Renaissance. How is it that the radicals of the Harlem Renaissance could develop unprecedented anti-sexist and anti-heterosexist cultural aesthetics and politics nearly six decades prior to the birth of rap music and hip hop culture, but yet the bulk of postmillennial rap music and hip hop culture remains as misogynistic and homophobic as the sky is blue and water is wet? This is a serious issue, and one that demands that those of us who identify as both hip hoppers *and* radical humanists interrogate immediately, as this is a matter of life or death—which is to say, hip hop's life or death.

To, once again, invoke the spirit of Claude McKay's classic poem, his weighted words should be taken to heart now more than ever: "If we must die, O let us nobly die!" I write all of this consciously bearing in mind that I/ we have been socialized in *sanitized or user-friendly sexist and heterosexist settings*: from the African American church to African American colleges and universities, from the expressions of African American entertainers to the awe-inspiring acrobatics of African American athletes. But, as I have illustrated above, in the midst of every major modern African American social and political movement there have been radical women and homosexuals, as well as radical male and heterosexual humanists who were willing to go against *the hegemony of heteronormativity, hyper-heterosexuality, and hyper-masculinity* and consciously contribute to heterosexual-homosexual alliances (Brandt 1999; Johnson and Henderson 2005; Sears and Williams 1997).

As within the wider world of the Harlem Renaissance, within the world of the Homo-Hop Movement (i.e., again, the Homosexual Hip Hop Movement), the artistry and activism of homosexual men have almost always eclipsed the artistry and activism of homosexual women. Hence, the conception of hip hop radical humanism articulated here does not give the *patriarchal homosexuality* and *internalized (hetero)sexism* promoted and practiced by many gay male rappers and hip hoppers a pass (Halberstam 1997, 1998, 2005; Piontek 2006; Wilton 1995). As with white supremacy and anti-black racism, patriarchy and misogyny are utterly evil and exploitive, no matter who the culprit is, whether black or white, male or female, heterosexual or homosexual (R.A. Ferguson 2004; Stockton 2006; Stokes 2001). In an effort to expose the historical roots of the prickly practice that privileges gay men's art and politics over that of lesbian women's art and politics, I now turn to A. B. Christa Schwarz's *Gay Voices of the Harlem Renaissance* (2003), where she revealingly wrote:

> To some extent, male same-sex interested Renaissance artists enjoyed a greater degree of freedom than other Harlemites who desired members of the same sex. They could partake in all aspects of Harlem's gay world—the lower-class world with speakeasies and buffet flats, the bohemian parties and studio meetings—and had their own gay networks offering protection, intimacy, and support. As evident in their correspondence, however, they never felt completely safe faced with vigilant black moral forces demanding performances of respectability in what [Alain] Locke generally described as a "dangerous environment." Same-sex-interested female Renaissance writers were in an overall less privileged position. Gloria Hull points to the existence of black lesbian circles, yet while these could offer support, they lacked the powerful presence of Renaissance "stars"—usually crowned by predominantly male critics and Renaissance intellectuals—and Renaissance leaders who could offer personal advice and boost careers. . . . It seems true that indiscretions on the part of male Renaissance artists were usually overlooked by the guardians of Harlem's morality if general standards of decency were adhered to—their homosexual inclinations were generally treated as "open secrets." (23; see also Hull 1987; Wall 1995)

After reading this, the logical question here has to do with the reasons why the "vigilant black moral forces demanding performances of respectability" would give gay male Renaissance "stars" a pass—of course, provided that "general standards of decency were adhered to"—but at the same time be extremely punitive, if not outright heterosexist *and* misogynist, toward lesbian female Renaissance "stars" (e.g., Georgia Douglas Johnson, Alice

Moore Dunbar-Nelson, and Angelina Weld Grimké). Although she was not directly commenting on the Harlem Renaissance, I believe that at least part of our answer can be found within the pages of bell hooks's classic *Talking Back: Thinking Feminist, Thinking Black* (1989), where she noted that often "homophobia directed at lesbians was [and remains] rooted in deep religious and moral belief that women define their womanness through bearing children. The prevailing assumption was that to be a lesbian was 'unnatural' because one would not be participating in child-bearing" (121).

I find African American heterosexists' reliance on "deep religious" doctrine to justify their discrimination against African American homosexuals particularly problematic because this same doctrinaire (mis)interpretation of the Bible, Jesus's teachings, and Christian ethics has been and continues to be used to justify African American males' supposedly God-given superiority in relationship to African American females' allegedly God-given inferiority. To put it plainly, African American Christians cannot hypocritically have it both ways. They cannot, on the one hand, habitually turn a blind eye to heterosexual black men's "backsliding" promiscuity, by claiming that "boys will be boys" and that "the brothers are simply 'sowing their wild oats'" (à la Psalm 25:7), and then, on the other hand, mercilessly condemn young black women's "out-of-wedlock" sexual activities and pregnancies.

On numerous occasions I have witnessed young women being called out and condemned from the pulpit, or called before the ever-watchful eyes and eager ears of the entire congregation to confess their "sins" and sincerely ask for forgiveness without one single word being directed at the usually older men who impregnated them. This, indeed, is a dastardly double-standard and, even more, one that actually goes against Jesus Christ's teachings, especially in John 8:1–11, where he forgave a woman caught in the act of adultery and who, based on the "Law of Moses," was condemned to be stoned. As is well known, Jesus replied quite calmly: "He that is without sin among you, let him first cast a stone at her" (John 8:7). Needless to say, "And they which heard it, being convicted by their own conscience, went out one by one, beginning at the eldest, even unto the last: and Jesus was left alone, and the woman was standing in the midst" (John 8:9).

In terms of the problems inherent in the African American church's position (or, rather, disposition) on homosexuality, truth be told, it is actually an untenable attitude that strikingly contradicts the church's longstanding and strong stance on civil rights and social justice. Even though many African American ministers preach about the "sexual immorality" of "Sodom and Gomorrah" (Jude 1:7) and often in the same breath ardently exclaim "we must hate the sin and love the sinner, as Jesus does!," they fail to comprehend how racism and heterosexism are intricately intertwined. As Johnnetta B. Cole and Beverly Guy-Sheftall importantly shared in *Gender Talk: The Struggle for Women's Equality in African American Communities* (2003):

"Just as white people have misused Biblical texts to argue that God supported slavery, and that being black was a curse, the Bible has been misused by African Americans to justify the oppression of homosexuals. It is ironic that while they easily dismiss the Bible's problematic references to black people, they accept without question what they perceive to be its condemnation of homosexuals" (120; on alleged pro-slavery and anti-blackness in the Bible, see Genesis 9:20–27; Exodus 21:7–11; Ephesians 6:5–8; Colossians 3:22–4:1; Titus 2:9–10). Is it possible that the Bible is wrong when and where we come to its pronouncements on blackness and slavery, but unreservedly right when and where we come to its alleged "judgments" against homosexuality? If so, this is some tricky magic, whether "Biblical" or otherwise.

Whether we are discussing religion or politics, aesthetics or athletics, an often hidden form of heterosexism makes it seem as though holding on to homophobia is a "natural" and "normal" part of what it means to be human in general, and American in particular. Where above Schwarz was commenting on the 1920s and 1930s, and hooks more or less on the 1950s and 1960s, and Cole and Guy-Sheftall on the ways in which "deep religious" reads of the Bible are frequently heterosexist, it is interesting to observe how almost a hundred years later Hip Hop Movement lesbians' lives seem to eerily echo Harlem Renaissance lesbians' lives. Here we have hit on not only another area where *hip hop's amnesia* rears its head, but also an area which, if engaged from the hip hop radical humanist perspective discussed above, could potentially shed a great deal of light on hip hop lesbians' lives and struggles.

Part of the point here is that just as African American heterosexuals call on all U.S. citizens—regardless of race, gender, class, sexual orientation, or religious affiliation—to contribute their voices, time, energy, and resources to our ongoing civil rights and social justice struggles, in the same spirit, African American lesbian, gay, bisexual, and transgender (LGBT) sisters and brothers call on *all* U.S. citizens to contribute to the ongoing LGBT struggles for human and civil rights. It should be stated outright and unequivocally: There is no such thing as "progressive" or "radical" African American politics that do not include a concerted and unmitigated critique of heterosexism and homophobia, not only within mainstream America, but especially within African America.

Post–Civil Rights Movement politics must be concerned with much more than civil rights. Post–Black Power Movement politics must be concerned with much more than rhetorically condemning "rednecks," "honkies," and "crackers," or critiquing the super-structural impact of anti-black racism and white supremacy on black and other non-white folk. Post–Women's Liberation Movement politics must be concerned with much more than condemning patriarchy and critiquing misogyny. This is all to say, hip hop's politics must

be more multi-issue and multivalent than any previous form of politics because, truth be told, the Hip Hop Generation may very well be the most
thoroughly "integrated"—albeit not truly "desegregated"—generation in
U.S. history. "To whom much is given, much is required," is the way my
grandmother repeatedly put it to me in her paraphrase of Luke 12:48.

The Hip Hop Generation's politics cannot simply revolve around race,
gender, and class as though they are nice and neat academic categories free
from the controversies surrounding sexuality, both heterosexual and homosexual. It would seem that I need not emphasize this considering the longstanding discussion surrounding *the hyper-sexualization of hip hop*, but
along with race, gender, and class hip hop's political agenda needs a
thorough conception and critique of sexuality that is not the same-old heteronormative and homophobic conception and conservative critique of sexuality
handed down to us by many of our great grandparents, grandparents, and
parents. It is only when we move beyond a heteronormative and homophobic
conception of sexuality that we can begin to really and truly acknowledge
and earnestly appreciate the humble humanity of our LGBT sisters and
brothers.

All of this is to say, if racism affects African Americans, then it affects *all*
people. If sexism affects women, then it affects *all* people. If heterosexism
affects homosexuals, then—in all honesty and on the highest humanist principles—it affects *all* people. We have to ask ourselves how really and truly
different is the Hip Hop Generation from previous generations of purportedly
"progressive" youth if, when it is all said and done, hip hoppers are perpetuating several of the very same regressive *and* repressive thoughts and practices that radical youth critiqued and combated nearly a hundred years ago?
This is obviously an uncomfortable question, but one that I honestly believe
each and every one of us must solemnly ask and answer ourselves. *Selah.*

The irony with respect to the continuation of the practice of privileging
African American gay males over African American lesbian females is that
many hip hoppers, both heterosexual and homosexual, do not understand that
hip hop culture cannot and will not develop to its fullest potential unless each
and every hip hopper is able to speak their special truths and offer up their
unique contributions to hip hop culture and the broader Hip Hop Movement.
Equally important here is the simple fact that gay male privilege is yet and
still a *male privilege* and, therefore, must be challenged because it is nothing
more than a supposedly kinder and gentler or seemingly "softer" form of
patriarchy—which, it could go without saying, there quite simply is no such
thing: any and all forms of patriarchy are hardcore and extremely callous.
There remains much within the world of hip hop, even within the world of
the Homo-Hop Movement, that is predicated on racism, sexism, heterosexism, and classism that—however subtle or seemingly innocent to most others—targets African American lesbians in ways that these systems of exploi-

tation, oppression, and violence do not any other group of African Americans—or, truth be told, any other group of Americans in general for that matter. As Patricia Hill Collins importantly pointed out in *Black Sexual Politics: African Americans, Gender, and the New Racism* (2005), a series of binaries predicated on the pretenses of "normal" and "abnormal," literally, "divides and conquers" African American lesbians' lives:

> When ideologies that defend racism and heterosexism become taken-for-granted and appear to be natural and inevitable, they become hegemonic. Few question them and the social hierarchies they defend. Racism and heterosexism both share a common cognitive framework that uses binary thinking to produce hegemonic ideologies. Such thinking relies on oppositional categories. It views race through two oppositional categories of whites and blacks, gender through two categories of men and women, sexuality through two oppositional categories of heterosexuals and homosexuals. A master binary of normal and deviant overlays and bundles together these and other lesser binaries. In this context, ideas about "normal" race (whiteness, which ironically, masquerades as racelessness), "normal" gender (using male experiences as the norm), and "normal" sexuality (heterosexuality, which operates in a similar hegemonic fashion) are tightly bundled together. In essence, to be completely "normal," one must be white, masculine, and heterosexual, the core hegemonic white masculinity. This mythical norm is hard to see because it is so taken-for-granted. Its antithesis, its Other, would be black, female, and lesbian, a fact that black lesbian feminist Audre Lorde pointed out some time ago. (96–97; see also Lorde 1984, 1988, 1996, 2004, 2009)

Here emphasis needs to be placed on the hegemonic oppositional logic that seemingly always and everywhere "divides and conquers" all who are not "white, masculine, and heterosexual." In this specific instance—and certainly not always and everywhere—corresponding with "white, masculine, and heterosexual" are the larger intersecting and interlocking systems of exploitation, oppression, and violence these adjectives stubbornly stand for: that is, "white" equates to racism; "masculine" equates to sexism, particularly patriarchy; and "heterosexual" equates to heterosexism and homophobia. Observe that as quiet as it has been kept, as with religion in the United States and almost anything else of consequence, sexuality historically has been and roguishly remains intensely racialized *and* colonized. This means, then, that white male heterosexuality represents the epitome of "normal" sexuality, whereas black female homosexuality represents the epitome of "abnormal" sexuality (Hull, Scott, and Smith 1982; James, Foster, and Guy-Sheftall 2009; McKinley and DeLaney 1995; Phillips 2006; B. Smith 1983).

This line of logic leads us to the often-overlooked fact that white homosexuality or any variation of white Lesbian, Gay, Bisexual, Transsexual, Transgender, and Queer (LGBTTQ) lifestyle is not considered nearly as sexually deviant and socially dissident as an African American lesbian lifestyle. It should also be observed in earnest that, even though African American men, both heterosexual and homosexual, must contend with commonplace caricatures of their sexuality which incessantly and sadomasochistically liken them to wild animals, criminals, sex addicts, and hereditary rapists, yet and still, their position on the overarching hegemonic hierarchy of the "master binary of normal and deviant" that Collins discussed above noticeably remains a notch higher than African American lesbians who register as the exact opposite of "white, masculine, and heterosexual." Collins resolutely continued:

> Within this oppositional logic, the core binary of normal/deviant becomes ground zero for justifying racism and heterosexism. The deviancy assigned to race and that assigned to sexuality becomes an important point of contact between the two systems. Racism and heterosexism both require a concept of sexual deviancy for meaning, yet the form that deviance takes within each system differs. For racism, the point of deviance is created by a *normalized white heterosexuality* that depends on a *deviant black heterosexuality* to give it meaning. For heterosexism, the point of deviance is created by this very same *normalized white heterosexuality* that now depends on a *deviant white homosexuality*. Just as racial normality requires the stigmatization of the sexual practices of black people, heterosexual normality relies upon the stigmatization of the sexual practices of homosexuals. In both cases, installing white heterosexuality as normal, natural, and ideal requires stigmatizing alternate sexualities as abnormal, unnatural, and sinful. (97; all emphasis in original)

The "normalized white heterosexuality"/"deviant black heterosexuality" dichotomy not only vilifies African American sexuality and perpetuates the continued *sexual colonization* of African Americans (even after enslavement), but it also excludes alternative sexualities outside of the hegemonic heterosexual orbit altogether. In other words, racial colonization is inextricable from sexual colonization in America, and this is one of the many reasons that there is a never-ending national conversation concerning the "abhorrent" sexual lives and sexual practices of adolescent black and brown youth, especially young non-white women in general. If white male heterosexuality surreptitiously serves as the "norm" by which society measures the sexual lives and sexual practices of all "Others" (most especially non-white "Others"), then where black heterosexuality is seen as deviant compared to white heterosexuality, black homosexuality is perceived as outright "abnormal, unnatural, and sinful" in the most extreme senses of these terms imaginable.

Truth be told, however, it is not merely heterosexuals who internalize the rubrics of racial, gender, and class normality predicated on *the white-bourgeois-heterosexual-male model*. Homosexuals also internalize the rubrics of racial, gender, and class normality predicated on *the white-bourgeois-hetero-*

*sexual-male model*, because neither their sexual identity nor their sexual orientation exists in some sort of raceless, genderless, and classless vacuum. All of this means that, even though the African American LGBTTQ community may be deeply committed to eradicating anti-black racism and homophobia, when it comes to sexism within the world of the African American LGBTTQ community, many of our gay brothers "hate on" our lesbian sisters just as much as the homophobic, hyper-heterosexual, muscles/penis/testicles–obsessed male rappers who are at the center of commercial rap music and hip hop culture. Speaking directly to this issue, in their groundbreaking article "Sista Outsider: Queer Women of Color and Hip Hop" (2007), Eric Pritchard and Maria Bibbs interrogate the patriarchal homosexuality and internalized (hetero)sexism of many gay male rappers, revealingly writing:

> In the advent of the movement called "Homo-Hop," which serves to frame gay hip hop within a term acknowledging the larger LGBT community that is a part of the culture, males benefit from being at the center of this "gay rapper" discourse while bisexual and lesbian women of color in the hip hop game remain maligned and subsequently ignored in media coverage and opportunities. In the popular news media, criticisms of homophobic rhetoric, the potential for "gay hip hop" to be a viable genre of hip hop culture, and even the homophobic rhetoric itself are all gendered male. We wish to stress here that this does not mean queer men are not marginalized in the hyper-masculine, heteronormative and homophobic discourse of hip hop, however, in order to present the collective and diverse voices of queer women of color in hip hop, it is necessary to critique the male privilege and sexism existing for queer men as well and how that affects women in the LGBT and hip hop communities. (22)[26]

Bisexual and lesbian non-white women are faced with a set of serious problems within the world of hip hop. On the one hand, they must confront the sexism and heterosexism of mainstream hyper-masculinist and heteronormative hip hop. On the other hand, they have to contest the patriarchal homosexuality of many gay male hip hoppers and critique the gender hierarchy within the Homo-Hop Movement. It is this double or triple bind, this "multiple jeopardy" as Deborah King (1988) contended, that makes bisexual and lesbian women's relationship with rap music, hip hop culture, and the wider Hip Hop Movement qualitatively different than any of the other members of the hip hop community.

Few dispute rap music's misogyny, or hip hop's sexism in general. However, it is a rare (a very rare) Hip Hop Studies scholar and/or activist who will break the longstanding silence surrounding hip hop's heterosexism and homophobia. Admittedly, considering my lack of intimate (or empirical) knowledge with regard to homosexuals' lives and struggles, I am not the ideal Hip Hop Studies scholar-activist to break the silence and broach this subject. But, as someone who identifies as both a hip hopper *and* a radical humanist, my conscience compels me to speak truth to power by using my male and heterosexual privilege in the interest of women's liberation *and* homosexual liberation. As a hip hop radical humanist—who also happens to be a specialist in black radical politics and critical social theory—there is also a sense in which I want to utilize my evolving interdisciplinary studies and ongoing emphasis on intersectionality to reach an audience who might not otherwise be aware of, or care for, what has come to be called "critical queer theory."[27]

Truth be told, I have gone back and forth over whether I should raise the issue of the hegemony of heteronormativity and hyper-heterosexuality in hip hop. I kept telling myself that there are so many other well-established Hip Hop Studies scholars who are certainly much more qualified than I to speak on the hegemony of heteronormativity and hyper-heterosexuality in hip hop. But, as I surveyed the postmillennial hip hop scene, I became increasingly aware of the excruciating pain and suffering that many homosexual hip hoppers, some of whom are close brother- and sister-comrades of mine, have experienced during the more than three decades of the Hip Hop Movement. It is not simply the silence surrounding homosexuality within the world of hip hop but, even more, the near erasure and/or invisibility of homosexuals as a result of the hegemony of heteronormativity and hyper-heterosexuality within U.S. society as a whole.

Recently one of my homosexual colleagues enthusiastically told me that she could not wait for me to complete my sequel to *Hip Hop's Inheritance*. I earnestly asked her why. Next she said something that has stuck with me since then. She patiently explained to me that my work, especially on the Homo-Hop Movement, would probably reach heterosexuals in ways that most homosexuals' hip hop criticism cannot. She, of course, was referring to me reaching African American heterosexuals and the ways in which African American homosexuals are silenced and, frequently, physically, psychologically, and verbally violated (e.g., Sakia Gunn, Rashawn Brazell, Duanna Johnson, Roger English, and Roberto Duncanson) within the African American community and wider world.

I gently shared with her that I know many African American heterosexuals who love—or, at the least, greatly appreciate—Langston Hughes, James Baldwin, Alvin Ailey, Audre Lorde, Essex Hemphill, and Angela Davis. Then, she solemnly and lovingly checked me with impunity. She said: "Listen, Brother Rabaka, I ain't never heard no straight black person talk about how Baldwin's gayness factored into his books, or how Angela Davis's lesbianism is linked to her political activism—especially, her post–Black Panther Party and post–Soledad Brothers activism."

I sat silent for a moment, staring into the sunset in the distance, carefully thinking things over. She was on point. She was right and, not that she needed to hear it from me, I humbly told her so. Her weighted words helped me to think about how the various identities we either reject or embrace influence our ability to appreciate aspects of others' identities, and develop deep sensitivities to their distinct identity formation processes and ongoing identity politics.

Bisexual and lesbian non-white women in the world of hip hop are regularly asked to choose between being homosexuals or hip hoppers, as well as homosexuals or members of their specific racio-cultural groups. The work of hip hop lesbian feminists has documented how gay men often play prominent roles in coercing bisexual and lesbian women to choose between their queer identities and their hip hop identities. In other words, this is what might be termed "gay-on-gay violence."[28]

Clearly, then, a gay man's sexual orientation does not automatically preclude him from practicing patriarchy anymore than a woman's gender somehow automatically precludes her from perpetuating patriarchy. For the record: Non-whites can, and often do, internalize white supremacy and racism. Women can internalize and frequently have internalized patriarchy and misogyny. And homosexuals can internalize and historically have internalized heterosexism and homophobia. This is precisely why anti-racism, in and of itself, solves only part of the problem; feminism, in and of itself, solves only part of the problem; and, anti-heterosexism, in and of itself, solves only part of the problem. Without emphasizing that racism, sexism, classism, and heterosexism are all extremely important intersecting and interlocking systems of exploitation, oppression, and violence that must be collectively combated, then all we are left with are drive-by, hit-or-miss movements meandering from one pressing issue to the next with no concrete or coherent radical humanist and authentically "universal" end-goal (Herek 1998; Jung and Smith 1993; Sears and Williams 1997; Wehbi 2004).

The Homo-Hop Movement gives us an almost ideal opportunity to explore the reasons why anti-racism, anti-sexism, anti-classism, and anti-heterosexism divorced from authentic radical humanism often yields little more than empty rhetoric and the continued social segregation of so-called "progressive" communities. How truly progressive are male anti-racists if they, whether consciously or unconsciously, dehumanize women? How truly progressive are white feminists if they, whether consciously or unconsciously, dehumanize non-white people, especially non-white women? How truly progressive are anti-heterosexist gay male activists if they, whether consciously or unconsciously, dehumanize and marginalize bisexual and lesbian women? What about the ways in which white homosexuals, whether con-

sciously or unconsciously, dehumanize and marginalize non-white homosexuals' lives and struggles (Brandt 1999; Johnson and Henderson 2005; E. S.
Nelson 1993; Somerville 2000; Stockton 2006; Stokes 2001)?

In her eye-opening essay, "'I Used to Be Scared of the Dick': Queer
Women of Color and Hip Hop Masculinity," Andreana Clay (2007a) critically discussed white and male supremacy in the ways in which homosexuality
is depicted in the United States and some of the reasons that non-white
(especially black and brown) bisexual and lesbian women continue to identify with hip hop culture. She rhetorically and revealingly asked: "So, who
and why do queer women identify with this culture that is known for its
homophobia and sexism? And, how do we continue to maintain queer feminist ideology and practice in this groove" (151)?

First, she asserted that as of late often when African American homosexuality is discussed the conversation almost immediately turns to the "on the
down low" phenomenon, which centers on bisexual black men's closeted sex
lives. Consequently, bisexual and gay black men's "promiscuity" and "un-
healthy sexual practices" dominate the discourse on African American
homosexuality. Secondly, she wrote, even though "the larger gay community
has pushed a national debate about same-sex marriage into the public eye . . .
[m]ost of the poster children for the same-sex marriage debate are white: gay
neighborhoods or scenes, like the Castro district in San Francisco, are predominantly white, male, and middle-class. In both of these contexts, queer
black desire and identity has been erased, especially for women" (152–53).
Clay continued, "[b]ecause we are absent from a discussion of black same-
sex sex on the one hand and one of gay and lesbian identity on the other, it's
no surprise that young, queer women of color find reprieve anywhere we
can—including the often sexist, homophobic, and hyper-masculine genre of
hip hop" (153).

Clay claimed that "queer engagement with hip hop masculinity is mad
full of complexity and contradiction" (160). This is so because, as Todd
Boyd argued in *Am I Black Enough for You?: Popular Culture from the
'Hood and Beyond* (1997), many black men have embraced the "nigga"
identity, and "the nigga is not interested with anything that has to do with the
mainstream, though his cultural products are clearly an integral part of mainstream popular culture" (33). In a sense, the "nigga" is mainstream America's unacknowledged alter ego, its "bastard" brother, sister, or—from mainstream America's paternalistic perspective—its "bastard" child. Therefore,
ironically, "[t]he nigga rejects the mainstream even though he has already
been absorbed by it" (33).[29]

In U.S. culture and society African American masculinity, as with
African American sexuality, is situated in a socio-cultural context that is
simultaneously within and without or, rather, inside and outside of mainstream heteronormativity, because black men and their blackness are always

being psychopathically and schizophrenically rejected *and* absorbed by mainstream American heteronormativity. Hip hop masculinity has been expressed through the guises of the nigga, the playa, the hustla, the thug, the pimp, the drug dealer, the prisoner, and the ex-con, among others. Each of these expressions of *hip hop anti-hero masculinity* has been much maligned by mainstream America. Therefore, one can comprehend why the sexually dissident bisexual and lesbian "sista outsiders" of the Hip Hop Generation could come to selectively embrace certain elements of rap music and hip hop culture. This is so because rap music and hip hop culture, despite its mainstream absorption and hyper-commercialization, continues to provide a, however "underground," polyvocal voice for the voiceless, a culture for the supposedly cultureless, and a sense of belonging for those who have been told in no uncertain terms that they do not belong, especially in mainstream America.

When it is all said and done, it is hip hop radical humanism that provides us—*all of us*—with a sense of belonging, with a "home-place" within the world of hip hop, regardless of our race, gender, class, sexual orientation, or religious affiliation (see hooks 1990, 41–51). Hip hop radical humanism has a special place in its heart for hip hop homosexuals because it critically comprehends that in order for the Hip Hop Generation to really and truly transform itself into a viable socio-political movement it must strongly stress that our struggle is not only a struggle against racial domination, gender discrimination, and economic exploitation, but also an earnest struggle *against* homophobia and *for* homosexual liberation. Heterosexism and homophobia are in fact fatal forms of domination and discrimination. Therefore, those of us genuinely and incorrigibly committed to social justice and human liberation must be, by default, committed to the freedom of sexual expression and homosexual liberation. With this in mind, we must hold bell hooks's hallowed words in *Talking Back: Thinking Feminist, Thinking Black* (1989) deep in our hearts:

> Significantly, attitudes toward sexuality and sexual preference are changing. There is greater acknowledgement that people have different sexual preferences and diverse sexual practices. Given this reality, it is a waste of energy for anyone to assume that their condemnation will ensure that people do not express varied sexual preferences. Many gay people of all races, raised within this homophobic society, struggle to confront and accept themselves, to recover or gain the core of self-love and well-being that is constantly threatened and attacked both from within and without. This is particularly true for people of color who are gay. It is essential that non-gay black people recognize and respect the hardships, the difficulties gay black people experience, extending love and understanding that is essential for the making of authentic black community. One way we show our care is by vigilant protest of homophobia. By acknowledging the union between black liberation struggle and gay libera-

tion struggle, we strengthen our solidarity, enhance the scope and power of our allegiances, and further our resistance. (125–26; see also Clarke 2006; Lorde 1996, 2004, 2009)

It is time for us to move beyond the politics of being "politically correct" and the incessant impulse to appeal to our enslavers, colonizers, and oppressors. At their origins rap music and hip hop culture represented something new: a new aesthetic, new music, new politics and, perhaps even, a new vision of American society and humanity. It would be really sad if years from now post–hip hop historians write that even though it initially ushered in new and novel approaches to music, dance, theater, film, fashion, art, poetry, literature, culture, politics, and social movement, ultimately hip hop culture degenerated into *a woman-hating and homosexual-hating culture* that can be best summarized by Langston Hughes's lyrical lines from his classic poem "Harlem," in his volume *Montage of a Dream Deferred* (1951), where he poignantly wrote of deferred dreams drying up like raisins in the sun, of sun-soaked dry dreams that fester like sores and stink like rotten meat. If, indeed, hip hop is dying, we need to calmly ask ourselves who is killing it and whether we are contributing to its life or complicit in its untimely death.

In order for hip hop to historically register as more than merely another youthful generation's decadent dream, hip hoppers—of all races, genders, classes, sexual orientations, and religious affiliations—must up their games and get hip to contemporary radical politics, radical anti-racism, radical feminism, and radical humanism. The steady Democratic Party and Republican Party diets of "American democracy" we have been force-fed since our births are not and never will be enough. To truly transcend ourselves and our society, to consciously continue our "struggle[s] to confront and accept [our]selves, to recover or gain the core of self-love and well-being that is constantly threatened and attacked both from within and without," we will need to radically *remix*—that is, radically recreate and re-articulate—a hip hop culture that is based on *love*—that is, *agápē* (unconditional love), *érōs* (passionate love), *philía* (friendly or brotherly and sisterly love), and *storgē* (familial love).

All hyperbole aside, over the last decade or so I sincerely believe that a lot of the love has been lost in rap music and hip hop culture. Instead of a hip hop culture predicated on woman-hating and homosexual-hating, hip hop radical humanism builds on and sincerely seeks to go beyond bell hooks's heartfelt contention that, "It is essential that non-gay black people recognize and respect the hardships, the difficulties gay black people experience, extending love and understanding that is essential for the making of authentic black community. One way we show our care is by vigilant protest of homophobia." The "vigilant protest of homophobia" by heterosexual hip hoppers, the unambiguous critique of patriarchy by male hip hoppers, the unrepentant confrontation of white supremacy by white hip hoppers, and the unyielding condemnation of capitalism by all hip hoppers, especially those who are "up out da 'hood and livin' good," are the core concerns of an authentic hip hop radical humanism; anything less does not deserve to be labeled humanism or "real" hip hop.

Similar to many of the homosexuals of the Harlem Renaissance, the homosexuals of the Hip Hop Generation have long demonstrated their ability to appreciate and contribute to "mainstream" hip hop culture. However, similar to many of their heterosexist antecedents, very few of the heterosexuals of the Hip Hop Generation have challenged the hegemony of hip hop's heterosexism and heteronormativity. As with the New Negro Movement at the turn of the twentieth century, either hip hop culture will consciously extend and expand itself to include the lives and struggles of homosexuals, completely freeing itself from heterosexism and heteronormativity, or else homosexual and radical humanist heterosexual hip hoppers are justified in leaving the world of hip hop and creating a new, radically humanist post–hip hop culture. Neither homosexuals, females and males, nor heterosexual women should have to tolerate hip hop's sexism and heterosexism one minute longer. It is time for hip hop to clean its house. "Out with the old, and in with the new," as the saying goes.

The expression "out with the old, and in with the new" is apropos here, as it could be said to perfectly capture my sincere belief that hip hoppers need to get past narcissistically celebrating themselves as the much-heralded "Hip Hop Generation" and move toward thinking of themselves, rap music, and hip hop culture as part of a larger multi-issue movement. Building on the above discussion concerning hip hop radical humanism, the concluding "remix" critically engages the longstanding tendency to privilege hip hop's aesthetics over its politics. Obviously the Hip Hop Generation is political, but precisely how its politics are distinguished from other youthful generations' politics is an issue rarely raised.

If we were to really press "progressive" hip hoppers to identify the major items on hip hop's political agenda—as I do annually in my Hip Hop Studies courses—it might shock and awe us to find that very few hip hoppers have a clear understanding of the major social and political issues and ills confronting the Hip Hop Generation. Even more, most hip hoppers seem to be completely oblivious to the ways in which many of their major social and political problems have origins in and, consequently, eerily mirror the crises that confronted classic blues, classic jazz, and bebop youth. Now that we have a *remixed* sense of what rap music and hip hop culture inherited from classic blues, classic jazz, and bebop, as well as the pre–Civil Rights Movement socio-political movements these musics served as soundtracks for, it is time for us to cogently and coherently connect classical black popular music and classical black popular movements to contemporary black popular music and contemporary black popular movements.

In an earnest effort to move away from hip hop aestheticism, narcissism, and individualism and toward hip hop humanism, altruism, and collectivism, the focus of the remaining "remix" will be on transforming the Hip Hop Generation and transitioning it into a multi-issue movement that does not merely incessantly celebrate itself through its unprecedented aesthetic innovations, but offers new, viable radical politics and social visions based on the highest humanist principles. As the previous "remixes" have demonstrated, classic blues was much more than merely music, but deeply connected to a movement. Classic jazz was much more than merely music, but also inextricable from the politics and aesthetics of a movement. Moreover, bebop was much more than merely music, but also the aural expression and sonic signature of a movement. Likewise, rap, neo-soul, and other forms of hip hop music are much more than merely music, but also the aural expression and sonic signature of not simply "hip hop culture" or the "Hip Hop Generation" but, even more, *the Hip Hop Movement*. Hence, it is time for us to humble ourselves and hail the emergence of the Hip Hop Movement!

## NOTES

1. For further discussion of Alain Locke's life and legacy, especially his philosophy of the Harlem Renaissance, and for the most noteworthy works that informed my analysis here, see Buck (2005), L. Harris (1999), Harris and Molesworth (2008), Linnemann (1982), Locke (1983, 1989, 1992, 2012), and J. Washington (1986, 1994).

2. For further discussion of the Red Summer of 1919, and for the most noteworthy works that informed my analysis here, see McWhirter (2011), Mellis (2008), Tuttle (1996), Voogd (2008), and Whitaker (2008).

3. For further discussion of the Great Migration of African Americans in the early twentieth century, and for the most noteworthy works that informed my analysis here, see Arnesen (2002), Grossman (1991), Hahn (2003), A. Harrison (1991), Lemann (1991), Marks (1989), Osofsky (1996), Redkey (1969), and Trotter (1991).

4. For further discussion of Claude McKay's life and legacy, as well as the major works consulted to develop my interpretation here, see Gayle (1972), Giles (1976), Holcomb (2007), Ramesh and Rani (2006), and Tillery (1992).

5. For further discussion of minstrelsy or, rather, the minstrel show in the early twentieth century, and for the most noteworthy works that informed my analysis here, see Bean, Hatch and McNamara (1996), Brundage (2011), Cockrell (1997), Mahar (1999), Nowatzki (2010), Springhall (2008), and Toll (1974, 1976).

6. Historically there has been a great deal of discussion concerning whether or not the revolts of enslaved Africans had any significant impact on bringing African American enslavement to an end. Often more attention is paid to the "white abolitionists" without also noting the "black abolitionists" (Quarles 1969). To get a sense of the significance of the revolts of the enslaved and their impact on toppling African American enslavement, see Aptheker (1983), D. B. Davis (2006), Hine and Gaspar (1996), Genovese (1992), H. Jones (1987), Rucker (2006), Sale (1997), E. R. Taylor (2006).

7. It may be difficult for many of my readers to comprehend the complexities and contradictions of what was commonly called the "Negro Problem" between the waning years of the Civil War through to the increased militancy of the Civil Rights Movement, a period roughly running from 1855 to 1965. However, it is extremely important to highlight this often-overlooked discourse within mainstream American and, especially, African American intellectual history and culture because it helped to shape and define the intellectual, artistic, and activist cultures of every major African American social and political movement from the turn of the twentieth century all the way through to the turn of the twenty-first century. Furthermore, the "Negro Problem" discourse, however surreptitiously, also influenced every major post-Emancipation African American cultural and aesthetic movement, from the Harlem Renaissance through to the Hip Hop Movement. For further discussion, please see chapter 1 of my book *Against Epistemic Apartheid*, where I engaged arguably one of the loudest and longest critics of the "Negro Problem" discourse, W. E. B. Du Bois, and most of his major works regarding the "Negro Problem" and its solution (see Rabaka 2010a).

8. For further discussion of whiteness within the American social, political, and cultural world, and for the most noteworthy works that informed my analysis here, see Delgado and Stefancic (1997), E. Lott (1993), Meer (2005), Olson (2004), and Roediger (2007).

9. Here I am, of course, drawing from the pioneering work of the Jamaican political philosopher, Charles Mills, who, in *The Racial Contract* (1997), famously contended: "The Racial Contract is that set of formal or informal agreements or meta-agreements (higher-level contracts *about* contracts, which set the limits of the contracts' validity) between the members of one subset of humans, henceforth designated by (shifting) 'racial' (phenotypical/genealogical/cultural) criteria . . . as 'white,' and coextensive (making due allowance for gender differentiation) with the class of full persons, to categorize the remaining subset of humans as 'non-white' and of a different and inferior moral status, sub-persons, so that they have a subordinate civil standing in the white or white-ruled politics the whites either already inhabit or establish or in transactions as aliens with these polities, and the moral and juridical rules normally regulating the behavior of whites in their dealings with non-whites or apply only in a qualified form (depending in part on changing historical circumstances and what particular variety of non-white is involved), but in any case the general purpose of the Contract is always the differential privileging of whites as a group with respect to non-whites as a group, the exploitation of their bodies, land, and resources, and the denial of equal socio-economic opportunities to them. All whites are *beneficiaries* of the Contract, though some whites are not *signatories* to it" (11, all emphasis in original). In other words, Mills's work accents the surreptitious nature of white supremacy within the contemporary world. The "racial contract" is not a thing of the past, but covertly continues to *racially colonize* almost each and every interaction in the (post)modern moment. Clearly, blackface minstrelism speaks volumes about the ways in which whites were considered human in juxtaposition to black and other non-white non-humans. Additionally, it is important to emphasize that *the diabolical dialectic of white superiority and black inferiority* did not end with the Emancipation Proclamation or the Civil War. It continued through Reconstruction, post-Reconstruction, the Black Women's Club Movement, the New Negro Movement, the Harlem Renaissance, World War I, World War II, the Civil Rights Movement, the Black Power Movement, and stubbornly remains here with us in the postmillennial moment of the Hip Hop Movement. In order for the Hip Hop Generation to really and truly disrupt its *amnesia* (historical, cultural, social, political, etc.), it will be necessary to engage white supremacy and anti-black racism, even though most white and, truth be told, many non-white hip hoppers believe that we are in a "post-racial" period, and that racism no longer exists or only flares up every now and then. For further discussion of the "racial contract" and the "racial polity," see Mills (1998, 1999, 2003a, 2003b). And, for a more detailed discussion of *the diabolical dialectic of white superiority and black inferiority*, see my previously mentioned *Against Epistemic Apartheid: W.E.B. Du Bois and the Disciplinary Decadence of Sociology*, as well as *Forms of Fanonism: Frantz Fanon's Critical Theory and the Dialectics of Decolonization* (Rabaka 2010a, 2010b).

10. The rising racial consciousness of the "New Negroes" was sparked by the infamous Hayes-Tilden compromise of 1877, which subsequently led to the 1896 Supreme Court "separate but equal" verdict in the *Plessy v. Ferguson* case. Between 1895 and 1940, African

Americans experienced an intense period of social transformation, which had an enormous impact on their social and political consciousness, and it is this evolution of African Americans' cultural, social, and political consciousness during the period ending the nineteenth century and beginning the twentieth century that is commonly called the New Negro Movement. As mentioned previously, African American historian Rayford Logan (1954) famously referred to the decade closing the nineteenth century as the "nadir" of African American history, and his work, along with the work of several other scholars, has brought to light more than three thousand documented lynchings during this unfortunate era (see Brundage 1993, 1997; Gonzales-Day 2006; Ifill 2007; Nevels 2007; Pfeifer 2004; Waldrep 2006; Zangrando 1980). The New Negro Movement culminated with the wide and varied cultural and artistic innovations of the Harlem Renaissance. In essence, the "New Negro" was distinguished from the "Old Negro" by resistance to African American re-enslavement and American apartheid. They rejected the *minstrelesque mischaracterizations* of African Americans and the white-washed revisionist interpretations of the African holocaust and African American enslavement, which made white enslavers appear as though they were patently pious, benevolent Christians who "civilized" and "Christianized" the "heathen," "barbarous," and "irreligious" Africans they ruled over on their palatial antebellum plantations. New Negro Studies, then, is an extremely important area of inquiry within African American Studies, even though it is frequently folded into Harlem Renaissance Studies. Undoubtedly New Negro Studies and Harlem Renaissance Studies discursively dovetail but, yet and still, it is important to distinguish between the two because, to put it plainly, the cultural and aesthetic innovations of the Harlem Renaissance are virtually incomprehensible without first engaging the historical, cultural, social, and political coming-to-critical consciousness that the New Negro Movement fostered. For my (re)interpretation of the New Negro Movement, and for the most noteworthy works that informed my analysis here, see A. E. Carroll (2005), Favor (1999), Foley (2003), Gates and Jarrett (2007), Hutchinson (1995, 2007), Lamothe (2008), D. L. Lewis (1989), Locke (1925), W. J. Maxwell (1999), Peplow and Davis (1975), and Wintz (1996b).

11.   For further discussion of the origins and evolution of the Black Women's Club Movement, from the National Federation of Afro-American Women to the National Association of Colored Women, see "remix" 2. And, for further discussion of African American women's contributions to the New Negro Movement and Harlem Renaissance, and for the most noteworthy works that informed my analysis here, see Egar (2003), Honey (1989), Hull (1987), Mitchell and Taylor (2009), Patton and Honey (2001), Roses and Randolph (1996), and Wall (1995).

12.   For further discussion of W.E.B. Du Bois's pioneering civil rights leadership and activism, especially with respect to the Niagara Movement and NAACP, and for the most noteworthy works that informed my analysis here, see Broderick (1959), D.L. Lewis (1993, 2000), Marable (1986), Meier (1963), Rabaka (2007, 2008, 2010a, 2010c), Rudwick (1960, 1968), and Wolters (2001).

13.   The body of research on the radicalism of the intellectuals and artists of the Harlem Renaissance has grown greatly over the last decade. This work helps to highlight why it is important to grasp and seriously grapple with the social and political influence of the New Negro Movement on the Harlem Renaissance prior to exploring its cultural and aesthetic innovations. Most members of the Renaissance, in one way or another, had connections to, or, at the least, affinities with, leftist, working-class, and/or populist mass movements. However, what distinguished the Renaissance radicals from both the turn of the twentieth century New Negroes and the white socialists, communists, and unionists of their epoch was their unapologetic critique of racism *and* capitalism. In this sense, then, it is both the political *and* artistic radicalism of the Harlem Renaissance that proves unprecedented in African American history, culture, and struggle. Hence, here we are given grounds to point to what could be called *New Negro critical social theory and counter-ideology*. For the most noteworthy works which have informed my interpretation of "New Negro critical social theory and counter-ideology," see Baldwin (2002), Foley (2003), W. James (1998), Maxwell (1999), Mullen and Smethurst (2003), Naison (2005), Smethurst (1999), and Solomon (1998).

14.  For further discussion of W. E. B. Du Bois's aesthetics and its impact on the Harlem Renaissance, and for the most noteworthy works that informed my analysis here, see Aptheker (1989), Kirschke (2007), D. L. Lewis (1993, 2000), Moses (1978, 2004), Rampersad (1990), and Wintz (1996a).

15.  For detailed discussions of the various 1960s and 1970s multi-issue movements that advocated for authentic multiracial and multicultural democracy in America that the Hip Hop Movement, whether consciously or unconsciously, has drawn from, see Anner (1996), Breines (2006), Churchill and Wall (1988), Haney-López (2003), D. A. Harris (1995), Maeda (2009, 2011), Mariscal (2005), Ogbar (2004), Rosales (1996), Roth (2004), and Springer (2005).

16.  In *When Harlem Was in Vogue* (1989), David Levering Lewis discussed the growing disdain that younger New Negroes developed in relation to the older New Negro civil rights establishment: "'Wallie' Thurman had become increasingly distressed by party-line art. Temporarily replacing [George] Schuyler in 1926 as editor of *The Messenger*, he lashed out repeatedly against the Victorian aesthetics of civil rights grandees—those whom he and novelist Zora Hurston later ridiculed as the 'Niggerati.' Before the end of the year, he decided to recruit younger artists and launch a magazine [i.e., *Fire!!!*] devoted to art for the artist's sake—and for the sake of the folk. His rent-free place on 136th Street—the infamous '267 House' . . . was the cradle of revolt against establishment arts. Thurman and Hurston also mocked themselves by calling 267 House 'Niggerati Manor,' and all the younger artists called Thurman their 'leader'—the fullest embodiment of outrageous, amoral independence among them. Thurman never doubted that, freed from the prim guidance of the leading civil rights organizations, the artists would recognize the need 'for a truly Negroid note' and would go to the proletariat rather than to the bourgeoisie for characters and material" (193). As can be easily detected, the intentionally outrageous and ironic term "Niggerati" is a portmanteau of "nigger" and "literati" meant to mock the black bourgeois pretentions and "Victorian aesthetics of [New Negro] civil rights grandees" and their mealy-mouthed minions. Although the "Niggerati" neologism took form as a rebuke of the Victorianism, conservatism, bourgeoisism, and unmitigated elitism of the New Negro civil rights establishment, observe how—similar to the artists and activists of both the Black Arts Movement and the Hip Hop Movement—a controversial new name and movement moniker was eventually embraced by the young radicals of the Harlem Renaissance. As the unrepentant "Niggerati" of the Harlem Renaissance, Hurston, Thurman, Langston Hughes, Helene Johnson, Richard Bruce Nugent, Gwendolyn Bennett, Jonathan Davis, and Aaron Douglass, among others, sought not only civil rights and social justice, but also democratic socialist and sexual revolution. For further discussion of the "Niggerati" of the Harlem Renaissance, and for the most noteworthy works that informed my analysis here, see Gates and Jarrett (2007), Hurston (1942, 1979), Marks and Edkins (1999), and Thurman (2003).

17.  For further discussion of what Nadall termed the "racial aesthetic" of the Harlem Renaissance and the "wide variety of nineteenth century literary and visual images of African Americans" that Renaissance radicals were deconstructing and reconstructing in their paintings, plays, poems, novels, dances, and music, and for the most noteworthy works that informed my analysis here, see Calo (2007), A. E. Carroll (2005), Earle (2007), Fleetwood (2011), Goeser (2007), Kirschke (1995, 2007), Powell and Bailey (1997), and Reynolds and Wright (1989).

18.  For further discussion of bisexuality, homosexuality, and transgressive sexuality within the world of the Harlem Renaissance, and for the most noteworthy works that informed my analysis here, see Chapman (2011), Haidarali (1997), Holcomb (2007), Hurston (1942), Nugent (2002), Pochmara (2011), Somerville (2000), Thurman (2003), J. F. Wilson (2010), and Woods (1998).

19.  For further discussion of the ways in which African American women challenged the colonization of their sexuality during the Harlem Renaissance, and for the most noteworthy works that informed my analysis here, see Chapman (2011), A. Y. Davis (1998b), Egar (2003), Haidarali (1997), Hull (1987), Roses and Randolph (1996), and Wall (1995).

20.  For further discussion of queer hip hop culture, homo-thugs, the Homosexual Hip Hop Movement, and what is alternatively called "queer" rap or "gay" rap, and for the most noteworthy works that informed my analysis here, see Amani (2007), Cannick (2006), Coleman and Cobb (2007), Hinton (2006), Lane (2011), Myhre (2007), Shimeles (2010), V. Stephens (2005), Rodriguez (2006), Tan (2006), T. T. West (2005), and D. M. Wilson (2007).

21.  Kalamka and West's critique of the ways in which African American masculinity, as publicly perceived and performed, is connected to a growing body of scholarly research that challenges African American heterosexual males' supposed monopoly on African American maleness and African American masculinity. For example, see B. K. Alexander (2006), Blount and Cunningham (1996), Byrd and Guy-Sheftall (2001), Carbado (1999), R. A. Ferguson (2004), Hine and Jenkins (1999, 2001), hooks (2004a, 2004b), R. L. Jackson (2006), Jackson and Hopson (2011), E. P. Johnson (2003), Lemelle (2010), and Mutua (2006). More specifically, Kalamka and West's words here help to highlight and critically turn us toward a *counterhistory of hip hop masculinity*, which is primarily based on African American male speaking, singing, rapping, dancing, and other styles, but which has increasingly become absorbed by the non-black males, both white and non-white, of the Hip Hop Generation. It is not simply young suburban white males who have embraced the mutilating machismo and often brutal braggadocio of hip hop masculinity, but also young, working-class white, Mexican American, Latin American, Asian American, Native American, and Caribbean, among other, "postmodern," "postcolonial," and/or "postmillennial" males. Accenting homosexual, "queer," or other transgressive masculinities within global, national, and local hip hop communities will only bring us one step closer to bridging the yawning chasm between hip hop's radical rhetoric concerning "freedom," "liberation," "peace," and "justice," and its actual prickly practices toward homosexuals—which is to say, its infamous homophobia and heterosexism. What we must do, I honestly believe, is expand the range and meaning of "manhood," "maleness," and "masculinity" for the Hip Hop Generation by deconstructing and reconstructing it, making it more multidimensional, multivalent, and unequivocally inclusive of what bell hooks, in *The Will to Change: Men, Masculinity, and Love* (2004b), has famously referred to as "alternative masculinities" (see "Feminist Manhood" in hooks [2004b], 107–24; see also, "Reconstructing Black Masculinity" in hooks [1991], 87–114 and "Feminist Masculinity" in hooks [2000a], 67–71). For further discussion, and for the most noteworthy works which have indelibly influenced my interpretation of hip hop masculinity, see T. J. Brown (2006), Greene (2008), Hagedorn (2008), K. M. Harris (2006), Hopkinson and Moore (2006), R. L. Jackson (2006), K. Powell (2003), E. Watson (2009), and V. A. Young (2007).

22.  For further discussion of heterosexism and homophobia in rap music and hip hop culture, and for the most noteworthy works that informed my analysis here, see Amani (2007), Cannick, (2006), Child (2006), Dean (2009), Hinton (2006), Myhre (2007), Shimeles (2010), and D. M. Wilson (2007).

23.  For further discussion of Audre Lorde's remarkable life and legacy, and for the most noteworthy works that informed my analysis here, see Abod (1990), De Veaux (2004), Griffin and Parkerson (1996), and Lorde (1988, 1996, 2004, 2009).

24.  It is important here to remind my readers that at the conceptual core of critical social theory is a commitment to justice, especially what has come to be called "social justice." My specific conception of critical social theory, "Africana critical theory," entails theorizing about the "social," "political," and "cultural" in the interest of racial, gender, sexual, economic, legal, educational, and religious justice. What makes critical social theory "critical" is its unconditional commitment to justice, not simply for one's own group, but also for other oppressed and struggling groups. Hence, my conception of critical social theory is humanist or, rather, *radically humanist* in that it extends beyond black folk, heterosexuals, and males—in other words, allegedly my "own group(s)." When confronted with a situation where group differences result in one group being privileged while others are oppressed, the radical humanism at the heart of my conception of critical social theory demands an unflinching and principled rejection of exploitation, oppression, and/or violence and an earnest embrace of justice and fairness. This means, then, that while individuals' human rights matter, my critical theory emphasizes justice and fairness in broader—communal, national, and international—terms, as a collective- or group-based phenomenon. Usually questions of justice and fairness fall outside of the orbit of

conventional social theory, but they are conspicuously at the conceptual core of critical social theory. For further discussion of my conception of critical social theory, see Rabaka (2007, 2008, 2009, 2010a, 2010b, 2011).

25.   For further discussion of my conception of "radical humanism" (as well as "revolutionary humanism"), which has been indelibly influenced by the insurgent intellectual and radical political legacies of W. E. B. Du Bois, C. L. R. James, Martin Luther King Jr., Jean-Paul Sartre, Frantz Fanon, Amilcar Cabral, Che Guevara, Audre Lorde, James Baldwin, Herbert Marcuse, Angela Davis, bell hooks, Michel Foucault, Raya Dunayevskaya, and Paulo Freire, among many others, see Rabaka (2007, 2008, 2009, 2010a, 2010b).

26.   My analysis throughout this section has greatly benefitted from systemic readings of several noteworthy works in Lesbian, Gay, Bisexual, Transsexual, Transgender, and Queer (LGBTTQ) Studies. For example, see Abelove, Barale, and Halperin (1993), Beemyn and Eliason (1996), Corrales and Pecheny (2010), Haggerty and McGarry (2007), Lovaas, Elia, and Yep (2006), Johnson and Henderson (2005), Meezan and Martin (2003), Richardson and Seidman (2002), and Seidman, Fischer, and Meeks (2006).

27.   The discourse on "critical queer theory" or "queer critical theory" has been developing since the 1990s, and some of the earliest articulations can be found in Steven Seidman's "Deconstructing Queer Theory, or the Under-Theorization of the Social and the Ethical" (1995), *Queer Theory/Sociology* (1996), and *Difference Troubles: Queering Social Theory and Sexual Politics* (1997). Major late-millennial/postmillennial contributions to critical queer theory include: Barber and Clark (2002), Driskill, Finley, Gilley, and Morgensen (2011), K. Floyd (2009), Foucault (1990a, 1990b, 1990c), Hames-Garcia (2001), Morton (1996), E. S. Nelson (1993), Plummer (2005), Seidman, Fischer, and Meeks (2006), and Sullivan (2003). Critical queer theory constitutes theorizing about queerness in the interest of justice and fairness for homosexuals. It accents and criticizes homophobia and heterosexism in social, political, and cultural thought, practices, and institutions.

28.   For further discussion of "gay-on-gay violence," or what is alternatively called "queer-on-queer violence," as well as other forms of LGBTTQ domestic and intimate partner violence, and for the most noteworthy works that informed my analysis here, see Girshick (2002), Island and Letellier (1991), Kaschak (2001), Lundy and Leventhal (1999), Renzetti (1992), Renzetti and Miley (1996), and Ristock (2002, 2011).

29.   For further discussion of many hip hoppers' embrace of the "nigga" identity and use of the "n-word," and for the most noteworthy works that informed my analysis here, see Asim (2007), Judy (1994), Kelley (1997), Kennedy (2002), T. L. Williams (2007), and V. A. Young (2007).

*Remix 5*

# The Hip Hop Movement

*From Merely Rap Music to a Major Multi-Issue Socio-Political Movement*

Influence of popular culture aside, the gains of the Civil Rights/Black Power generation were so large and transformative that that historic period has come to define what activism is. The Civil Rights Movement is extensively debated and taught in our schools and is commemorated during holidays and observances like Martin Luther King Jr. Day and Black History Month, year after year. Future movements are impossible to conceive and activism that produced significant social gains prior to the 1950s and 1960s has been all but forgotten. Current forms of struggle that go outside of the civil rights box are ignored or deemed meaningless. —Bakari Kitwana, *The Hip Hop Generation: Young Blacks and the Crisis in African American Culture*, 153

## HIP HOP: FROM GENERATION TO MOVEMENT

To invoke hip hop as a "movement," rather than merely a "generation" is to conjure up and conceive of hip hop culture as both politics *and* aesthetics. To speak of hip hop as a "movement" also means circumventing the longstanding—and, at this point, very tired—tendency to privilege hip hop's aesthetics over hip hop's politics. Several scholars have bemoaned the contemporary propensity to assess the Harlem Renaissance almost exclusively in light of its novels, short stories, poems, plays, paintings, and sculptures while woefully overlooking its music, often leaving the music to Eurocentric Jazz Age scholars who have been routinely inclined to view classic blues and classic jazz as

231

nothing more than "jungle sounding" background music (i.e., muzak) for the "troubled geniuses" of the Lost Generation. For instance, in *Black Music in the Harlem Renaissance* (1990), music scholar Samuel Floyd observed:

> The Harlem Renaissance has been treated primarily as a literary movement, with occasional asides, contributed as musical spice, about the Jazz Age and the performances of concert artists. But music's role was much more basic and important to the movement. In fact, the stance of black leadership and scattered brief comments about music during the period suggest the primacy of music to Renaissance philosophy and practice. The idea that black music was America's only distinctive contribution to American and world musical culture was accepted and emphasized by Renaissance leaders and by some of the rank and file. (3)

In *The New Negroes and Their Music: The Success of the Harlem Renaissance* (1997), musicologist Jon Michael Spencer joined Floyd in complete agreement, sternly stating: "Ragtime, blues, and jazz were the wells to which the Renaissance artists went for the substance—the themes, rhythms, and 'feel'—of their 'high' art. This is true whether we are speaking of the musical composition or the novel, painting, or anthology of poetry or folklore" (xx). Hence, we witness here the often-overlooked fact that, even though most studies of the Harlem Renaissance have almost exclusively focused on it as a literary movement, it was in fact much more. Related to the narrow read of the Harlem Renaissance as purely a literary movement is the frequently glossed over fact that the New Negro Movement was arguably as much a cultural aesthetic movement as it was a socio-political movement.

African American movements historically have been and unrepentantly remain much more complicated and complex than most historians and sociologists of social movements have been willing to concede. All of this is to say that here when I write of the "Hip Hop Movement," I am invoking a momentous movement that is much like the early twentieth century African American movements that, whether acknowledged or not, provide the Hip Hop Generation with not merely its aesthetics, musical or otherwise, but with the firm foundations upon which it has built its history, culture, politics, and social visions. Moreover, here by summoning the "Hip Hop Movement" I wish to move the conversation concerning hip hop culture forward, above and beyond critiques—constructive or otherwise—about rap music's bourgeoisism, sexism, and heterosexism, and turn our attention anew toward the ways in which one-dimensional discussions that crudely collapse hip hop culture into rap music, or vice versa, erase or, at the very least, render invisible not only hip hop's other major artistic areas (e.g., visual art, dance, theater, film, fashion, and literature), but also its distinct politics and social visions.

When and where hip hop cultural critics speak or write of the "Hip Hop Generation" there is a marked tendency to focus almost exclusively on rap music, especially rap music's "mean-mugging," "bitching-beating," "pimp-slapping," "ho-smacking," and "homosexual-hating." Furthermore, if the Hip Hop Generation's politics and social visions are engaged they are most frequently examined utilizing rap music as their primary point of departure, as if the body scholarship that constitutes Hip Hop Studies, the countless high-caliber documentaries, and the other important *extra-musical* aspects of hip hop culture do not exist. In a sense, erstwhile interpreters of hip hop culture invert the common (mis)interpretation of the Harlem Renaissance.

In other words, *where the Harlem Renaissance is commonly conceived of as a literary movement, the Hip Hop Movement is primarily perceived to be a musical movement.* Rarely do critics discuss the music that not only served as the soundtrack for the literary works of the Harlem Renaissance, but also the radical New Negro—or, rather, "Niggerati"—politics and social visions of the artist-activists of the Harlem Renaissance. Conversely, rarely do critics examine and emphasize the politics and social movements that not only inform rap, neo-soul, and the other major musical forms of the Hip Hop Movement, but also the literature, dance, theater, film, fashion, and visual art of the Hip Hop Movement.

As we witnessed in "remix" 2 with the connections between classic blues and the Black Women's Club Movement, and in "remixes" 3 and 4 with the connections between classic jazz, the Harlem Renaissance, and the New Negro Movement, African American cultural and aesthetic movements are rarely, if ever, divorced from African American social and political movements. Hence, there are several precedents that give us grounds to invoke and engage hip hop as both a distinct music *and* a movement, poetics *and* politics, aesthetics *and* activism. Hip hop, in other words, will not be anyone's one-trick-pony—even though, truth be told, it is the Hip Hop Generation's "Signifying Monkey."[1] It is a lot more multidimensional and multivalent than its erstwhile interpreters—both its fanatics and critics—seem to currently comprehend. Even if we were to focus on the major forms of rap music in our initial efforts to gauge the connections between hip hop's aesthetics and hip hop's politics, many may be shocked to find that the major genres of rap music—their points of origin and early evolution—seem to remarkably reflect the major social events and political episodes in African American history, culture, and struggle roughly between 1980 and the present.

This "remix" challenges interpretations of hip hop culture that routinely reduce it to the issues and ills of rap music. Although extremely important, here rap music is not privileged over hip hop's other important extra-musical elements, especially its politics and social visions. Undeniably reflective of many of the core concerns and core contradictions of the Hip Hop Generation, rap music can be conceived of as a sonic representation of hip hop's politics and social visions, but should not in any way be understood to be indicative of the totality, wide range, and wide reach of hip hop's politics and social visions. In other words, this "remix" seeks to challenge the terse tendency to privilege hip hop's aesthetics over its politics, especially the incessant inclination to coarsely collapse the unprecedented dynamism and important extra-musical innovations of hip hop culture into its most popular and "mainstream" social symbol: rap music.

Above we have witnessed how damaging one-dimensional interpretations of multidimensional movements can be. Hence, to reiterate, even though there were many musical, theatrical, dance, film, fashion, and visual art innovations during the Harlem Renaissance's heyday, it is most commonly understood to be a momentous literary movement. Harlem Renaissance radicalism has been frequently reduced to "aesthetic radicalism," as if the communist and socialist currents sweeping the nation during and after both World War I and World War II had little or no effect on African America; as if W. E. B. Du Bois did not join the Socialist Party in 1911; as if Chandler Owen and A. Philip Randolph did not publish their Socialist Party–supported *Messenger* magazine; as if Cyril Briggs's African Blood Brotherhood did not publish its Communist Party–supported *Crusader* magazine; as if Langston Hughes, one of the leading lights of the Harlem Renaissance, did not go through an eye-opening and jaw-dropping radical period where he composed some of the most scathing attacks on America's anti-black racism and embrace of vampiric capitalism in U.S. history—works which were later collected in the unfortunately out-of-print volume *Good Morning Revolution: Uncollected Writings of Social Protest* (1973).[2]

One-dimensional interpretations of multidimensional movements not only reduce the movements to the lame linear logic that only one element of the movement really matters, but it also robs movement members of their multidimensionality, of their distinct personalities and politics. In a sense, by making multidimensional movements appear to be one-dimensional, multidimensional movement participants are robbed of their distinct humanity and, in other words, dehumanized and de-politicized. Ultimately, this kind of misinterpretation of multidimensional movements, whether willful or not, makes it seem as though many African American movements have one goal instead of, as is most often the case, a series of goals—some short-term, others long-term.

Hip hop culture is often spoken of and written about as if it exists outside of space and time, as if the major social events and political episodes in mainstream American and African American history and culture between 1980 and the present have had little or no impact on its origins and ongoing evolution. However, the Hip Hop Movement—as opposed to the more nebulous notions of the "Hip Hop Generation"—is invoked and articulated here to conceptually capture the Hip Hop Generation's unique place in the continuum of African American movements. And, in light of the longstanding tendency toward dehumanization and de-politicization in African American movement scholarship, it is important for Hip Hop Studies scholars in specific, and the Hip Hop Generation in general, to consciously steer clear of any interpretation of hip hop culture that privileges one aspect of the culture over all others.

Rap music, and hip hop culture in general, is more or less a sonic symbol of the best and worst—the good, the bad, and the ugly—of African American history, culture, and politics between 1980 and the present. But the inclination to raise rap music up out of the context of hip hop culture, and the propensity to divorce almost the whole of hip hop culture from late twentieth century African American social and political movements and struggles, means that once again African American aesthetics are, in most instances, understood to be the opposite of African American politics instead of two mutually related and unerringly inextricable expressions of a long-oppressed and long-exploited people. As was discussed in the previous "remix," a similar tendency to downplay and diminish the connections between the New Negro Movement's politics and the Harlem Renaissance's aesthetics continues to plague analyses of both of those classic movements. All of which is to say, an insidious "either/or" and linear logic has conceptually "divided and conquered" early twentieth century African American movements' politics from their aesthetics, and vice versa. Here, by invoking the Hip Hop Movement, I sincerely seek to connect or, rather, *reconnect* hip hop's aesthetics and hip hop's politics without privileging one over the other.

Part of what makes the present invocation and articulation of the Hip Hop Movement distinctive is that it seeks to combat *hip hop's amnesia* by reconnecting the Hip Hop Movement with its aesthetic and political roots in the major African American musics and movements of the first half of the twentieth century: classic blues and the Black Women's Club Movement; classic jazz and the New Negro Movement and the Harlem Renaissance; and bebop and the Bebop Movement and the Hipster Movement. My next book, *The Hip Hop Movement*, will treat the Hip Hop Movement's more obvious and openly acknowledged contributions from rhythm & blues and the Civil Rights Movement, soul music and the Black Power Movement, and funk, gogo, disco and the Black Women's Liberation Movement—roughly covering the years 1955 through to the emergence of rap music and the Hip Hop Movement circa 1980. Considering the detailed discussions of what the Hip Hop Generation has inherited from the African American musics and movements of the first half of the twentieth century in the previous "remixes," here our focus will be on, first and foremost, identifying the Hip Hop Movement's political agenda and social visions and, secondly, connecting hip hop's politics and aesthetics to those of the above mentioned classic musics and classic movements.

What lessons can hip hoppers learn from classic blues, the Black Women's Club Movement, classic jazz, the New Negro Movement, the Harlem Renaissance, bebop, the Bebop Movement, and the 1940s and 1950s Hipster Movement? Here we consciously combat *hip hop's amnesia* by disrupting the "let's-reinvent-the-wheel" mindset of seemingly most hip hoppers by exploring *hip hop's inheritance* from classic blues, the Black Women's Club Movement, classic jazz, the New Negro Movement, the Harlem Renaissance, bebop, the Bebop Movement, and the 1940s and 1950s Hipster Movement— that is to say, from the turn of the twentieth century through to the end of the Bebop Movement and the Hipster Movement, essentially from 1895 through to 1955. We begin, then, by exploring the Hip Hop Movement's political agenda and social visions, much of which is ironically mirrored in rap music.

## HIP HOP: FROM MERELY RAP MUSIC TO A MAJOR MULTI-ISSUE SOCIO-POLITICAL MOVEMENT

In one of the first scholarly books on rap music, *Black Noise: Rap Music and Black Culture in Contemporary America* (1994), Tricia Rose asserted that rap music "brings together a tangle of some of the most complex social, cultural, and political issues in contemporary American society" (2). As was discussed in the previous "remixes," something very similar could be said about classic blues, classic jazz, and bebop. African American music, even in its earliest manifestations, registers the complexities and contradictions of African American life and struggles in ways that few other art forms have been able to, or conceivably can. Much has been made of the contradictions of hip hop culture, especially rap music, which, on the one hand, has been undeniably used to raise the Hip Hop Generation's historical, cultural, social, and political consciousness, but, on the other hand, has been also used to big-up bourgeoisism, celebrate sexism, and hail heterosexism.

However, as Rose emphasized, "[r]ap's contradictory articulations are not signs of absent intellectual clarity" or political naïveté on the part of hip hoppers. But, truth be told, "they are a common feature of community and popular cultural dialogues that always offer more than one cultural, social, or political viewpoint. These unusually abundant polyvocal conversations seem irrational when they are severed from the social contexts where everyday struggles over resources, pleasure, and meanings take place" (2).

Special mention should be made of Rose's contention that rap's contradictions are actually "a common feature of community and popular cultural dialogues that always offer more than one cultural, social, or political viewpoint." This means that *there is no single and central point of view that each and every African American adheres to or operates from*, and hip hoppers must be granted artistic license just as the most controversial artists histori-cally have been. Think about the state of aesthetic realism and fantasy if, say, Shakespeare's raunchier plays had been censored as opposed to celebrated, or Picasso's *Guernica* had been banned because it controversially depicted the fascist bombing of a small Basque town in April of 1937, or Leon Go-lub's *Interrogation III* had been disallowed in the early 1980s because it depicted a hooded nude woman strapped to a chair with her legs cocked open so as to reveal her genitals, surrounded by two ominous-looking male tor-mentors dressed in military clothes.

Let's be real here: a lot of rap is okay, more of it is good, but very little of it is genuinely great or will one day be considered "classic" music. However, the same could be truthfully said about any genre of music, especially any genre of black popular music. We must bear in mind here that all forms of African American music (including the spirituals) have been assailed from both within and without—that is to say, attacked from both inside and out-side of African America at one time or another.[3]

If nothing else, "remixes" 2 through 4 allowed us to see that classic blues, classic jazz, and bebop were all at one time or another perceived as indecent, immoral, and irreligious influences on U.S. youth, especially black and white youth. In other words, black popular music and black popular culture have long been considered corrupting forces, furiously fueling the wildfires and untamed youthful passions of America's "impressionable" and "troubled" youth. Therefore, it is important for pre–Hip Hop Generation elders to steer clear of *African American musical nostalgia*, which is to say, *the now com-mon custom of claiming that earlier forms of black popular music were somehow free from controversy and contradiction*. To put it plainly, *African American musical nostalgia* entails waxing poetic and nostalgic about a time when African American music allegedly offered a "purer" aesthetic and a "higher" moral vision—it is, quite simply, to yearn for a time in African American history and culture, musical or otherwise, that has never really existed.

To break this down even further, I am saying as simply and sincerely as I possibly can that all black popular music seems to have an innovative aes-thetic appeal and insightful moral vision that, initially and with ironic regu-larity, is either over-looked or assailed from both within and without African America. But, it must be observed, the same music that is criticized and demonized in its infancy is usually eventually seen as a serious aural innova-tion and cultural contribution. Hence, when the formerly disliked and demon-ized genre falls from the lofty heights of musical popularity among black youth ultimately it too is bemoaned, if not mourned, and in time juxtaposed and privileged over the following newfangled, supposedly "degenerate" and demonized form of black popular music.

Just as African American political thought and social movements seem to come and go in cycles, so too does black popular music seem to come and go in cycles, albeit *sonic cycles*. This is, in part, I honestly believe, because African American music and African American movements are much more inextricable and intensely intertwined than most African American music critics and African American movement scholars have fully fathomed.[4] What is truly distinctive about the Hip Hop Movement, especially when compared and contrasted with previous African American movements, is the widespread consciousness of the centrality and passionate belief in the singularity of its newfangled music in relationship to its overarching social, political, and cultural movement.[5]

Where the members of the Black Women's Club Movement more or less rejected the classic blues queens; where the members of the New Negro Movement more or less denounced classic jazz and bebop; where many of the more moderate members of the Civil Rights Movement railed against the new expressions of black sexuality in rhythm & blues; and where many of the more militant members of the Black Power Movement perceived certain aspects of soul music to be nothing more than corporate America's continued commercialization and commodification of African American culture—most members of the Hip Hop Movement openly embrace some form of rap music, whether old school rap, party rap, pop rap, political rap, jazz rap, gangsta rap, conscious rap, alternative rap, rock rap, reggae rap, Latin rap, Reggaeton, Christian rap, Dirty South rap, Mid-West rap, West Coast rap, underground rap, or hardcore rap. When the various forms of early twentieth century black popular music are carefully placed within the context of the major African American movements of their specific moment of musical popularity we are able to calmly conclude that the classic blues queens were the equivalent of contemporary female rappers, neo-soul divas, b-girls, and, yes, video vixens (Hayes 2010; Hayes and Williams 2007). Classic bluesmen equate to contemporary rappers, neo-soul Romeos, b-boys and, yes, hip hop "hoodlums."

Likewise, ragtime, with its raunchy-to-respectable meteoric rise, initially occupied a place very similar to contemporary rap music in the American social imagination. Classic jazz, as Kathy Ogren observed in *The Jazz Revolution* (1989), was once thought to seduce U.S. youth with its intriguing "jungle" rhythms and sultry sounds, and tantalizing tall-tales of "hard luck and good times, of lust and loneliness" (12). All of this is to say that almost all of the black popular music that is now raised up and highly revered as undeniably noble expressions of African American—if not mainstream American—culture were, in their own unique ways during their heydays, once understood to be notorious—and, let it be said openly and honestly, notorious "nigger noise," as U.S. historical and cultural records reveal (Lhamon 1998; E. Lott 1993; Miller 2011).

As with the musics and movements discussed in the previous "remixes," rap music and hip hop culture as a whole undeniably harbor many controversies and contradictions. However, instead of placing hip hop outside of the African American movement orbit, these "controversies and contradictions," conversely, place it squarely within the African American movement tradition. As Rose (1994) remarked, the "unusually abundant polyvocal conversations" that historically have been and remain at the heart of African American movements "seem irrational when they are severed from the [distinct] social," political, historical, and cultural contexts that gave rise to them and fueled their forward motion. As the major soundtrack for the contemporary African American movement, the Hip Hop Movement, rap music registers African Americans' ambitions in and frustrations with post–Civil Rights Movement, post–Black Power Movement, post–Women's Liberation Movement, postfeminist and, indeed, postmodern America (Boyd 2002; P. H. Collins 2006; Keyes 2002; Reeves 2008; D. Sullivan 2011).

A lot of rap music—especially what is variously called "conscious" rap, "political" rap, or "message" rap—critiques ongoing anti-black racism and questions the social, political, and economic gains of the Civil Rights Movement and the Black Power Movement. In this sense, although often overlooked, rap also voices hip hoppers' intra-racial critiques of both Civil Rights Movement moderates and Black Power Movement militants. Instead of the prosperity and remixed democracy they believed they were promised by Civil Rights moderates and Black Power militants many hip hoppers experienced firsthand new, virtually unprecedented forms of callousness and poverty as they came of age in the last quarter of the twentieth century. [6] Directly commenting on the generational and "intra-racial class division" between the Civil Rights moderates, Black Power militants, and hip hoppers, in *Reflecting Black: African American Cultural Criticism* (1993), Michael Eric Dyson declared:

> In this regard, rap music is emblematic of the glacial shift in aesthetic sensibilities between blacks of different generations, and it draws attention to the severe economic barriers that increasingly divide ghetto poor blacks from middle- and upper-middle-class blacks. Rap reflects the intra-racial class division that has plagued African American communities for the last thirty years. The increasing social isolation, economic hardship, political demoralization, and cultural exploitation endured by most ghetto poor communities in the past few decades have given rise to a form of musical expression that captures the terms of ghetto poor existence. I am not suggesting that rap has been limited to the ghetto poor, but only that its major themes and styles continue to be drawn from the conflicts and contradictions of black urban life. (7)

Whether we like it or not, taken as a whole rap music represents the aspirations and idiosyncrasies of the Hip Hop Generation, as well as the ambitions and eccentricities of the wider world of African America between 1980 and the present. This is a point that should not be glossed over to please the "siddity" whims and wishes of the contemporary black bourgeoisie, who has long been embarrassed and enraged by rap music (especially gangsta rap and hardcore hip hop), if not the whole of the Hip Hop Generation. But, as emphasized above, hip hop culture should not be roguishly reduced to rap music, and especially not gangsta rap and hardcore hip hop. Without in anyway disavowing or diminishing the sonic or social significance of gangsta rap and hardcore hip hop it is important to unequivocally state that these forms of rap music and hip hop culture, with their unambiguous embrace of *the thug/pimp/prostitute paradigm* and junior high school–like smutty and slutty sadomasochistic fantasies, seem to have eclipsed all other elements of hip hop culture, especially hip hop's politics and more progressive poetics.

The Hip Hop Generation is not the first generation of young black folk to be raised up and called out as especially egregious examples of what is outright wrong with African America, if not America in general. In "remix" 2, we witnessed the controversy surrounding the classic blues queens in particular, and young black blues people in general. In "remix" 3, we observed the contentious relationship most Americans, including many African Americans, had with classic jazz and bebop. In "remix" 4, we took note of the war of words that seemingly assailed the "Niggerati" radicals of the Harlem Renaissance from every side. In each instance cited here it was—to employ Dyson's words from the passage above—the rise of a "form of musical expression that capture[d] the terms of ghetto poor existence."

Furthermore, it was—as allegedly with the "Niggerati"—the supposed celebration of "ghetto poor existence" that was frowned on by the black and white upper and middle classes. Even though the black and white upper and middle classes historically have only seemed willing to help the ghetto poor when it is convenient for them (i.e., the black and white upper and middle classes), which is very rarely, notice how they have a great deal of disdain toward the ghetto poor when they, the poor and poverty-stricken, creatively express their lives and loves, their ambitions and frustration, their trials and tribulations in their own time and on their own terms. We have here, then, one of the first major issues the *Hip Hop Movement* (as opposed to merely the Hip Hop Generation) seeks to address: the ghetto, and the poor and poverty-stricken, working class and underclass who, often humbly and enduring many hardships, dwell therein.

The Hip Hop Movement's politics should not be expected to mindlessly mirror the Civil Rights Movement or the Black Power Movement's politics. At first issue is the simple fact that such a position is nostalgic in the worst way, yearning for an era that currently only exists in history books. The Hip

Hop Movement must be allowed to emerge in its own time and on its own terms. However, as was witnessed with the emergence of the classic blues queens during the Black Women's Club Movement years and the "Niggerati" during the Harlem Renaissance years, the impulse on the part of nostalgic "New Negro" elders and black bourgeois conservatives to control and quarantine African American youth militancy is not new and, in truth, has been a repetitive part of African American history, culture, and struggle for more than a century. In fact, what is strikingly new and novel about the Hip Hop Movement, not only compared with the Black Women's Club Movement and the New Negro Movement but also with respect to the Civil Rights Movement and the Black Power Movement, is that it registers as both an African American movement *and* an unprecedented *multicultural, multi-racial, multi-national, multi-lingual, and multi-religious youth movement.*[7]

The Hip Hop Movement is obviously an African American movement insofar as its primary points of departure are previous African American movements and many of its goals are identical to those of previous African American movements. As argued throughout this study, whether consciously or unconsciously, the Hip Hop Movement has indeed inherited a great deal from the major early twentieth century African American movements: from the Black Women's Club Movement and the New Negro Movement, to the Harlem Renaissance and the Bebop Movement. The Hip Hop Movement's roots in the Civil Rights Movement and Black Power Movement are more readily acknowledged. However, even when and where its emergence in the aftermath of the Civil Rights Movement and Black Power Movement is acknowledged, few have taken the time to do more than merely mention or make passing references to these historic connections.

What is needed now, especially in light of the hyper-commercialization of rap music and hip hop culture, are more nuanced archaeologies and alternative histories of hip hop's origins and evolution. Where *Hip Hop's Inheritance* offered an alternative history of hip hop by focusing on the cultural aesthetic movements that provided it with its aesthetic foundation, *Hip Hop's Amnesia* engages early twentieth century African American social and political movements, and their respective soundtracks, which provided the Hip Hop Movement with its musical, political, and rhetorical foundations. My next book, *The Hip Hop Movement*, will examine the Hip Hop Generation's "inheritance" from and "amnesia" with regard to rhythm & blues and the Civil Rights Movement through to the disintegration of disco and the Black Women's Liberation Movement, roughly around 1980. In other words, *The Hip Hop Movement* will explore the influence of the major African American musics and movements of the second half of the twentieth century on rap music and hip hop culture, essentially covering the years 1955 through 1980.

*The Hip Hop Movement* will also explore the Hip Hop Movement as an unprecedented *multicultural, multi-racial, multi-national, multi-lingual, and multi-religious youth movement.* From 1980 through to the present, black popular music and black popular culture have achieved a high level of visibility and, in several senses, respectability that ushered in an entirely new ethos in both contemporary popular culture *and* contemporary political culture. Various aspects of hip hop culture, especially breakdance and rap music, "crossed over" to mainstream America in ways that built on and went well beyond major record labels and record companies such as Mercury, Motown, Atlantic, Stax/Volt, Chess, Vee Jay, Brunswick, Hi, Minit/Instant, Malaco, and Philadelphia International in the 1960s and 1970s.[8]

In his eye-opening book, *Other People's Property: A Shadow History of Hip Hop in White America* (2007), Jason Tanz decidedly declared, "over the past couple of decades, just about every element of mainstream American culture has, in one way or another, fucked with hip hop" (x). He wryly went on, "[o]ur television shows are spiced with hip hop humor, presidential candidates drop knowing references to the Atlanta hip hop duo Outkast, and gangsta rapper Snoop Dogg appears next to Lee Iacocca in advertisements for Chrysler automobiles. Just like previous paradigm-shifters before it— from jazz to rock to punk—hip hop culture, which once felt alien and potentially revolutionary, has been fully integrated into American life" (x). Any doubts about what the Hip Hop Movement "inherited" from the Civil Rights Movement can be quickly laid to rest, although I am certain distinguished folk like Rosa Parks and Martin Luther King had a different kind of "integration" in mind when they risked their lives for social justice and to redefine American democracy.

Tanz's work is telling, especially when he emphasized that, even though hip hop "once felt alien and potentially revolutionary" to most of mainstream America (including the black bourgeoisie), by the turn of the twenty-first century it had been "fully integrated into American life." Rap music and hip hop culture have, literally, achieved entry into mainstream American society in ways that the African American youth who, for the most part, initiated and intensely evolved the music and culture have not. This brings us to the question of how truly "integrated" and "desegregated" is twenty-first century America, especially under the Obama administration and Tea Party hateration?

As was discussed in "remixes" 2 through 4, even within the context of Jim Crow laws and wholesale segregation black popular music and black popular culture often "crossed over" to white America.[9] Even more, to continue questioning, we must ask how truly new and novel are rap music and hip hop culture if they occupy positions suspiciously similar to each and every form of black popular music and black popular culture that preceded them? In other words, contemporary black popular music and black popular culture, arguably best represented by rap music and hip hop culture, are more or less *aesthetically accepted* but *politically rejected.*

As Tanz hinted at above, rap music and hip hop culture really register within mainstream America when and where they appear to be politically neutral, "black" or "racial" in white user-friendly or Eurocentrically acceptable ways, and "gendered" or "feminine" in ways which do not challenge misogyny and patriarchy (i.e., *not* à la Sarah Jones's jaw-dropping "Your Revolution," a.k.a. "Your Revolution Will Not Happen Between These Thighs!" [in A. Olson 2007, 8–10]). Tanz (2007) characteristically continued his "shadow history" tongue-in-cheek critique of white folks'—especially suburban white youths'—fascination with rap music and hip hop culture:

> It is, in a sense, an old story. The artistic expression of black struggle has always captivated white listeners, ever since groups of slaves converted their plantation woes into musical lamentations. The urge of sheltered suburban kids to turn to abrasive, foreign music—from rock to punk to techno—as an outlet for their own frustrations and fantasies is almost as old as the suburbs themselves. And every generation has discovered new technology by which to infuriate and befuddle its parents, a goal that rap music has proven singularly successful at achieving. But hip hop is a unique phenomenon. Unlike rock, which did not gain a foothold in popular culture until Elvis Presley gave a white face to its potentially threatening rhythms, rap's performers and narratives have remained defiantly black for more than two decades. Even more importantly, it is understood to be more than mere entertainment. More than any other musical form before it, hip hop promises to provide insight into the lives and thoughts of an entire community of black Americans.
>
> If our culture is an expression of our deepest fears, anxieties, and fantasies, then what does it say that hip hop has become our national soundtrack? In 1970, Tom Wolfe coined the expression "radical chic" to describe a cadre of moneyed white elites that entertained itself by throwing dinner parties for the Black Panthers. Today, that prospect seems neither radical nor particularly chic. To an unprecedented degree, our popular culture consists of white people entertaining themselves with—and identifying with—expressions of black people's struggles and triumphs. Racial dissonance has become an immutable fact of our everyday life. Rappers Method Man and Redman shill for Right Guard deodorant; soccer moms shout "you go, girl!" at one another; white kids wear FUBU, a black-owned clothing label whose name stands for "For Us, By Us." (x–xi; see also 99–199; Wolfe 1970) [10]

After importantly acknowledging the African American roots of rock music, Tanz emphasized that what might be the most extraordinary aspect of rap music and hip hop culture—especially in light of the hardcore *vanillaization* and commercialization of blues, jazz, and rock—may very well be the fact that "rap's performers and narratives have remained defiantly black for more than two decades." Rap's "defiantly black" discourse is actually what makes it "more than mere entertainment." Even with all of the blackface minstrelesque motifs in contemporary rap music and hip hop culture, yet and still, there remains remnants of both black conservatism *and* black radicalism that sometimes harks back to the Black Women's Club Movement and the New Negro Movement and, at other times, evokes the aesthetic exoticism and artistic activism of the Harlem Renaissance and the Bebop Movement.

Observe that Tanz's work squarely places rap music and hip hop culture within both the African American music and the African American movement traditions, and I could not agree with him more when he stated, "[m]ore than any other musical form before it, hip hop promises to provide insight into the lives and thoughts of an entire community of black Americans." Hence, rap frequently blurs the lines between aesthetics and politics by being "defiantly black" and decidedly ghetto-centered (or, rather, "ghettocentric") in an era—1980 to the present—where most of mainstream America and the African American middle-class sought to distance themselves from discussions of race, racial oppression, and racialized economic exploitation (i.e., the longstanding anti-black racist nature of U.S. capitalism). Instead of sounding like leftover or "lost" tracks from a Last Poets or Watts Prophets album, rappers' engagement of race, racism, class, and capitalism is sometimes serious and sometimes playful, sometimes inspiring and, truth be told, sometimes extremely infuriating. However, what should be emphasized after all of rap's critics and defenders have had their say is that rap has unrepentantly remained "defiantly black" and decidedly ghettocentric in post–Civil Rights Movement and post–Black Power Movement America, even as most hip hoppers' parents and grandparents seemed to retreat from race, race-consciousness, and serious critiques of racial oppression and economic exploitation between 1980 and the present. Here we have yet another distinguishing feature of the Hip Hop Movement and its admittedly problematic aesthetics, acoustics, poetics, and politics.

Special attention should be paid to the often-overlooked fact that although the Hip Hop Movement's politics do not rotely resemble the Black Women's Club Movement or the New Negro Movement's politics, it is, in its own unique way, political—in fact, I would go so far to say, *extremely political*, insofar as its politics were initially and currently continue to be put forward during a so-called "post-racial," "post-feminist," "post-Marxist," "post–Civil Rights Movement," "post–Black Power Movement," and "post–Women's Liberation Movement" period. To be "defiantly black" in an era of anti-black racist and anti-poor people Reaganism and Bushism is to challenge the very foundations on which modern America was built. To be "defiantly black" in the last quarter of the twentieth century—which is to say, even after the unprecedented black radicalism of the Black Power Movement—is to challenge the very foundations on which modern African America was built.

And, lastly, to be "defiantly black" in Obama's America is to challenge the long-lingering myth and lily-white lie that African American life actually improved simply because an African American was elected the president of the United States of America.

If the Hip Hop Movement surreptitiously inherited nothing else from the "Niggerati" of the Harlem Renaissance and the beboppers of the Bebop Movement it has been its ability to distinguish between black conservatism and black radicalism, which is to say, African American upper-class and middle-class policies and programs and African American working-class and underclass-focused policies and programs. One doesn't have to be Cornel West, Michael Eric Dyson, or Tavis Smiley to see that many of Obama's policies and programs actually do not speak to the special needs of working-class and poor people, especially working-class and poor black folk. The concern here has nothing to do with the color of Obama's skin, who his parents were, or where he was born, but—and here's the real rub—it has more to do with the ongoing poor quality of the majority of African Americans' births, lives, and deaths during his presidency and administration. It would seem that Jean-Baptiste Alphonse Karr's old adage "plus ça change, plus c'est la même chose"—that is, "the more it changes, the more it's the same thing" or, the more noted translation, "the more things change, the more they stay the same"—is applicable to African America now more than ever before.

Tanz was completely correct when he contended, "[t]o an unprecedented degree, our popular culture consists of white people entertaining themselves with—and identifying with—expressions of black people's struggles and triumphs. Racial dissonance has become an immutable fact of our everyday life." Let's "keep it real" and, even more importantly, *keep it critical* here: Wasn't blackface minstrelsy a tell-tale sign of "racial dissonance" in antebellum, Civil War, Reconstruction, and post–Reconstruction America? Wasn't the artistry and activism of the Harlem Renaissance indicative of the "racial dissonance" in America between 1920 and 1940? Wasn't the rise of rhythm & blues in the 1950s and 1960s a sonic symbol of the national struggle against "racial dissonance" in America, undoubtedly best embodied by the Civil Rights Movement? Who can deny that the soul music of the 1960s and 1970s, by *de-commercializing* and *re-politicizing* rhythm & blues, served as an obvious aural rebellion against "racial dissonance" in America and an extremely intimate and innovative soundtrack for the Black Power Movement? It might be uncomfortable for many of my readers to sincerely grapple with and seek to grasp the physical, psychological, spiritual, and emotional implications of the longstanding reality of "white people entertaining themselves with—and identifying with—expressions of black people's struggles and triumphs," but it is only when we earnestly engage this issue that we can come to terms with both the sonic and social salience of rap music and hip hop culture. In short, the Hip Hop Movement represents a kind of continuation of African American social commentary and political critique via one of the only avenues black youth have available to them to make such commentary and critique.

In so many words, Tanz and I are saying that black suffering and black social misery, black oppression and black exploitation, have become a major part—if not the motor inside of the merciless, macabre-making machine—of the U.S. entertainment industry. From nineteenth century blackface minstrelism all the way through to the twenty-first century frequently minstrelesque musings of gangsta rappers and hardcore hip hoppers, African Americans' lives and labors, African Americans' hardships and historic endurance of racial hatred, and African Americans' historic trauma and contemporary drama have all at one time or another ironically entertained white America. This point hits home even harder when we seriously consider the ways in which white youth have been and remain utterly entertained by "hardcore," "dirty," and, especially, "gangsta" rap.

Here at the outset of our discussion of the more controversial aspects of rap, primarily "gangsta rap" (and its correlate "hardcore hip hop culture"), it is important to openly acknowledge all the heated debates and hyper-critical reactions to this music—almost all of which seem to regularly negate its variety and vast cultural, social, and political significance. If for no other reason, gangsta rap is important because it rose from and continues to give voice to the lives and struggles, the aspirations and frustrations, of a long-oppressed people during an epoch of intense social, political, and economic transformation and manipulation.[11]

However, by the same token, the meteoric rise and "cross-over" success of rap music and hip hop culture also resonated with suburban white youth coming of age in post–Civil Rights Movement America. Herein lies one of the great ironies of rap music and hip hop culture: it not only sonically symbolizes the aspirations and frustrations of black ghetto youth, but also, and rather ironically I believe, white suburban youth. No matter how my more black nationalist–minded readers may feel about this, 1980s and 1990s "gold" (at least half a million albums sold), "platinum" (one million albums sold), and "multi-platinum" (two million or more albums sold) album sales speak volumes about the ways in which white suburban youth identified— albeit often from an anti-black racist exotic and erotic frame of reference— with rap music and hip hop culture. In other words, here I wish to openly acknowledge that rap music and hip hop culture have both particular *and* universal elements—which is to say, elements that simultaneously speak to the special epochal needs of black ghetto youth *and* white suburban youth. The duality of hip hop discourse, in my mind, lucidly demonstrates the continued centrality of African American thought, culture, and struggles within the wider context of contemporary American culture, politics, and society.

As with the more moderate Civil Rights Movement youth and the more militant Black Power Movement youth, Hip Hop Movement youth must be allowed to develop strategies and tactics that they believe directly speak to their specific cultural, social, and political struggles. The social and political problems of the past, quite simply said, are not the social and political problems of the present, and the ongoing centrality of African American thought, culture, and struggles within the Hip Hop Movement speaks volumes about the ways in which hip hoppers, in their own unique way, are raising awareness about historic and current issues impacting African America. "Instead of corrupting young whites," optimistically exclaimed Bakari Kitwana in *Why White Kids Love Hip Hop: Wankstas, Wiggers, Wannabes, and the New Reality of Race in America* (2005), "hip hop is helping usher in a new racial politics that has come into its own with the post–Baby Boom Generation" (19). Hip hop, Kitwana continued, is a "framework," a "culture that has brought young people together and provides a public space that they can communicate within unrestricted by the old obstacles" (78).

The "old obstacles" Kitwana hints at here obviously have something to do with pre–Hip Hop Generation racial segregation, economic exploitation, and perhaps even gender domination. As they come to maturity the Hip Hop Generation is coming to realize that it is *the first generation of U.S. citizens not born into or forced to come of age in a racially segregated U.S. society.* There is a palpable new freedom in the air, and even our most hard-nosed cultural critics and political pundits have been forced to concede that "young whites are engaging with black youth culture just as corporate culture has become a tool for marketing everything, even blackness, via pop culture. In short, America has changed" (78–79). In many ways what I am wont to call the "Hip Hop Movement" is preoccupied with many of the exact same issues—racial, cultural, sexual, gender, and economic issues—that engrossed its musical antecedents and movement ancestors. However, what truly distinguishes the Hip Hop Movement from previous African American musics and movements might actually have more to do with the unique historical moment in which it emerged and rapidly evolved.

Although the Hip Hop Movement is arguably preoccupied with either the exact same or extremely similar issues as previous major African American movements, what ultimately distinguishes it is its unique utilization of digital and telecommunications technology, new forms of social networking and social media, and—many might argue, most importantly—the hard historical fact that the gains of the Civil Rights Movement and the Black Power Movement seem to have hit some kind of reset button that has miraculously enabled an entire generation of U.S. citizens to side-step the unspeakable horrors, hindrances, and hard feelings that have historically accompanied en-slavement, racial colonization, racial segregation, lynching, Jim Crow laws, Black Codes, and outright American apartheid. It is undeniable that many hip hoppers—especially, ironically, both conscious *and* gangsta rappers—feel that contemporary society is particularly discouraging for and inhospitable to working-class and poor black people, especially black ghetto youth. Howev-er, many of these same hip hoppers are quick to concede that, if things are bad for black people now, then they were worse prior to the Civil Rights Movement and Black Power Movement. Indeed, as was exclaimed above, "America has changed," but not enough to where institutional racism or anti-black economic exploitation are things of the past, or somehow artifacts that only exist in history books and the dated footage in historical documentaries.

Perhaps what has really changed has more to do with white suburban youth's open admission of their fascination with black ghetto youth popular music and popular culture. Whether we agree or disagree with white subur-ban youth hyper-consumption of black ghetto youth popular music and popu-lar culture, the fact remains that there is indeed a "new racial reality" in America. Kitwana importantly identified what he understood to be the "five primary variables" that helped to usher in the Hip Hop Movement's "new racial politics":

> A new racial politics has been unfolding in the post–Baby Boom Generation that before now has not been adequately discussed. Five primary variables helped create the climate for this new racial politics to emerge: the rise of the global economy and a resulting sense of alienation among young whites in the 1980s and 1990s; significant ruptures in the popular music scene; a further shifting American economy at the turn of the millennium, which was accom-panied by a declining sense of white privilege; the institutionalization of key aspects of the Civil Rights Movement; and finally the socio-political range of post-1960s black popular culture. (23)

Here it is important to observe Kitwana's emphasis on race, culture, politics, and economics. From his point of view, the breakthroughs of the Civil Rights Movement, the "socio-political range of post-1960s black popular culture," and the "rise of the global economy" all factor into the Hip Hop Movement's "new racial politics." Notice that Kitwana was careful not to over-aestheti-cize hip hop culture's roots. Deftly demonstrating that hip hop culture is much more than rap music, by highlighting the Hip Hop Movement's roots in the Civil Rights Movement he turned his readers' attention to the often under-discussed fact that the Civil Rights Movement not only altered African Americans' relationship with the U.S. government and legal system, but also with white America, especially white youth. Kitwana importantly continued his discourse on the Hip Hop Movement's "new racial reality":

This new reality influenced the degree to which white youth have engaged hip hop. The narratives of the Civil Rights Movement in history textbooks, the telling and re-telling of the same in documentaries and feature films, the endless replaying of audio and video footage of [Martin Luther] King's speeches on radio and television year after year (following the establishment of the King holiday and strong pockets of resistance to it) have all helped familiarize white kids with distant or unknown aspects of black culture. For the first time, most young white Americans came of age with a fair degree of awareness of African American culture. At the same time, public acceptance of old stereotypical assumptions was diminishing. (38)

Although I do not share Kitwana's belief that "[f]or the first time, most young white Americans came of age with a fair degree of awareness of African American culture," because I believe it is important to critically question which aspects of African American culture white youth are familiar with (i.e., mostly black popular music and black popular culture), I do agree with his assertion that the Civil Rights Movement has garnered a singular place within contemporary American culture and society. In addition, even though I disagree with Kitwana's contention that "public acceptance of old stereotypical assumptions [is] diminishing," because even a cursory listen to the latest gangsta, hardcore, "commercial," or "pop" rap—for example, 50 Cent's *Get Rich or Die Tryin'* (2003), Lil' Wayne's *Tha Carter II* (2005), Snoop Dog's *The Blue Carpet Treatment* (2006), The Game's *Doctor's Advocate* (2006), Nicki Minaj's *Pink Friday* (2010), Kanye West's *My Beautiful Dark Twisted Fantasy* (2010), or Rick Ross's *Teflon Don* (2010)—will demonstrate loud and clear that many of the main motifs of blackface minstrelism, 1970s blaxploitation films, and the pimpisms of Dolemite, Iceberg Slim, and, of course, Donald Goines continue to haunt rap music, hip hop culture, and the Hip Hop Movement.

To be fair to Kitwana, who is a much-respected colleague and comrade of mine, it should be pointed out that he only engaged gangsta rap and hardcore hip hop in passing. However, this could be seen, yet and still, as a problematic omission in a book provocatively titled *Why White Kids Love Hip Hop.* Call me pessimistic, if you must, but I'm not sufficiently convinced that "white kids'" relationship with hip hop actually constitutes "love" (and certainly not "real love," in a Mary J. Blige hip hop neo-soul sense), as much of it looks, sounds, smells, tastes, and feels a lot like *lust*—of course, *love* and *lust* are both four letter words that begin with "l" but, needless to say, there is a big, yawning chasm of difference between them. To invoke "lust" here also takes us back to African American enslavement (e.g., recall the systematic rape of enslaved black girls and black women by oppressing, exploiting, and violating white men); the Lost Generation invasion (seeking sexual gratification) of uptown nightclubs and other haunts during the Harlem Renaissance years; white America's obsession with jazz music and jazz dance during the

1930s; and the Beat Generation's (and later the beatniks') fascination with bebop music and the militant politics of the Bebop Movement during the 1950s.

After teaching Hip Hop Studies courses for more than a decade and a half, I remain suspicious of what white youth really and truly know about African American culture *beyond black popular music and black popular culture*. Indeed, I will readily agree with Kitwana that white youth seem to have sound-bite knowledge of the Civil Rights Movement, but when I press them—as I always do—in my classes and in my lectures around the country, most often white youth's knowledge of the Civil Rights Movement seems to have been gathered from what they were able to glean from *Wikipedia*, Twitter, Facebook, MySpace, miscellaneous blogs, primetime sitcoms, the nightly news, or Hollywood movies. Here I am faithfully following W. E. B. Du Bois, bell hooks, Frantz Fanon, Malcolm X, Paulo Freire, Gloria Ladson-Billings, and Henry Giroux by making a critical distinction between *information* and bona fide *education*: information is most often desultory and superficial, where education is deep and significant.

Truth be told, most white youth have a superficial or referential relationship with the Civil Rights Movement, and almost every other aspect of African American culture, because "mature" mainstream white America— meaning, their ancestors, great-grandparents, grandparents, and parents— historically has had and currently continues to have artificial or *amnestic* relationships with African American history, culture, and struggle. In other words, I am saying as simply and sincerely as I possibly can, *hip hop's amnesia is not wholly or inherently the Hip Hop Generation's alone, but it has been, however unheralded, handed down from previous generations and movements to the Hip Hop Generation and, by default, the newfangled Hip Hop Movement*. Not to put too fine a point on it, but I honestly believe that if we would really like to answer the question, "why do white youth love hip hop?"—to paraphrase Kitwana—we will have to more thoroughly engage the genre of rap music and style of hip hop culture that has consistently caught their eyes, ears, emotions, and, at times, hard-earned money: gangsta rap and hardcore hip hop culture.

## "NIGGAZ WITH ATTITUDE!": ON THE SADOMASOCHISTIC AND SCHIZOPHRENIC PROGRESSIVE/REGRESSIVE TENDENCIES IN GANGSTA RAP AND HARDCORE HIP HOP CULTURE

The term "hardcore hip hop" generally refers to those aspects of hip hop culture, especially gangsta rap and non-gangsta-related "reality" rap, that highlight and harangue the "hardcore" or harsh conditions of ghetto life and struggles. It is essentially a subgenre within the world of hip hop that first developed on the East Coast hip hop scene in the mid-1980s. It quickly spread to the West Coast "gang-banging" and crack-infested hip hop scene. [12]

Often characterized as "confrontational" and "aggressive"—that is, lyric-wise, beatwise, and with its inclusion of "noisy" sampling and production—included among the pioneers of hardcore rap music and hip hop culture are acclaimed rap artists and rap groups such as Schoolly D, Spoonie Gee, Kool G Rap, Ice-T, Boogie Down Productions, Run-D.M.C., and Public Enemy. [13] Emerging in the midst of Reaganism, hardcore hip hop's confrontational lyricism and decidedly political poetics mostly mirrored the lived-experiences and life-struggles of black male ghetto youth, providing a long-muted, and long-thought to be mindless, mass with a national—and soon international—voice. Hardcore hip hop culture spawned two major genres of rap: conscious rap and gangsta rap.

As a precursor to conscious and gangsta rap, in the 1980s what was then called "hardcore rap" eschewed the early rap and hip hop fascinations with and themes of partying and bragging (à la the Sugarhill Gang, Grandmaster Flash and the Furious Five, the Treacherous Three, Whodini, U.T.F.O., Kurtis Blow, and Roxanne Shanté). Hardcore rappers in the 1980s rhymed about the harsh reality, grim experiences, and bleak future prospects of black youth life in the ghettoes they grew up in and, for the most part, still lived in. They rhymed about reality, *their* reality, which was filled with nagging parents (mostly mothers), players, pimps, prostitutes, preachers, prisoners, schoolteachers, drug dealers, hustlers, and hoodlums. Their rhymes reflected an America—a *black America*—that Ronald Reagan and his rightwing cronies consistently turned a blind eye to and woefully turned their backs on (Hudson and Davies 2008; Rousseas 1982; Schaller 1992).

Hardcore rap was both streetwise and beatwise—meaning, it had high quality lyrics and bumping beats. It was in-your-face tough talk backed by big, booty-shaking, and trunk-rattling rhythms. Much of it was menacing and mean-spirited, but a lot of it was also quite humorous. Which is also to say, in its own way 1980s hardcore rap continued the African American tragicomic tradition that—as we witnessed in the previous "remixes"—harks back to our enslaved ancestors' work songs and field hollers, as well as classic blues, classic jazz, and bebop (Banfield 2010; Grassian 2009; T. L. Stanley 2009).

Although gangsta rap is currently the most famous—or, rather, most infamous—contemporary manifestation of hardcore rap, not all hardcore rap revolves around or relies on gangsta themes—which is to say, primarily *the ghetto-gangsta-nigga-pimp-thug theme.* However, it should be emphasized, much of it overlaps with the reality rap lyrics of most "conscious," "message," or "political" rap. Moving away from party rhymes and braggadocio, and big boasts about their microphone skills and sexual prowess, 1980s hardcore rappers' music and lyrics eventually began to reflect the gritty and most often grating inner-city surroundings in which it was created and initially enjoyed.

Prior to the gangsta rap *ghetto-gangsta-nigga-pimp-thug theme* formula that found fame and fortune in the 1990s—back when Boogie Down Productions released *Criminal Minded,* Public Enemy dropped *Yo! Bum Rush the Show!,* and Ice-T hit hard with *Rhyme Pays,* all in 1987—the lyrical lines between gangsta and conscious rap were extremely blurred. The common thread between these albums has to do with the fact that each contains political rhymes and what would now be considered "gangsta" rhymes. For instance, even Public Enemy, undoubtedly the undisputed "Kings of Conscious Rap," had seemingly gangsta-themed tracks on their debut *Yo! Bum Rush the Show!;* just listen to the songs "Sophisticated Bitch," "Miuzi Weighs A Ton," and "Timebomb."[14]

All of this is to say, even in its first decade of development, rap music and hip hop culture harbored serious political contradictions and sordid social thoughts, as well as seemingly *sadomasochistic and schizophrenic progressive/regressive tendencies.* On the one hand, 1980s hardcore rappers understood themselves to be exposing the harsh realities of life in *the hood.* By exposing the issues and ills of the ghetto many hardcore rappers honestly believed that more people, especially those folk who did not live in the ghetto and could relatively easily access much-needed resources, would get involved and altruistically work to change the "Third World" or "undeveloped" country-like conditions most African Americans lived in. On the other hand, hardcore rappers also felt the need to make connections between what was happening in the ghetto and what was happening in the wider public sphere (i.e., increasing unemployment, rising crime rates, the slashing of social services, and the under-funding of public education—in short, virtually *a war on the poor*).[15]

In other words, 1980s hardcore rappers offered up their own homespun super-structural critique and political commentary on rising anti-black racism and increased economic exploitation during the rightwing-ruling Reagan years. Additionally, hardcore rappers also sought to deliver messages directly to ghetto youth and express their own distinct ghettocentric worldviews. Undeniably, their worldviews seemed to be preoccupied with sex, drugs, violence, and profanity. But the exact same thing could be said about suburban white youth in the 1980s and 1990s. We have to be careful here not to demonize black ghetto youth for the exact same things that the larger society gives white suburban youth a pass on and pat on the wrist for.

Admittedly, I can understand why so many on both the "right" and the "left" have accused rap music of promoting profanity, drug abuse, alcoholism, sexism, and heterosexism, among other issues and ills. But I cannot in good conscience understand why so many obviously intelligent adults have a tendency to make little or no distinctions between gangsta rap and the plethora of other genres of rap music—especially, "conscious," "political," "message," "alternative," "underground," or "reality" rap.[16] It really sickens me that many of the same "obviously intelligent adults" hypocritically rail against youth who do not make distinctions between, say, the progressive jazz of John Coltrane and the smooth jazz of Kenny G, or the progressive rock of Led Zeppelin and the pop rock of the Bee Gees, but yet insult the whole of the Hip Hop Generation by belittling and making a mockery of a music that clearly means so much to us and says so much about the world as we are experiencing (or, rather, *enduring*) it.

As quiet as it has been kept, gangsta rap and hardcore hip hop actually say a great deal about American culture, politics, society, race relations, gender relations, class struggle, and sexuality between the late 1980s and the present. For instance, in *Rap Music and the Poetics of Identity* (2000), music scholar Adam Krims contended that the years between 1988 and 1996 constituted the "classic gangsta rap" era (46–92). If nothing else, then, late 1980s and 1990s gangsta rap provides us with a window into rap music and hip hop culture's evolution at a time when black popular music and black popular culture unrepentantly reflected the underbelly and undesirable elements of late twentieth century America's ongoing apartheid, oppression of women, exploitation of its workers, and dastardly disregard for its poor.

In often complex ways, the issues and ills as a consequence of a combination of destructive government policies and programs, devastating de-industrialization, intense political disaffection, persistent poverty, unabating unemployment, putrid police repression, the rise of the prison industrial complex, the drug trade, and increased gang activity all, in one way or another, informed the subjects, sights, sounds, semantics, and sadomasochism of gangsta rap and its correlate hardcore hip hop culture. Early gangsta rap classics—including Ice-T's *Power* (1988), *The Iceberg/Freedom of Speech* (1989), and *O.G.: Original Gangster* (1991); Too Short's *Life Is . . . Too Short* (1988), *Born To Mack* (1989), and *Short Dog's in the House* (1990); N.W.A.'s *Straight Outta Compton* (1988) and *Niggaz4Life* (1991); The D.O.C.'s *No One Can Do It Better* (1989); Ice Cube's *AmeriKKKa's Most*

*Wanted* (1990), *Death Certificate* (1991), and *The Predator* (1992); Dr. Dre's *The Chronic* (1992); Tupac Shakur's *2Pacalypse Now* (1991) and *Strictly 4 My Niggaz* (1993); and, of course, Snoop Dogg's *Doggystyle* (1993) and *Tha Doggfather* (1996)—all in their own unique way seem to eerily reflect black ghetto youth experiences, if not the experiences of black America as a whole, during the dark days of the Reagan and Bush administrations. In a sense, by the time Bill Clinton was elected president and Dr. Dre dropped *The Chronic* in 1992, gangsta rap, with its homespun hip hop–styled hedonism and sadomasochism, was all but considered part and parcel of rap music and hip hop culture, and Snoop's game-changing *Doggystyle* ushered in a whole new, even higher pop culture profile for gangsta rap and hardcore hip hop.

The irony here is, of course, that black ghetto youth's harrowing experiences during the Reagan and Bush years, along with a penchant for classic rhythm & blues, classic soul, classic funk, classic gangster films, classic kung fu films, and classic blaxploitation films, provided the first wave of gangsta rappers with the provocative prose, poetic license, and captivating commentary that they ingeniously "remixed" and translated into a "multi-billion-dollar-a-year global industry, influencing fashion, lifestyles and language while selling everything from SUVs to personal computers" (Jones and Gundersen 2007, 2). It has been said that crime pays, but here it would seem that poetically licensed lyrical rhymes about crime, violence, and sex is what really pays. Consequently, from its debut in 1987 under the guise of the above-mentioned hardcore or proto-gangsta rap albums by Boogie Down Productions, Public Enemy, and Ice-T through to the assassinations of Tupac Shakur in 1996 and the Notorious B.I.G. in 1997, gangsta rap and hardcore hip hop were an extraordinary commercial successes. Their sudden and, for most highbrow music critics, inexplicable success thrust them to the center of not only the music industry, but of the wider world of the U.S. entertainment, film, and culture industries.

It became quite common for gangsta rap albums to achieve "gold," "platinum," or very often "multi-platinum" sales status during its heyday between 1987 and 1997. Albums by classic gangsta rap artists and groups—such as Ice-T, N.W.A., Ice Cube, Dr. Dre, the D.O.C., Snoop Dogg, Tupac Shakur, Compton's Most Wanted, Above the Law, Too Short, the Geto Boys, Scarface, the Notorious B.I.G., Bone Thugs-N-Harmony, Da Lench Mob, DJ Quick, and Master P.—sold by the hundreds of thousands, some even sold by the millions, in essence, eclipsing almost all other forms of rap music in the public eye. For instance, even if we were to focus exclusively on Death Row Records, undeniably the leading gangsta rap record label in the 1990s, their extraordinary album sales mirror the emergence and staying power of gangsta rap in the 1990s: Dr. Dre's *The Chronic* (1992), Snoop Dogg's *Doggystyle* (1993) and *Tha Doggfather* (1996), the *Above the Rim* (1994) soundtrack, the *Murder Was the Case* (1994) soundtrack, Tha Dogg Pound's *Dogg Food* (1995), Tupac's *All Eyez On Me* (1996) and *Makaveli/The Don Killuminati* (1996), and the *Gang-Related* (1997) soundtrack were all certified "multi-platinum" by the Recording Industry Association of America (RIAA).[17]

Between 1987 and 1997 gangsta rap registered as more than merely a new, decidedly more decadent direction in rap music and hip hop culture. It also, however morally repugnant and roguishly, represented African American youth's—especially black ghetto youth's—increasing frustration with what they perceived to be the antiquated and incessant employment of the Civil Rights Movement model in the interest of achieving social justice at the turn of the twenty-first century. Eithne Quinn, in *Nuthin' But a "G" Thang: The Culture and Commerce of Gangsta Rap* (2005), asserted that gangsta rap between 1987 and 1997 was "a self-consciously, timely (though largely non-progressive) rejection of traditional modes of cultural and political protest" (13).

The question begs: Why would black ghetto youth reject "traditional modes of cultural and political protest," whether they were being put forward by white or black "adult" America? Because, as gangsta rap seems to emphasize with each and every rhyme, it was "adult" America's august "traditions" and "social conventions" that created the crippling cauldron, the socially segregated, derisively and greatly despised ghettos and slums in which black ghetto youth were imprisoned and callously left to rot by both the black and white bourgeoisies, by both black and white politicians, and by both black and white preachers and teachers.

Gangsta rap is nothing else if it is not *African American youth angst* and a tell-tale semantic and sonic sign that black ghetto youth think and feel very deeply about the wicked world they inherited from their political predecessors, social movement ancestors, pop culture precursors, and, of course, musical antecedents. By poeticizing, packaging, and mercilessly marketing "the ghetto," gangsta entrepreneurs "ironically created a saleable product out of their own region's de-industrialization," contended Quinn (13). In the 1980s and 1990s gangsta rap was "grounded in difficult and extreme material conditions," but, Quinn continued, "it was also deeply informed by topical discourses and sensational images of urban America."

Between 1980 and 1992, both Ronald Reagan and George H. W. Bush "exploited poor black Americans by mobilizing opportunist discourses of race, and, in a circular move, used such discourses to justify their policies of federal withdrawal and penal escalation" (13). From Reagan and Bush's hardcore Republican points of view, at least based on the policies and programs their respective administrations put forward, black America in the 1980s and early 1990s seemed like and was, thus, treated like a long-lost wasteland or de-industrialized desert. And, along with the critical, hyper-

critical, and sometimes even hateful responses by Jesse Jackson, Louis Farrakhan, and Khalid Muhammad, among many others, gangsta rappers registered post–Civil Rights Movement black America's riposte to the rising tide
of extreme rightwing Republicanism and carpetbagger capitalist racism
sweeping across the United States between 1980 and 2000.

Once gangsta rap is situated within the callous and crippling 1980s and
early 1990s context in which it initially emerged and evolved, when we
sincerely take to heart the above contention that gangsta rap represents
*African American youth angst* and a sure semantic and sonic sign that black
ghetto youth think and feel very deeply about the decadent and divisive
world they inherited, then, and perhaps only then, does gangsta rap reveal
itself to be an expression of the Hip Hop Generation's skewed and schizophrenic, hedonistic and extremely problematic, aesthetics *and*—most importantly here—politics. Admittedly, gangsta rap's politics may not look or
sound like the Civil Rights Movement's politics as expressed through 1950s
and 1960s rhythm & blues—for example: "A Change Is Gonna Come" by
Sam Cooke; "Promised Land" by Chuck Berry; "Our Day Will Come" by
Ruby and the Romantics; "Move on Up," "Keep on Pushing," "People Get
Ready," "It's All Right," "Amen," "Choice of Colors," and "This is My
Country" by Curtis Mayfield and the Impressions; "Mississippi Goddam" by
Nina Simone; "Just My Soul Responding" by Smokey Robinson and the
Miracles; "Gotta Get A Job" and "Working in a Coalmine" by Allen Tous-
saint; "I Wish Someone Would Care" by Irma Thomas; and, of course,
"We're Gonna Make It" by Little Milton.

Moreover, gangsta rap's politics may not look or sound like the Black
Power Movement's politics as expressed through 1960s and 1970s soul mu-
sic—for example: "Say It Loud—I'm Black and I'm Proud" by James
Brown; "What's Goin' On?" and "Inner-City Blues (Make Me Wanna Hol-
ler)" by Marvin Gaye; "Respect" and "Natural Woman" by Aretha Franklin;
"The Ghetto" and "Someday We'll All Be Free" by Donny Hathaway; "Big
Brother," "Living for the City," "Higher Ground," "Jesus Children of Ameri-
ca," "They Won't Go When I Go," "You Haven't Done Nothin'," "Village
Ghetto Land," and "Black Man" by Stevie Wonder; "Mighty Mighty" by
Earth, Wind and Fire; "(For God's Sake) Give More Power to the People" by
the Chi-Lites; "Ship Ahoy" and "Give the People What They Want" by the
O'Jays; "Brother's Gonna Work It Out" and "Life's No Fun Living in the
Ghetto" by Willie Hutch; "Fight the Power" by the Isley Brothers; "Message
From a Black Man" and "Slave" by the Temptations; "The Revolution Will
Not Be Televised" by Gil Scott-Heron; "Am I Black Enough For You?" by
Billy Paul; "Is It Because I'm Black?" by Syl Johnson; "My People . . . Hold
On" by Eddie Kendricks; "To Be Young, Gifted, and Black" and "Four
Women" by Nina Simone; "Chocolate City" by Parliament; "One Nation
Under a Groove" by Funkadelic; and, of course, "Ain't No Stoppin' Us

Now" by McFadden & Whitehead. Even though its politics often seem to be in outright opposition to many (although certainly not all) of the aforementioned songs, no mistake should be made about it, gangsta rap is—however sick and twisted—an expression of the Hip Hop Generation's aesthetics *and* politics. Helping to corroborate my claim, and continuing her expert analysis, Quinn importantly observed:

> With its confrontational and darkly humorous themes, the form [i.e., gangsta rap] elicited great affective investment from its fan base, but also outraged and affronted others. Discursively, then, gangsta's importance rested on its generation a staggering amount of controversy, leading to intense soul-searching and outcry. The genre provoked sharp debate both within and beyond the black community, from the FBI's writing an official letter in 1989 to express concern about NWA's single "Fuck tha Police" (from *Straight Outta Compton*) to the 1993 bulldozing of rap CDs by Calvin Butts III, black minister of the Abyssinian Baptist Church in Harlem, and the 1995 congressional hearings on censorship, which focused on Death Row Records. In the face of heightened public and political responses, gangsta rappers drew attention to, toyed with, and often purposefully exacerbated social divisions. Such discursive reflection helped energize gangsta's artistry. . . . . In content and form, gangsta rap lyrics explore how groups and individuals negotiate their social positioning and, as artists, their own roles as cultural mediators, commercial producers, and musical personas. (12)

As an understandable consequence of its hyper-masculinity, hyper-misogyny, hyper-materialism, and frequent hyper-homophobia, gangsta rap is rarely probed for the ways in which its *texts* shrewdly reflect its *contexts*.[18] What I seek to do here is bring gangsta rap's aesthetics and politics together, exploring why and to what extent classic gangsta rap's content and form was ambivalent, self-conscious, possibly progressive on certain issues, regrettably regressive on others, and all the while trenchantly transgressive in the *context* of 1980s and 1990s America. By looking at gangsta rappers as artists, not simply "high school drop-out hoodlums," "street hustlers," and "unredeemable thugs" we can calmly come to understand why Quinn contended that "[i]n the face of heightened public and political responses, gangsta rappers drew attention to, toyed with, and often purposefully exacerbated social divisions." Lots of artists "push buttons" and controversially raise issues that society seeks to gloss over or sweep under the rug. It is undeniable that America—yes, even after the Civil Rights Movement, the Women's Liberation Movement, and the Lesbian, Gay, Bisexual & Transgender Liberation Movement—continues to have several serious "social divisions" that are horribly (albeit often realistically) reflected in gangsta rap and, however unheralded and unflattering, have come to haunt the Hip Hop Generation as a whole.

What if Quinn is really and truly onto something when she asserted that gangsta rap lyrics "explore how groups and individuals negotiate their social positioning and, as artists, their own roles as cultural mediators, commercial producers, and musical personas"? I would like to audaciously suggest that the same could be said about each and every form of rap music. In its own often-warped and often-wicked way rap music reflects both the Hip Hop Generation's aesthetics *and* politics. In many ways it is sort of the "Rosetta Stone" of the Hip Hop Movement, possibly providing future interpreters of hip hop culture with a key to discursively decipher the many mysteries of hip hop as both music *and* movement.

Whether we like it or not, gangsta rappers are artists. Indeed, they are "cultural mediators, commercial producers, and musical personas." However, what frequently distinguishes them from other American and non-American artists is the fact that they and their beloved artistry—that is to say, their aesthetic *texts*—initially emerged and evolved within the unforgiving *context* of U.S. ghettos, hoods, barrios, slums, and government housing projects. There is, indeed, a cruel and heart-breaking irony to be poor and extremely poverty-stricken in a country that has been long-touted to be the most affluent and politically progressive on the face of God's green earth. As with the *amnesia* we have been plagued with, narcissism is not the Hip Hop Generation's alone. If nothing else, America is a narcissistic nation chock-full of folk who hold extremely gnarly beliefs about how much better they are than the hard-working and humble humanity who make up the majority of the human species.

Often within the world of the ghetto the issues and ills of the larger society play themselves out in the extreme: for example, instead of masculinity there is hyper-masculinity; instead of misogyny there is hyper-misogyny; instead of materialism there is hyper-materialism; instead of heterosexism there is hyper-heterosexism; and instead of violence there is hyper-violence, etc. However, bear in mind that much of the ghetto's "hyper-ness," if you will, is informed by its ragged relationship with mainstream and moneyed America. The ghetto does not exist in a vacuum and, although most folk in America suffer from an acute form of *amnesia* when and where we come to the ghetto, rappers—and, yes, even the most morally repugnant and ethically reprehensible gangsta rappers—frequently develop schizophrenic progressive/regressive ghettocentric discourses that far outrun abstract academic and *bourgeois chic* discourses concerning "the ghetto problem" and "the immigration issue" in America.[19] In "Listening to Learn and Learning to Listen: Popular Culture, Cultural Theory, and American Studies" (1990a), George Lipsitz suggested that it is often artists, rather than scholars and critics, who are "the most sophisticated cultural theorists in America":

Indeed, one might argue that the most sophisticated cultural theorists in America are neither critics nor scholars, but rather artists—writers Toni Morrison, Leslie Marmon Silko, Rudolfo Anaya, and Maxine Hong Kingston or musicians Laurie Anderson, Prince, David Byrne, and Tracy Chapman. Their work revolves around the multiple perspectives, surprising juxtapositions, subversions of language, and self-reflexivities explored within cultural theory. It comes from and speaks to contemporary cultural crises about subjectivity and nationality. Issues that critics discuss abstractly and idealistically seem to flow effortlessly and relentlessly from the texts of popular literature and popular culture. (627; see also Lipsitz 1990b, 1994, 2007)

Following Lipsitz's lead, I would like to suggest that rappers' work "revolves around the multiple perspectives, surprising juxtapositions, subversions of language, and self-reflexivities explored within cultural theory." Also, it "comes from and speaks to contemporary cultural crises about subjectivity and nationality." Moreover, "[i]ssues that critics discuss abstractly and idealistically seem to flow effortlessly and relentlessly from the texts" of rap music, and hip hop culture in general. When hip hop's aesthetics and politics are brought together and placed into critical dialogue with the wider political cultures of both turn of the twenty-first century African America and mainstream America, then hip hop music and the Hip Hop Movement may be interpreted as a grassroots youth movement. That is to say, in many senses, the Hip Hop Movement is *simultaneously an aesthetic, cultural, social, and political multi-issue movement* in the interests of Sly and Family Stone's "Everyday People" and Arrested Development's remixed "People Everyday," replete with their collective references to peace, love, freedom, freakiness, fairness, and justice.

To push this line of logic even further, I am suggesting that even the most controversial forms of rap music—in this instance gangsta rap—are simultaneously a dissident kind of "everyday people's" political culture—with trappings of the age-old "hidden transcript" of oppressed communities—*and*, rather ironically, a hyper-visible and hyper-corporatized mainstream commercial musical form—*and*, on top of all of that, yet and still, contemporary black popular music. Rap music contains both the traditional subversions of authority predicated on African Americans' history of domination and discrimination, and it also offers a highly commodifiable and sometimes pseudo-radical chic variety of youth protest, early twenty-first century youth angst, and black youth's ongoing anti-racist rebellion and search for social justice.

The fact that rap music is marketed and hyper-consumed—and that even the most masculinist, misogynist, materialist, and heterosexist rappers requisition the folklore, tales, toasts, jive, jokes, colloquialisms, mannerisms, and musics of the august African American rhetorical and musical traditions for explicitly commercial ends—reinflicts, even distorts and "dumbs down," but does not in any way whatsoever negate, the rich colloquial and cultural traditions deeply embedded within it. All of this, of course, might be one of the main reasons rap music has not been *European Americanized* and over-run by a bunch of modern-day Elvis Presleys, Bill Haleys, Buddy Hollys, and countless other blonde-haired and blue-eyed rock and soul Romeos—although, I gotsta keep it real, *word is bond*, mad props to the Beastie Boys, 3rd Bass, House of Pain, 311, Linkin Park, Limp Bizkit, Rage Against the Machine, Kid Rock, and, of course, Eminem.

Perhaps one of the reasons the deceptively deep and sometimes hidden history of rap music's "remixed" archetypal representations has been often-overlooked in even the most scholarly and critical treatments of the music is the simple but frequently ignored fact that overly academic engagements of rap music have routinely downplayed and diminished *the socio-political dimensions of hip hop discourse*. In other words, when hip hop is acknowledged as both *a new form of music* and *a new form of socio-political movement*, then we can easily see that rap music's "remixed" archetypal representations of poor black folk come uncomfortably close to the conventional anti-black racist categories that poverty-stricken black people have long been cast in by "conservative," "liberal," and sometimes even allegedly "radical" white America. These extremely controversial *colored-Negro-nigger-black-African American archetypes* once commercially constructed—not in the black ghetto but in the bourgeois boardrooms of corporate America, and then sent out to lily-white suburban audiences gleefully on *inner-city safari* far removed from the initial point of aesthetic origin and political performance (à la Edward Said's [1999, 2000] "traveling theory")—discursively and dangerously overlap with longstanding racial myths and sexual stereotypes about African Americans.

At the center of the more searing claims leveled against rap, especially gangsta rap, is its purported reinforcing of negative and "niggardly" stereotypes about African Americans. Although corporate America is certainly complicit in spreading "negative and 'niggardly' stereotypes about African Americans" via rap music, what makes gangsta rap stand out and extra explosive, even amongst other contentious forms of rap music, is that it is primarily young, poor, black males who conjure up and recreate the extremely controversial *colored-Negro-nigger-black-African American archetypes* that lie at the heart of gangsta rap and hardcore hip hop culture. Gangsta rap complicates the conventional critiques coming out of African American Studies, American Studies, Ethnic Studies, Cultural Studies, and Postcolonial Studies concerning misrepresentations of black folk and blackness predominantly generated by Eurocentric and bourgeois white male theorists, critics, artists, and producers. For instance, even the negative and "niggardly" representations of black folk and blackness incessantly circulated in 1970s blaxploitation films, for the most part, could be chalked up to the radical chic and erstwhile exploitative practices of wealthy white male screenwriters, directors, and producers.[20]

However, and this is one of the reasons it is so controversial, rap—especially gangsta rap—offered one of the first mainstream consumer-friendly and mass commercial forms in which mostly young black cultural workers generated images that were often blatantly associated with anti-black racist myths and sexual stereotypes about black folk and blackness. By flagrantly courting controversy, in its own sick and twisted way, rap music deftly demonstrates that the Hip Hop Generation's politics are probably just as—if not even more—complicated and contradictory as its music and overarching aesthetics. Hence, here I am strongly suggesting that it is time to acknowledge hip hop for what it really is or, at the least, for what it has actually heuristically become over the last three and a half decades of its existence: both *a new form of music* and *a novel form of socio-political movement*—that is, *the Hip Hop Movement*.

There is a very serious sense in which rap music's controversies and contradictions are actually emblematic of the wider Hip Hop Movement's controversies and contradictions. Hence, even as I summon the Hip Hop Generation to move beyond its seemingly incessant and extremely narcissistic celebrations of its sexual prowess, "sick whips," music, money, movies, and mansions, at the very same moment I openly and honestly admit the contradictions and controversies of my most beloved generation. In fact, I would go so far as to say that the Hip Hop Generation seems prone to contradiction and controversy, and this propensity for contradiction and controversy manifests itself loud and clear in the Hip Hop Movement's sometimes progressive, and sometimes regressive and extremely problematic politics and social visions.

Just as rappers—the "unofficial" mouthpieces of the Hip Hop Movement—routinely send schizophrenic progressive/regressive mixed messages, frequently on the same song, the Hip Hop Movement's politics and social visions seem to constantly and chameleonically shift. For instance, it is quite common for rappers to one moment feign a posture of peace, benevolence, and non-violence, then the next moment metaphorically mean-mug and sonically saber-rattle so as to invoke the black buck/badman/trickster black folk hero who is seemingly always unerringly heading down a murderous bloodbath warpath. Rappers often one moment mercilessly critique American capitalism and all of its ills and then the very next moment boldly brag about their rags-to-riches unapologetic embrace of the American Dream and their extraordinary Booker T. Washington–style bootstrap-uplift achievements, replete with copious references to multiple mansions, Maybachs, "baby-mamas," and other material (and, let it be said, sadomasochistic) comforts. Moreover, rappers are renowned for one moment praising their mothers and grandmothers, but then in the very next moment calling seemingly almost all Hip Hop Generation women "hood rats," "hoochie mamas," "chickenheads," "skeezers," "tricks," "tramps," "gold-diggers," "hussies," "heifers," "bitches," and "hos," etc. In what has now become a characteristic double-move in the rap game (if not in hip hop culture in general), the Hip Hop Movement's overtly "radical" gestures and "political" posturing are frequently as self-conscious, self-serving, and even opportunist as its often reactionary, anti-liberal, and at times even anti-radical *amnestic* assertions.

Rappers—again, representing the "unofficial" mouthpieces of the Hip Hop Movement—in their own often-unwitting ways frequently register the Hip Hop Movement's very serious problems with the discernible decrease in nationally networked African American protest movements and social justice struggles between 1980 and the present. In this sense, it could be said that rap music reveals that the Hip Hop Movement's real political energies and ongoing efforts actually lay in the struggle to come to terms with an age in which there has been a dramatic decline in popular protest politics, and this has been all the more devastating and dispiriting in light of African Americans' long history of political protest and freedom fighting: from the Abolitionist Movement and Black Women's Club Movement, to the New Negro Movement and Harlem Renaissance; from the Bebop Movement and Civil Rights Movement to the Black Power Movement and Black Women's Liberation Movement.

Most rap music, to a certain extremely salient extent, may reflect hip hoppers' post–Civil Rights Movement, post–Black Power Movement, post–Women's Liberation Movement, and post–Lesbian, Gay, Bisexual & Transgender Liberation Movement inertia and disappointment. Can it be honestly denied that inertia, anger, angst, disappointment, and even anti-radicalism have come to be part and parcel of most rap music, and—however unnerving this all may be for many of us—this discontent and exasperation is somehow as aesthetically and politically important and inexplicably invigorating as the music's more obvious expressions of ambition, optimism, radicalism, and other progressive pronouncements? Rap music does more than merely convey the hyper-misogyny and hyper-materialism of the Hip Hop Generation. It also communicates extremely important social and political thought that frequently reflects the socio-political pulse of the Hip Hop Movement. Moreover, rap exhibits an acute awareness—often buried beneath a barrage of braggadocio, bourgeoisism, profanity, misogyny, homophobia, and banging beats—of the promises that have not been fulfilled in the aftermaths of the Civil Rights Movement, Black Power Movement, Women's Liberation Movement, and Lesbian, Gay, Bisexual & Transgender Liberation Movement. In short, at its core rap music is a *discourse on declension*—which is to say, it is a discourse on *political decline, social decay, cultural crisis, sexual subversion, and moral deterioration.*

# THE HIP HOP MOVEMENT: A NEW MUSICAL MOVEMENT *AND* A NEW SOCIO-POLITICAL MOVEMENT

In many ways the Hip Hop Generation's angst seems to be connected more to the much-misunderstood Black Power Movement and its correlate Black Arts Movement than the Civil Rights Movement. Recall that many hip hoppers' discontent and political depression revolve around the excruciating feelings of abandonment, frustration, and repulsion mentioned above. Clearly, Black Power militants felt that the Civil Rights Movement did not go far enough in its efforts to eradicate anti-black racism and anti-black economic exploitation at the hands of U.S. capitalism.

As witnessed in myriad rappers'—especially "conscious," "message," or "political" rappers'—rhymes, similar to the Black Power militants, the Hip Hop Generation has articulated almost identical sentiments concerning the advances *and* setbacks of the Civil Rights Movement. In *The Hip Hop Generation: Young Blacks and the Crisis in African American Culture* (2002), Bakari Kitwana contended that hip hoppers' frustrations with the Civil Rights Movement stem from what they understand to be "America's unfulfilled promise of equality and inclusion" (xx). After all of the demonstrations, protests, marches, sit-ins, and freedom rides of the 1960s, the Hip Hop Generation, similar to the Black Power proponents, has recurringly called into question the concrete gains of the Civil Rights Movement. As a matter of fact, Kitwana claimed, African Americans in the twenty-first century continue to be plagued by racism and the crude anti-black racist calculus of U.S. capitalism that the 1950s and 1960s civil rights struggle was valiantly waged against.

All too often various forms of *amnesia* seem to rear their heads when and where discussions concerning the gains of the 1950s and 1960s civil rights struggle fail to acknowledge the truly troubling state of African America since the late 1960s. "Ignored is the grim reality," Kitwana cautioned, "that concrete progress within the civil rights arena has been almost nil for nearly four decades. Neither acknowledged are the ways persisting institutionalized racism has intensified for Hip Hop Generationers despite 1950s and 1960s civil rights legislation" (xx–xxi).

With all due respect, then, politically conscious hip hoppers have refused to romanticize and mythologize the social gains of the Civil Rights Movement because they know all too well that those advances were not the end-all and be-all in terms of African Americans' ultimate achievement of a truly democratic and multicultural society free from racism, patriarchy, heterosexism, religious intolerance, and the evils of capitalist political economy. In other words, it seems that the politically conscious amongst the hip hoppers have come to the uncomfortable conclusion that no matter how "great" and "groundbreaking" the Civil Rights Movement's achievements were, African Americans' search for social justice must go on unabated in the twenty-first century—*a luta continua*, to solemnly invoke the motto of the FRELIMO Movement during Mozambique's war for independence. Highlighting how the hip hoppers' struggles against racism and capitalism differ from those of both the Civil Rights moderates and Black Power militants, Kitwana sternly stated:

> The 1950s and 1960s brought many changes in law, and the early 1970s ushered in an age of black elected officials, but the 1980s and 1990s were void of any significant movement around which young blacks could organize at the national level. For us, in part due to the previous generation's victories, to-day's "enemy" is not simply white supremacy or capitalism. White supremacy is a less likely target at a time when lynchings aren't commonplace (in the traditional sense) and when blacks can vote and are not required by law to sit in the back of the bus. To deem capitalism the enemy when financial success and the righteousness of the free market have become synonymous with patri-otism is hardly popular. (148–49)

It is understood, then, that the Hip Hop Generation has its own distinct versions of racism and capitalism that it must critique and contend with. What is less understood, however, is that many of the strategies and tactics of past social movements do not automatically offer viable solutions to our problems in the present. Obviously there are myriad ways in which the racism and capitalism of the twenty-first century are inextricable from the racism and capitalism of the twentieth century. But, simply acknowledging how they are inextricable without also critically acknowledging their *ideo-logical evolution* over the last fifty years does not help hip hop critical theorists and activists *identify*, *critique*, and *contend with* contemporary— often even more insidious and abominable—expressions of racism and capi-talism (and, not to mention, sexism and heterosexism as well).[21]

This means, then, that in the final analysis even the Black Power Move-ment and its aesthetic arm, the Black Arts Movement, can only provide the Hip Hop Movement with paradigms and points of departure that raise our awareness of *why* the preceding generation struggled and *what* they struggled against. It is up to hip hoppers to determine *when* and *how* we will struggle against the most pressing issues of our epoch. However, the main point is that there must be ongoing and increased insurgent struggle, not merely rhyming rhetorical radicalism, vocal acrobatics, and word-wizardry about the new struggles of African Americans and the other wretched of the earth in the twenty-first century.

As Kitwana bemoaned above, "the 1980s and 1990s were void of any significant movement around which young blacks could organize at the na-tional level," and, sadly, something very similar could be said for young folk of other colors and cultures. How has coming of age in an era "void of any significant [national] movement" depoliticized or, at the least, politically depressed the Hip Hop Generation? Or, at the very least, how has it caused hip hoppers' entire approach to politics and social movement to be drastically different from any generation of Americans, especially African Americans, in post–Civil War history?

Eithne Quinn (2005) went so far as to say that gangsta rappers "are nothing if not charged symbols of post–Civil Rights malaise" (37). Growing up in the long shadow cast by our grandparents and parents' Civil Rights moderatism and Black Power militantism, respectively and respectfully, most hip hoppers' "malaise" has caused them to resent and reject traditional forms of African American political protest and social movement. However, as Kitwana (2002) astutely observed, even though the Hip Hop Generation does not have a "broad national movement, we are not without smaller-scale activist movements" (149). Thus, as it often seems to me, more than any other segment of the hip hop community it historically has been and remains the rappers who have consistently taken up the responsibility to boldly speak the special truth of contemporary black ghetto youth. Rappers, although often ridiculed, register hip hoppers' anger, angst, and rejection of the more moderate elements of our grandparents and parents' youth culture, politics, and social visions, as well as the more mainstream conventions and values that dehumanize black and other poor and marginalized people.

Even though it has been often-ignored, as rap music has matured it has also been used as a tool to constructively critique and comment on the major issues and ills of the Hip Hop Movement. It is interesting to observe that, among the "smaller-scale activist movements" that Kitwana asserted that the Hip Hop Movement is composed of, several of these micro-movements have produced rappers (and spoken-word artists) who have offered up their particular micro-movement's (and often micro-movements', in the plural sense) valuable criticisms of the wider Hip Hop Movement, its rap music and version of hip hop culture. Hence, the Hip Hop Movement's myriad mini-movements articulate the Hip Hop Generation's political critiques and social commentary in terms of U.S. culture, politics, and society as a whole *and* frequently does the same with respect to the dominant hip hop culture, politics, and community as a whole.[22]

"It seems logical that a force from within the hip hop cultural movement," quipped Kitwana, "would be the most sound vehicle to bring the Hip Hop Generation's political interest into the mainstream political process" (187). However, it is additionally important for us not to overlook the ways in which the Hip Hop Generation also constructively or, rather, self-reflexively critiques its own exacerbation and perpetuation of many of the issues and ills it is critical of in the wider world of U.S. culture, politics, and society. As is quite well known, for instance, the Hip Hop Movement has, however in-

choate, collectively articulated critiques of: racism; capitalism; class struggle; electoral politics; government bias in favor of the rich; government
disaster response with respect to poor non-white communities; the military's
over-recruitment of the poor, especially poor non-white people; war and
American imperialism abroad; employment discrimination; housing discrimination; the horrors of low-income housing; the immigration issue; environmental racism; corporate corruption; police brutality; and the prison industrial complex (especially, mandatory minimum sentencing and the death penal-
ty) within the world of mainstream U.S. culture, politics, and society.

The Hip Hop Movement has matured to the point where it has a, however
unheralded, highly developed self-reflexive critical culture. Of all its critics,
ironically it would seem that the hip hoppers themselves have consistently
offered rap music and hip hop culture the most useful evaluations of both its
contradictions *and* its authentic contributions. For example, insightful criticisms from the Hip Hop Women's Movement have been given voice by
incomparable rappers (a.k.a. "femcees") and spoken-word artists such as
Sarah Jones, Mecca the Ladybug, Eve, Michelle Tea, Missy Elliot, Lenelle
Moïse, Lauryn Hill, Aya de León, Leah Harris, Jill Scott, Jessica Care
Moore, Bahamadia, Meliza Bañales, Alix Olson, Queen Latifah, Ursula
Rucker, Medusa, Mystic, Jean Grae, and, of course, Me'Shell Ndegéocello.
Moreover, criticism aimed at the wider Hip Hop Movement emerging from
the Homosexual Hip Hop Movement has been articulated by extraordinarily
gifted rappers and spoken-word artists such as Aggracycst, Alicia Leafgreen
(a.k.a. White Lesbian Rapper [WLR]), Code Red, DaLyrical, Damashai,
Deadlee, Deep Dickollective, Buttaflysoul, Dutchboy, God-dess & She,
Hissy Fitt, Johnny Dangerous, Juba Kalamka, Jwahari, Katastrophe, Mack
Mistress, Miss Money, Q-Boy, QPid (a.k.a. Yung Shortee), Smokey Da Ban-
dit, Smut Stud, Storietella the Female Beast, Sugur Shane, Tim'm West, and
Tori Fixx.

Needless to say, as the previous "remixes" have illustrated, homosexual
hip hoppers are concerned with more than merely hip hop's homophobia and
heterosexism, just as hip hop feminists are concerned with more than rap
music's misogyny and incessant pandering to patriarchy. At this point, hip
hop's internal politics and self-reflexive critical culture plays itself out in
ways that challenge most conventional conceptions of politics, social movement, and self-reflexivity. Similar to most rap music, hip hop's politics frequently touch on a wide range of topics, and, truth be told, the novel ways
hip hop has both collapsed and combined pressing social problems has con-
founded several of the more sophisticated contemporary social and political
theorists, who brazenly insist on utilizing twentieth century social movement
models and political paradigms in their efforts to interpret the Hip Hop
Movement's unprecedented and solidly twenty-first century *multicultural,*

*multi-racial, multi-national, multi-lingual, multi-religious, and extremely multi-issue politics and social movement.* Again, Kitwana offered his expert insight on this issue:

> Influence of popular culture aside, the gains of the Civil Rights/Black Power generation were so large and transformative that that historic period has come to define what activism is. The Civil Rights Movement is extensively debated and taught in our schools and is commemorated during holidays and observances like Martin Luther King Jr. Day and Black History Month, year after year. Future movements are impossible to conceive and activism that produced significant social gains prior to the 1950s and 1960s has been all but forgotten. Current forms of struggle that go outside of the civil rights box are ignored or deemed meaningless. (153).

Indeed, a major part of the problem most pre–Hip Hop Generation folk have with rap music and hip hop culture has something to do with its seemingly incessant celebrations of sex, sexism, drugs, alcoholism, and materialism, among other ills. But, by lopsidedly focusing all of their attention on commercial or pop rap music and the other more popular aspects of hip hop culture (e.g., hip hop slang, film, fashion, dance, and graffiti, etc.), hip hop's unequivocal critics often downplay and diminish hip hop's political culture and, by default, the multi-issue politics and social movement of the broader Hip Hop Movement altogether. This is not simply unfortunate, but it is also extremely disingenuous, as it negates the principled and politically progressive elements of hip hop culture—again, not to mention the wider world of the Hip Hop Movement.

In so many words in *The Hip Hop Generation* Kitwana seems to be saying that Civil Rights and Black Power generationers, if not Baby Boomers in general, seem to be suffering from an acute case of *political nostalgia.* For most folk born after World War II the Civil Rights Movement represents the *condicio sine qua non*, which is to say, the only "real" and "right" way to wage a struggle for civil rights and social justice. All social movements before and after do not register because they were not or, as in the case of the Hip Hop Movement, they absolutely are not the Civil Rights Movement—or one of the other "great" and groundbreaking movements of the 1960s.

As Kitwana correctly put it, movements that emerged in the aftermath of the Civil Rights Movement—such as the myriad mini-movements that make up the Hip Hop Movement—or, even further, post–Hip Hop Movement future movements "are impossible to conceive." And, what is more, "activism that produced significant social gains prior to the 1950s and 1960s has been all but forgotten." This, of course, is to say that the Abolitionist Movement, the Women's Suffrage Movement, the Black Women's Club Movement, the New Negro Movement, the Harlem Renaissance, the Hipster Movement, and the Bebop Movement, for all intents and purposes, have been "all but forgotten" by most hip hoppers' grandparents and parents, who seem to remain preoccupied with the Civil Rights Movement of the 1950s and 1960s. Here we have in black and white, and in clear and concise prose, precisely and exactly what I am referring to as *hip hop's amnesia*. Again, *hip hop's amnesia* is not simply about what the Hip Hop Generation has forgotten but should remember, but also about what generations prior to ours—and possibly even what the generations that will surely follow after ours—have forgotten, or will forget, but should remember about rap music, hip hop culture, and the unique historical, cultural, social, political, and economic moment in which this novel music and culture emerged and unnerved.

Kitwana could not have hit the nail on its head any harder than when he asserted that "[c]urrent forms of struggle that go outside of the civil rights box are ignored or deemed meaningless." How much of the Hip Hop Movement, which obviously goes "outside of the civil rights box," is for all intents and purposes either altogether "ignored or deemed meaningless"? How has this "benign neglect"—in the Moynihanian and Nixonian senses—further complicated and continued the contradictions and crises of the Hip Hop Movement's already complicated *multicultural, multi-racial, multi-national, multi-lingual, multi-religious, and extremely multi-issue politics and social movement*?[23] How might *hip hop's amnesia* and the *amnesia surrounding hip hop* be remedied by openly acknowledging not only the Civil Rights Movement, but also the Abolitionist Movement, the Women's Suffrage Movement, the Black Women's Club Movement, the New Negro Movement, the Harlem Renaissance, the American Labor Movement, the Lost Generation, the Hipster Movement, the Bebop Movement, the Beat Generation, the Black Power Movement, the Hippie Movement, the Free Speech Movement, the Women's Liberation Movement, the New Left Movement, the Anti-War Movement, the Sexual Liberation Movement, the American Indian Movement, the Chicano Movement, the Asian American Movement, the Lesbian, Gay, Bisexual & Transgender Liberation Movement, the Political Prisoners Movement, the Disability Rights Movement, the Animal Rights Movement, and the Environmental Justice Movement, among many others too numerous to name?

The Hip Hop Movement, when it is all said and done, is *simultaneously a multicultural, multi-racial, multi-national, multi-lingual, multi-religious, and extremely multi-issue musical and socio-political macro-movement composed of several often seemingly uncoordinated micro-movements*. In its own sometimes warped and sometimes wicked ways, it embodies both what might be considered the "best" and the "worst" of the historic movements mentioned above. Moreover, it is important here to bear in mind something that Robin D. G. Kelley, in *Freedom Dreams: The Black Radical Imagina-*

*tion* (2002), perceptively wrote: "the desires, hopes, and intentions of the people who fought for change cannot be easily categorized, contained, or explained" (ix).

Let's face it. Social and political movements are invariably messy affairs. Each movement mentioned above had its "messy"—if not, outright maddening—moments. The Hip Hop Movement, being composed of several mini-movements, might be messier and more maddening than any previous movement; this much I am willing to humbly concede. But what I am not willing to concede or overlook is the historical fact that there were high levels of almost each and every major allegedly "negative" aspect of rap music and hip hop culture at the heart of most, if not all, of the aforementioned movements: from the use of profanity to widespread promiscuity; from sexism to materialism; and from alcoholism to drug addiction.

The Hip Hop Movement admittedly may be unlike any previous social movement in its composition and seemingly uncoordinated political aspirations but, make no mistake about it, it is a movement nonetheless. Furthermore, for those who would quickly and flippantly label the Hip Hop Movement a bravura flop, I want to caution them to keep in mind Kelley's caveat when he warned us against judging whether a movement was a "success" or a "failure" based on whether or not it was able to achieve *all* of its goals. To speak candidly here, serious social and political movements, as well as insurgent cultural aesthetic movements, are often not so much about eradicating each and every ill on their respective agendas as much as they are about critical consciousness-raising and decolonizing and radicalizing the wretched of the earth, inspiring them to begin their processes of self-transformation *and* social transformation. Kelley insightfully contended:

> Unfortunately, too often our standards for evaluating social movements pivot around whether or not they "succeeded" in realizing their vision rather than on the merits or power of the visions themselves. By such a measure, virtually every radical movement failed because the basic power relations they sought to change remain pretty much intact. And yet it is precisely these alternative visions and dreams that inspire new generations to continue to struggle for change. (ix)

I would be one of the first to admit the Hip Hop Movement's "failures." But, even as we observe what hip hoppers did not do, it is extremely important to point to what they did—and, even more, what they are doing now. This thought is connected to the all too American tendency to sanctimoniously stand tall and tell the world what we are *against* but never really state what we are *for*, what we really and truly believe in. Undeniably, the Hip Hop Movement has inherited a great deal of political ambivalence from the preceding socio-cultural movements, and there are lists long enough to wrap around the surface of the globe several times detailing each and every despicable and dastardly deed committed in the name of the "Hip Hop Generation" or, rather, the "Hip Hop Movement."

Yet and still, I honestly believe that there will come a time in the not too distant future where there will be a reappraisal of rap music, hip hop culture, and the overarching Hip Hop Movement, and, if nothing else, it will be acknowledged for its contributions to both aesthetics *and* politics—which is to say, it will finally be recognized as *a musical and socio-political multi-issue movement*. For instance, according to my colleague Adam Bradley, in *Book of Rhymes: The Poetics of Hip Hop* (2009), "[t]hanks to the engines of global commerce, rap is now the most widely disseminated poetry in the history of the world" (xiii). He went further to incisively observe:

> Of course, not all rap is great poetry, but collectively it has revolutionized the way our culture relates to the spoken word. Rappers at their best make familiar the unfamiliar through rhythm, rhyme, and wordplay. They refresh the language by fashioning patterned and heightened variations of everyday speech. They expand our understanding of human experience by telling stories we might not otherwise hear. The best MCs—like Rakim, Jay-Z, Tupac, and many others—deserve consideration alongside the giants of American poetry. We ignore them at our own expense. (xiii)[24]

However strange it might seem for us to admit it, there are people who have never read or even heard of William Wordsworth and Walt Whitman, or Pablo Neruda and Langston Hughes, but who can recite to you verbatim and with little difficulty the latest Lil' Wayne or Nicki Minaj rhyme. Rap music and hip hop culture have definitely had an impact on America, if not the world, and that impact has not been always and everywhere negative. This is where hip hop's critics demonstrate the lopsided and often lame nature of many of their blanket condemnations of rap music, where they frequently refuse to give credence to any form of rap music.

For many of rap music's more wild-eyed and, I am wont to say, "hardcore" critics there quite simply is no difference between Will Smith and Lil' Wayne, Lauryn Hill and Lil' Kim, or Common and 2 Live Crew. Rap music, as has long been said of the ghetto youth who invented and initially evolved it, is all the same, filled with cliché rhyme after cliché rhyme concerning the ghetto, guns, hot girls, drinking, and drugs. The fact that rap music, and hip hop culture in general, is actually much more nuanced and its politics much more complicated and complex than the simple "what you see is what you get" figments of "mature"—and mostly upper- and middle-class—folks' imaginations seems to rarely dawn on them.

In other words, rap music is seemingly a soundtrack to an underworld that the well-to-do and relatively wealthy in America want nothing whatsoever to do with—unless, of course, it is a Friday or Saturday night and they are down at a party or up in the club. Then, and perhaps only then, do the well-to-do and relatively wealthy wanna hang out in the hood and kick it with the "hoodlums" of the Hip Hop Generation. Needless to say, the "thug passion" is palpable even all the way up here from the cultural confines of, and ongoing twenty-first century American apartheid conditions in, Denver and Boulder, Colorado.

As the most popular expression of hip hop culture, rap music's resonance with the wider public speaks volumes about the ways in which the Hip Hop Movement has impacted the contemporary public sphere. To go back to the statement that essentially rap "expand[s] our understanding of [the] human experience by telling stories we might not otherwise hear," it is equally important to acknowledge that not all of the stories that rap shares are negative or about the ghetto, guns, hot girls, drinking, and drugs. As a matter of fact, rap has consistently proven to be a provocative tool to push the envelope and press issues that might otherwise have fallen through the cracks and crevices of contemporary "polite" culture, politics, and society. In its own unique way rap also registers as the Hip Hop Generation's deconstruction and reconstruction of what it means to be black or white, male or female, rich or poor, straight or gay, et cetera, at the turn of the twenty-first century. However, while rap is undeniably "new school" music, it is also undeniably "old school" poetry.

Most of rap's fans and critics seem to have forgotten that at its core *rap is poetry*, and poetry is a textual and, at times, oral form that can lyrically express both love *and* hate, the sacred *and* the secular, comedy *and* tragedy, and ecstasy *and* agony. Rap's fans and critics would do well to remember that "[r]ap is public art," as Bradley (2009) insisted, and that "rappers are perhaps our greatest public poets, extending a tradition of lyricism that spans continents and stretches back thousands of years" (xiii). He candidly continued:

> Rap is poetry, but its popularity relies in part on people not recognizing it as such. After all, rap is for good times; we play it in our cars, hear it at parties and at clubs. By contrast, most people associate poetry with hard work; it is something to be studied in school or puzzled over for hidden insights. Poetry stands at an almost unfathomable distance from our daily lives, or at least so it seems given how infrequently we seek it out. (xii)

Here, then, it is important for us to emphasize *hip hop's amnesia* and the *amnesia surrounding hip hop* with respect to the highbrow approach to poetry and the lowbrow interpretation of rap. This obvious highbrow/lowbrow double standard seems to almost perfectly mirror how hip hop's multi-issue politics are treated or, rather, ill-treated. Compared to previous movements' politics, the Hip Hop Movement's multi-issue politics are juxtaposed as merely "juvenile gibberish" and not worthy of being taken seriously, even though hundreds and hundreds of "conscious," "political," and "message" rappers have innovatively articulated hip hop culture's complex and complicated multi-issue politics and social movement in searing song after song. But the fact that there are increasingly more and more books being written that explore "rap as poetry" or the "poetic dimensions of rap" bodes well for hip hop's aesthetics, even if, truth be told, much of this work is extremely ambivalent with respect to hip hop's multi-issue politics and social movement beyond rap music and hip hop's poetics.

That being said, here it is important for us to conclude our discussion— and this book—by emphasizing what might be loosely termed "rap's radical side" or, rather, the "rhetorical radicalism of rap music." In terms of internal critiques of the Hip Hop Generation's hyper-materialism and general bourgeois radicalism (if one must refer to it as "radicalism" at all), several "conscious," "message," "political," democratic socialist, and democratic socialist-sounding (or, rather, pseudo-democratic socialist) rappers have rhetorically put hip hop's bourgeoisisms and capitalist pretensions on blast. Inspired by 1960s and 1970s political poets and spoken-word artists, such as Amiri Baraka, Sonia Sanchez, Haki Madhubuti, Nikki Giovanni, the Last Poets, the Watts Prophets, Jayne Cortez, Gil Scott-Heron, and Millie Jackson, "message rap" took its name from Grandmaster Flash and the Furious Five's 1982 rap classic "The Message."

The song's first verse seems to deftly demonstrate why it resonated, and continues to resonate, so deeply with black ghetto youth: "Broken glass everywhere/ People pissing on the stairs, you know they just don't care/ I can't take the smell, can't take the noise/ Got no money to move out, I guess, I got no choice/ Rats in the front room, roaches in the back/ Junkies in the alley with a baseball bat/ I tried to get away, but I couldn't get far/ Cause the man with the tow-truck repossessed my car." It would seem that "mature" and mainstream America frequently focuses more on violence, misogyny, and homophobia in rap music and hip hop culture than on the cries of desperation and perceptive critiques of the crushing and crippling nature of ghetto life emanating from "conscious," "political," and "message" rap music.

As anyone who has earnestly read the previous "remixes" will be able to calmly comprehend, the need to critique violence, misogyny, and homophobia in rap music and hip hop culture remains paramount. However, I honestly believe that it is also just as important for us to acknowledge the ways in which hip hoppers are politically progressive and offer principled critiques of both hip hop *and* America's violence, hyper-masculinism, hyper-heterosexism, hyper-materialism, and open embrace of capitalist vampirism. "The Message" influenced countless early rappers, and the genre (i.e., "message rap") that the song spawned continues to the present moment—although corporate America obviously does not believe that message rap is as profitable as violent, materialistic, misogynistic, and homophobic rap.

Arguably more than any other form of rap music, message rap articulates the Hip Hop Movement's mission and multi-issue socio-political agenda. Even as I write all of this, however, I know all too well that I must proceed with caution, that rejecting each and every aspect of rap music and hip hop culture that doesn't jive with some highfalutin, "polite," and "politically correct" conception of culture, politics, and society will leave us with a very short list of "principled" and "progressive" rap music and hip hop culture. But, by the same token, we have to honestly ask ourselves whether there has ever been a youth movement with perfect or pristine politics, especially in America? As we witnessed in the previous "remixes," neither the Black Women's Club Movement nor the New Negro Movement, and neither the Lost Generation nor the Beat Generation, can claim to have had perfect and always and everywhere "principled" and "progressive" politics. The exact same thing could be said about the Civil Rights Movement, the Black Power Movement, the Hippie Movement, the Anti-War Movement, the New Left Movement, the Women's Liberation Movement, and the Lesbian, Gay, Bisexual & Transgender Liberation Movement, among the many other movements that followed in their wake.

We have to ask ourselves whether it is purely a coincidence that many of the more principled and politically progressive rap artists have turned to producing, packaging, marketing, and distributing their own work—à la many of the blues people of the classic blues era, the "Niggerati" of the Harlem Renaissance, and several of the beboppers of the Bebop Movement—because they simply do not want to deal with the backwards bourgeois culture and incessantly anti-black racist super-exploitative practices of corporate America?[25] Or whether contemporary corporate America has been stuck-on-stupid so long that they honestly cannot see how unbalanced and lyrically lopsided their artist rosters are, with gangsta, commercial, and pop rappers almost exclusively having access to high-profile production teams, high-end marketing programs, and prestigious concert venues that only corporate-connected music industry moguls can lavish their artists with. Even though I wholeheartedly agree with Kitwana (2002) when he declared, "to date most [of hip hop's politics] have been steeped in political naïveté, partisan politics, or petty-bourgeois radicalism," yet and still, I believe it is important for us to acknowledge those rap artists and hip hoppers who have broken with and boldly gone beyond the old moderatism of the Civil Rights Movement and the angry militantism of the Black Power Movement, as well as the inertia and complacency that seem to have so many hip hoppers in a social and political holding pattern (188).

Although controversial and contradictory—similar to almost every other aspect of hip hop culture—conscious, political, and message rappers have consistently challenged, decolonized, and repoliticized the Hip Hop Movement, if not much of postmodern America. Like the gangsta rappers, message rappers have primarily focused on black ghetto youth, and poverty-stricken people in general. This is important to point out because there has been a longstanding tendency for both the white and black bourgeoisies to turn a blind eye on the high levels of human suffering and social misery emerging from deep within the bowels of the barrios, slums, and ghettos.

Arguably beginning with Public Enemy's *Yo! Bum Rush the Show* in 1987 and KRS-One and Boogie Down Production's *By All Means Necessary* in 1988, message rap exploded. It rhetorically rallies on behalf of ghetto youth, collectively combining an innovative—and often extremely unnerving for many—mix of black nationalism, anarchism, Marxism, Leninism, Maoism, Fanonism, Guevaraism, Castroism, Zapatistaism, Buddhism, socialism, feminism, and womanism, among many other political and ideological perspectives. The remarkable political and ideological range and reach of conscious, political, and message rappers deftly demonstrate the Hip Hop Movement's unique *multicultural, multi-racial, multi-national, multi-lingual, multi-religious, and extremely multi-issue politics and social visions.*

Obviously what qualifies such a varied group of artists and activists as rappers or hip hoppers is their unyielding use of rap music and hip hop culture as their primary points of departure. Along with other subgenres of rap music, such as "alternative," "underground," and "jazz" rap, one of the major preoccupations of conscious, political, and message rappers is their emphasis on social critique and social commentary. However, one thing that clearly distinguishes most conscious, political, and message rappers from alternative, underground, and jazz rappers is the fact that frequently the former group of rappers embrace and articulate what might be deemed "radical" political views and agendas, in contrast to the more generalized kind of "drive-by" social critique and social commentary typical of the latter.

In other words, most conscious, political, and message rappers also double as political activists or, rather, *raptivists* (i.e., rappers *and* socio-political activists), whose rhymes reflect specific "radical" plans or progressive political programs aimed at transforming—not merely "drive-by" critiquing or cleverly commenting on—contemporary society—especially what is happening in the hood, the barrios, the slums, and the ghettos coast to coast. This is precisely where and why conscious, political, and message rappers can be said to connect with the wider world of contemporary radical politics and critical social theory. After all, didn't Karl Marx quip in his *Theses on Feuerbach*: "The philosophers have only interpreted the world in various ways, but the damned point is to change it?"

How many seemingly hundreds and hundreds of rappers are merely "interpret[ing] the world in various ways" without coming to the realization that "the damned point is to change it"? Here, I am once again, in the most heartfelt manner imaginable, hailing the Hip Hop Movement. I honestly believe that when taken together—and when we do not summarily disqualify folk simply because we do not agree with each and every thing they call or claim to be "hip hop"—we are so much more than merely a "generation" in some sort of generalized or sociologically succinct and academically acceptable way.

Unlike the commercial and pop rappers' whose work, for the most part, often seems to glamorize the ghetto, most conscious, political, and message rappers understand themselves to be "telling it like it is" and "kickin' reality" in their rhymes. Indeed, they rhyme about the ghetto, guns, hot girls, drinking, and drugs arguably just as much as gangsta, commercial, and pop rappers. But the difference is that conscious, political, and message rappers rhyme about these things to raise awareness, to remind the ghetto, the nation, and even the globe that close to 150 years after President Abraham Lincoln issued the Emancipation Proclamation African Americans continue to be enslaved and shackled and chained by anti-black racism, poverty, poor housing, horrid healthcare, unabated unemployment, ongoing substandard education, over-representation in the armed services, and penal escalation.[26]

In short, socially and politically conscious rappers, in their own often-warped and often-wicked ways, actually represent the conscience of the Hip Hop Movement. The messages in their music often have morals and provide principles without being overly didactic. As a matter of fact, the best and most provocative conscious, political, and message rappers are the ones whose politics and social visions *challenge* and *change* their audiences surreptitiously—that is to say, in seemingly secretive and unwitting ways.

Major conscious, political, and message rappers include: Arrested Development; Basehead; Big Will; the Blue Scholars; Boogie Down Productions; Brand Nubian; Browny Loco; Commendante; Common (a.k.a. Common Sense); the Coup; Dead Prez; Def Jef; Del tha Funkee Homosapien; De La Soul; Digable Planets; the Disposable Heroes of Hiphoprisy; Divary; Dream Warriors; Elegal; Missy Elliott; Michael Franti; Freestyle Fellowship; the Fugees; Gang Starr; Guru; Genocide; the Goats; Goodie Mob; Cee-Lo Green; Lauryn Hill; Immortal Technique; Intelligent Hoodlum; Sick Jacken & Cynic; Wyclef Jean; Jedi Mind Tricks; Sarah Jones; the Jungle Brothers; Jurassic 5; Kemo the Blaxican; KRS-One; Little Brother; Lupe Fiasco, Main Source; Mos Def; MRK; the Native Guns; Sole; Talib Kweli; the Narcicyst; Olmeca; Outkast; Paris; the Perceptionists; the Pharcyde; Pharoache Monch; Poor Righteous Teachers; Public Enemy; Psycho Realm; Queen Latifah; Q-Tip; Rage Against the Machine; Rakim; Rebel Diaz; Zack de la Rocha; Rockin' Squat; the Roots; Hasan Salaam; Lakim Shabazz; Sister Souljah; Spearhead; Strate Crooked; Success-N-Effect; Amir Sulaiman; Tohil; Tolteca; A Tribe Called Quest; the Visionaries; Saul Williams; and X-Clan, among many others. Obviously this is not a list of conscious, political, and message rappers that would be acceptable to those who wish to listen to rap music completely free from *the ghetto-gangsta-nigga-pimp-thug theme* that seems to saturate so many aspects of hip hop culture.

Again, cutting loose each and every rapper who, however momentarily, gives into *the ghetto-gangsta-nigga-pimp-thug theme* will ultimately leave us with an extremely limited and short playlist. I honestly believe that what is most important here is for us to not only listen for the negative and vulgar in rap music, but also the positive, the edifying, and the uplifting. We need to begin to listen for the love as opposed to the hate, and develop the ability to not simply critique but also appreciate rap music.

I can say with some certainty that anyone who sincerely listens to any of the above conscious, political, and message rappers will hear sonic deconstructions of *the ghetto-gangsta-nigga-pimp-thug theme* and aural reconstructions of what it means to be African American and poor, African American and male, African American and female, African American and heterosexual, African American and homosexual, African American and Christian, African American and Muslim, African American and from a specific city, state, or region, and, even more, what it means to transcend the tried and true conceptions of what it means to be African American. All of this is to say, that very often it is not gangsta, commercial, or pop rap that reveals what lies at the heart of the Hip Hop Movement but—seemingly unbeknownst to all but the most ardent critics, fans, and students of hip hop culture—conscious, political, and message rap. In short, conscious, political, and message rap frequently challenges both external and internal misconceptions about what it means to be a hip hopper and, most importantly here, what it means to be relatively young, struggling, humble, and hard-working human beings who are valiantly confronting the various issues and ills facing black folk and the Hip Hop Generation as a whole at the turn of the twenty-first century.

The Hip Hop Movement may not even remotely resemble previous social and political movements, but it is a movement. The Hip Hop Movement may not have all the hallmarks of a "progressive" movement, but—as the conscious, political, and message rap noted above reveals—there are principled and politically progressive hip hoppers—sensitive human souls with unquenchable commitments to continuing the fight for freedom that has been nobly handed down from generation to generation, movement to movement, and suffering soul to suffering soul. For those of us deeply disturbed by what is going on in our global warming and war-torn world, for those of us compassionately concerned about the perilous path that the Hip Hop Generation and Tea Party–terrorized America is heading down, for those of us still desperately searching for solutions to our most pressing social and political problems—conscious, political, and message rap and socially and politically conscious hip hop culture remain a beacon of light, boldly illuminating the cold and corrupt, dark and discontent world we inherited.

Conscious, political, and message rappers cannot rupture the Hip Hop Generation's relationship with the pre-existing violence, racism, sexism, heterosexism, capitalism, colonialism, militarism, alcoholism, drug addiction, and religious intolerance by themselves. Each and every one of us must, on the most hallowed humanist principles, make whatever sacrifices necessary to transform ourselves and our society, our kinfolk and our community, our friends and even, truth be told, our enemies. Real humanism—what I am wont to call "radical humanism"—does not start and stop with our family and friends, our specific race and gender, our fellow citizens and soldiers, or our religious brethren and sistren, but transcends all of the trappings of, literally, "man-made" contemporary nation-states, religions, languages, politics, economics, culture, and society.

So much of contemporary rap music and hip hop culture seem to revolve around a repetition of the present. We hear again and again and over and over about "what's hot!" and "what's not!" It is all about the right here and right now: the next sadomasochistic rendezvous, the next *ménage à trios*, the next trite tryst, the next train, the next gangbang, and on and on *ad infinitum*. Meanwhile, hip hoppers are left with no real sense of history, of their unique heritage, and, consequently, most hip hoppers seem to have no real prospects for the future—that is to say, the future beyond this Friday's paycheck and that off-da-hook house party they heard gonna happen over the weekend.

There is an old adage, frequently attributed to Marcus Garvey, that says: "If you don't know your past, you will never know your future." I could not agree with the esteemed Mr. Garvey more. I would only like to add the cold, hard fact that no real future can evolve out of a present that is incessantly repeating itself over and over again: cliché rhyme after cliché rhyme, and cliché video after cliché video about the ghetto, guns, hot girls, drinking, and drugs. From where I stand, there is so much more to rap music and hip hop culture.

I honestly believe that we all have our contributions to make to the Hip Hop Movement, and if I didn't I couldn't have made the innumerable sacrifices necessary to research and write this book. Just as the classic blues queens had their fun but made their contributions, just as the "Niggerati" of the Harlem Renaissance had their fun but made their contributions, and just as the beboppers of the Bebop Movement had their fun but made their contributions, hip hoppers can have their fun but need to make sure that they are making serious and seminal contributions—not only sonic and aesthetic contributions, but also social and political contributions. Each of the previous aesthetic movements coincided with wider social and political movements. And, it is important to observe that frequently the artistic and political leaders were often one and the same, if not, at the least, in deep dialogue concerning the most pressing social and political problems facing black folk. Without hip hoppers beginning to consciously come together as a *movement*—again, which is more than merely a "generation"—it is almost certain that the Hip Hop Generation will go down in history as one of the most violent, profane, materialistic, misogynistic, and homophobic generations in American history, if not possibly in world history.

When I listen to India.Arie, the Roots, Jill Scott, Mos Def, Talib Kweli, Erykah Badu, Common, Macy Gray, Michael Franti, Me'Shell Ndegéocello, Immortal Technique, and Dead Prez, among many others, I am uplifted. I am inspired. I am energized and given the strength to continue the struggle for freedom and social justice. However, their more principled, prudent, and progressive work also reminds me that *real struggle grows out of love* or, rather, *real and righteous struggle is love-inspired*: love for God; love for our ancestors; love for our family and friends; love for our culture; love for our community; love for our city, state, and country; love for oppressed and exploited people around the world; and, lastly, a humble and non-narcissistic love for ourselves.

Again, I would like to state as simply and sincerely as I possibly can that each and every one of us has our own distinct contributions to make to the forward flow of the Hip Hop Movement and the decolonization and re-politicization of the Hip Hop Generation. Moreover, it should also be emphasized that *hip hop's amnesia* and the *amnesia surrounding hip hop* will never really and truly come to an end unless and until we are all able to make our special contributions to hip hop culture without regard to our race, gender, class, sexual orientation, religious affiliation, or nation of origin. In this sense, I would like to suggest that Dead Prez's searing song "It's Bigger Than Hip Hop!" serve as one of the major mottos of the Hip Hop Movement from this point forward. Indeed, the Hip Hop Movement is "bigger than hip hop" and involves our entire country, if not the entire world. What we do right here and right now will have an impact on the future: our individual future and our collective future.

I have chosen to think, teach, research, write, lecture, and engage in critical dialogue because the world we live in desperately requires—more than ever before—that we contribute, however we are best suited, to the ongoing struggle for human freedom, social justice, creativity, and future growth. We must face the world we currently live in and continue to dream of the liberated future world we want and deserve to live in. This book was researched, written, and remixed in the spirit of both *critical* and *appreciative love*, as well as *affirmational* and *transformational love*, and I humbly pray that my most beloved readers will accept it in both of the spirits in which it was earnestly offered and intended. *Lift Every Voice and Sing. Nkosi Sikelel' iAfrika. A luta continua. Selah.*

# NOTES

1. In terms of rap music and hip hop culture representing a continuation and contemporary (re)articulation of "Signifyin(g)" and the "Signifying Monkey" trope that reaches back to African American enslavement, here I am obviously referencing Henry Louis Gates's research in his classic *The Signifying Monkey: A Theory of African American Literary Criticism* (1988), especially where he explained:

> Tales of the Signifying Monkey seem to have had their origins in slavery. Hundreds of these have been recorded since the early twentieth century. In black music, Jazz Gillum, Count Basie, Oscar Peterson, the Big Three Trio, Oscar Brown Jr., Little Willie Dixon, Snatch and the Poontangs, Otis Redding, Wilson Pickett, Smokey Joe Whitfield, and Johnny Otis—among others—have recorded songs about either the Signifying Monkey or, simply, Signifyin(g). The theory of Signifyin(g) is arrived at by explicating these black cultural forms. Signifyin(g) in jazz performance and in the play of black language games is a mode of formal revision, it depends for its effects on troping, it is often characterized by pastiche, and, most crucially, it turns on repetition of formal structures and their differences. Learning how to Signify is often part of our adolescent education.
>
> Of the many colorful figures that appear in black vernacular tales, perhaps only Tar Baby is as enigmatic and compelling as is that oxymoron, the Signifying Monkey. The ironic reversal of a received racist image of the black as simian-like, the Signifying Monkey, he who dwells at the margins of discourse, is our trope for repetition and revision, indeed our trope of chiasmus, repeating and reversing simultaneously as he does in one deft discursive act. If Vico and Burke, or Nietzsche, de Man, and Bloom, are correct in identifying four and six "master tropes," then we might think of these as the "master tropes," and of Signifyin(g) as the slave's trope, the trope of tropes, as Bloom characterizes metalepsis, "a trope-reversing trope, a figure of a figure." Signifyin(g) is a trope in which are subsumed several other rhetorical tropes, including metaphor, metonymy, synecdoche, and irony (the master tropes), and also hyperbole, litotes, and metalepsis (Bloom's supplement to Burke). To this list we could easily add aporia, chiasmus, and catachresis, all of which are used in the ritual of Signifyin(g). (51–52)

After reading all of this, it would seem that rap music, with its emphasis on pastiche, repetition, revision, aporia, chiasmus, catachresis, metaphor, metonymy, irony, hyperbole, synecdoche, litotes, and metalepsis, amazingly embodies what I am wont to call twenty-first century "Signifyin(g)." As will be discussed in detail below, similar to the age-old African American trope of the Signifying Monkey, a wide range of rappers provide tongue-in-cheek critiques of contemporary culture, politics, and society. However, because most of "mature" and "mainstream" America has it in their minds that rap music is purely party or pornographic music, the deep political dimensions of rap music and hip hop culture have been buried beneath a barrage of tall tales and often unfounded criticisms. Consequently, this "remix" essentially seeks to demonstrate that hip hop is much more than merely rap music, and that rap is quite simply nothing more than the soundtrack for a broader Hip Hop Movement, which is simultaneously a cultural aesthetic *and* socio-political movement.

2. For further discussion of the communist and socialist currents running through the New Negro Movement and Harlem Renaissance, and for the most noteworthy works that informed my analysis here, see Baldwin (2002), Briggs (1987), Bynum (2010), W. James (1998), Kornweibel (1975, 1998, 2002), Makalani (2004, 2011), Mullen and Smethurst (2003), Naison (2005), Pfeffer (1990), Samuels (1977), Solomon (1998), Smethurst (1999), and S. K. Wilson (2000).

3. Many may understandably assume that even the great "Negro spirituals" have always been the celebrated and much sought-after songs that they are today. However, nothing could be further from the truth. As W. E. B. Du Bois famously and revealingly wrote in *The Souls of Black Folk* (1903b):

> Little of beauty has America given the world save the rude grandeur God himself stamped on her bosom; the human spirit in this new world has expressed itself in vigor and ingenuity rather than in beauty. And so by fateful chance the Negro folk-song—the rhythmic cry of the slave—stands to-day not simply as the sole American music, but as the most beautiful expression of human experience born this side the seas. It has been neglected, it has been, and is, half despised, and above all it has been persistently mistaken and misunderstood; but notwithstanding, it still remains as the singular spiritual heritage of the nation and the greatest gift of the Negro people. (251)

Emphasis should be placed on Du Bois's comment that even as late as 1903 African American music—"the Negro folk-song—the rhythmic cry of the slave"—had been shunned by both blacks and whites. For many—especially upper-class and middle-class—blacks it served as an aural embarrassment because it was so closely associated with enslavement. For many whites it sounded like nothing more than "musical primitivism" or, rather, sonic frenetic foolishness. Ultimately, for these reasons, and many more too numerous to mention here, early African American music, including the much revered spirituals and gospel music, was "neglected," it was "half despised, and above all," similar to rap music, it was "persistently mistaken and misunderstood." For further discussion of the origins and evolution of the spirituals, and for the critical research that influenced my analysis here, see Abbington (2001), Darden (2004), Mapson (1984), J. M. Spencer (1990, 1995), and W. T. Walker (1979). Special mention must be made of the critically acclaimed documentaries on the spirituals and gospel music that indelibly influenced my interpretation here. Along with the scholarly books on the spirituals and gospel music, I would implore my readers to view George Nierenberg's *Say Amen, Somebody!: A History of Gospel Music* (1982), Andrew Dunne and James Marsh's *The Story of Gospel Music* (2004), and Larry Bograd and Coleen Hubbard's *I Can Tell the World: The Spirituals Project* (2010).

4. For further discussion of the (inter)connections between African American music and African American movements (including rap music and the Hip Hop Movement), and for the most noteworthy works that informed my analysis here, see Baraka (1963), Gilroy (1993), Goodman (2009), Guttentag and Sturman (2010), Moten (2003), M. A. Neal (1998, 2002, 2003), Rabaka (2011, forthcoming), Spence (2011), and Ward (1998).

5. For further discussion of the ways in which rap, neo-soul, and other forms of hip hop music serve as the central soundtracks for the myriad contemporary African American (*and* multicultural American) youth movements (i.e., the overarching Hip Hop Movement between 1980 and the present), and for the most noteworthy works that informed my analysis here, see Butler (2009), Bynoe (2004), Goff (2008), Hill (2009), Ogbar (2007), Perry (2004), Rabaka (2011, forthcoming), and Watkins (2005).

6. For fuller discussions of the racial, social, political, economic, and cultural climate during rap music and hip hop culture's formative years between 1975 and 2000, and for the most noteworthy works that informed my analysis here, see Bonilla-Silva (2001, 2003), Bonilla-Silva and Doane (2003), Bulmer and Solomos (2004), Essed and Goldberg (2001), Goldberg (1990, 1993, 1994, 1997, 2001, 2008), Goldberg and Solomos (2002), Massey and Denton (1993), Oliver and Shapiro (1995), Omi and Winant (1994), and Winant (1994, 2001, 2004). Moreover, here I specifically have in mind what renowned black feminist sociologist Patricia Hill Collins (1998, 2000, 2005) dubbed the "new racism" that emerged at the turn of the twenty-first century.

7. With regard to my contention that the Hip Hop Movement actually registers as both an African American movement *and* an unprecedented *multicultural, multi-racial, multi-national, multi-lingual, and multi-religious youth movement*, my interpretation here is based on a number of scholarly works in "Global Hip Hop Studies" or, rather, "International Hip Hop Studies"

(Alim, Ibrahim and Pennycook 2009; A. K. Harrison 2009; Higgins 2009; Kato 2007; Mitchell 2001; Neate 2004; Spady, Alim, and Samir 2006; Terkourafi 2010; Toop 1991, 2000). Moreover, I have consulted more geographically and culturally specific scholarly research, for instance, in Native American/American Indian Hip Hop Studies (Browner 2002, 2009; Hisama and Rapport 2005; Miles and Holland 2006); Chicano and Latino Hip Hop Studies (G. Baker 2011; Dennis 2011; Fernandes 2006; Flores 2000; McFarland 2008; Pardue 2008, 2011; Rivera 2003; Rivera, Marshall, and Hernandez 2009); African and Caribbean Hip Hop Studies (Charry 2012; C. J. Cooper 2004; Diouf and Nwankwo 2010; Henriques 2011; Hinds 2002; Ntarangwi 2009; Osumare 2007; Saucier 2011; Stolzoff 2000; Weiss 2009); Asian, South Asian, and Islamic Hip Hop Studies (Cooke and Lawrence 2005; Condry 2006; Malik 2009; Nair and Balaji 2008; Neate 2004; Nieuwkerk 2011; Sharma 2010); and European Hip Hop Studies (Durand 2002; Feiereisen and Hill 2011; Kaya 2001; Lapiower 1997; I. Maxwell 2003; Pacoda 2000; Toop 2000).

    8. This is an extremely important point because much of *hip hop's amnesia* can be easily attributed to the Hip Hop Generation's often ragged relationship with not simply the Civil Rights Movement and Black Power Movement, but also with the predominantly rhythm & blues, soul, and funk soundtracks of the aforementioned movements. If we have consensus on the general notion that African American music frequently contains coded social and political messages that coincide with broader African American socio-political movements, then we would do well to attend to the history of both African American musics *and* African American socio-political movements in our efforts to combat *hip hop's amnesia*. As previously mentioned, this will be the core concern of my forthcoming book, *The Hip Hop Movement*, which will essentially pick up where *Hip Hop's Amnesia* concludes by exploring African American musics and movements from the Civil Rights Movement and Black Power Movement to the Women's Liberation Movement and Lesbian, Gay, Bisexual & Transgender Liberation Movement—roughly engaging rhythm & blues and soul to funk and disco or, rather, roughly covering the years 1955 to 1980. In the meantime, for the scholarly research that has indelibly influenced my thought in terms of the 1960s and 1970s "cross-over" phenomenon of rhythm & blues, soul, funk, and disco, especially with respect to major record labels and record companies such as Mercury, Motown, Atlantic, Stax/Volt, Chess, Vee Jay, Brunswick, Hi, Minit/ Instant, Malaco, and Philadelphia International, see Abbott (2000), Andriote (2001), Bernard (1996), Bolden (2008), Bowman (1997), Broven (1978), Dahl (2001), Danielsen (2006), Early (2004), Echols (2010), Freeland (2001), Gamson (2005), George (1988, 2007), Goosman (2005), Guralnick (1986), Hannusch (1985, 2001), Haralambos (1975), Hoskyns (1987), J. A. Jackson (2004), O. A. Jackson (1995), Lornell and Stephenson (2001), J. Morgan (2011), Phinney (2005), Posner (2002), Pruter (1991, 1993, 1996), Ripani (2006), P. Shapiro (2005b), D. Thompson (2001), R. Vincent (1996), Ward (1998, 2001), and Werner (2004, 2006).

    9. For further discussion of the "cross-over" phenomenon in African American musical history and culture, especially the ways in which black popular music has influenced white popular music, and for the most noteworthy works that informed my analysis here, see Awkward (2007), Guralnick (1999), Kempton (2003), Phinney (2005), Ripani (2006), A. Shaw (1970, 1978, 1986), and Werner (2006).

    10. Tanz's telling reference to African Americans' invention of or, at the least, key contributions to the origins and early evolution of rock & roll should not be overlooked. There is a very tired tendency to view rock music as the exclusive domain of and soundtrack for white America, negating the historical fact that at its outset it was almost wholly a black creation. As countless musicologists have reported, rock & roll's primary musical points of departure were blues, folk, jazz, country, gospel, jump blues, boogie-woogie, doo-wop, and rhythm & blues. If, indeed, rock began primarily as a synthesis of the aforementioned musics, and if the bulk of its early pioneers were in fact African Americans (e.g., Sister Rosetta Tharpe, Ike Turner and the Kings of Rhythm, Big Mama Thornton, Chuck Berry, Bo Diddley, Etta James, Fats Domino, Little Richard, the Ink Spots, the Mills Brothers, the Platters, the Coasters, and the Drifters), then it is important to highlight the African American origins and early evolution of rock & roll. For further discussion of the African American origins and early evolution of rock & roll, especially the ways in which early rock & roll musically mirrored early rhythm & blues, and

for the most noteworthy works that informed my analysis here, see Altschuler (2003), Aquila (2000), Bertrand (2000), Crazy Horse (2004), M. Fisher (2007), Guralnick (1986, 1989, 1999), Mahon (2004), Merlis and Seay (1997), Othello (2004), and Redd (1974).

11.   For further discussion of gangsta rap and hardcore hip hop culture, and for the most noteworthy works that informed my analysis here, see Canton (2006), Dyson (1997, 2002, 2007), Grant (2002), Hagedorn (2008), Haugen (1998, 2003), Kitwana (1994), Osayande (1996, 2008), E. Quinn (2000a, 2000b, 2005), M. Quinn (1996), Riley (2005), Ro (1996), and Rose-Robinson (1999).

12.   For further discussion of West Coast rap music and hip hop culture, and for the most noteworthy works that informed my analysis here, see Basu (1992), Cross (1993), Grant (2002), A. K. Harrison (2009), Jiménez (2011), Mayne (2000), Miller, Vandome, and McBrewster (2011), M. H. Morgan (2009), E. Quinn (2005), W. Shaw (2000a, 2000b, 2000c), and T. L. Williams (2002).

13.   For further discussion of these, among other, primarily East Coast "old school" pioneers of hardcore rap music and hip hop culture, and for the most noteworthy works that informed my analysis here, see McCoy (1992), Nelson and Gonzales (1991), P. Shapiro (2005a), Wang (2003), and Woodstra, Bush, and Erlewine (2008).

14.   For further discussion of Public Enemy, their early gangsta-themed songs, and popularization of what we now call "conscious rap," and for the most noteworthy works that informed my analysis here, see Danielsen (2008), Eiswerth (1996), Hamrick (1991), Myrie (2008), Walser (1995), and Weingarten (2010).

15.   For further discussion of the "war on the poor" (as opposed to what is commonly called the "war on poverty"), and for the most noteworthy works that informed my analysis here, see E. Anderson (1981, 1990, 1999, 2008), Farmer (2003), Gans (1995), and Katz (1989).

16.   For further discussion of the various genres of rap music, and for the most noteworthy works that informed my analysis here, see Bogdanov, Woodstra, Erlewine and Bush (2003), Bradley (2009), Bradley and DuBois (2010), Bynoe (2006), Hess (2007a, 2007b, 2010), Krims (2000), and P. Shapiro (2005a).

17.   For further discussion of Death Row Records and its dominance of the gangsta rap genre in the 1990s, and for the most noteworthy works that informed my analysis here, see J. Brown (2002), Miller, Vandome and McBrewster (2011), Ro (1996, 1998), Savidge (2001), and R. Sullivan (2002).

18.   My emphasis here on *rap texts* being reflective of *hip hop contexts*—and broader U.S. economic, social, political, and cultural contexts—has been undeniably influenced by Murray Forman's brilliant book *The Hood Comes First: Race, Space, and Place in Rap and Hip Hop* (2002), as well as several other cutting-edge works in cultural geography and racial geography, such as Dwyer and Bressey (2008), Flint (2004), Harvey (1989, 1996, 2006, 2009), McKittrick and Woods (2007), Schein (2006), and N. Smith (1984).

19.   My analysis here has been informed by several noteworthy works in the sociology of the ghetto—or, rather, "ghetto studies"—that primarily focus on African American life and struggles in the ghetto. For example, see Hannerz (1969), Hilfiker (2002), N. Jones (2010), Meier (1976), Stanley-Niaah (2010), Venkatesh (2000), Warren (2008), D. Wilson (2007), and Winant (2001).

20.   For further discussion of late 1960s and 1970s blaxploitation (i.e., "black exploitation") films, and for the most noteworthy works that informed my analysis here, see Dunn (2008), Koven (2001, 2010), Lawrence (2007), Sieving (2011), Sims (2006), and Walker, Rausch and Watson (2009).

21.   For further discussion of the *ideological evolution* of the various forms of racism and capitalism—as well as sexism and heterosexism—that are in many ways specific to the Hip Hop Generation and turn of the twenty-first century America, and for the most noteworthy works that informed my analysis here, see Alexander (2010), Bonilla-Silva (2001, 2003), P. H. Collins (2005, 2006), Desmond and Emirbayer (2010), Gallagher (2008), D. T. Goldberg (1997, 2001, 2008), Oliver and Shapiro (1995), Omi and Winant (1994), and Winant (2004).

22.   For further discussion of what might be termed "contemporary African American micro-politics," as well as the Hip Hop Movement's new "micro-movement politics," please see Gillespie (2010), A. K. Harrison (2009), Jeffries (2011), C. Johnson (2007), Junn and Haynie (2008), Laraña, Johnston, and Gusfield (1994), Ogbar (2007), Pattillo (2007), Spence (2011), and Venkatesh (2006).

23.   By "benign neglect" here, I wish to invoke the insidious policy that was introduced by New York Senator Daniel Patrick Moynihan. Serving as an advisor on "urban affairs," in 1970 Moynihan sent a memorandum to President Richard Nixon suggesting that "the issue of race could benefit from a period of 'benign neglect.'" He went on to say: "The subject has been too much talked about" and "[w]e may need a period in which Negro progress continues and racial rhetoric fades." Obviously, the "benign neglect" policy was put forward to quell the ongoing racial conflicts and national crisis in the aftermath of the Civil Rights Movement. As the heightened militantism of the Black Power Movement surely showed, African Americans knew full well that civil rights legislation, especially the Civil Rights Act of 1964 and the Voting Rights Act of 1965, meant little or nothing until they were implemented and actually trickled down to working-class and poverty-stricken black folk. In light of the Watts Rebellion in 1965 and the allegedly "widespread arson" in the South Bronx and Harlem in the late 1960s and early 1970s, Moynihan argued that firemen should not have to risk their lives in a "futile war" fighting fires in inner-city neighborhoods. In so many words, he suggested that urban arson was one of the many social pathologies caused by the heated "racial rhetoric" of Black Power militants. Senator Moynihan ultimately believed that his "benign neglect" policy would not only curb the heated "racial rhetoric," but also cure the overcrowding of the ghettos by forcing poor people to flee as a result of arson or the ever-looming threat of arson at the time. For further discussion of the Moynihanian and Nixonian policy of "benign neglect," see Bartol (1992), Eichengreen (2000), Entman and Rojecki (2000), L. Harris (1973), Upchurch (2008), and Wills (1970).

24.   For further discussion of rap as poetry and the poetics of hip hop, and for the most noteworthy works that informed my analysis here, see Bradley and DuBois (2010), Buckholz (2010), Dorsey (2000), Pate (2010), Perry (2004), Sitomer and Cirelli (2004), and L. A. Stanley (1992).

25.   Blues people and the "Niggerati's" producing, packaging, marketing, and distribution of their own work were discussed in "remixes" 2 and 4, respectively. However, in terms of beboppers producing, packaging, marketing, and distributing their own work I have in mind here Charles Mingus and Max Roach's often-overlooked Debut Records venture. The record label was established in 1952 with the express intent of circumventing the slew of aesthetic compromises Mingus, Roach, and many other beboppers felt they had to endure when they recorded their compositions for major record companies. Between 1952 and 1957, Debut captured the musical magic of Mingus, Roach, Bud Powell, Dizzy Gillespie, Charlie Parker, Miles Davis, J.J. Johnson, Kenny Clarke, Dexter Gordon, Kenny Dorham, Pepper Adams, Hank Mobley, Bennie Green, Louis Bellson, Tal Farlow, Walter Bishop, Paul Bley, Thad Jones, John Lewis, Hank Jones, Wynton Kelly, Duke Jordan, Teddy Charles, Elvin Jones, Roy Haynes, Lee Konitz, Barry Galbraith, and Mal Waldron, among many others. For further discussion of Debut Records and its significance with regard to "bebop radicalism" and "bebop aesthetic independence," see DeVeaux (1997), Michel (1997), Mingus (1971, 1990), Owens (1995), and Weiler (1994).

26.   For further discussion of the ways in which African Americans continue to be enslaved and shackled and chained by anti-black racism, poverty, poor housing, horrid healthcare, unabated unemployment, ongoing substandard education, over-representation in the armed services, and penal escalation, and for the most noteworthy works that informed my analysis here, see M. Alexander (2010), Blackmon (2008), Massey and Denton (1993), Oliver and Shapiro (1995), T. M. Shapiro (2004), and W. J. Wilson (1987, 1997, 1999, 2009).

# Bibliography

## NOTE ON THE BIBLIOGRAPHY

The unique interdisciplinary and intersectional nature of this book necessitated idiosyncratic authorial and bibliographic decisions—decisions that will not make any self-respecting environmentalist shudder. My personal commitment to our fragile ecology and the economic realities of making this volume affordable demanded economy of expression and citation wherever possible. As a consequence, I have eliminated citations that are obvious. For example, popular music and popular film citations have been altogether omitted. Musicologists and Film Studies scholars are likely to cringe, but I suspect non-academic intellectuals, artists, and activists will greatly appreciate a more affordable and eco-friendly volume.

Abbington, James. (Ed.). (2001). *Readings in African American Church Music and Worship.* Chicago, IL: GIA Publications, Inc.

Abbott, Kingsley. (2000). *Calling Out Around the World: A Motown Reader.* London: Helter Skelter.

Abbott, Lynn, and Seroff, Doug. (2002). *Out of Sight: The Rise of African American Popular Music, 1889–1895.* Jackson: University Press of Mississippi.

———. (2007). *Ragged But Right: Black Traveling Shows, "Coon Songs," and the Dark Pathway to Blues and Jazz.* Jackson: University Press of Mississippi.

Abelove, Henry, Barale, Michele Aina, and Halperin, David M. (Eds.). (1993). *The Lesbian and Gay Studies Reader.* New York: Routledge.

Abod, Jennifer. (Director). (1990). *Edge of Each Other's Battles: The Vision of Audre Lorde.* Long, Beach, CA: Profile Productions.

Abu-Lughod, Janet L. (2007). *Race, Space, and Riots in Chicago, New York, and Los Angeles.* New York: Oxford University Press.

Adams, Terri, and Fuller, Douglas. (2006). "The Words Have Changed But the Ideology Remains the Same: Misogynistic Lyrics in Rap Music." *Journal of Black Studies* 36 (6): 938–57.

Ahmed, Feroz. (1992). *Infant Mortality Among Black Americans*. Washington, DC: Institute for Urban Affairs and Research, Howard University.

Albertson, Chris. (1979). *Jelly Roll Morton*. Alexandria, VA: Time-Life Books.

———. (2003). *Bessie*. New Haven: Yale University Press.

Aldridge, Daniel W. (2011). *Becoming American: The African American Quest for Civil Rights, 1861–1976*. Wheeling, IL: Harlan Davidson.

Aldridge, John W. (1985). *After the Lost Generation: A Critical Study of the Writers of Two Wars*. New York: Arbor House.

Alexander, Bryant K. (2006). *Performing Black Masculinity: Race, Culture, and Queer Identity*. Lanham, MD: AltaMira.

Alexander, Michelle. (2010). *The New Jim Crow: Mass Incarceration in the Age of Color-Blindness*. New York: New Press.

Alford, Lucy. (Ed.). (1984). *Break-Dancing*. London: Hamlyn.

Alim, H. Samy. (2004). *You Know My Steez: An Ethnographic and Sociolinguistic Study Of Style-Shifting in a Black American Speech Community*. Durham: Duke University Press.

———. (2005). *Real Talk: Language Culture & Education in the Hip Hop Nation*. New York: Routledge.

———. (2006). *Roc the Mic Right: The Language of Hip Hop Culture*. New York: Routledge.

Alim, H. Samy, Ibrahim, Awad, and Pennycook, Alastair. (Eds.). (2009). *Global Linguistic Flows: Hip Hop Cultures, Youth Identities, and the Politics of Language*. New York: Routledge.

Allen, William Francis. (Ed.). (1995). *Slave Songs of the United States*. New York: Dover.

Altschuler, Glenn C. (2003). *All Shook Up: How Rock 'n' Roll Changed America*. New York: Oxford University Press.

Alvarez, Luis. (2008). *The Power of the Zoot: Youth Culture and Resistance During World War II*. Berkeley: University of California Press.

Amani, Khalil. (2007). *Hip Hop Homophobes: Origins and Attitudes Towards Gays and Lesbians in Hip Hop Culture*. Bloomington, IN: iUniverse, Inc.

Amatokwu, Onyekambuashie N. (2009). "An Afrocentric Analysis of Hip Hop Musical Art Composition and Production: Roles, Themes, Techniques, and Contexts." Ph.D. dissertation, Department of African American Studies, Temple University, Philadelphia.

Anderson, Elijah. (1981). *Place on the Corner*. Chicago: University of Chicago Press.

———. (1990). *Streetwise: Race, Class, and Change in an Urban Community*. Chicago: University of Chicago Press.

———. (1999). *Code of the Street: Decency, Violence, and the Moral Life of the Inner-City*. New York: Norton.

———. (Ed.). (2008). *Against the Wall: Poor, Young, Black, and Male*. Philadelphia: University of Pennsylvania Press.

Anderson, Iain. (2007). *This Is Our Music: Free Jazz, the Sixties, and American Culture* Philadelphia: University of Pennsylvania Press.

Anderson, Jervis. (1993). *This Was Harlem: A Cultural Portrait, 1900–1950*. New York: Farrar, Straus & Giroux.

Anderson, Thomas Jefferson, III. (2004). *Notes to Make the Sound Come Right: Four Innovators of Jazz Poetry*. Fayetteville: University of Arkansas Press.

Andriote, John-Manuel. (2001). *Hot Stuff: A Brief History of Disco*. New York: HarperEntertainment.

Anner, John. (Ed.). (1996). *Beyond Identity Politics: Emerging Social Justice Movements in Communities of Color*. Boston: South End Press.

Aptheker, Herbert. (1983). *American Negro Slave Revolts*. New York: International Publishers.

———. (1989). *The Literary Legacy of W.E.B. Du Bois*. White Plains, NY: Kraus International.

Aquila, Richard. (2000). *That Old-Time Rock & Roll: A Chronicle of an Era, 1954–1963*. Chicago: University of Illinois Press.

Argyle, Ray. (2009). *Scott Joplin and the Age of Ragtime*. Jefferson, NC: McFarland.

Armstrong, Louis. (1957). "Louis Armstrong, Barring Soviet Tour, Denounces Eisenhower and Gov. Faubus." (September 19): 23. Retrieved from www.nytimes.com/books/97/08/03/reviews/armstrong-eisenhower.html.

———. (1999). *Louis Armstrong, In His Own Words: Selected Writings* (Thomas David Brothers, Ed.). New York: Oxford University Press.

Arnesen, Eric (2002). *Black Protest and the Great Migration: A Brief History with Documents.* Bedford: St. Martin's Press.

Arsenault, Raymond. (2006). *Freedom Riders: 1961 and the Struggle for Racial Justice.* New York: Oxford University Press.

Asante, Molefi Kete. (1988). *Afrocentricity.* Trenton, NJ: Africa World Press.

———. (1990). *Kemet, Afrocentricity, and Knowledge.* Trenton, NJ: Africa World Press.

———. (1998). *The Afrocentric Idea.* Philadelphia: Temple University Press.

———. (1999). *The Painful Demise of Eurocentricism.* Trenton, NJ: Africa World Press.

———. (2007). *An Afrocentric Manifesto.* Oxford, UK: Polity Press.

Asim, Jabari. (2007). *The N Word: Who Can Say It, Who Shouldn't, and Why.* Boston: Houghton Mifflin.

Austerlitz, Paul. (2005). *Jazz Consciousness: Music, Race, and Humanity.* Middletown, CT: Wesleyan University Press.

Austin, Joe. (2001). *Taking the Train: How Graffiti Art Became an Urban Crisis in New York City.* New York: Columbia University Press.

Awkward, Michael. (2007). *Soul Covers: Rhythm & Blues Remakes and the Struggle for Artistic Identity (Aretha Franklin, Al Green, Phoebe Snow).* Durham: Duke University Press.

Babb, Tracie. (2002). *The Treatment of Women in the Hip Hop Community: Past, Present, and Future.* New York: Fordham University.

Bailey, Julius. (Ed.). (2011). *Jay-Z: Essays on Hip Hop's Philosopher King.* Jefferson, NC: McFarland.

Baker, Geoffrey. (2011). *Buena Vista in the Club: Rap, Reggaeton, and Revolution in Havana.* Durham: Duke University Press.

Baker, Houston A., Jr. (1984). *Blues, Ideology, and Afro-American Literature: A Vernacular Theory.* Chicago: University of Chicago Press.

———. (1993). *Black Studies, Rap, and the Academy.* Chicago: University of Chicago Press.

Balaji, Murali. (2010). "Vixen Resistin': Redefining Black Womanhood in Hip Hop Music Video." *Journal of Black Studies* 41 (1): 5–20.

Baldwin, Katherine A. (2002). *Beyond the Color-Line and the Iron Curtain: Reading Encounters Between Black and Red, 1922–1963.* Durham: Duke University Press.

Ball, Jared. (2009). "FreeMix Radio: The Original Mixtape Radio Show." *Journal of Black Studies* 39 (4): 614–34.

———. (2011). *I Mix What I Like!: A Mixtape Manifesto.* New York: AK Press.

Banfield, William C. (2010). *Cultural Codes: Makings of a Black Music Philosophy—An Interpretive History from Spirituals to Hip Hop.* Lanham, MD: Scarecrow Press.

Banjoko, Adisa. (2004). *Lyrical Swords: Hip Hop and Politics in the Mix.* San Jose, CA: YinSumi Press.

Baraka, Amiri. (1961). *Preface to a Twenty Volume Suicide Note.* New York: Totem Press.

———. (1963). *Blues People: Negro Music in White America.* New York: Morrow.

———. (1969). *Black Magic: Collected Poetry, 1961–1967.* Indianapolis: Bobs-Merrill.

———. (1970a). *It's Nation Time.* Chicago: Third World Press.

———. (1970b). *In Our Terribleness (Some Elements and Meaning in Black Style).* Indianapolis: Bobs-Merrill.

———. (1972). *Spirit Reach.* Newark: Jihad Productions.

———. (1975). *Hard Facts.* Newark: Congress of Afrikan People.

———. (1978). *The Selected Poetry of Amiri Baraka/LeRoi Jones.* New York: Morrow.

———. (1995). *Transbluesency: The Selected Poems of Amiri Baraka/LeRoi Jones.* New York: Marsilio Publishers.

Barber, Stephen M., and Clark, David L. (Eds.). (2002). *Regarding Sedgwick: Essays on Queer Culture and Critical Theory.* New York: Routledge.

Barfield, Ray E. (1996). *Listening to Radio, 1920–1950*. Westport, CT: Praeger.

Barnes, Sandra L. (2010). *Black Mega-Church Culture: Models for Education and Empowerment*. New York: Lang.

Barnett, LaShonda K. (2007). *I Got Thunder: Black Women Songwriters on Their Craft*. New York: Thunder's Mouth Press.

Barongan, Christy, and Hall, Gordon C. N. (1995). "The Influence Of Misogynous Rap Music On Sexual Aggression Against Women." *Psychology of Women Quarterly* 19: 195–207.

Barrett, Marvin. (1959). *The Jazz Age*. New York: Putman.

Bartol, Frank R. (1992). *A Season of Benign Neglects and Other Essays*. Munising, MI: Bayshore Press.

Basu, Dipannita. (1992). "Rap Music, Hip Hop Culture, and the Music Industry in Los Angeles." *The Center for Afro-American Studies Report* 15 (1&2): 20–25.

Basu, Dipannita, and Lemelle, Sidney J. (Eds.). (2006). *The Vinyl Ain't Final: Hip Hop and the Globalization of Black Popular Culture*. London: Pluto Press.

Battle, Juan, and Barnes, Sandra L. (Eds.). (2010). *Black Sexualities: Probing Powers, Passions, Practices, and Policies*. New Brunswick: Rutgers University Press.

Bayles, Martha. (1994). *Hole in Our Soul: The Loss of Beauty and Meaning in American Popular Music*. New York: Free Press.

Bean, Annemarie, Hatch, James V., and McNamara, Brooks. (Eds.). (1996). *Inside the Minstrel Mask: Readings in Nineteenth Century Blackface Minstrelsy*. Hanover, NH: Wesleyan University Press.

Beardsworth, Richard. (1996). *Derrida & Political*. New York: Routledge.

Bebey, Francis. (1999). *African Music: A People's Art*. New York: Lawrence Hill Books.

Beemyn, Brett, and Eliason, Mickey. (Eds.). (1996). *Queer Studies: A Lesbian, Gay, Bisexual & Transgender Anthology*. New York: New York University Press.

Bell, Caryn Cossé. (1997). *Revolution, Romanticism, and the Afro-Creole Protest Tradition in Louisiana, 1718–1868*. Baton Rouge: Louisiana State University Press.

Bender, Wolfgang. (1991). *Sweet Mother: Modern African Music*. Chicago: University of Chicago Press.

Bergreen, Laurence. (1997). *Louis Armstrong: An Extravagant Life*. New York: Broadway Books.

Berland, Jody. (1998). "Locating Listening: Technological Space, Popular Culture, and Canadian Meditations." In Andrew Leyshon, David Matless, and George Revill (Eds.), *The Place of Music* (129–50). New York: Guilford Press.

Berlin, Edward A. (1980). *Ragtime: A Musical and Cultural History*. Berkeley: University of California Press.

———. (1994). *King of Ragtime: Scott Joplin and His Era*. New York: Oxford University Press.

Berliner, Brett A. (2002). *Ambivalent Desire: The Exotic Black Other in Jazz Age France*. Amherst: University of Massachusetts Press.

Bernard, Regina A. (2009). *Black & Brown Waves: The Cultural Politics of Young Women of Color and Feminism*. Boston, MA: Sense Publishers.

Bernard, Shane K. (1996). *Swamp Pop: Cajun and Creole Rhythm & Blues*. Jackson: University Press of Mississippi.

Bertrand, Michael T. (2000). *Race, Rock, and Elvis*. Urbana: University of Illinois Press.

Bhui, Hindpal Singh. (Ed.). (2009). *Race and Criminal Justice*. Los Angeles: Sage.

Billingsley, Andrew. (1999). *Mighty Like a River: The Black Church and Social Reform*. New York: Oxford University Press.

Black Public Sphere Collective. (Eds.). (1995). *The Black Public Sphere: A Public Culture Book*. Chicago: University of Chicago Press.

Blackmon, Douglas A. (2008). *Slavery by Another Name: The Re-Enslavement of Black Americans from the Civil War to World War II*. New York: Doubleday.

Blair, Karen J. (1980). *The Clubwoman as Feminist: True Womanhood Redefined, 1868–1914*. New York: Holmes & Meier Publishers.

Blassingame, John W. (1973). *Black New Orleans, 1860–1880*. Chicago: University of Chicago Press.

Bleser. Carol K. R. (1991). *In Joy and in Sorrow: Women, Family, and Marriage in the Victorian South, 1830–1900*. New York: Oxford University Press.

Blodgett, Geoffrey, and Howe, Daniel W. (Eds.). (1976). *Victorian America*. Philadelphia: University of Pennsylvania Press.

Blount, Marcellus, and Cunningham, George P. (Eds.). (1996). *Representing Black Men*. New York: Routledge.

Boardman, Fon Wyman. (1968). *America and the Jazz Age: A History of the 1920s*. New York: H.Z. Walck.

Bogazianos, Dimitri A. (2011). *5 Grams: Crack Cocaine, Rap Music, and the War on Drugs*. New York: New York University Press.

Bogdanov, Vladimir, Woodstra, Chris, and Erlewine, Stephen Thomas. (Eds.). (2002). *All Music Guide to Jazz: The Definitive Guide to Jazz Music*. San Francisco: Backbeat Books.

———. (Eds.). (2003a). *All Music Guide to Blues: The Definitive Guide to Blues*. San Francisco: Backbeat Books.

———. (Eds.). (2003b). *All Music Guide to Soul: The Definitive Guide to R&B and Soul*. San Francisco: Backbeat Books.

Bogdanov, Vladimir, Woodstra, Chris, Erlewine, Stephen Thomas, and Bush, John. (Eds.). (2003). *All Music Guide to Hip Hop: The Definitive Guide to Rap & Hip Hop*. San Francisco: Backbeat Books.

Bogle, Donald. (2000). *Toms, Coons, Mulattoes, Mammies, and Bucks: An Interpretive History of Blacks in American Films*. New York: Continuum.

———. (2001). *Primetime Blues: African Americans on Network Television*. New York: Farrar, Straus & Giroux.

———. (2005). *Bright Boulevards, Bold Dreams: The Story of Black Hollywood*. New York: One World/Ballantine Books.

Bograd, Larry, and Hubbard, Coleen. (Directors). (2010). *I Can Tell the World: The Spirituals Project*. Los Angeles, CA: Vanguard.

Bolden, Tony. (2008). *The Funk Era and Beyond: New Perspectives of Black Popular Culture*. New York: Macmillan.

Bonilla-Silva, Eduardo. (2001). *White Supremacy and Racism in the Post–Civil Rights Era*. Boulder, CO: Lynne Rienner.

———. (2003). *Racism Without Racists: Color-Blind Racism and the Persistence of Racial Inequality in the United States*. Lanham, MD: Rowman and Littlefield.

Bonilla-Silva, Eduardo, and Doane, Ashley. (Eds.). (2003). *White Out: The Continuing Significance of Racism*. New York: Routledge.

Bonner, Pat E. (1996). *Sassy Jazz and Slo' Draggin' Blues: Music in the Poetry of Langston Hughes*. New York: Lang.

Boone, Margaret S. (1989). *Capital Crime: Black Infant Mortality in America*. Newbury Park: Sage.

Boone, William Edward. (2008). "The Beautiful Struggle: An Analysis of Hip Hop Icons, Archetypes, and Aesthetics." Ph.D. dissertation, Department of African American Studies, Temple University, Philadelphia.

Bost, Suzanne. (2001). "'Be Deceived If Ya Wanna Be Foolish': (Re)constructing Body, Genre, and Gender in Feminist Rap." *Postmodern Culture* 12 (1). doi: 10.1353/pmc.2001.0017.

Bourgeois, Anna Stong. (2004). *Blueswomen: Profiles of 37 Early Performers, with an Anthology of Lyrics, 1920–1945*. Jefferson, NC: McFarland.

Bowen, Patrick D. (2011). "The Search for 'Islam': African American Islamic Groups in NYC, 1904–1954." *The Muslim World*. doi: 10.1111/j.1478-1913.2011.01372.x.

Bowleg, Lisa. (2008). "When Black + Lesbian + Woman ≠ Black Lesbian Woman: The Methodological Challenges of Qualitative and Quantitative Intersectionality Research." *Sex Roles* 59 (5–6): 312–25.

Bowman, Robert M. J. (1997). *Soulsville, U.S.A.: The Story of Stax Records*. New York: Schirmer Books.

Boyd, Todd. (1997). *Am I Black Enough for You?: Popular Culture from the 'Hood and Beyond*. Indianapolis: Indiana University Press.

————. (2002). *The New H.N.I.C.: The Death of Civil Rights and the Reign of Hip Hop*. New York: New York University Press.

————. (2003). *Young, Black, Rich, and Famous: The Rise of the NBA, the Hip Hop Invasion and the Transformation of American Culture*. New York: Doubleday.

Boykin, Keith. (1996). *One More River to Cross: Black and Gay in America*. New York: Anchor Books/Doubleday.

Bracey, Earnest N. (2003). *On Racism: Essays on Black Popular Culture, African American Politics, and the New Black Aesthetics*. Lanham, MD: University Press of America.

Bradley, Adam. (2009). *Book of Rhymes: The Poetics of Hip Hop*. New York: Basic/Civitas.

Bradley, Adam, and DuBois, Andrew. (Eds.). (2010). *The Anthology of Rap*. New Haven: Yale University Press.

Braithwaite, Ronald L., and Taylor, Sandra E. (Eds.). (1992). *Health Issues in the Black Community*. San Francisco: Jossey-Bass.

Bramwell, David, and Green, Jairus. (2003). *Breakdance: Hip Hop Handbook*. New York: Street Style Publications.

Branch, Enobong H. (2011). *Opportunity Denied: Limiting Black Women to Devalued Work*. New Brunswick: Rutgers University Press.

Brandt, Eric. (Ed.). (1999). *Dangerous Liaisons: Blacks, Gays, and the Struggle for Equality*. New York: New Press.

Breines, Winifred. (2006). *Trouble Between Us: An Uneasy History of White and Black Women in the Feminist Movement*. New York: Oxford University Press.

Briggs, Cyril V. (1987). *The Crusader* (6 Volumes; Robert A. Hill, Ed.). New York: Garland.

Broderick, Francis L. (1959). *W.E.B. Du Bois: Negro Leader in a Time of Crisis*. Palo Alto, CA: Stanford University Press.

Brooks, Daphne. (2006). *Bodies in Dissent: Spectacular Performances of Race and Freedom, 1850–1910*. Durham: Duke University Press.

————. (2008). "'All That You Can't Leave Behind': Black Female Soul Singing and the Politics of Surrogation in the Age of Catastrophe." *Meridians: Feminism, Race, Transnationalism* 8 (1): 180–204.

Brooks, Tim. (2004). *Lost Sounds: Blacks and the Birth of the Recording Industry, 1890– 1919*. Urbana: University of Illinois Press.

Brothers, Thomas David. (2006). *Louis Armstrong's New Orleans*. New York: Norton.

Broven, John. (1978). *Rhythm and Blues in New Orleans*. Gretna, LA: Pelican.

Browder, Laura. (2000). *Slippery Characters: Ethnic Impersonators and American Identities*. Chapel Hill: University of North Carolina Press.

Brown, Jake. (2002). *Suge Knight: The Rise, Fall, and Rise of Death Row Records—The Story of Marion "Suge" Knight*. Phoenix, AZ: Colossus Books.

Brown, Jayna. (2008). *Babylon Girls: Black Women Performers and the Shaping of the Modern*. Durham: Duke University Press.

Brown, Ruth Nicole. (2008). *Black Girlhood Celebration: Toward a Hip Hop Feminist Pedagogy*. New York: Lang.

Brown, Sterling A. (1932). *Southern Road: Poems*. Boston: Beacon Press.

Brown, Timothy J. (2006). "Welcome to the Terrordome: Exploring the Contradictions of Hip Hop Black Masculinity." In Athena D. Mutua (Ed.), *Progressive Black Masculinities* (191–214). New York: Routledge.

Browner, Tara. (2002). *Heartbeat of the People: Music and Dance of the Northern Pow-Wow*. Urbana: University of Illinois Press.

————. (Ed.). (2009). *Music of the First Nations: Tradition and Innovation in Native North America*. Urbana: University of Illinois Press.

Brundage, W. Fitzhugh. (1993). *Lynching in the New South: Georgia and Virginia, 1880–1930*. Urbana: University of Illinois Press.

————. (Ed.). (1997). *Under Sentence of Death: Lynching in the South*. Chapel Hill: University of North Carolina Press.

————. (2011). *Beyond Blackface: African Americans and the Creation of American Popular Culture, 1890–1930*. Chapel Hill: University of North Carolina Press.

Brun-Lambert, David. (2009). *Nina Simone: The Biography* (Paul Morris and Isabelle Villancher, Trans.). London: Aurum.

Buck, Christopher. (2005). *Alain Locke: Faith and Philosophy*. Los Angeles: Kalimat.

Buckholz, William. (2010). *Understand Rap: Explanations of Confusing Rap Lyrics You & Your Grandma Can Understand*. New York: Abrams Image.

Budds, Michael J. (Ed.). (2002). *Jazz & the Germans: Essays on the Influence of "Hot" American Idioms on 20th Century German Music*. Hillsdale, NY: Pendragon Press.

Bulmer, Martin, and Solomos, John. (Eds.). (2004). *Researching Race and Racism*. New York: Routledge.

Buntin, Denise M. (1988). "Sexually Transmitted Diseases in Blacks." *Dermatologic Clinics* 6 (3): 443–56.

Burke, Patrick L. (2008). *Come In and Hear the Truth: Jazz and Race on 52nd Street*. Chicago: University of Chicago Press.

Burnim, Mellonee V., and Maultsby, Portia K. (Eds.). (2006). *African American Music: An Introduction*. New York: Routledge.

Burroughs, William S. (1959). *Naked Lunch*. New York: Olympia Press/Grove Press.

Butler, Paul. (2009). *Let's Get Free: A Hip Hop Theory of Justice*. New York: New Press.

Bynoe, Yvonne. (2004). *Stand and Deliver: Political Activism, Leadership, and Hip Hop Culture*. Brooklyn, NY: Soft Skull Press.

———. (Ed.). (2006). *Encyclopedia of Rap and Hip Hop Culture*. Westport, CT: Greenwood Press.

Bynum, Cornelius L. (2010). *A. Philip Randolph and the Struggle for Civil Rights*. Urbana: University of Illinois Press.

Byrd, Rudolph P., and Guy-Sheftall, Beverly. (Eds.). (2001). *Traps: African American Men on Gender and Sexuality*. Indianapolis: Indiana University Press.

Calo, Mary Ann. (2007). *Distinction and Denial: Race, Nation, and the Critical Construction of the African American Artist, 1920–1940*. Ann Arbor: University of Michigan Press.

Campbell, James. (2001). *This is the Beat Generation: New York, San Francisco, Paris*. Berkeley: University of California Press.

Cannick, Jasmyne A. (2006). "Hip Hop's Homophobia and Black Gay America's Silence." *Pride Source Media Group /Pridesource.com*. Retrieved from www.pridesource.com/article.html?article=18369.

Canton, David A. (2006). "The Political, Economic, Social, and Cultural Tensions in Gangsta Rap." *Reviews in American History* 34 (2): 244–57.

Capeci, Dominic J. (1977). *Harlem Riot of 1943*. Philadelphia: Temple University Press.

Capeci, Dominic J., and Wilkerson, Martha Frances. (1991). *Layered Violence: The Detroit Rioters of 1943*. Jackson: University of Mississippi.

Caplan, Patricia. (1987). *The Cultural Construction of Sexuality*. New York: Tavistock.

Caponi-Tabery, Gena. (Ed.). (1999). *Signifyin(g), Sanctifyin' & Slam Dunking: A Reader in African American Expressive Culture*. Amherst: University of Massachusetts Press.

———. (2008). *Jump for Joy: Jazz, Basketball, and Black Culture in 1930s America*. Amherst: University of Massachusetts Press.

Carbado, Devon W. (Ed.). (1999). *Black Men on Race, Gender, and Sexuality: A Critical Reader*. New York: New York University Press.

Carbado, Devon W., McBride, Dwight A., and Weise, Donald. (Eds.). (2002). *Black Like Us: A Century of Lesbian, Gay, and Bisexual African American Fiction*. San Francisco: Cleis Press.

Carby, Hazel. (1991). "In Body and Spirit: Representing Black Women Musicians." *Black Music Research Journal* 11 (2): 177–92.

———. (1998). "It Jus Be's Dat Way Sometime: The Sexual Politics of Women's Blues." *Radical America* 20 (4): 9–24.

Carney, Court. (2009). *Cuttin' Up: How Early Jazz Got America's Ear*. Lawrence: University Press of Kansas.

Carroll, Ann Elizabeth. (2005). *Word, Image, and the New Negro: Representation and Identity in the Harlem Renaissance*. Bloomington: Indiana University Press.

Carroll, Rebecca. (Ed.). (2003). *Saving the Race: Conversations on Du Bois from a Collective Memoir of* The Souls of Black Folk. New York: Harlem Moon.

———. (Ed.). (2006). *Uncle Tom or New Negro?: African Americans Reflect on Booker T. Washington and* Up From Slavery *One Hundred Years Later*. New York: Broadway Books/ Harlem Moon.

Carson, Clayborne, Garrow, David J., Gill, Gerald, Harding, Vincent, and Hine, Darlene Clark. (Eds.). (1997). *The Eyes on the Prize Civil Rights Reader*. New York: Penguin.

Carter, J. Kameron. (2008). *Race: A Theological Account*. New York: Oxford University Press.

Cash, Floris Loretta. (1986). "Womanhood and Protest: The Club Movement Among Black Women, 1892–1922." Ph.D. dissertation, State University of New York, Stony Brook.

———. (2001). *African American Women and Social Action: The Clubwomen and Volunteerism from Jim Crow to the New Deal, 1896–1936*. Westport, CT: Greenwood Press.

Castleman, Craig. (1982). *Getting Up: Subway in New York*. Cambridge: Massachusetts Institute of Technology Press.

Chadwick, Whitney, and Latimer, Tirza T. (Eds.). (2003). *The Modern Woman Revisited: Paris Between the Wars*. New Brunswick: Rutgers University Press.

Chang, Jeff. (2005). *Can't Stop Won't Stop: A History of the Hip Hop Generation*. New York: St. Martin's Press.

———. (Ed.). (2006). *Total Chaos: The Art And Aesthetics of Hip Hop*. Cambridge, MA: Basic/Civitas Books.

Chapman, Erin D. (2011). *Prove It On Me: New Negroes, Sex, and Popular Culture in the 1920s*. New York: Oxford University Press.

Charles, Helen. (1990). *Womanism: Recognizing "Difference"—One Direction for the Black Woman Activist*. Canterbury, England: University of Kent.

Charnas, Dan. (2010). *The Big Paycheck: The History of the Business of Hip Hop*. New York: New American Library.

Charry, Eric S. (Ed.). (2012). *Hip Hop Africa: New African Music in a Globalizing World*. Bloomington: Indiana University Press.

Charters, Ann. (Ed.). (1983). *The Beats, Literary Bohemians in Post-War America* (2 Volumes). Detroit: Gale.

———. (1986). *Beats & Company: A Portrait of a Literary Generation*. Garden City, NY: New York: Doubleday.

———. (Ed.). (1993). *The Penguin Book of the Beats*. New York: Penguin.

———. (1994). *Kerouac: A Biography*. New York: St. Martin's Press.

———. (Ed.). (2001). *Beat Down to Your Soul: What Was the Beat Generation?* New York: Penguin Books.

———. (Ed.). (2003). *The Portable Beat Reader*. New York: Penguin Classics.

Charters, Ann, and Charters, Samuel Barclay. (2010). *Brother-Souls: John Clellon Holmes, Jack Kerouac, and the Beat Generation*. Jackson: University Press of Mississippi.

Charters, Samuel Barclay. (1963). *The Poetry of the Blues*. New York: Oak Publications.

———. (1975). *The Country Blues*. New York: Da Capo Press.

———. (1977). *The Legacy of the Blues: A Glimpse into the Art and the Lives of Twelve Great Bluesmen*. New York: Da Capo.

———. (1981). *The Roots of the Blues: An African Search*. New York: Putnam.

———. (2005). *Walking a Blues Road: A Selection of Blues Writing, 1956–2004*. New York: Marion Boyars Publishers.

———. (2008). *A Trumpet Around the Corner: The Story of New Orleans Jazz*. Jackson: University Press of Mississippi.

Chase, Christopher W. (2010). "Prophetics in the Key of Allah: Towards an Understanding of Islam in Jazz." *Jazz Perspectives* 4 (2): 157–81.

Cheney, Charise L. (2005). *Brothers Gonna Work It Out: Sexual Politics in the Golden Age of Rap Nationalism*. New York: New York University Press.

Chernoff, John Miller. (1979). *African Rhythm and African Sensibility: Aesthetics and Social Action in African Musical Idioms*. Chicago: University of Chicago Press.

Chevannes, Barry. (Ed.). (1998). *Rastafari and Other African-Caribbean Worldviews.* New Brunswick, NJ: Rutgers University Press.

Chevigny, Paul. (2005). *Gigs: Jazz and the Cabaret Laws in New York City.* New York: Routledge.

Child, Abigail. (Director). (2006). *On the Downlow.* Los Angeles: Docurama/New Video.

Chilton, John. (1990). *The Song of the Hawk: The Life and Recordings of Coleman Hawkins.* Ann Arbor: University of Michigan Press.

Christensen, Jeanne. (2003). "The Philosophy of Reasoning: The Rastafari of Jamaica." Ph.D. dissertation, University of Colorado at Boulder.

Churchill, Ward, and Wall, Jim V. (1988). *Agents of Repression: The FBI's Secret Wars Against the Black Panther Party and the American Indian Movement.* Boston: South End Press.

Clarke, Cheryl. (2006). *The Days of Good Looks: The Prose and Poetry of Cheryl Clarke, 1980 to 2005.* New York: Carroll & Graf Publishing.

Clay, Adreana. (2007a). "'I Used to be Scared of the Dick': Queer Women of Color and Hip Hop Masculinity." In Gwendolyn D. Pough, Elaine Richardson, Aisha Durham, and Rachel Raimist (Eds.), *Home Girls Make Some Noise!: The Hip Hop Feminism Anthology* (148–65). Mira Loma, CA: Parker Publishing.

———. (2007b). "Like an Old Soul Record: Black Feminism, Queer Sexuality, and the Hip Hop Generation." *Meridians: Feminism, Face, Transnationalism* 8 (1): 53–73.

Cockrell, Dale. (1997). *Demons of Disorder: Early Blackface Minstrels and Their World.* Cambridge: Cambridge University Press.

Cohen, Cathy J. (1999). *The Boundaries of Blackness: AIDS and the Breakdown of Black Politics.* Chicago: University of Chicago Press.

Cohen, Tom. (Ed.). (2001). *Jacques Derrida and the Humanities: A Critical Reader.* Cambridge: Cambridge University Press.

Cohodas, Nadine. (2010). *Princess Noire: The Tumultuous Reign of Nina Simone.* New York: Pantheon.

Cole, Johnnetta B., and Guy-Sheftall, Beverly. (2003). *Gender Talk: The Struggle for Women's Equality in African American Communities.* New York: Ballantine.

Coleman, Robin R. M., and Cobb, Jasmine. (2007). "No Way of Seeing: Mainstreaming and Selling the Gaze of Homo-Thug Hip Hop." *Popular Communication* 5 (2): 89–108.

Collier, Graham. (1975). *Jazz Lecture Concert.* Cambridge: Cambridge University Press.

Collier, James Lincoln. (1983). *Louis Armstrong, An American Genius.* New York: Oxford University Press.

———. (1987). *Duke Ellington.* New York: Oxford University Press.

Collier-Thomas, Bettye. (2010). *Jesus, Jobs, and Justice: African American Women and Religion.* New York: Knopf..

Collier-Thomas, Betty, and Franklin, V. P. (Eds.). (2001). *Sisters in the Struggle: African American Women in the Civil Rights–Black Power Movement.* New York: New York University Press.

Collins, Catherine Fisher. (Ed.). (2006). *African American Women's Health and Social Issues.* Westport, CT: Praeger.

Collins, Patricia Hill. (1998). *Fighting Words: Black Women and the Search for Social Justice.* Minneapolis: University of Minnesota Press.

———. (2000). *Black Feminist Thought: Knowledge, Consciousness, and the Politics of Empowerment* (Second Edition). New York: Routledge.

———. (2003). "Some Group Matters: Intersectionality, Situated Standpoints, and Black Feminist Thought." In Tommy L. Lott and John P. Pittman (Eds.), *A Companion to African American Philosophy* (205–30). Malden, MA: Blackwell.

———. (2005). *Black Sexual Politics: African Americans, Gender, and the New Racism.* New York: Routledge.

———. (2006). *From Black Power to Hip Hop: Racism, Nationalism, and Feminism.* Philadelphia: Temple University Press.

————. (2007). "Pushing Boundaries or Business as Usual?: Race, Class, and Gender Studies and Sociological Inquiry." In Craig J. Calhoun (Ed.), *Sociology in America: A History* (572–604). Chicago: University of Chicago Press.

Collins, Sharon M. (1997). *Black Corporate Executives: The Making and Breaking of a Black Middle-Class*. Philadelphia: Temple University Press.

Comissiong, Solomon W. F. (2007). *Mining the Positive Motivators from Hip Hop to Educate: How I Met Knowledge & Education thru Hip Hop Culture*. Philadelphia, PA: Xlibris.

Condry, Ian. (2006). *Hip Hop Japan: Rap and the Paths of Cultural Globalization*. Durham: Duke University Press.

Cone, James H. (1969). *Black Theology and Black Power* . New York: Seabury.

————. (1970). *A Black Theology of Liberation* . Philadelphia: Lippincott.

————. (1972). *The Spirituals and The Blues: An Interpretation* . New York: Seabury.

————. (1975). *God of the Oppressed* . New York: Seabury.

Cone, James H., and Wilmore, Gayraud S. (Eds.). (1993). *Black Theology: A Documentary History* (2 Volumes). Maryknoll, NY: Orbis.

Coner-Edwards, Alice F., and Spurlock, Jeanne. (Eds.). (1988). *Black Families in Crisis: The Middle-Class*. New York: Brunner/Mazel.

Conrad, Kate, Dixon, Travis L., and Zhang, Yuanyuan. (2009). "Controversial Rap Themes, Gender Portrayals and Skin Tone Distortion: A Content Analysis of Rap Music Videos." *Journal of Broadcasting & Electronic Media* 53 (1): 134–56.

Constantine-Simms, Delroy. (Ed.). (2001). *The Greatest Taboo: Homosexuality in Black Communities*. Los Angeles, CA: Alyson Books.

Cook, Bruce. (1971). *The Beat Generation: The Tumultuous '50s Movement and Its Impact on Today*. New York: Scribner.

Cooke, Mervyn, and Horn, David. (Ed.). (2002). *The Cambridge Companion to Jazz*. New York: Cambridge University Press.

Cooke, Miriam, and Lawrence, Bruce B. (Eds.). (2005). *Muslim Network from Hajj to Hip Hop*. Chapel Hill: University of North Carolina Press.

Cooper, Carolyn J. (1995). *Noises in the Blood: Orality, Gender, and the "Vulgar" Body of Jamaican Popular Culture*. Durham: Duke University Press.

————. (2004). *Sound Clash: Jamaican Dancehall Culture at Large*. New York: Macmillan, 2004.

Cooper, Martha, and Chalfant, Henry. (1984). *Subway Art*. New York: Holt, Rinehart and Winston.

Cooper, Wayne F. (1987). *Claude McKay: Rebel Sojourner in the Harlem Renaissance, A Biography*. Baton Rouge: Louisiana State University Press.

Corbould, Clare. (2009). *Becoming African Americans: Black Public Life in Harlem, 1919–1939*. Cambridge, MA: Harvard University Press.

Cornwell, Anita. (1983). *Black Lesbian in White America*. Tallahassee, FL: Naiad Press.

Corrales, Javier, and Pecheny, Mario. (2010). *The Politics of Sexuality in Latin America: A Reader on Lesbian, Gay, Bisexual, and Transgender Rights*. Pittsburgh: University of Pittsburgh Press.

Cortez, Jayne. (1969). *Pisstained Stairs and the Monkey Man's Wares*. New York: Phrase Text.

Cose, Ellis. (1993). *The Rage of a Privileged Class*. New York: HarperCollins.

Covington, Jeanette. (2010). *Crime and Racial Constructions: Cultural Misinformation About African Americans in Media and Academia*. Lanham, MD: Lexington Books.

Cowley, Malcolm. (1973). *A Second Flowering: Works and Days of the Lost Generation*. New York: Viking.

Crawford, Richard. (2005). *America's Musical Life: A History*. New York: Norton.

Crawford, Vicki L., Rouse, Jacqueline A., and Woods, Barbara. (Eds.). (1990). *Women in the Civil Rights Movement: Trailblazers and Torchbearers*. Brooklyn, NY: Carlson.

Crazy Horse, Kandia. (Ed.). (2004). *Rip It Up: The Black Experience in Rock & Roll*. New York: Macmillan, 2004.

Cross, Brian. (1993). *It's Not About a Salary: Rap, Race, and Resistance in Los Angeles*. New York: Verso.

Crowther, Bruce, and Pinfold, Mike. (1986). *The Jazz Singers: From Ragtime to the New Wave*. New York: Blandford Press.

Curtis, Susan. (1994). *Dancing to a Black Man's Tune: A Life of Scott Joplin*. Columbia: University of Missouri Press.

Dahl, Bill. (2001). *Motown: The Golden Years, The Stars and Music That Shaped a Generation*. Iola, WI: Krause.

Dance, Stanley. (2000). *The World of Duke Ellington*. New York: Da Capo Press.

Daniels, Douglas H. (1985). "Lester Young: Master of Jive." *American Music* 3 (3): 313–28.

———. (2002). "Los Angeles Zoot: Race 'Riot,' the Pachuco, and Black Music Culture." *Journal of African American History* 87, 98–118.

Danielsen, Anne. (2006). *Presence and Pleasure: The Funk Grooves of James Brown and Parliament*. Middletown, CT: Wesleyan University Press.

———. (2008). "The Musicalization of 'Reality': Reality Rap and Rap Reality on Public Enemy's *Fear of a Black Planet*." *European Journal of Cultural Studies* 11 (4): 405–21.

Dannin, Robert. (2002). *Black Pilgrimage to Islam*. New York: Oxford University Press.

Darden, Bob. (2004). *People Get Ready!: A New History of Black Gospel Music*. New York: Continuum.

Davenport, Stephen. (1995). "Queer Shoulders to the Wheel: Beat Movement as Men's Movement." *Journal of Men's Studies* 3 (4): 297–307.

Davis, Angela Y. (1981). *Women, Race and Class*. New York: Vintage.

———. (1989). *Women, Culture, and Politics*. New York: Vintage.

———. (1998a). "Afro-Images: Politics, Fashion, and Nostalgia." In Monique Guillory and Richard C. Green (Eds.), *Soul: Black Power, Politics, and Pleasure* (23–32). New York: New York University Press.

———. (1998b). *Blues Legacies and Black Feminism: Gertrude "Ma" Rainey, Bessie Smith, and Billie Holiday*. New York: Pantheon.

Davis, David Brion. (2006). *Inhuman Bondage: The Rise and Fall of Slavery in the New World*. Oxford: Oxford University Press.

Davis, Elizabeth L. (1996). *Lifting As They Climb: The National Association of Colored Women*. New York: G.K. Hall.

Davis, Francis. (1988). *In the Moment: Jazz in the 1980s*. New York: Oxford University Press.

———. (1990). *Outcats: Jazz Composers, Instrumentalists, and Singers*. New York: Oxford University Press.

———. (1992). "Man with a Horn." *Atlantic Monthly* 269 (3): 116.

———. (1995). *The History of the Blues*. New York: Hyperion.

Davis, Jack E. (Ed.). (2001). *The Civil Rights Movement*. Malden, MA: Blackwell.

Davis, Nathan T. (1996). *African American Music: A Philosophical Look at African American Music in Society*. Needham Heights, MA: Simon & Schuster.

Dawson, Michael C. (2001). *Black Visions: The Roots of Contemporary African American Political Ideologies*. Chicago: University of Chicago Press.

———. (2011). *Not in Our Lifetimes: The Future of Black Politics*. Chicago: University Of Chicago Press.

Dean, Terrance. (2009). *Hiding in Hip Hop: On the Down Low in the Entertainment Industry, from Music to Hollywood*. New York: Atria.

Delgado, Richard, and Stefancic, Jean. (Eds.). (1997). *Critical White Studies: Looking Behind the Mirror*. Philadelphia: Temple University Press.

Demers, Joanna Teresa. (2001). "'Brothers Gonna Work It Out?': Echoes of Blaxploitation Sound in Hip Hop." *Music Research Forum* 16: 2–19.

———. (2002). "Sampling as Lineage in Hip Hop." Ph.D. dissertation, Princeton University.

———. (2003). "Sampling the 1970s in Hip Hop." *Popular Music* 22 (1): 41–56.

Dennis, Christopher. (2011). *Afro-Colombian Hip Hop: Globalization, Transcultural Music, and Ethnic Identities*. Lanham, MD: Lexington Books.

Dent, Gina. (Ed.). (1992). *Black Popular Culture*. Seattle: Bay Press.

Derrida, Jacques. (1967). *De la grammatologie*. Paris: Les Éditions de Minuit.

———. (1976). *Of Grammatology* (Gayatri Chakravorty Spivak, Trans.). Baltimore: Johns Hopkins University Press.

Desmond, Matthew, and Emirbayer, Mustafa. (2010). *Racial Domination, Racial Progress: The Sociology of Race in America.* New York: McGraw-Hill Higher Education.

De Veaux, Alexis. (2004). *Warrior Poet: A Biography of Audre Lorde.* New York: Norton.

DeVeaux, Scott K. (1988). "Bebop and the Recording Industry: The 1942 AFM Recording Ban Reconsidered." *Journal of the American Musicological Society* 41 (1): 126–65.

———. (1997). *The Birth of Bebop: A Social and Musical History.* Berkeley: University of California Press.

Dickson, Lynda Faye. (1982). "The Early Club Movement Among Black Women in Denver, 1890–1925." Ph.D. dissertation, University of Colorado at Boulder.

Dill, Bonnie Thornton. (1994). *Across the Boundaries of Race and Class: An Exploration of Work and Family Among Black Female Domestic Servants.* New York: Garland.

DiMeglio, John E. (1973). *Vaudeville U.S.A.* Bowling Green, OH: Bowling Green University Popular Press.

Dimitriadis, Greg. (2009). *Performing Identity/Performing Culture: Hip Hop as Text, Pedagogy, and Lived Practice.* New York: Lang.

Diouf, Mamadou, and Nwankwo, Ifeoma Kiddoe. (Eds.). (2010). *Rhythms of the Afro-Atlantic World: Rituals and Remembrances.* Ann Arbor: University of Michigan Press.

Dolan, Marc. (1996). *Modern Lives: A Cultural Re-Reading of "The Lost Generation."* West Lafayette, IN: Purdue University Press.

Donalson, Melvin Burke. (2007). *Hip Hop in American Cinema.* New York: Lang.

Donnelly, Mabel Collins. (1986). *The American Victorian Woman: The Myth and the Reality.* New York: Greenwood.

Doreski, Carole. (1998). *Writing America Black: Race Rhetoric in the Public Sphere.* New York: Cambridge University Press.

Dorsey, Brian. (2000). *Spirituality, Sensuality, Literality: Blues, Jazz, and Rap as Music and Poetry.* Vienna, Austria: Braumüller.

Douglas, George H. (1987). *The Early Days of Radio Broadcasting.* Jefferson, NC: McFarland.

Driggs, Frank, and Lewine, Harris. (1982). *Black Beauty, White Heat: A Pictorial History of Classic Jazz, 1920–1950.* New York: Morrow.

Driscoll, Kevin Edward. (2009). "Stepping Your Game Up: Technical Innovation Among Young People of Color in Hip Hop." Master of Science, Department of Comparative Media Studies, Massachusetts Institute of Technology.

Driskill, Qwo-Li, Finley, Chris, Gilley, Brian J., and Morgensen, Scott L. (Eds.). (2011). *Queer Indigenous Studies: Critical Interventions in Theory, Politics, and Literature.* Tucson: University of Arizona Press.

Dublin, Thomas, Arias, Franchesca, and Carreras, Debora. (2003). *What Gender Perspectives Shaped the Emergence of the National Association of Colored Women, 1895–1920?* Alexandria, VA: Alexander Street Press.

Du Bois, W.E.B. (1903a). "Possibilities of the Negro: The Advance Guard of the Race." *Booklover's Magazine* 2 (1): 3–15.

———. (1903b). *The Souls of Black Folk: Essays and Sketches.* Chicago, IL: McClurg.

———. (1903c). "The Talented Tenth." In Booker T. Washington (Ed.), *The Negro Problem: A Series of Articles by Representative American Negroes Today* (33–75). New York: James Pott & Co.

———. (1911). *The Quest of the Silver Fleece: A Novel.* Chicago: McClurg.

———. (1920). *Darkwater: Voices From Within the Veil.* New York: Harcourt Brace.

———. (1924). *The Gift of Black Folk: The Negroes in the Making of America.* Boston: Stratford.

———. (1928). *Dark Princess: A Romance.* New York: Harcourt Brace.

———. (1934). *William Monroe Trotter.* New York: Crisis Publishing.

———. (1964). *The Selected Poems of W.E.B. Du Bois.* Accra, Ghana: University of Ghana Press.

———. (1968). *The Autobiography of W.E.B. Du Bois: A Soliloquy on Viewing My Life from the Last Decade of Its First Century.* New York: International Publishers.

———. (1977). *Book Reviews by W.E.B. Du Bois* (Herbert Aptheker, Ed.). Millwood, NY: Kraus-Thomson.

————. (1985). *Creative Writings by W.E.B. Du Bois: A Pageant, Poems, Short Stories and Playlets* (Herbert Aptheker, Ed.). Millwood, NY: Kraus-Thomson.

————. (1986). *Du Bois: Writings* (Nathan Irvin Huggins, Ed.). New York: Library of America Press.

————. (1995a). *Black Reconstruction in America, 1860–1880*. New York: Touchstone.

————. (1995b). *W.E.B. Du Bois Reader* (David Levering Lewis, Ed.). New York: Henry Holt.

Dudden, Faye E. (2011). *Fighting Chance: The Struggle Over Woman Suffrage and Black Suffrage in Reconstruction America*. New York: Oxford University Press.

Dunn, Stephane. (2008). *"Baad Bitches" and Sassy Supermamas: Black Power Action Films*. Urbana: University of Illinois Press.

Dunne, Andrew, and Marsh, James. (Directors). (2004). *Story of Gospel Music: The Power in the Voice*. Burbank, CA: BBC/Warner Home Video.

Durand, Alain-Philippe. (Ed.). (2002). *Black, Blanc, Beur: Rap Music and Hip Hop Culture in the Francophone World*. Lanham, MD: Scarecrow Press.

Dwyer, Claire, and Bressey, Caroline. (Eds.). (2008). *New Geographies of Race and Racism*. Burlington, VT: Ashgate.

Dyer, Joel. (2000). *Perpetual Prisoner Machine: How America Profits from Crime*. Boulder, CO: Westview.

Dyson, Michael Eric. (1993). *Reflecting Black: African American Cultural Criticism*. Minneapolis: University of Minnesota Press.

————. (1997). *Between God and Gangsta Rap: Bearing Witness to Black Culture*. New York: Oxford University Press.

————. (2002). *Holler If You Hear Me: Searching for Tupac Shakur*. New York: Basic Civitas.

————. (2005). *Is Bill Cosby Right?: Or Has the Black Middle Class Lost Its Mind?* New York: Basic Civitas.

————. (2006). *Come Hell or High Water: Hurricane Katrina and the Color of Disaster*. New York: Basic Civitas.

————. (2007). *Know What I Mean?: Reflections on Hip Hop*. New York: Basic Civitas.

Dyson, Michael Eric, and Daulatzai, Sohail. (Eds.). (2010). *Born to Use Mics: Reading Nas's Illmatic*. New York: Basic Civitas.

Earle, Susan Elizabeth. (Ed.). (2007). *Aaron Douglas: African American Modernist*. New Haven: Yale University Press.

Early, Gerald L. (2004). *One Nation Under a Groove: Motown and American Culture*. Ann Arbor: University of Michigan Press.

Eaton, Kalenda C. (2008). *Womanism, Literature, and the Transformation of the Black Community, 1965–1980*. New York: Routledge.

Echols, Alice. (2010). *Hot Stuff: Disco and the Remaking of American Culture*. New York: Norton.

Egar, Emmanuel E. (2003). *Black Women Poets of the Harlem Renaissance*. Lanham, MD: University of America Press.

Ehrman, John. (2005). *The Eighties: America in the Age of Reagan*. New Haven, CT: Yale University Press.

Eichengreen, Barry J. (2000). *From Benign Neglect to Malignant Preoccupation: U.S. Balance-of-Payments Policy in the 1960s*. Cambridge, MA: National Bureau of Economic Research.

Eiswerth, Joseph P. (1996). "Rap Music as Protest: A Rhetorical Analysis of Public Enemy's Lyrics." Master's thesis, University of Nevada, Las Vegas.

Elam, Harry J., and Jackson, Kennell A. (Eds.). (2005). *Black Cultural Traffic: Crossroads in Global Performance and Popular Culture*. Ann Arbor: University of Michigan Press.

Ellington, Duke. (1973). *Music Is My Mistress*. Garden City, NY: Doubleday.

————. (1993). *The Duke Ellington Reader* (Mark Tucker, Ed.). New York: Oxford University Press.

Ellison, Mary. (1989). *Lyrical Protest: Black Music's Struggle Against Discrimination*. New York: Praeger.

Ellison, Ralph W. (1943). "Editorial Comment." *Negro Digest* 1 (4): 300–1.
———. (1970). "What Would America Be Like Without Blacks?" *Time Magazine* (April 6): 54–55.
———. (1995). *Collected Essays of Ralph Ellison* (John F. Callahan, Ed.). New York: Modern Library.
———. (2001). *Living With Music: Ralph Ellison's Jazz Writings* (Robert G. O'Meally, Ed.). New York: Modern Library.
Emerson, Rana A. (2002). "'Where My Girls At?': Negotiating Black Womanhood in Music Videos." *Gender and Society* 16 (1): 115–35.
Entman, Robert M., and Rojecki, Andrew. (2000). *The Black Image in the White Mind: Media and Race in America*. Chicago: University of Chicago Press.
Epstein, Dena J. P. (2003). *Sinful Tunes and Spirituals: Black Folk Music to the Civil War*. Urbana: University of Illinois Press.
Erbsen, Wayne H. (1986). "The Seekers: The Beat Generation and Psychedelic Drugs." Master's thesis, University of Wisconsin, Madison.
Erenberg, Lewis A. (1998). *Swingin' the Dream: Big Band Jazz and the Rebirth of American Culture*. Chicago: University of Chicago Press.
Essed, Philomena, and Goldberg, David Theo. (Eds.). (2001). *Race Critical Theories: Texts and Contexts*. Malden, MA: Blackwell.
Eure, Joseph D., and Spady, James G. (Eds.). (1991). *Nation Conscious Rap: The Hip Hop Vision*. New York: PC International Press.
Evans, Mike. (1999). *Jazz Singers*. London: Hamlyn.
Evans, Nicholas M. (2000). *Writing Jazz: Race, Nationalism, and Modern Culture in the 1920s*. New York: Garland.
Ewens, Graeme. (1992). *Africa O-Ye!: A Celebration of African Music*. New York: Da Capo.
Fanon, Frantz. (1967). *Black Skin, White Masks*. New York: Grove.
———. (1968). *The Wretched of the Earth*. New York: Grove.
Fanusie, Fatimah. (2007). "Ahmadi, Beboppers, Veterans, and Migrants: African American Islam in Boston, 1948–1963." In Theodore Louis Trost (Ed.), *The African Diaspora and the Study of Religion* (67–97). New York: Macmillan.
Farmer, Paul. (2003). *Pathologies of Power: Health, Human Rights, and the New War on the Poor*. Berkeley: University of California Press.
Farrell, Walter C., and Johnson, Patricia A. (1981). "Poetic Interpretations of Urban Black Folk Culture: Langston Hughes and the 'Bebop' Era." *MELUS* 8 (3): 57–72.
Fauset, Jessie Redmon. (1924). *There is Confusion*. New York: Horace Liveright.
———. (1928). *Plum Bun: A Novel Without a Moral*. New York: Frederick A. Stokes Publishing.
———. (1931). *The Chinaberry Tree*. New York: Frederick A. Stokes Publishing.
Favor, Martin J. (1999). *Authentic Blackness: The Folk in the New Negro Movement*. Durham, NC: Duke University Press.
Feagin, Joe R., and Sikes, Melvin P. (1994). *Living with Racism: The Black Middle-Class Experience*. Boston: Beacon Press.
Feiereisen, Florence, and Hill, Alexandra M. (Eds.). (2011). *Germany in the Loud Twentieth Century: An Introduction*. Oxford: Oxford University Press.
Feinstein, Elaine. (1985). *Bessie Smith*. New York: Viking.
Feinstein, Sascha. (1997). *Jazz Poetry: From the 1920s to the Present*. Westport, CT: Greenwood.
Feinstein, Sascha, and Komunyakaa, Yusef. (Eds.). (1991). *The Jazz Poetry Anthology : First Set*. Bloomington: Indiana University Press.
———. (Eds.). (1996). *The Jazz Poetry Anthology: Second Set*. Bloomington: Indiana University Press.
Felisbret, Eric, and Felisbret, Luke. (2009). *Graffiti New York*. New York: Abrams.
Ferguson, Roderick A. (2004). *Aberrations in Black: Toward a Queer of Color Critique*. Minneapolis: University of Minnesota.
Fernandes, Sujatha. (2006). *Cuba Represent!: Cuban Arts, State Power, and the Making of New Revolutionary Cultures*. Durham, NC: Duke University Press.

Ferris, William. (2009). *Give My Poor Heart Ease: Voices of the Mississippi Blues*. Chapel Hill: University of North Carolina Press.

Fisher, Marc. (2007). *Something in the Air: Radio, Rock, and the Revolution that Shaped a Generation*. New York: Random House.

Fisher, Miles Mark. (Ed.). (1998). *Negro Slave Songs in the United States*. New York: Citadel.

Fitzgerald, F. Scott. (1922). *Tales of the Jazz Age*. New York: Scribner.

Fitzgerald, Kevin. (Director). (2004). *Freestyle: The Art of Rhyme*. New York: Palm Pictures.

Fleetwood, Nicole R. (2011). *Troubling Vision: Performance, Visuality, and Blackness*. Chicago: University of Chicago Press.

Flint, Colin. (Ed.). (2004). *Spaces of Hate: Geographies of Discrimination and Intolerance in the U.S.A.* New York: Routledge.

Flores, Juan. (2000). *From Bomba to Hip Hop: Puerto Rican Culture and Latino Identity*. New York: Columbia University Press.

Floyd, Kevin. (2009). *Reification of Desire: Toward a Queer Marxism*. Minneapolis: University of Minnesota Press.

Floyd, Samuel A. (1990). *Black Music in the Harlem Renaissance: A Collection of Essays*. New York: Greenwood.

———. (1995). *Power of Black Music: Interpreting its History from Africa to the United States*. New York: Oxford University Press.

Foley, Barbara. (2003). *Spectres of 1919: Class and Nation in the Making of the New Negro*. Urbana: University of Illinois Press.

Forman, Murray. (2002). *The Hood Comes First: Race, Space, and Place in Rap and Hip Hop*. Middletown, CT: Wesleyan University Press.

Forman, Murray, and Neal, Mark Anthony. (Eds.). (2012). *That's the Joint!: The Hip Hop Studies Reader* (2nd Edition). New York: Routledge.

Foucault, Michel. (1977a). *Language, Counter-Memory, Practice: Selected Essays and Interviews by Michel Foucault* (Donald F. Bouchard, Ed.). Ithaca: Cornell University Press.

———. (1977b). *Power/Knowledge: Selected Interviews and Other Writings, 1972–1977* (Colin Gordon, Ed.). New York: Pantheon.

———. (1988). *Politics, Philosophy, Culture: Interviews and Other Writings, 1977–1984* (Lawrence D. Kritzman, Ed.). New York: Routledge.

———. (1990a). *The History of Sexuality, Volume 1: The Will to Knowledge*. New York: Vintage.

———. (1990b). *The History of Sexuality, Volume 2: The Use of Pleasure*. New York: Vintage.

———. (1990c). *The History of Sexuality, Volume 3: The Care of the Self*. New York: Vintage.

Fox, Stephen R. (1970). *Guardian of Boston: Williams Monroe Trotter*. New York: Atheneum.

Franklin, Eric N., and Watkins, William H. (1984). *Breakdance*. Chicago: NTC/Contemporary Publishing.

Franklin, Vincent P. (1984). *Black Self-Determination: A Cultural History of the Faith of the Fathers*. Westport, CT: Lawrence Hill.

Frazier, E. Franklin. (1962). *The Black Bourgeoisie: The Rise of a New Middle-Class in the United States*. New York: Collier.

Fredrickson, George M. (1987). *The Black Image in the White Mind: The Debate on Afro-American Character and Destiny, 1817–1914*. Hanover, NH: Wesleyan University Press.

Freeland, David. (2001). *Ladies of Soul*. Jackson: University Press of Mississippi.

Freeman, Richard B., and Holzer, Harry J. (Eds.). (1986). *The Black Youth Employment Crisis*. Chicago: University of Chicago Press.

Fricke, Jim, and Ahearn, Charlie. (Eds.). (2002). *Yes Yes Y'all: The Experience Music Project Oral History of Hip-Hop's First Decade*. New York: Da Capo Press.

Friedwald, Will. (1996). *Jazz Singing: America's Great Voices from Bessie Smith to Bebop and Beyond*. New York: Da Capo.

———. (2010). *A Biographical Guide to the Great Jazz and Pop Singers*. New York: Pantheon.

Frost, Richard. (1999). "Jazz and Poetry." *Antioch Review* 57 (3): 386–401.

Fulop, Timothy, and Raboteau, Albert J. (Eds.). (1996). *African American Religion: Interpretive Essays in History and Culture*. New York: Routledge.

Fulwood, Sam. (1996). *Waking from the Dream: My Life in the Black Middle-Class*. New York: Anchor Books.

Gabbard, Krin. (2004). *Black Magic: White Hollywood and African American Culture*. New Brunswick, NJ: Rutgers University Press.

Gabbidon, Shaun L. (2010). *Race, Ethnicity, Crime, and Justice: An International Dilemma*. Los Angeles: Sage.

Gallagher, Charles A. (Ed.). (2008). *Racism in Post-Race America: New Theories, New Directions*. Chapel Hill, NC: Social Forces Publishing.

Gammond, Peter. (1975). *Scott Joplin and the Ragtime Era*. New York: St. Martin's.

Gamson, Joshua. (2005). *The Fabulous Sylvester: The Legend, the Music, the Seventies in San Francisco*. New York: Henry Holt.

Gan, Su-Lin, Zillmann, Dolf, and Mitrook, Michael. (1997). "Stereotyping Effect of Black Women's Sexual Rap on White Audiences." *Basic and Applied Social Psychology* 19 (3): 381–99.

Gans, Herbert J. (1995). *The War Against the Poor: The Underclass and Anti-Poverty Policy*. New York: Basic.

Gastman, Roger, and Neelon, Caleb. (2010). *The History of American Graffiti*. New York: Harper Design.

Gates, Henry Louis, Jr. (1988). *The Signifying Monkey: A Theory of African American Literary Criticism*. New York: Oxford University Press.

———. (1993). "The Black Man's Burden." In Michael Warner (Ed.), *Fear of a Queer Planet: Queer Politics and Social Theory* (230–39). Minneapolis: University of Minnesota Press.

Gates, Henry Louis, Jr., and Jarrett, Gene Andrew. (Eds.). (2007). *The New Negro: Readings in Race, Representation, and African American Culture, 1892–1938*. Princeton, NJ: Princeton University Press.

Gatewood, Willard B. (1990). *Aristocrats of Color: The Black Elite, 1880–1920*. Bloomington: Indiana University Press.

Gayle, Addison. (1972). *Claude McKay: The Black Poet at War*. Detroit: Broadside.

Genovese, Eugene D. (1992). *From Rebellion to Revolution: Afro-American Slave Revolts in the Making of the Modern World*. Baton Rouge: Louisiana State University Press.

George, Nelson. (1988). *The Death of Rhythm & Blues*. New York: Pantheon.

———. (1994). *Blackface: Reflections on African Americans and the Movies*. New York: HarperCollins.

———. (1999). *Hip Hop America*. New York: Viking.

———. (2007). *Where Did Our Love Go?: The Rise and Fall of the Motown Sound*. Urbana: University of Illinois Press.

George-Warren, Holly. (Ed.). (1999). *The Rolling Stone Book of the Beats: The Beat Generation and American Culture*. New York: Hyperion.

Gerard, Charley. (1998). *Jazz in Black and White: Race, Culture, and Identity in the Jazz Community*. Westport, CT: Greenwood.

Gere, Anne Ruggles. (1997). *Intimate Practices: Literacy and Cultural Work in U.S. Women's Clubs, 1880–1920*. Urbana: University of Illinois Press.

Gewirtz, Isaac. (2007). *Beatific Soul: Jack Kerouac on the Road*. London: Scala Publishers.

Giddings, Geoffrey Jahwara. (2003). *Contemporary Afrocentric Scholarship: Toward a Functional Cultural Philosophy*. Lewiston, NY: Mellen Press.

Giddings, Paula. (1984). *When and Where I Enter: The Impact of Black Women on Race and Sex in America*. New York: Quill.

Giddins, Gary. (1985). *Rhythm-a-ning: Jazz Tradition and Innovation in the '80s*. New York: Oxford University Press.

———. (1988). *Satchmo*. New York: Doubleday.

———. (1998). *Visions of Jazz: The First Century*. New York: Oxford University Press.

Giddins, Gary, and DeVeaux, Scott K. (2009). *Jazz*. New York: Norton.

Giles, James R. (1976). *Claude McKay*. Boston: Twayne.

Gillespie, Andra. (2010). *Whose Black Politics?: Cases in Post-Racial Black Leadership*. New York: Routledge.

Gillespie, Dizzy. (1979). *To Be, or Not . . . To Bop* (with Al Fraser). New York: Da Capo.

Gilmore, Glenda E. (1996). *Gender and Jim Crow: Women and the Politics of White Supremacy in North Carolina, 1896–1920*. Chapel Hill: University of North Carolina Press.

Gilroy, Paul. (1993). *Small Acts: Thoughts on the Politics of Black Cultures*. New York: Serpent's Tail.

Ginsberg, Allen. (1956). *Howl, and Other Poems*. San Francisco: City Lights Books.

Ginwright, Shawn A. (2004). *Black in School: Afrocentric Reform, Urban Youth & the Promise of Hip Hop Culture*. New York: Teachers College Press.

Gioia, Ted. (1988). *The Imperfect Art: Reflections on Jazz and Modern Culture*. New York: Oxford University Press.

———. (2011). *The History of Jazz*. New York: Oxford University Press.

Girshick, Lori B. (2002). *Woman-to-Woman Sexual Violence: Does She Call It Rape?* Boston: Northeastern University Press.

Gitler, Ira. (1985). *Swing to Bop: An Oral History of the Transition in Jazz in the 1940s*. New York: Oxford University Press.

———. (2001). *The Masters of Bebop*. New York: Da Capo.

Glasgow, Douglas G. (1981). *The Black Underclass: Poverty, Unemployment, and Entrapment of Ghetto Youth*. New York: Vintage.

Glaude, Eddie S., Jr. (Ed.). (2002). *Is it Nation Time?: Contemporary Essays on Black Power and Black Nationalism*. Chicago: University of Chicago Press.

Goeser, Caroline. (2007). *Picturing the New Negro: Harlem Renaissance Print Culture and Modern Black Identity*. Lawrence: University Press of Kansas.

Goff, Keli. (2008). *Party Crashing: How the Hip Hop Generation Declared Political Independence*. New York: Basic.

Gold, Robert S. (1957). "The Vernacular of the Jazz World." *American Speech* 32 (4): 271–82.

Goldberg, David Joseph. (1999). *Discontented America: The United States in the 1920s*. Baltimore: Johns Hopkins University Press.

Goldberg, David Theo. (Ed.). (1990). *Anatomy of Racism*. Minneapolis: University of Minnesota Press.

———. (1993). *Racist Culture: Philosophy and the Politics of Meaning*. Cambridge, MA: Blackwell.

———. (Ed.). (1994). *Multiculturalism: A Critical Reader*. Cambridge, MA: Blackwell.

———. (1997). *Racial Subjects: Writing on Race in America*. New York: Routledge.

———. (2001). *The Racial State*. Malden, MA: Blackwell.

———. (2008). *The Threat of Race: Reflections on Racial Neoliberalism*. Malden, MA: Blackwell.

Goldberg, David Theo, and Solomos, John. (Eds.). (2002). *A Companion to Racial and Ethnic Studies*. Malden, MA: Blackwell.

Goldschmidt, Henry. (2006). *Race and Religion Among the Chosen Peoples of Crown Heights*. New Brunswick, NJ: Rutgers University Press.

Gomez, Michael Angelo. (2005). *Black Crescent: The Experience and Legacy of African Muslims in the Americas*. New York: Cambridge University Press.

Gonzales-Day, Ken. (2006). *Lynching in the West, 1850–1935*. Durham: Duke University Press.

Goodall, Nataki H. (1994). "Depend on Myself: T.L.C. and the Evolution of Black Female Rap." *Journal of Negro History* 79 (1): 85–93.

Gooding-Williams, Robert. (Ed.). (1993). *Reading Rodney King/Reading Urban Uprising*. New York: Routledge.

Goodman, Jon. (Director). (2009). *Let Freedom Sing: How Music Inspired the Civil Rights Movement*. Fairfax, VA: Time-Life Video.

Goosman, Stuart L. (2005). *Group Harmony: The Black Urban Roots of Rhythm & Blues*. Philadelphia: University of Pennsylvania Press.

Gordon, Ann D., and Collier-Thomas, Bettye. (Eds.). (1997). *African American Women and the Vote, 1837–1965*. Amherst: University of Massachusetts Press.

Gossett, Thomas F. (1985). *Uncle Tom's Cabin and American Culture*. Dallas: Southern Methodist University Press.

Gourse, Leslie. (1984). *Louis' Children: American Jazz Singers*. New York: Morrow.

———. (1999). *Wynton Marsalis: Skain's Domain—A Biography*. New York: Schirmer..

Graham, Lawrence. (1999). *Our Kind of People: Inside America's Black Upper-Class*. New York: HarperCollins.

———. (2006). *The Senator and the Socialite: The True Story of America's First Black Dynasty*. New York: HarperCollins.

Grandt, Jürgen E. (2009). *Shaping Words to Fit the Soul: The Southern Ritual Grounds of Afro-Modernism*. Columbus: Ohio State University Press.

Grant, Elizabeth. (2002). "Gangsta Rap: The War on Drugs and the Location of African American Identity in Los Angeles, 1988–1992." *European Journal of American Culture* 21 (1): 4–15.

Grassian, Daniel. (2009). *Writing the Future of Black America: Literature of the Hip Hop Generation*. Columbia: University of South Carolina Press.

Gray, Cecil C. (2001). *Afrocentric Thought and Praxis: An Intellectual History*. Trenton, NJ: Africa World Press.

Gray, Herman S. (1995). *Watching Race: Television and the Struggle for "Blackness."* Minneapolis: University of Minnesota Press.

———. (2005). *Cultural Moves: African Americans and the Politics of Representation*. Berkeley: University of California Press.

Grazian, David. (2003). *Blue Chicago: The Search for Authenticity in Urban Blues Clubs*. Chicago: University of Chicago Press.

Green, Adam. (2009). *Selling the Race: Culture, Community, and Black Chicago, 1940–1955*. Chicago: University of Chicago Press.

Green, Harvey, and Perry, Mary-Ellen. (Eds.). (1983). *The Light of the Home: An Intimate View of the Lives of Women in Victorian America*. New York: Pantheon.

Green, Lisa J. (2002). *African American English: A Linguistic Introduction*. New York: Cambridge University Press.

Greene, Jasmin S. (2008). *Beyond Money, Cars, and Women: Examining Black Masculinity in Hip Hop Culture*. Newcastle, NE, UK: Cambridge Scholars.

Griffin, Ada G., and Parkerson, Michelle. (Directors.). (1996). *Litany for Survival: The Life and Work of Audre Lorde*. New York: Third World Newsreel.

Griffiths, David. (1998). *Hot Jazz: From Harlem to Storyville*. Lanham, MD: Scarecrow Press.

Grime, Kitty. (1983). *Jazz Voices*. New York: Quartet Books.

Grimes, Sara. (2000). *Backwater Blues: In Search of Bessie Smith*. Amherst, MA: Rose Island Publishing.

Grossman, James R. (1991). *Land of Hope: Chicago, Black Southerners, and the Great Migration*. Chicago: University of Chicago Press.

Guerrero, Ed. (1993). *Framing Blackness: The African American Image in Film*. Philadelphia: Temple University Press.

Gundaker, Grey. (1998). *Signs of Diaspora/Diaspora of Signs: Literacies, Creolization, and Vernacular Practice in African America*. New York: Oxford University Press.

Guralnick, Peter. (1986). *Sweet Soul Music: Rhythm & Blues and the Southern Dream of Freedom*. New York: Harper & Row.

———. (1989). *Lost Highway: Journeys & Arrivals of American Musicians*. New York: Harper & Row.

———. (1999). *Feel Like Going Home: Portraits in Blues & Rock 'n' Roll*. Boston: Little Brown.

Gushee, Lawrence. (2005). *Pioneers of Jazz: The Story of the Creole Band*. New York: Oxford University Press.

Guttentag, Bill, and Sturman, Dan. (Directors). (2010). *Soundtrack for a Revolution*. New York: Docurama Films/New Video.

Guy-Sheftall, Beverly. (1990). *Daughters of Sorrow: Attitudes Toward Black Women, 1880–1920*. Brooklyn, NY: Carlson.

————. (Ed.). (1995). *Words of Fire: An Anthology of African American Feminist Thought.* New York: Free Press.

Gwaltney, John Langston. (1980). *Drylongso: A Self-Portrait of Black America.* New York: Random House.

Hadley, Susan, and Yancy, George. (Eds.). (2011). *Therapeutic Uses of Rap and Hip Hop.* New York: Routledge.

Hagedorn, John. (2008). *World of Gangs: Armed Young Men and Gangsta Culture.* Minneapolis: University of Minnesota Press.

Hager, Steven. (1984). *Hip Hop: The Illustrated History of Break-Dancing, Rap Music, and Graffiti.* New York: St. Martin's.

Haggerty, George E., and McGarry, Molly. (Eds.). (2007). *Companion to Lesbian, Gay, Bisexual, Transgender, and Queer Studies.* Malden, MA: Blackwell.

Hahn, Steven. (2003). *A Nation Under Our Feet: Black Political Struggles in the Rural South, from Slavery to the Great Migration.* Cambridge, MA: Harvard University Press.

Haidarali, Laila. (1997). "'The Weird, Faded Glory of Black Girls': Deconstructing Black Female Sexuality in the Harlem Renaissance, 1920–1930." Master's thesis, University of Windsor, Canada.

Hajdu, David. (1996). *Lush Life: A Biography of Billy Strayhorn.* New York: Farrar, Straus & Giroux.

Halberstam, Judith. (1997). "Mack-Daddy, Superfly, Rapper: Gender, Race, and Masculinity in the Drag King Scene." *Social Text* 52/53: 104–31.

————. (1998). *Female Masculinity.* Durham: Duke University Press.

————. (2005). *In a Queer Time and Place: Transgender Bodies, Subcultural Lives.* New York: New York University Press.

Hall, Diane, Cassidy, Elaine, and Stevenson, Howard. (2008). "Acting 'Tough' in a 'Tough' World: An Examination of Fear Among Urban African American Adolescents." *Journal of Black Psychology* 34 (3): 381–98.

Hames-Garcia, Michael. (2001). "Can Queer Theory Be Critical Theory?" In William S. Wilkerson and Jeffrey Paris (Eds.), *New Critical Theory: Essays on Liberation* (201–22). Lanham, MD: Rowman & Littlefield.

Hamlet, Janice D. (1998). *Afrocentric Visions: Studies in Culture and Communication.* Thousand Oaks, CA: Sage.

Hampton, Robert L., Gullotta, Thomas P., and Crowel, Raymond L. (Eds.). (2010). *Handbook of African American Health.* New York: Guilford.

Hampton, Sylvia, and Nathan, David. (2004). *Nina Simone: Break Down and Let It All Out.* London: Sanctuary.

Hamrick, Kevin Robert. (1991). "'Fight the Power!': An Ideographic Analysis of the Rhetoric of Public Enemy." Master's thesis, Department of Speech Communication and Theater Arts, Wake Forest University.

Haney-López, Ian. (2003). *Racism on Trail: The Chicano Fight for Justice.* Cambridge, MA: Belknap.

Hannel, Susan L. (2002). "The Africana Craze in the Jazz Age: A Comparison of French and American Fashion, 1920–1940." Ph.D. dissertation, Ohio State University.

————. (2006). "'Africana' Textiles: Imitation, Adaptation, and Transformation During the Jazz Age." *Textile: The Journal of Cloth and Culture* 4 (1): 68–103.

Hannerz, Ulf. (1969). *Soulside: Inquiries into Ghetto Culture and Community.* New York: Columbia University Press.

Hannusch, Jeff. (1985). *I Hear You Knockin': The Sound of New Orleans Rhythm and Blues.* Ville Platte, LA: Swallow Publications.

————. (2001). *The Soul of New Orleans: A Legacy of Rhythm and Blues.* Ville Platte, LA: Swallow Publications.

Haralambos, Michael. (1975). *Soul Music: The Birth of a Sound in Black America.* New York: Da Capo.

Harding, Vincent. (1981). *There Is A River: The Black Struggle for Freedom in America.* New York: Harcourt Brace Jovanovich.

Harlan, Louis R. (1972). *Booker T. Washington: The Making of a Black Leader, 1856–1901*. New York: Oxford University Press.
———. (1982). "Booker T. Washington and the Politics of Accommodation." In John Hope Franklin and August Meier (Eds.), *Black Leaders of the Twentieth Century* (1–18). Chicago: University of Illinois Press.
———. (1983). *Booker T. Washington: The Wizard of Tuskegee, 1901–1915*. New York: Oxford University Press.
Harper, Michael S. (1970). *Dear John, Dear Coltrane*. Chicago: University of Illinois Press.
Harris, Angelique C. (2009). "Marginalization by the Marginalized: Race, Homophobia, Heterosexism, and 'the Problem of the 21st Century.'" *Journal of Gay and Lesbian Social Services* 21 (4): 430–48.
Harris, Cheryl I. (1993). "Whiteness as Property." *Harvard Law Review* 106 (8): 1707–91.
Harris, Dean A. (Ed.). (1995). *Multiculturalism From the Margins: Non-Dominant Voices on Difference and Diversity*. Westport, CT: Bergin & Garvey.
Harris, Keith M. (2006). *Boys, Boyz, Bois: An Ethics of Black Masculinity in Film and Popular Media*. New York: Routledge.
Harris, Leonard. (Ed.). (1999). *The Critical Pragmatism of Alain Locke: A Reader on Value, Theory, Aesthetics, Community, Culture, Race, and Education*. Lanham, MD: Rowman & Littlefield.
Harris, Leonard, and Molesworth, Charles. (2008). *Alain L. Locke: Biography of a Philosopher*. Chicago: University of Chicago Press.
Harris, Louis. (1973). *The Anguish of Change*. New York: Norton.
Harris, Oliver C. G. (1999). "Queer Shoulders, Queer Wheel: Homosexuality and Beat Textual Politics." *European Contributions to American Studies* 42: 221–40.
Harris, Paisley Jane. (1994). "I'm as Good as Any Woman in Your Town: The Interconnections of Gender, Race, and Class in the Blues of Ma Rainey and Bessie Smith." Master's thesis, University of Minnesota.
Harris-Perry, Melissa V. (2004). *Barbershops, Bibles, and BET: Everyday Talk and Black Political Thought*. Princeton: Princeton University Press.
———. (2011). *Sister Citizen: Shame, Stereotypes, and Black Women in America*. New Haven: Yale University Press.
Harrison, Alferdteen. (Ed.). (1991). *Black Exodus: The Great Migration from the American South*. Jackson: University Press of Mississippi.
Harrison, Anthony Kwame. (2009). *Hip Hop Underground: The Integrity and Ethics of Racial Identification*. Philadelphia: Temple University Press.
Harrison, Daphne Duval. (1988). *Black Pearls: Blues Queens of the 1920s*. New Brunswick, NJ: Rutgers University Press.
Hartman, Charles O. (1991). *Jazz Text: Voice and Improvisation in Poetry, Jazz, and Song*. Princeton: Princeton University Press.
Harvey, David. (1989). *The Urban Experience*. Baltimore: Johns Hopkins University Press.
———. (1996). *Justice, Nature, and the Geography of Difference*. Cambridge, MA: Blackwell.
———. (2006). *Spaces of Global Capitalism*. New York: Verso.
———. (2009). *Social Justice and the City*. Athens: University of Georgia Press.
Hasse, John Edward. (1985). *Ragtime: Its History, Composers, and Music*. New York: Schirmer.
———. (1993). *Beyond Category: The Life and Genius of Duke Ellington*. New York: Simon & Schuster.
———. (2000). *Jazz: The First Century*. New York: Morrow.
Haugen, Jason D. (1998). "Some Socio-Cultural Functions of Deixis in Gangsta Rap Discourse." *Texas Linguistic Forum* 42: 145–57.
———. (2003). "'Unladylike Divas': Language, Gender, and Female Gangsta Rappers." *Popular Music & Society* 26 (4): 429–44.
Haupt, Adam. (2008). *Stealing Empire: P2P, Intellectual Property and Hip Hop Subversion*. Cape Town: Human Sciences Research Council.
Hayes, Eileen M. (2010). *Songs in Black and Lavender: Race, Sexual Politics, and Women's Music*. Urbana: University of Illinois Press.

Hayes, Eileen M., and Williams, Linda F. (Eds.). (2007). *Black Women and Music: More Than the Blues*. Urbana: University of Illinois Press.

Hayes, Reginald B. (2008). *Evolution of the Club and Juke Joints In America: A Social Renaissance*. New York: BookSurge Publishing.

Hazzard-Gordon, Katrina. (1990). *Jookin': The Rise of Social Dance Formations in African American Culture*. Philadelphia: Temple University Press.

Heilmann, Ann. (Ed.). (2003). *Feminist Forerunners: New Womanism and Feminism in the Early Twentieth Century*. Chicago: Pandora.

Heise, Thomas. (2011). *Urban Underworlds: A Geography of Twentieth Century American Literature and Culture*. New Brunswick, NJ: Rutgers University Press.

Hendershott, Heidi A. (2004). "School of Rap: The Politics and Pedagogies of Rap Music." Ph.D. dissertation, Pennsylvania State University.

Henderson, Stephen. (1973). *Understanding the New Black Poetry: Black Speech and Black Music as Poetic References*. New York: Morrow.

Hendricks, Wanda A. (1998). *Gender, Race, and Politics in the Midwest: Black Clubwomen in Illinois*. Bloomington: Indiana University Press.

Hennessey, Thomas J. (1994). *From Jazz to Swing: African American Jazz Musicians and Their Music, 1890–1935*. Detroit: Wayne State University Press.

Henriques, Julian. (2011). *Sonic Bodies: Reggae Sound Systems, Performance Techniques, and Ways of Knowing*. New York: Continuum.

Herek, Gregory M. (Ed.). (1998). *Stigma and Sexual Orientation: Understanding Prejudice Against Lesbians, Gay Men, and Bisexuals*. Thousand Oaks, CA: Sage.

Hersch, Charles. (2007). *Subversive Sounds: Race and the Birth of Jazz in New Orleans*. Chicago: University of Chicago Press.

Hess, Mickey. (2005). "Metal Faces, Rap Masks: Identity and Resistance in Hip Hop's Persona Artist." *Popular Music & Society* 28 (3): 297–311.

———. (Ed.). (2007a). *Icons of Hip Hop: An Encyclopedia of the Movement, Music, and Culture*. Westport, CT: Greenwood.

———. (2007b). *Is Hip Hop Dead?: The Past, Present, and Future of America's Most Wanted Music*. Westport, CT: Praeger.

———. (2010). *Hip Hop in America: A Regional Guide* (2 Volumes). Santa Barbara, CA: Greenwood.

Hewitt, Nancy A. (Ed.). (2010). *No Permanent Waves: Recasting Histories of U.S. Feminism*. New Brunswick, NJ: Rutgers University Press.

Higginbotham, Evelyn Brooks. (1993). *Righteous Discontent: The Women's Movement in the Black Baptist Church, 1880–1920*. Cambridge, MA: Harvard University Press.

Higgins, Dalton. (2009). *Hip Hop World*. Berkeley, CA: Groundwood Books.

Hilfiker, David. (2002). *Urban Injustice: How Ghettos Happen*. New York: Seven Stories Press.

Hill, Marc Lamont. (2009). *Beats, Rhymes, and Classroom Life: Hip Hop Pedagogy and the Politics of Identity*. New York: Teachers College Press.

Hilmes, Michele, and Loviglio, Jason. (Eds.). (2002). *Radio Reader: Essays in the Cultural History of Radio*. New York: Routledge.

Hindman, Matthew S. (2009). *The Myth of Digital Democracy*. Princeton: Princeton University Press.

Hinds, Selwyn Seyfu. (2002). *Gunshots in My Cook-up: Bits and Bites from a Hip Hop Caribbean Life*. New York: Atria Books.

Hine, Darlene Clark. (Ed.). (1990a). *Black Women in American History: From Colonial Times Through the Nineteenth Century* (Vols. 1–4). Brooklyn, NY: Carlson.

———. (Ed.). (1990b). *Black Women in American History: The Twentieth Century* (Vols. 5–8). Brooklyn, NY: Carlson.

Hine, Darlene Clark, and Gaspar, David B. (Eds). (1996). *More Than Chattel: Black Women and Slavery in the Americas*. Bloomington: Indiana University Press.

———. (Eds.). (2004). *Beyond Bondage: Free Women of Color in the Americas*. Urbana: University of Illinois Press.

Hine, Darlene Clark, and Jenkins, Earnestine. (Eds.). (1999). *A Question of Manhood: A Reader in U.S. Black Men's History and Masculinity* (Volume 1). Bloomington: Indiana University Press.

———. (Eds.). (2001). *A Question of Manhood: A Reader in U.S. Black Men's History and Masculinity* (Volume 2). Bloomington: Indiana University Press.

Hine, Darlene Clark, King, Wilma, and Reed, Linda. (Eds.). (1995). *We Specialize in the Wholly Impossible: A Reader in Black Women's History*. Brooklyn: Carlson.

Hine, Darlene Clark, and Thompson, Kathleen. (1998). *A Shining Thread of Hope: The History of Black Women in America*. New York: Broadway Books.

Hinton, Alex. (Director). (2006). *Pick Up the Mic!: The (R)Evolution of the Homo-Hop Movement*. Los Angeles: Planet Janice/Rhino Films.

Hirsch, Arnold R., and Logsdon, Joseph. (Eds.). (1992). *Creole New Orleans: Race and Americanization*. Baton Rouge: Louisiana State University Press.

Hisama, Ellie M., and Rapport, Evan. (2005). *Critical Minded: New Approaches to Hip Hop Studies*. Brooklyn, NY: Institute for Studies in American Music.

Hobsbawm, Eric John. (1993). *The Jazz Scene*. New York: Pantheon.

Hobson, Janell. (2003). "The 'Batty' Politic: Toward an Aesthetic of the Black Female Body." *Hypatia* 18 (4): 87–105.

Holcomb, Gary E. (2007). *Claude McKay, Code Name Sasha: Queer Black Marxism and the Harlem Renaissance*. Gainesville: University Press of Florida.

Honey, Maureen. (Ed.). (1989). *Shadowed Dreams: Women's Poetry of the Harlem Renaissance*. New Brunswick, NJ: Rutgers University Press.

hooks, bell. (1981). *Ain't I A Woman: Black Women and Feminism*. Boston: South End.

———. (1984). *Feminist Theory: From Margin to Center*. Boston: South End.

———. (1989). *Talking Back: Thinking Feminist, Thinking Black*. Boston: South End.

———. (1990). *Yearning: Race, Gender, and Cultural Politics*. Boston: South End.

———. (1991). *Black Looks: Race and Representation*. Boston: South End.

———. (1994a). *Outlaw Culture: Resisting Representation*. New York: Routledge.

———. (1994b). *Teaching to Transgress: Education as the Practice of Freedom*. New York: Routledge.

———. (2000a). *Where We Stand: Class Matters*. New York: Routledge.

———. (2000b). *Feminism is for Everybody: Passionate Politics*. New York: Routledge.

———. (2004a). *We Real Cool: Black Men and Masculinity*. New York: Routledge.

———. (2004b). *The Will to Change: Men, Masculinity, and Love*. New York: Atria.

Hopkinson, Natalie, and Moore, Natalie Y. (2006). *Deconstructing Tyrone: A New Look at Black Masculinity in the Hip Hop Generation*. San Francisco: Cleis Press.

Horne, Gerald. (1995). *Fire This Time: The Watts Uprising and the 1960s*. Charlottesville: University Press of Virginia.

Hornsby, Alton. (Ed.). (2005). *A Companion to African American History*. Malden, MA: Blackwell.

Horricks, Raymond. (1984). *Dizzy Gillespie and the Bebop Revolution*. New York: Hippocrene.

Hoskyns, Barney. (1987). *Say It One Time for the Broken-Hearted: The Country Side of Southern Soul*. London: Fontana Collins.

Houde, Mary Jean. (1989). *Reaching Out: A Story of the General Federation of Women's Clubs*. Chicago: Mobium Press.

Howland, John Louis. (2009). *"Ellington Uptown": Duke Ellington, James P. Johnson & the Birth of Concert Jazz*. Ann Arbor: University of Michigan Press.

Hudson, Cheryl, and Davies, Gareth. (Eds.). (2008). *Ronald Reagan and the 1980s: Perceptions, Policies, Legacies*. New York: Macmillan.

Hudson-Weems, Clenora. (1995). *Africana Womanism: Reclaiming Ourselves*. Boston: Bedford.

———. (2004). *Africana Womanist Literary Theory*. Trenton, NJ: Africa World Press.

Huggins, Nathan I. (1971). *The Harlem Renaissance*. New York: Oxford University Press.

———. (Ed.). (1976). *Voices from the Harlem Renaissance*. New York: Oxford University Press.

Hughes, Langston. (1926). *The Weary Blues*. New York: Knopf.
———. (1927). *Fine Clothes to the Jew*. New York: Knopf.
———. (1942). *Shakespeare in Harlem*. New York: Knopf.
———. (1951). *Montage of a Dream Deferred*. New York: Holt.
———. (1961). *Ask Your Mama: 12 Moods for Jazz*. New York: Knopf.
———. (1973). *Good Morning Revolution: Uncollected Social Protest Writings* (Faith Berry, Ed.). New York: Lawrence Hill Books.
———. (1997). "The Negro Artist and the Racial Mountain." In William L. Van Deburg (Ed.), *Modern Black Nationalism: From Marcus Garvey to Louis Farrakhan* (52–58). New York: New York University Press.
Hughes, Langston, and Mingus, Charles. (1958). *Weary Blues*. New York: Verve.
Hull, Gloria T. (1987). *Color, Sex & Poetry: Three Women Writers of the Harlem Renaissance*. Bloomington: Indiana University Press.
Hull, Gloria T., Scott, Patricia Bell, and Smith, Barbara. (Eds.). (1982). *All the Women Are White, All the Blacks Are Men, But Some of Us Are Brave: Black Women's Studies*. New York: Feminist Press.
Hunter, Marcus Anthony. (2010). "The Nightly Round: Space, Social Capital, and Urban Black Nightlife." *City and Community* 9 (2): 165–86.
Hunter, Tera W. (1997). *To 'Joy My Freedom: Southern Black Women's Lives and Labors After the Civil War*. Cambridge, MA: Harvard University Press.
Huntington, Carla S. (2007). *Hip Hop Dance: Meanings and Messages*. Jefferson, NC: McFarland & Co.
Hurston, Zora Neale. (1937). *Their Eyes Were Watching God: A Novel*. Philadelphia: Lippincott.
———. (1942). *Dust Tracks on a Road: An Autobiography*. Philadelphia: Lippincott.
———. (1979). *I Love Myself When I Am Laughing . . . And Then When I Am Looking Mean and Impressive: A Zora Neale Hurston Reader* (Alice Walker, Ed.). Old Westbury, NY: Feminist Press.
Hurt, R. Douglas. (Ed.). (2003). *African American Life in the Rural South, 1900–1950*. Columbia: University of Missouri Press.
Hutchinson, George. (1995). *The Harlem Renaissance in Black and White*. Cambridge, MA: Harvard University Press.
———. (Ed.). (2007). *The Cambridge Companion to the Harlem Renaissance*. Cambridge: Cambridge University Press.
Ifill, Sherrilyn A. (2007). *On the Courthouse Lawn: Confronting the Legacy of Lynching in the Twenty-First Century*. Boston: Beacon.
Imes, Birney. (2003). *Juke Joint*. Jackson: University Press of Mississippi.
Inciardi, James A. (Ed.). (1980). *Racial Criminology: The Coming Crises*. Beverly Hills: Sage.
Ipiotis, Celia. (Director). (1984). *Popular Culture in Dance: the World of Hip Hop*. New York: ARC Videodance.
Irvin, Dona L. (1992). *The Unsung Heart of Black America: A Middle-Class Church at Mid-Century*. Columbia, MO: University of Missouri Press.
Island, David, and Letellier, Patrick. (1991). *Men Who Beat the Men Who Love Them: Battered Gay Men and Domestic Violence*. New York: Harrington Park Press.
Israel. (Director). (2002). *The Freshest Kids: A History of the B-Boy*. Los Angeles: QD3 Entertainment.
Iton, Richard. (2008). *In Search of the Black Fantastic: Politics and Popular Culture in the Post–Civil Rights Era*. New York: Oxford University Press.
Izant, Eric M. (2008). "Altered States of Style: The Drug-Induced Development of Jack Kerouac's Spontaneous Prose." Master's thesis, Department of English, Brigham Young University.
Jackson, Buzzy. (2005). *A Bad Woman Feeling Good: Blues and the Women Who Sing Them*. New York: Norton.
Jackson, John A. (2004). *House on Fire: The Rise and Fall of Philadelphia Soul*. New York: Oxford University Press.
Jackson, Oscar A. (1995). *Bronzeville: A History of Chicago Rhythm & Blues*. Chicago: Heno.

Jackson, Ronald L. (2006). *Scripting the Black Masculine Body: Identity, Discourse, and Racial Politics in Popular Media*. Albany: State University of New York Press.

Jackson, Ronald L., and Hopson, Mark C. (Eds.). (2011). *Masculinity in the Black Imagination: Politics of Communicating Race and Manhood*. New York: Lang.

Jackson, Sherman A. (2005). *Islam and the Black American: Looking Toward the Third Resurrection*. New York: Oxford University Press.

James, G. Winston. (Ed.). (2007). *Voices Rising: Celebrating 20 Years of Black Lesbian, Gay, Bisexual & Transgender Writing*. Washington, DC: RedBone Press.

James, Stanlie M., Foster, Frances Smith, and Guy-Sheftall, Beverly. (Eds.). (2009). *Still Brave: The Evolution of Black Women's Studies*. New York: Feminist Press.

James, Winston. (1998). *Holding Aloft the Banner of Ethiopia: Caribbean Radicalism in Early Twentieth-Century America*. New York: Verso.

———. (2000). *Fierce Hatred of Injustice: Claude McKay's Jamaica and His Poetry of Rebellion*. New York: Verso.

Jeffries, Michael P. (2011). *Thug Life: Race, Gender, and the Meaning of Hip Hop*. Chicago: University of Chicago Press.

Jemie, Onwuchekwa. (1976). *Langston Hughes: An Introduction to the Poetry*. New York: Columbia University Press.

Jenkins, Henry. (2006). *Convergence Culture: Where Old and New Media Collide*. New York: New York University Press.

———. (2009). *Confronting the Challenges of Participatory Culture: Media Education for the 21st Century*. Cambridge, MA: Massachusetts Institute of Technology Press.

Jenkins, Maude T. (1984). "The History of the Black Women's Club Movement in America." Ed.D. dissertation, Teachers College, Columbia University.

Jenkins, Todd S. (Eds.). (2004). *Free Jazz and Free Improvisation: An Encyclopedia*. Westport, CT: Greenwood.

Jewell, Derek. (1977). *Duke: A Portrait of Duke Ellington*. New York: Norton.

Jiménez, Gabriela. (2011). "'Something 2 Dance 2': Electro Hop in 1980s Los Angeles and Its Afro-Futurist Link." *Black Music Research Journal* 31 (1): 131–44.

Johnson, Cedric. (2007). *Revolutionaries to Race Leaders: Black Power and the Making of African American Politics*. Minneapolis: University of Minnesota Press.

Johnson, E. Patrick. (2003). *Appropriating Blackness: Performance and the Politics of Authenticity*. Durham, NC: Duke University Press.

———. (2008). *Sweet Tea: Black Gay Men of the South*. Chapel Hill: University of North Carolina Press.

Johnson, E. Patrick, and Henderson, Mae G. (Eds.). (2005). *Black Queer Studies: A Critical Anthology*. Durham, NC: Duke University Press.

Johnson, James Weldon. (1912). *The Autobiography of an Ex-Colored Man*. New York: Sherman, French & Co.

———. (1917). *Fifty Years & Other Poems*. Boston: Cornhill.

———. (1927). *God's Trombones: Seven Negro Sermons in Verse*. New York: Viking.

———. (2000). *The Complete Poems* (Sondra K. Wilson, Ed.). New York: Penguin.

Johnson, James Weldon, and Johnson, J. Rosamond. (Ed.). (2002). *The Books of American Negro Spirituals: Including the Book of American Negro Spirituals and the Second Book of Negro Spirituals*. New York: Da Capo.

Johnson, Joan Marie. (2004). *Southern Ladies, New Women: Race, Region, and Clubwomen in South Carolina, 1890–1930*. Gainesville: University Press of Florida.

Johnson, Marilynn S. (1998). "Gender, Race, and Rumours: Re-Examining the 1943 Race Riots." *Gender & History* 10 (2): 252–77.

Jones, Charisse, and Shorter-Gooden, Kumea. (2003). *Shifting: The Double-Lives of Black Women in America*. New York: HarperCollins.

Jones, Howard. (1987). *American Abolition, Law, and Diplomacy*. New York: Oxford University Press.

Jones, Jacqueline. (1985). *Labor of Love, Labor of Sorrow: Black Women, Work and the Family from Slavery to the Present*. New York: Basic.

Jones, Max, and Chilton, John. (1971). *Louis: The Louis Armstrong Story, 1900–1971*. Boston: Little, Brown.

Jones, Meta DuEwa. (2011). *The Muse is Music: Jazz Poetry from the Harlem Renaissance to Spoken Word*. Urbana: University of Illinois Press.

Jones, Nikki. (2010). *Between Good and Ghetto: African American Girls and Inner-City Violence*. New Brunswick, NJ: Rutgers University Press.

Jones, Steve, and Gundersen, Edna. (2007). "Can Rap Regain Its Crown?" *USA Today* (June 15): 1–6. Retrieved from www.usatoday.com/life/music/news/2007-06-14-rap-decline_N.htm.

Jordan, Matthew F. (2010). *Le Jazz: Jazz and French Cultural Identity*. Urbana: University of Illinois Press.

Jordan, Winthrop D. (1968). *White Over Black: American Attitudes Toward the Negro, 1550–1812*. Chapel Hill: University of North Carolina Press.

Joseph, Peniel E. (Ed.). (2006a). *Black Power Movement: Rethinking the Civil Rights–Black Power Era*. New York: Routledge.

———. (2006b). *Waiting 'Til the Midnight Hour: A Narrative History of Black Power in America*. New York: Henry Holt.

Jost, Ekkehard. (1981). *Free Jazz*. New York: Da Capo.

Judy, R. A. T. (1994). "On the Question of Nigga Authenticity." *boundary 2* 21 (3): 211–30.

Jung, Patricia B., and Smith, Ralph F. (1993). *Heterosexism: An Ethical Challenge*. Albany: State University of New York.

Junn, Jane, and Haynie, Kerry L. (Eds.). (2008). *New Race Politics in America: Understanding Minority and Immigrant Politics*. New York: Cambridge University Press.

Kalamka, Juba, and West, Tim'm. (2006). "It's All One: A Conversation." In Jeff Chang (Ed.), *Total Chaos: The Art and Aesthetics of Hip Hop* (198–208). New York: Basic/Civitas.

Kaplicer, Brett I. (2001). "Rap Music and De Minimis Copying: Applying the Ringgold and Sandoval Approach to Digital Samples." *Communication Abstracts* 24 (2): 155–296.

Kaschak, Ellyn. (2001). *Intimate Betrayal: Domestic Violence in Lesbian Relationships*. Binghamton, NY: Haworth Press.

Kater, Michael H. (1992). *Different Drummers: Jazz in the Culture of Nazi Germany*. New York: Oxford University Press.

Kato, M. T. (2007). *From Kung Fu to Hip Hop: Globalization, Revolution, and Popular Culture*. Albany: State University of New York Press.

Katz, Michael B. (1989). *The Undeserving Poor: From the War on Poverty to the War Welfare*. New York: Pantheon.

Kaya, Ayhan. (2001). *Sicher in Kreuzberg/Constructing Diasporas: Turkish Hip Hop Youth in Berlin*. Piscataway, NJ: Transaction Publishers.

Keil, Charles. (1991). *Urban Blues*. Chicago: University of Chicago Press.

Kelley, Robin D.G. (1997). *Yo' Mama's Disfunktional!: Fighting the Culture Wars in Urban America*. Boston: Beacon.

———. (2002). *Freedom Dreams: The Black Radical Imagination*. Boston: Beacon.

Kelley, Robin D. G., and Lewis, Earl. (Ed.). (2000). *To Make Our World Anew: A History of African Americans*. New York: Oxford University Press.

Kempton, Arthur. (2003). *Boogaloo: The Quintessence of American Popular Music*. New York: Pantheon.

Kennedy, Randall. (2002). *Nigger: The Strange Career of a Troublesome Word*. New York: Pantheon.

Kennedy, Rick. (1994). *Jelly Roll, Bix, and Hoagy: Gennett Studios and the Birth of Recorded Jazz*. Bloomington: Indiana University Press.

Kerouac, Jack. (1957). *On the Road*. New York: Viking.

———. (1958). "Aftermath: The Philosophy of the Beat Generation." *Esquire Magazine* (March): 24–25.

———. (2007). *The Portable Jack Kerouac* (Ann Charters, Ed.). New York: Penguin.

Keyes, Cheryl L. (2000). "Empowering Self, Making Choices, Creating Spaces: Black Female Identity via Rap Music Performance." *Journal of American Folklore* 113 (449): 255–69.

———. (2002). *Rap Music and Street Consciousness*. Urbana: University of Illinois Press.

King, Deborah K. (1988). "Multiple Jeopardy, Multiple Consciousness: The Context of a Black Feminist Ideology." *Signs* 14 (1): 42–72.

Kirchner, Bill. (Ed.). (2000). *The Oxford Companion to Jazz*. New York: Oxford University Press.

Kirschke, Amy Helene. (1995). *Aaron Douglas: Art, Race, and the Harlem Renaissance*. Jackson: University Press of Mississippi.

———. (2007). *Art in Crisis: W.E.B. Du Bois and the Struggle for African Identity and Memory*. Bloomington: Indiana University Press.

Kitwana, Bakari. (1994). *The Rap on Gangsta Rap, Who Run It?: Gangsta Rap and Visions of Black Violence*. Chicago: Third World Press.

———. (2002). *The Hip Hop Generation: Young Blacks and the Crisis in African American Culture*. New York: Basic/Civitas.

———. (2005). *Why White Kids Love Hip Hop: Wangstas, Wiggers, Wannabes, and the New Reality of Race in America*. New York: Basic/Civitas.

Kline, Wendy. (2001). *Building a Better Race: Gender, Sexuality, and Eugenics from the Turn of the Century to the Baby Boom*. Berkeley: University of California Press.

Knight, Michael Muhammad. (2007). *The Five Percenters: Islam, Hip Hop, and the Gods of New York*. Oxford: Oneworld.

Knopf, Terry Ann. (2006). *Rumors, Race, and Riots*. New Brunswick, NJ: Transaction.

Knupfer, Anne Meis. (1996). *Toward a Tender Humanity and a Nobler Womanhood: African American Women's Clubs in Turn-of-the-Century Chicago*. New York: New York University Press.

———. (2006). *The Chicago Black Renaissance and Women's Activism*. Urbana: University of Illinois Press.

Koch, Lawrence O. (1988). *Yardbird Suite: A Compendium of the Music and Life of Charlie Parker*. Bowling Green, OH: Bowling Green State University Press.

Koehler, Lyle. (1980). *A Search for Power: The "Weaker Sex" in Seventeenth Century New England*. Urbana: University of Illinois Press.

Kofsky, Frank. (1970). *Black Nationalism and the Revolution in Music*. New York: Pathfinder.

———. (2008). (1998). *John Coltrane and the Jazz Revolution of the 1960s*. New York: Pathfinder.

———. (2008). *Black Music, White Business: Illuminating the History and Political Economy of Jazz*. New York: Pathfinder.

Kolawole, Mary Ebun Modupe. (1997). *Womanism and African Consciousness*. Trenton, NJ: Africa World Press.

Komunyakaa, Yusef. (2002). "Langston Hughes + Poetry = The Blues." *Callaloo* 25 (4): 1140–43.

Korall, Burt. (2002). *Drummin' Men: The Heartbeat of Jazz: The Bebop Years*. New York: Oxford University Press.

Kornweibel, Theodore. (1975). *No Crystal Stair: Black Life and the Messenger, 1917–1928*. Westport, CT: Greenwood.

———. (1998). *Seeing Red: Federal Campaigns Against Black Militancy*. Bloomington: Indiana University Press.

———. (2002). *"Investigate Everything": Federal Efforts to Compel Black Loyalty During World War I*. Bloomington: Indiana University Press.

Koven, Mikel J. (2001). *The Pocket Essential Blaxploitation Films*. Harpenden, UK: Pocket Essentials.

———. (2010). *Blaxploitation Films*. Harpenden, UK: Kamera.

Krims, Adam. (2000). *Rap Music and the Poetics of Identity*. Cambridge: Cambridge University Press.

Kubik, Gerhard. (1999). *Africa and the Blues*. Jackson: University Press of Mississippi.

Kugelberg, Johan. (Ed.). (2007). *Born in the Bronx: A Visual Record of the Early Days of Hip Hop*. New York: Rizzoli.

Lacy, Karyn R. (2007). *Blue-Chip Black: Race, Class, and Status in the New Black Middle-Class*. Berkeley: University of California Press.

LaFollette, Marcel C. (2008). *Science on the Air: Popularizers and Personalities on Radio and Early Television*. Chicago: University of Chicago Press.

Lake, Obiagele. (1998). *Rastafari Women: Subordination in the Midst of Liberation Theology*. Durham, NC: Carolina Academic Press.

Lamothe, Daphne M. (2008). *Inventing the New Negro: Narrative, Culture, and Ethnography*. Philadelphia: University of Pennsylvania Press.

Landry, Bart. (1987). *The New Black Middle-Class*. Berkeley: University of California Press.

Lane, Nikki. (2011). "Black Women Queering the Mic: Missy Elliott Disturbing the Boundaries of Racialized Sexuality and Gender." *Journal of Homosexuality* 58 (6–7): 775–92.

Lapiower, Alain. (1997). *Total Respect: La Generation Hip Hop en Belgique*. Brussels: Fondation Jacques Gueux/EVO.

Laraña, Enrique, Johnston, Hank, and Gusfield, Joseph R. (Eds.). (1994). *New Social Movements: From Ideology to Identity*. Philadelphia: Temple University Press.

Larsen, Jane Kathrine. (2006). "Sexism and Misogyny in American Hip Hop Culture." Ph.D. dissertation, University of Oslo.

Lawlor, William. (Ed.). (2005). *Beat Culture: Icons, Lifestyles, and Impact*. Santa Barbara, CA: ABC-CLIO.

Lawrence, Novotny. (2007). *Blaxploitation Films of the 1970s: Blackness and Genre*. New York: Routledge.

Lawson, R. A. (2010). *Jim Crow's Counterculture: The Blues and Black Southerners, 1890–1945*. Baton Rouge: Louisiana State University Press.

Lee, Benson. (Director). (2008). *Planet B-Boy: Break-Dancing Has Evolved*. New York: Arts Alliance America.

Lees, Gene. (1994). *Cats of Any Color: Jazz Black and White*. New York: Oxford University Press.

Leland, John. (2004). *Hip: The History*. New York: HarperCollins.

Lemann, Nicholas. (1991). *The Promised Land: The Great Black Migration and How It Changed America*. New York: Vintage.

Lemelle, Anthony J. (2010). *Black Masculinity and Sexual Politics*. New York: Routledge.

Leonard, Neil. (1962). *Jazz and the White Americans: The Acceptance of a New Art Form*. Chicago: University of Chicago Press.

———. (1986). "The Jazzman's Verbal Usage." *Black American Literature Forum* 20 (1/2): 151–60.

Leur, Walter van de. (2002). *Something to Live For: The Music of Billy Strayhorn*. New York: Oxford University Press.

Levine, Lawrence. (1977). *Black Culture and Black Consciousness: Afro-American Folk Thought from Slavery to Freedom*. New York: Oxford University Press.

Lewis, David Levering. (1989). *When Harlem Was In Vogue*. New York: Oxford University Press.

———. (1993). *W.E.B. Du Bois: Biography of a Race, 1868–1919*. New York: Henry Holt.

———. (Ed). (1994). *The Portable Harlem Renaissance Reader*. New York: Viking.

———. (2000). *W.E.B. Du Bois: The Fight for Equality and the American Century, 1919–1963*. New York: Henry Holt.

Lewis, George. (2008). *A Power Stronger Than Itself: The AACM and American Experimental Music*. Chicago: University of Chicago Press.

Lewis, Pete. (2009). "Guru & MC Solar Interview." *Blues & Soul* (May). Retrieved from www.bluesandsoul.com/feature/411/guru_and_solar_team_talk/.

Lewis, Robert M. (2003). *From Traveling Show to Vaudeville: Theatrical Spectacle in America, 1830–1910*. Baltimore, MD: Johns Hopkins University Press.

Lhamon, W. T. (1998). *Raising Cain: Blackface Performance from Jim Crow to Hip Hop*. Cambridge, MA: Harvard University Press.

———. (Ed.). (2003). *Jump Jim Crow: Lost Plays, Lyrics, and Street Prose of the First Atlantic Popular Culture*. Cambridge, MA: Harvard University Press.

Lieb, Sandra R. (1981). *Mother of the Blues: A Study of Ma Rainey*. Amherst: University of Massachusetts Press.

Light, Alan. (Ed.). (1999). *The Vibe History of Hip Hop*. New York: Random House.

Lincoln, Eric C., and Mamiya, Lawrence H. (Ed.). (1990). *The Black Church in the African American Experience*. Durham, NC: Duke University Press.

Linden, Amy. (2004). "The Last Maverick: Me'Shell Ndegeocello and the Burden of Vision." In Kandia Crazy Horse (Ed.), *Rip It Up: The Black Experience in Rock 'n' Roll* (185–89). New York: Macmillan.

Linnemann, Russell J. (Ed.). (1982). *Alain Locke: Reflections on a Modern Renaissance Man*. Baton Rouge: Louisiana State University Press.

Lipsitz, George. (1990a). "Listening to Learn and Learning to Listen: Popular Culture, Cultural Theory, and American Studies." *American Quarterly* 42 (4): 615–36.

———. (1990b). *Time Passages: Collective Memory and American Popular Culture*. Minneapolis: University of Minnesota Press.

———. (1994). *Dangerous Crossroads: Popular Music, Postmodernism, and the Poetics of Place*. New York: Verso.

Litwack, Leon F. (1979). *Been in the Storm So Long: The Aftermath of Slavery*. New York: Vintage.

———. (1998). *Trouble in Mind: Black Southerners in the Age of Jim Crow*. New York: Knopf.

Litweiler, John. (1984). *The Freedom Principle: Jazz after 1958*. New York: Morrow.

———. (1992). *Ornette Coleman: A Harmolodic Life*. New York: Morrow.

Locke, Alain L. (Ed.). (1925). *The New Negro*. New York: Boni.

———. (1936). *Negro Art: Past and Present*. Washington, DC: Howard University Press.

———. (1983). *The Critical Temper of Alain Locke: A Selection of His Essays on Art and Culture* (Jeffrey C. Stewart, Ed.). New York: Garland Publishing.

———. (1989). *The Philosophy of Alain Locke: Harlem Renaissance and Beyond* (Leonard Harris, Ed.). Philadelphia: Temple University Press.

———. (1992). *Race Contacts and Interracial Relations: Lectures on the Theory and Practice of Race* (Jeffrey C. Stewart, Ed.). Washington, DC: Howard University Press.

———. (2012). *The Works of Alain Locke* (Charles Molesworth, Ed.). New York: Oxford University Press.

Logan, Rayford W. (1954). *The Negro in American Life and Thought: The Nadir, 1877–1901*. New York: Dial Press.

Loiacano, Darryl K. (1989). "Gay Identity Issues among Black American: Racism, Homophobia, and the Need for Validation." *Journal of Counseling and Development* 68 (1): 21–25.

Lomax, Alan. (1973). *Mister Jelly Roll: The Fortunes of Jelly Roll Morton, New Orleans Creole and Inventor of Jazz*. Berkeley: University of California Press.

Long, Alecia P. (2004). *The Great Southern Babylon: Sex, Race, and Respectability in New Orleans, 1865–1920*. Baton Rouge: Louisiana State University Press.

Long, John. (2005). *Drugs and the "Beats": The Role of Drugs in the Lives and Writings of Kerouac, Burroughs, and Ginsberg*. College Station, TX: Virtual Bookworm Publishing.

Longstreet, Stephen. (1965). *Sportin' House: A History of the New Orleans Sinners and the Birth of Jazz*. Los Angeles: Sherbourne Press.

———. (1986). *Storyville to Harlem: Fifty Years in the Jazz Scene*. New Brunswick, NJ: Rutgers University Press.

Lorde, Audre. (1984). *Sister Outsider: Essays and Speeches by Audre Lorde*. Freedom, CA: The Crossing Press Feminist Series.

———. (1988). *A Burst of Light: Essays by Audre Lorde*. Ithaca, NY: Firebrand.

———. (1996). *The Audre Lorde Compendium: Essays, Speeches, and Journals*. London: Pandora.

———. (2004). *Conversations with Audre Lorde* (Joan Wylie Hall, Ed.). Jackson: University Press of Mississippi.

———. (2009). *I Am Your Sister: The Collected and Unpublished Writings of Audre Lorde* (Rudolph P. Byrd, Johnnetta B. Cole, and Beverly Guy-Sheftall, Eds.). New York: Oxford University Press.

Lornell, Kip, and Stephenson, Charles C. (2001). *The Beat: Go-Go's Fusion of Funk and Hip Hop*. New York: Billboard Books.

Lott, Eric. (1988). "Double V, Double-Time: Bebop's Politics of Style." *Callaloo* 36 (Summer): 597–605.

———. (1993). *Love and Theft: Blackface Minstrelsy and the American Working Class*. New York: Oxford University Press.

———. (1995). "Double V, Double-Time: Bebop's Politics of Style." In Krin Gabbard (Ed.), *Jazz Among the Discourses* (243–55). Durham, NC: Duke University Press.

Lott, Tommy L. (1999). *The Invention of Race: Black Culture and the Politics of Representation*. Malden, MA: Blackwell.

Lovaas, Karen, Elia, John P., and Yep, Gust A. (Eds.). (2006). *LGBT Studies and Queer Theory: New Conflicts, Collaborations, and Contested Terrain*. New York: Harrington Park Press.

Lundy, Sandra E., and Leventhal, Beth. (1999). *Same-Sex Domestic Violence: Strategies for Change*. Thousand Oaks, CA: Sage.

MacAdams, Lewis. (2001). *Birth of the Cool: Beat, Bebop, and the American Avant-Garde*. New York: Free Press.

Macias, Anthony. (2010). "'Detroit Was Heavy!': Modern Jazz, Bebop, and African American Expressive Culture." *Journal of African American History* 95 (1): 44–70.

Maeda, Daryl J. (2009). *Chains of Babylon: The Rise of Asian America*. Minneapolis: University of Minnesota Press.

———. (2011). *Rethinking the Asian American Movement*. New York: Routledge.

Magee, Jeffrey. (2005). *The Uncrowned King of Swing: Fletcher Henderson and Big Band Jazz*. New York: Oxford University Press.

Maggin, Donald L. (2005). *Dizzy: The Life and Times of John Birks Gillespie*. New York: HarperCollins.

Mahar, William J. (1999). *Behind the Burnt Cork Mask: Early Blackface Minstrelsy and Antebellum American Popular Culture*. Urbana: University of Illinois Press.

Mahon, Maureen. (2004). *Right to Rock: The Black Rock Coalition and the Cultural Politics of Race*. Durham, NC: Duke University Press.

Mailer, Norman. (1957). *The White Negro : Superficial Reflections on the Hipster*. San Francisco: City Lights Books.

Makalani, Minkah. (2004). "For the Liberation of Black People Everywhere: The African Blood Brotherhood, Black Radicalism, and Pan-African Liberation in the New Negro Movement." Ph.D. dissertation, University of Illinois at Urbana-Champaign.

———. (2011). *In the Cause of Freedom: Radical Black Internationalism from Harlem to London, 1917–1939*. Chapel Hill: University of North Carolina Press.

Malik, Abd Al. (2009). *Sufi Rapper: The Spiritual Journey of Abd al Malik*. New York: Inner-Traditions.

Mandel, Howard. (2007). *Miles, Ornette, Cecil: How Miles Davis, Ornette Coleman, and Cecil Taylor Revolutionized the World of Jazz*. New York: Routledge.

Mapson, J. Wendell. (1984). *Ministry of Music in Black Church*. Valley Forge, PA: Judson Press.

Marable, Manning. (1983). *How Capitalism Underdeveloped Black America*. Boston: South End.

———. (1986). *W.E.B. Du Bois: Black Radical Democrat*. Boston: Twayne.

———. (2007). *Race, Reforms, and Rebellion: The Second Reconstruction and Beyond in Black America, 1945–2006*. Jackson: University Press of Mississippi.

Marable, Manning, and Aidi, Hishaam D. (Eds.). (2009). *Black Routes to Islam*. New York: Macmillan.

Marable, Manning, and Clarke-Avery, Kristen. (Eds.). (2008). *Seeking Higher Ground: The Hurricane Katrina Crisis, Race, and Public Policy Reader*. New York: Macmillan.

Marable, Manning, and Mullings, Leith. (Eds.). (2000). *Let Nobody Turn Us Around: Voices of Resistance, Reform, and Renewal—An African American Anthology*. Lanham, MD: Rowman & Littlefield.

Margolick, David. (2007). "The Day Louis Armstrong Made Noise." *New York Times* (September 23). Retrieved from www.nytimes.com/2007/09/23/opinion/23margolick.html?pagewanted=all.

Mariscal, George. (2005). *Brown-Eyed Children of the Sun: Lessons from the Chicano Movement, 1965–1975*. Albuquerque: University of New Mexico Press.

Marks, Carole. (1989). *Farewell, We're Good and Gone: The Great Black Migration*. Bloomington: Indiana University Press.

Marks, Carole, and Edkins, Diana. (Eds.). (1999). *Power of Pride: Style-Makers and Rule-Breakers of the Harlem Renaissance*. New York: Crown.

Marler, Regina. (2004). *Queer Beats: How the Beats Turned America On to Sex*. San Francisco: Cleis Press.

Marquis, Donald M. (2005). *In Search of Buddy Bolden: First Man of Jazz*. Baton Rouge: Louisiana State University Press.

Marshall, Wayne. (2006). "Giving Up Hip Hop's Firstborn: A Quest for the Real After the Death of Sampling." *Callaloo* 29 (3): 868–92.

Martin, Bradford D. (2011). *The Other Eighties: A Secret History of America in the Age of Reagan*. New York: Hill & Wang.

Martin, Theodora P. (1987). *The Sound of Our Own Voices: Women's Study Clubs, 1860–1910*. Boston: Beacon.

Masotti, Louis H., and Bowen, Don R. (Eds.). (1968). *Riots and Rebellion: Civil Violence in the Urban Community*. Beverly Hills, CA: Sage.

Massey, Douglas S., and Denton, Nancy A. (1993). *American Apartheid: Segregation and the Making of the Underclass*. Cambridge, MA: Harvard University Press.

Massood, Paula J. (2003). *Black City Cinema: African American Urban Experiences in Film*. Philadelphia: Temple University Press.

Materson, Lisa G. (2009). *For the Freedom of Her Race: Black Women and Electoral Politics in Illinois, 1877–1932*. Chapel Hill: University of North Carolina Press.

Mathew, Sujarani. (2007). *Womanism: Off the Feminist Track*. Bangalore: Dharmaram Publications.

Mathieson, Kenny. (1999). *Giant Steps: Bebop and the Creators of Modern Jazz 1945–1965*. Edinburgh: Payback.

Maxwell, Ian. (2003). *Phat Beats, Dope Rhymes: Hip Hop Down Under Comin' Upper*. Middletown, CT: Wesleyan University Press.

Maxwell, William J. (1999). *New Negro, Old Left: African American Writing and Communism Between the Wars*. New York: Columbia University Press.

Maynard, John A. (1991). *Venice West: The Beat Generation in Southern California*. New Brunswick, NJ: Rutgers University Press.

Mayne, Heather J. (2000). "The Wild, Wild West: Images of California in Contemporary Rap Music." *California History* 79 (1): 70–75.

Mazama, Ama. (2002). *The Afrocentric Paradigm*. Trenton, NJ: Africa World Press.

Mazón, Mauricio. (1984). *The Zoot Suit Riots: The Psychology of Symbolic Annihilation*. Austin: University of Texas Press.

Mazzola, Guerino, and Cherlin, Paul B. (2009). *Flow, Gesture, and Spaces in Free Jazz*. New York: Springer-Verlag.

McCann, Paul. (2008). *Race, Music, and National Identity: Images of Jazz in American Fiction, 1920–1960*. Madison, NJ: Fairleigh Dickinson University Press.

McClellan, Lawrence. (2004). *The Later Swing Era, 1942–1955*. Westport, CT: Greenwood.

McCloud, Aminah Beverly. (1995). *African American Islam*. New York: Routledge.

McCoy, Judy. (1992). *Rap Music in the 1980s: A Reference Guide*. Metuchen, NJ: Scarecrow Press.

McCree, Donna H., Jones, Kenneth T., and O'Leary, Ann. (Eds.). (2010). *African Americans and HIV/AIDS: Understanding and Addressing the Epidemic*. New York: Springer.

McDarrah, Fred W., and McDarrah, Gloria S. (2001). *Beat Generation: Glory Days in Greenwich Village*. New York: Schirmer.

McFarland, Pancho. (2008). *Chicano Rap: Gender and Violence in the Post-Industrial Barrio*. Austin: University of Texas Press.

McKay, Claude. (1912a). *Constab Ballads*. London: Watts.

———. (1912b). *Song of Jamaica*. Kingston, Jamaica: A.W. Gardner.

———. (1928). *Home to Harlem*. New York: Harper & Brothers.

————. (1929). *Banjo: A Story Without a Plot*. New York: Harper & Brothers.

————. (1933). *Banana Bottom*. New York: Harper & Brothers.

————. (1937). *A Long Way from Home*. New York: Arno Press.

————. (1953). *Selected Poems of Claude McKay*. New York: Harcourt Brace Jovanovich.

————. (1973). *The Passion of Claude McKay: Selected Poetry and Prose, 1912–1948* (Wayne F. Cooper, Ed.). New York: Schocken.

————. (1995). *Romance in Marseilles*. Exeter, UK: University of Exeter Press.

————. (2004). *Complete Poems* (William J. Maxwell, Ed.). Urbana: University of Illinois Press.

McKinley, Catherine E., and DeLaney, L. Joyce. (Eds.). (1995). *Afrekete: An Anthology of Black Lesbian Writing*. New York: Anchor Books.

McKittrick, Katherine, and Woods, Clyde Adrian. (Eds.). (2007). *Black Geographies and the Politics of Place*. Cambridge, MA: South End Press.

McQuillar, Tayannah L. (2007). *When Rap Music Had a Conscience: The Artists, Organizations, and Historic Events That Inspired and Influenced the "Golden Age" of Hip Hop, from 1987 to 1996*. New York: Thunder's Mouth Press.

McRae, Rick. (2001). "'What Is Hip?' and Other Inquiries in Jazz Slang Lexicography." *Music Library Association Notes* 57 (3): 574–84.

McWhirter, Cameron. (2011). *Red Summer: The Summer of 1919 and the Awakening of Black America*. New York: Henry Holt.

Meadows, Eddie S. (2003). *Bebop to Cool: Context, Ideology, and Musical Identity*. Westport, CT: Greenwood.

Meeder, Christopher. (2008). *Jazz: The Basics*. New York: Routledge.

Meer, Sarah. (2005). *Uncle Tom Mania: Slavery, Minstrelsy, and Trans-Atlantic Culture in the 1850s*. Athens: University of Georgia Press.

Meezan, William, and Martin, James I. (Eds.). (2003). *Research Methods with Gay, Lesbian, Bisexual, and Transgender Populations*. Binghamton, NY: Harrington Park Press.

Meier, August. (1963). *Negro Thought in America, 1880–1915: Racial Ideologies in the Age of Booker T. Washington*. Ann Arbor: University of Michigan Press.

————. (1976). *From Plantation to Ghetto*. New York: Hill and Wang.

Mellis, Delia Cunningham. (2008). "The Monsters We Defy: Washington, D.C. in the Red Summer of 1919." Ph.D. dissertation, City University of New York.

Merlis, Bob, and Seay, Davin. (1997). *Heart & Soul: A Celebration of Black Music Style in America, 1930 – 1975*. New York: Stewart, Tabori & Chang.

Mezzrow, Mezz. (1990). *Really the Blues*. New York: Citadel Press/Carol Publishing.

Michel, Ed. (Producer). (1997). *The Debut Records Story* (4 Compact Disc Set). Berkeley, CA: Debut Records/Fantasy Records.

Miles, Tiya, and Holland, Sharon P. (Eds.). (2006). *Crossing Waters, Crossing Worlds: The African Diaspora in Indian Country*. Durham, NC: Duke University Press.

Miller, Frederic P., Vandome, Agnes F., and McBrewster, John. (Eds.). (2011). *Rap West Coast*. Paris: Alphascript Publishing.

Miller, Karl Hagstrom. (2010). *Segregating Sound: Inventing Folk and Pop Music in the Age of Jim Crow*. Durham, NC: Duke University Press.

Miller-Young, Mireille. (2008). "Hip Hop Honeys and Da Hustlaz: Black Sexualities in the New Hip Hop Pornography." *Meridians: Feminism, Race, Transnationalism* 8 (1): 261–92.

Mills, Charles W. (1997). *The Racial Contract*. Ithaca, NY: Cornell University Press.

————. (1998). *Blackness Visible: Essays on Philosophy and Race*. Ithaca, NY: Cornell University Press.

————. (1999). "The Racial Polity." In Susan E. Babbitt and Susan Campbell (Eds.), *Racism and Philosophy* (13–31, [endnotes] 255–57). Ithaca, NY: Cornell University Press.

————. (2003a). *From Class to Race: Essays in White Marxism and Black Radicalism*. Lanham, MD: Rowman & Littlefield.

————. (2003b). "White Supremacy." In Tommy L. Lott and John P. Pittman (Eds.), *A Companion to African American Philosophy* (269–84). Malden, MA: Blackwell.

Mingus, Charles. (1971). *Beneath the Underdog: His Words as Composed by Mingus*. New York: Knopf.

————. (1990). *Charles Mingus: The Complete Debut Recordings* (12 Compact Disc Set). Berkeley, CA: Debut Records/Fantasy Records.

Minkler, Meredith, and Roe, Kathleen M. (1993). *Grandmothers as Caregivers: Raising Children of the Crack Cocaine Epidemic.* Newbury Park, CA: Sage.

Mitchell, Angelyn, and Taylor, Danille K. (Eds.). (2009). *Cambridge Companion to African American Women's Literature.* Cambridge: Cambridge University Press.

Mitchell, J. Paul. (Ed.). (1970). *Race Riots in Black and White.* Englewood Cliffs, NJ: Prentice-Hall.

Mitchell, Tony. (Ed.). (2001). *Global Noise: Rap and Hip Hop Outside the USA.* Hanover, NH: University Press of New England.

Miyakawa, Felicia M. (2005). *Five Percenter Rap: God Hop's Music, Message, and Black Muslim Mission.* Bloomington: Indiana University Press.

Mockus, Martha. (2007). "Me'Shell Ndegeocello: Musical Articulations of Black Feminism." In Christa D. Acampora and Angela L. Cotton (Eds.), *Unmaking Race, Remaking Soul: Transformative Aesthetics and the Practice of Freedom* (81–102). Albany: State University of New York Press.

Monk, Craig. (2008). *Writing the Lost Generation: Expatriate Autobiography and American Modernism.* Iowa City: University of Iowa Press.

Mook, Richard. (2007). *Rap Music and Hip Hop Culture: A Critical Reader.* Dubuque, IA: Kendall/Hunt.

Moore, Lisa C. (Ed.). (1997). *Does Your Mama Know?: An Anthology of Black Lesbian Coming Out Stories.* Decatur, GA: RedBone Press.

Morgan, Bill. (2010). *The Typewriter is Holy: The Complete, Uncensored History of the Beat Generation.* New York: Free Press.

Morgan, Francesca. (2005). *Women and Patriotism in Jim Crow America.* Chapel Hill: University of North Carolina Press.

Morgan, Joan. (1995). "Fly-Girls, Bitches, and Hoes: Notes of a Hip Hop Feminist." *Social Text* 45: 151–57.

————. (1999). *When Chickenheads Come Home to Roost: A Hip Hop Feminist Breaks It Down.* New York: Simon & Schuster.

Morgan, Johnny. (2011). *Disco.* New York: Sterling.

Morgan, Marcyliena H. (2005). "Hip Hop Women Shredding the Veil: Race and Class in Popular Feminist Identity." *South Atlantic Quarterly* 104 (3): 425–44.

————. (2009). *The Real Hip Hop: Battling for Knowledge, Power, and Respect in the L.A. Underground.* Durham, NC: Duke University Press.

Morris, Aldon. (1981). "Black Southern Student Sit-in Movement: An Analysis of Internal Organization." *American Sociological Review* 46 (6): 744–67.

————. (1984). *The Origins of the Civil Rights Movement: Black Communities Organizing for Change.* New York: Free Press.

Morton, Donald. (Ed.). (1996). *Material Queer: A LesBiGay Cultural Studies Reader.* Boulder, CO: Westview.

Moses, Wilson Jeremiah. (1978). *The Golden Age of Black Nationalism, 1850–1925.* New York: Oxford University Press.

————. (2004). *Creative Conflict in African American Thought: Frederick Douglass, Alexander Crummell, Booker T. Washington, W.E.B. Du Bois, and Marcus Garvey.* Cambridge: Cambridge University Press.

Moten, Fred. (2003). *In the Break: The Aesthetics of the Black Radical Tradition.* Minneapolis: University of Minnesota Press.

Mullen, Bill V., and Smethurst, James. (Eds.). (2003). *Left of the Color Line: Race, Radicalism, and Twentieth Century Literature of the United States.* Chapel Hill: University of North Carolina Press.

Mumford, Kevin J. (2007). *Newark: A History of Race, Rights, and Riots in America.* New York: New York University Press.

Muñoz-Laboy, Miguel, Weinstein, Hannah, and Parker, Richard. (2007). "The Hip-Hop Club Scene: Gender, Grinding and Sex." *Culture, Health & Sexuality* 9 (6): 615–28.

Murray, Dufferin A. (1998). "From the Word Up: The Poetic Message of Rap Music." Ph.D. dissertation, University of Western Ontario.

Mutua, Athena D. (Ed.). (2006). *Progressive Black Masculinities*. New York: Routledge.

Myhre, Kyle. (2007). "Conscious Rappers and Homophobia." *Why Is Guante So Angry?* Retrieved from http://www.guante.info/2007/02/article-conscious-rappers-and.html.

Myrie, Russell. (2008). *Don't Rhyme for the Sake of Riddlin': The Authorized Story of Public Enemy*. New York: Canongate Books.

Myrsiades, Kostas. (Ed.). (2002). *The Beat Generation: Critical Essays*. New York: Lang.

Nadell, Martha Jane. (2004). *Enter the New Negroes: Images of Race in American Culture*. Cambridge, MA: Harvard University Press.

Nair, Ajay, and Balaji, Murali. (Eds.). (2008). *Desi Rap: Hip Hop and South Asian America*. Lanham, MD: Lexington Books.

Naison, Mark. (2005). *Communists in Harlem During the Depression*. Urbana: University of Illinois Press.

Neal, Larry. (1969). *Black Boogaloo: Notes on Black Liberation*. San Francisco: Journal of Black Poetry Press.

Neal, Mark Anthony. (1998). *What the Music Said: Black Popular Music and Black Public Culture*. New York: Routledge.

———. (2002). *Soul Babies: Black Popular Culture and the Post-Soul Aesthetic*. New York: Routledge.

———. (2003). *Songs in the Key of Black Life: A Rhythm and Blues Nation*. New York: Routledge.

Neate, Patrick. (2004). *Where You're At?: Notes from the Frontline of a Hip Hop Planet*. New York: Riverhead Books.

Negus, Keith. (1999). *Music Genres and Corporate Cultures*. New York: Routledge.

Nelsen, Hart M., Yokley, Raytha L., and Nelsen, Anne K. (Eds.). (1971). *The Black Church in America*. New York: Basic.

Nelson, Emmanuel S. (Ed.). (1993). *Critical Essays: Gay and Lesbian Writers of Color*. London: Haworth Press.

Nelson, Havelock, and Gonzales, Michael A. (1991). *Bring the Noise: A Guide to Rap Music and Hip Hop Culture*. New York: Harmony Books.

Nelson, Stanley. (Director). (2011). *Freedom Riders*. Brighton, MA: PBS Video.

Nevels, Cynthia S. (2007). *Lynching to Belong: Claiming Whiteness Through Racial Violence*. College Station: Texas A&M University Press.

Newman, Louise Michele. (1999). *White Women's Rights: The Racial Origins of Feminism in the United States*. New York: Oxford University Press.

Newton-Matza, Mitchell. (Ed.). (2009). *Jazz Age: People and Perspectives*. Santa Barbara, CA: ABC-CLIO.

Nicholson, Stuart. (1995). *Jazz: The 1980s Resurgence*. New York: Da Capo.

———. (2005). *Is Jazz Dead?: (Or Has It Moved to a New Address)*. New York: Routledge.

Nielsen, Aldon Lynn. (1997). *Black Chant: Languages of African American Postmodernism*. Cambridge: Cambridge University Press.

Nielsen, Amie, Martinez, Ramiro, and Rosenfeld, Richard. (2005). "Firearm Use, Injury, and Lethality in Assaultive Violence." *Homicide Studies* 9 (2): 83–108.

Nierenberg, George T. (Director). (1982). *Say Amen, Somebody!* Carmel, CA: Pacific Arts Video Records.

Nieuwkerk, Karin van. (Ed.). (2011). *Muslim Rap, Halal Soaps, and Revolutionary Theater: Artistic Developments in the Muslim World*. Austin: University of Texas Press.

Nketia, J. H. Kwabena. (1974). *The Music of Africa*. New York: Norton.

Nowatzki, Robert. (2010). *Representing African American in Trans-Atlantic Abolitionism and Blackface Minstrelsy*. Baton Rouge: Louisiana State University Press.

Ntarangwi, Mwenda. (2009). *East African Hip Hop: Youth Culture and Globalization*. Urbana: University of Illinois Press.

Nugent, Richard Bruce. (2002). *Gay Rebel of the Harlem Renaissance: Selections from the Work of Richard Bruce Nugent* (Thomas H. Wirth, Ed.). Durham, NC: Duke University Press.

Nyongó, Tavia Amolo Ochieng'. (2009). *The Amalgamation Waltz: Race, Performance and the Ruses of Memory.* Minneapolis: University of Minnesota Press.
Oakley, Giles. (1997). *The Devil's Music: A History of the Blues.* New York: Da Capo.
Oboe, Annalisa, and Scacchi, Anna. (Eds.). (2008). *Recharting the Black Atlantic: Modern Cultures, Local Communities, Global Connections.* New York: Routledge.
Ogbar, Jeffrey O. G. (2004). *Black Power: Radical Politics and African American Identity.* Baltimore: Johns Hopkins University Press.
———. (2007). *The Hip Hop Revolution: The Culture and Politics of Rap.* Lawrence: University of Kansas Press.
Ogg, Alex. (2001). *The Hip Hop Years: A History of Rap* (with David Upshal). New York: Fromm International.
Ogren, Kathy J. (1989). *The Jazz Revolution: Twenties America & the Meaning of Jazz.* New York: Oxford University Press.
Oliphant, Dave. (Ed.). (1994). *The Bebop Revolution in Words and Music.* Austin: University of Texas Press.
———. (2002). *The Early Swing Era, 1930 to 1941.* Westport, CT: Greenwood.
Oliver, Melvin L., and Shapiro, Thomas M. (1995). *Black Wealth/White Wealth: A New Perspective on Racial Equality.* New York: Routledge.
Oliver, Paul. (1960). *The Meaning of the Blues.* New York: Collier.
———. (1970). *Aspects of the Blues Tradition.* New York: Oak Publications.
———. (2006). *Broadcasting the Blues: Black Blues in the Segregation Era.* New York: Routledge.
———. (2009). *Barrelhouse Blues: Location Recording and the Early Traditions of the Blues.* New York: BasicCivitas Books.
Olson, Alix. (Ed.). (2007). *Word Warriors: 35 Women Leaders in the Spoken-Word Revolution.* Emeryville, CA: Seal Press.
Olson, Joel. (2004). *The Abolition of White Democracy.* Minneapolis: University of Minnesota Press.
Olsson, Bengt. (1970). *Memphis Blues and Jug Bands.* London: Studio Vista.
Olsson, Göran. (Director). (2011). *Black Power Mixtape: 1967–1975.* New York: IFC Films.
O'Meally, Robert G. (Ed.). (1998). *The Jazz Cadence of American Culture.* New York: Columbia University Press.
O'Neal, Hank. (2009). *The Ghosts of Harlem: Sessions with Jazz Legends.* Nashville: Vanderbilt University Press.
Omi, Michael, and Winant, Howard. (1994). *Racial Formation in United States: From the 1960s to the 1990s.* New York: Routledge.
Osayande, Ewuare X. (1996). *Gangsta Rap is Dead: Ciphers, Poems and Prophecies on the War for Hip Hop Culture.* Philadelphia, PA: Talking Drum Communications.
———. (2008). *Misogyny & The Emcee: Sex, Race & Hip Hop.* Philadelphia, PA: Talking Drum Communications.
Osofsky, Gilbert. (1996). *Harlem, The Making of a Ghetto: Negro New York, 1890–1930.* Chicago: Ivan R. Dee.
Oster, Harry. (1969). *Living Country Blues.* Detroit: Folklore Associates.
Ostransky, Leroy. (1978). *Jazz City: The Impact of Our Cities on the Development of Jazz.* Englewood Cliffs, NJ: Prentice-Hall.
Osumare, Halifu. (2007). *The Africanist Aesthetic in Global Hip Hop.* New York: Macmillan.
Othello, Javon. (2004). *The Soul of Rock & Roll: A History of African Americans in Rock Music.* Oakland, CA: Regent Press.
Oware, Matthew. (2009). "A 'Man's Woman'?: Contradictory Messages in the Songs of Female Rappers, 1992–2000." *Journal of Black Studies* 39 (5): 786–802.
———. (2011). "Brotherly Love: Homosociality and Black Masculinity in Gangsta Rap Music." *Journal of African American Studies* 15 (1): 22–39.
Owens, Thomas. (1995). *Bebop: The Music and Its Players.* New York: Oxford University Press.
Pacoda, Pierfrancesco. (2000). *Hip Hop Italiano: Suoni e Scanari del Posse Power.* Torino: Einaudi.

Pagán, Eduardo Obregón. (2003). *Murder at the Sleepy Lagoon: Zoot Suits, Race, and Riot in Wartime L.A.* Chapel Hill: University of North Carolina Press.

Painter, Nell Irvin. (2006). *Creating Black Americans: African American History and Its Meanings, 1619 to the Present.* New York: Oxford University Press.

Palmer, Robert. (1981). *Deep Blues.* New York: Penguin.

Panish, Jon. (1997). *The Color of Jazz: Race and Representation in Post-War American Culture.* Jackson: University Press of Mississippi.

Parasecoli, Fabio. (2007). "Bootylicious: Food and the Female Body in Contemporary Black Pop Culture." *Women's Studies Quarterly* 35 (1): 110–25.

Pardue, Derek. (2008). *Ideologies of Marginality in Brazilian Hip Hop.* New York: Macmillan.

———. (2011). *Brazilian Hip Hoppers Speak from the Margins: We's on Tape.* New York: Macmillan.

Parker, Alison M., and Cole, Stephanie. (Eds.). (2000). *Women and the Unstable State in Nineteenth Century America.* College Station: Texas A & M University Press.

Parmar, Priya. (2009). *Knowledge Reigns Supreme: The Critical Pedagogy of Hip Hop Activist KRS-ONE.* Rotterdam, The Netherlands: Sense Publishers.

Parrish, Lydia. (Ed.). (1992). *Slave Songs of the Georgia Sea Islands.* Athens: University of Georgia Press.

Parsonage, Catherine. (2005). *The Evolution of Jazz in Britain, 1880–1935.* Burlington, VT: Ashgate.

Pastras, Philip. (2001). *Dead Man Blues: Jelly Roll Morton Way Out West.* Berkeley: University of California Press.

Pate, Alexs D. (2010). *In the Heart of the Beat: The Poetry of Rap.* Lanham, MD: Scarecrow Press.

Patterson, Anita Haya. (2000). "Jazz, Realism, and the Modernist Lyric: The Poetry of Langston Hughes." *MLQ: Modern Language Quarterly* 61 (4): 651–82.

Pattillo, Mary E. (2000). *Black Picket Fences: Privilege and Peril Among the Black Middle-Class.* Chicago: University of Chicago Press.

———. (2007). *Black on the Block: The Politics of Race and Class in the City.* Chicago: University of Chicago Press.

Patton, Venetria K., and Honey, Maureen. (Eds.). (2001). *Double-Take: A Revisionist Harlem Renaissance Anthology.* New Brunswick, NJ: Rutgers University Press.

Payne, Charles M., and Green, Adam. (Eds.). (2003). *Time Longer Than Rope: A Century of African American Activism, 1850–1950.* New York: New York University Press.

Peplow, Michael W., and Davis, Arthur Paul. (Eds.). (1975). *The New Negro Renaissance: An Anthology.* New York: Holt, Rinehart and Winston.

Peretti, Burton W. (1992). *The Creation of Jazz: Music, Race, and Culture in Urban America.* Urbana: University of Illinois Press.

———. (2009). *Lift Every Voice: The History of African American Music.* Lanham, MD: Rowman & Littlefield.

Perry, Imani. (2004). *Prophets of the Hood: Politics and Poetics in Hip Hop.* Durham, NC: Duke University Press.

Peterson, Lloyd. (2006). *Music and the Creative Spirit: Innovators in Jazz, Improvisation, and the Avant-Garde.* Lanham, MD: Scarecrow Press.

Pfeffer, Paula F. (1990). *A. Philip Randolph: Pioneer of the Civil Rights Movement.* Baton Rouge: Louisiana State University Press.

Pfeifer, Michael J. (2004). *Rough Justice: Lynching and American Society, 1874–1947.* Urbana: University of Illinois Press.

Phillips, Layli. (Ed.). (2006). *The Womanist Reader.* New York: Routledge.

Phillips, Layli, Reddick-Morgan, Kerri, and Stephens, Dionne P. (2005). "Oppositional Consciousness Within an Oppositional Realm: The Case of Feminism and Womanism in Rap and Hip Hop, 1976–2004." *Journal of African American History* 90 (3): 253–77.

Phillips, Lisa. (Ed.). (1995). *Beat Culture and the New America, 1950–1965.* New York: Whitney Museum of American Art.

Phillips, Susan A. (1999). *Wallbangin': Graffiti and Gangs in L.A.* Chicago: University of Chicago Press.

Phinney, Kevin. (2005). *Souled American: How Black Music Transformed White Culture*. New York: Billboard Books.

Phipps, Cyrille. (Director). (1992). *Respect is Due!: Black Women in Rap Lyrics and Music Videos*. New York: Third World Newsreel.

———. (Director). (1993). *Our House: Lesbians and Gays in the Hood*. New York: Third World Newsreel.

Pinn, Anne H., and Pinn, Anthony B. (2002). *Fortress Introduction to Black Church History*. Minneapolis, MN: Fortress Press.

Pinn, Anthony B. (1998). *Varieties of African American Religious Experience*. Minneapolis, MN: Fortress Press.

———. (Ed.). (2003). *Noise and Spirit: The Religious and Spiritual Sensibilities of Rap Music*. New York: New York University Press.

———. (2006). *The African American Religious Experience in America*. Westport, CT: Greenwood.

———. (2009). "Rap Music, Culture and Religion: Concluding Thoughts." *Culture and Religion* 10 (1): 97–108.

———. (2010). *Understanding & Transforming the Black Church*. Eugene, OR: Cascade Books.

Pinn, Anthony B., and Valentin, Benjamin. (Eds.). (2009). *Creating Ourselves: African Americans and Hispanic Americans on Popular Culture and Religious Expression*. Durham, NC: Duke University Press.

Piontek, Thomas. (2006). *Queering Gay and Lesbian Studies*. Urbana: University of Illinois Press.

Plummer, Ken. (2005). "Living with the Tensions: Critical Humanism and Queer Theory. In Norman K. Denzin and Yvonna S. Lincoln (Eds.), *The Sage Handbook of Qualitative Research* (357–75). Thousand Oaks, CA: Sage.

Pochmara, Anna. (2011). *The Making of the New Negro: Black Authorship, Masculinity, and Sexuality in the Harlem Renaissance*. Amsterdam: Amsterdam University Press.

Pollard, Sam. (Producer). (1999). *I'll Make Me a World : African-American Artists in the 20th Century* (6 Episodes). Alexandria, VA: PBS Video.

Porter, Bruce, and Dunn, Marvin. (1984). *The Miami Riot of 1980: Crossing the Bounds*. Lexington, MA: Lexington Books.

Porter, Eric. (1999). "'Dizzy Atmosphere': The Challenge of Bebop." *American Music* 17 (4): 422–46.

———. (2002). *What Is This Thing Called Jazz?: African American Musicians as Artists, Critics, and Activists*. Berkeley: University of California Press.

Potter, Russell A. (1995). *Spectacular Vernaculars: Hip Hop and the Politics of Postmodernism*. Albany: State University of New York Press.

Posner, Gerald L. (2002). *Motown: Music, Money, Sex, and Power*. New York: Random House.

Pough, Gwendolyn. (2002). "Love Feminism But Where's My Hip Hop?: Shaping a Black Identity." In Daisy Hernández and Bushra Rehman (Eds.), *Colonize This!: Young Women of Color on Today's Feminism* (85–98). New York: Seal Press.

———. (2003). "Do the Ladies Run This…?: Some Thoughts on Hip Hop Feminism." In Rory Dicker and Alison Piepmeier (Eds.), *Catching a Wave: Reclaiming Feminism for the 21st Century* (232–43). Boston: Northeastern University Press.

———. (2004). *Check It While I Wreck It: Black Womanhood, Hip Hop Culture, and the Public Sphere*. Boston: Northeastern University Press.

Powell, Catherine Tabb. (1991). "Rap Music: An Education with a Beat from the Street."*Journal of Negro Education* 60 (3): 245–59.

Powell, Kevin. (2003). *Who Gonna Take the Weight?: Manhood, Race, and Power in America*. New York: Three Rivers Press.

Powell, Richard J., and Bailey, David A. (Eds.). (1997). *Rhapsodies in Black: Art of the Harlem Renaissance*. Berkeley: University of California Press.

Pride, Felicia. (2007). *The Message: 100 Life Lessons from Hip Hop's Greatest Songs*. New York: Thunder's Mouth/Running Press.

Pritchard, Eric, and Bibbs, Maria. (2007). "Sista Outsider: Queer Women of Color and Hip Hop." In Gwendolyn D. Pough, Elaine Richardson, Aisha Durham, and Rachel Raimist (Eds.), *Home Girls Make Some Noise!: The Hip Hop Feminism Anthology* (19–40). Mira Loma, CA: Parker Publishing.

Pruter, Robert. (1991). *Chicago Soul.* Urbana: University of Illinois Press.

———. (Ed.). (1993). *Blackwell Guide to Soul Recordings.* Cambridge, MA: Blackwell.

———. (1996). *Doo-Wop: The Chicago Scene.* Urbana: University of Illinois Press.

Quarles, Benjamin. (1969). *Black Abolitionists.* Oxford: Oxford University Press.

Quinn, Eithne. (2000a). "Black British Cultural Studies and the Rap on Gangsta." *Black Music Research Journal* 20 (2): 195–216.

———. (2000b). "'Who's the Mack?': The Performativity and Politics of the Pimp Figure in Gangsta Rap." *Journal of American Studies* 34 (1): 115–36.

———. (2005). *Nuthin' But A "G" Thang: The Culture and Commerce of Gangsta Rap.* New York: Columbia University Press.

Quinn, Michael. (1996). "'Never Shoulda Been Let out the Penitentiary': Gangsta Rap and the Struggle over Racial Identity." *Cultural Critique* 34: 65–89.

Rabaka, Reiland. (2007). *W.E.B. Du Bois and the Problems of the Twenty-First Century: An Essay on Africana Critical Theory.* Lanham, MD: Lexington Books.

———. (2008). *Du Bois's Dialectics: Black Radical Politics and the Reconstruction of Critical Social Theory.* Lanham, MD: Lexington Books.

———. (2009). *Africana Critical Theory: Reconstructing the Black Radical Tradition, from W.E.B. Du Bois and C.L.R. James to Frantz Fanon and Amilcar Cabral.* Lanham, MD: Lexington Books.

———. (2010a). *Against Epistemic Apartheid: W.E.B. Du Bois and the Disciplinary Decadence of Sociology.* Lanham, MD: Lexington Books.

———. (2010b). *Forms of Fanonism: Frantz Fanon's Critical Theory and the Dialectics of Decolonization.* Lanham, MD: Lexington Books.

———. (Ed.). (2010c). *W.E.B. Du Bois: A Critical Reader.* Surrey, UK: Ashgate Publishing.

———. (2011). *Hip Hop's Inheritance: From the Harlem Renaissance to the Hip Hop Feminist Movement.* Lanham, MD: Lexington Books.

———. (forthcoming). *The Hip Hop Movement: From R&B and the Civil Rights Movement to Rap and Obama's America.* Lanham, MD: Lexington Books.

Raboteau, Albert J. (1978). *Slave Religion: The "Invisible Institution" in the Antebellum South.* New York: Oxford University Press.

———. (1995). *A Fire in the Bones: Reflections on African American Religious History.* Boston: Beacon.

———. (1999). *Canaan Land: A Religious History of African Americans.* New York: Oxford University Press.

Radano, Ronald M. (2000). *Music and the Racial Imagination.* Chicago: University of Chicago Press.

———. (2003). *Lying Up a Nation: Race and Black Music.* Chicago: University of Chicago Press.

Rahn, Janice. (2002). *Painting Without Permission: Hip Hop Graffiti Subculture.* Westport, CT: Bergin & Garvey.

Railton, Diane, and Watson, Paul. (2011). *Music Video and the Politics of Representation.* Edinburgh: Edinburgh University Press.

Ramesh, Kotti S., and Rani, Kandula N. (2006). *Claude McKay: The Literary Identity from Jamaica to Harlem and Beyond.* Jefferson, NC: McFarland.

Ramey, Lauri. (2008). *Slave Songs and the Birth of African American Poetry.* New York: Macmillan.

Rampersad, Arnold. (1990). *The Art and Imagination of W.E.B. Du Bois.* New York: Schocken.

———. (2002a). *The Life of Langston Hughes: I, Too, Sing America, 1902–1941, Vol. 1* (2nd Edition). New York: Oxford University Press.

———. (2002b). *The Life of Langston Hughes: I Dream a World, 1941–1967, Vol. 2* (2nd Edition). New York: Oxford University Press.

Ramsey, Guthrie P. (2003). *Race Music: Black Cultures from Be-Bop to Hip Hop*. Berkeley: University of California Press.

Raskin, Jonah. (2004). *American Scream: Allen Ginsberg's Howl and the Making of the Beat Generation*. Berkeley: University of California Press.

Rattenbury, Ken. (1990). *Duke Ellington: Jazz Composer*. New Haven: Yale University Press.

Ray, Ella Maria. (1998). "Standing in the Lion's Shadow: Jamaican Rastafari Women Reconstructing their African Identity." Ph.D. dissertation, Johns Hopkins University.

Redd, Lawrence N. (1974). *Rock Is Rhythm & Blues: The Impact of Mass Media*. East Lansing: Michigan State University Press.

Redkey, Edwin S. (1969). *Black Exodus: Black Nationalist and Back-to-Africa Movements, 1890–1910*. New Haven, CT: Yale University Press.

Reeves, Marcus. (2008). *Somebody Scream!: Rap Music's Rise to Prominence in the Aftershock of Black Power*. New York: Farber & Farber.

Reich, Howard, and Gaines, William. (2003). *Jelly's Blues: The Life, Music, and Redemption of Jelly Roll Morton*. Cambridge, MA: Da Capo.

Reid-Brinkley, Shanara R. (2008). "The Essence of Res(ex)pectability: Black Women's Negotiation of Black Femininity in Rap Music and Music Video." *Meridians: Feminism, Race, Transnationalism* 8 (1): 236–60.

Reisner, Robert G. (1977). *Bird: The Legend of Charlie Parker*. New York: Da Capo.

Renzetti, Claire M. (1992). *Violent Betrayal: Partner Abuse in Lesbian Relationships*. Newbury Park, CA: Sage.

Renzetti, Claire M., and Miley, Charles H. (Eds.). (1996). *Violence in Gay and Lesbian Domestic Partnerships*. New York: Harrington Park Press.

Resnick, Michael. (2006). "BurnList: The Digital 'Mix Tape' Comes of Age." Retrieved from www.events-in-music.com/burnlist-mix-tapes.html.

Reynolds, Gary A., and Wright, Beryl J. (Eds.). (1989). *Against the Odds: African American Artists and the Harmon Foundation*. Newark, NJ: Newark Museum Press.

Riccardi, Ricky. (2011). *What a Wonderful World: The Magic of Louis Armstrong's Later Years*. New York: Pantheon.

Richardson, Diane, and Seidman, Steven. (Eds.). (2002). *Handbook of Lesbian and Gay Studies*. Thousand Oaks, CA: Sage.

Rickford, John R. (1999). *African American Vernacular English: Features, Evolution, Educational Implications*. Malden, MA: Blackwell.

Rickford, John R., Mufwene, Salikoko S., Bailey, Guy, and Baugh, John. (Eds.). (1998). *African American English*. New York: Routledge.

Rickford, John R., and Rickford, Russell J. (2000). *Spoken Soul: The Story of Black English*. New York: Wiley.

Riley, Alexander. (2005). "The Rebirth of Tragedy Out of the Spirit of Hip Hop: A Cultural Sociology of Gangsta Rap Music." *Journal of Youth Studies* 8 (3): 297–311.

Riley, Charles A. (2004). *The Jazz Age in France*. New York: Abrams.

Ripani, Richard J. (2006). *The New Blue Music: Changes in Rhythm & Blues, 1950–1999*. Jackson: University Press of Mississippi.

Ristock, Janice L. (2002). *No More Secrets: Violence in Lesbian Relationships*. New York: Routledge.

———. (Ed.). (2011). *Intimate Partner Violence in LGBTQ Lives*. New York: Routledge.

Rivera, Raquel Z. (2003). *New York Ricans from the Hip Hop Zone*. New York: Macmillan.

Rivera, Raquel Z., Marshall, Wayne, and Hernandez, Deborah P. (Eds.). (2009). *Reggaeton*. Durham, NC: Duke University Press.

Ro, Ronin. (1996). *Gangsta: Merchandizing the Rhymes of Violence*. New York: St. Martin's.

———. (1998). *Have Gun Will Travel: The Spectacular Rise and Violent Fall of Death Row Records*. New York: Doubleday.

Roberts, Robin. (1991). "Music Videos, Performance and Resistance: Feminist Rappers." *Journal of Popular Culture* 25 (2): 141–52.

———. (1994). "Ladies First: Queen Latifah's Afrocentric Feminist Music Video." *African American Review* 28 (2): 245–57.

Robertson, Gil L. (Ed.). (2006). *Not in My Family: AIDS in the African American Community.* Chicago: Agate.

Robinson, Cedric J. (2007). *Forgeries of Memory and Meaning: Blacks and the Regimes of Race in American Theater and Film Before World War II.* Chapel Hill: University of North Carolina Press.

Rocchio, Vincent F. (2000). *Reel Racism: Confronting Hollywood's Construction of Afro-American Culture.* Boulder, CO: Westview.

Rodriguez, Richard T. (2006). "Queering the Homeboy Aesthetic." *Aztlan: A Journal of Chicano Studies* 31 (2): 127–37.

Rodriquez, Jason. (2006). "Color-Blind Ideology and the Culture Appropriation of Hip Hop." *Journal of Contemporary Ethnography* 35 (6): 645–68.

Roediger, David R. (2005). *Working Toward Whiteness: How America's Immigrants Became White—The Strange Journey from Ellis Island to the Suburbs.* New York: Basic.

———. (2007). *The Wages of Whiteness: Race and the Making of the American Working-Class.* New York: Verso.

Rojas, Maythee. (2009). *Women of Color and Feminism.* Berkeley, CA: Seal Press.

Roland, Paul. (Ed.). (2000). *Jazz Singers: The Great Song Stylists in Their Own Words.* New York: Billboard Books.

Rollins, Judith. (1985). *Between Women: Domestics and Their Employers.* Philadelphia: Temple University Press.

Rosales, Francisco A. (1996). *Chicano!: The History of the Mexican American Civil Rights Movement.* Houston, TX: Arte Público Press.

Rose, Tricia. (1994). *Black Noise: Rap Music and Black Culture in Contemporary America.* Middletown, CT: Wesleyan University Press.

———. (2008). *The Hip Hop Wars: What We Talk About When We Talk About Hip Hop—and Why It Matters.* New York: Basic/Civitas.

Rose-Robinson, Sia. (1999). "A Qualitative Analysis of Hardcore and Gangsta Rap Lyrics, 1985–1995." Ph.D. dissertation, Howard University, Washington, DC.

Roses, Lorraine E., and Randolph, Ruth E. (Eds.). (1996). *Harlem's Glory: Black Women Writing, 1900–1950.* Cambridge, MA: Harvard University Press.

Ross, Catherine. (2003). *Twenties London: A City in the Jazz Age.* New York: Macmillan/St. Martin's.

Roth, Benita. (1999a). "Race, Class, and the Emergence of Black Feminism in the 1960s and 1970s." *Womanist Theory and Research* 2:1 (Fall).

———. (1999b). "The Vanguard Center: Intra-movement Experience and the Emergence of African-American Feminism." In Kimberly Springer (Ed.), *Still Lifting, Still Climbing: Contemporary African American Women's Activism* (70–90). New York: New York University Press.

———. (2004). *Separate Roads to Feminism: Black, Chicana and White Feminist Movements in America's Second Wave.* New York: Cambridge University Press.

Rousseas, Stephen William. (1982). *The Political Economy of Reagonomics: A Critique.* Armonk, NY: Sharpe.

Rovai, Alfred P., Gallien, Louis B., Stiff-Williams, Helen R. (Eds.). (2007). *Closing the African American Achievement Gap in Higher Education.* New York: Teachers College Press.

Royle, Nicholas. (2003). *Jacques Derrida.* New York: Routledge.

Rucker, Walter C. (2006). *River Flows On: Black Resistance, Culture, and Identity Formation in Early America.* Baton Rouge: Louisiana State University Press.

Rucker, Walter C., and Upton, James N. (Eds.). (2007). *Encyclopedia of American Race Riots.* Westport, CT: Greenwood.

Rudwick, Elliot M. (1960). *W.E.B. Du Bois: A Study in Minority Group Leadership.* Philadelphia: University of Pennsylvania.

———. (1968). *W.E.B. Du Bois: Propagandists of the Negro Protest.* New York: Atheneum.

Runell, Marcella. (Ed.). (2008). *Conscious Women Rock the Page: Using Hip Hop Fiction to Incite Social Change.* New York: Sister Outsider Entertainment.

Runell, Marcella, and Diaz, Martha. (2007). *The Hip Hop Education Guidebook*. New York: Hip Hop Association Publications.

Russell, Jamie. (2001). *Queer Burroughs*. New York: Palgrave.

Russell, Ross. (1996). *Bird Lives!: The High Life and Hard Times of Charlie (Yardbird) Parker*. New York: Da Capo Press.

Russell, Tony, and Smith, Chris. (Eds.). (2006). *The Penguin Guide to Blues Recordings*. New York: Penguin.

Said, Edward W. (1999). "Traveling Theory Reconsidered." In Nigel C. Gibson (Ed.), *Rethinking Fanon* (197–214). Amherst, NY: Humanity Books.

———. (2000). "Traveling Theory." In Moustafa Bayoumi and Andrew Rubin (Eds.), *The Edward Said Reader* (195–217). New York: Vintage.

Salamone, Frank A. (2009). *The Culture of Jazz: Jazz as Critical Culture*. Lanham, MD: University Press of America.

Sale, Maggie M. (1997). *Slumbering Volcano: America Slave Ship Revolts and the Production of Rebellious Masculinity*. Durham, NC: Duke University Press.

Salem, Dorothy. (1990). *To Better Our World: Black Women in Organized Reform, 1890–1920*. Brooklyn, NY: Carlson.

Sales, Grover. (1984). *Jazz: America's Classical Music*. New York: Da Capo.

Samuels, Wilfred David. (1977). *Five Afro-Caribbean Voices in American Culture 1917–1929: Hubert H. Harrison, Wilfred A. Domingo, Richard B. Moore, Cyril V. Briggs, and Claude McKay*. Boulder, CO: Belmont Books.

Sanchez, Sonia. (1969). *Home Coming*. Detroit: Broadside Press.

Sandke, Randy. (2010). *Where the Dark and the Light Folks Meet: Race and the Mythology, Politics, and Business of Jazz*. Lanham, MD: Scarecrow Press.

Sanger, Kerran L. (1995). *"When the Spirit Says Sing!": The Role of Freedom Songs in the Civil Rights Movement*. New York: Garland.

Sansevere, John R., and Farber, Erica. (1993). *Post-Bop Hip Hop: A Tribe Called Quest*. Racine, WI: Western Publishing.

Saucier, Paul Khalil. (Ed.). (2011). *Native Tongues: An African Hip Hop Reader*. Trenton, NJ: Africa World Press.

Savage, Barbara D. (1999). *Broadcasting Freedom: Radio, War, and the Politics of Race, 1938–1948*. Chapel Hill: University of North Carolina Press.

Savidge, Leigh. (Director). (2001). *Welcome to Death Row*. Santa Monica, CA: Xenon Pictures.

Saxton, Alexander. (1990). *The Rise and Fall of the White Republic: Class Politics and Mass Culture in Nineteenth Century America*. New York: Verso.

Schafer, William J. (2008). *The Original Jelly Roll Blues: The Story of Ferdinand Lamothe, a.k.a. Jelly Roll Morton, The Originator Of Jazz, Stomps and Blues*. London: Flame Tree Publishing.

Schafer, William J., and Allen, Richard B. (1977). *Brass Bands and New Orleans Jazz*. Baton Rouge: Louisiana State University Press.

Schafer, William J., and Riedel, Johannes. (1973). *The Art of Ragtime: Form and Meaning of an Original Black American Art*. Baton Rouge: Louisiana State University Press.

Schaller, Michael. (1992). *Reckoning with Reagan: America and Its President in the 1980s*. New York: Oxford University Press.

Schein, Richard H. (Ed.). (2006). *Landscape and Race in the United States*. New York: Routledge.

Schiele, Jerome H. (2000). *Human Services and the Afrocentric Paradigm*. New York: Haworth Press.

Schlereth, Thomas J. (1992). *Victorian America: Transformations in Everyday Life, 1876–1915*. New York: HarperPerennial.

Schloss, Joseph G. (2004). *Making Beats: The Art of Sample-Based Hip Hop*. Middletown, CT: Wesleyan University Press.

———. (2009). *Foundation: B-Boys, B-Girls and Hip Hop Culture in New York*. New York: Oxford University Press.

Schuller, Gunther. (1986). *Early Jazz: Its Roots and Musical Development.* New York: Oxford University Press.

———. (1989a). *The History of Jazz.* New York: Oxford University Press.

———. (1989b). *The Swing Era: The Development of Jazz, 1930–1945.* New York: Oxford University Press.

Schulman, Bruce J. (2001). *The Seventies: The Great Shift in American Culture, Society, and Politics.* New York: Free Press.

Schumacher, Thomas G. (1995). "'This is a Sampling Sport': Digital Sampling, Rap Music and the Law in Cultural Production." *Media Culture Society* 17 (2): 253–73.

Schur, Richard L. (2009). *Parodies of Ownership: Hip Hop Aesthetics and Intellectual Property Law.* Ann Arbor: University of Michigan Press.

Schwartzman, David. (1997). *Black Unemployment: Part of Unskilled Unemployment.* Westport, CT: Greenwood.

Schwarz, A. B. Christa. (2003). *Gay Voices of the Harlem Renaissance.* Bloomington: Indiana University Press.

———. (2007). "Transgressive Sexuality and the Literature of the Harlem Renaissance." In George Hutchinson (Ed.), *The Cambridge Companion to the Harlem Renaissance* (141–54). Cambridge: Cambridge University Press.

Scott, Michelle R. (2008). *Blues Empress in Black Chattanooga: Bessie Smith and the Emerging Urban South.* Urbana: University of Illinois Press.

Scott-Heron, Gil. (1971). *Pieces of a Man.* New York: RCA/Flying Dutchman.

Sears, James T., and Williams, Walter L. (Eds.). (1997). *Overcoming Heterosexism and Homophobia: Strategies That Work.* New York: Columbia University Press.

Seidel, Samuel Steinberg. (2011). *Hip Hop Genius: Remixing High School Education.* Lanham, MD: Rowman & Littlefield Education.

Seidman, Steven. (1995). "Deconstructing Queer Theory, or the Under-Theorization of the Social and the Ethical." In Linda J. Nicholson and Steven Seidman (Eds.), *Social Postmodernism: Beyond Identity Politics.* Cambridge: Cambridge University Press.

———. (Ed.). (1996). *Queer Theory/Sociology.* Cambridge, MA: Blackwell.

———. (1997). *Difference Troubles: Queering Social Theory and Sexual Politics.* Cambridge: Cambridge University Press.

Seidman, Steven, Fischer, Nancy, and Meeks, Chet. (Eds.). (2006). *Handbook of New Sexuality Studies.* New York: Routledge.

Sengstock, Charles A. (2004). *That Toddlin' Town: Chicago's White Dance Bands and Orchestras, 1900–1950.* Urbana: University of Illinois Press.

Shack, William A. (2001). *Harlem in Montmartre: A Paris Jazz Story Between the Great Wars.* Berkeley: University of California Press.

Shapiro, Edward S. (2006). *Crown Heights: Blacks, Jews, and the 1991 Brooklyn Riot.* Waltham, MA: Brandeis University Press.

Shapiro, Nat, and Hentoff, Nat. (1966). *Hear Me Talkin' To Ya: The Story of Jazz and the Men Who Made It.* New York: Dover.

Shapiro, Peter. (Ed.). (2001). *Hip Hop: The Mini-Rough Guide.* London: Rough Guides.

———. (Ed.). (2005a). *The Rough Guide to Hip Hop* (2nd Edition). London: Rough Guides.

———. (2005b). *Turn the Beat Around: The Secret History of Disco.* New York: Faber and Faber.

Shapiro, Thomas M. (2004). *The Hidden Cost of Being African American: How Wealth Perpetuates Inequality.* New York: Oxford University Press.

Sharma, Nitasha Tamar. (2010). *Hip Hop Desis: Asian Americans, Blackness, and a Global Race Consciousness.* Durham, NC: Duke University Press.

Sharpley-Whiting, Tracy D. (2007). *Pimps Up, Ho's Down: Hip Hop's Hold on Young Black Women.* New York: New York University Press.

Shaw, Arnold. (1970). *The World of Soul: Black America's Contributions to the Pop Music Scene.* New York: Cowles Book Co.

———. (1977). *52nd Street: The Street of Jazz.* New York: Da Capo.

———. (1978). *Honkers and Shouters: The Golden Years of Rhythm & Blues.* New York: Macmillan.

———. (1986). *Black Popular Music in America: From the Spirituals, Minstrels, and Ragtime to Soul, Disco, and Hip Hop.* New York: Schirmer Books.

———. (1987). *The Jazz Age: Popular Music in the 1920s.* New York: Oxford University Press.

———. (1998). *Let's Dance: Popular Music in the 1930s* (Ed. By Bill Willard). New York: Oxford University Press.

Shaw, Stephanie J. (1991). "Black Club Women and the Creation of the National Association of Colored Women." *Journal of Women's History* 3 (2): 1–25.

Shaw, William. (2000a). *Westsiders: Stories of Boys in the Hood.* London: Bloomsbury.

———. (2000b). *Westside: The Coast-to-Coast Explosion of Hip Hop.* New York: Cooper Square.

———. (2000c). *Westside: Young Men and Hip Hop in L.A.* New York: Simon & Schuster.

Shelton, Maria L. (1997). "Can't Touch This! Representations of the African American Female Body in Urban Rap Videos." *Popular Music and Society* 21 (3): 107–16.

Sherrard-Johnson, Cherene. (2007). *Portraits of the New Negro Woman: Visual and Literary Culture in the Harlem Renaissance.* New Brunswick, NJ: Rutgers University Press.

Shimeles, Nebeu. (2010). "I Love My Niggas No Homo: Homophobia and the Capitalist Subversion of Violent Masculinity in Hip Hop." *CTSJ: Journal of Undergraduate Research* 1 (1): 1–26.

Shipton, Alyn. (1999). *Groovin' High: The Life of Dizzy Gillespie.* New York: Oxford University Press.

———. (2007). *A New History of Jazz.* New York: Continuum.

Shirky, Clay. (2008). *Here Comes Everybody: The Power of Organizing Without Organizations.* New York: Penguin.

Shreffler, Anne C. (1997). "Classicizing Jazz: Concert Jazz in Paris and New York in the 1920s." In Herman Danuser (Ed.), *Klassizistiche Moderne: Paul Sacher Stiftung Basel April 1996* (55–71). Winterthur: Amadeus.

Shuker, Roy. (2001). *Understanding Popular Music.* New York: Routledge.

Sieving, Christopher. (2011). *Soul Searching: Black-Themed Cinema from the March on Washington to the Rise of Blaxploitation.* Middletown, CT: Wesleyan University Press.

Silverman, Hugh J. (Ed.). (1989). *Derrida and Deconstruction.* New York: Routledge.

Simone, Nina. (1966). *Wild is the Wind.* Universal City, CA: Verve Music/Philips.

———. (2003a). *Four Women: The Nina Simone Philips Recordings* (4 Compact Disc Set). Universal City, CA: Verve.

———. (2003b). *I Put A Spell On You: The Autobiography of Nina Simone* (with Stephen Cleary). New York: Da Capo.

———. (2008). *To Be Free: The Nina Simone Story* (4 Compact Disc/1 Digital Video Disc Set). New York: RCA/Legacy.

Simpson, Henri Lee. (2004). "Critical Incidents Relating to High School Drop-Out of Identified Young Adult Black Males." Ph.D. dissertation, University of Texas at Austin.

Sims, Yvonne D. (2006). *Women of Blaxploitation: How the Black Action Film Heroine Changed American Popular Culture.* Jefferson, NC: McFarland.

Singer, Merrill, and Mirhe, Greg. (2006). "High Notes: The Role of Drugs in the Making of Jazz." *Journal of Ethnicity in Substance Abuse* 5 (4): 1–38.

Singh, Nikhil Pal. (2004). *Black Is A Country: Race and the Unfinished Struggle for Democracy.* Cambridge, MA: Harvard University Press.

Sitomer, Alan L., and Cirelli, Michael. (Eds.). (2004). *Hip Hop Poetry and the Classics: Connecting Our Classic Curriculum to Hip Hop Poetry Through Standards-Based Language Arts Instruction.* Beverly Hills, CA: Milk Mug.

Skeggs, Beverley. (1993). "Two Minute Brother: Contestation Through Gender, 'Race' and Sexuality." *Innovation: The European Journal of Social Sciences* 6 (3): 299–323.

Skerl, Jennie, and Lydenberg, Robin. (Eds.). (1991). *William S. Burroughs at the Front: Critical Reception, 1959–1989.* Carbondale: Southern Illinois University Press.

Small, Christopher. (1998a). *Music of the Common Tongue: Survival and Celebration in African American Music.* Hanover, NH: University Press of New England.

————. (1998b). *Musicking: The Meanings of Performing and Listening.* Hanover, NH: Wesleyan University Press.

Smethurst, James Edward. (1999). *The New Red Negro: The Literary Left and African American Poetry, 1930–1946.* New York: Oxford University Press.

Smith, Barbara. (Ed.). (1983). *Home Girls: A Black Feminist Anthology.* New York: Kitchen Table Press.

Smith, Danyel. (1994). "Gang Starr: Jazzy Situation." *Vibe* (May): 88.

Smith, Efrem, and Jackson, Phil. (2005). *The Hip Hop Church: Connecting with the Movement Shaping Our Culture.* Downers Grove, IL: InterVarsity Press.

Smith, John David. (2000). *Black Judas: William Hannibal Thomas and* The American Negro. Athens: University of Georgia Press.

Smith, Neil. (1984). *Uneven Development: Nature, Capital, and the Production of Space.* New York: Blackwell.

Smith, R. J. (2006). *The Great Black Way: L.A.'s Central Avenue in the 1940s and the Shaping of African American Culture.* London: Perseus Running.

Smith, Susan Lynn. (1986). "The Black Women's Club Movement: Self-Improvement and Sisterhood, 1890–1915." Master's thesis, University of Wisconsin, Madison.

Smith-Rosenberg, Carroll. (1985). *Disorderly Conduct: Visions of Gender in Victorian America.* New York: Knopf.

Smith-Shomade, Beretta E. (2003). "'Rock-a-Bye, Baby!': Black Women Disrupting Gangs and Constructing Hip Hop Gangsta Films." *Cinema Journal* 42 (2): 25–40.

Smitherman, Geneva. (1975). *Black Language and Culture: Sounds of Soul.* New York: Harper & Row.

————. (1986). *Talkin' and Testifyin': The Language of Black America.* Detroit: Wayne State University Press.

————. (2000). *Talkin' That Talk: Language, Culture and Education in African America.* New York: Routledge.

————. (2006). *Word From the Mother: Language and African Americans.* New York: Routledge.

Smulyan, Susan. (1994). *Selling Radio: The Commercialization of American Broadcasting, 1920–1934.* Washington, DC: Smithsonian Institution Press.

Solomon, Mark I. (1998). *The Cry Was Unity: Communists and African American, 1917–1936.* Jackson: University Press of Mississippi.

Somerville, Siobhan B. (2000). *Queering the Color-Line: Race and the Invention of Homosexuality in American Culture.* Durham, NC: Duke University Press.

Sondergard, Sid. (2003). "Unable to Queer the Deal: William S. Burroughs's Negotiations with 'Eugene Allerton.'" *Critique: Studies in Contemporary Fiction* 44 (2): 144–56.

Sotiropoulos, Karen. (2006). *Staging Race: Black Performance in Turn of the Century America.* Cambridge, MA: Harvard University Press.

Southern, Eileen. (1997). *Music of Black Americans: A History.* New York: W. W. Norton.

Spady, James G., Alim, H. Samy, and Meghelli, Samir. (Ed.). (2006). *The Global Cipha: Hip Hop Culture and Consciousness.* Philadelphia, PA: Black History Museum Press.

Spady, James G., Dupres, Stefan, and Lee, Charles G. (Eds.). (1995). *Twisted Tales: In the Hip Hop Streets of Philly.* Philadelphia, PA: UMUM/LOH Publishers.

Spady, James G., Lee, Charles G., and Alim, H. Samy. (1999). *Street Conscious Rap.* Philadelphia, PA: Black History Museum Press/LOH Publishers.

Spellman, A. B. (1965). *The Beautiful Days.* New York: Poets Press.

Spence, Lester K. (2011). *Stare in the Darkness: The Limits of Hip Hop and Black Politics.* Minneapolis: University of Minnesota Press.

Spencer, Frederick J. (2002). *Jazz and Death: Medical Profiles of Jazz Greats.* Jackson: University Press of Mississippi.

Spencer, Jon Michael. (1990). *Protest & Praise: Sacred Music of Black Religion.* Minneapolis: Fortress Press.

————. (Ed.). (1991). "The Emergency of Black and the Emergence of Rap." *Black Sacred Music: A Journal of Theomusicology* 5 (1): 1–94.

————. (1993). *Blues & Evil.* Knoxville: University of Tennessee Press.

———. (1995). *The Rhythms of Black Folk: Race, Religion, and Pan-Africanism*. Trenton, NJ: Africa World Press.

———. (1997). *The New Negroes and Their Music: The Success of the Harlem Renaissance*. Knoxville: University of Tennessee Press.

Spirer, Peter. (Director). (1997). *Rhyme & Reason: A History of Rap Music*. Burbank, CA: Buena Vista Home Entertainment.

———. (Director). (2005). *The MC: Why We Do It*. Chatsworth, CA: Image Entertainment.

———. (Director). (2006). *The Art of 16 Bars: Get Ya' Barz Up*. Chatsworth, CA: Image Entertainment.

Sportis, Yves. (1990). *Free Jazz*. Paris: Editions de l'Instant.

Springer, Kimberly. (Ed.). (1999). *Still Lifting, Still Climbing: Contemporary African American Women's Activism*. New York: New York University Press.

———. (2001). "The Interstitial Politics of Black Feminist Organizations." *Meridians: Feminism, Race, Transnationalism* 1 (2): 155–91.

———. (2002). "Third Wave Black Feminism?" *Signs: Journal of Women in Culture and Society* 27 (4): 1059–82.

———. (2005). *Living for the Revolution: Black Feminist Organizations, 1968–1980*. Durham, NC: Duke University Press.

Springhall, John. (2008). *Genesis of Mass Culture: Show Business Live in America, 1840 to 1940*. New York: Macmillan.

St. Jean, Yanick, and Feagin, Joe R. (1998). *Double Burden: Black Women and Everyday Racism*. Armonk, NY: Sharpe.

Stambler, Irwin, and Stambler, Lyndon. (Eds.). (2001). *Folk and Blues: The Encyclopedia*. New York: Thomas Dunne Books.

Stanley, Lawrence A. (Ed.). (1992). *Rap: The Lyrics*. New York: Penguin.

Stanley, Tarshia L. (Ed.). (2009). *Encyclopedia of Hip Hop Literature*. Westport, CT: Greenwood.

Stanley-Niaah, Sonjah Nadine. (2010). *Dancehall: From Slave Ship to Ghetto*. Ottawa: University of Ottawa Press.

Steele, Valerie. (1985). *Fashion and Eroticism: Ideals of Feminine Beauty from the Victorian Era to the Jazz Age*. New York: Oxford University Press.

Steinschneider, Janice. (1994). *An Improved Woman: The Wisconsin Federation of Women's Clubs, 1895–1920*. Brooklyn, NY: Carlson.

Stephens, Dionne P., and Few, April L. (2007a). "The Effects of Images of African American Women in Hip Hop on Early Adolescents' Attitudes Toward Physical Attractiveness and Interpersonal Relationships." *Sex Roles* 56 (3–4): 251–64.

———. (2007b). "Hip Hop Honey or Video Ho: African American Preadolescents' Understanding of Female Sexual Scripts in Hip Hop Culture." *Sexuality & Culture* 11 (4): 48–69.

Stephens, Ronald J. (1996). "Keepin' It Real: Toward an Afrocentric Aesthetic Analysis of Rap Music and Hip Hop Subculture." Ph.D. dissertation, Department of African American Studies, Temple University, Philadelphia.

Stephens, Vincent. (2005). "Pop Goes the Rapper: A Close Reading of Eminem's Genderphobia." *Popular Music* 24 (1): 21–36.

Sterk, Claire E. (1999). *Fast Lives: Women Who Use Crack Cocaine*. Philadelphia: Temple University Press.

Sternfeld, Joshua. (2007). "Jazz Echoes: The Cultural and Socio-Political Reception of Jazz in Weimar and Nazi Berlin, 1925–1939." Ph.D. dissertation, University of California, Los Angeles.

Sterritt, David. (2004). *Screening the Beat: Media Culture and the Beat Sensibility*. Carbondale: Southern Illinois University Press.

Stewart, Jeffrey C. (2007). "The New Negro as Citizen." In George Hutchinson (Ed.), *The Cambridge Companion to the Harlem Renaissance* (13–27). Cambridge: Cambridge University Press.

Stewart-Baxter, Derrick. (1970). *Ma Rainey and the Classic Blues Singers*. New York: Stein and Day.

Stimpson, Catharine R. (1983). "The Beat Generation and the Trials of Homosexual Libera-
tion." *Salmagundi* 58/59: 373–92.
Stockton, Kathryn B. (2006). *Beautiful Bottom, Beautiful Shame: Where "Black" Meets
"Queer."* Durham, NC: Duke University Press.
Stokes, Mason B. (2001). *Color of Sex: Whiteness, Heterosexuality, and the Fictions of White
Supremacy.* Durham, NC: Duke University Press.
Stolzoff, Norman C. (2000). *Wake the Town and Tell the People: Dancehall
Culture in Jamaica.* Durham, NC: Duke University Press.
Stone, Amy, and Ward, Jane. (2011). "From 'Black People Are Not a Homosexual Act' to
'Gay is the New Black': Mapping White Uses of Blackness in Modern Gay Rights Cam-
paigns in the United States." *Social Identities* 17 (5): 605–24.
Stone, Ruth M. (Ed.). (2008). *The Garland Handbook of African Music.* New York: Garland.
Stowe, David W. (1994). *Swing Changes: Big Band Jazz in New Deal America.* Cambridge,
MA: Harvard University Press.
———. (2004). *How Sweet the Sound: Music in the Spiritual Lives of Americans.* Cambridge,
MA: Harvard University Press.
———. (2010). "Both American and Global: Jazz and World Religions in the United States."
*Religion Compass* 4 (5): 312–23.
Stowe, Harriet Beecher. (1852). *Uncle Tom's Cabin.* Boston: John P. Jewett and Company.
Strausbaugh, John. (2006). *Black Like You: Blackface, Whiteface, Insult & Imitation in Ameri-
ca Popular Culture.* New York: Penguin.
Strode, Timothy F., and Wood, Tim. (Eds.). (2008). *The Hip Hop Reader.* New York: Pearson
Longman.
Studlar, Gaylyn. (1996). *This Mad Masquerade: Stardom and Masculinity in the Jazz Age.*
New York: Columbia University Press.
Such, David Glen. (1993). *Avant-Garde Jazz Musicians: Performing "Out There."* Iowa City:
University of Iowa Press.
Sudhalter, Richard M. (1999). *Lost Chords: White Musicians and Their Contribution to Jazz,
1915–1945.* New York: Oxford University Press.
Suisman, David. (2009). *Selling Sounds: The Commercial Revolution in American Mu-
sic.*Cambridge, MA: Harvard University Press.
Sullivan, Denise. (2011). *Keep On Pushing: Black Power Music from Blues to Hip Hop.*
Chicago: Lawrence Hill Books.
Sullivan, Nikki. (2003). *A Critical Introduction to Queer Theory.* New York: New York Uni-
versity Press.
Sullivan, Randall. (2002). *LAbyrinth: A Detective Investigates the Murders of Tupac Shakur
and Notorious B.I.G., The Implication of Death Row Records' Suge Knight, and the Origins
of the Los Angeles Police Scandal.* New York: Grove Press.
Sulton, Anne T. (Ed.). (1996). *African American Perspectives on Crime Causation, Criminal
Justice Administration, and Crime Prevention.* Boston: Butterworth Heinemann.
Summers, Martin Anthony. (2004). *Manliness and its Discontents: The Black Middle-Class
and The Transformation of Masculinity, 1900–1930.* Chapel Hill: University of North Caro-
lina Press.
Tan, Joël Barraquiel. (2006). "Homothugdragsterism." In Jeff Chang (Ed.), *Total Chaos: The
Art and Aesthetics of Hip Hop* (209–18). New York: Basic/Civitas.
Tanz, Jason. (2007). *Other People's Property: A Shadow History of Hip Hop in White America.*
New York: Bloomsbury.
Taylor, David John. (2009). *Bright Young People: The Lost Generation of London's Jazz Age.*
New York: Farrar, Straus & Giroux.
Taylor, Eric R. (2006). *If We Must Die: Shipboard Insurrections in the Era of the Atlantic Slave
Trade.* Baton Rouge: Louisiana State University.
Taylor, Frank C., and Cook, Gerald. (1987). *Alberta Hunter: A Celebration in Blues.* New
York: McGraw-Hill.
Taylor, Henry Louis, and Hill, Walter. (Eds.). (2000). *Historical Roots of the Urban Crisis:
African Americans in the Industrial City, 1900–1950.* New York: Garland.

Taylor, Shawn. (2007). *People's Instinctive Travels and the Paths of Rhythm*. New York: Continuum.

Teachout, Terry. (2009). *Pops: A Life of Louis Armstrong*. Boston: Houghton Mifflin Harcourt.

Tenaille, Frank. (2002). *Music is the Weapon of the Future: Fifty Years of African Popular Music*. Chicago: Lawrence Hill Books.

Terborg-Penn, Rosalyn. (1998). *African American Women in the Struggle for the Vote, 1850–1920*. Bloomington: Indiana University Press.

Terkourafi, Marina. (2010). *Languages of Global Hip Hop*. New York: Continuum.

Thernstrom, Stephan, and Thernstrom, Abigail. (1997). *American in Black and White*. New York: Simon & Schuster.

Thomas, William Hannibal. (1901). *The American Negro: What He Was, What He Is, and What He May Become*. New York: Macmillan.

Thompson, Dave. (2001). *Funk*. San Francisco: Backbeat Books.

Thompson, Lisa B. (2009). *Beyond the Black Lady: Sexuality and the New African American Middle Class*. Urbana: University of Illinois Press.

Thompson, Robert Farris. (1974). *African Art in Motion: Icon and Act*. Los Angeles: University of California Press.

———. (1983). *Flash of the Spirit: African and Afro-American Art and Philosophy*. New York: Random House.

Thompson, Shirley Elizabeth. (2009). *Exiles at Home: The Struggle to Become American in Creole New Orleans*. Cambridge, MA: Harvard University Press.

Thurman, Wallace. (2003). *Collected Writing of Wallace Thurman: A Harlem Renaissance Reader* (Amritjit Singh and Daniel M. Scott III, Eds.). New Brunswick, NJ: Rutgers University Press.

Tillery, Tyrone. (1992). *Claude McKay: A Black Poet's Struggle for Identity*. Amherst: University of Massachusetts Press.

Toll, Robert C. (1974). *Blacking Up: The Minstrel Show in Nineteenth Century America*. Oxford: Oxford University Press.

———. (1976). *On With the Show!: The First Century of Show Business in America*. New York: Oxford University Press.

Tolson, Gerald H., and Cuyjet, Michael J. (2007). "Jazz and Substance Abuse: Road to Creative Genius or Pathway to Premature Death." *International Journal of Law and Psychiatry* 30 (6): 530–38.

Toop, David. (1991). *Rap Attack 2: African Rap to Global Hip Hop*. London: Serpent's Tail.

———. (2000). *Rap Attack 3: African Rap to Global Hip Hop*. London: Serpent's Tail.

Touré, Askia M. (1970). *Juju: Magic Songs for the Black Nation*. Chicago: Third World Press.

Townsend, Peter. (2000). *Jazz in American Culture*. Jackson: University Press of Mississippi.

Toynbee, Jason. (2000). *Making Popular Music: Musicians, Creativity and Institutions*. New York: Oxford University Press.

Tracy, Steven C. (Ed.). (1999). *Write Me a Few of Your Lines: A Blues Reader*. Amherst: University of Massachusetts Press.

———. (2001). *Langston Hughes & the Blues*. Urbana: University of Illinois Press.

A Tribe Called Quest. (1991). *The Low End Theory*. New York: Jive/BMG Music.

Troka, Donna. (2002). "'You Heard My Gun Cock': Female Agency and Aggression in Contemporary Rap Music." *African American Research Perspectives* 8 (2): 82–89.

Trotter, Joe William, Jr. (Ed.). (1991). *The Great Migration in Historical Perspective: New Dimensions of Race, Class, and Gender*. Bloomington: Indiana University Press.

———. (2001). *The African American Experience*. Boston: Houghton Mifflin.

Tuck, Stephen G. N. (2010). *We Ain't What We Ought To Be: The Black Freedom Struggle, from Emancipation to Obama*. Cambridge, MA: Belknap.

Tucker, Linda G. (2007). *Lockstep and Dance: Images of Black Men in Popular Culture*. Jackson: University Press of Mississippi.

Tucker, Susan. (1988). *Telling Memories Among Southern Women: Domestic Workers and Their Employers in the Segregated South*. Baton Rouge: Louisiana State University Press.

Tucker-Worgs, Tamelyn. (2011). *The Black Mega-Church: Theology, Gender, and the Politics of Public Engagement*. Waco, TX: Baylor University Press.

Tumpak, John R. (2008). *When Swing Was the Thing: Personality Profiles of the Big Band Era.* Milwaukee, WI: Marquette University Press.
Turner, Richard Brent. (2003). *Islam in the African American Experience.* Bloomington: Indiana University Press.
Tuttle, William M. (1996). *Race Riot: Chicago in the Red Summer of 1919.* Urbana: University of Illinois Press.
Tye, Larry. (2004). *Rising from the Rails: Pullman Porters and the Making of the Black Middle-Class.* New York: Henry Holt.
Upchurch, Thomas. (2008). *Race Relations in the United States, 1960–1980.* Westport, CT: Greenwood.
Utley, Ebony A. (2012). *Rap and Religion: Understanding the Gangsta's God.* Westport, CT: Praeger.
Vail, Ken. (2003). *Dizzy Gillespie: The Bebop Years, 1937–1952.* Lanham, MD: Scarecrow Press.
Van Deburg, William L. (1992). *New Day in Babylon: The Black Power Movement and American Culture, 1965–1975.* Chicago: University of Chicago Press.
Vance, Carole S. (1984). *Pleasure and Danger: Exploring Female Sexuality.* Boston: Routledge & K. Paul.
Vaz, Kim Marie. (Ed.). (1995). *Black Women in America.* Thousand Oaks, CA: Sage.
Venkatesh, Sudhir Alladi. (2000). *American Project: The Rise and Fall of a Modern Ghetto.* Cambridge, MA: Harvard University Press.
———. (2006). *Off the Books: The Underground Economy of the Urban Poor.* Cambridge, MA: Harvard University Press.
Vergara, Camilo J. (1995). *The New American Ghetto.* New Brunswick, NJ: Rutgers University Press.
Vincent, Rickey. (1996). *Funk: The Music, the People, and the Rhythm of the One.* New York: St. Martin's Griffin.
Vincent, Theodore G. (Ed.). (1990). *Voices of a Black Nation: Political Journalism in the Harlem Renaissance.* Trenton, NJ: Africa World Press.
Vogel, Shane. (2009). *The Scene of Harlem Cabaret: Race, Sexuality, Performance.* Chicago: University of Chicago Press.
Vogel, Todd. (Ed.). (2001). *The Black Press: New Literary and Historical Essays.* New Brunswick, NJ: Rutgers University Press.
Voogd, Jan. (2008). *Race Riots & Resistance: The Red Summer of 1919.* New York: Lang.
Waagbø, Janne. (2007). "'Dancehall!—A Serious Thing!': Performing Gender in Jamaican Dancehall." Ph.D. dissertation, University Of Oslo.
Walcott, Rinaldo. (1996). "Performing the Postmodern: Black Atlantic Rap and Identity in North America." Ph.D. dissertation, University of Toronto.
Waldrep, Christopher. (Ed.). (2006). *Lynching in America: A History in Documents.* New York: New York University Press.
Waldron, Edward E. (1971). "The Blues Poetry of Langston Hughes." *Negro American Literature Forum* 5 (4): 140–49.
Walker, David, Rausch, Andrew J., and Watson, Chris. (2009). *Reflections on Blaxploitation: Actors and Directors Speak.* Lanham, MD: Scarecrow Press.
Walker, Klive. (2005). *Dubwise: Reasoning from the Reggae Underground.* Toronto: Insomniac Press.
Walker, Tshombe R. (1998). "The Hip Hop Worldview: An Afrocentric Analysis." Ph.D. dissertation, Department of African American Studies, Temple University, Philadelphia.
Walker, Wyatt Tee. (1979). *"Somebody's Calling My Name": Black Sacred Music and Social Change.* Valley Forge, PA: Judson Press.
Walker-Hill, Helen. (2007). *From Spirituals to Symphonies: African American Women Composers and Their Music.* Chicago: University of Illinois Press.
Wall, Cheryl A. (1995). *Women of the Harlem Renaissance.* Bloomington: Indiana University Press.
Wallenstein, Barry. (1980). "The Jazz-Poetry Connection." *Performing Arts Journal* 4 (3): 122–134.

————. (1991). "Poetry and Jazz: A Twentieth-Century Wedding." *Black American Literature Forum* 25 (3): 595–620.

Walrond, Eric. (1924). "Enter the New Negro, A Distinctive Type Recently Created by the Colored Cabaret Belt in New York" (with Miguel Covarrubias). *Vanity Fair* (December): 59–62.

Walser, Robert. (1995). "Rhythm, Rhyme and Rhetoric in the Music of Public Enemy." *Ethnomusicology: Journal of the Society for Ethnomusicology* 39: 193–217.

Walters, Ronald W. (1993). *Pan-Africanism in the African Diaspora: An Analysis of Modern Afrocentric Political Movement*. Detroit: Wayne State University Press.

Wang, Oliver (Ed.). (2003). *Classic Material: The Hip Hop Album Guide*. Chicago: ECW Press.

Ward, Brian. (1998). *Just My Soul Responding: Rhythm & Blues, Black Consciousness, and Race Relations*. Berkeley: University of California Press.

————. (Ed). (2001). *Media, Culture, and the Modern African American Freedom Struggle*. Gainesville: University Press of Florida.

————. (2004). *Radio and the Struggle for Civil Rights in the South*. Gainesville: University Press of Florida.

Ward, Geoffrey C. (2000). *Jazz: A History of America's Music*. New York: Knopf.

Warner, Simon. (2007). *Text, Drugs and Rock 'n' Roll: The Beats and Rock, from Kerouac to Cobain*. New York: Continuum.

Warren, Roland L. (Ed.). (2008). *Politics and African American Ghettos*. New Brunswick, NJ: Aldine Transaction.

Washington, Booker T. (Ed.). (1900). *A New Negro for a New Century: An Accurate and Up-to-Date Record of the Upward Struggles of the Negro Race*. Chicago: American Publishing House.

————. (1901). *Up from Slavery: An Autobiography*. Garden City, NY: Doubleday.

Washington, Johnny. (1986). *Alain Locke and Philosophy: A Quest for Cultural Pluralism*. New York: Greenwood Press.

————. (1994). *A Journey Into the Philosophy of Alain Locke*. New York: Greenwood Press.

Watkins, S. Craig. (1998). *Hip Hop Culture and the Production of Black Cinema*. Chicago: University of Chicago Press.

————. (2005). *Hip Hop Matters: Politics, Pop Culture, and the Struggle for the Soul of a Movement*. Boston, MA: Beacon.

————. (2009). *The Young and the Digital: What the Migration to Social-Network Sites, Games, and Anytime, Anywhere Media Means for Our Future*. Boston: Beacon.

Watson, Elwood. (Ed.). (2009). *Pimps, Wimps, Studs, Thugs, and Gentlemen: Essays on Media Images of Masculinity*. Jefferson, NC: McFarland.

Watson, Steven. (1995a). *The Birth of the Beat Generation: Visionaries, Rebels, and Hipsters, 1944–1960*. New York: Pantheon.

————. (1995b). *Harlem Renaissance: Hub of African American Culture, 1920–1930*. New York: Pantheon.

Webb, Gary. (1998). *Dark Alliance: The CIA, the Contras, and the Crack Cocaine Explosion*. New York: Seven Stories Press.

Wehbi, Samantha. (Ed.). (2004). *Community Organizing Against Homophobia and Heterosexism: The World Through Rainbow-Colored Glasses*. New York: Harrington Park Press.

Weiler, Uwe. (1994). *The Debut Label: A Discography*. Norderstedt: Weiler Press.

Weingarten, Christopher R. (2010). *It Takes a Nation of Millions to Hold Us Back*. New York: Continuum.

Weiss, Brad. (2009). *Street Dreams and Hip Hop Barbershops: Global Fantasy in Urban Tanzania*. Bloomington: Indiana University Press.

Weitz, Rose. (1998). *The Politics of Women's Bodies: Sexuality, Appearance, and Behavior*. New York: Oxford University Press.

Weitzer, Ronald, and Kubrin, Charis. (2009). "Misogyny in Rap Music." *Men and Masculinities* 12 (1): 3–29.

Welbon, Yvonne. (Director). (1993). *Sisters in the Life: First Love*. New York: Third World Newsreel.

Wells, Mildred White. (1953). *Unity in Diversity: The History of the General Federation of Women's Clubs.* Washington, DC: General Federation of Women's Clubs Publishing.

Welter, Barbara. (1976). *Dimity Convictions: The American Woman in the Nineteenth Century.* Athens: Ohio University Press.

Werner, Craig H. (2004). *Higher Ground: Stevie Wonder, Aretha Franklin, Curtis Mayfield, and the Rise and Fall of American Soul.* New York: Crown.

———. (2006). *Change is Gonna Come: Music, Race & the Soul of America.* Ann Arbor: University of Michigan Press.

Wesley, Charles H. (1984). *The History of the National Association of Colored Women's Clubs: A Legacy of Service.* Washington, DC: National Association of Colored Women.

West, Cornel. (1993). *Race Matters.* New York: Random House.

West, Tim'm T. (2005). "Keepin' It Real: Disidentification and Its Discontents." In Harry J. Elam, Jr., and Kennell Jackson (Eds.), *Black Cultural Traffic: Crossroads in Global Performance and Popular Culture* (162–84). Ann Arbor: University of Michigan Press.

Whitaker, Robert. (2008). *On the Laps of Gods: The Red Summer of 1919 and the Struggle for Justice That Remade a Nation.* New York: Crown.

White, Deborah Gray. (1999). *Too Heavy A Load: Black Women in Defense of Themselves, 1894–1994.* New York: Norton.

White, E. Frances. (2001). *Dark Continent of Our Bodies: Black Feminism and the Politics of Respectability.* Philadelphia: Temple University Press.

White, Kevin. (2000). *Sexual Liberation or Sexual License?: The American Revolt Against Victorianism.* Chicago: Ivan R. Dee.

White, Shane, and White, Graham J. (1998). *Stylin': African American Expressive Culture From Its Beginnings to the Zoot Suit.* Ithaca, NY: Cornell University Press.

White, Walter Francis. (1924). *The Fire in the Flint.* New York: Knopf.

———. (1926). *Flight.* New York: Knopf.

Whitehead, Kevin. (2011). *Why Jazz?: A Concise Guide.* New York: Oxford University Press.

Wilkerson, Isabel. (2010). *The Warmth of Other Suns: The Epic Story of America's Great Migration.* New York: Random House.

Williams, Juan. (1987). *Eyes on the Prize: America's Civil Rights Years, 1954–1965.* New York: Viking.

Williams, Justin A. (2010a). "The Construction of Jazz Rap as High Art in Hip Hop Music." *Journal of Musicology* 27 (4): 435–59.

———. (2010b). "Musical Borrowing in Hip Hop Music: Theoretical Frameworks and Case Studies." Ph.D. dissertation, University of Nottingham.

Williams, Martin T. (1959). *The Art of Jazz: Essays on the Nature and Development of Jazz.* New York: Oxford University Press.

———. (1960). *King Oliver.* London: Cassell.

———. (1962). *Jelly Roll Morton.* London: Cassell.

———. (1967). *Jazz Masters of New Orleans.* New York: Macmillan.

———. (1970a). *Jazz Masters in Transition, 1957–1969.* New York: Macmillan.

———. (1970b). *The Jazz Tradition.* New York: Oxford University Press.

———. (1985). *Jazz Heritage.* New York: Oxford University Press.

———. (1989). *Jazz In Its Time.* New York: Oxford University Press.

———. (1992). *Jazz Changes.* New York: Oxford University Press.

Williams, Richard. (2002). *Nina Simone: Don't Let Me Be Misunderstood.* Edinburgh: Canongate Books.

Williams, Todd Larkins. (Director). (2002). *Tha Westside.* San Mateo, CA: Niche Entertainment/Image Entertainment.

———. (Director). (2007). *The N Word.* Port Washington, NY: Koch Releasing.

Willis, Deborah, and Williams, Carla. (2002). *The Black Female Body: A Photographic History.* Philadelphia: Temple University Press.

Wills, Garry. (1970). *Nixon Agonistes: The Crises of the Self-Made Man.* Boston: Houghton Mifflin.

Wilmer, Valerie. (1992). *As Serious as Your Life: John Coltrane and Beyond.* London: Serpent's Tail.

Wilmore, Gayraud S. (1983). *Black Religion and Black Radicalism: An Interpretation of the Religious History of Afro-American People.* Maryknoll, NY: Orbis.
————. (Ed.). (1989). *African American Religious Studies: An Interdisciplinary Anthology.* Durham, NC: Duke University Press.
Wilson, Bianca. (2009). "Black Lesbian Gender and Sexual Culture: Celebration and Resistance." *Culture, Health & Sexuality* 11 (3): 297–313.
Wilson, D. Mark. (2007). "Post-Pomo Hip Hop Homos: Hip Hop Art, Gay Rappers, and Social Change." *Social Justice San Francisco* 34 (1): 117–40.
Wilson, David. (2007). *Cities and Race: America's New Black Ghetto.* New York: Routledge.
Wilson, James F. (2010). *Bulldaggers, Pansies, and Chocolate Babies: Performance, Race, and Sexuality in the Harlem Renaissance.* Ann Arbor: University of Michigan Press.
Wilson, Peter Niklas. (1999). *Ornette Coleman: His Life and Music.* Berkeley, CA: Berkeley Hills Books.
Wilson, Sondra K. (Ed.). (2000). *The Messenger Reader: Stories, Poetry, and Essays from the Messenger Magazine.* New York: Modern Library.
Wilson, William J. (1987). *The Truly Disadvantaged: The Inner City, the Underclass, and Public Policy.* Chicago: University of Chicago Press.
————. (1997). *When Work Disappears: The World of the New Urban Poor.* New York: Knopf/Random House.
————. (1999). *The Bridge Over the Racial Divide: Rising Inequality and Coalition Politics.* Berkeley: University of California Press.
————. (2009). *More Than Just Race: Being Black and Poor in the Inner City.* New York: Norton.
Wilton, Tamsin. (1995). *Lesbian Studies: Setting an Agenda.* New York: Routledge.
Wimsatt, William Upski. (2003). *Bomb the Suburbs: Graffiti, Race, Freight-Hopping and the Search for Hip Hop's Moral Center.* New York: Soft Skull Press.
Winant, Howard. (1994). *Racial Conditions: Politics, Theory, Comparisons.* Minneapolis: University of Minnesota Press.
————. (2001). *The World is a Ghetto: Race and Democracy Since World War II.* New York: Basic.
————. (2004). *The New Politics of Race: Globalism, Difference, Justice.* Minneapolis: University of Minnesota Press.
Wintz, Cary D. (Ed.). (1996a). *African American Political Thought, 1890–1930: Washington, Du Bois, Garvey, and Randolph.* Armonk, NY: Sharpe.
————. (Ed.). (1996b). *The Politics and Aesthetics of "New Negro" Literature.* New York: Garland.
Wipplinger, Jonathan Otto. (2006). "The Jazz Republic: Music, Race, and American Culture in Weimar Germany." Ph.D. dissertation, University of Michigan, Ann Arbor.
Wohl, Robert. (1979). *The Generation of 1914.* Cambridge, MA: Harvard University Press.
Woideck, Carl. (1996). *Charlie Parker: His Music and Life.* Ann Arbor: University of Michigan Press.
Wolfe, Tom. (1970). *Radical Chic & Mau-Mauing the Flak-Catchers.* New York: Farrar, Straus & Giroux.
Wolters, Raymond. (2001). *Du Bois and His Rivals.* Columbia: University of Missouri Press.
Wondrich, David. (2003). *Stomp and Swerve: American Music Gets Hot, 1843–1924.* Chicago: Chicago Review Press.
Wood, David. (Ed.). (1992). *Derrida: A Critical Reader.* Cambridge, MA: Blackwell.
Woods, Gregory. (1998). *The History of Gay Literature: The Male Tradition.* New Haven, CT: Yale University Press.
Woodstra, Chris, Bush, John, and Erlewine, Stephen Thomas. (Eds.). (2008). *Old School Rap and Hip Hop.* New York: Backbeat Books.
Work, John W. (Ed.). (1998). *American Negro Songs: 230 Folk Songs and Spirituals, Religious and Secular.* Mineola, NY: Dover.
Wormser, Richard. (Producer). (2002). *The Rise and Fall of Jim Crow: A Century of Segregation* (4 Episodes). San Francisco, CA: California Newsreel.

Worthy, Ruth. (1952). "Negro in Our History: William Monroe Trotter, 1872–1934." Master's thesis, Department of History, Columbia University.

Wright, Laurie. (Ed.). (1993). *The Jug Bands of Louisville*. Essex, England: Storyville Publications.

Wright, Richard. (1940). *Native Son*. New York: Harper & Brothers.

Yaffe, David. (2006). *Fascinating Rhythm: Reading Jazz in American Writing*. Princeton, NJ: Princeton University Press.

Yanow, Scott. (2000a). *Bebop*. San Francisco: Miller Freeman Books.

———. (2000b). *Swing*. San Francisco: Miller Freeman Books.

———. (2001a). *Classic Jazz*. San Francisco: Backbeat Books.

———. (2001b). *The Trumpet Kings: The Players Who Shaped the Sound of Jazz Trumpet*. San Francisco: Backbeat Books.

———. (2008). *The Jazz Singers: The Ultimate Guide*. New York: Backbeat Books.

Young, Vershawn A. (2007). *Your Average Nigga: Performing Race, Literacy, and Masculinity*. Detroit: Wayne State University Press.

Zangrando, Robert L. (1980). *The NAACP Crusade Against Lynching, 1909–1950*. Philadelphia: Temple University Press.

Zhang, Yuanyuan, Dixon, Travis L., and Conrad, Kate. (2009). "Rap Music Videos and African American Women's Body Image: The Moderating Role of Ethnic Identity." *Journal of Communication* 59 (2): 262–78.

———. (2010). "Female Body Image as a Function of Themes in Rap Music Videos: A Content Analysis." *Sex Roles* 62 (11): 787–97.

Zimmerman, Marc A., Steinman, Kenneth J., and Rowe, Karen J. (1999). "Violence Among Urban African American Adolescents: The Protective Effects of Parental Support." *Violence & Abuse Abstracts* 5 (4): 78–103.

Zott, Lynn M. (Ed.). (2003). *The Beat Generation: A Gale Critical Companion*. Detroit: Gale.

# Index

Adderley, Cannonball, 122, 141, 145
African: holocaust, 25, 180–181, 225n10;
    music, 28–30, 35, 70, 95n10
African American: enslavement, xvi, xix,
    xxxn4, 15, 20, 25, 29–30, 34, 45–48,
    56, 93n5, 95n11, 158, 169, 176, 189,
    216, 224n6, 225n10, 249, 279n1,
    280n3; history, 54–59, 64–69, 98n37,
    114–117, 137–138, 162n13, 188–189,
    225n10, 235–237; movement music,
    xv–xx, xxv, 231–278
African American women : poor, 21–27,
    40–52, 60, 77–83, 88, 94n8, 98n35;
    underclass, 23, 31, 93n3, 94n8, 96n22;
    working-class, 20–42
African Blood Brotherhood, 194, 234
Afro-boho, 151–154
Afrocentricity, 69–71, 97n30, 121,
    143–144
Aggracycst, 266
Albertson, Chris, 97n34
alchemy: aesthetic, 28, 115; aural, xxii
Allen, Red, 107
Ambrosius, Marsha, 78
American: apartheid, 16, 29–34, 95n12,
    105, 181–182, 225n10, 247, 270;
    imperialism, 9–10, 265; Victorianism,
    50, 95n20
the American Dream, 44, 261
*The American Negro What He Was What
    He Is and What He May Become*

(Thomas), 45–48, 73
Ammons, Gene, 118, 133
amnesia, xvi; musical, 158
Anaya, Rudolfo, 259
Anderson, Carleen, 147
Anderson, Laurie, 259
Angelou, Maya, 152
anti-black: ghetto youth impulse, 4, 17n2;
    racist sexism, 49; racist violence, 30,
    64, 172–175, 189; sexism, 8, 21–28, 49,
    75–77
Arie, India. *See* India.Arie
Armatrading, Joan, 82
Armstrong, Louis, 99–100, 104, 105,
    106–107, 117, 120, 141, 143
artistic activism, 100, 169–171, 192–198
artistic license, 140, 171, 236
Atlantic Records, 15, 242
Aunt Chloe, 195
Aunt Jemima, 195
avant-gardism, 125

Baby Boomer Generation, 156, 267
*Back to the Old School* (Just-Ice), 1
Badu, Erykah, 71, 78, 84, 148, 157, 278
Bahamadia, 71, 147, 266
Bailey, Buster, 107
Bailey, Ida, 185
Bailey, Mildred, 35
Baker, Chet, 133
Baker, Josephine, 71, 183, 200

337

Baldwin, James, 218
Ball, Jared, xxiii
Bambaataa, Afrika, xxixn3, 144
Bañales, Meliza, 266
Bandy, Robert, 127
Baraka, Amiri, xv, 4, 139, 152, 272; *Blues People*, xv, 4
Barnes, Paul, 106
Bartz, Gary, 145
Bashir, Jamil. *See* Jaki Byard
Beat Generation, 130, 132–138, 139, 152
beauty standards, 74–75, 97n34
bebop, 117–131
Bebop Movement, 117–138
Bechet, Sidney, 105, 109, 112
Bellson, Louie, 283n25, 118, 123
"benign neglect", 268, 283n23
Bennett, Gwendolyn, 170, 227n16
Bentley, Gladys, 62, 81, 86
Berland, Jody, 10
Berry, Chuck, 256, 281n10
Berry, Chu, 107, 110
Bibbs, Maria, 216–217
Bigard, Barney, 105, 106
Biggie Smalls, 4
Bilal, 148
Bilbo, Theodore, 173
bisexuality, 82, 170, 199–200, 207–208
Bishop, Walter, 123, 283n25
black: "angry black woman" stereotype, 79–80; bourgeoisie, 21–28, 40–92, 93n3, 93n6, 96n22, 128–129, 183–184, 200, 240; church, 26–27, 38–42, 48–52, 54–56, 61; classical political culture, 2–16, 167–208; classical popular culture, 2–16; classical popular music, 28–42, 99–161; classical social movements, 2–16, 19–28, 42–92, 167–208; clubwomen, 19–28, 42–54, 58–59, 62, 87–92; expressive culture, 33, 52, 67–68, 96n21, 170, 177, 189; feminism, 21–28, 37, 40, 42–54, 58–92, 94n8–94n9, 147, 182, 184, 280n6; feminist nationalism, 22; ghetto youth, xvi, xxiii, xxv, xxixn3, 3–6, 9, 10, 17n2–17n3, 246, 248, 251, 252–256, 265, 270, 272, 273–274; male supremacy, 45, 72, 89; masculinist nationalism, 22; masculinity, 31, 182,

200–202, 220, 228n21; nationalism, 144, 155, 168, 175, 191, 274; newspapers, 49, 86; pop music divas, 58, 68, 71, 84, 148, 238; popular culture, xvi–xx, 1–16, 19–42, 54–92, 99–161, 237–262; popular music, 1–16, 19–42, 54–92, 99–161, 237–262; protest, 63–68, 76–80, 83, 120, 255–262; public sphere, 54–58, 96n23; radicalism, 6–10, 167–224; women's standpoint, 25–27. *See also* film
Black Arts Movement, xxxn5, 101, 103, 129–130, 149, 153, 168, 177, 190–191, 199, 207, 227n16, 263, 264
Black Codes, 29, 64, 104–105, 180, 182, 187, 247
Black Panther Party, 58, 243
Black Power Movement, 164n33, 168, 190–191, 197, 207, 225n9, 235, 238–239, 240–245, 247–250, 262–269
Black Sheep, 144
Black Thought (rapper), xii, xxiii, xxxn7
Black Women's Club Movement, 19–28, 42–92
Black Women's Liberation Movement, 33, 45, 68, 235, 241, 262
Blake, Eubie, 109
Blakey, Art, 118, 122–123, 141, 142, 145
Blige, Mary J., 249
Blow, Kurtis, 251
blues, 19–42, 54–92; queens, 19–42, 54–92; women, 19–42, 54–92
*Blues Ideology and Afro-American Literature* (Baker), 52
*Blues & Soul* , 148–149
Blumenthal, Bob, 108
body image, 75, 151
Bogan, Lucille, 35
Bolden, Buddy, 105, 106, 112
Bolshevik Revolution, 175
Boogie Down Productions, 251, 252, 254, 274, 275
boogie-woogie piano, 108, 117, 281n10
bop talk, 99, 150, 152, 158
bourgeoisism, 50, 52–54, 57, 61, 91, 93n3, 94n8, 170, 184, 227n16, 232, 236, 262, 272
Bowser, Clarence, 109
Boxley, George, 177

10, 80, 258–259, 260; Cultural Studies, xxii, 10, 80, 89, 260; Global Hip Hop Studies, 280n7; International Hip Hop Studies, 280n7; Islamic Hip Hop Studies, 280n7; Lesbian Gay Bisexual Transsexual Transgender and Queer (LGBTTQ) Studies, 215, 216–218, 229n26, 229n28; Popular Music Studies, xv–xxiii, 80, 231–278; Postcolonial Studies, 260; Postmodern Studies, xxii, 10–16; Women's Studies, xxii, 10, 20, 25, 39, 70, 80, 81, 89–90
Edwards, Teddy, 118
Eisenhower, Dwight, 120
Elam, Keith Edward. *See* Guru
Eldridge, Roy, 107, 110, 118
Ellington, Edward Kennedy "Duke", 99, 107, 108–110
Elliott, Missy, 72, 151, 275
Ellis, Herb, 118, 123
Ellis, Pee Wee, 145
Ellison, Ralph, 115, 129
embourgeoisement, 25
English, Roger, 218
Etheridge, Melissa, 80
Eurocentrism, 25, 50–54, 170, 204
European American black music scholars, 63–67
European classical music, 32–33, 103, 105, 116–117
Evans, Bill, 141
Evans, Stomp, 106
Eve (rapper), 78
Évora, Césaria, 28

Fab 5 Freddie, 152
Fanon, Frantz, 89, 104, 250; "The Black Man and Language", 104
Farrakhan, Louis, 149, 255
Farrell, Joe, 146
Farris, Dionne, 71
fashion, 72, 116, 132, 134, 162n17
Fauset, Jessie, 110, 169
Feloni (rapper), 82
female rappers. *See* women rappers
femcees (female MCs), 266
feminism, 19–92
Ferlinghetti, Lawrence, 139
field hollers, 29, 35, 56, 103, 251

Fields Geechie, 106
film, 116, 141, 153, 156, 249, 254, 282n20; blaxploitation, 153, 254; hood, 141
*Fire!!!* (magazine), 208, 227n16
Fitzgerald, Ella, 104, 110, 118
Fixx, Tori, 266
Floyd, Samuel, 232
Foucault, Michel, xxi
Foxx, Jamie, 48
Franklin, Aretha, 15, 84
Franti, Michael, 275, 278
Frazier, E. Franklin, 96n22
FRELIMO (Frente de Libertação de Moçambique) Movement, 263
Fuller, Curtis, 141
funk, xviii, xxiv, 17n2, 23, 33, 84, 105, 112, 157, 158, 201, 235, 254, 281n8
Fu-Schickens, 144

The Game (rapper), 249
Gangsta Boo, 86
Gang Starr, 100, 143, 146, 151, 275
Garvey, Amy Jacques, 183
Garvey, Marcus, 174, 194, 277
Gates, Henry Louis, 188–189, 193, 208, 279n1
gender justice, 27, 54–92
Genet, Jean, 136–137
genteelism, 24, 184, 198
Getz, Stan, 133
ghetto, 144, 184, 239–240, 244–278; music, xvi–xxv, 105, 113, 244–278
ghetto-gangsta-nigga-pimp-thug theme, 252, 275–276
Gillespie, Dizzy, 99–100, 118–123, 124, 126, 132, 135, 141, 153
Ginsberg, Allen, 132, 133, 136; *Howl*, 132–133
Giovanni, Nikki, 22, 152, 272
Giroux, Henry, 250
Glasper, Robert, 155
God-dess & She, 266
Goines, Donald, 249
Golub, Leon, 236
Goodie Mob, 4, 275
Gordon, Jimmie, 65
gospel, xxiv, 35, 38–40, 41, 79, 280n3
Grae, Jean, 79, 266
graffiti-writing, xxixn3, 76, 201, 267

Hi-Tek (DJ), 15
Hodges, Johnny, 109–110
Holiday, Billie, 84, 104, 110, 118, 153, 157
Holiday, Frank, 109
Holmes, John Clellon, 136
*Home Girls Make Some Noise!*, 90
homoeroticism, 82, 199–203
homophobia, 209–224
Homosexual Hip Hop Movement, 209–224
homosexuality, 192–224
hooks, bell, 22, 25, 94n8, 211, 221–222, 228n21
Hope, Elmo, 118
Hope, John, 185
Hopkins, Claude, 109
Hopkins, Pauline, 173, 189
Howard, Darnell, 106
Howard, Ronald Ray, 126
Hubbard, Freddie, 141, 142, 145, 147
Huddleston, William Emanuel. *See* Yusef Lateef
Huggins, Nathan, 204
Hughes, Langston, 99–100, 110, 139, 159, 160, 164n39, 170, 175, 209–210, 218, 222, 227n16, 234, 270; "The Negro Artist and the Racial Mountain," 209–210; *The Weary Blues*, 139, 159
Hugo, Chad, 148
Hull, Gloria, 211
humanism: radical, 5–6, 211, 219–223, 228n24, 277
Humphrey, Bobbi, 147
Hunter, Alberta, 35, 38
Hurricane Katrina, 127
Hurston, Zora Neale, 110, 170, 183, 192, 193, 200, 227n16

*I'll Make Me a World* (documentary), 93n5
Ice Cube, 72, 253–254
Ice-T, 251, 252, 253–254
Iceberg Slim, 249
illness: AIDS (Acquired Immune Deficiency Syndrome), 5, 17n3, 23, 71, 100; alcoholism, 36, 62, 132, 253, 267, 269, 277; Center for Disease Control and Prevention, 5, 18n4; HIV/AIDS, 5, 17n3, 23, 71, 100
Immortal Technique, 275, 278
India.Arie, 71, 75, 278

interracial: heterosexual-homosexual alliances, 171–224; relationships, 170–171
Ipiotis, Celia, xxixn3
Isis, 71
Israel (filmmaker), xxixn3
Ivy Queen, 69

Jacki-O, 86
Jacks, James W., 48, 73
Jackson, Buzzy, 74
Jackson, Cliff, 109
Jackson, Jesse, 149, 255
Jackson, Millie, 272
Jackson, Milt, 145
Jackson, Willis, 136–137
Jacquet, Illinois,.32
Jamal, Ahmad, 122–123
James, Etta, 84, 281n10
Jarrett, Gene Andrew, 188–189, 196
Jarrett, Keith, 141
jazz, 99–161; concert, 140; controversy, 113–117, 135; creole musicians, 104–105; films, 156; language, 124; poetry, 99–102, 110–118, 138–161; vocals, 104
Jazz Age, 110–117, 232
Jazz Gillum, 279n1
Jazz Messengers, 122, 142, 145
Jay-Z, 14, 151, 270
J Dilla, 148
Jean, Wyclef, 151, 275
Jefferson, Hilton, 107
Jigga. *See* Jay-Z
Jim Crow laws, 29, 173, 180, 182, 187, 242, 247
jingoism, 9
jive, 99, 104, 124, 150, 152, 259, 273
J.J. Fad, 72
Johnny Dangerous, 266
Johnson, Charles, 110
Johnson, Charles Spurgeon, 194
Johnson, Duanna, 218
Johnson, Georgia Douglas, 211
Johnson, Helene, 227n16
Johnson, J. J., 118, 141, 283n25
Johnson, James P., 109
Johnson, James Weldon, 169, 172
Johnson, Walter, 107

LL Cool J, 61
Lô Cheikh, 28
Locke, Alain, 110, 167–169, 193, 195, 199, 211
Logan, Rayford, 173, 225n10
Lorde, Audre, 152, 206–208, 215
Lost Generation, 110–117, 130, 132, 133–137, 172, 231, 249, 268, 273
Lott Eric, 124–125
Love Monie, 72, 144–145, 148
L'Trimm, 72
Lucie, Lawrence, 106
lynching, 29, 64, 170, 173, 174, 182, 188, 189, 195, 247, 264

Maal Baaba, 28
Mack Mistress, 266
Madhubuti Haki, 152, 272
Main Source, 100, 275
Makeba, Miriam, 28
Malaco Records, 242
Manor, Chatham, 177
Mapfumo, Thomas, 28
Marsalis, Branford, 146, 147, 155
Marsalis, Wynton, 140, 142–143
Marsh, James, 280n3
Marshall, Kaiser, 107
Martin, Sarah, 35, 41
Marx, Karl, 153
Marxism, 89, 153
Mayfield, Curtis, 14–15, 149–150, 256
McCann, Les, 145
McClure, Michael, 139
McDaniel, Hattie, 79
McDuff, Jack, 145
McGhee, Frederick, 185
McGhee, Howard, 118
MC Hammer, 143
McKay, Claude, 110, 160, 173–176, 193, 199, 207, 210; "If We Must Die", 174–175, 210
McLean, Jackie, 118, 123, 133, 141
MC Lyte, 72, 79, 94n9
McShann, Jay, 110, 118
McWhorter, John, 22
Mecca the Ladybug. *See* Ladybug
medicine shows, 20, 32, 41, 106, 119
Medusa (rapper), 71, 266
the Meters, 154

Method Man, 243
Mezzrow Mezz, 132
Mia X, 86
Middle Passage, 11, 181
Miles, Lizzie, 41
Miley, James "Bubber", 109–110
militarism, 9, 21, 40, 114, 277
Millennial Generation, 102, 114, 156
Miller, Glen, 110
Miller, Irvin C., 97n34
Miller, Kelly, 45
Mills, Charles, 225n9
Minaj, Nicki, 86, 249, 270
Mingus, Charles, 99, 118, 139, 153, 283n25
Minit/Instant Records, 242, 281n8
minstrel shows, 176–181, 224n5; blackface, 23, 93n2, 176, 181, 204, 225n9, 245–246, 249
minstrelism, postmillennial, 23
Minton's Playhouse, 124
misogyny, 6–10, 18n5, 54–92, 192–208, 211–224, 251–262
missionary societies, 51
Miss Money, 266
Mitchell, George, 106
mixtape, xxi–xxviii
Mobley, Hank, 123, 141, 153, 283n25
Mockus, Martha, 83
Modern Jazz Quartet, 122
Moïse, Lenelle, 266
Monk, Thelonious, 118, 123, 124–125, 126, 141, 146, 153
Monroe's Uptown House, 124
Montgomery Bus Boycott, 67
Montgomery, Wes, 141
Moore, Jessica Care, 75, 266
Morgan, Frank, 118
Morgan, Gertrude, 185
Morgan, Joan, 94n8–94n9
Morgan, Lee, 141
Morris, Leo. *See* Muhammad, Idris
Morrison, Toni, 259
Morton, Benny, 107
Morton Jelly Roll, 106, 107, 112, 141, 162n6
Mos Def, 144, 275, 278
Motown Records, 15, 242, 281n8

97n30, 138–161, 231–278; Dirty South, 238; East Coast, 251–252, 282n13; feminist, 59–92; gangsta, 251–278, 282n11; hardcore, 251–278, 282n11; homosexual, 209–224; jazz, 99–102, 110–118, 138–161, 164n39, 164n45; Latin, 238; luxury, 14; message, 1–16, 97n30, 138–161, 202, 231–278; Mid-West, 238; old school, 197, 238; political, 236–250, 252, 263–278; queer, 209–224; reggae, 238; rock, xvi, 238; soul, 148; underground, xxiv, 23, 40, 117, 138–139, 158–161, 238, 253, 274; West Coast, 238, 282n12; women-centered, 54–92, 97n30, 98n38, 98n40
rape, 46–48, 249
Reagan, Ronald, 149, 244, 251, 252, 253–254, 255
Recording Industry Association of America (RIAA), 150, 254
Reconstruction, 29, 33, 38, 55–69, 167–208
Redding, Otis, 14
Redman (rapper), 243
Redman, Don, 107–108
Reeves, Gerald, 106
Reflection Eternal (rap group), 15
reggae, xxiv, 69, 84, 97n29, 157, 158; womanist, 69
reggaeton, xvi, 238
religion, xxii, 8, 28, 32, 36, 41–45, 49–55, 61–62, 67, 96n26, 121–123, 179, 211–215, 228n24; Christianity, 121; intolerance, 9, 205, 211–215, 263, 277; Islam, 121–123, 163n24–163n25; Islamophobia, 9; Nation of Islam, 67, 153
Resnick, Michael, xxiv
The Re-Up Gang, xxiv
Rexroth, Kenneth, 139
rhythm & blues, 2, 10, 13, 19, 23, 33, 35, 41, 58, 79–80, 84, 85, 105, 108, 129, 135, 143, 147, 149, 157–158, 235, 238, 241, 245, 254, 256, 281n8, 281n10
Rich, Buddy, 118, 123
Richardson, Elaine, 90
Rihanna, 78
riots: Crown Heights (1991), 127, 128; Harlem (1943), 126–127, 163n27; Los

Angeles (1992), 127, 128; Miami (1980), 127; New York City (1977), 127; Newark (1967), 127; Red Summer (1919), 172–176, 224n2; St. Louis (1917), 174; zoot suit, xxvii, 100, 128–130, 163n31; Watts (1965), 127, 283n23. *See also* race
Roach, Max, 99, 118, 141, 153, 283n25
the roaring twenties, 110–114, 135
Roberts Robin, 69–71
Roberts, Luckey, 109
Robinson, Smokey, 256
Robinson, Sylvia, 202–203
Rochester, Joe, 109
rock & roll, 19, 23, 35, 83–84, 85, 135, 281n10
Rock Steady Crew, 152
Rodney Red, 118
Rollins, Sonny, 133, 141, 153
The Roots, xxiii, xxxn7, 148, 157, 275, 278
Rose, Tricia, 8–10, 76, 94n9, 236, 239; *Black Noise*, 8–9, 94n9, 236–237
Ross, Rick, 249
Rosolino, Frank, 118
Rossiter, Red, 106
Roxanne Shanté, 251
Ruby and the Romantics, 256
Rucker, Ursula, 266
Ruffin, Josephine, 88
Run-D.M.C., 251
Rushing, Jimmy, 104

Said, Edward, 260
Salaam, Liaquat Ali. *See* Clarke, Kenny
Salem, Dorothy, 44, 48–50
Salt-N-Pepa, 72
Sample, Joe, 145
sampling, 147–149, 151, 165n46, 251
Sanchez, Sonia, 22, 139, 152, 272
Santana, Juelz, xxiv
Sartre, Jean-Paul, 136–137, 153
Saud, Sulaimon. *See* Tyner, McCoy
Savage, Augusta, 110
Savoy Ballroom, 131
Saxton, Alexander, 178–179
Schoolly D, 251
Schwarz A. B. Christa, 199–200, 206–207, 211–212, 213; *Gay Voices of the Harlem Renaissance*, 199, 211

# About the Author

**Reiland Rabaka** is an associate professor of African, African American, and Caribbean studies in the Department of Ethnic Studies and Humanities Program at the University of Colorado at Boulder, where he is also an affiliate professor in the Women and Gender Studies Program and a research fellow at the Center for Studies of Ethnicity and Race in America (CSERA). He also holds graduate faculty appointments in the College of Music, School of Education, Department of Sociology, and Department of Religious Studies at the University of Colorado at Boulder. His research has been published in the *Journal of African American Studies, Journal of Black Studies, Western Journal of Black Studies, Africana Studies Annual Review, Ethnic Studies Review, Jouvert: A Journal of Postcolonial Studies, Socialism & Democracy,* and *Journal of Southern Religion,* among others. He is an editorial board member of the *Journal of African American Studies, Journal of Black Studies,* and *Africana Studies Annual Review.*

Rabaka is the editor of the *Critical Africana Studies* book series, which is published by the Rowman & Littlefield Publishing Group, and he has published ten books, including *W.E.B. Du Bois and the Problems of the Twenty-First Century* (2007); *Du Bois's Dialectics: Black Radical Politics and the Reconstruction of Critical Social Theory* (2008); *Africana Critical Theory* (2009); *Forms of Fanonism: Frantz Fanon's Critical Theory and the Dialectics of Decolonization* (2010); *Against Epistemic Apartheid: W.E.B. Du Bois and the Disciplinary Decadence of Sociology* (2010); *Hip Hop's Inheritance: From the Harlem Renaissance to the Hip Hop Feminist Movement* (2011); and *The Hip Hop Movement: From R&B and the Civil Rights Movement to Rap and the Hip Hop Generation* (forthcoming). In addition, he is the editor of *W.E.B. Du Bois: A Critical Reader* (2010) and coeditor (with Arturo Aldama, Elisa Facio, and Daryl Maeda) of *Telling Our Stories: Ethnic Histories and Cultures of Colorado* (2011).

His research has been recognized with several awards, including funding from the National Science Foundation, the Eugene M. Kayden Book Award, the Cheikh Anta Diop Book Award, and the National Council for Black Studies' W.E.B. Du Bois–Anna Julia Cooper Award for Outstanding Publications in Africana Studies.

Rabaka has conducted archival research and lectured extensively both nationally and internationally, and has been the recipient of numerous community service citations, distinguished teaching awards, and research fellowships. His cultural criticism, social commentary, and political analysis have been featured in print, radio, television, and online media venues such as NPR, PBS, BBC, ABC, NBC, BET, *The Tom Joyner Morning Show*, *The Philadelphia Tribune*, and *The Denver Post*, among others. He is also an award-winning poet, spoken-word artist, and multi-instrumentalist.